An Exposition of First John

An Exposition of First John

John Cotton

**Sovereign Grace Publishers, Inc.
P.O. Box 4998
Lafayette, IN 47905**

Exposition of First John, John Cotton
Paperback edition
Copyright © 2001
By Jay P. Green, Sr.
All Rights Reserved
ISBN: 1-58960-134-3

Reader,

To satisfy the importunity of some friends, rather than out of any presumption that my testimony can prove any credit to this excellent piece, I have ventured to give thee my poor judgment concerning it. I observed in the whole such a blessed marriage between piety and art, such a sweet condescension to the meanest capacities, such a spiritual handling of spiritual truths, and such clear discoveries of the state of nature and the state of grace, that (even if the work had not borne the name Cotton) I could not but conclude that the author was a workman that need not be ashamed.

Let me tell thee by experience that such a blessed gale of the Spirit of grace (who assisted the author) doth accompany the religious perusal of this book, that I am very confident, if there is the least spark of grace in thy heart, it will make thy smoking flax break forth into a heavenly flame of light and love. While I perused it to correct the many errors of the former impression, its heavenly matter pointed at (and, I hope, corrected) more and greater errors in my heart. If thou be bad it may make thee good,* but if thou be good, I am sure it will make thee better. This is the hearty prayer of him who is,

> Thy soul's friend, and the servant of thy faith,
> Roger Drake

Feb. 26, 1657.

*It is the author's teaching that the word read does not convert. In this I must at least question, if not disagree.

I John 1:1, 2

"That which was from the beginning, which we have heard, which we have seen with our eyes, which we have looked upon, and our hands have handled, of the Word of Life; (for the life was manifested, and we have seen it and bear witness, and show unto you that eternal life which was with the Father and was manifested unto us)."

The children of God are exercised in the whole course of their lives with many conflicts of conscience; especially at the beginning of their course of Christianity, they are exercised with this doubt, whether they indeed do belong to the election of grace and are indeed among the number of those that belong unto God.

And, because faith is usually then very weak in them, it comes to pass that their doubtings are strong. They have many doubts of their state; and from doubtings arise trouble of mind and terror of conscience.

When the sun is in its full strength and shines brightly, there arise no clouds or mists or vapors, but only when it is low. So it is with faith and doubting; and St. John, moved by the Holy Ghost, penned this epistle for pacifying our consciences with the peace of God and filling our hearts with joy in the Holy Ghost (1:4). And because our joy cannot be full unless we enjoy union with him and communication with his children, therefore he also opens that (v. 3).

And these are both begun and preserved, first, by receiving the truth of doctrine, and second, by walking in holiness of life. Contrariwise they are hindered and interrupted, first, by error in doctrine and, second, by wickedness and uncleanness of life. Therefore he inserts instructions everywhere; first, for enlightening our minds with truth of doctrine, and second, for directing our steps with precepts of holiness of life. And from both he teaches us to gather to ourselves marks of our states with God, so that our joy may be full.

In the text he instructs us in the knowledge of doctrine, what we are to think and believe concerning the doctrine of the apostles, whether preached or written. Concerning this doctrine two things are here delivered.

I. The subject of it, Christ Jesus
   A. In Himself
      1. As God, from the beginning eternal
      2. As man, as being heard, seen, and grasped by the senses
   B. As in himself to us, the word of life (v. 1)
II. The end and scope of it
   A. Subordinate, fellowship with the apostles and saints, and with God (v. 3)
   B. Supreme, our fullness of joy (v. 4).

"That which was from the beginning."

-1. Why is it said here, "that which was from the beginning," rather than "he who was from the beginning"? It is here said, "that which was from the beginning," to signify and set forth unto us a double nature in one and the same word of life, in one and the same person of Christ. If he had said," he who was from the beginning, whom we have seen," it might have been thought that the same word of life was in one and the same nature; or else that one person was from the beginning, another person seen and heard. But when he says, "that word of life which was from the beginning and which we have heard and seen," he plainly insinuates that there is a distinction of properties in the word of life.

There was something of the word of life which was from

the beginning, namely, his Godhead. And again there was something in the same word of life that was heard and seen, namely his manhood. If there is something both eternal and approachable by the senses, then there is no confusion of properties in the person of Christ. The apostles preach a Christ in whom is both something from the beginning, and something heard and seen; and that in the word which was from the beginning is not that in the word which was sensible; and that in the word which was sensible is not that in the word which was eternal. And therefore those who teach the flesh of Christ to be everywhere (as the Germans) or everywhere in the sacraments (as the Papists), they do not observe the distinction here made by the apostle.

-2. What does it mean, to be "from the beginning"? The phrase is ambiguous and must be interpreted according to the nature of the thing to which it is attributed. It sometimes signifies:
   -1. The beginning of the story of Christ Luke 1:2).
   -2. The time of the delivery of the law (1 John 2:7).
   -3. The institution of a thing (Matt. 19:8).
   -4. The fall (John 8:44).
   -5. The creation (Joel 2:2).

But none of these is meant here: not the first nor second, for before Abraham was, he was (John 8:58). Not the third, fourth, or fifth, for he himself created all things (John 1:3).

There is another "from the beginning," which is higher than all these, namely from the beginning of eternity — which, lacking beginning, implies that he was before all beginnings (Prov. 8:23).

Doct. And because there cannot be two eternals, but one eternal, and that is God; therefore Christ also is eternal, God with the Father and Holy Ghost.

This is not to be omitted because it is plain, but to be preached because it is certain; especially since some have lately been so far bewitched by Satan as to seal the contrary with their blood. It is proved:

-1. By the names and titles given to him. (a) God (1 John 5:20; Rom. 9:5) (b) Jehovah (Exod. 3:2, 4, 6). (c) Saviour (Matt. 1:21), which is none but God (Isa. 43:11, Hos. 13:4). And who was able to save us from sin by satisfying God's wrath but God?

-2. By the essential properties of the Godhead agreeing to him. (a) Knowing the heart and reins (Jer. 11:20; Rev. 21:23), yea all things (John 21:17) (b) Omnipotence (John 5:19) (c) Omnipresence (Matt. 18:20) (d) Eternity (John 8:58, 17:5) (e) Equality with his Father, without sacrilege (Phil. 2:6).

-3. By his works of (a) Power (i. creation, Heb. 1:2, Col. 1:16, and that for his glory; ii. providence, Heb. 1:3; iii. miracles, John 14:11) (b) Grace (i. election, John 15:16; ii. redemption, Gal. 3:13) (c) Giving of the Spirit (John 4:10) (d) Giving of eternal life (John 10:28; Rom. 6:23).

-4. By the worship ascribed to him. (a) Prayer (Acts 7:60) (b) Faith in him, for else how could we call on him? (Rom. 10:14; John 1:12; Ps. 2:12)

Use 1. To confute all those blasphemous heresies by which Satan has labored to overthrow the truth of the Godhead of Christ; as those of the Cerinthians, Ebonites, and Arians, who taught that he was only pure man, and had no being before the virgin Mary, or at most before the creation.

Use 2. To terrify all who are enemies of his kingdom (Ps. 2:12; Luke 19:14, 27).

Use 3. To comfort all who are Christ's (John 10:28; Ps. 23:1; Isa. 43:1, 2) because they were elected in Christ (Eph. 1:4) and our life is hid with him (Col. 3:3). Therefore it is both sure and unchangeable, for he is so.

Use 4. To exhort us to worship him (Matt. 28:9) as an eternal God, God from the beginning. Moses reproved the Israelites for worshipping new gods (Deut. 32:17), gods whom their fathers did not know. But Christ they knew and worshipped; Moses himself (Deut. 33:16), Jacob (Hos. 12:4; Gen. 48:15, 16), and Abraham (Gen. 22:11, 12).

Now his worship consists in the duties of faith and repentance, for those are the parts of God's worship which he has revealed to us and requires from us.

-1. The duties of faith (John 14:1).

a. Do you receive anything from God? Receive it remembering your own unworthiness in yourself, for thus you worship him through whom God accepts you and pours his blessings upon you (Eph. 1:3), for none but God could receive them for us from all eternity.

b. Do you give anything to God? Do you offer up any obedience? Do so remembering your own imperfection, for thus you worship him through whom our lame sacrifices are acceptable (Col. 3:17); for none but God could do this for us.

c. Do you want anything? Seek unto God in the name of Jesus Christ, and believe that you shall receive it. In this way you honor him (John 16:23, 24), for none but God can procure this for us.

d. Do you doubt the truth of any of the promises of God through unbelief? Believe that they are yea and amen in him (2 Cor. 1:20), and so you worship him; for only God can call things that are not, as though they were.

-2. The duties of repentance.

a. Do you at any time (though you should continually) remember your old sin? O remember also that he whom you crucified by them was the eternal God, the Lord of glory; and that will work a godly sorrow (Zech. 12:10).

b. Does Satan tempt you to commit any sin? O remember that thereby you should trample under foot the blood of the Son of God, who has saved you from your sins (Heb. 10:29).

"That which we have heard." As there was something in the word of life which was eternal from the beginning, so there was something which was manifest to the senses; and this was -1. heard, -2. seen and looked upon, -3. handled.

I. What is the word which we have heard? Not a word of rumor, but -1. His doctrine (John 6:68). -2. The testimony which his Father gave of him (Matt. 17:5, 6; 2 Pet. 1:17).

II. What is the word which we have seen?

-1. His flesh (John 1:14).

-2. His works, especially his miracles (John 2:11).

-3. His state of humiliation. (a) His poor and despicable life (Matt. 8:20). (b) His agony (Matt. 26:37). (c) His accusation and arraignment (Matt. 26:55-57; John 20:12). (d) His death (Luke 23:46, 47). (e) His burial (Mark 15:47; John 19).

-4. His state of exaltation. (a) A preamble to it (Matt. 17:2, 3). (b) His resurrection (John 20:8, 20). (c) His ascension (Acts 1:9, 10). (d) His sitting at the right hand of God (Acts 7:55).

-5. John saw many of these things in a more familiar manner than most of the apostles; as Christ took with him only Peter and James and John to behold: (a) His raising Jairus' daughter to life (Mark 5:37); (b) His glory in the mount (Matt. 17:1); (c) His agony in the garden (Matt. 26:37).

III. What is the word which we have handled with our hands? This adds an emphasis of certainty, as before. (a) He caught Peter by the hand (Matt. 14:31). (b) He washed their feet (John 13:5). (c) John leaned on his breast (John 13:15).

Doct. He who was from the beginning truly God, was in the fullness of time truly man.

A plain doctrine, you will say, and well known to the least in this congregation. Be it so, yet it is fit to put you in remembrance of it (2 Pet. 1:12, 13; Rom. 15:14, 15).

But you will say to me, Is it not much better to speak of the person of Christ and of the benefits which we receive by him, as justification, adoption, sanctification by the Spirit of God, faith love, hope, repentance? I answer, take heed lest this be one kind of spiritual harlotry and adultery. If you see a maid betrothed to a man, who desires to hear and speak of the gifts and presents he will bestow upon her, as rings, bracelets, jewels, etc.; and has no mind at all to hear or speak of his person, would you not say she loved his gifts more than himself?

Now the manhood of Christ is proved by two reasons.

-1. By the titles given to him. He is called: (a) Flesh (John 1:14; Rom. 1:3: Heb. 2:14). (b) Man (Acts 17:31). (c) Son of man (Luke 19:10). (d) Seed of David (2 Tim. 2:8), Abraham (Gal. 3:16), the woman (Gen. 3:15). (e) Emmanuel (Isa. 7:14; Matt. 1:23).

-2. By the properties of a man in him. (a) Being born of woman (Matt. 1:25). (b) Hunger (Matt. 21:18) and thirst (John 19:28). (c) Weariness (John 4:6). (d) Grief and sorrow (Isa. 53:3,4,10; Matt. 26:38) and with it weeping (John 11:35). (e) Bleeding and sweating (Luke 22:44). (f) Dying (John 19:30).

Now for the reasons why Christ became man.

-1. That he might be a middle person, or of a middle nature, between the persons offending and the persons offended. If he had still remained God alone, he would have been the person offended with us; or if only man, then he would have been the party offending; and therefore that he might be of a middle condition, it was needful that he should take upon him our nature.

-2. That our nature, which had transgressed, might make satisfaction. If he had not taken on him our nature, he could not have satisfied for our sins (Heb. 2:16).

-3. That he might be able to suffer death for us (Heb. 2:9), which God could not do.

-4. That he might be more compassionate on our infirmities (Heb. 2:17,18).

Use 1. To confute the heresies of Eutyches and the Manichees, who taught that Christ had only an imaginary body.

Use 2. To stir us up to meditation.

a. Concerning God. First, concerning his justice, so severe against sin that all the mere men in the world could not satisfy for it, and therefore Christ became man; and that is the reason why the damned are tormented, because they cannot satisfy. Second, concerning his mercy and love to us;

the Father to abase his Son, the Son to abase himself for us. Third, concerning his wisdom, to find out such a means to save us, when he passed by the more glorious angels.

b. Concerning ourselves, who were in so wretched a condition that the blood of bulls and goats could not save us; men and angels could not save us; the Son of God must empty himself of glory and majesty and become man for us. If therefore you have no part in Christ Jesus, the same sins which plucked Christ from heaven to earth will pluck you from earth to hell.

Use 3. To teach us Christian practice.

a. To teach us humility (Phil. 2:6, 7). First, by considering our own state, and the misery of it, if it caused him to take upon him the form of a servant. Second, by considering his example. He took upon himself the form of a servant to be serviceable to us; so we also ought to abase ourselves to be serviceable to our brethren.

b. To stir us up to labor to be united to his nature, as he was to ours (2 Pet. 1:4). He became the son of man so that we might become the sons of God; we cannot answer the intent of his incarnation better.

c. To move us to a holy thankfulness and joyfulness in the Lord. Zacharias blessed the Lord for this (Luke 1:68); Mary magnified him (Luke 1:46); John leaped for joy in his mother's belly (Luke 1:41); Abraham long before saw it in the promise (John 8:56) and laughed (Gen. 17:16, 17) and thereupon called his son Isaac; and lastly the angels, who have less benefit than we, praised God for it (Luke 2:14).

Doct. If the apostles saw and heard these things, then blessed were they (Luke 10:22, 23).

-1. By this means they had a greater measure of knowledge. He expounded to them the secrets of the kingdom of God (Matt. 13:11, 16; Mark 4:34). As Solomon's servants were happy (1 Kings 10:8), so much more Christ's disciples, for they saw and heard a greater than Solomon.

-2. Their faith also was strengthened by this means in the promise of the Messiah, which had been deferred so long. It is many times an exercise for faith, to be commanded to believe what we do not see; but to see what we do not believe is a great strenfthening to a weak faith (John 20:29). Again, a greater measure of knowledge is a notable means of a greater measure of faith. And if you object Heb. 11:1 against this, I answer that the meaning of the verse is somewhat different: though things are not yet seen, yet faith makes them evident; not that whatever we believe by faith is not seen. Stephen saw and believed the same (Acts 7:55).

-3. Their peace of conscience also was more settled and established (Luke 2:29, 30), for they saw now that Christ had come to accomplish that work of reconciliation which was promised before. In this regard the glory of the second temple was greater than that of the first (Hag. 2:9). The second temple lacked five things of the former: Aaron's rod, the pot of manna, Urim and Thummim, and fire from heaven; and yet it was greater than the former. Why? Because these three, knowledge, faith, and peace of conscience, were so much increased, not to a few as before, but widely, even to the simple.

Use 1. Here we have just occasion to meditate of our blessedness also, above that of the old church; for all those grounds of the apostles' blessedness remain to us; as: (a) Means of knowledge clearer to us than to the old church; by the apostles' preachings and writings we even see Christ crucified (Gal. 3:10). (b) Means of stronger faith, because of greater means of knowledge and because that which they hoped for is already accomplished to us. (c) Means of settling greater peace, since Christ has not only come to make our peace (as he came to Simeon), but had already done it. And therefore it were a shame for us to be more ignorant, faithless, and perplexed in conscience than they were.

Use 2. To stir us up to pity the states of such poor people as still sit in darkness and in the shadow of death, having no means of knowledge, of faith, of peace (John 7:49).

Use 3. How great then is that blessedness prepared for us in heaven! We shall see Christ as he is, and then: (a) Our knowledge shall be perfect (1 Cor. 13:12). (b) Our faith shall be joined with fruition; yea, we shall see what we believe (1 Cor. 13:12). (c) Our peace shall be passing understanding (Phil. 4:7), unspeakable and glorious (1 Pet. 1:8).

It is good to feed on these spiritual joys, and then carnal delights will soon grow out of taste and relish.

Doct. Christ in himself, and to us, is the word of life.

Here we shall show in what respects he is called, first, a word, and second, a word of life.

Christ is called a word in four respects, as he is the wisdom, image, interpreter, and promise of the Father.

-1. The wisdom of the Father. As reason flows from the soul or mind of man, and is of the same nature with it, so Christ (who is the wisdom and reasoning of the Father) flowed from the Father, was begotten of him, and is of the same nature with him. Hence he is called the wisdom that dwells with God (Prov. 8:1, 3, 24-30, 34, 35; 1 Cor. 1:24).

-2. As the words or speech of a man is a character of his mind, for "Out of the abundance of the heart the mouth speaks," so Christ is the character or engraven form of the Father's person (Heb. 1:3).

-3. As the speech or word of a man declares the will and meaning of the speaker, so does Christ of the Father (John 1:18; Matt. 11:27).

-4. Christ may very well be called the word of God, or the speech of God, because he it was through whom the Lord spoke from the beginning; that is, the word of promise which he made to Adam, to Abraham, to Isaac, to Jacob, to David, etc.; hence Christ is called the Promise (Heb. 11:39). Hence he who is called a servant (1 Chron. 17:19) is called the word (2 Sam. 7:21), that is, a servant spoken of or promised.

Christ is called a word of life for two reasons.

-1. Because he has special life in himself (John 1:4).

-2. Because he communicates life.

a. He communicates natural life, which to us men is the light of reason (John 1:4); this we have from him as an author, these following as a head or root.

b. Spiritual life.

First, by dying for us, for his death is our life; by his wounds we are healed (Isa. 53:5). Now the life we live by Christ's death is justification (Col. 1:14) and mortification (Rom. 6:6; Gal. 2:19).

Second, Christ also communicates spiritual life to us by rising for us; for as we have been like him in dying to sin by his death, so do we live to God by his life (Rom. 6:5, 10, 11). Now the life we live by his resurrection is vivification or newness of life, since Christ now lives in us by his spirit (Gal. 2:20; 1 Cor. 6:17) and resurrection to glory (Rom. 8:11); hence he is called a quickening spirit (1 Cor. 15:45).

Use 1. If Christ is a word of life, then men out of Christ have no life in them; they have neither the life of justification, nor mortification, nor vivification, nor resurrection to glory, but are stark dead men to grace and glory.

Use 2. If Christ is a word of life, then we who profess ourselves to be Christians, to be members of Christ, are to live no life but his. We life a threefold life (natural, spiritual, and carnal, by which we live the life of reason, of grace, and of sin). The former two we may live, and indeed are to live, because we receive both these lives from Christ the word of life. The last, however, we are not to live, for the members can live no life but the life of their head, the branches no life but the life of the root; hence Paul lived not, but Christ in him (Gal. 2:20). Now that we may do this, we must esteem and carry ourselves as dead men to all things else, so that we may wholly live and move and have our being in him. We are not to live in our old sins; we are not to live to our own friends, riches, or honor; and we are not to live to our own reason and will.

Use 3. If Christ is a word of life, a living and a quickening word, then when we find our hearts dead and dull and indisposed to good duties, let us run and seek him for life and quickening (Ps. 119:37, 40).

1 John 1:2

"For the life appeared, and we have seen it and bear witness, and show unto you that eternal life which was with the Father and was manifested unto us."

-1. Note the dependence of this verse upon the former. It contains an answer to an objection. If Christ was from the beginning, eternal, God, how then could he be seen and heard? "No man has seen God at any time" (John 1:18). The apostle answers that that eternal Word of life was in fullness of time made manifest in the flesh.

-2. Note the order of the words in themselves. In the order of the original they stand thus: "For that life, that eternal life, which was with the father, and which we have seen, and whereof we bear witness, and which we show (or declare) unto you, appeared, appeared I say, unto us."

-3. Note the meaning of the words. This is best opened by handling five distinct propositions, which are explicit in the text. Three concern Christ, two concern the apostles.

-1. Christ is life, life eternal.

-2. This eternal life, Christ, was with the Father.

-3. This eternal life, which was with the Father, appeared to the apostles.

-4. The apostles and disciples saw this eternal life.

-5. The apostles and disciples bore witness unto, and declared, this eternal life unto the church of God.

I. Christ is life. Thus he is called the word of life (John 1:1). He is called 'eternal life' (1 John 5:20), and is so because, first, he himself lives forever (Rev. 1:17, 18; Prov. 8:23); and second, because he is to us the author of eternal life (Heb. 5:9; John 18:28).

Use 1. From this the Godhead of Christ is argued, for no creature is eternal, but all had their beginning in time.

Use 2. Thus we see a reason: (a) For the saying, "All who hate me love death" (Prov. 8:36); such are all who will not be ruled by him (Luke 19:14). (b) For what is said in Eph. 2:1-5, men out of Christ are dead. (c) Why ungodly and wicked men die eternally. They are out of Christ (John 15:6, where is to be translated, not men, but angels, Matt. 13:49, 50). Whomever the angels find out of Christ, they cast into eternal death; not so much because they have deserved it (for so have the godly), but because they are out of Christ. (d) Why some for a time make a fair profession, yet do not hold out; their life of grace is a torrent for a time, but not fed by any living spring (John 4:14). (e) Why the children of God forsake all for him (Matt. 19:27; Job 2:4). (f) Why the children of God live forever (John 14:19).

Use 3. This teaches everyone to labor to find Christ, for in finding him we find eternal life (Prov. 8:35).

II. The eternal life, Christ, was with the Father.

-1. He was with the Father as a nourisher of the creature, sustaining all (Heb. 1:3), and sustaining his church especially, preserving for us that spiritual life which he conveyed unto us. Thus Eph. 1:3 says "all blessings;" as election (ver. 4), adoption (ver. 5). But when were these? "Before the world began" (2 Tim. 1:9). Hence he is called "the everlasting Father (Isa. 9:6).

-2. He was with the Father as a source of delight, both to the Father (John 17:24; Matt. 3:17) and to the creature (Prov. 8:31 rightly translated). If the creature can fill and ravish us with servile delights, how much more can the persons of the blessed Trinity delight one another, yea and us also. The many delights which are scattered in the creation (as food, drink, company, recreation, etc.) are not nearly so delightful as Christ (Ps. 4:6, 7; Ps. 16:11).

Use 1. And if this life was with the Father, then they were together from all eternity; and because there cannot be two eternals, but one eternal, therefore they must needs be conjoined and united in the same essence. And yet because the one was with the other, there must be some distinction between them. Because it cannot be essential, for their essence is one; neither can it be accidental, for there are no accidents in God, this distinction must be personal.

Use 2. If Christ was with the Father in the manner before declared (as a nourisher and a delight), then here is an answer to that vain cavilling question of atheists. If the world was created but five thousand years ago, they say, what did God do in the ages before? I answer, he did two things. (a) The persons in the Godhead were nourishing, delighting, and solacing each other. (b) God was ordaining Christ to be a nourisher and solacer of his church (1 Pet. 1:20).

Use 3. If Christ was with the Father, in whose presence is fullness of joy and pleasure forevermore (Ps. 16:11), then how unspeakable was the love of Christ to such wretches as we! For our sakes he would leave his Father, to take part of our miseries so that we might be partakers of his pleasure. O where are our hearts, that they can delight no more in him?

Use 4. If Christ was with the Father, then the children of God may comfort themselves that we shall also be with God too, to behold the glory which Christ had with the Father. Christ is now where he was from eternity (John 16:28); and where he now is, he has prayed that we also may be (John 17:24), and so prays until this day (Rom. 8:34); and the Father hears him always (John 11:42).

III. This eternal life which was with the Father, appeared unto the apostles and disciples.

What is meant by 'appeared,' or, more exactly, 'was made manifest'? How was he made manifest? In the flesh (1 Tim. 3:16). Christ had been made manifest in days past to the patriarchs; and that by three ways. -1. By apparition, in the appearance and shape of flesh (Gen. 18:17, where he is called (Jehovah), to Hagar (Gen. 16:7, 13), to Moses (Exod. 3:2, 4, 6). -2. By preaching (Gen. 3:15). -3. By faith, which makes things appear which appear not, which makes things evident which are not seen (Heb. 11:1; Gen. 17:17).

Doct. The incarnation of Christ, and his conduct in the world, was the manifestation of him to the apostles and church of God.

"Becoming manifest" here is called his manifestation (2 Tim. 1:10). It is called his "appearing," which is a metaphor, as if it were the breaking forth of the sun from under a cloud. See also John 12:46.

This incarnation of Christ was the manifestation of him to the apostles and church of God.

-1. To the outward man. His divine person, being before that time invisible and unapproachable, became visible and palpible by his incarnation (John 1:18).

-1. To the inward man. They knew him to be both God (Ps. 2:7, 8; mark our Saviour's urging that passage in Matt. 22:44, 45) and man (Gen. 3:15). They knew him to be prophet (Deut. 18:18; John 4:25), priest (Ps. 110:4), and king (Ps. 2: 7-9) over his church; yet they knew not how these things should be, Luke 1:34. Though they had known his benefits before (Luke 10:22-24), yet it had been obscurely and darkly, as wrapped up in a shadow (2 Cor. 3:13), as seen afar off (Heb. 11:13); but they were now brought to light by his incarnation and coming into the world (2 Tim. 1:10).

Use 1. For instruction.

a. Here we learn the meaning of that difficult place, Heb. 9:7, 8. Why was that way into the most holy place shut up from the sight of God's people? Because the way into heaven was not yet manifest, the one being a type of the other. But what was that way into heaven? It was Christ, incarnate, living, and dying among us (Heb. 10:19, 20); hence at Christ's death the veil of the temple was rent in twain, and so the way into the most holy place was opened (Matt. 27:51).

b. We learn the reason why the apostles and saints of God who lived in those times were endued with a greater and larger measure of gifts and graces than ever before or since. Christ left his apostles behind him to be his almsgivers, as it were; to bestow his largesse on the church. We see also the reason why there was a greater measure of light of the knowledge of salvation shed abroad into the world in those times than ever before; it was because of Christ's coming in the flesh, which was his manifestation; when the sun rises, should not the light break forth more gloriously than before? Five thousand were converted at two sermons (Acts 2:41, 4:4).

c. We learn the reason for ceasing of oracles in the apostles' time. Christ had appeared; his light had broken through, and "what communion hath light with darkness?" (2 Cor. 6:14) They were devils (1 Cor. 10:20). When Christ's kingdom was partly outward in solemn sacrifices and ceremonies, he allowed the devil to erect the like. But when Christ's kingdom became in a manner wholly spiritual (as it did from the time of his appearing in the flesh) he would not allow his enemy to enjoy any other kingdom but spiritual in the hearts and souls of men.

d. We learn a difference in perceptions. Christ was made manifest in the flesh, yet some knew him not (John 1:5; 1 Cor. 2:8), while others did (John 1:14). And the reason why some saw him not is threefold: -1. They shut their own eyes (Acts 28:27). -2. The devil blinded their eyes (2 Cor. 4:4). -3. God blinded them (John 12:37-40).

Use 2. To reprove all Christians who are yet ignorant of Christ and know him not. They are now without excuse (2 Cor. 4:3; John 15:22). If the veil had still lain over Christ, there might have been some pretense, but now there is none.

Use 3. If Christ's first coming was such a manifestation of him, what a glorious manifestation his second coming will be (1 Cor. 13:12; 2 Cor. 3:18).

IV. The apostles saw this eternal life made manifest in the flesh.

The truth of this is apparent from John 1:14. The observations arising from hence are: -1. The truth of our Saviour's incarnation. -2. The blessedness of the apostles in seeing what others desired and could not; but of these we have spoken before.

V. The apostles bore witness and declared this eternal life unto the church of God.

The meaning of these two phrases, to bear witness to Christ and to declare him to the church, is one; they bore witness by declaring, and they declared by bearing witness. Hence it was that when he appointed them to declare and publish his gospel to all the world, he appointed them only to bear witness to him (Acts 1:8). Again, witnessing is put for declaring in Acts 20:21.

To confirm this proposition (not to heap many references to support a clear truth) take only two passages, Acts 10:34, 40, 41; Acts 5:32.

But how could the apostles bear witness to Christ, since he received not the testimony of men? (John 5:33, 34) The testimonies of men are of two sorts: for confirmation, and these the Saviour refuses, because he has greater (John 5: 36, 37), and for declaration; and these the Saviour embraces, appointing his disciples to that end. Had he wanted witnesses for confirmation, would he not rather have sent Solomon in all his royalty than poor fishermen? If therefore the Pope and his clergy were not greater than the apostles, they would not claim for themselves power to give authority to the Scriptures; for are not such men for confirmation?

But why would our Saviour have such poor and simple men to be his witnesses, and to declare and preach him, rather than Gamaliel and the other rabbins of the Jews?

-1. To magnify his power, for he was able to persuade the whole world to embrace him and his doctrine by such weak instruments (2 Cor. 4:7; Acts 4:13).

-2. To take away and prevent a slander, which might otherwise have been raised upon the gospel — that it had been the device of a man's brain, a human policy devised by great men to keep the rest in awe (1 Cor. 2:6, 8). Many profane atheists are ready now so to think and speak; how much more if great men and princes had embraced it and set it forward at first. At first Satan hindered religion by persuading the world that its professors were enemies of the state (Acts 16:20, 21); but when long experience proved that none were more faithful, now he goes about to persuade that princes devised it for their own ends.

-3. To teach all ministers, both how to become most able and sufficient preachers of the gospel, and how to deliver the gospel as to be most for God's glory. If learning and skill in human knowledge would have made us most able ministers of his gospel, he would either have chosen such to be his witnesses, or have made them so by instructing them during that three years when he abode with them. But he found them ignorant fishermen and left them thus, very raw and rude in knowledge, yea even of the principles of religion (Acts 1:8); and yet in one hour, fifty days later, by sending the Holy Spirit, he made them more able ministers than all the prophets before them. And again: being such simple men, the apostles were fitted to deliver it so as might be most for God's glory, not in excellency of words but in evidence of the Spirit (1 Cor. 2:4, 5). And therefore Paul, a learned man, imitated their simplicity (1 Cor. 2:12, 13).

Use 1. Behold then the great and fearful unthankfulness of the world, who put most of these men to death for declaring unto them eternal life.

Use 2. If the apostles show unto us eternal life, it is easy to discern how far from eternal life those must be, who do not receive their witness; alas, how many poor souls through the greatest part of the world, Jews, Turks, and all the rest of the pagans and infidels, are by this means cut off from all hope of eternal life! How true are our Saviour's words, many there are who go in the broad way to destruction (Matt. 7:13).

Use 3. Then how much to blame are the wolves (not shepherds) of the church of Rome, who shut and lock up from the people in a strange tongue the writings of the prophets and apostles! Is this not one way to bar them from eternal life?

Use 4. Then we are all to be exhorted diligently to be conversant in the writings of the apostles. What the Saviour said of the writings of the prophets (John 5:39), my text also says of the writings of the apostles; they bear witness of Christ and show us eternal life. Ministers most of all are to be conversant in their writings, because we succeed the apostles in bearing witness unto Christ; and we must declare him without differing from their message, or else we bring a curse upon our heads (Gal. 1:8).

Use 5. Then we are to praise the Lord's goodness unto us, for he has granted unto us their writings (as Ps. 147:12, 19, 20). It was a great preferment to the Jews to have the writings of the prophets (Rom. 3:1, 2); but their witness to Christ is much more dark and obscure than this of the apostles. Without their writings, we should but have groped after God (Acts 17:27); and as for Christ, this eternal life, we should never have dreamed of him. May the Lord make us more thankful and more careful to walk worthy of these blessings, lest he take them from us.

I John 1:3

"That, I say, which we have seen and heard, we declare unto you, that you also may have fellowship with us; and truly our fellowship is with the Father and with his Son Jesus Christ."

In these two verses we have of the apostles' doctrine: -1. The subject repeated, "That which we have seen and heard." -2. The subject declared. -3. Two ends: subordinate, fellowship with the apostles, and supreme, fullness of joy.

The subject is repeated for explanation or plainness, and for confirmation of what he had said before. He thrice repeats, "That which we have seen," and doubles, "That which we have heard," to show that he did not doubt of what he spoke, but was most confident and resolute in it.

Observe hence the certainty and undoubted truth of the doctrine of the apostles.

-1. The apostles taught nothing but what was manifest to their senses (2 Pet. 1:16). Sense took away doubting even from unbelieving Thomas (John 20:25-28).

-2. The apostle again and again repeats here that what they taught was manifest to their senses; now repetitions are for confirmation (Gen. 41:32; Gal. 1:8,9). This shows again how confident he was of it himself; therefore we should not be surprised at what he says (John 21:24).

-3. The efficacy of that doctrine, or the power of it, argues its certainty. For that doctrine which gives us union with God, communion with the saints of God, and fullness of joy in ourselves, must be a most certain doctrine of heavenly truth; there is no persuasion to settle a man's conscience greater than this.

-4. For a fourth reason, consider another branch of the power of this doctrine. The apostles who declared it were, for the most part, poor and simple and unlearned men; the doctrine itself was but of a crucified Saviour, harsh to carnal ears (1 Cor. 1:23). The times were such that it was not only everywhere spoken against (Acts 28:22), but also grievously persecuted throughout the Roman empire. And yet, so powerfully did it work that in the time of Tertullian (the next age after Christ) there were more Christians everywhere than of all other professions besides.

Use 1. If the apostles' doctrine were so certain that they preached nothing but what they had seen and heard, then we see why they were so bold and zealous and diligent in preaching (Acts 4:20; 2 Pet. 1:15,16). Fables are best at first hearing; but comfortable, sound and certain truths are more profitable the oftener they are heard.

Use 2. Then all of us are to receive their testimony, for upon this ground our Saviour complains bitterly for not being received (John 3:11), as does John Baptist (John 3:32).

Use 3. Then the children of God who repose their hopes

upon the apostles' doctrine may hence comfort themselves. We build not upon uncertainties, as those in Isa. 28:15; if our faith and hope were built upon the doctrines and traditions of men, we might justly fear and stand in doubt lest they might fail and deceive us in the end. But they are not.

Use 4. If the apostles preached nothing but what they were most certain of, then it must be our care also to preach to the people of God no uncertainties.

    a. We must preach nothing but what we have good warrant for from Scripture; for the scriptures are of certain truth (1 Cor. 4:6; Acts 26:27).

    b. We must have our hearts established with grace (Heb. 13:9; 2 Pet. 1:20, 21); for if no scripture is of any private interpretation; being written by the Spirit, they are by him best interpreted. See also 1 Cor. 2:11, 16, 17.

Then follow the ends of the apostles' writings, which are: -1. Fellowship with the apostles and disciples. -2. Union with God (v. 3). -3. Fullness of joy (v. 4).

Before we come to speak of these individually, some things may be gathered from them all jointly, touching the nature of the scriptures.

-1. The perfection of the Scripture. If the apostles declared what they had heard and seen, to the end that we might have fellowship with God and with them, and fullness of joy, then either they failed of their end, or else we by their doctrine (written for that purpose, v. 4) may have all things necessary for salvation. Yea, what is salvation itself but these very ends? Our Saviour calls it eternal life to know him (John 17:3); and what more comfortable knowledge of him than this? (This is a good conclusion of the whole Bible; for this gospel was written last of all, to stop the mouths of Ebion, Cerinthus, etc., who then began to urge human traditions in time of his banishment.) Hence also John 20:30. Let us away then with Popish traditions.

-2. The profit of the scripture. That doctrine by which we come to have such comfortable and excellent benefits (yea, none greater) must needs be of singular profit and goodness; yea, none greater (Matt. 16:26; Ps. 19:10). When we have found it to have wrought these heavenly things in us, we shall come to desire it, to practice it indeed, and to labor for these things by it.

-3. The power of the doctrines of the scripture. That which must bring us from having fellowship with Satan and the unfruitful works of darkness, to have fellowship with the saints, yea with God himself, and to enjoy fullness of joy — what admirable efficacy must it have! (Rom. 1:16; 2 Cor. 10:4). This word must needs be stronger than Satan (Luke 11:21, 22).

Use 1. This reproves the practice of those who will profess that the word of God takes place in them and has power in them; and yet they still keep their old fellowship with Satan, with the wicked of the world, and with the unfruitful works of darkness. See John 5:38.

Use 2. Then fellowship with God and with the saints, and fullness of joy may be obtained; else why did the apostles preach and write of Christ to that end? Satan keeps many from seeking these things, because they think them impossile to attain, as the Jews (John 6:52, 66). Though at first Nicodemus could not conceive such a mystery as this, yet at length he came to Jesus by night to have it explained, and his doctrine took place in him (John 3:9, 7:50, 52, 19:39).

Use 3. Then great reason have we all to attend to the doctrine of the apostles. Ministers especially are to be careful and diligent. "Preach the word, be instant" (2 Tim. 4:2; Eccl. 11:6).

"That you also might have fellowship with us, and truly our fellowship is with the Father and with his Son Jesus Christ."

In handling these three ends of the apostles' doctrine, communion with saints, union with God, and fullness of joy, it is to be shown: -1. What each of them is in its order. -2. How the apostles' doctrine procures them for us.

-3. Some uses for each one.

By fellowship 'with us,' the apostle means himself and all the saints of God.

I. The communion of the saints is a spiritual conjunction of the saints with Jesus Christ and one another, in which Christ partakes of our infirmities, and we in common partake of benefits and communicate them to one another.

-1. I call it a spiritual conjunction, to distinguish it from: (a) Natural, as the three persons of the Trinity are joined in one nature and essence. (b) Personal, as the two natures of Christ are in one person. (c) Moral, as man and wife are in law one flesh by God's ordinance. For this is a conjunction of men's persons, not by an outward bond (such as God's ordinance is to marriage) but by an inward bond, one Spirit resting in Christ above measure and in the saints according to their measure (1 Cor. 6:17; 1 Jhn 4:13; Rom. 8:9). Hence it is that the same mind is in us which was in Christ (Phil. 2:5), and all the members are alike affected and disposed toward God, Christ, their own sins, good works, and one another.

-2. I call it the communion of saints. Now by saints I do not mean only saints canonized by the Pope, nor only the saints departed, but the saints also on earth; for their conjunction with Christ and with one another is mentioned in John 15:5; Eph. 5:30; 1 Cor. 12:13; John 17:20, 21.

-3. Christ partakes of our infirmities. And the infirmities of which he takes part are of three sorts: (a) Of nature, flesh, and blood (Heb. 2:14; Phil. 2:7). (b) Of corruption, all our sins being imputed to him (2 Cor. 5:21; 1 Pet. 2:24). (c) Of condition, taking all our afflictions and miseries (Acts 9:4; Col. 1:24).

-4. We in this communion partake of Christ's benefits. Now these are six: (a) Adoption (Gal. 4:4-6); hence we are said in the text to have fellowship with God. (b) The righteousness of Christ imputed (2 Cor. 5:21). The Papists deride this, thinking it the same as saying one man may be wise or learned by another man's wisdom, but Christ was not another man to us. (c) Holiness (1 Cor. 1:30), which stands in mortification (Rom. 6:6) and in vivification or fruitfulness (John 15:5). Creatures which are dead all winter live again when they lie in the sun at springtime. (d) Protection of angels (Ps. 91:11, 12; Heb. 1:14). (e) Dominion over the creatures (Heb. 2:7, 8; 1 Cor. 3:22, 23). (f) The right to a glorious inheritance (Gal. 4:7; Col. 1:12).

-5. We communicate these benefits to one another. (a) In heart, mutually praying for one another (Eph. 6:18). Hence a Christian man, as a rich merchant, has agents dealing for him with God in every country. (b) In voice, by mutual instruction (2 Tim. 2:25, 26; Acts 18:25, 26) and mutual reproof (Gal. 6:1, 2), and mutual consolation (1 Thess. 5:14). (c) In action, by a good example of Christian life (Matt. 5:16; Phil. 2:15) and by liberal bestowing of outward things upon them (Gal. 6:10).

Now since it is a spiritual conjunction of the saints with Christ and one with another, this communion is compared to marriage (Eph. 5:23, 30) and vine-branch nourishment (John 15:5). Since it is a communicating of our goods to one another, it is a brotherhood (Col. 1:3).

II. How does the apostles' doctrine procure and preserve this union and communion? By these means:

-1. By making known to us that by nature we were strangers and enemies to God (Col. 1:21; Acts 26:18; Eph. 2:2; 2 Tim. 2:26). This fellowship which all natural men have with Satan consists in three things. (a) In resemblance. Both sin with one continued act (1 John 3:8; John 8:44; Acts 13:10), and they have fellowship one with another. (b) In subjection of the natural man to the government and guidance of Satan (Eph. 2:2; Tim. 2:26). All God's children are led by his Spirit (Rom. 8:14); so natural men are led by that wicked spirit. He works first upon the mind, deluding and blinding them (2 Cor. 4:4), and then he carries the heart and affections whither it pleases him (John 13:27; Eph. 2:2). (c) In undergoing the same punishment (Matt. 25:41).

-2. By working upon our hearts a remorse (κατανύσσω) of conscience with the knowledge of this (Acts 2:37). (This word remorse, κατάνυξις, is translated 'slumber' and used in a contrary sense in Rom. 11:8, where it signifies not compunction, but the deep slumber in which natural men feel no compunction. The spirit thus afflicted is called wounded (Prov. 18:14), broken (Ps. 51:17), weary (Matt. 11: 28). This remorse comes not alike to all; to some it is more terrible and makes a deeper impression (Job 6:2-4; 13:24); to others it is not so grievous, as to Lydia (Acts 16:14, 15).

But why must we be thus wounded before we are made whole? (a) To make us like Christ, for he was so (Matt. 26: 37; Luke 22:44; Matt. 27:46), and we must be like him (Rom. 8:29). (b) To make us value Christ and his benefits at a higher rate (Matt. 9:12; Prov. 27:7). The lack of this is the reason why Christ is so little esteemed among many (c) To tame our wanton hearts, and make us more pliable to the yoke of Christ and to any course of service which he shows (Acts 9:6; 16:30; 2:37). Our Saviour can soon persuade heavy-laden and weary souls to think that his yoke is easy and his burden light, when they have felt the burden of sin. How heavy is sin! (Ps. 38:4) But it is a hard matter to persuade others to think so.

-3. By revealing Christ unto us and working in our hearts a sound and earnest desire to seek and enjoy him (Matt. 5:6). And because Christ is ours only by faith (John 3:16) and faith is ours only by the Holy Spirit, therefore we must not rest until, by pouring out our earnest desires to God, we have obtained him (Luke 11:13).

-4. The same doctrine works faith, by which we are united to Christ (Rom. 10:17; Gal. 3:7).

III. The uses are three.

Use 1. Hence then it is easy to discern what state natural men are in, out of fellowship with God and his saints. If by nature we had fellowship with them, why should we need the apostles' doctrine to bring us to it? Those who defy the devil in their own strength, and cannot bear to hear that they ever had any fellowship with him, have as yet no fellowship with God.

Use 2. Then fellowship with God and his saints is a thing that may be attained. Satan deludes men to the contrary as an effectual means to keep them from seeking it.

Use 3. Then all have great cause with diligence to attend upon the apostles' doctrine, for it is the power of God unto salvation (Rom. 1:16).

1 John 1:4

"And these things we write unto you, that your joy may be full."

For the meaning of these words, note: -1. what is here meant by joy; -2. How this joy is said to be full.

I. What is here meant by joy?

Some by joy understand that glorious state of delight and pleasure which the saints in heaven enjoy, and which we ourselves hope for after this life, according to the promise (Ps. 16:11); but here I take to be meant that joy in the Holy Spirit which those who have fellowship with Christ enjoy in this life (though the former is not excluded, but follows upon the other). The reasons why I think so are two.

-1. Though there is fullness of joy in heaven, yet to my remembrance heaven is nowhere in scripture called full of joy. Yea, in the apostle's writing there is another on this side heaven which is called full joy (John 15:11, 16:24).

-2. Now since fullness of joy is a purpose of St. John in writing, what he intends may easily be conjectured by the means he uses to procure it to us. Now if you will notice, the whole course of his writing is really nothing else but laying down certain marks by which we may examine ourselves and discern whether we have fellowship with God or not; whether we are in the state of grace or not. See 1:6-9; 2:3. Now these marks do not so directly tend to procure us fullness of joy in heaven, as to settle our hearts now in the assurance that we are in the state of grace. So by full joy I understand the apostle to mean joy in the Holy Spirit.

What is this joy?

Joy in the Holy Spirit is a spiritual affection arising from peace of conscience, by which we rejoice in our union with Christ with joy unspeakable and full of glory. Or joy in the Holy Spirit is a spiritual affection by which the heart is unspeakably and gloriously enlarged and ravished upon the solid apprehension of union and communion with Christ.

-1. It is a spiritual joy, not only because the objects of it are spiritual good things (union with Christ) and the benefits which we reap from it (adoption, righteousness, holiness, protection of angels, dominion over the creatures, a right to a glorious inheritance); but also and principally, it is spiritual because it is wrought in us by the Holy Spirit. Hence it is called joy in the Holy Ghost (Rom. 14:17); hence he is called the Comforter (John 15:26). When God and Christ are said to dwell in the hearts of faithful men, nothing else is meant but the Holy Spirit dwelling in them and working this joy (John 14:23; Rev. 3:20; John 14:8 compared with John 16:7, 22).

-2. This joy arises from peace of conscience (Rom. 14:17; Rom. 5:1-3). Now peace of conscience is a work of the Holy Spirit which arises from being conscious of our righteousness or our justification before God; for to be justified before God is not enough to pacify the conscience, unless it is felt. See David's example (Ps. 51:8-12).

-3. By this joy we receive our union with Christ (1 Pet. 1:8,;', whom we do believe and rejoice, yea rejoice in him whose we are by faith (Gal. 6:4). This is also shown in that it arises from peace and peace in turn arises from righteousness, by union with Christ.

-4. This union is with joy unspeakable and glorious (1 Pet. 1:8). These words may seem to express some accidental things to this joy; because the nature of it cannot be well declared in itself, these words outline the nature of it. This joy is unspeakable, because, like bodily health, it is better felt than expressed. It is glorious, because it is a glimpse of the glory and joy of heaven. Hence the Spirit who works it is called "the earnest of our inheritance" (Eph. 1:14). It is glorious too, because it triumphs gloriously against all causes of grief and sorrow (Rom. 5:3; Acts 20: 23, 24).

II. How is this joy said to be full?

-1. In opposition to that joy which arises from the things of this life; this is more full than that (Ps. 4:6, 7). The joys of this world are empty joys when compared to those of the next, as witness: (a) The variety of them. If there were full joy to be had by them, what need we seek for variety? Why does the bee suck so many flowers, if she could find honey enough in one? (b) The mixture of sorrow in them. (c) The shortness of them. That which would be full joy to an eternal soul must be eternal, whereas these are not.

-2. In opposition to that lesser joy which Christians have in Christ Jesus, but yet it is often eclipsed and in the wane through manifold doubtings of our state (1 Pet. 1:6).

III. Uses of the whole.

Use 1. If full joy may be had by the apostles' doctrine, then there is no need of traditions; if joy may be full by the word written, what then can they add?

Use 2. Then they who seek joy in earthly things embrace an empty shadow of joy, an empty pit (Jer. 2:13). Though the stars should shine always to us, yet if we had no greater light, still we should have continual darkness.

Use 3. Then the hearty embracing of the apostles' writings and finding the fruits of them, brings not melancholy and dumpishness, as the world thinks, but fullness of joy.

Use 4. Then let us search the apostles' writings and find full joy in them. This our Saviour teaches us (John 5:39).

1 John 1:5

"This then is the message which we have heard of him, and declare unto you, that God is light, and in him is no darkness at all."

In the four former verses we had the apostles' doctrine, or the doctrine of the gospel, described: -1. By the subjects of it, Christ Jesus in his human and divine nature (vv. 1, 2). -2. By the ends of it; subordinate, communion with God (v. 3) and supreme, fullness of joy (v. 4). Here the same doctrine is described: -1. By a triple adjunct of it. It is: (a) A message, (b) Heard of Christ, (c) Declared to the church. -2. It is also described by part of the content of it: "God is light, and in him is no darkness."

The second and third points have been spoken of before (vv. 1, 2). The parts then of these words are two: -1. The nature of the doctrine of the gospel. It is a message. -2. The nature of God: he is light, and in him is no darkness at all.

Doct. 1. The doctrine of the gospel is a message.

This appears: -1. By the title of it, Evangelium, a good message (Rom. 10:16). -2. By the names of the penmen of it, Evangelists, bearers of good tidings. -3. By the names of the first preachers of it. They were Apostles, Messengers (Rom. 10:15), Tidings-bearers of good things. -4. By the names of the later ministers of it to this day. They are Angels (Rev. 2:1), that is, Messengers (Job 33:23).

Observations here concerning ministers are these.

-1. If the gospel or the apostles' doctrine is a message, then it does not receive its authority from such as deliver it; for it is not the messenger's part to judge or ratify his message, but rather to declare it.

Use. Against the Papists, who make their judges and clergy to be judges of the scriptures.

-2. Then ministers are not to run with the gospel in their mouths, before they are sent (Rom. 10:15; Heb. 5:4; Exod. 4:10-13; Jer. 1:6). This is not spoken to quench the timely zeal of those who, furnished and sanctified with gifts, undertake the function when they are called, for the prophet Isaiah offered himself when his lips were touched (Isa. 6:8). Likewise Paul immediately (Gal. 1:16). This observation, however, is given to stay the too soon ripe forwardness of such as run on the Lord's errand before he sends them.

-3. Then ministers are to be well instructed in the knowledge of the gospel (Mal. 2:7). Else we shall run without our errand, as Ahimaaz did (2 Sam. 18:22, 23, 29), and so we shall bring nothing but confused tumultuous notions.

-4. Then ministers are to be faithful in delivery (Prov. 13:17, 25:13); which stands in two things. -1. In delivering their whole message (as Paul, Acts 20:26, 27) and no more (Jer. 23:28; Prov. 30:6). -2. In applying it as the sender intended.

Use. To refute the Papists, who add traditions to their message, and against those who deliver no message at all, who make the hearts of the righteous sad (see Ezek. 13:22).

-5. Then ministers are to be diligent (Prov. 10:26). The Lord's errand is his work, which when negligently done brings a curse (Jer. 48:10; though that be to kill, yet this to save). Sloth makes waste in every work (Prov. 18:9); so here especially it makes waste of souls (Prov. 29:18).

-6. If the apostles' doctrine is the Lord's message, then purity is needful in the messengers. That mouth should not be given to rotten and unsavory speeches, which is the Lord's interpreter to the people. All the vessels of the ministry to the Lord were holy in the old tabernacle; how much more ought the ministers who are chosen vessels unto him? Earthen vessels they are indeed (2 Cor. 4:7); yet when they are clean and sweet, we do not despise to eat and drink from them.

-7. Then the apostles' doctrine, the doctrine of the gospel, must not be received as the doctrine of men, but as a message from God; and that is: (a) With attentive hearts. (b) With reverence (Judg. 3:20; Ps. 66:2). (c) With believing and faithful hearts (Acts 27:25; Heb. 4:2; Luke 1:45).

Doct. 2. God is light, and in him is no darkness at all.

The parts of these words are two: -1. The condition of

God: "he is light." -2. The perfection or purity of that condition: "in him is no darkness." In opening the meaning of the words, I must show you: -1. In what respect God is called 'light.' -2. Why it is added, "In him is no darkness at all."

-1. For the first, there are three attributes of light. (a) It is bright and shining. Hence it is put for knowledge (Matt. 4:16; Eccl. 2:13). Hence ministers having knowledge are called lights (Matt. 5:14; Rom. 2:19). (b) It is pure and clear; thus it is used to picture purity and holiness of life (2 Cor. 6:14; Matt. 5:16). Your light is your doctrine and holy life; hence also godly men are called lights for their holy conversation (Phil. 2:15). (c) It is pleasant and cheerful (Eccl. 11:7). Thus it is put for joy and comfort (Ps. 112:4).

Now God is said to be light in all these three respects, but the last is not here intended. A man may have fellowship with God without walking always in joy and cheerfulness, but we cannot have fellowship if we walk in ignorance and uncleanness.

God is said to be light for two reasons: (a) He is so in himself. He knows all things (Heb. 4:13; Ps. 147:5), and he is holy (Lev. 11:44; Hab. 1:13). (b) He is said to be light because he makes us so; men of knowledge, scattering the darkness of ignorance (Ps. 91:10), and holy men (Lev. 20:8). Hence at our first creation, God's image consisted in knowledge (Col. 3:10) and holiness (Eph. 4:24). And by our regeneration we are again made light (Eph. 5:8).

God is not said to be light metaphorically, because these things are in him, but properly, because he is light, that is, wisdom and holiness itself. For God is essentially knowledge, and so his holiness is himself.

-2. In God is said to be no darkness at all. This is spoken: (a) To confirm what he said before, for so St. John usually, as soon as he affirms a truth, denies the contrary falsehood (1 John 4:2-3, 7-8). As Pharaoh's repeated dreams, these repeated statements are for confirmation (Gen. 41:32; Gal.

1:8, 9). (b) By way of opposition to our knowledge (1 Cor. 13:12) and holiness (1 John 1:8).

Use 1. Observe God's simplicity of nature; he is in the light, the light is in him; he is light itself, which shows that whatever is in him is himself. Though light is in the sun, yet the sun is not light itself.

Use 2. Then no wonder if we cannot see the full wisdom of the ways of God; who can look upon the sun in its full strength? Yet the sun is not light itself; whose eyes will not be dazzled by his glorious light? (1 Tim. 6:16;;Rom. 11:33, 34).

Use 3. If in God's light there is not a dram of darkness or ignorance, then he knows all things (John 21:17). Four things especially: (a) Events (Isa. 41:2 , 23; 44:7); and therefore he is not subject to after counsels. From this we know that though God is said to repent, as of creating man and choosing Saul, yet both are said as of a man, when he went about to do otherwise (Gen. 6:6; 1 Sam. 15:11; Numb. 23:19). How needful then is it to consult with him and seek his direction in all our counsels! (b) The most secret sins that are committed (Ps. 139:11, 12; Isa. 29:15). (c) The inmost heart of man (Jer. 17:9, 10); how vain then is the hypocrite! How he dances in a net before God (Heb. 4:13; 1 Sam. 16:7). (d) The wants of his children (Matt. 6:32); hence we are eased of destructful and distrustful care (v. 31).

Use 4. Then those who live in ignorance and uncleanness are without God in the world, for he is light (Eph. 4:18, 19); then we are to labor to be light, in all manner of knowledge and holy conversation (1 Pet. 1:15, 16).

Use 5. Then we are to seek to him to enlighten our darkness; he is the fountain of light, light itself; he alone scatters the mists of our darkness, ignorance, and pollutions (Ps. 119:33; Ps. 5:8).

1 John 1:6

"If we say that we have fellowship with him, and walk in darkness, we lie, and do not the truth."

In the first four verses St. John had declared the subject of his doctrine, and his purpose in writing them of it. The subject was God-man; that which was seen and heard was man, the word of life, both God and man. The end of his doctrine was also double: -1. Subordinate, to bring Christians on to fellowship with the apostles; and lest they should despise them, he tells them their fellowship was not base; it was with the Father and his Son Jesus Christ. -2. The supreme and main end was that their joy might be full. Fullness of joy in the Spirit is the main end and purpose of this epistle.

Then in ver. 5 he comes to a particular of that subject which he had handled before in general. He tells them one thing that he had heard of Christ, and that was that God is light, and in him is no darkness at all; this was one part of the message he was to deliver.

Some understand it of Christ; so he is called the Light that enlightens everyone that comes into the world (John 1:9); but he here speaks of Christ as the Son of that light, and therefore he speaks here of the Father. We have heard that God is light, and in him is no darkness.

Now we come to the application of it. Desiring to train them up in the fullness of joy, he desires to clear all doubts; therefore this is his method. He tells you of some things he heard from Christ, and then he gives signs of their fellowship with Christ, so that everyone might know what part he has in this joy.

From this St. John gathers a double note of our fellowship with God, by which we may know it, that our joy may be full (v. 6). Negatively, for if God is light, then he who says he has fellowship with God and yet walks in darkness is a liar. Then on the other side affirmatively (v. 7). If we walk in the light, we have fellowship with one another, and so with God.

Doctrine 1. Opinion and profession of fellowship with God is no certain sign of true fellowship with him; opinion of religion is no certain sign of religion.

"If we say." Now saying includes three things: -1. To think; a man may say it in his heart, when he thinks so, and that is his opinion. "The fool hath said in his heart, There is no God." (Ps. 14:1; see also Exod. 2:14; Ps. 30:6). -2. To speak in outward words. -3. In outward manner, to make show and profession in walking (Rom. 1:22). All these are meant here; to carry oneself as if one were a Christian, and yet to walk in darkness, is hypocrisy. "Not everyone who says, Lord, lord" (Matt. 7:21-23). It is not thinking nor saying that carries it, nor walking so outwardly; for we may do so and still have no fellowship with Christ.

Why is profession of Christianity no sign of grace?

-1. Because opinion may spring from presumption, as Haman's opinion that the king would honor no man as much as himself (Esther 6:6). Many times out of self-love, we think we wish well to God and he to us, when there is no such matter in truth.

-2. Opinion may spring from common graces, such as may be in hypocrites (Matt. 7:21-23). They wondered why they were not received, because they had done many good works and prophesied in his name, and cast out devils, etc., and therefore they doubted not that they would be accepted; so from these common gifts we often have a good conceit of ourselves that God will accept us.

And for outward appearance, a man may so conduct himself as if he were a good Christian. -1. A man may profess religion for worldly respects, as many became Jews (Esther 8:17). It may be for fear of the laws, or friends; many loved Christ for loaves, for profit, because there is fullness in Christ (John 6:26). -2. Common graces may make us profess religion; as a man that has been enlarged at the world, he is willing to come to it; as those in John 5:35, who were yet thorns (Mark 4:18) and the stony ground. -3. Some are drawn on through mere compulsion of conscience, and yet live in darkness; some have gifts of prayer and preaching and zeal, as Jehu had, and joy in the word as Herod; yet, because they walked in darkness, they had no fellowship with God.

Use 1. A ground of comfort to those who are afraid that they are hypocrites, and are much discouraged, and think they have no fellowship with God. If there are some who say they have fellowship with the Father and have none, so contrarily there are some who think and say they have no fellowship with him, and yet may have.

Use 2. It confutes the Papists, who say we teach that men's opinion is faith, and a man is justified by persuasion. But we do not say that every opinion and persuasion is a good argument for justifying faith, but only that kind of persuasion and opinion that is built upon God's testimony, upon the testimony of the Word and Spirit. Otherwise we say many a man's persuasion is built on selflove or some common graces.

Use 3. It may teach us to consider seriously whether we are well grounded, for a man may be deceived in it. If we say we have fellowship and yet walk in darkness, we lie. A man would hardly be comforted with a piece of gold in such a condition; what are thousands of gold and silver, what is it to have his estate current and body strong, and to have his heart unsound and counterfeit — all current but his own soul. What greater confusion is there than the cutting off of a man's hopes? For a man to live all his days in a good hope, and at death to have his hopes to fail him, this confounds his spirit; therefore take not for gold all that glitters.

Use 4. It teaches us not forthwith to be deluded with the opinion of another, but consider whether they are not deceived whom he takes to be good, or sound whom he takes to be hypocrites. Do not easily take them to be our brethren and sisters who carry a show; the church never had more wrong than by false brethren who have spied out their liberty and informed against them. Take not every professor for a brother; men may say they have fellowship with God, and yet walk in darkness; therefore take heed of entertaining such into your good opinion and fellowship.

It was a commendable practice of the apostles (Acts 9:26) not to admit Paul easily; and it is commonly said, if a man or woman carries a Bible or comes to good duties, why, they begin to be esteemed; but others who make not such a show are less respected.

Doct. 2. A life led in ignorance and uncleanness is a certain sign of hypocrisy; a profession of religion joined with a life led in ignorance and ungodliness, is a sure sign of hypocrisy.

Darkness implies both ignorance and ungodliness; darkness has a fourfold signification. -1. Sometimes it is put for ignorance (Matt. 4:16). -2. It is put for profaneness and ungodliness; every sin is called darkness (2 Cor. 6:14; Eph. 5:8). -3. Sometimes it is put for horror of conscience and confusion of spirit (Isa. 50:10). -4. Sometimes for obscurity, dishonor, and desolation (Prov. 20:12).

The last two are not meant here. -1. A man may walk in much discomfort and yet have fellowship with God (Isa. 50:10). "The bruised reed will he not break" (Matt. 12:20). A man in such a condition walks in darkness, and yet God will not break and quench such. -2. Many a child of God walks in much dishonor and baseness, and yet has fellowship with God (1 Cor. 4:13; Ps. 22:6). David complains he was a worm and no man, a reproach and scorn of men, and yet was a good man and had fellowship with God. Therefore it cannot be meant of these two, for those who are in such a condition are ordinarily most sound and sincere, whereas others with more comfort walk more loosely and carelessly.

But if we live in uncleanness or ignorance, we have no fellowship with God (Prov. 19:2). God is a God of light, omniscient, and how can he have fellowship with God, if he has no light in him? (Hos. 4:6, "My people perish for want of knowledge.") Ignorance is a certain note of destruction. "Where no vision is, the people perish" (Prov. 29:18), that is, where there is no means of seeing (Matt. 15:14).

Why are ignorance and ungodliness signs of hypocrisy?

-1. Where there is no knowledge, the light of the word is lacking. Ignorance cannot stand with the fellowship of God. Now the word is a light and a lantern; one in a house cannot do work without light, especially a stranger who knows not what to do; so a man is a stranger within himself if he has no light; and how can he order himself, tell what to do, if he has no light in him? Many think their states good; but if they had light, they would not think so. Others think their states bad, but cannot get out of this; they have no light to get out of it, and therefore cannot have fellowship with God.

-2. Uncleanness and ungodliness cannot stand with the fellowship of God (2 Cor. 6:14; Ps. 94:20; Ps. 5:4. Hab. 1:13).

a. Because of the nature of God, who is of pure eyes and cannot endure to behold any iniquity.

b. Because of the power of all saving graces; they purify and cleanse the heart. So faith purifies the heart (Acts 15:9); so hope (1 John 3:3), so love; you who love God depart from iniquity.

c. Because of the power of the Spirit in him who has fellowship with God (1 Cor. 6:17; Ezek. 36:27).

Use 1. It shows that ignorance is no mother of devotion, for what is devotion but a stricter and nearer fellowship with God? It shows therefore the dangerous state of wicked ignorant men, who think their ignorance will plead for them; but they are deceived. "Through want of knowledge my people perish"; God takes no pleasure in fools. You may think you have fellowship with God and yet live in ignorance and darkness, but you deceive yourself. Can a man live in the sun and have neither light nor heat? So what fellowship has that man with God, who has neither light of knowledge nor warmth of grace from him?

Use 2. It may be a trial of our state. If we have no knowledge of God, we have no fellowship with him. It is true, many there are who desire knowledge and yet cannot attain it; and regarding such, God will accept of their desire or give them knowledge; but such as please themselves in their ignorance have no fellowship with God (2 Tim. 2:21). They are sealed up to damnation. If a man walks in darkness and says he has fellowship with God, he lies.

Who then can say his heart is clean? Have not the best of God's children their failings? I answer, it is true they have their failings, but do they walk in them? It is one thing to step into a way, and another thing to walk in that way. David stepped into the way of adultery and murder, but he did not continue in it. A man who walks in a good way may be turned out of it by a wild beast or a storm or carelessness, but when he sees he is wrong, he turns into the right path again. So it is with a godly heart; he may be carried out of the way by the violence of temptation, etc., but he returns again as soon as he sees his error.

Use 3. To teach men, if ever they desire to have fellowship with God, to cleanse themselves from ignorance and ungodliness. If you desire to have fellowship with God, you must: (a) Avoid ignorance and labor for knowledge; desire to know his will, and they who love light are loved by God. (b) Do not turn aside to any dark crooked way (Ps. 125:5). The Israel of God have no crooked ways to walk in (2 Cor. 6:17, 18 with 7:1). This scripture shows us that if we desire fellowship with God, we must look into all dark corners and cast out all uncleanness; and if you do thus strive to reform yourself, you are not in darkness. If you cleanse yourself from dark and crooked and unclean ways, you may assure yourself that you have fellowship with God.

1 John 1:7

"But if we walk in the light as he is in the light, we have fellowship one with another; and the blood of Jesus Christ cleanses us from all our sins."

The scope of the apostle St. John was to deliver what he had heard and seen from Christ; to this end, that their joy might be full.

His first message was that God is light (v. 5); and from there he gathers a certain sign of our fellowship with God, or lack of it. He lays down a sign of the lack in v. 6, "He who walks in darkness has no fellowship with him." Now in the seventh verse he lays down a sign of our enjoying this fellowship with God.

In this verse we have two parts: -1. A certain sign of our fellowship with God, namely, "if we walk in the light." -2. The privilege of such a state, "the blood of Christ cleanses us from our sins;" so here is the mark of a true Christian, and his privilege.

Doct 1. To walk in the light is a certain mark of true fellowship with God; that is, God's fellowship with us, and ours with him.

But what is light? Light is sometimes taken for light of knowledge, holiness, comfort, glory. -1. It is taken for light of knowledge (Matt. 4:16). Light is clear, and so is knowledge. -2. It is taken sometimes for light of holiness (Eph. 5:8). Light is clean; so is holiness. -3. Sometimes for comfort (Ps. 97:11). -4. For glory. Now darkness is contrary to all these; so to walk in the light is to walk in the ways of knowledge, purity, comfort, and glory.

What is it to walk? It is commonly taken for the whole course of a Christian life, but in figurative speech the term is very significant. It implies: -1. That a Christian course is a voluntary motion. A man is not said to walk if he is pulled and dragged; there is no motion more voluntary than walking. -2. It is a continued motion; not a step or two can make a walk. -3. Walking gains ground. Standing still covers no ground, but walking does; so a Christian goes about Christian duties not only voluntarily but continually. He grows up in them. Is this not implied in the doctrine? To lead a Christian course voluntarily, continually, and increasingly, is a sign of fellowship with God. Now that those who thus walk do have fellowship with God is evident. "Ye were sometimes darkness, but now ye are light in the Lord; walk therefore as children of light" (Eph. 5:8); that is, children of God, for God is light. Those who walk in truth and not in error and heresy, they are children of God (Ps. 1:1, 2). The law of God is the way of holiness and truth; and if he who walks in the way is blessed, then he has fellowship with God, for in his fellowship is all blessedness (Ps. 119:1, 2).

There are two reasons to establish the doctrine:

-1. Our nature is insufficient to walk in these ways without the Spirit of God in us and directing us (Ezek. 36:27; John 15:5). Without Christ we can do nothing (Hos. 14:8); if any good fruit is growing in a Christian it is from the Spirit of God; otherwise the fruit of a carnal fruit is carnal (John 3:6). We cannot be holy without God's Holy Spirit, nor bring forth any good fruit. Further, as we cannot be good without his Spirit, so we cannot do good without him (2 Cor. 3:5). Christ thinks it an impossible thing for a carnal man's heart to be well (Matt. 15:19).

-2. Such as do walk in light have recovered the image of God. Now this image consisted in light (John 1:4), light of knowledge and holiness (Col. 3:10; Eph. 4:24). The fellowship which Adam had with God in paradise, the same also have all who walk in the ways of truth and holiness.

But one will say, Do you not see many true Christians who have true grace and yet walk in much darkness; how then do they have fellowship with God? "He who fears the Lord, and hearkens to the voice of his servants, who walks in darkness, and sees no light" (Isa. 50:10); this, it is said, shows that a man may still fear the Lord and hearken to the voice of his servants, and still walk in darkness. I answer, such a one walks not in any gross ignorance, or error and heresy, or in darkness of uncleanness and profaneness; but he may walk in darkness and discomfort and dishonor, and yet have true fellowship with God. No Christian walks more in light than they who walk most in darkness; those who walk most discouraged walk more carefully and fearfully, whereas many who walk in more comfort walk more loosely and scandalously.

But why must they walk in discomfort if they walk in the light? Does not all discomfort arise from ignorance, from not knowing their own state and God's nature and love towards them? I answer, it is true that they walk in darkness, and that is the reason they walk so uncomfortably; for if they were truly enlightened in the nature of God and their own state, they would have more comfort. But yet this is no affected ignorance, but ignorance of infirmity and weakness and lack of experience. It is one thing to be in a way, and quite another thing to walk in that way; such a man does not walk in that darkness because it is not voluntary; neither is it continual, but at length he grows to be further enlightened.

Use 1. Of refutation against the Papists, who say we deny good works. We do disclaim all works as any cause or merit of justification (Ps. 130:3); but we do not disclaim good works in themselves. We do not discourage any from good works, but indeed encourage them. Is this no encouragement to walk in the light, when we say that all such shall have fellowship with God and be cleansed by the blood of Christ? These are strong motives to good works. We maintain good works (as the apostle says) for necessary uses (Tit. 3:14).

What are these necessary uses? -1. For us, that we may have fellowship with God. -2. To glorify God (Matt. 5:16, "Let your good works so shine before men," etc.) -3. To stop slanders of vain men (Tit. 1:11). -4. To lead others by our good works to a Christian course. A good conversation is a good means of the conversion of others.

We further say that good works justify us, in St. James' sense (James 2:14). There is a double justification: -1. Of a man from sin in the sight of God. -2. Of a Christian from hypocrisy in the sight of both God and man. In the first way a man is justified only by the blood of Christ; in the second way he may be justified by good works. For we know that a man's conscience has two burdens: -1. "My sins are great and liable to damnation; how shall I be freed from that?" From this our own works cannot justify us; it is done only by the blood of Christ. -2. "Yes, but the blood of Christ cleanses only true Christians who are in Christ and have true grace. But I am a hypocrite; how shall I be free from the imputation of hypocrisy?" From that I am justified by my good works. Let it appear to myself and others that I have lived in all uprightness (2 Cor. 1:12). Thus my justification from hypocrisy before God and man is by the witness of my upright and unblameable life, so that I am justified 6rom a double accusation, from the one by the one way, from the other by a second way. I am a sinner; that I cannot deny; my best works are sinful, and therefore I can be justified from sin only by the blood of Christ.

But Christ's blood does not belong to you, if you are a hypocrite. Now how shall you know the sincerity of faith but from the fruits, that is, a holy and righteous life? If we walk so, we justify ourselves from that imputation. How does Hezekiah defend himself when God spoke bitter things? "Remember how I have walked before thee with an upright heart" (1 Kings 3:6). Therefore we say that a holy life is an evident sign of our fellowship with God; it glorifies God, it stops slanders and leads to the conversion of others. And above all, it will justify us from hypocrisy.

Use 2. To try whether we have fellowship with God or not. We do, if we walk in the light (Isa. 50:10). If a man walks in light of truth and holiness, in knowledge of God's will and obedience to it; if he continues in it and grows in grace, and goes forward from step to step, from strength to strength (Ps. 84:11), it is a true sign of fellowship with God. There is no corrupt nature that can have such desires, at least not continue and grow up in them.

But may a Christian not be carried out of his way, as David into adultery, Noah into drunkenness, and Peter into denial of Christ? Yes, they were indeed ways of darkness, but: -1. They did not turn to them voluntarily, but through violence of temptation and corruption. -2. They continued not in them. -3. They did not grow up in them; that is, they took no pleasure in them. A man is not judged by a step or two, but according to his walk and the whole drift of his course. He may take a step or two out of the way, but yet if he recovers himself, we say the other is his way. God does not judge of a man's spirit by a step or two, for then who could be justified? There is no Christian but sometimes steps awry, and it may be three or four steps; as David, into idleness, into adultery, into drunkenness, into murder (2 Sam. 11). So on the contrary, a wicked man may take a step or two into a godly course; he may read some good book, pray, hear the word. Thus there cannot be a just judgment of a man on either part by a step or two, but we must judge of men by their walks.

If a man's Christian course is voluntary, constant, and growing, a step or two out of the way will not condemn him. The wise men came a long journey to seek Christ, and went out of their way to Jerusalem to inquire. But when the star left them, they did not stay there, but went to their way again; and then the star appeared to them again. So when a godly man goes to seek Christ, yet he may turn out of the way and leave God's word; yet he does not stay there but goes into the way again, and then he has God's word to direct him once more.

Will you judge a man to be good if he is in good company? Many a man will go out of his way for company's sake; so we must not judge what they do by a start, but by their constant voluntary growing course; what way they hold to, that is their way. The heart of a good man in evil company is not quiet; it is no voluntary motion; and so with the wicked in good company.

Use 3. This will teach men not to content themselves in any ignorance or uncleanness or wicked course. You cannot walk in darkness and have fellowship with God; therefore if you would claim fellowship with God, disclaim fellowship with sin.

Use 4. To teach Christians that it is not enough to be holy and true, but God requires that you should walk in light and holiness (Eph. 5:8; Gal. 5:25). If you would be a man of knowledge and piety, it is needful that you walk in that course.

It is not enough to set an instrument in tune, but it must sound forth; it is not enough to have our hearts in a good frame, but we must walk in that frame. "Thy word is a lamp unto my feet, and a light unto my path" (Ps. 119:105). What, to look upon? No, but to be a guide to his steps. We should order our steps according to his word. A Christian must not only have gifts and graces, but walk accordingly. He is a distempered Christian who has the feet of a Christian and yet walks not. He is only the image of a Christian. An image has the exact parts of a man, but makes no use of them. It has eyes and sees not, ears and hears not, feet and walks not (Ps. 115:5-7). So he is only the image of a Christian, he who has parts and gifts and does not walk accordingly.

Use 5. Of comfort to such Christians as are walking and doing, though they cannot go on as fast as they would. A man who walks does not go as fast as he who gallops; but yet if you only walk in a good way, you do make progress, and you shall come to your journey's end at last.

"The blood of Jesus Christ his son cleanses us from all sin."

Doct. 2. Such as walk in the light, the blood of Christ purges them from all their sins.

The verse sets down two privileges of those who walk in the light. Not only do they have fellowship with God, but with Christ as well. This fellowship is in his mediation, and that in cleansing us from all our sins.

What is meant by "the blood of Christ"? The blood of Christ here means not only that blood shed upon the cross, but his whole death, signified by blood which was the effect of his death, for blood poured out after his death (John 19:33, 34; Rom. 5:8). And the death of Christ is not all, for he suffered many things besides; so that it comprehends all his sufferings (1 Pet. 3:18). But there is a further synecdoche; sometimes his blood and passion are put for his whole obedience (Rom. 5:18, 19); for it is attributed to his entire obedience, that it makes us free from sin. All his desertions of spirit were sufferings of Christ, tending to cleanse us from sin. Blood includes all his sufferings and obedience; and indeed the very blood of Christ, had it not been offered in obedience and humility, would have done no good; for the promise is to him who does something, "Do this and live" (John 10:18). His passion was done in obedience (Phil. 2:7, 8).

But why is our cleansing from sin ascribed most to his blood, if it reached to his whole death and passion and obedience? Why is his blood mentioned in Matt. 26:28; Rom. 5:9; Heb. 9:14; 1 Pet.1:19; and why is salvation most attributed to his blood? There are three reasons: -1. Because death was the wages of sin (Rom. 6:23; Gen. 3:17); therefore we or our surety must satisfy that. -2. His death is the foundation of the whole covenant; the legacy is of no force without the death of the testator (Heb. 9:17). -3. Blood is most mentioned because it is an evident testimony of death, for in blood is life; and because it accomplished all the legal types (Heb. 9:22).

Why is it called "the blood of Jesus Christ his son"? Because the Christ who shed his blood was the son of God, and that added efficacy to it (Heb. 10:14); it was not the blood of sinful man, and therefore it must be of infinite power (Acts 20:28).

How is this blood said to cleanse? -1. It juyifies us. By his blood we are cleansed (Rom. 5:9; Eph. 1:7). We are justified by it because it frees us from the guilt and punishment of sin. (a) From the guilt of sin; guilt is that by which we are liable to the curse. (b) From the punishment of sin, so that now there is no condemnation to us (Rom. 8:1; Rom. 4:25; 1 Pet. 2:24). -2. It sanctifies us. We are cleansed from sin by a sanctifying power in the death of Christ. Our consciences being sprinkled by it, we are freed from the stain and lust of sin (Heb. 9:14), and are endued with supernatural grace so that we are afraid to commit any sin.

What is meant in the text by 'all sin'? -1. From all kinds of sin, as (a) From original and actual sins. (b) From sins of omission and of commission. (c) From the sins of our

birth and of our life; of youth and of riper years (Rom. 5:9).
-2. From all sins against us and upon our conscience. Now we could not be justified if any sin were unpardoned (Heb. 9:14). If it is a dead work or sin of omission, our conscience is purged from it; for if the blood of bulls and goats cleansed all sins of the flesh, much more the blood of Christ cleanses from all sin. There is no sin from which men cannot be cleansed by the blood of Christ, except the sin against the Holy Ghost (Heb. 10:26); because they tread under foot the blood of the covenant (Heb. 10:29).

Lastly, how can Christ's blood cleanse from all sin?

-1. The wonderful efficacy of Christ's blood is taken from the divinity of his person; the reason it is so effectual is that it is the blood of the son of God (Heb. 9:14).

-2. He stood in our persons on the cross, through the acceptation of God. God accepted him as a surety for us (Heb. 7:22; 1 Peter 2:24). Therefore it is as much as if we had done it in our own persons (John 10:11). He had no need to shed his blood for himself, for he had never sinned.

Use 1. To reprove the Papists, who teach that the mass, being celebrated for the dead and living, justifies from sin. But if the blood of Christ cleanses us from all sin, there is no need of the mass to cleanse us from any sin. Further, they teach that the mass is an unbloody sacrifice; but it must be a bloody sacrifice if it will cleanse (Heb. 10:10, 14). And if it is often offered, it does not exceed the sacrifices of the law (Heb. 10:1-5).

Use 2. To refute the Popish purgatory. If Christ's blood cleanses us from all sin, why do we need a purgatory to expiate any sin? This is a blasphemy against Christ's blood.

But do not temptation and affliction, and word and sacraments, and faith and other graces, purge us from sin, and purify us? The scripture itself says it of afflictions (Heb. 12:11). It is true that there are many means to purge us from sin; but there is no efficacy in any of them except by virtue of Christ's blood. Therefore those in hell have no benefit, because Christ's blood does not reach there; and if any are bettered by afflictions or word or sacraments, it is from the virtue of Christ's blood; and if Christ's blood be sprinkled on purgatory, we will not reject it.

Use 3. Of refutation against the opinion of many godly divines, that we are purified from the sin of our birth by the purity of Christ's birth; from sins of omission by his active and complete obedience; and from sins of commission by his passive obedience. True, there is much in the purity of his birth, in his obedience, in his passion, which makes us fit to be cleansed; but we must hold that the blood of Christ cleanses us from all sin, for the latter brings the former to perfection. A lamb defiled in the old law was never accepted, though it were slain for a sacrifice; but if it had not been slain, though spotless, it would not have been accepted either. So, had Christ not been a lamb spotless and undefiled, his death would not have cleansed us from our sins; and, though he were spotless and undefiled, yet he must be slain, or else we could not be cleansed either. The purity of Christ's nature, without his death, does not cleanse us from sin; but we must take all jointly together. All his active obedience was passive, and all his passive obedience was active. It was part of his passion that he was obedient to the law (Gal. 4:4, 5); and by the obedience of Christ to the death, we are cleansed from all sin.

Use 4. To refute some who say we are justified by faith because it is itself a work in us. They say we are not justified by the works of the law but by our faith (Rom. 11:5, 6). But if we are justified by faith, and if it is a work in us, how then does the blood of Christ cleanse us from sin? But faith justifies us by laying hold of the blood of Christ.

Use 5. To comfort all those who walk in the light; let them not be discomforted. You will say, my heart is full of impatience, covetousness, and uncleanness; these are great sins indeed, but the blood of Christ cleanses from all sin; there is no measure, number, or limit.

But one will say, He does not cleanse all men; how shall I know whether my sins are cleansed?

Why, do you walk in the light as God is in the light? If you do, then his blood cleanses you from all sin. Therefore if a man would have comfort, he must consider whether he lives in any sin voluntarily and walks in darkness. If he does, he has no part in Christ's blood; but if there is no sin which he is not willing to avoid; no duty which he does not desire to perform, and amend all, it is a sign that he is walking in light. If you see what is amiss and labor to correct it, it is a sign you walk in the light; and then assure yourself that the blood of Christ will cleanse you from all your sins.

Use 6. If Christ's blood cleanses from all sin, then no sin is venial. Is that sin venial which can only be cleansed by Christ's blood?

Use 7. To show us the reason why the blood of Christ is called precious (1 Pet. 1:19). It is more precious than the blood of bulls and goats; and more precious than silver and gold, for all in the world cannot remit one sin or save one soul from hell (Ps. 49:6-8; Heb. 12:24).

Use 8. To teach Christians to walk boldly in a Christian course, notwithstanding all former sins. We are much troubled in our spirits because of our sins, because of their multitude and greatness; but let us be bold (Heb. 10:19-23). We may be bold to approach to God's throne, bold to enter heaven. Let no sin discourage us, for his blood cleanses

Use 9. All ordinances, word, prayer, sacrament, communion of saints, all holy duties, will do no good without his blood. Therefore desire God that every ordinance may be sprinkled with his blood. As water alone does not cleanse without soap, so it is that all the waters of Jordan cannot cleanse us from dead works without the blood of Christ intermingled. Let us not rest in any ordinance or performance, in any prayer or fast, or in all of them; but though you would spend your own blood to cleanse your soul from sin, all will be in vain unless it is mixed with the blood of Christ. Therefore pray that the word and sacrament, and every ordinance, may be sprinkled with Christ's blood to justify and sanctify. The blood of Christ has procured sentence of absolution from God, and virtue from the Spirit of grace, to wash away all our sins. Therefore lay hold on it. This is to lay hold upon the horns of the altar; therefore in all Christian consideration and duties, look chiefly and principally to him, or else all will be in vain.

1 John 1:8, 9

"If we say that we have no sin, we deceive ourselves, and the truth is not in us. If we confess our sins, he is faithful and just to forgive us our sins, and to cleanse us from all unrighteousness."

From the former verse St. John gathers a twofold mark of our state. First (v. 8), If the blood of Christ cleanses us from all sin, then they are liars who say they have no sin. Second (v. 9), Christ is faithful to forgive us our sins if we but confess them.

If we say: -1. In heart (Ps. 14:1), where such a thought is. -2. In speech. -3. In manner; to speak a thing is to profess so, to carry ourselves so as may manifest our opinion.

Doct. Opinion and profession of perfect holiness is an error willful, pernicious, and dangerous.

-1. It is an error and delusion, for it is contrary to God's express word (Prov. 20:9; Eccl. 7:22; 1 Kings 8:46; James 3:2). In many things we sin all, both in matter and manner.

-2. It is a willful error. A man does not learn it from others, but he persuades himself so. (a) If any read the scriptures, he shall find their teaching to be contrary (Ps. 130:3; Ps. 143:2). (b) Though a man never read the scriptures, he shall meet with daily crosses, and his own heart will tell him it is for his sin (Job 14:1). (c) There is none but finds he has need of pardon for sin (Zech. 11:4; John 16: 8, 9). If the Holy Spirit is to convince the world of sin (as the latter place says), there is not a man in the world who is not convinced to be a sinner. Therefore to say he has no sin must be willful error.

-3. It is a dangerous error, because it drives out all truth of grace. Where this conceit is, there can be no truth of grace.

a. Where there is truth of grace, it always expresses itself in three things regarding sin: every godly man first renounces his own righteousness (Phil. 3:7, 8); he complains bitterly of sin (Rom. 7:24); and he fights against sin to the death (Heb. 12:4). Now if every godly man does this, how can there be any truth of grace in a man who either thinks or professes he has no sin?

b. Where there is truth of grace, it expresses itself in two things regarding the blood of Christ. He prizes it above all blessings in the world (Gal. 6:14; 1 Cor. 2:2); and why need he prize it so much if he has no sin? He desires further to bathe himself daily in that blood (Zech. 13:1); why need he do that, if he have no sin?

c. Where there is truth of grace, it expresses itself regarding perfection of holiness. He strives after perfection earnestly every day (Phil. 3:12-14); why does the Christian need mortification if there is no sin?

Use 1. This truth shows many to be in a dangerous state, devoid of grace. (a) Such were the Pharisees, who counted themselves just and holy. Such were the Essenes, who counted themselves strict observers of the law of Moses. Such a one was that young man who came to Christ (Matt. 19:20), but Christ convinced him that he was not perfect. Such were the Catharists of old, a sect in the church who thought themselves pure from all sin. (b) It likewise reproves the Libertines, who counted themselves perfect keepers of the law. (c) Such are the Papists, who say the virgin Mary was without sin. She does not say it herself; she acknowledged a Saviour, and therefore she had sin. (d) And such are they who live as if they were free from sin, who have a good opinion of themselves in a carnal state. And such is the body of the world. They will, it may be, say they are sinners; but why then do they not mourn and repent for sin? Why, they see no need of that; "I have lived honestly all my life, and I hope my state is good;" and so they deceive themselves.

Use 2. Hence we see a necessity laid on ministers to preach the law; or else how shall people see their sins? By the law sin comes to be revived (Rom. 7:7).

Use 3. Do you believe you are guilty indeed of many sins? Why then confess it, and conduct yourself so; renounce your sins inwardly and mourn for them; strive against them; for otherwise you do not profess yourself to be a sinner, unless your heart prizes the blood of Christ and desires to be bathed in it. And if you think yourself to be a sinner, daily get hold of grace; you are yet sinful and miserable, and therefore need more grace.

Use 4. If we are all sinners, then let us learn to bear God's hand patiently (Micah 7:9). Is any froward and impatient man in affliction? He professes he is no sinner; he who practices impatience professes innocency. If a man is indeed innocent, he will be ready for the storm; but the man who takes crosses impatiently, thinks they fall on him undeservedly.

Use 5. Learn not to be censorious, not to reject others for sin. We ought not to despise them lightly, but for wallowing and walking in sin; for in many things we sin all. Truly if we are over-censorious, we profess ourselves to be no sinners; for if we were, we would pity them and be careful for ourselves (Matt. 7:5, 6).

If we say we have no sin, we have no truth in us.

"If we acknowledge our sins, he is faithful and just to forgive us our sins, and to cleanse us from all unrighteousness." (v. 9)

Doct. Unfeigned confession of our sins to God is the ready way to the pardon and healing of them. Confession is the ready way to justification and sanctification, pardoning of sin, and cleansing from sin.

Bellarmine takes this passage as proof of auricular

confession; he says it is meant, not of confession to God, but to the priest. And what is his ground? That to this confession is added a promise of pardon, but nowhere in Scripture is there a promise of pardon given for confession to God; only to the apostles and ministers of Christ (John 20:23).

But it is a notorious falsehood to say that no promise is made to him who confesses to God (Prov. 28:13). We understand this verse of confession to God; he denies it, because the writer speaks of confession to him from whom sin may be hidden, which it cannot be from God. But yet many a man hides his sin from himself, and will not search his own heart, and labors to hide it from God (Isa. 29:15). And it is apparent that the place in Proverbs speaks of confession to God, for he speaks of confessing to him from whom he might find mercy; but confession to man often brings ruin. I would further ask them: Is there no place which expresses pardon to him who confesses his sins toward the temple? (Ps. 32:5, 6; Job 33:27, 28). And the whole prayer of Solomon (1 Kings 8) runs on promise of pardon to him who confesses to God, and God answers to that petition (9:3). And now that Solomon's temple is destroyed, we have a greater than the temple, yea, one of whom the temple was but a type. If we confess our sins and offer our prayers in the name of Christ, our sins shall be pardoned and healed.

In John 20:23 there is no mention of confession, but they have power to remit them without confession. In Acts 9:17 Ananias comes to Paul without hearing a word from him. Paul's sins were not remitted by confessing them to Ananias, but by calling on the name of the Lord (Acts 22:16); indeed if a man is burdened in conscience, it is meet that he should confess his faults to the faithful ministers of God and request their help and prayers (James 5:16, which is meant of ministers as well as laymen; of Christians in general, Mal. 2:7).

But, it may be asked, what difference will you make between ministers and laymen, if you say we may confess our faults to laymen in private? I answer, when Christ says of his ministers, "whose sins you remit, they are remitted," it is not meant that they have judicial power to absolve them and say, "Your sins are forgiven, in the name of the Father, and of the Son, and of the Holy Spirit;" but he has given them a ministerial power to declare remission of sins to those who are penitent; if they see them penitent and humble, they may declare some promise to which pardon is affixed.

This in turn leads to another question. If common Christians may do thus (and it is certain they may), is there no difference between ministers and them? I answer, God is more wont to bless a minister's discerning of a man and his applying comfort, than that of common Christians (Rom. 10:14, 15). The ordinary way of faith, and of comfort by faith, is by the ministry of the gospel.

What is it to forgive sin?

To forgive sin is to free a man from sin and punishment, and to remit it (Jer. 31:33). To cleanse from sin is to mortify sin and quicken grace.

The necessity of confession may be seen from the following reasons:

-1. In respect to God. (a) Confession does a great honor to his justice. No man confesses his sin to God without glorifying God's justice; though he deal ever so hardly with him, yet his justice should be magnified (Ps. 51; Neh. 9:33; Dan. 9:7). (b) It sanctifies the name of God's grace; the apostle's reason for showing the sinfulness of all men (Rom. 2 & 3) is to magnify the riches of God's grace. It shows that if men have any mercy, it is from free grace.

-2. In respect to ourselves. (a) It exceedingly humbles us and makes us willing to accept any hand of God (Lev. 26:41, 42). How do men come to be humbled? If they confess their sins and the sins of their fathers, that will humble them. (b) Confession of sin to God restrains us from commission of sin; for if a man considers that he must come before God and break his heart for a sin, he will be more ashamed of his sin before God than before men. In David's case, "Against thee, against thee only have I sinned," was what most affected him. (c) Confession of sin makes us examine ourselves, and that is very profitable. When a man comes and considers the frame of his heart and life, it afflicts him much. Probing a wound causes anguish to the body, and yet is healthful; so examination of ourselves brings spiritual health in the wake of its anguish.

Now for the properties of this confession. It must be serious and sincere, and with a resolution to do so no more. When a man confesses his sins with grief of heart for offending God, and resolves never to do the like again, this is very effectual.

Use 1. This serves to teach us that in scripture the repentance of an humble sinner goes before justification and sanctification. Many a man comes to be humbled, and is yet confident that his sin is neither forgiven nor his heart sanctified. If confession is the way to pardon, what need a man confess his sins, if he is truly persuaded they are forgiven? We grant therefore that repentance is the way to pardon, to the fence of it at least.

It is a question whether repentance goes before faith or faith before repentance. I answer, if you take it practically, there is no man who believes his sin pardoned or healed before he is brought to humiliation, contrition, and sorrow.

Use 2. To teach all who stand either in need of pardon or of cleansing from sin, what course to take. The best have need to increase it; but if you have not found pardon or cleansing at all, here is a plain promise: "If we confess our sins, he is faithful and just to forgive us our sins"; as if he should say, If we should confess our sins truly, and yet find no pardon, it would violate the faithfulness and righteousness of God.

You will say, I have confessed my sins often before God and yet have found no pardon. I answer, have you confessed your chief sins, those by which you have dishonored God most? If you hold any back, no wonder God also holds back comfort; he who hides his sins shall not prosper (Prov. 28:13).

But you will say, I have dealt plainly with God, as far as I can tell. I ask you, has your confession been serious, heartily grieving for dishonoring God, and giving him the praise of his justice, that you have deserved nothing but hell? And do you praise his mercy and humble your soul? Why, in this case you may not have the feeling of pardon, but you are in the way to pardon. Would you commit again those sins you confess? Do you hate and abhor them? Then you are cleansed from them. If sin is your greatest burden, then it is pardoned. Indeed the Lord does not limit the time; he may make good this promise to some sooner, to some later; but there is none to whom he will never make it good, if they will but wait upon him.

Use 3. Of consolation to every soul who does confess sin unto God, who does truly and seriously confess, and grieve and mourn for those sins by which he has most dishonored God and wounded his own soul (1 Sam. 12:19). If you do this, God will certainly pass by all your transtressions; if God has pawned his faith and truth and justice on it, he will certainly do it. An honest man will not fail in such a case; how much less will God. And thus, though you should find in yourself many corruptions, yet you may conclude you are in the way to further comfort and cleansing.

Therefore let everyone who desires to find comfort in the pardon of his sin, and cleansing from it, confess his sin to God. God has promised to do it; therefore if you desire to find pardon and cleansing increased, you must look up to him, so that you may have your sins pardoned and cleansed through Christ.

"And to cleanse us from all unrighteousness." From this scripture we may deduce the following doctrine.

Doct. It is a filthy thing to lie in sin unpardoned. Or, sin unpardoned is filthiness and uncleanness; it is an unclean and filthy thing Ezek. 36:25; Zech. 13:1).

There is a fountain set open for sin and for uncleanness (2 Cor. 7:1). Here St. Paul calls sin "filthiness and uncleanness"; there are in scripture many other expressions of this kind.

God is willing to possess men with the truth of the exceeding sinfulness of sin; therefore he compares it to the most filthy things. -1. To mire and dirt which the sea casts out (Isa. 57:20); this is a means of casting forth sinfulness. -2. To vomit and to a sow's wallowing in the mire (2 Pet. 2:22), which is loathsome. -3. To scum which is cast into the fire or into ashes (Ezek. 24:6). -4. To the carcass of detestable and abominable things (Jer. 16:18); hence it is that our best duties are sometimes compared to a menstruous cloth (Isa. 64:6). -5. To uncircumcision (Col. 2:14). -6. To dung (Ps. 83:10). God says he will cast the dung of their solemn feasts upon their faces (Mal. 2:3); that is, their sinful observance of holy ordinances.

Thus God would have us look at sin as a congress of all filthiness; if you would put it all together, sin would comprehend all. Hence it is that the best performances of wicked men are unclean (Titus 1:15), and the sacrifices of the wicked are an abomination (Prov. 28:9).

Why is sin so loathsome? Because it is that which comes naturally from man corrupt; it is the natural issue of corrupt nature, therefore loathsome. Now the excrement of a clean person is loathsome; much more of a corrupt person; and this is the issue of a corrupt nature (Lev. 15:8; John 3:6; Job 14:4; Job 25:5).

Use 1. This is a ground of reproof to any who boast in sin. If it is indeed as mire or scum or dung or vomit, how vainly do they glory! They glory in their shame (Phil. 3:19); they glory in their dung, in their vomit, in their base filthiness (Isa. 3:9). It is a woeful thing to profess filthiness openly; if men do thus, woe unto them.

Use 2. It should stir us up not to lie in sin, no, not for a day. If a child should lie in its dung, or if we should, we would think we were unfit for civil company; yet such we are, as long as we lie in sin unpardoned. This should therefore spur us on to repentance, not to rest until we get sin pardoned. We shall then be washed from our filthiness.

Use 3. To move us to help one another out of sin. We should count it beastly and brutish if we should let a child lie in its filth; so are we if we let any whom we can help, lie in their own defilements of sin. And were our minds so quick to smell as our bodies, we should as much loathe the smell or presence of sin as of filthy dung; it is through lack of spiritual faculties that we are content with it.

Use 4. To provoke us to more earnest wrestling for cleansing from sin; when we have defiled ourselves with sin, none can help us out but God; others may help the work forward, but none can effectually cleanse us except God. Therefore we should come before God as the saints have done (Ezra 9:6; Jer. 31:18,19; Dan. 9:7). We must not come before God with extenuation, as Adam. We should be ashamed to come into company with defiled bodies; we would not say it is our infirmity or our pastime; and indeed we have our pastime in God, in prayer, in our callings, in holy duties. This is a loathsome thing, to pretend lightness or infirmity in filthiness; therefore let us take shame to ourselves and strive for cleansing. See Ps. 51:7; David would be thoroughly cleansed.

Use 5. It may stir us up to take heed of evil company without, and corruption within. A man should loathe to keep company with base filthy unclean fellows, as drunkards or swearers (2 Cor. 6:17); and Paul also exhorts us to cleanse ourselves from all filthiness within (2 Cor. 7:1). We would be loath to have any filthy unclean thing about us; so we should cleanse ourselves from all sin, because it is a remnant of filthiness.

Use 6. It may show us the wonderful preciousness of the blood of Christ, and the no less wonderful favor and love of God towards us. If Christ's blood were not of wonderful efficacy, it could not cleanse such base, filthy, sinful lusts; and likewise, if God's favor were not wonderful, he would not take upon him such a homely office. If women were not mothers, they would not take upon them such homely offices as cleansing their children from their filth; and if God's love for us were not divine in its strength, he would not cleanse us from our filthiness. To cleanse us, he pours clean water upon us. It is with us as with young infants who would lie in their defilements if their mothers did not make them clean; and so we would even wallow in the defilements of sin if God did not cleanse us. Therefore admire God's love and mercy toward us.

"And cleanse us from all unrighteousness."

Doct. 2. All sin is unrighteousness.

Sin and righteousness are uniformly mentioned together (Rom. 6:13); the one explains the other. Sometimes unrighteousness is limited to the sins of the second table, and thus contrasted with unholiness, the sins of the first; but sometimes righteousness is used to comprehend the whole course of a Christian, and unrighteousness by contrast comprehends all sins. Every sin wrongs either God, others, or ourselves; righteousness gives everyone his due. If we sin in excess and intemperance, we debase and defile ourselves; if we sin in theft or slander, we wrong others in their goods or good names; and if we do not worship God as God, if we do not keep his sabbaths, or if we profane his name, we wrong God.

Use 1. This shows the error of those who think, if they pay every man his own, they are righteous men. What? Do you commit no wrong? Are you not a sinner? Yes, they will say. Well, then, you are not righteous; for every sin does wrong to God, to ourselves, or to others.

Others say if they wrong any, it is themselves. Very well; it is unrighteousness to wrong yourself.

Use 2. As you love innocence, live righteously; do God no wrong, yourself no wrong, and others no wrong; for else you are unrighteous.

Use 3. For comfort to any who have their souls cleansed

by the blood of Christ from all filthiness. We are holy; we are set at liberty from all filthiness and all unrighteousness.

Doct. 3. Sin, when pardoned, is forever cleansed; whatever sin God pardons, the same sin he also cleanses.

It is shown in Heb. 9:14; the same blood that pardons, cleanses us from sin. This is manifest from the death of Christ, for his death serves not only to procure pardon of sin, but likewise healing for sin. His blood is offered up as a ransom for sin, and thus it is pardoned; but not only so, it is also a means to kill and mortify sin (Rom. 6:6). There is in it a destructive power to kill sin, as well as a meritorious power to pardon sin.

His death is said to mortify sin in us in the following ways: -1. As an example; for if Christ is dead, we also shall die with him to sin (Rom. 6:9, 11). -2. It has a natural efficacy, since it is an object fearful and formidable. When sin presents itself, we look at it as crucifying Christ; and then can we look upon it without mourning? (Zech. 12:10) Shall we wrong him so much as to crucify him again? -3. His blood cleanses sin, in obtaining at God's hand a spirit of sanctification, which makes the death of the head reach to the lowest members of the body. When the head dies, the members die; so the death of Christ obtained for us the spirit of God; and if he our head dies, then we shall die to sin. As the resurrection of Christ procures our life to righteousness, so the death of Christ grants our death to sin (Gal. 4:4, 5).

But you will say, if sin is always mortified when it is pardoned, how does it come to pass that godly men often fall into the same sin? Does not David confess that there was a way of lying in him? (Ps. 119:29) He says, "Remove from me the way of lying"; which implies that it was not one act, but a way, a course of habit that he walked in. So Jonah was froward before he went to Nineveh, and he was froward afterward. How is it then that sin may be cleansed and yet renew itself; and, if it renew itself, how is it cleansed?

I answer, it is with sin in this respect as with Samson's hair: it may be cut, but it will grow again. Sin may be mortified in some ways and at some times, but yet renewed again, because sin in this life is mortified only in part. Pride, wantonness, and covetousness are mortified in part, but in part remain alive; and if we neglect the practice of mortification, we shall fall again into some sin we had gotten some mastery over. If sin breaks out again, it is because we neglect those means by which we should mortify sin. The apostle does not say, "The blood of Christ has cleansed us," but, "cleanses;" does now cleanse us. He implies by this that cleansing is a continued act. The blood of Christ is a perfect medicine to heal sin and purge from filthiness, but if a man neglects to apply this medicine to his soul, it cannot be as effectual as it would.

Use 1. For trial, whether our sins are pardoned or not. Would you know whether your sin is pardoned? Why, if it is, it is also cleansed; but if your sin is not cleansed in some measure, it is not pardoned at all. Therefore look at your sins. If they are healed, then they are certainly pardoned, for it is the same blood of Christ that both heals and pardons sin (Hos. 14:4). God does not only love freely and pardon graciously, but he heals also. Therefore consider: do you find your sins healed? That is, do they not have that power which they had before? Do they seem loathsome to you, whereas you delighted in them before? Do you not hate them in heart and avoid them in practice? Then those sins are pardoned. And if he pardons one sin, he pardons all, for his pardons are universal. But if a man still lives in sin and loves it well, and is no more ashamed than he formerly had been, but goes on in the same sin, then truly it is not healed nor pardoned.

But some godly one will say, I feel my sin so far from being mortified that it grows stronger and more vigorous; what then shall I think? I answer: -1. It may grow stronger in our feeling, when it is not so in itself. It is not because sin is stronger, but because our feelings are livelier. A man in extremity of sickness feels no pain, but when he begins to recover, he feels more pain — this is not because the disease is stronger, but because his senses are sharper. -2. Do you not find in such a case that sin is more loathsome and bitter to you? Then it is in some measure mortified. Mortifying is a borrowed expression from a surgeon's mortifying or deadening a wound. They bind a joint and stop all flow of blood, so that it is made insensible to pain; so if we have stopped the freeness of our spirits to sin, we are not so lively to run to sin, and this itself is a sign that corruption is mortified. If you are as lively and ready, and you delight as much in sin as before, then it is not mortified; but if it grows loathsome and bitter, this is a sign of mortification.

Use 2. To direct us how to make good use of the blood of Christ; not only to pardon our sins, but also to heal them. We must not stop when we have made use of it for pardon, but we must make use of it for healing as well; else we take the blood of Christ in vain, for it was sent to heal as well as to pardon. Therefore do not pray God only to pardon your sins through Christ's blood, but to lay his blood warm to your heart every day, that you may have your heart and ways cleansed. This cleansing is a continued act, not of one day or two, but throughout our whole life we should make use of Christ's blood to cleanse us.

How may we do this? -1. Consider what great things he did for us, the just for the unjust, and the meditation of this will make us ashamed of sin. -2. Pray to God for the quickening work of his Spirit, that the same blood of Christ which has procured pardon may also procure healing for us.

Use 3. This teaches us all to labor to grow in cleanness of heart and life, for the blood of Christ cleanses us (Zech. 13:1). If a fountain runs into a channel that is muddy, it will at length cleanse it by continual flowing; so, though Christ should find our spirits muddy and defiled, yet we should let his blood flow daily upon us and be ever rinsing our hearts at the fountain.

Use 4. Comfort to all God's servants who have had any experience of the pardon of their sins. You shall certainly in time feel and find healing and cleansing from your sins. If you see a clear fountain running into a filthy channel, the stream itself is made filthy and muddy for the present; but afterwards both stream and channel are pure and clean. So Christ's blood may run into muddy spirits, and may at first stir up the corruption and make your spirit seem more foul; you may find more pride, and vanity, and uncleanness. But will it remain so? No, truly; in cleansing it will cleanse, and will go on until it has purged all corruption.

1 John 1:10

"If we say that we have not sinned, we make him a liar, and his word is not in us."

These words are a repetition of the former verse, but with some additions. St. John magnifies this sin; hypocrites do not only make themselves liars, but they make God a liar as well. And this is not only blasphemous but heretical; it extirpates all the truth of the word.

Doct. Opinion and profession of perfect righteousness, even in those who are cleansed by the blood of Christ, is not only an error, but a blasphemous and heretical error; it is sacrilegious and heretical.

But why does St. John repeat this? Did he not say enough before? I answer:

-1. It might be thought that he spoke of carnal men before. Therefore to make it manifest that even those who had confessed their sins and were cleansed from unrighteousness, even those, if they should say they had no sin, should make both themselves and God liars; therefore he repeats it.

-2. He saw that men were ready to cleanse themselves from sin sinfully. If we can, we are ready by any pretense to free ourselves from a judgment of sinfulness. Therefore he presses his doctrine: if we say the contrary, we are indeed so foul that we have no spark of religion in us. Not one spark of the word then dwells in us.

-3. It is a point of great necessity to believe this truth, and therefore he enjoins this conclusion again.

One may say either in heart, in word, or in manner. To say this in any of these ways is to make God a liar and no God; for if he is not a God of truth, he is not God.

Why does such a one make God a liar?

-1. Because God has given his Son Christ to cleanse us from all sin; and why would he send Christ to cleanse sin if we had no sin? He who says he has no sin, overthrows the coming of Christ and the cleansing power of his blood.

-2. Because God has often said that all men are sinners (Rom. 3:23; Gal. 3:22; Job 15:14; Job 7:20). David, though a holy man, yet professes himself a sinner (Ps. 130:3; 143:2). The most perfect of God's servants have testified of themselves that they are sinners; therefore if we say we have not sinned, we make both them and God liars.

What is meant when he says, "The word is not in him"? -1. It is not in his judgment, for he is not persuaded of its truth. -2. It is not in his heart, for he does not trust in it, nor does he receive it and its saving efficacy in love. He who says he has no sin does not receive the word (Acts 20:32; 1 Thess. 2:13; 2 Tim. 3:15).

Now the word is said not to be in a man when there is not in him enough of the word to save him. He may be ignorant of some divine truths and yet have the word of God in him; but if he lacks the knowledge and faith of those things which he must have to be saved, the word does not dwell in him.

Now he who denies sin to be in him does not only deny that one truth; but the word is not in him because he is void of all saving truth. The saving truths of God are four: repentance for sin, faith for pardon, mortification of sin, and sanctification from sin. If a man is without sin, to what purpose are all such exhortations to repentance? To what purpose are all scriptures pointing to faith in Christ? To what purpose are those which tend to mortification or sanctification? So then he who denies sin to be in him, not only sins against God and makes him a liar, but he does also heretically err in overthrowing all saving truth; the doctrine of repentance, of mortification, of faith, of sanctification, all these are overthrown.

If a man professes perfection in himself, it is impossible for him to have any truth of grace, believing he has no need of repentance, or faith in Christ, or mortification, or sanctification. This is a frightening doctrine. St. John may well be called Boanerges, a son of thunder, for these are thundering speeches. He who says he has no sin is a liar against himself and against God, a blasphemer, and a heretic.

Use 1. To confute the heresy of perfect obedience to the law. This heresy may be manifest in three ways.

    a. The Papists hold that justification is by works. Had they no other error but this, it is blasphemous, atheistic, and heretical; and it overturns the foundation of religion. What is the foundation of religion but the doctrine of repentance and faith? And if any are justified by works, they have neither need of repentance or faith. If righteousness is by the law, then Christ died in vain and his blood is of no effect (Gal. 5:4). Therefore that opinion is vain, that the Popish religion and ours may be reconciled. Let St. John give his judgment: he tells you that he who says he has no sin, that he has fulfilled the law and is justified by works, has no truth in his religion at all.

Therefore it is impossible that he should have any saving religion in him, he who holds justification by works and merits. He makes God a liar, and his word is not in him. For then God would have sent his Son in vain (Gal. 2:19, 20), and then Christ himself would have come in vain. Further, he would teach us to lie; for he teaches us to pray, "Forgive us our debts"; and if we have none, Christ lies in saying so. Again, the Holy Spirit should be a liar; for if he is sent to convince us of sin (John 16:15) when there is none in us, he lies to us.

    (b) This wicked heresy is also manifested by those

who say the virgin Mary had no sin. She said the contrary herself; and indeed, had she professed sinlessness, she would have been a liar and no truth would have been in her.

c. The heresy was manifested by the Catharists of old.

Use 2. Daily let us take up such a meditation as this: this day we sin, this day we have need of Christ and faith. We must daily take up such a meditation, or else we have no saving faith in our hearts. And if every day we are possessed with a persuasion that we are subject to sins, not only venial but mortal; that we have need of Christ, of repentance, and of faith; and that we can never say, this is a day in which I have not sinned — if we are thus persuaded, it will lead us on to all that saving knowledge of God and of the word, which will keep our hearts always in a holy frame. Such a man will be ready to think: I need to renew my repentance today; I need to lay hold upon Christ; I have need of mortification. Therefore the apostle would have us take up daily a continual remembrance that we are sinners. We are daily to consider in ourselves wherein we have failed; we are to renew our repentance and to look up to God for pardon of such and such sins and for sanctification. Otherwise we shall begin to drift from the saving truths of God's word and from their power in our hearts. Many Christians indeed do drift from this truth; but so far as we do it, we dishonor God and weaken our grace.

Use 3. It will serve to teach us that whoever walks in the remembrance of his own sinfulness, whoever is possessed of it and conscious of it, glorifies God's truth and magnifies the power of the word in his own heart. God has said, and we bear witness of it in our hearts, that Christ and the Holy Spirit were not sent in vain. Christ says that the publicans and harlots entered into the kingdom of God ahead of the Pharisees (Matt. 21:31); and why? Because publicans and harlots were conscious of their sinfulness, and so would soon acknowledge their need of repentance, faith, mortification, and sanctification; whereas the Pharisees thought themselves just, and were not conscious of their sinful state and of their need for repentance.

Use 4. St. John writes this epistle that their joy may be full; that it may be always like the full moon, never in wane and eclipse. Therefore if any Christian desires such fullness of joy, let him daily remember his sin. What is the reason many Christians fail in their confidence and fall into doubts concerning their state? I would ask them whether they have walked in a daily consciousness of their sins. If not, no marvel if their joy is clouded and eclipsed. St. John would have us strongly persuaded of this: "If we say we have no sin, we make God a liar;" and therefore if any Christian can go all the day with no sense of remorse for sin, without being startled by his heart, no wonder his joy is eclipsed. On the contrary, if you go on continually in a sensible apprehension of your sinfulness, and so renew your repentance, faith, and mortification, this will make you to keep on cleansing yourself daily, and so your joy would be renewed daily. We never had cause to complain of our state except by reason of hardness of heart. And how are our hearts hardened? Sin gets within us and we do not perceive it; and so we are hardened by it, and then our joy is overclouded (Heb. 12:12-15; Heb. 3:13). Therefore if we would keep our hearts from hardness, let us labor to spy out our sins and be humble for them daily, and so we will keep a soft heart, and a soft heart is always peaceable.

1 John 2:1

"My little children, these things I write unto you that you sin not. And if any man sin, we have an advocate with the Father, Jesus Christ the righteous.

To the former points there might arise two objections, to encourage men to sin. -1. If confession of sins is a means to have them pardoned, and if the blood of Christ cleanses us from all unrighteousness, then we need only go to God confessing our sins after we have sinned, and we shall be pardoned. -2. Since he says, "If we say we have no sin, we deceive ourselves and the truth is not in us," then why should we strive against sin, since do what we may we shall still fall into it?

Against both these objections he shows that he does not write these things to embolden them in sin, but to discourage them from it. "These things I write unto you, that you sin not."

The parts of the words are three: -1. A loving compellation, "my little children." -2. A declaration of the end of his writing, "that you sin not." -3. A consolation to those who, notwithstanding, fall into sin; he tells them that Christ is both an advocate and an atonement.

I. We begin with the compellation, "my little children." He speaks not of natural but of spiritual children, such as are justified (v. 12) and sanctified (v. 13). When he calls them, "my little children," it implies that his ministry helped beget them to God.

Doct. They who are the instruments under God of our conversion, justification, and sanctification, they are to us as spiritual fathers; and we are to them as little children.

It is an expression often used by the apostle, as 1 Cor. 4:15, where he prefers himself to all other teachers they had. So he calls Timothy (1 Tim. 1:2), Titus (Titus 1:4), and

Onesimus (Philemon 2, 22). As natural parents beget children of the seed which they infuse, so ministers beget children of the immortal seed of the word (1 Pet. 1:23-25). As in natural seed, so in spiritual, there is a material and a spiritual part. The material part is the letter of the word; the spiritual part is the Spirit conveyed in it. Now because ministers, together with the word, convey the Spirit, therefore they beget children by the word. Thus they are called fathers, and those so begotten are called children.

But does not Christ say, "Call no man father upon the earth"? (Matt. 23:9) True; but he does not forbid us to call such ministers spiritual fathers. What he does forbid is: -1. The affectation of such titles. Many affect to be called fathers of the church, who never begot any to God, as the Pharisees did. -2. Attempting to be the father of a sect or faction, to draw disciples after them (1 Cor. 1:12). Some are anxious to be called Calvinists or Lutherans, because they have taken up their doctrine. The domination of factions and sects is forbidden in scripture, but we should look at all Christians as members of one Christ and all ministers as servants of the same Christ (1 Cor. 3:5-9). What is forbidden is that men be divided, some of Paul and some of Apollos. -3. It is not forbidden to call ministers such, but to have confidence in their sayings as more ancient and to prefer them to the scriptures or to the sayings of others of equal graces and gifts. -4. Ministers are forbidden to take up such titles, to be called Rabbi or Master. This is forbidden, but we see Christ did not universally forbid such titles.

Use 1. Of direction to ministers, or to those who intend to enter the ministry. What is it to which their main endeavors should be directed? To be fruitful; to beget children to God. It is good for a minister to look at the good respect of the people and at his living and maintenance; but he is chiefly to desire and bend his endeavors to beget children to God, to beget to God those whom he may respect as children, with the like care and diligence. Preferment, or credit, or wealth are but the husks of his calling. The true end of his endeavor is to beget children.

How may that be done?

a. He is to be certain that he grows strong himself, for weak men in nature are not prolix. Therefore ministers must labor to grow strong in grace. A man without grace seldom begets any to God; therefore they must first mortify sin and increase in grace.

b. There may be strength in ministers, yet a disproportion between them and their people. Therefore ministers and people must strive to keep a proportion and correspondence. A minister must see how he may accommodate himself to the temper of his people; he must, with Paul, become all things to all men, that he may beget some. In everything that is lawful he must accommodate, but he must by no means comply with the evil whims of his people (Jer. 15:19), for then he brings contempt upon his doctrine.

c. Look that your seed be spiritual; that is, the pure word dispensed in the Spirit and power. Mingle no traditions or tricks of your wit with it; if you do, your seed is corrupt and lacks vigor. A velvet scabbard dulls the edge of the sword; it hinders the power of it. What has the chaff to do with the wheat? (Jer. 23:28, 29) You must not mingle the word with the dreams and fancies of men, but dispense the word in the power and evidence of the Spirit. Labor to have the word sealed in your heart, that you may speak out of the heart and inward affection. That word which comes from the heart, sooner goes to the heart.

Use 2. This truth may teach hearers how to hear the word of God aright. If ministers are so to dispense the seed of the word that they may beget children to God, then hearers must learn to apply themselves to their ministers. You must not content yourself with having gotten a good minister, and with your respect for him (though these are very good); but labor until you are spiritual children to him, if you were not so before; or if you were, be nursed by him, suck nourishment from him, grow in grace under him, and labor to receive stronger meat from him, that you may become a father to others (Heb. 5:12). It yields much comfort to a man's spirit when he can say the seed of such and such a sermon converted him; and contrariwise, it often fills a man with many doubts when he has not discerned the power of the word.

Use 3. It may teach both ministers and people to carry themselves towards one another as fathers and children. Many times a mariner carries a king over the sea; in that case, though he is a prince, yet he must be ruled by the mariner. So a minister may teach princes and great men, and they in this case must be as children to him.

a. We are to give our teachers such respect as children owe to parents (Gal. 4:14, 15).

b. Children owe parents imitation in any good thing, and the more they see the image of God in them, the more they are to imitate them. So people are to follow their ministers in any good counsel; that is the duty of children to their spiritual fathers (1 Cor. 4:15, 16).

c. Obedience in the Lord is required of hearers. Speaking of Timothy, the apostle says, "You know the proof of him, how as a son with the father he served with me in the gospel" (Phil. 2:22). He makes it his commendation that he never commanded any duty to him without receiving his obedience as a child to its father. He showed obedience to the Gospel of Christ; so people are to yield obedience to the gospel of Christ which they receive from their ministers.

Use 4. Now on the other side, it also teaches ministers how to show their fatherhood to their people. Begetting them is the least part of paternity. But further:

a. They are not to leave them, for still there are some corruptions cleaving to children from the womb; and if they are not helped from them, they will perish (Ezek. 16:4). So ministers will be murderers if, when they have begotten children by the seed of the word, they leave them to their own rawness and corruptions of their hearts, do not help them against them, and do not help them to grow in grace and make progress in Christianity.

b. Parents train up their children in all knowledge they

can, either in learning or in trades; so ministers are to adorn their people with such graces and ornaments that they may give them up to Christ, brides fit for him (2 Cor. 11:2, 3).

c. Ministers are to provide for them an eternal inheritance (2 Cor. 12:14). Parents lay up for their children; they labor to get an estate to leave to their posterity; so ministers are to lay up an eternal weight of glory for their people, not only to get them into heaven, but to load them with an eternal weight of glory and fill them with patience, humility, and all the graces of God's Spirit, for the spirit of glory rests upon such. The minister should help them to grow in grace, that they might be filled with glory.

How is the minister to do this?

a. Labor to help them to grow in humility. A man must lay down all ambitious thoughts, or else he will never come to heaven (Matt. 18:2, 3). David could not get a kingdom until he had learned to be like a weaned child (Ps. 131; Jer. 45). The way to be exalted in heaven is to be humble here on earth. An humble spirit shall be a glorious soul; before honor goes humility.

b. Labor to help them with patience and constance; for if they are patient in suffering with well-doing, and if they are ready to run through all conditions for Christ's cause and for the gospel, great is their reward in heaven (Matt. 5:10, 11). O rest not when you have begotten them and see some truth of grace wrought in them; but lay up for them a plentiful treasure in heaven. Help them to be rich in grace, that they may be rich in glory at the end.

Three graces especially go to the attaining of excellence of glory: zeal in doing God's will, patience in suffering, and humility in both. And zeal breeds fruitfulness. What was the reason one gained a greater reward in the parable? Because he was more fruitful with his talents (Luke 19:17-19). Therefore it should be the care of ministers to help their people (as much as they are able) to grow in these graces.

II. We come now to the second part, viz. the apostle's

declaration of the end of his writing. "These things I write unto you that you sin not." From his declaration comes this point.

Doct. The end of dispensing any promise or proof of our sinful state is not to give liberty to sin, but to prevent sin in us.

For here the apostle answers an objection which might arise: If the blood of Christ cleanses us from all sin, then we may be bold to sin. We need only run to Christ's blood, and we shall be cleansed from all our sins. But he says, "I write these things that you sin not;" therefore he implies that neither law nor gospel should encourage us to sin, but should restrain us.

-1. The law shows us the impossibility of not sinning, but does not teach us how to sin. It shows us sin (Rom. 3:20); and to show sin is not to teach us how to sin but how to avoid it. Further, it shows us not only the nature of sin, but also convinces us of sin and its danger (Rom. 7:14; Gal. 3:10).

-2. And the gospel teaches that the blood of Christ cleanses us from all our sins. (a) It shows a remedy against sin, the blood of Christ, and the means, "If we confess our sins." But it shows at the same time that if we fall headlong and willingly into sin, we most ungratefully, profanely tread underfoot the blood of Christ (Heb. 10:29). We account it prodigality to despise precious things; how much more desperate is it to despise the most precious blood of Christ. (b) The gospel teaches us to use the blood of Christ to mortify sin, and not only to get it mortified but cleansed; for the use of the gospel is to mortify sin, and therefore it does not lead us to the commission of sin. First, it begets faith, which purifies the heart (Acts 15:9). Second, it begets hope, and that also purifies (1 John 3:3). Third, it begets love, and that love constrains us to good and restrains us from evil (2 Cor. 5:14).

Thus both law and gospel admonish us to flee sin.

Use 1. To direct ministers what course to take.

    a. If any misconstruction may arise from your

teaching, you should wisely prevent it. St. John saw that here would arise an encouragement to sin from one doctrine he had delivered, and a discouragement from fighting sin from another. Therefore he tells them, "These things I write that you sin not."

b. Another direction is to frame yourselves to dispense milk to babes. St. John was a son of thunder and a pillar among the apostles (Gal. 2:9). Yet he was writing to babes, and tells them, "My little children, these things I write unto you that you sin not." It seems a weak line for such a man, but he tempers his teaching according to their strength. We would perhaps be ready to think it poor homely stuff to say the like; who could not have said as much? Yet even an apostle does not think it too base for him.

Use 2. Of reproof to the Papists, who lock up St. John's writings from the people, so that they may not be allowed to read them. If he wrote these things so that they might not sin, then they give free rein to sin who deny leave and liberty to read them.

Use 3. To teach us the poisonous corruption of our natures. Out of the purest, soundest doctrine we gather poison. St. John foresaw that from his doctrine they would be ready to gather false conclusions. So when St. Paul had delivered the doctrine of free justification, see what use, or misuse rather, they made of it (Rom. 5:20). He taught that, as sin abounded, so did grace much more abound; he saw that they would be ready to gather false conclusions from it and therefore prevents it. "Shall we then sin, that grace may abound? God forbid" (6:1). Therefore it must wean us from love for ourselves. The commonest meats are most nourishing and good; other rare meats commonly breed distempers; but some stomachs will corrupt any meat. So the plainest doctrines of religion are the soundest and best, but such is the corruption of our nature that it is ready to gather poison even out of them.

Use 4. To teach us when we have made a good use of the apostles' writings. When they divert us from sin, when we are restrained and kept back from sin by them, we then make good use of them. St. John wrote this epistle that they might not sin; labor therefore by reading it to be made more cautious against sin. We must try, if we can, to do no sin; but if we do sin, let us repent and hate it, and so it will be as no sin to us.

III. We now come to the third point, viz. the consolation. "If any man sin, we have an advocate with the Father." He had taught the contrary, and told them he wrote these things that they might not sin; but yet for all that, notwithstanding their best care and endeavor, it would not be that they would continue without sinning. But here is the comfort: "If any man sin, we have an advocate with the Father." He does not say that every man has an advocate with the Father, but I and you, and such as we are; we have an advocate with the Father.

Now what is an advocate? Sometimes the name is applied to the Holy Spirit, sometimes to the Son. In John 14:16, the name is given to the Spirit; he is called the Paraclete because he is a comforter and an advocate. How? Not by pleading our case before the Father, but by pleading in our hearts, in giving us the spirit of grace and supplication, as the apostle says (Rom. 8:26). In law, anyone may be said to be our advocate who draws our petitions for us. The Holy Spirit does not plead for us in heaven, but he draws up our petitions for us so that they are accepted in heaven (Rom. 8:27). He speaks good things from God to us, and good things from us to God (1 Cor. 2:3). He tells us of our peace with God and our comfort, and helps us to plead with God.

But properly it is the office of the Son to be an advocate. An advocate in court is a more special pleader in behalf of another whose cause is to be judged; and so Christ is our advocate in a special manner with the Father.

Doct. Every sinner has enemies who plead against him before the Father in heaven.

We should not need an advocate to plead for us if we had none to accuse us and plead against us. We no sooner sin than we have accusations put up in heaven against us, and so our advocate puts in his arguments for us.

What are these adversaries?

-1. Our own sins plead against us and accuse us day and night. Some sins plead against us in a special way, and those are crying sins. The murder of Abel was a crying sin (Gen. 4:10); the sins of Sodom cried (Gen. 18:20); and there are four things in Sodom mentioned, which cried to heaven for vengeance: pride, idleness, intemperance, and unmercifulness to the poor (Ezek. 16:49). So detaining the laborer's wages is a crying sin (James 5:4); so also oppression (Exod. 22:22, 27). These are special crying sins, because they will give God no rest until he has avenged them in this world. They will not stay until the last judgment, but call for present judgment; but all our sins speak in the Lord's ear, and all call for vengeance against us.

-2. Another adversary that accuses us is the righteous law of God, which we have broken, that the word may not be in vain (John 5:45).

-3. The third enemy is Satan, who accuses us night and day (Rev. 12:10). So he accused Job (Job 1:9-11). He accused him of hypocrisy; because he had no real reason to accuse him, therefore he fabricated one.

-4. Our own conscience accuses us, and that is as a thousand witnesses (Rom. 2:15).

Use 1. To take heed how we make bold with any sin. You may commit them upon a pretense of pleasure, or profit, or credit; but there is no sin we commit which does not plead against us, yes and stir up the law and Satan and our own consciences to plead against us too.

Use 2. It teaches us the miserable state of a poor sinner who goes on in sin and never takes any steps to get Christ as an advocate for him. He may hope that Christ pleads for him in heaven, but this is a vain hope. As long as he goes on in sin, he may be sure that sin and Satan and the law and his conscience accuse him; and since he has none to plead for him, what a woeful case he is in!

Use 3. It will stir us up to get an advocate who may plead for us against our accusers.

Doct. Every child of God has the Lord Jesus Christ in heaven to plead his cause for him.

"If any man sin, we have an advocate with the Father, Jesus Christ the righteous." He does not say that every man who sins has an advocate, but we — that is, you and I, and such as are the children of God (Rom. 8:34) — we have an advocate with the Father. He "makes intercession for us;" that is, he interrupts the accusation and strikes in for us. Because he has not only died for us, but risen for us, he follows the business to the utmost, until it is accomplished (Heb. 7:25).

How does he make intercession for us?

-1. He does not fall down at the Father's feet, but he acts the part of an advocate by his presence at the throne of grace, so that his very presence cuts off many accusations. Since it is known that he is our friend and stands for us, they dare not be so bold (Heb. 9:24).

-2. He not only pleads for us by his presence, but he intercedes for us by the merit of his blood; and that pleads for us more powerfully than either sin, or the law, or Satan, or our own consciences, can plead against us. His blood speaks better things than that of Abel (Heb. 12:24); that blood cried for condemnation, this for absolution.

-3. He pleads for us by giving us leave to use his name for our help, and giving us his Spirit also to draw up our petitions for us and help us to plead for ourselves in his name. He is our chief advocate; he sends the Spirit (John 16: 23, 24); therefore though the Spirit is indeed our advocate, yet he himself is sent by Christ (John 14:16, 17).

-4. He is our advocate by expressing his good will towards us to his Father. He declares his will to be that we may be cleared from all doubts and be where he is, to behold his glory. This he did upon earth (John 17:24), and this same petition he expresses for us in heaven. The reason of it is given in Rom. 8:34, where his mediation is made a distinct work from his death, resurrection, ascension, and sitting at his Father's right hand. Besides all these, he makes requests for us in his own person, pleading to God for us for all good things, as Moses did often for the people (Exod. 32:21, 32). And as it was with Moses, so it was to be with Christ (Deut. 18:18); as Moses, a mediator, put in a word of peace for the people, so does Christ.

But does he thus intercede for every sinner? No, he does not say every man has an advocate, but only 'we.' He did not intercede for all when he was upon the earth ("I pray not for the world," John 17:9); for if Christ should have prayed for all men, God would have heard him for all men, and then his death would have been effectual for all men; for he says, "Thou hearest me always" (John 11:42). Christ is not an advocate for all, but only for the children of God.

Use 1. To direct a Christian who sins. He must look up to heaven for an advocate who may stand to plead for him, when sin and Satan and conscience and the law plead against him. When a poor soul has his conscience pleading horror against him, why, look up to heaven for an advocate. First get into the state of the children of God; it is not any man, but we who are as little children, begotten to God by the ministers of his word (1 Cor. 4:15). If we are such, we have an advocate.

Use 2. Of consolation to all whose consciences strike and gall them, who are disquieted with the bitterness of their sins. When sin accuses, the law accuses, and Satan and conscience accuse, what will comfort a poor soul in this case? Why, that we have an advocate with the Father.

But now may I know that he prays and pleads for me? (a) If you are a little child to God, give up yourself to him and to his ministers, and be obedient to his ordinances. (b) If he sends his Spirit into your heart and helps you to draw your petitions, it is a sign that he himself is about the work. By our sins we dampen his spirit; but if God renews his Spirit in us, it is a sign that Christ has our cause in hand.

1 John 2:2

"And he is the propitiation for our sins, and not for ours only, but also for the sins of the whole world."

In these words we have Jesus Christ described: -1. By his external function, as being an advocate and a propitiation for our sins. -2. By his inward qualification, as being righteous. We have studied his office of advocate; we come now to his second office. "He is the propitiation for our sins, and not for ours only, but for the sins of the whole world."

Doct. Jesus Christ is the propitiation for the sins not only of believing Jews, but likewise of believing Christians all the world over.

Some translations render it, "He is the reconciliation"; but that does not express the full meaning. Propitiation includes three things.

-1. It requires that he should expiate our sins, that is, make satisfaction for them. A man may be a means of reconciliation without satisfaction, but he cannot be a propitiation without offering satisfaction for the wrong done. Now Christ did make satisfaction for our sins (Heb. 2:17); and to make satisfaction, he offered a satisfactory sacrifice for our sins (1 Pet. 2:24). Since he bore the sin and punishment due to it, it is as much as if we had done it.

-2. To be a propitiation it is required that he make peace and reconciliation; for though a man sometimes may recompense and satisfy a wrong, yet the party wronged will not be at peace with him. But Christ has taken it upon him to reconcile God to us, so that his wrath is turned from us and his favor restored (Col. 1:21). Now this reconciling implies three things: that once we were friends with God, that we fell out with God, and that, having fallen out, we are reconciled again and made at peace with him. Now this last is procured by Christ; whereas we were once friends with God in Paradise, and fell from him and his favor, Christ has come and made up that breach and reconciled us again.

-3. When Christ is said to be a propitiation for our sins, it implies that he has procured the manifestation of God's favor to us. Suppose a friend makes satisfaction for another, and gets reconcilement with another with whom he is fallen out; yet if the man does not know it, his heart is as heavy as ever. But Christ has not only procured us God's favor, but he also tells us that his Father is reconciled with us and at peace with us (Job 33:23, 26). This is the effect of Christ's propitiation: we shall see God's face with joy, and we shall pray to him with comfort. He says himself, "He who loves me shall be loved of my Father" (John 14:21); he will bring them together, and there shall be a mutual expression of love to one another and refreshment in one another. God shall take comfort in us and we in him (Rev. 3:20), for Christ goes further in this case than any man can.

Absalom had offended his father in slaying his brother Ammon, so he flew away from his father's court. Joab procured a reconcilement, but he would not satisfy for the blood he had shed. He did indeed procure so much that Absalom was sent home; but yet says David, "Let him return to his own house; he shall not see my faie" (2 Sam. 14:24). Joab could not satisfy for his blood, and thus the king would not see his face; so there lacked complete satisfaction and manifestation of the king's favor. Afterwards manifestation was procured; but still there lacked propitiation, because satisfaction could not be made. Christ, however, has not only procured favor, but satisfaction as well, and has declared his favor to us in so doing.

Now further, Christ has done this not only for the believing Jews, but all Christians the world over. To whom does he speak here? To "little children"; and who were they? They were Jews, as appears in v. 7, for they from the first giving of the law were commanded to love one another. Now besides these weak Jews, the apostle says he is not only the propitiation for their sins, but for the sins of the whole world.

Now 'world' is diversely used in scripture. -1. It is sometimes put for the frame of nature (Acts 17:24). -2. It is sometimes taken for the pleasure and profits of the world (1 John 2:16). -3. It is sometimes put for the wicked of the world (John 15:19). -4. It is sometimes taken for the Gentiles in opposition to the Jews (Rom. 11:12). -5. It is sometimes taken for the believers of the world (2 Cor. 5:19). Though it may sometimes have further extent, it is taken in this passage in opposition to Christian Jews; that is, he is not only a propitiation for the Jews, but also for the believing Gentiles.

But further, Christ is not only a propitiation for his children, but for the whole world; that is, the whole body of the creation. By Adam's fall the whole world was cursed; so Christ by his death renewed the blessing to the world again (Rom. 8:20). Therefore it is said, the whole body of the creation waits for the liberty which the sons of God have. We have a type of this in Noah (Gen. 8:20, 21). Noah, as a type of Christ, makes atonement for the world by sacrifice; and God smelled a sweet savor and promised that he would no more curse the earth for man's sake. And what was done typically in him is perfectly procured in Christ. Christ is now lord of all; he has bought not only us, but our ground and cattle and houses, and our children. And he has so purchased it that the world shall be a blessing to the church; the tumults and disorders shall be for the good of his people.

Has Christ made any propitiation for the wicked? For reprobates? If not, then how for all the world?

-1. You must distinguish between the wicked and the rest of the world. In this they all agree, that Christ is lord over all, wicked and good; he has bought all (2 Pet. 2:1), so that they are vassals to be ruled by Christ's dominion. He has bought them for the church's service, to do them good.

-2. I say that Christ has laid down a sufficient price for all, and to this degree he has procured God's patience to forbear them, and his bounty to lead them to repentance

(Rom. 2:4, 5). Yea, he has procured for them not only gifts fitting them for rule and ministry, and the common gifts and graces, but many sanctifying gifts as well (Heb. 10:29).

But is he then a propitiation for them? I answer, to make propitiation it is required not only that a satisfaction and reconciliation be made, but that they lay hold of it. Under the old law, who had an atonement made by the sacrifices they offered? Only those who laid their hands on the head of the sacrifice (Lev. 1:4). So then this is nothing for the propitiation of the wicked; they do not lay hold on the head of Christ, they do not take hold on him as an advocate and propitiation, and therefore they are left inexcusable. This point is likewise handled by Paul (Rom. 3:25; 2 Cor. 5:19). The whole world was out of fellowship with God, and Christ purchased something for all.

Use 1. This shows that it is a wicked opinion of the Papists, to say that the bread in the sacrament is a propitiatory sacrifice for the sins of the world. Thus they wrong Christ both in his advocation and in his propitiation. If there had been need of another propitiation, his had been insufficient (Heb. 10:10). But they ascribe propitiation to the sacramental bread, to purgatory, and to afflictions; they say their own voluntary devotions are satisfactin, as whippings and pilgrimages and fastings. But if Christ is the propitiation, we need none more but him.

It is objected that we allow one friend to pray for another here on earth, and to intreat God for him; then may not saints in heaven pray for us, as well as saints on earth? I answer, -1. We have both commands and examples for the one (James 5:16, and Paul desires the prayers of the churches), but we have neither command nor example for the other. -2. We desire those to pray for us who know of our cases. But it is uncertain that the angels or the saints in heaven know us or our wants; and it is certain they do not know our thoughts. -3. And when we desire other men here on earth to pray for us, we do not make them advocates as they do angels and saints. First, we do not desire them to pray in their own merits and name, as they do the angels and saints. Second, they pray to the virgin Mary for graces; so they ask spiritual gifts of the saints, gifts which God alone can give. Third, they ascribe to them certain proper works, make them patrons of nations, and distribute among them several offices. They pray to one for healing one disease, and to another for another.

Use 2. If Christ is our reconciliation, then it shows us what we are outside of Christ; enemies to God, and such enemies that if all the angels and saints in heaven should plead for us, they could not make propitiation for us. It is Christ's prerogative (Col. 1:21; Rom. 5:20; Eph. 2:5). We are enemies and strangers to God, and all the imaginations of our hearts are wholly evil continually. We delude ourselves by saying, "I hope I am not so far from the favor of God," but we are all so by nature.

Use 3. It should teach us, when we do find and feel that we are sinners, to think upon Christ's reconciliation and propitiation.

Someone will say, "I do believe that Christ has made an atonement for sinners and reconciled all believers; but how shall I know whether or not I am among that number?" I answer, has Christ ever brought you to see God's face with comfort? If you have ever beheld the face of God with joy and comfort, know that this could not be unless Christ had been a propitiation for you.

You will say, "Oh, I had comfort once, but now it is all gone again." I say, no man who is brought into the king's presence does always stand before him, but there is a time for the king to separate himself. So there is no Christian who stands always in the presence of God's face. It is enough that you have been brought to kiss God's hand and taste of his favor. You will say, "But I have never felt any comfort and joy in prayer and other ordinances." I reply: (a) Have you fallen out with your sins? If you have, you love God and are loved by him (Ps. 97:10). (b) Do you feel that you love God much, for you have been a great sinner, and yet God has had mercy upon you? This is a sign that much is forgiven you. (c) Do you find your heart compassionate with other men's sins? It is a sign yours are forgiven (Eph. 4:32).

Use 4. If we find that we are enemies to God and our peace is not made with him, it is to our wisdom to pacify God. Do as Adonijah did when he had offended King Solomon. He ran and took hold of the horns of the altar (1 Kings 1:50); so we should run and take hold of Christ. He who had any benefit by a sacrifice was to lay his hands on its head; so, would you have any benefit by Christ? Lay hold on him, confess your sins over him, and entreat him to make your peace with God.

But how may we know whether we lay hold on Christ? (a) Every man who lays hold on Christ takes him for better or for worse; he takes him to be a Ruler as well as a Saviour. You must give up yourself to be guided by his will, as well as to receive benefit by him. (b) If you find your heart wholly resting on Christ, and none but him; if this is the frame of your heart, that you desire none in heaven or earth in comparison to him (Ps. 73:25); then you have laid hold upon him.

Use 5. This may be of help to Christians who have their sins pardoned and are in Christ. Though you be such, yet you are not to think that you have no need of Christ; for if you were as St. John and the apostles — pillars — yet you would still have need of an advocate and propitiation; for in many things you would sin daily and fall out with God. If God would fall out with us as often as we fall out with him, we would never have peace. Therefore go to Christ and entreat him to be your atonement from day to day. Christ is not only a peacemaker but a peacekeeper; we daily offend God or ourselves, and therefore we stand daily in need of Christ's mediation. Likewise we have much need of Christ's Spirit to help us in our prayers.

Use 6. Of consolation to every Christian soul. Consider that even in the midst of your sins you have Christ for your propitiation, to keep your peace with God. Not a day passes over our heads in which we do not fall out with God; and if Christ would not intercede for us, what would become of us? But here is the comfort: Christ is truly our propitiation, and therefore it is certain and sure that he is more able to keep our peace than we are to break it. And besides, he has taken it upon him to be an atonement between God and us. Here is also further comfort: he has not only been a means of reconciliation, but he has also manifested it unto us; he has brought us to see God's face with comfort.

But this is not all. Here is matter of further comfort: since he is made a propitiation for the whole world, the whole world shall be at peace with us; there is also a reconciliation between me and all the creatures. I have comfort from every blessing, by Christ's propitiation (John 5:19, 23); so whatever a Christian meets with, whether good deeds or bad, even in persecution, this is his comfort: the whole world shall be for his good. Though I meet with crosses and afflictions, it shall be for my good; and this is the reason, that Christ is a propitiation for the whole world.

Use 7. If God has made so large an atonement for all, then let us draw one another to take heed of sin, to run to Christ, to make use of Christ's atonement. Old Eli made this use: "If one man sin against another, the judge shall judge it; but if a man sin against the Lord, who shall plead for him?" (1 Sam. 2:25). If you fall out with God and walk in sin, who shall make your peace with him? That is a work no friend you have can do; no means you can use can make up that breach — none but Christ — and you must not presume upon Christ's mediation. He will not be a cover for anyone's sin; that is a sign of reprobation, to turn God's grace into wantonness (Jude 4). And take heed you do not offend Christ; it is a notable counsel which God gives to Moses to deliver to the people: "Behold, I send an angel before you (that is, Christ, the angel of the covenant); beware of him, provoke him not; he will not spare your misdeeds, for my name is in him" (Exod. 23:20-22). If you do willingly sin against him, he will not pardon you. Therefore encourage all the friends you have to make use of Christ's reconciliation. He is a propitiation for little children (v. 1), for young men, for old men (the following verses), for all who are willing to lay hold on him. Paul makes this use (2 Cor. 5:19-21), and it is the chief point of the gospel, that God has made Christ a propitiation for sin. Therefore we beseech you to make use of it; take not Christ's blood in vain; beware of offending his grace and mercy; and labor to bring all men to Christ. Since the propitiation is so general, and since there is such a fountain set open, let us draw to it for ourselves and our children; let us teach our children that Christ is a propitiation for their sins.

We have heard Christ described from his external offices, as an advocate and a propitiation. We come now to his internal virtue or qualification: "Jesus Christ the righteous."

Doct. Jesus Christ is the righteous Lord; or, Jesus Christ, in either his office of an advocate or of a reconciler, is Jesus Christ the righteous.

The scripture testifies this (Heb. 4:15; 1 Peter 3:8; 1 Pet. 2:22). Pilate, who condemned him, gave him this testimony: "I am innocent of the blood of this just man" (Matt. 27:24). Yea, from his birth he had this testimony by the angel (Luke 1:35), "that holy thing," in opposition to all others, who are sinners from the very womb. He was holy in his birth, in his life, in his death. It is said that he knew no sin (2 Cor. 5:19); that is, he had experience of none. But the Father made him sinful by imputation, that we might be made just by imputation.

It was necessary that he should be righteous without sin, that he might be our reconciler and our advocate. If he had had any sin, he could have been neither of these.

-1. It was meet that he should be righteous; for had he been sinful himself, he could not have made atonement for sin. It was required that all the sacrifices should be without blemish (Lev. 1:3, 10), for else they would not have been accepted, as the Lord tells them (Mal. 1:8). All things defiled with sin are abominable to God (Heb. 7:25, 26), unless some atonement was made. Now had Christ been sinful, he could not have made an atonement for our sins. He who knew no sin was imputed a sinner for us, that we might be imputed righteous for his sake (2 Cor. 5:19-21).

-2. It was meet that he should be righteous, that he might be our advocate. "God hears not sinners" (John 9:31). The blind man was not so blind that he could not see that. But God hears Christ always; and we need such an advocate to prevail continually with God. Look at all the parts of his advocation for us, and it is meet that he should be righteous. (a) He appears for us in the sight of God. If he had been a sinner, his person would have been odious in God's sight. (b) He advocates by pleading the merits of his own death. Now how could it have been meritorious if he died as a malefactor? (c) He gives us his name and Spirit to use in our prayers; but to use his name would have been of no effect, had he been a sinner. (d) He prays for us and makes known his will to the Father concerning us. But this would do no good if he had been a sinner.

-3. It is meet he would be righteous, that he might be our justifier. Our justification comes by his obedience, for his righteousness is imputed to us. Now his righteousness could not have been imputed to us if it had been imperfect.

Use 1. It is a ground of much consolation to those who lay hold of Christ, and have him for their advocate and reconciler; for he is one who is just and righteous, and therefore fit to prevail for us.

What then will hinder the joy of a Christian? (a) "I have many doubts of the pardon of my sins; could I be sure of that, I would be joyful." I answer, you have a reconciler who is just and righteous, and therefore he will procure pardon for you. (b) "But I am still unjust and unrighteous." I answer, your Reconciler is not so; and it is not required that the reconciled should be righteous, but only the reconciler. (c) "I cannot pray; my prayers are heartless and faithless." Perhaps; but we have an advocate who is holy and just, and he prays and intercedes for us; and we shall find and receive the benefits of his righteousness. Though we fall daily into much unrighteousness, yet Jesus Christ our mediator is righteous.

Use 2. To teach us to be righteous, as he is righteous. God would have us conformable to the image of his son (Rom. 8:29); and that consists in holiness and righteousness. God would have us so walk that our surname might be justice; we must be righteous toward God, to give him his due; righteous toward others, to give them their due; and righteous toward ourselves.

To be called Christians and yet not to be righteous, is to be called Christians and still to be no Christians. Why are we called Christians, if not because we are anointed with the unction of Christ? If a man professes himself a Christian, and is not righteous, he is not a Christian; he has not the Spirit of Christ, and is therefore none of his. We may fail, of course, but it is required that the current and bent of our hearts and ways be to walk righteously. We aim at righteousness, though sometimes we miss the mark.

Use 3. This may quiet us if we fear evil in well doing. How? Because Christ was most righteous, and yet he suffered much unrighteousness in a righteous cause. We think we have much wrong if for righteousness' sake we meet with unrighteous treatment. If we meet with crosses, and fires and fagots, in innocence, we cry out; but it was so with Christ, and so we must not think it strange to suffer ill for well-doing, not only to be reviled, but to lose our goods and our lives. If we should meet with death, it is no more than Christ suffered. It was the scoff of atheists in old times, Why do the righteous suffer and the wicked prosper, if there is a God who governs the earth? But we must consider that God is patient as well as just, and therefore many times forbears punishment.

1 John 2:3

"And hereby we do know that we know him, if we keep his commandments."

The apostle John had shown in the former verses that Christ is our advocate and propitiation; and here his little children might reason, "But how shall I know that Christ is my advocate and reconciler? Though he is both, yet how shall I know that he is so to me?" He answers, "Hereby we know that we know him, if we keep his commandments."

St. John here speaks of the knowledge which we call acquaintance, familiarity, and fellowship. "I know you not" (Matt. 7:23); that is, I have no acquaintance and fellowship with you. Hereby we know that we have fellowship with Christ if we keep his commandments; by this you may know whether or not you have fellowship with Christ. The third verse, then, shows our fellowship with Christ in his mediation.

Doct. 1. A man who knows Christ may and should come to know that he does know him, and may and should come to have fellowship and communion with him.

"Hereby we know that we know him"; here is a reflex action. The senses do not reflect by themselves; the eye sees other men's faces, but cannot see its own without reflection in a glass. So in our spiritual knowledge we may more readily discern our spiritual state than our faces; for we do not see our face except in another medium, but we know our spiritual things directly; we not only know, but we know that we know what is meant by them.

To know Christ means more than to know his nature and person and offices, and that he is God-man, and that he is our advocate and reconciler and propitiation. The devil knows this much. A spiritual knowledge is not superficial but operative; it is not dead but lively; not naked but clothed with acquaintance; not idle but working us to obedience (Ps. 19: 9-11); and that works us to mortification (Gal. 6:14).

This knowledge makes all the world dead to us; as when a man has set his affections on a woman, it deadens his affection to all others. The sons of Eli did not know the Lord (1 Sam. 2:12), nor did Pharaoh (Exod. 5:2); that is, they did not have this lively operative knowledge joined with obedience.

Thus true knowledge is operative, and begets trust and confidence and joy in God (Jer. 10:23), and it is joined with obedience (1 Chron. 28:9). So then it is such a knowledge as makes us -1. trust in him, -2. fear him, -3. honor him, -4. serve him, -5. cleave to him, and -6. yield obedience to him. "I have seen the oppression wherewith the Egyptians oppress my people Israel" (Exod. 3:9); that is, I have not only looked on it, but have had compassion and intend to deliver them. "Remember thy creator"; that is, bend your affections to him and honor him. So to know Christ is to affect him, to honor him, to cleave to him, to obey him, to acquaint ourselves with him; for by knowledge is here meant familiarity and acquaintance.

What is this knowledge, to know that we know him?

It is an act of understanding by which, upon good grounds, we discern that we do know God and have fellowship with him. No man calls that knowledge which is only a conjecture; but this knowledge is more than a true faith. Though knowledge and faith are two distinct things, they stand together; "We have known and believed" (1 John 4:16). So this knowledge is more than faith, for faith is a persuasion or trust taken by man upon divine testimony. If I believe something upon man's testimony, that is credulity; when I take it upon God's authority, that is faith, a higher step; but here is a higher still, for we know and believe. This is more than opinion or faith.

So then we may know that we know him.

Doct. 2. A man who knows Christ may not only think so, and have such an opinion, and believe so, but he may know he knows Christ.

He may know it by two effects.

-1. By feeling in his own heart that, though he has been oppressed with sin, he now finds his soul brought to peace. If he finds Christ pacifying his soul, he knows that he knows Christ. A man whose spirit has been oppressed with the consciousness of sin, if his soul is comforted and pacified, then knows that he knows Christ. Now he is acquainted with Christ in experience. One who was never troubled with sin does not know the worth and virtue of Christ; but a man who has been afflicted in conscience for sin, and is now pacified, he knows Christ. He had heard of him before, but now he sees him plainly (Job 42:5). He now sees his worth and excellency (Cant. 5:10). A man knows that this is Christ, because he knows that nothing in heaven or earth could pacify him but Christ.

-2. He knows that he knows Christ, not only by having his conscience pacified but by having it purified (Acts 15:9); purified from the lusts of sin. Whereas we were covetous before, now we are heavenly minded; whereas vain before, now we are serious in serious matters, and look at trifles as trifles; whereas intemperate before, now temperate; unclean before, now holy and chaste. We were disordered before, but now our hearts are cast into another mold and frame; both the inward and outward man are purified; the words and actions are purified. Thus we know that we know him if we keep his commandments; that they who know Christ may say, I know that I know him.

Use 1. To refute that Popish doctrine which teaches that none can be certain of his salvation. They say it is heretical presumption; many worldlings think it is impossible, and others think it needless to be obtained; but such may be convinced by this doctrine. What says the apostle Peter? "Give all diligence to make your calling and election sure" (2 Pet. 1:10). How shall we make it sure, if we know that we know it? God gives us his spirit so that we may see the grace he has given us (1 Cor. 2:12; 1 John 3:24). St. John speaks it here of little children, that they may know it; thus this knowledge is both possible and necessary, and may be certain.

The Papists say we may have a conjectural knowledge, but no certainty of faith. But this implies a contradiction: if it is conjectural, it is not knowledge. We do not know what we only conjecture. If I ask you, "Do you know such a one?" you do not say you think you know him. If you do, you do not know him at all. So when they say we cannot have knowledge of faith, we do not say they may only believe it, but they may have certainty of feeling. Faith may admit much doubting, but knowledge excludes all doubting.

Use 2. To consider whether we can say that we know we know him. Do you know that you have acquaintance and fellowship with Christ? Do you believe it? If so, on what grounds? (a) Have you found Christ pacifying your conscience by his blood? If so, then you know that you know him (Phil. 4:7). (b) Do you find your conscience purified? Do you find your corruption mortified? Do your lusts grow abominable? Do you find your heart cleansed from wrath and impatience? Certainly then you know that you know Christ, for none else could pacify and purify your heart. If you are in such a frame that you dare not sin, that you seek peace and pursue it, then you may know that you have Christ; but if the signs are lacking, especially purifying, then you know him not.

Use 3. To exhort us never to rest until we know that we have acquaintance with Christ. If a man had all the knowledge in the world, what comfort would it afford him if he did not know whether he had fellowship with Christ? Never think you know anything if you know not Christ, and do not rest there until you know you know him. Animals see and hear, but they do not know they do so, because they are irrational and lack the faculty of reflection. In spiritual things a carnal heart is blind; but a Christian may know Christ, and know he knows him. We must not rest in men's good opinions or in their good words concerning us, but we must never rest until we know that Christ dwells in us and we in him; we may know this by pacifying and purifying our consciences.

Use 4. Of consolation to those who sin and fall daily, and find their own emptiness. Their knowledge, is small, their experience little, their outward comforts shallow; but this is a great consolation, that a man knows Christ and knows he knows him. God never gives us a blessing without being willing that we should know it. If he sets up a light in our minds, he would have us discern that light and walk in its brilliance; therefore let us thankfully knowledge it and comfort ourselves in it.

We come now to the evidence by which we come to know that we know Christ. Hereby we know we know him, if we keep his commandments. To understand this we must know that: -1. There is a perfect keeping of the commandments, without sin. St. John disclaimed that before (1:8,10). -2. There is another keeping of the commandments which is not perfect without sin, but perfect without dissimulation or hypocrisy; and that is here meant.

Doct. 3. Sincere obedience, or keeping the commandments of Christ, is a certain sign and argument for our undoubted and known fellowship with Christ.

What is it to keep his commandments? The keeping of his commandments is usually expressed in scripture by comparisons.

-1. Sometimes it is expressed by keeping the commandments as a man would keep his way, turning neither to the right hand nor to the left (Josh. 1:7). Then we must look at the commandments as our path; a traveller does not go out of his way, and if forced out he returns to it as quickly as he can.

-2. Sometimes it is expressed by keeping jewels. We should keep them as our treasure, set our hearts upon them (Prov. 6:20, 21). This verse, "bind them about thy heart," implies that they are to be regarded as our greatest treasure and worn about our necks. He would have us look at them as our ornaments. Many men would be rich, but they would not always have it known; but a Christian is not only to look at Christ's commandments as his treasure, but as his ornaments and credit. A man is said to keep the commandments when he looks at them as his treasures and ornaments. He is not ashamed to let it appear that he keeps Christ's commandments; he is not ashamed to wear them about him openly.

-3. It is compared to keeping the apple of a man's eye (Prov. 7:2). A man keeps the apple of his eye very tenderly;

he would not have the least mote come into his eye. So it is true of keeping God's commandments; the least offense or scruple against God's commandments is bitter and noisome to him, as motes to the apple of his eye. He cares not what the world thinks of it; if it is against the law of God it is noisome to him.

-4. It is expressed by keeping the commandments as a man would keep his soul (Prov. 19:16). If it comes to this, either break the commandments or lose your life, a Christian will keep the commandments and lose his life. A man must be willing to give up his life for Christ (Luke 14:26). Now if we thus keep his commandments, it is an evident sign that we know that we know him.

But it will be said, Such keeping is very strict and hard to be obtained; who can do this? In many things we offend all, and who is it who goes not astray? I answer, a Christian may keep the commandments as his way, when he intends to go on; and if he is out of the way it is beside his intention. He may keep them as his treasure, though sometimes upon some temptation he may part with some of them; yet he mourns for it when he knows of it, and it is the grief of his heart. And though a Christian may sometimes be ashamed of his profession, yet afterwards he is ashamed of his shame, as Peter; and though a Christian sometimes offends against the commandment, yet he is never well until he has gotten out this mote. Sometimes a man may rather choose his life, as Peter, but afterwards he grieves and weeps bitterly, and would rather part with his life than with the commandment. If it is thus with you, it is a sign your keeping is sincere.

But how is obedience such a certain sign of our acquaintance with Christ?

-1. This sincere keeping of the commandments is regarded by the Saviour as an act of friendship with him (John 15:14). We take it as a point of special friendship when a man is ready at our command and willing to do what we would have him; yes, and the Saviour takes it not only as love, but as constant abiding love (John 15:10); and if it springs from our love to Christ, it must first spring from Christ's love to us, for we could not have loved him unless he loved us first (1 John 4:19, 5:3). No man keeps anything that is grievous. A man may have fire about his house, or a mote in his eye; but he does not keep it, for it is grievous. When he keeps the commandments as his way, his treasure, his eye, his life, this is not grievous to him. Every duty, be it ever so bad, seems easy because he loves Christ dearly; as Jacob's seven years of service for Rachel seemed but a little time because he loved her (Gen. 29:20). If there is such mutual love, it is a certain sign of acquaintance with Christ.

-2. This keeping of his commandments is a sign of our abiding in Christ and so of our acquaintance with him (John 15:1; Hos. 14:8, "Upon me is my fruit found"); otherwise we are barren. It is Christ who puts forth any fruit in us (Ezek. 36:27). How does it come to pass that a man keeps God's laws and judgments, if not because he has his Spirit within him? He keeps us, and then we keep his commandments.

Use 1. To refute Popish errors. (a) That a man may keep the commandments perfectly without sin. (b) That, though he can thus keep them, yet he cannot be sure of his salvation. These are contradictory; hereby we know that we know him, if we keep his commandments; so that is either certain that they do not keep his commandments, or if they do, that they may be certain of their fellowship with Christ and of salvation by him. (c) It refutes them in this: they say we discourage men from good works. We do indeed say that none can be justified by the works of the law, but we do not discourage men from good works; for we say that if men keep God's commandments, which is to perform good works, by this they may come to know that they know Christ. We say more: not only a perfect keeping of them, but a sincere keeping of them (though imperfectly, yet with respect and care), though it does not justify us, yet it does justify the truth of our state, and this is no small matter. Yea, we challenge them for discouraging men from good works; for they will not grant that we know we know him by them, but they still leave a man in doubt. We grant much comfort from good works, for though they do not justify us, yet by them we know that we are justified.

Use 2. To confute the Arians. This shows a plain reason for the divinity of Christ, because by keeping his commandments we may come to know him. Now this would not hold if he did not have authority to command with God himself. "There is one lawgiver" (James 4:12); therefore if Christ is our lawgiver, he is one with God the Father; and his commandments are of the same authority and benefit as the Father's commandments.

Use 3. This shows the cause why many men do not know that they know Christ.

a. Those cannot know Christ who do not know his commandments; for if they do not know them, how can they keep them? God's ways are too hard to be found in the night, in ignorance or darkness.

b. Though a man knows them, yet he may divide them; some he will keep and some he will not keep; if he does this, he cannot come to know that he knows Christ, because he does not keep his commandments. If you are content to live in the least known sin; if you do not as gladly root out any sin as you would pull a mote out of your eye, you cannot know Christ or come to know that you know him.

c. There are others who know Christ, and yet they do not know that they know him. Why? Because they do not keep his commandments as their way; they do not look at them as their treasure, as their ornaments; they do not keep them as the apple of their eye, but swallow many motes; this does much hinder their souls. Many would do much for religion, but would not have it come to light; then no wonder if they do not see their states. If motes are in our eyes, we cannot see as otherwise we might; so if sin lies in our souls, no wonder if we are so blind that we cannot see our state in Christ or know that we know him.

Use 4. This shows us a ready way to peace of conscience.

Would we know that we have our consciences at peace? Why, then, we must labor to know that we know Christ, and that will pacify the conscience. Indeed this is peace of conscience, if we are acquainted with Christ. But how shall we know that? Keep the commandments of Christ as our way, as our treasure, as the apple of our eye, as our life; then we may know that we know him, and that we have fellowship with him. And then our consciences will be quiet both in life and death, if we keep the commandments as our way and are troubled when we are out of the way; if we keep it as our treasure and are grieved at the loss of it as at the loss of our ornaments; if we cannot allow any sin to be in our souls without being afflicted for it. But if we keep the commandments carelessly, we keep the peace of our consciences loosely. It may be that we walk in God's ways, but not so closely and carefully as we should; this hinders our own peace.

When his hypocrisy had been found out, speaking now in a good temper, Jonah said, "They that follow lying vanities forsake their own mercies" (Jonah 2:8); they who follow any comfort of the world, any treasure, any ornament, any life that they prize above the commandments of God, find it at the end to be a lying vanity, a deluding thing, and by following it they forsake their own mercies, that is, the portion of mercy which God had appointed them. Jonah spoke from woeful experience; he clung to his credit, a lying vanity, and thought he would prevent his discredit. But God found him out, and he found it out by experience: those who stick to any pleasure more than to God, forsake their own mercies. He might have had mercy if he had been obedient, but now he saw no hope of mercy, in this world at least; therefore it may teach us to take heed of trusting to any deluding vanity.

Use 5. Of consolation to constant keepers of God's commanements. Sometimes a man may keep them and still be in fear and doubts of his state. Well then, go on in that way still; keep them as your way, your treasure, and the apple of your eye; as your life, that is, as the way to comfort; and be it known unto you that if you do this, you do know Christ.

For if you did not love God, you would never go on in a constant course of keeping his commandments; and you could not love him unless he loved you first. Further, you could not keep his commandments but by his Spirit dwelling in you, and that argues acquaintance with him. It is said, "In keeping his commandments there is great reward" (Ps. 19:11), greater than gold or silver; and a man may still lack a quiet conscience and yet have that, but a man who keeps God's commandments shall have both (Ps. 119:72). Thousands of gold and silver will not keep a man's heart warm and comfortable, but the keeping of God's commandments will; and if you are about your calling, no business of your calling shall hinder your peace, and no commandment of God hinders your peace. Indeed if you go about things unwarranted in the commandment, in the world or in your calling, if you look at your own profit and pleasure, and not at God's commandments, you will lose your peace and lack it in that day's business. But if you go about things in view of the commandment, never fear; your calling will never hinder your peace. Keep the commandment and you keep your peace.

1 John 2:4

"He that saith, I know him, and keepeth not his commandments, is a liar, and the truth is not in him."

It is St. John's usual course to propound the truth both affirmatively and negatively: affirmatively in v. 3, negatively in v. 4. In v. 5 he amplified the keeping of Christ's commandment by a double benefit. -1. In him who does so, the love of God is perfect. -2. By this we know that we are in him. Then in v. 6 he passes this conclusion, urging us to conform our lives to the life of Christ.

"He who says, I know him." To say may be in heart, in word, or in outward carriage. The knowledge spoken of here is acquaintance; so then, he who says he has acquaintance with God, and keeps not his commandments (as his way, his treasure, his ornaments, his eye, his life), -1. He is a liar. That is, he not only speaks falsely, but he knows he speaks falsely; for that is the difference between a mere untruth and a lie. -2. There is no truth in him: not one true grace, not one true act of repentance and faith.

Doct. Professing the knowledge of Christ, without keeping his commandments, is an undoubted sign that a man is a liar, and the best grace in him is counterfeit; he has no true grace in him.

To say in the heart is opinion; to say in the tongue or manner is profession; and if he does the latter, he is a liar. "They profess they know God, but in their works they deny him" (Tit. 1:15, 16); such a one is "abominable, disobedient, and to every good work reprobate"; that is, he goes about it untowardly, is unskillful in it, has no sincerity, and his work is rejected of God as reprobate counterfeit silver.

How is such a man said to be a liar and have no truth in him? A man may be a liar sometimes, and yet have some truth in him; but such a one has no truth, for: -1. He speaks folly. -2. He speaks against conscience. -3. No truth is in him.

-1. He speaks folly. This appears from the efficacy of all true knowledge of Christ, which brings forth obedience. If a man knows Christ, he knows him and loves him and obeys him (Matt. 7:22, 23). All saving knowledge stirs us up to obedience to God and to righteousness towards man. If a man is a son of Belial, he does not know God; those who do not obey him never knew him (1 Chron. 29:9). Those who do not serve him never knew him (John 14:21). And further, no man knows God who has not known the depth and danger of sin; if he does not know his estrangement and absence from God, he knows not God.

After such a one knows sin, he comes to know Christ and his mediation. He is sensible of his former misery and knows the excellence of Christ; he has been so stricken with sin that he looks upon it as the most heinous thing, and the keeping of God's commandments as the sweetest thing, in all the world. God's commandments are not grievous to him. Such knowledge springs from experience of our former misery, and therefore they who never come to this never knew Christ.

-2. He speaks against conscience. Why is he a liar? Because he is convicted by the testimony of that light which shines in his heart (John 16:9). There is a spirit of convicion in all those who live in the church, for others do not contend that they know Christ; but those who so profess are convinced of their sins, of their unbelief and disobedience, and of the wickedness of their hearts and lives.

But are there not many who live carnally and wickedly, and yet are not convinced of their sins? It is true that there are such; but, living in such a course, they do not trespass against their consciences; they think they keep the law, and so think well of themselves; and they are at peace and secure.

But though he walk thus civilly and conformably, yet such a man's conscience is uncertain about his state. He is convinced that he lacks something, but he cannot tell what it is until he is thoroughly convinced by God's Spirit. Thus it was in Matt. 19:18-20; Mark 10:19, 20. The young man told Christ, "All these have I kept from my youth; what lack I yet?" His conscience guided him to feel that he lacked something. Though he had kept the law in the outward letter, yet he saw that something was missing, and his conscience was not at rest. Thus the man who says he knows Christ and yet keeps not his commandment, speaks against the conviction of his conscience, and therefore is a liar. I do not speak of Christians who lack peace because they do not keep God's commandments, but of those who think they keep his commandments solely because they have peace.

-3. No truth is in such a man. Why? Because all graces are conjoined with obedience; every true grace of God is either the cause of obedience, or a companion of obedience, or the effect of obedience. Faith works by love (Gal. 5:6), and love is the fulfilling of the law (Rom. 13:10; 1 Tim. 1:5); and so hope (1 John 3:3). Patience is joined with obedience, and meekness springs from obedience; and from the spiritual experience of a man's weakness and experience of Christ's power comes humility. So all graces either spring from obedience, or serve to it, or accompany it.

Even those very graces that are more in the understanding and speculation either spring from obedience or help to obedience. The knowledge of a Christian is not unfruitful (2 Pet. 1:8); and it brings forth fruits of obedience. Every gift a Christian has, he considers what good he may do with it; and if he sees it is not serviceable he does not regard it. So then, if every grace either breeds, nurses, or accompanies obedience, then whoever professes he knows God and does not keep his commandments, has no truth nor true grace.

Use 1. To try the truth of our profession. Would you know the truth of your grace, of your repentance, of your faith, of your humility? You shall know it by your fruitfulness. What use do you make of your graces? Would you know whether your repentance or love is sound? Consider then, do they make you obedient, and careful to keep God's commandments as your way, your treasure, your ornaments, your eye, your life? If any grace is fruitful and makes you faithful in keeping God's commandments, that is a witness of the truth of that grace. A painted tree, though ever so fair, yet bears no fruit; but a living tree bears fruit. You have cause to suspect your grace if it does not make you more fruitful and more careful to please God. If grace makes you obedient, it is sincere. But if a man has ever so many gifts and graces, and they do not lead him to obedience, then truly they are but counterfeit, and there is no true grace in him. If wisdom caused them to rebel (Isa. 47:10), there is no truth in their wisdom; if any grace leaves you more corrupt, or less fruitful, there is no truth in it.

Use 2. It exhorts us to a careful and diligent keeping of God's commandments. Hereby: (a) We shall keep our profession true, our consciences void of offense, and shall have an evidence that we know Christ. If a man says he knows God and yet does not keep his commandments, his profession is not true; but he who both says and does so, his profession is sincere. (b) It will keep your conscience in peace. When your conscience does not check you, but bears you witness that you desire to do God's will in truth, this brings great peace. (c) It keeps your grace sound. The more you are obedient and fruitful, the more grace increases. A Christian who lets his grace lie at rest will soon find it rusty, and he may doubt the truth of his grace. If metal lies up and rusts, we may justly suspect it to be brittle and weak; but if it is kept in continual use, we do not suspect it. Take a Christian who does not exercise himself in grace; he grows so rusty that he suspects the truth of his grace. But put your grace to employment, let it be in continual use, and you shall easily see that it is good metal. The employment of graces proves the truth of them; therefore as we desire to keep our profession true, or our consciences clean, or our graces sound, let us keep in a daily course of obedience, always doing good.

Use 3. Of consolation to all who take a good course and labor to keep God's commandments, when they sometimes suspect all their grace is counterfeit and there is no sincerity in them. If there is no sincerity in you, you cannot keep God's commandments as your way; but you endeavor it, and it is the grief of your soul when you go out of the way. Do you keep them as your treasure and ornament, and the apple of your eye, and life? Why then, there is truth of grace in you; truth of sincerity, though not of perfection. You must not expect to keep them perfect without sin, but if you desire to keep them as the most precious thing, as your treasure, your ornament, your life, the apple of your eye, your grace is sound. If it were counterfeit you would not keep God's commandments. "Wickedness says to the wicked, there is no fear of God before his eyes" (Ps. 36:1); how does that appear By his fruits he knows him; and it is plain he has no sear of God before his eyes. If you set yourself in no good way, your profession cannot be true; but if your way is good, and if you do not take it up when it is not, then your profession is true and your grace sound.

It is a question whether Solomon fell finally, whether or not his graces were true. You may know his repentance was true, because he found his lust for women as bitter as death (Eccl. 7:26). Well then, if an adulterous or idolatrous wife was as bitter as death to him, then it is an evident sign that he looked at his transgression as death; then he looked at the commandment as life, and his repentance was sincere. So then if a man finds his sin as bitter as death, it is a sign his repentance is true.

But here we must distinguish between the horror of sin and sin itself. The horror of sin may be as bitter to us as death, but not the sin itself. For Judas, the horror of sin was so bitter that for it he hanged himself; but had he been troubled with the sin itself in his conscience, as he was with the horror of his conscience, he would not have gone about to help one sin by another. Had he hated sin for itself, he would have hated murder as sin. So then, would you know whether it is horror of sin that troubles you? If it be horror, you will seek to drive it away by more sin, as some do by merry company and merry books. This is a plain sign that sin troubles them not, for then they would not seek to help one sin by another. But if you regard the breach of the law as the loss of your way, as the losing of your treasure, as a mote in your eye, as losing your life, then you may have comfort; your profession is true, your conscience clear, your profession sincere and sound.

1 John 2:5

"But whoever keeps his word, in him verily is the love of God perfected. Hereby we know that we are in him."

These words declare a double comfort for all who keep the commandments of Christ Jesus. -1. God's love is perfect in them. -2. By their obedience they know that they are in him. So he who keeps his commandments, if he looks in himself, will find perfect love; if he looks outside himself, he will find he is in Christ; yea, and more, he knows it too. Thus the apostle concludes, v. 16, that he who says he is in Christ ought so to walk as Christ also walked.

To keep his word or commandments, as I told you, is a borrowed expression from many things which we keep with great care, as our way, our treasure, our ornament, the apple of our eye, our life. What is such a man's benefit? First, the love of God is perfected in him, and second, he knows he is in Christ.

The love here spoken of is not the love with which God loves us, but the love by which we love God, and that is perfected in us.

Doct. Keeping God's commandments is undoubtedly and truly the perfection of our love to God.

What is here meant by perfection? There is a double perfection: -1. Perfection complete, without all lack or imperfection, and that is denied to any man in this world. "Not as though I had already attained, either were already perfect; but I follow after" (Phil. 3:12); that is, not exempt from all weaknesses. Our knowledge is imperfect and our love is imperfect; there is a continual reluctance (Gal. 3:3, 4). -2. Perfection without falsehood, hypocrisy, dissimulation, or guile; and such a perfection is found in all true believers who keep God's commandments. "The love of God is perfected in them;" that is, without hypocrisy, dissimulation, or guile. Thus Noah was a perfect man (Gen. 6:9), and Asa (1 Kings 15). Asa's heart was perfect, that is, sincere, though he had many and great failings. Hezekiah says, "Remember how I have walked before thee with a perfect heart" (1 Kings 20:3). The phrase is usual in scripture, to call that "perfect" which is sincere and true.

But how may it be called perfect? Sincerity of obedience is called perfect, because whatever is lacking is covered in the blood of Christ; and if a man's sin is covered, it is as if he had no sin (Ps. 32:1, 2). When there is so much uprightness in a man's heart that he walks without any guile, to him the Lord imputes no sin.

But is there any in whose heart there is no guile?

-1. There is none that they tolerate or justify, none that they nourish or maintain. If they have any they strive against it and are not quiet until they are rid of it. They have no guile that their judgments allow and that their wills consent to; blessed are such to whom no sin is imputed, in whose spirit there is no guile.

-2. They strive after perfection, and if they have a willing heart the Lord accepts it, according to what a man has, and not according to what he has not (2 Cor. 8:12). See how Christ approved the two mites of the poor widow, because she had a heart to give all her estate. Christ says, she gave more than they all; so if a man gives all his heart to God, and would give more if he had more, why, God accounts it as perfect.

But how does such a keeping of the commandments argue love to be perfect?

A thing is said to be perfect three ways: -1. When there is a perfecting of all parts, with none lacking. -2. A man is called perfect who is ready and skillful, and nimble at any business. -3. A thing is said to be perfect when it will hold constant, as we call those colors perfect which will hold their hue in every weather. Now such a perfection of love to God is in all who keep God's commandments.

-1. There is a perfection of all the parts of love in all such men; there is none of the parts wanting. The parts of love are two: an affection to fellowship with Christ, and an affection to be doing good to him. If we love anything completely, we desire communion with it, and we desire to communicate good to it; if we are able we rejoice, and if we are unable we earnestly desire it. How does a man know his love to his friend? By desire of communion with him and communication of good to him.

Now such a man as keeps Christ's commandments thus loves Christ. (a) He is broken off from the love of all other things, and he has an unfeigned affection to have fellowship with him. And to get that, he keeps his commandments and so dwells in Christ, and Christ in him (John 14:21, 22). (b) He desires to communicate good to Christ. Our works cannot profit God; yet if we are willing to do God any service, to be about his commandment at any time, then the love of God is perfect in us; for we desire fellowship with him and desire to do him the best service we can.

-2. Again, in perfection there is a readiness to work. So, the man who keeps God's commandments shows his love to be ready; he is quick to perform every good duty, because it is a commandment of God. He is a willing person (Ps. 110:3; 2 Cor. 8:12); you need not stand urging him, but he is willing to do God's will. His tongue is as the pen of a ready writer (Ps. 45:1).

-3. There is a perfect love in him, because it is constant and durable, and will not change. Such a man's love is the same in health and sickness, in the church and at home, in prosperity and adversity; and if it is in any way disturbed at any time, it will return again to its former constant course.

But you will say, how may I know how it appears that if I keep God's commandment, my love is perfect? From two reasons:

-1. From the adversity of our natural tempers to any commandment. If you see anyone willing and ready to be at God's command, you may say certainly the love of God has overcome him; the commandments of God cross his will, cross his affections, cross his profit and pleasure. Thus if you see him giving himself up to keep God's commandments, it is an undoubted sign that the love of God is in him, for it constrains him to do what nature would not do.

-2. From the growth of love in such a one. Whatever weak beginnings of love you find in him as he begins to keep

God's commandments, he grows more perfect every day; he grows in fruitfulness, he grows ready to every good work (John 15:2), so that the love of God is perfected in him by obedience. As a fruitful tree grows faster when its root is deeper in the ground, so a Christian grows faster as he sticks his root into Christ. And as the husbandman will take more care with a fruitful tree, to dress and prune it, than with a sour unfruitful tree, so when a man is fruitful in God's commandments, he does not only sink his root, his faith and hope, deeper and deeper in Christ, but the Lord himself is willing to cut down all those noisome lusts that suck away the sap of grace. If God sees a man set fully to follow God, and keep his commandments, the Lord will cut off all cumbrances, all corruptions, all things that hinder the growth of grace.

Use 1. For trial of our love to God, whether or not it is perfect, whether sincere or counterfeit. How do you find your heart affected to God's commandments? Do you look at them as your way? Does it grieve you to be out of them? Do you look at them as your treasure, as most profitable to you? Do you look at them as your ornaments, as most honorable to you? Do you look at them as the apple of your eye, as your life, most near and dear and precious to you? If you do, you have in you that love which is perfect without guile, perfect in every part of love and in readiness and constancy. But if a man looks at God's commandments as a by-path, as taking him out of the way; if he looks at them as unprofitable and dishonorable, if he can break them without any scruple, if he would rather part with them than with his life, verily the love of God is not perfect in him.

Use 2. For direction to all who desire perfection of love to Christ. Do you desire to love the Lord Jesus in perfection, not only in parts and degrees? Why then, this is the way; keep his commandments, and take heed of breaking any of them.

What is the reason we deceive ourselves in our love to Christ? We think it is love to Christ if we only keep a solemn feast to him at the time of his nativity; but is there no better argument nor furtherance of your love for Christ than this? Take heed of it; if Christ has commanded us to deck our bodies and houses, if Christ has commanded us to feast and be liberal, you will find it a great help to further your love to Christ, and an evidence thereof. But if you go on in any course without a commandment, take heed lest you fall from religion to civility, from civility to intemperance and wantonness; and what is the reason? Because we have the custom of our fathers for it, and not the commandment of Christ. If it were Christ's commandment, the more you would find your love perfected, the more forward you would be to good; your spirit would grow from one grace to another. But because men look at custom, they begin in the Spirit and end in the flesh.

Take a Christian in the beginning of the Sabbath; he finds his heart impatient with spiritual duties, but before it is over, he is so enlarged that he is sorry it is complete. Why? Because he obeys a commandment. But if we do anything out of custom, we shall find it goes from better to worse, so that Christ has not more dishonor the rest of the twelve months than he has these last twelve days. But if you would have your love perfected, then frame your life and course according to God's commandments, and then the more you practice the more you may. You shall find your grace growing, and your love perfected to every good work.

Use 3. Of consolation to all who apply themselves to doing God's commandments. Do you find yourself ordering your ways according to a commandment? If you find it so delightful to you that you would still walk in it; if you think of it as your way, your treasure, your ornament, etc., why, this is your comfort: the love of God is perfect in you, and will grow more perfect; so perfect that God covers all your infirmities; so perfect that it grows up high to perfection, even to all its parts; so perfect that God sees you willing and ready to be doing his will; so perfect that you resolve to hold on and be constant; if God sees you thus molded to a commandment and not to customs, God will uphold you and help you and strengthen you, until he makes you perfect. And this is no small comfort to a soul.

1 John 2:5, 6

"Hereby we know that we are in him. He that saith he abideth in him, ought even so to walk as he walked."

In v. 5 you have an obedient Christian pictured: -1. By his practice: he keeps Christ's commandment. -2. By his privilege, which is double: first, his love is perfected, and second, he knows that he is in Christ.

In v. 6 a duty is enjoined to all who would profess fellowship with Christ, namely, imitation of Christ. They ought to walk as he has walked. From the first part of the fifth verse, we have observed that to observe Christ's commandments is to perfect our love to him. These next words show how to honor him and ourselves together, rightly. He honors us, first, by knowledge of our fellowship with Christ, and second, by our duty to walk as he has walked.

"Hereby we know that we are in him." By what? By the love in us? No, but by keeping his commandments we know that we have fellowship with him, though love and obedience are coincident. So then here is a promise not only of their being in Christ, but of knowing that they are in him.

Doct. Sincere obedience to the word of Christ is both a certain and evident sign of our blessed state in Christ. "Hereby," that is, by keeping his commandments, "we know that we are in him."

What is it to be in Christ?

We are said in scripture to be in Christ in three degrees.

-1. They are said to be in Christ who submit themselves to the ordinances of God, hear the word, receive the sacrament, use prayer and other good duties, and live unblameably before his people. In 1 Cor. 7:39 he gives liberty to any Christian woman, to marry whom she will if her husband is dead, but "only in the Lord"; and in 1 Tim. 5:11 he forbids Timothy to receive the younger widows, because "when they have begun to wax wanton against Christ, they will marry"; this is not here meant, though it is a part of it.

-2. There is a further being in Christ by participating in some graces, though not sanctifying graces. These may fit them for many Christian offices, as for the magistry (as Jehu) and for the ministry (as Judas). Still is it true, "Every branch in me that beareth not fruit he taketh away" (John 15:2). There can be no man truly in Christ and yet bringing forth no fruit; he must suck some sap and nourishment from Christ. But even those out of Christ may show common grace, as the zeal of Jehu, the trembling of Felix, the joy of Herod.

-3. Men are said to be in Christ when they participate in such graces as accompany salvation, such graces as make them true members of Christ; as faith, humility, hope, and patience. And of such fruits St. John here speaks: by such fruits we may know that we are in Christ.

And thus we are said to be in Christ partly from all eternity, in the purpose of God (Eph. 1:4); not actually, but virtually. God looked at us as members to be in Christ in time; and notwithstanding this decree, these do not as yet live in obedience to any commandment and have as yet no fellowship with Christ.

But there is another being in Christ which is actual; namely of such as are called out of the state of nature and bring forth the fruits of new obedience. The apostle speaks of those who "were in Christ before me" (Rom. 16:7); not elected before him, but called before him; he was a persecutor when they were professors. Thus we are said to be in Christ when we lay hold of him by faith (John 1:12).

What is it to know that we are in Christ?

It is more than opinion or thinking so, for we are never said to know that which we only think to be true. No man knows this to be gold or silver, if he only thinks it is so. No man bases his knowledge upon conjecture; indeed opinion always comes from conjecture, that is, it may be true or false; but knowledge is on sure grounds. It is then faith? No; they go together, yet they differ much; there is as much difference between them as between hearing and feeling. "Faith comes by hearing." When we assent to anything upon divine testimony, as if God has given us some word, we believe it; but when we see a thing by sense or experience, or by some certain arguments from God's dealing with us, then we not only know it from God's word, but we plainly see it by experience in our hearts from some love of God. Again, we find that our hearts have been proud and unclean; but now pride and uncleanness fall down, and we begin to conform ourselves to God's will; now we know that Christ is in us, or else we could not have turned ourselves to any good thing.

Why is such obedience a certain sign and evidence of our good state in Christ? How can we know by it that we are in Christ?

-1. Our natures are wonderfully insufficient to keep any commandment of God without it (2 Cor. 3:5; Matt. 12:34, 35; Rom. 3:12). We of ourselves are altogether fruitless in the works of righteousness, until Christ's love dwells in us (Ezek. 36:25-27). How can men keep God's law, except by the Spirit of God who dwells in them? Look at men in the state of nature; their fairest fruits are but the vines of Sodom and grapes of Gomorrah (Deut. 32:32, 33). They seem as fair as any, but their clusters are bitter; and so the best fruits of all natural men are bitter. Our very honey is like gall and wormwood, and our best actions are full of corruption and bitterness. If a man then finds his grapes savory (his words, thoughts, and actions gracious and sweet), so that he is now fruitful in obedience, it is an evident sign that he is in Christ; for else he would not have been able to do anything which is good.

-2. If it were not for the love of Christ that constrains

us, we would never be willing to deny ourselves. Do you see a man willing to submit himself to Christ and to his ordinances? It would not be but by the love of Christ, which constrains us to deny ourselves.

Use 1. Of refutation of that Popish error by which it is impossible that anyone should know his state in Christ, or be certain that he shall be saved. It is one of their canons. Why then does the apostle speak to little children, babes in Christ, for this purpose, "that they may know they are in Christ," if it were impossible to be known? Therefore in concluding it is impossible for a man to know that he is in Christ, they go against the doctrine of the apostles and against Christ. If any man preach another gospel than that which St. John delivered, let him be accursed (Gal. 1:7).

Use 2. To refute an unjust complaint they make against us. They say that we discourage men from good works; this complaint is unjust. For though we say good works do not justify us, yet by them we know that we are justified, and that is no small encouragement. My good works do not justify me, but they do justify my justification. Further, we say to them that they discourage men from good works; for they say, when a man has done what he can and fulfilled the whole law, yet he cannot certainly know that he is in Christ; and so what profit will it be for a man to obey the law, if afterwards he still does not know whether God loves him? But we say if a man walks in a constant course of obedience to God's commandments, he may thereby know that he is in Christ; and this is an encouragement to good works.

Use 3. To try whether we keep God's commandments, and whether we are in Christ or not. Would you know whether you keep God's commandments as you should? Do you keep them as your way, your treasure, etc.? If you do, I declare unto you that you are in Christ; and you either know Christ or shall know him. And if you desire to know whether you are in Christ, why, you may know it; keep God's commandments.

Use 4. Consolation to every soul who keeps God's commandments; you are in Christ, and you know it. If you are in Christ, you have no condemnation belonging to you (Rom. 8:1). And you may know it also. How ill then do they deal with their own souls, those who know they are in Christ and yet are put off by every discouragement! It is a shame that such Christians, who have a privilege of being in Christ and knowing it, should be discouraged; therefore those who would keep a continual festival unto Christ, let them get into Christ and learn to know that they are in Christ, and this will be a comfort to them against all discouragements.

Doct. It is the duty of all who profess fellowship with Christ, to walk as Christ walked; or, the profession of fellowship with Christ ought to be joined with imitation of Christ.

What is it to walk as Christ walked? Christ has walked: -1. As God, -2. As mediator, God and man, and -3. As man.

-1. He wrought some works as God. He fasted forty days and forty nights; he fed five thousand with five loaves and two fishes; he walked on the water. God never calls us to imitate him in these works, but he calls, "Learn of me, for I am meek and lowly".

-2. He did some works as mediator. Does he call us to imitate him in these? Not in the same kind, but in resemblance to them. As he died for us and rose again, so in resemblance he calls us to die to sin and to rise again to the life of grace. He calls us to die to the world as he died to nature, and to rise to newness of life as he rose from the dead (Rom. 6:4).

Christ was in his mediation a prophet, priest, and king unto God. So he would have us as kings to rule over our temptations, to rule over our families, to rule over our tongues, to rule over our hearts. Likewise he has called us to be priests; to offer up sacrifices of prayer and praise, and alms, and to offer up our bodies and souls, an acceptable sacrifice unto him (Hosea 14:3; Heb. 13:16, 17; Rom. 12:1, 2). As prophets he bids us to teach our children and servants and families, and to instruct them (Acts 2:17; Deut. 6:7).

–3. Christ wrought some works as man; and here he was either a minister, a good man, or a suffering servant of God.

a. Ministers are to seek their calling from him, as he did from God. He saw God's call and was sent by his Father; so must we see his call, for to undertake the ministry without a call from him is the way to bring a curse on ourselves. Further, in his calling he performed his ministry with all faithfulness. He brought in the straying, healed the sick, instructed the ignorant (Ezek. 34:16); and his first care was "that they might have life, and that they might have it more abundantly" (John 10:10,11). So ministers should dispense the word of life, strive to beget the life of grace in the hearts of their people, help the weak, comfort the distressed, inform the ignorant, etc.

b. As a private Christian, a good man, we must imitate him in his doing and suffering. (i) For the matter of his doing, it was always God's command (John 14:31). (ii) For the manner of his doing, it was done in obedience to God's command (John 5:30); it was done with cheerfulness, for it was his meat and drink to do God's will; and it was done for God's glory (John 17:4). Here we are to imitate him especially.

c. So for his sufferings: they were all in innocence (1 Pet. 2:21); they were all with much patience (2 Pet. 2:23); and they were all with much profit, for he learned obedience by his temptations and sufferings (Heb. 5:8). He profited by his agony, by his despising, by his buffetings, by his crucifying; and in these we should imitate and follow him.

NOTE: As he has before set before us God as light for an example, he now calls us also to Christ, that we may imitate Him. Yet he does not simply exhort us to imitate Christ; but from the union we have with Him, he proves that we ought to be like Him. He says, A likeness in life and deeds will prove that we abide in Christ. But from these words he passes on to the next clause, which he immediately adds, respecting love to the brethren.--JOHN CALVIN

Why should we be like him? -1. God has decreed that we should be like him. -2. We have near fellowship with him; it is fitting that the members should be conformable to the head, the branch to the root.

Use 1. This is an evident refutation of that Popish doctrine of the merit of works, and their satisfaction and supererogation. If, when we have done all we can and walk as Christ walked, yea, if we could, as perfectly as he did; then we would have done no more than our duty. God has no reason to thank us, and we deserve nothing (Luke 17:9, 16). What is our duty? To walk as he walked. Now a servant does not look for thanks for his day's work; so we have not merited thanks for the works we have done. We cannot do more than we ought, and so we are far from supererogation.

Likewise for satisfaction: if our best works are our debts, then we cannot satisfy for our sins by our duties. Suppose a man owed another a great debt, and furthermore owed him all service for some great benefit, as for redeeming him from captivity. Doing his service would not satisfy his debt, because he owed him that besides. So we were all captives to Satan, and God through Christ delivered us, and for that we owe God all we have. If moreover we were in debt besides by our sins, then all our service will not satisfy for our sins, for we owe that besides; and one debt will not pay another.

Use 2. Of direction and exhortation for all who desire to walk according to the knowledge they have. Do you desire to be in Christ, and do you know that you are in Christ? Why, conform yourself to walk as Christ walked; and if you do, then you may keep a good Christmas all your life. You shall keep Christ's honor in remembrance all your life, if you walk as Christ walked. Christ died that we might die to sin (1 Pet. 4:1, 2); therefore whatever corruption is in you, let it die. Mortify pride, and anger, and uncleanness, and covetousness; learn to die to them and live to God. Make it your chief pleasure to do God's will; rise from all deadness and sluggishness of spirit. Have you been unable to rule over your spirit? Now put on the spirit of a king; overrule your passions and corruptions; rule your family; be as a priest to offer up sacrifices of prayer and praise and alms, to offer up body and soul to God's service. Do every work in obedience to God's commandment; do it with cheerfulness and meekness; do it to God's glory; and if you are called on to suffer, suffer innocently, not for any sinful act as murder or theft, but for righteousness' sake; and then suffer patiently and meekly. And whatever you suffer, be sure that you profit by it, by temptation, by crosses, by persecution. Learn obedience, and so you shall walk as Christ walked.

1 John 2:7

"Brethren, I write not a new commandment unto you, but an old commandment which you have had from the beginning. The old commandment is the word which you have heard from the beginning."

In the sixth verse the apostle had taught that it is the duty of all Christians to walk as Christ walked. Now he amplifies this commandment, first, by denying the newness of it (v. 7), though he admits it may be new in some respects (v. 8).

In this seventh verse we have these parts: -1. A loving compellation, "brethren." -2. A denial of the newness of this commandment: "I write not to you a new commandment." -3. The antiquity of it. -4. A declaration how it shall not appear to be new. All the doctrine which you have heard from the beginning is no other but this, that all must walk as Christ has walked.

Doct. The ministers of Christ are to acknowledge even their little children as their brethren.

Compare this verse with the first. There he calls them "little children," and here "brethren." So Paul expresses himself (Rom. 15:14; 1 Cor. 2:1; 2 Cor. 1:8).

Why are they to acknowledge them as brethren? Because

they and their minister partake in all things in which natural brethren partake. -1. They have the same God and Father who begets them (Eph. 4:6; James 1:17, 18). -2. They have one mother, the church (Gal. 4:26). St. Paul speaks of Jerusalem on earth, though he calls it Jerusalem which is from above, because it is above an earthly condition. And John himself was a little child to some, as they were to him (Gal. 4:19). And so sometimes private Christians labor and travail in begetting children to God. It is a wonder to see many times how some are put to pangs to beget their friends to God; sometimes by prayer, by exhortation, by reproof; by all means they use much pains. Therefore the church is called, "the mother of us all," because some in the church beget us. -3. They all partake in one immortal seed by which they are begotten unto God (1 Pet. 1:23). For the material part of this immortal seed, it is the word; for the spiritual part, it is the spirit of God (John 3:5). So it is not so much the letter of the word as the Spirit of God, by which all are begotten to God. -4. Both ministers and people are begotten to the same eternal inheritance (1 Pet. 1:4); and thus they are all called brethren.

Use 1. This will teach ministers so to look at their spiritual fatherhood as not to forget their spiritual brotherhood. Ministers must not show dominion over them, as lords over them (2 Cor. 1:24; 1 Pet. 5:2-4); so then their fatherhood must not make them lords, but the name of brotherhood must bind them to communion. They indeed have a kind of power, but not to bind the spirits of their people, not to make them believe as they do, except as they are like Christ (1 Cor. 11:1).

Use 2. This must teach both ministers and people to maintain brotherly love and affection. If you are brethren, "let brotherly love continue" (Heb. 13:1; 1 Pet. 2:17). Therefore the kind of desire and comfort there is in brotherly communion, the mutual joy when they meet, the same should be in Christian ministers and people.

Now the fruits of brotherly love are chiefly three:
a. Unity; that they should "keep the unity of the

Spirit in the bond of peace" (Eph. 4:3; Col. 3:14).

b. Equality; not to take away differences, but to make ourselves equal to others in affection. We must remember that though we have more gifts, yet they may have less corruption; they may not have so much grace, but they may make better use of it. e should always conceive of others as equal to or better than ourselves.

c. Spiritual communion; that is, mutual giving of help to one another; of exhortation, admonition, consolation, and reproof (Lev. 19:17;;1 Thess. 5:14). And in temporal things we should be helpful to one another, not quarreling (1 Cor. 6:5, 6), pardoning one another's failings, being helpful to the poor brethren (Rom. 15:1). We must not neglect or despise one another, or carry ourselves as strangers to one another. Is this brotherly love, to carry ourselves strangely toward them, and not care for their communion and company, and never help them? This is not brotherly love. And indeed the sacrament invites us to brotherly love, for we are moulded up as it were into one loaf, and we drink of the same cup (1 Cor. 10:17). Therefore if there is any strangeness or quarreling or contempt between us, we sin against this ordinance.

If God is the God of peace, then Satan is the author of discord; how comely a thing it is for brethren to live together in unity (Ps. 133:1-3). The Psalmist compares it to the most precious ointment that was poured on the head and ran down upon Aaron's beard and the skirts of his garments; and so the grace that is poured upon the most eminent Christian must run down to the lowest.

Use 3. This reproves the ministers who dishearten and make sad those whom God would not have made sad. Many times ministers are most bitter against their best hearers (Ezek. 13:22). Neither let people make sad the hearts of their ministers; brethren should not thus carry themselves, but should rather comfort one another.

Use 4. It also reproves the quickness of many to prefer the company of natural carnal men; their only delight is in them, and they are soon done with fellowship in the things of Christ. This also is contrary to St. John's precept.

"I write no new commandment."

Doct. The ministers of Christ must carefully avoid all suspicions of novelty in all the doctrines they teach, whether of faith or manners.

Thus when St. John saw that it might seem a new commandment to walk as Christ has walked, he told them, It is no new commandment that I write unto you (Jer. 6:16; Job 8:8-10). Moses sharply reproved the Israelites for serving new gods (Deut. 32:17; Acts 26:22). St. John continues witnessing no other truth but what Moses and the prophets had delivered before him.

But is it not said that it is the part of a good scribe to bring forth things both new and old? (Matt. 13:52) True, he is to bring forth new things, but: -1. T they are to be new to the people, not new to the word;;such as they never heard of, for it is their duty to bring their sheep to new fresh green pastures (Ps. 23:2). But it must not be new in itself, but anciently delivered by the prophets and apostles. -2. A minister who delivers an old doctrine, and known to the people, must yet bring it in a new manner, so that it may affect them the more, being dressed in a new manner. The appetite desires new dishes; as for our Saviour, he taught no new doctrine, but he spoke it in such a manner, in such parables, that it seemed strange to them. -3. The minister should have enough respect to newness as to bring out all old doctrines with a new vigor of spirit; not with the old spirit, but with a new affection and vigor, so that the people may be more affected by it. He must deliver the same matter with a new spirit; he must drink a new draught of the wine of the sanctuary; but he must not teach anything that is new to the scripture.

Why must he not? Because the scripture is perfect (Ps. 19:7). God's perfection is more seen in this than in any other of his works; the world is perfect in its kind (Ps. 19:6). But how perfect is the word of God! (Ps. 19:7) Now, it were a foolish thing to go about to create new creatures; as there is not a new creature in the world, so let a man survey all the doctrines, and he shall find them to be the same doctrines which were from the creation.

Use 1. To mortify a new-fangled trick of ministers and people, when the minister fits their itching ears with new doctrine, and the people take up new doctrine. This is against the apostles' practice here (2 Tim. 4:2, 3). Those at Mars hill thought Paul came in with new matters (Acts 17:19-21), and they were affected with news; but though this doctrine was new to them, it was not new to the word.

Use 2. To reprove the Popish religion. It is new; some are Franciscans and some Dominicans. These are new. We never read of them in the scripture. Neither do we read of Jesuits or monks or abbots; they never had any footsteps in the scripture. Some of them confess in their matters of difference from us that they have no ground in Scripture for purgatory or prayer for the dead; but what says St. John? "I write unto you no new commandment."

Use 3. To assemblies and synods. Take heed what you impose on the church; no new traditions must be thrust upon us. If it is not from God, let it be abandoned.

"But that which you have had from the beginning."

Doct. True antiquity in all doctrines of the apostles or ministers is that which has its original from the beginning.

That which has had its original merely from old times is not always safe (Matt. 5:27, 33). It is not true antiquity, because it was not from the beginning. The devil had his lying from the beginning (John 8:44), yet not from the first beginning; he was not created a liar, but he made himself so.

True antiquity is twofold: -1. From the first institution of a thing (Matt. 19:8), and that is a good antiquity. -2. From God, even though manifest in later times; for he is Alpha and Omega (Rev. 1:8), the beginning and end of all things.

Truth is always from the beginning. This is true for two reasons: -1. From the nature of evil, for it is always an aberration from the first good state. If there is any corruption in marriage, as polygamy or adultery, from the beginning it was not so. If the devil is a liar, from the beginning he was not so. -2. From the nature of truth and good things which come from God. They have the nature of God stamped on them; and he is the ancient of days, so are they. Though baptism and the Lord's supper were not in the world before Christ's coming in the flesh, yet being from God they have true antiquity; they are derived from the ancient of days.

Use 1. This reveals the vanity of the Popish allegation of antiquity. They claim antiquity of a thousand years; alas, many errors concerning circumcision and denial of the resurrection have been standing six thousand years! Yet their claim is nothing, for they were not from the beginning. The true doctrine is that which is from the beginning, or else from God immediately; all other antiquity is but vain. Therefore when the Papists pretend antiquity, it their religion is not as ancient as the Ancient of days, and if it does not come rom him, it is not true antiquity.

They will tell you too that these feasts which we celebrate in memory of Christ's nativity have great antiquity, four hundred years after Christ's time; but this is as yesterday if it does not come from Christ or the apostles, for God has revealed his whole mind in Christ (Heb. 1:2). Thus what does not come from Christ is vain. Ignatius says, "My antiquity is Christ."

Use 2. To show the ungrounded confidence of scholars in the Fathers. If it comes from the Fathers, it sinks deeply; yet truly if it has no higher source than the fathers, it is too young; no other writings besides the scriptures can plead true antiquity. Whatever it is, if it does not come from Christ or the first institution, it is too late, because it is not the same as we have had from the beginning.

And indeed there is just cause to suspect the fathers. (a) Many of them had no skill in the original, and therefore they must see by other men's eyes, that is, by translations, for few knew the meaning of the Scripture in the original tongues. None knew the Hebrew but Jerome and Origen. (b) Most of them were converted from heathenism, and so brought in many errors, as purgatory and festivals, etc., which the Papists take from them. (c) They lived in times in which many said they had their doctrine from the apostles' mouth. One said antichrist would be a Jew and live at Jerusalem, and, he says, was John's disciple. This is a gross error, and came from him who gave us Peter's supremacy. (d) They lived in those days when Popery came in, when the bottomless pit was opened and frogs arose; but later writers lived when these were dispelled. Therefore take heed of them. Many of course spoke very well, yet there is a difference. (e) Observe generally that God did not give them the

spirit of interpretation except weakly; and if they lacked such a spirit, how could they open the scriptures? Since then other and later writers had a clearer discerning, therefore it will be of more use to read wholesome later writers.

Use 3. To teach Christians what kind of life and manners to take up. You will say you do not love newness; why then, live ancient lives. Your obedience must be guided by an old rule. Walk in the way; walk not in ways of superstition, of covetousness, of vanity, of uncleanness. Every sin is a novelty, though it be ever so old a custom.

The old commandment is the word that they had from the beginning.

Doct. The commandment to walk after Christ's example is the doctrine, the old doctrine, that was taught to the church in all ages since the beginning of the world.

He tells them that this was no new doctrine, but such as they had from the beginning. In the time of innocence Adam was made after the image of God, and Christ is the image of God (Col. 1:15). After Adam fell, the first sermon that he heard was that the seed of the woman should break the serpent's head (Gen. 3:15), and this promise was renewed to

Abraham (Gen. 22:18). In later times, when the Lord led Israel out of Egypt, he sent the angel of the covenant to go before them (Exod. 23:20, 21; Deut, 18:18). From the beginning it was thus made possible to walk after the Lord; and whatever pattern they had from God, it was from Christ, the second person in the trinity (John 1:18; Lev. 19:8). And he charged them to be holy as he was; that is the same as this message of St. John here, to walk as Christ has walked. Christ is the same yesterday, today, forever (Heb. 13:8); the same before and under the law, the same today in the time of the gospel, and the same forever (1 Cor. 10:1-5; Acts 15:10, 11). They in the old covenant held the hope of being saved by faith, and by faith lived all the saints of old (Heb. 11:1 to 12:3).

Use 1. To justify the antiquity of Christian religion. There is nothing in Christian religion which we do not have either from commandment or promise or pattern of Christ. The death of Christ was shadowed in the sacrifices in the old law, and promised in paradise; and when Christ would convince them, he does it from here (Luke 24:26, 27). All our forefathers believed and died in the same religion that we do.

Use 2. If the imitation of Christ be of so great antiquity, then it convinces those who blame the Christian religion of novelty. Why, there is no Christian who walks as Christ walks, who walks not also as Abel and Noah and Abraham did. Therefore it is not a novelty, but a religion from the ancient of days and from the beginning.

Use 3. It may encourage every Christian to walk as Christ walked, when we consider that the patriarchs and prophets and apostles, since the world began, have gone before us in the same steps and in the same faith. If we cannot show a higher ground and longer antiquity for our doctrine than the Papists show for any Popish tradition, we will renounce it; but we take up no other religion than that which came from the Ancient of days, and was from the first institution. The care which a Christian takes to prepare himself for receiving the sacrament is ancient; the apostle reproved the lack of it in his time (1 Cor. 11:28, 29), and they set the lamb aside three days before the Passover, to prepare themselves (Exod. 12:3, 6). Therefore let every one of us examine our failings, humble ourselves, and entreat for pardon and cleansing, and for strength of grace to walk as Christ walked.

1 John 2:8

"Again, a new commandment I write unto you, that which is true in him, and also in you; for the darkness is past, and the true light now shines."

In this verse he amplifies his doctrine by a contrary argument of newness. -1. He describes the old commandment by another adjunct of newness. -2. He sets down in what respect it is new, and this in a double respect: in respect to Christ, and in respect to itself. -3. He propounds the reason for it, because Christ has scattered light among them and has driven the darkness away.

Doct. The commandment and doctrine of the imitation of Christ is a new commandment, both in regard to Christ and in regard to believers the members of Christ.

-1. It is new in regard to Christ. First, it is a new commandment; Christ has expressly commanded it. This was his common expression: "Follow me" (as Matt. 4:19; if the word is not a word of conversion, yet at least of new conversion, Matt. 9:9). And it is a general rule (Luke 9:23, where by following Christ is meant imitating Christ). Thus it is new in regard to Christ's commandment. Second, it is a new work, in regard to Christ's efficacy and power working in our hearts (v. 9). It is wrought and stamped in us by a new work of Christ in the spirits of his followers, so that they do indeed set their hearts to follow Christ.

-2. It is new in regard to us believers. In regard to the outward hearing of the ear it is new; it was never so plainly spoken before. "Follow me"; in all the Old Testament there is not such an express command. Second, it is new in rerard to that new work wrought in the hearts of Christians. "Put on the new man" (Eph. 4:24); that is, put on such a frame of holiness and righteousness that you may resemble the new Adam, the new man Christ.

Use 1. As we ought not to affect novelty, so we ought not to loathe and reject newness. Before St. John carefully avoided novelty, but here he commands newness.

The reason for the difference is: (a) Whatever comes from God, the Ancient of days, is always new and never waxes old. And as it is always new, so it is always old. (b) If it comes from God, the newer it is the better, because our old nature and corruptions and habits should always be abhorred by us; but grace, and the new man, and new ways of holiness, should always be acceptable to us. (c) If it is new and comes from God, it is a greater manifestation of God. We may see a greater light in it than ever before.

Use 2. Never look to fulfill this commandment to imitate Christ until you become a new man; for it is a new commandment, and a new commandment requires new obedience, and new obedience requires a new spirit and a new man. Therefore do not think to follow Christ with an old spirit.

So much for the newness of the commandment and the obedience required; now follows the reason, "for the darkness is past, and the true light now shineth."

Doct. The state of the children of God in this life is as darkness passing and the true light now shining.

This is an excellent description of a godly man's state from his first conversion forward. The word in the original signifies passing or driving away; it is not so well translated "past."

For the opening of the point consider that there is a threefold darkness and a corresponding threefold light. There is a darkness of ignorance (Matt. 4:16), of uncleanness (2 Cor. 6:16), and of affliction or discomfort (Ps. 112:4). Accordingly, there is a light of knowledge (Matt. 4:16), of holiness (2 Cor. 6:14; Eph. 5:8), and of comfort (Ps. 92:11).

It may be spoken of all here, but chiefly of the two first

pairs. Darkness of ignorance and uncleanness are passing away in a Christian, and light of knowledge and of holiness are shining forth daily more and more in his heart. As in Rom. 13:12, "The day is at hand"; that is, not yet come but still near at hand, "and the night is far spent," i.e. almost gone and spent, yet not so far spent as wholly gone; the shadows of the night still remain, but the day begins to dawn (2 Pet. 1:19). The dawning of the day is when the shadows of darkness are not yet clearly vanished; and he does not say the sun is rising, but the day star, whic rises a good while before the sun. There he describes the state of the church until the day of resurrection; the light of the gospel does not yet clearly and fully shine, but is only dawning. Christ in his children, as a day star, gives them comfortable light, but the sun is not yet in its strength (Prov. 4:18). It is not yet perfect day with us, no, not with the best Christians under heaven; but it grows by degrees until it is perfect day with them. This perfection comes only at the day of their death, like the earthen pitchers of Gideon's men (Judg. 7:16, 20). When they broke their pitchers, the lamps gloriously shone forth and dazzled their eyes. Thus it is with us Christians: when these earthen pitchers and carcasses are broken, our light will shine forth gloriously; and in the meantime we have light. We have lamps, but they are in pitchers, shining very dimly.

But if we had been perfected the first day, and the light had shined gloriously forth from the first, would it not have been better? Yes, if God had been pleased to have done it so; but God would not have it so, and therefore it would not have been better. God rather sees fit that we should carry our light in earthen vessels in which is partly darkness and partly light (2 Cor. 4:7). For what reason? For reasons known fully to him only; but we may mention these in part.

-1. That God might show his power in our weakness (2 Cor. 12:9, 10). We should never have known Christ's virtue, the power of grace, or the depth of our own corruptions, if we had been perfected the first day after our conversion. As God made the world by degrees and described it so, because he would have us discern his power, so God displays the power of his grace by perfecting it in us by degrees and not all at once.

-2. That God might teach us to war with spiritual enemies. He left Canaanites among those Israelites who were untaught in the wars of Canaan, to prove them and to know whether they would hearken to his commandments (Judg. 3:1-4); so he leaves his children some inbred enemies still in their souls, to humble them and to prove them, and to try if they will cling to him. Besides, Jesus Christ takes delight in ruling in the midst of his enemies (Ps. 110:2); in the midst of our corruptions. Faith rules in the midst of unbelief; humility rules in the midst of pride; meekness rules in the midst of anger. Grace gains ground in the face of corruption, which is to the glory of Jesus Christ.

-3. To prevent the multiplication of the beasts of the field among us. God left Canaanites among the Israelites for that purpose (Exod. 23:29, 30). If there were not weaknesses in us, it would not be possible for us to live in this world. The world would not bear with us, for you know it would not bear with Christ, who walked as meekly as might be. Satan found nothing in Christ (John 14:30), no corruption for him to work upon; if Christians had a full and clear light of grace breaking forth at once, the world would cry, Away with them, they are not worthy to live.

Use 1. See a ground of the great difference between Christian and Christian. They differ in faith, they differ in manners; some are comfortably persuaded of their states, but others are full of fears and doubts. How does this come about? Truly it is with Christians as with mornings of the day; some mornings are a good deal more bright than others; some are more dusky and dark. You will say, Why should a soul not come to a settled peace? True, we may for a time; but it will never be perfect day with us. St. John was an old Christian, and you see what he says; even for him the darkness was still going, and the light yet coming; by degrees we get hold of God, and gain strength against corruption. You have some summer mornings which are brighter than all the days of the year before them; so with Christians. In the morning of their first conversion, some see more clearly their states by far than others in their whole conversation; and though all have partly darkness and partly light, yet some get more light in one thing, some in another. Perhaps one Christian will not get hold of peace; yet he gets firm hold on some corruptions, as wantonness, pride, covetousness, and gets greater hold of the contrary graces. As it was with the pillar of the cloud (Ex. 14:20, to which the apostle alludes, Heb. 12:1), so it is with the spirits of God's servants; there is something in them that is cloudy, and there is something in them that is light. Peter would not have gone to martyrdom and yet he would (John 21:18); partly willing and partly unwilling. So it is with the spirit even of the best Christian; he has some unwillingless to some good duty that God calls him unto

Use 2. To teach us somewhat more to bear with one another's infirmities and eclipses (James 3:1, 2). Do not be of an unruly, imperious, and censious spirit, censoriously judging others. As we have streams of light, so streams of darkness; therefore bear with and nourish one another, and help one another out of this darkness. As in a lantern there can be a pane of light and a pain of darkness; so in every good quality we all have some darkness. In Rev. 12:1 the church is compared to the moon; and the moon is fullest of spots when it is at the full. But we do not neglect the moon because she has spots, but make use of her because she has light; so do not neglect any Christian because of his spots, but make use of his light, of the good which he has. Also be somewhat forbearing of carnal men, for you were sometimes darkness as they are (Titus 3:1-3).

Use 3. Let no man's life be an absolute pattern for you to follow, but only so far as they are light in the Lord. See how the text proves what the apostle speaks of in 1 Cor. 11:1. Follow Christ, and why? Because even our perfection is imperfect; we are but darkness passing. If you follow us in all things, you may take us on the blind side and so fall.

Use 4. To teach us to be driving away darkness and to be going out of it. With a candle, the least snuff not only dims the light but wastes the candle as well; so it is with our spirits. The least snuff of corruption wastes that oil of grace which is in our hearts, and dims and dampens the light which is in us. Therefore let us snuff our hearts often; let us take the thief out of the candle; let us take care to show forth the virtues of him who has called us out of darkness into his marvelous light (1 Pet. 2:9; Eph. 5:8). Away with darkness, all darkness of doubtings, of unbelief, or pride; this darkness is passing away from us, and we must not call it back again. Do not draw again the curtains of darkness about you. When the sun has risen, and a man begins to sleep and draw the curtains about him again, it is a sign that he intends to play the sluggard; so when new light shines in our hearts and we draw our old corruptions around us again, it is a shame to us (Gal. 3:1, 2; 2 Pet. 3:18). Help one another out of darkness; help your wife and children, and servants and friends and neighbors out of it. We cannot practice better than we know, but we know in part (1 Cor. 13:9, 12). Therefore pray, admonish, exhort; cleanse yourself and cleanse others from the mist and shadow of darkness, as much as you may.

Use 5. A Christian may then take comfort: (a) In troubles which many undergo because of darkness of spiritual state. It is a common thing for Christians to complain of darkness, of pride, of unbelief, of dullness. Fear lies upon us; and with what may we comfort ourselves? We think no one else is so; but here is some comfort for us, all are so in some measure. It is so with the best; they have but a mixed state, one crossing and thwarting another. The fairest day has dark clouds. (b) Is our darkness deeper than others? It may be, but do you not yet find it passing away? Do you not find more faith, more obedience, than before? Do you not make more conscience of your thoughts, words, and actions? This is a comfort; your darkness is going away, it wafts apace. (c) Here is a comfort against death. The time will come when all darkness will vanish away. Death will be but the breaking of our earthen pitchers, so that our light may break forth. Epictetus came one day and saw a woman mourning for her pitcher; the next day he came and saw another weeping for her son; and he said, "yesterday an earthen pitcher broken, and today a mortal body dead"; as if it were the same to have a pitcher broken and to die.

Use 6. To try our states. Would you know whether your grace is true or not? Do you find your darkness passing away and the light shining? A man may walk in a condition of darkness, and see no light of peace and comfort (Isa. 50: 10); but do you not then walk in a greater light of innocence and watchfulness and obedience? When a man is in the dark, he goes slowly and warily, and lifts his feet up high every step (Prov. 14:16); a godly man is afraid of something in his way, but a wicked man goes on boisterously and confidently. He knows his way as well as you can tell him, but he is a fool for his labor.

1 John 2:9-11

"He that says he is in light and hates his brother is in darkness until this time. He who loves his brother abides in the light, and there is no occasion of evil in him. But he who hates his brother is in darkness, and walks in darkness, and knows not where he goes, because darkness has blinded his eyes."

It is the custom of the apostle St. John, after he has delivered any doctrine, to make some application of it for the joy of God's children; for the end of his writing to them was that their joy might be full (1:4). And so he does here. Having said in the former verse that in the children of God darkness is passing and the true light now shining, he proceeds in these verses to give a description of him who hates his brother, and of him who loves his brother.

He describes the first by these four things: he is in darkness, he was always in darkness, he walks in darkness, and he knows not where he goes. The latter is amplified by giving a cause, "Darkness hath blinded his eyes."

Doct. He who hates his brother, whether he professes the light or not, is in darkness and always was in darkness, and knows not where he is or where he goes.

By brother is here meant chiefly a Christian brother, as in v. 7. It is chiefly meant of spiritual brethren, but there is a truth in it even towards natural brethren, or those of one kindred, or those of the same country.

To hate is here opposed to love, which as we noted consists in two things: desire for communion, and desire to communicate good to him whom we love. Therefore hatred desires neither of these, but consists in strangeness and enmity; in strangeness because they do not desire communion with them, and in enmity because they are not willing to communicate good to them. Sometimes it goes further, even to desiring positive evil to one (Lev. 19:17).

Now he who thus hates his brother, though it were but one whom he hates, is in a fourfold condition of darkness. -1. He is yet in darkness of ignorance and of wickedness. -2. Such a one was always in darkness; he is in darkness even until now. -3. He walks in darkness; that is, there is no action of his which is not a work of darkness, a sinful action; he makes not one good prayer or one good sermon. -4. He knows not where he is nor where he goes; that is, he knows not what state he is in before God, nor whither he goes, whether to heaven or hell, nor what his end will be, whether comfort or woe.

Now for the proof of the point: you may see it in 1 John 4:7, 8. -1. God is love (1 John 4:16), and therefore he who is not in love is not in God. God is not only loving, but love itself (Ps. 145:9). God communicates good to every creature according to its condition. -2. Hatred puts a distemper upon both our judgments and our affections in every action (1 John

2:11). It blinds us so that we cannot see that good which is in our brother, because of which we should love him; and it puts false opinions and surmises upon everything we see him do. -3. Hatred makes every duty we perform to God abominable to him, and therefore we walk in darkness if we hate (Matt. 5:23, 24; James 1:20). Because Cain hated his brother, his sacrifice would not burn (Gen. 4:4); it would not enter into God's acceptation.

Use 1. To refute an opinion of the Popish doctors. They say men may fall away from grace, and they prove it by the examples of Saul and Judas, who (they say) were in the state of grace. But it will be easily decided whether or not they were in the state of grace. Did not Saul hate his brother, that is, hate David? If he did, St. John here gives his judgment that he was always in darkness. And of Judas you may see Ps. 109:5, 8, which is applied to him (Acts 1:20).

Use 2. From this everyone may take a survey of his own state. Do we hate our brother; any brother, whether spiritual or natural, or any other man? Then we are in darkness.

But may not a man hate those who hate God with a perfect hatred? (Ps. 139:22) David indeed makes it a sign of a citizen in heaven (Ps. 15:4). But let us take heed. If a man hates God and maligns goodness, we must consider whether he does it of ignorance or of malice. If he does it of malice, we may and should hate him (Matt. 15:12-14); and of these David speaks. But if they sin of ignorance, we must not hate them with a perfect hatred. We must not indeed have fellowship and communion with them, but to communicate good to them is another matter; and that we may and must do upon all occasions. We must pray for them and admonish them. Christ prayed for those who crucified him (Luke 23:34), as did Stephen for his murderers (Acts 7:60); and it is thought by learned divines that that prayer was a means of Saul's conversion. And we may admonish such a one (1 Thess. 5:14, 15). But if a man sins in malice, we are neither to pray for him nor to admonish him.

Use 3. This teaches us that if we would have a sign of

our good state in Christ, we must love every brother; every brother in Christ, in nature, or in civil society (Gal. 6:10).

But may not good men sometimes be bitter against some brother? It may be so, but: -1. They do not know them to be brethren. -2. They do not hate them with the whole heart, but only partly, as far as they are unregenerate and will not repent of it when they know it. But however, if we do not hate any brother, we shall know certainly that we are in a good state.

Use 4. This is a ground of comfort to God's servants. God will not have one of them unloved; the world hates them (John 15:18), and if God would allow his servants to hate them, who would love them? Nay, but God would have every man to love his brethren; in v. 9 he speaks of professors, and in v. 11 he does not restrain it, even speaking of false professors. Now this should be our comfort, and this should make us careful to walk so as to be beloved.

Doct. He who loves his brother, walks constantly and inoffensively in the state of grace.

You may see that they walk constantly and persevere (John 13:35; Heb. 6:9,10; 1 John 3:14). That they walk inoffensively appears from the truth that love covers a multitude of sins (1 Pet. 4:8).

How and why do they do so? -1. God is love, and therefore all who dwell in love dwell in God, and God in them (1 John 4:16). Now if God dwells in them and they in God, they must needs walk constantly and inoffensively. -2. There is a power in love to fit us to dispense God's ordinances willingly, and likewise to have them dispensed to us willingly; and this power helps us exceedingly to walk constantly and inoffensively (1 Thess. 3:12,13). Love is apt to interpret all things well (1 Cor. 13:7); and it is for lack of this that men withdraw themselves from one another and so do not exhort one another; and therefore they are subject to fall away (Heb. 10:24-26). Every good duty establishes us in grace; and love is strong in good duties, and therefore it turns out that he who loves his brother walks constantly and inoffensively in the state of grace. -3. There is a holy light that shines about love; in the light one may see and avoid all stumblingblocks.

Use 1. To remove a false slander cast upon godly men, that they are the most bitter envious and malicious men, the truest cut-throats that are. You see from this that they are in the light, and thus are of another temper. Such malicious and envious men may say that they are in the light, but if they were they would love their brethren. Therefore these you speak of are either not so uncharitable as you say, or if they are they are not yet the children of light.

Use 2. This shows us a way to help cultivate the settledness and inoffensiveness of our state. If we are unsettled or offensive, it is for lack of love to our brethren (Prov. 13:20). If we keep full love and communion with God's children, we shall find grace secretly increase to establishment. If we ever were in the light and now find ourselves as it were in darkness, we are at a loss; we do not know where we are. But let us consider the first rise of it, and we shall find it was lack of love (Rom. 13:10).

Use 3. This will comfort those who love God and his children. If we cannot discern any other grace in ourselves, yet if we know certainly that there is never a brother whom we do not love with all our hearts, this is an evident sign that we are in the light, and that we shall walk constantly and inoffensively in the state of grace. And by this we shall abide in the light.

1 John 2:12

"I write unto you, little children, because your sins are forgiven you for his name's sake."

"Because your sins are forgiven you for his sake." For whose sake? There is no name mentioned either before or after, closer than the sixth verse. This verse therefore has reference to ver. 6. "I write unto you because your sins are forgiven you for his name's sake," that is, for Christ's sake. He now amplifies the commandment to walk after Christ, by giving them the motive to stir them up to it. And that motive is taken from pardon of sins. "Little children"; τεκνία not παιδία not "babes", as in v. 13. So then this word τεκνία is of three sorts; fathers, young men, and babes.

In the verse we have: -1. A loving compellation, "little children." -2. An office of love: "I write unto you." -3. A reason for his former exhortation. Walk as Christ has walked, because he has forgiven your sins.

Doct. The children of God, no matter of what growth or strength in Christ, must be as little children, whether old men, young men, or babes.

As this benefit of forgiveness of sins reaches to all, so does this title of children.

But why must we be as little children?

-1. We must be like them in modesty. Children are free from ambition; and therefore our Saviour, to wean his disciples from ambition, tells them that they must be as little children, or else they shall never inherit the kingdom of God.

-2. We must be like them in innocence, free from malice and revenge (1 Cor. 14:20). Vex a child ever so much, and he will tell you, "I will tell my father"; he will not do so without great cause, but if he does, that is all. So it should be with Christians; they should not complain easily, and if they do, let this be all, make known your wrongs. Though children are angry, they will not seek to revenge themselves.

-3. We hould be like them in simplicity, preferring plain simple food (1 Pet. 2:1). A Christian should not affect polish, but should seek the sincere milk of the word.

-4. Let us be like them in being weaned from the world. David could be content to be without his kingdom which before he had sought (Ps. 131:2). So should we be.

-5. Children are content with promises and hopes. Tell a child something; only let his father say he will buy him such a thing at London, or he has it laid up for him, and the child rests well pleased. So would God have us be content with promises and hopes. When we cry to God for this and that blessing or grace, he tells us that we shall have it when he sees fit; it is laid up for us in heaven, and in the meantime we should sit down content (Ps. 131:2, 3).

Use 1. To examine our own estates, whether or not we are God's children. If we are, we are as little children; not ambitious of outward honor, more careful how to use it than how to get it, and not contending for it if we have it not. And for innocence, we will be like little children; for revenge, we will lay it down and conduct ourselves without malice. Until you are in such a frame you cannot enter into God's kingdom. If you are covetous, or ambitious, or malicious, if you rise up either with ambition or malice, you shall never enter into God's kingdom. And as for simplicity, do you pretend to be curious? Is your heart murmuring and repining for the world, if you cannot get it? Why truly then, you are not as a little child. Can you be content with promises and hopes, and what is laid up in heaven for us; or in Christ, in whom our life is hid? (Col. 3:3) If you can be thus content, it is a good sign you are God's child.

Use 2. If saints are as little children, then take heed how you offend them. Parents will be more offended if you hurt their smaller children than if you hurt the bigger, because a little injury does them more harm. The angels are ready to come from heaven to help God's little children (Matt. 18:6-11).

"I write unto you."

Doct. The apostles of Christ, when they could not be present with the children of God, were willing to advise them by writing of things needful.

So Paul wrote his epistles when he was absent, and Peter and James, and Christ himself to the seven churches. -1. They write first to help their knowledge and to make them wise, so that they may know their duties (1 Tim. 3:15). -2. They wrote to them to help their memories (2 Pet. 1:12-14). -3. They wrote to establish them in knowledge received, and to confirm them. -4. To stir them up to practice those things they knew and remembered, and were established in (2 Pet. 1:12, 13). -5. Moses gave the reason why he would have the king to read the book of the law (Deut. 17:19, 20); that is, that he might learn to fear God and keep his commandments. -6. They wrote that by this means the joy of their hearers might be full. When they thus understood and remembered, it would increase their joy. This was the purpose for which St. John wrote this epistle.

Use 1. To refute the Papists, who withhold these writings from the common people. To what end then did they write them, if little children might not read them? Fathers, young men, babes; St. John wrote to all and would have all read them.

Use 2. To stir us up to constant reading of the scripture daily. How often? Why, the greatest man in the kingdom must read them once a day at least (Deut. 17:19). It will help our knowledge, help our memories, establish us, stir us up in practice, help us to fear God, and to grow in joy and fullness of consolation. What a help it was to the Bereans, that they read daily! It wonderfully helped their faith and comfort, for many of them believed and were confirmed in grace. But what if we are in a journey or sick; what then? In this case we are to meditate in the law of God (Ps. 1:2).

Doct. All the children of God have their sins forgiven them (Acts 10:43; Eph. 1:7).

-1. Sometimes remission of sin is called the covering of sin (Ps. 32:1, 2), and if sin is covered it is forgiven; it is not imputed unto us. -2. Sometimes it is called the throwing of them into the bottom of the sea (Micah 7:18, 19). When he forgives iniquity and sin, God drowns them as deep and as far out of sight as things in the bottom of the sea. -3. Sometimes it is called changing them, as in Isa. 1:18. "Though your sins be as scarlet, they shall be as white as snow"; they are quite changed. Though they were deep scarlet sins, yet they shall be made as white as snow. -4. Sometimes it is called washing away sin. "Wash me with hyssop, and I shall be clean" (Ps. 51:7), is an allusion to the blood of the law sprinkled with hyssop; so when we are sprinkled with Christ's blood, our sins are washed away. -5. Sometimes it is called a blotting out of sin; "as a thick cloud I have blotted out your sins" (Isa. 44:22). When the sun appears in its brightness, the cloud suddenly vanishes; so when our sins are forgiven, they are remembered no more (Isa. 43: 25; Jer. 31:34). When God pardons sin, he does so utterly blot it out, and it so vanishes, that it is no more to be found; there is no such thing in existence.

But how does it come about that when our sins are forgiven, they are so strongly purged? Because all sins are washed away in Christ; our sins are imputed to him, and his righteousness is imputed to us (Isa. 53:5; 2 Cor. 5:19). Our sins are his, and his righteousness is ours.

Use 1. To reprove the opinion of the Papists, who teach that the sins of the godly, though forgiven, are not completely forgiven. God, they say, reserves a temporal punishment, partly here and partly in purgatory. But it is a false doctrine; for if God covers them and washes them away, if he throws them into the bottom of the sea, if he blots them out with a thick cloud, if he remembers them no more, then they are thoroughly forgiven without any reservation of punishment.

Use 2. It reproves the doctrine that the afflictions of God's children are punishment for sin. But we know that if sins are not accounted ours, then our punishments must be of another nature; if sins are changed, then punishments also. All the sins of God's children are no longer counted as sins, but are diseases of the soul; and likewise all the afflictions of God's servants are not punishments but are medicines and purges to root out our distempers (Dan.

11:35). For the servant of God, afflictions are not given in justice as a way of revenge, but in mercy as a way of cure.

Use 3. This doctrine confutes purgatory. If God so pardons sins as to remember them no more, what need have we of purgatory to punish the remains of sin in God's children?

Use 4. It will teach all who desire to have their sins forgiven, to be of childlike dispositions, free from ambition and malice and revenge; to frame themselves in humility and innocence and meekness and simplicity and contentment, resting upon promises and hopes. If we are in this frame of mind, God will pardon our sins; and what is the reason we doubt our remission, but because we fail in this condition?

Use 5. It will comfort all God's children; they have this white stone, that is, absolution for sin, and a new name written in the stone, that is, adoption. And if we are of a meek, humble, innocent, simple frame of heart, we have this comfort.

Use 6. To exhort. (a) If God has thus freely given us, let it teach us freely to forgive others; and this will be an argument for our own remission (Matt. 6:11, 12). (b) We must be careful to offend God no more, if God has forgiven our sins and remembers them no more (1 John 5:18). When a woman's clothes are washed very white, she is loath that they should be spotted or mired; so after God has made us white as snow, let us take heed of polluting our consciences any more. It is a good sign that our consciences are pure, when we are afraid to spot them. (c) This will teach us to walk fruitfully and to be abundant in God's service (Luke 7: 47). (d) Lastly, it will teach us to be exceedingly thankful to God who has thus forgiven us (Ps. 103).

Doct. God forgives the iniquity of his saints for his name's sake (Isa. 43:25).

For his own sake he blots out our sins: -1. For his own glory, that his name might be magnified and feared (Ps. 130: 4; Ps. 103:1-3). -2. For the honor of Christ, that he may be honored through Christ (Eph. 1:5, 6). -3. For his own sake, that is, without any desert of ours, yea sometimes without any desire of ours (Isa. 43:22-25).

Use 1. This will teach us to be more abundantly thankful to God, to fear him more, to love him more, to honor and praise him more, since he for his own sake has blotted out our iniquities. If we had gone further into debt to another man than we should ever be able to get out, and if he freely forgave it, we would be loath to offend him. We would honor him and be ready to do him the best service we could. So, since God has forgiven us so great a debt, we should take heed that we do not run further arrears; that is, that we do not dishonor or offend that God who for his own sake has so freely forgiven us.

Use 2. This will teach all of us who have any experience of the forgiveness of our sins, to walk even as Christ walked; for St. John presses the truth on this ground. It should be our meat and drink to do his will, to glorify him in all our course, as it was Christ's care (John 17:4); for that is the end which God aims at in forgiving our sins, that we should walk as Christ walked.

Use 3. For consolation. If our sins are forgiven for Christ's name, then we need not fear that they will again be charged to us. If he had forgiven us for our own sake, we might justly have feared that he might afterwards, through our defaults, lay them again to our charge. But he has forgiven us for Christ's sake. He has not forgiven for the sake of our prayers, for our sins were pardoned before we called on him (Isa. 65:24). Indeed the reason your prayers grew so zealous was that God had forgiven your sins (Isa. 43:25, 26); and therefore God will not cancel our pardon, because he did it for his name's sake, for the glory of his own grace.

1 John 2:13

"I write unto you, fathers, because you have known him who is from the beginning."

In verse six he commended this duty to all Christians, to walk even as Christ walked. He amplifies this duty from the antiquity of it (v. 7) and from its newness (v. 8). Third, he mentions one special duty from the commandment, that is, love for the brethren (vv. 9-12). Fourth, he amplifies it by a benefit or motive to walk as he has walked; and that is from the pardon of sin generally granted to all Christians. Walk as Christ walked, because he has forgiven your sins. And now, v. 13, these τεχνία, or little children, he distinguishes into three sorts: fathers, young men, and babes. "Little children" is the name of all Christians, but babes are newly born to Christ; now all these should walk as Christ walked.

In this verse we have three parts: -1. An enumeration or distribution to the various ages of children to whom he commends this duty. -2. A ministerial duty of love which he tenders to them; that is, he writes to them. -3. A reason for each age why he urges this duty upon them: fathers, "because you have known him that is from the beginning"; young men, "because you have overcome the wicked one"; children, "because you have known the Father."

What is meant here by fathers, young men, and babes?

Some think it is meant of the varying statures of grace that Christians grow to; some are fathers, some are young men, and some are babes. But we never see these so divided; an old man in Christ is also a strong man in Christ, for grace does not grow weaker but stronger in old age; and the elder in grace are the more wise, the more fruitful, the more gracious. Therefore I think by fathers he means ancient Christians; they are of course old men too, but he has respect to their natural age. And by young men he means men young in years, yet stronger in grace; and by babes those who are tender in years, and babes in Christ too. Therefore it may well be understood of the natural difference in ages.

This interpretation may be confirmed by the reason he gives, taken from the differing delights of natural ages.

-1. Old age takes pleasure in study and rehearsing things that are long past; so you, fathers, have known the Ancient of days. You have known how Christ has been imparted from the beginning, so that in your natural desire for old things you have turned to the antiquity of Christ. -2. And so for young men: they have natural strength, and strive to show it in fightings and combats; therefore he says, "I write unto you because you have overcome the wicked one," because you have turned your strength to fighting against sin, satan, and the world, and have overcome them. -3. And for babes: though they know little, yet they do know their parents, and they express their joy in them. So he says, "I write unto you, babes, because you have learned to know the Father."

Since he writes to all sorts of Christians, observe:

Doct. God has his children among all sorts of ages of men; some of them are aged, some are young, and some are babes in nature and in grace.

God has a company of all ages calling on him, justified and sanctified.

-1. Among old men and women we read of Abraham and Sarah, a couple old and stricken in years; of Isaac and Rebecca, an ol couple also, and knowing the promises made of Christ (John 8:56), as indeed Sarah rejoiced in the promised Seed. We have also the examples of Moses, and David, and Zacharias and Elizabeth, who continued until they were old both in age and grace. There were some such among the priests, as Aaron and Jehoiada (2 Chron. 24:15). Likewise for the soldiers; there were some old soldiers of Christ, and old kings and nobles, who knew him who was from the beginning.

-2. For young men, famous is the example of Phineas (Numb. 25). In his youth he was full of zeal. Such was Josiah (2 Chron. 34:1-3), who at sixteen years of age sought the Lord God of his fathers, and at twenty years was so strong that he carried before him the whole state, though they were then strongly corrupted and given over to idolatry.

Being strong in the Spirit, he carried them to justice and reformation; he cleansed the land from Dan to Beersheba, and he stands to this day as a notable encouragement to young men, to be vigorous in zeal and grace.

-3. And for children, we mention Samuel, who ministered to the Lord when he was but a child (1 Sam. 2:18). So John the Baptist was filled with the Holy Spirit from his mother's womb; and of Timothy it is said that he knew the scriptures from a child (2 Tim. 1:5, 3:15), so that in this family there were all degrees. His grandmother Lois was an old woman, his mother Eunice a young woman, and he almost a child. Lois teaches Eunice; both teach Timothy; and from a very babe he knew the scripture.

But why does God desire to have some of all sorts to be servants to him?

-1. So that the grace of Christ might be extended to all sorts of men, as largely as the sin of Adam had extended to all ages and degrees (Rom. 5:12-18). If Adam had defiled all sorts, and if Christ had restored but some sorts of men, as only young men, then Adam's sin would have been more powerful to destroy than Christ's righteousness to save. It was therefore fit, as Adam had defiled all ages, that Christ should restore all ages and sanctify them. It is shown in Jer. 7:17, 18 that all ages are wholly corrupted: the father kindles the fire, the woman kneads the dough, and the children gather sticks, to make cakes to the queen of heaven. Now as all sorts are thus corrupted, so it is meet that there should be some of all sorts sanctified; why should God not have all sorts to serve him, as well as the queen of heaven?

-2. That distinctive honor might be returned to God by the various ages.

a. Old men bring this honor to God, whether they were called in old age or before, if they hold on.

(i) By this means God glorifies the truth of his promise that length of days is in the right hand of wisdom (that is, the fear of the Lord). On this ground Solomon encourages his son to wisdom (Prov. 3:16). Therefore, so that God might justify this promise, he will have some old men stand up before him, that it might be seen that wisdom does not make them so melancholy that they shorten their days. Religion harms no man; godly sorrow never wasted our days, but worldly sorrow.

(ii) When you see old men continue in their profession to their old age, they put an honor on religion. If only young men and children should profess religion, you would take it as indiscretion and hotness of spirit, but this objection flies when you see a grave old man take up a Christian walk. That God may make it known that wisdom and discretion are to be found in the ways of grace (Prov. 16:31), therefore he will have some old men walk in them, so that grey hairs may honor religion and religion may be a crown to them. Ignatius says, "Eighty-six years I have served God, and never found him to be a hard master"; so when Christians can say, I have served God so many years, it implies that they have found some comfort and joy in it. If it had been such a wearisome course they would have shaken it off during the years, but they hold out in it. Further, if men are converted in old age, it will be said that they now see by experience the vanity of all other courses; they see it is best to die a Christian and to spend their last days in Christianity; old men would never fall into it unless they saw that there is no way so comfortable and peaceable as that way is.

b. So for young men; it is a great honor to religion when they are converted.

(i) They make the power of Christ's grace manifest, that it is able to overcome the heat and power of youthful lusts. There is no age so violent and boisterous in corruption, so headstrong, so indiscreet and rash; with all their unruliness, stubbornness, vanity, pleasure, they are most indisposed to religion, and will not be converted. Therefore if God takes hold of their spirits and establishes them, when they by God's grace are able to rule their spirits, their lusts, their hearts, this argues the strength of grace.

If neither wise counsel nor magistrate can rule them, yet if the grace of God can rule them and their passions so that they can put forth their strength against the enemy (their own corruptions or the abuses of others), what an honor to Christ's grace (Ps. 119:9; Eccl. 11:9). When the elders sit still, sometimes a young Phineas rises up and shows his zeal for Christ.

(ii) Another honor they bring to God is their boldness and courage in a good cause. Though wise, old men are sometimes too cautious and backward; but young men have in zeal what is lacking in experience, and thus are always eager in any service for God.

c. And for babes and children; if they are brought to grace, God thereby casts shame on older men (Ps. 8:2), when they see babes giving more savory words than old men. Sometimes God confounds the folly of ancient men by the wisdom and grace in children. When Christ came riding into Jerusalem, the children cried out, "Hosanna," and prais him. The high priests disdained it; but Christ told them, "Have you not read, Out of the mouths of babes and sucklings thou hast perfected praise?" (Matt. 21:16, 17). This is to still the enemy and avenger (Ps. 8:2); they also shame you who are elders and priests, because of your backwardness.

Thus we see that God will have all sorts and ages of men to do him service.

Use. This may serve to teach all sorts of men.

a. Old men. If God has his number among all ages and conditions of men, then God expects to have his number among you who are old men. Do not say, I have now lived long enough in another course, but come on to a Christian course; or if you began before, go on. "You have known him that was from the beginning"; it will seem becoming to you to talk of the ancient promises and mercy of God.

b. Young men. Do not think it too soon to enter on a Christian course; and if you have begun, grow up in grace. What an honor it will be! As you have been strong in outward strength, so now be strong in grace, strong in the Spirit.

What an honor it will be to see you strong, subduing your corruptions! What an honor it will be to see your zeal and courage, stirring up old men's discretion, so that what is lacking in them may be supplied by you. What an honor it will be to God's grace, to see your strength turned against sin and lust, to see you sober and temperate and chaste, to see you zealous and quickened in grace. "Remember now thy creator in the days of thy youth" (Eccl. 12:1), for God takes pleasure then in your service. If you remember him then, he will be most ready to remember you in your old age.

c. Little children. If God has his number among babes, then do not let the parents say, "It is too soon for them to learn anything; they are too young; they cannot understand." Why, can we not teach them to know their Father? Tell them that he is able to do more for them and give them better things than you can do. Take no comfort in them until they take comfort in God; train them up to know God's ways, so that they may rejoice and solace themselves in God and good things, and that the firstfruits of their age may be consecrated to God. And if you do, you will consecrate the whole lump; for if the firstfruits are holy, so the vintage is holy; if the root is holy, so are the branches.

Consider that these babes are flexible and easily bent; it is far easier to train them in good things now than in their youth and riper years; therefore labor now to incline them to God and to good things. God will make them instruments to confound older, stronger men.

Doct. The ministers of Jesus Christ are to apply themselves and their doctrine to the sorts and ages of men they have to deal with.

So St. John here carves out several portions for fathers, for young men, and for babes. So does Paul (Titus 2:1-10). So with John the Baptist; when he had pressed the necessity of repentance, first the people came and asked, "Master, what shall we do?" And then the publicans and soldiers came and asked, "What shall we do?" And he answered them according to their various conditions (Luke 3:10-14). Further, God has put ministers in offices which demand that they should observe the differences among their people. They are stewards, to give everyone his portion (Luke 12:42). They are physicians (Jer. 8:22), and the physician does not dispense one salve to several sores. They are shepherds, and the shepherd dispenses himself according to the varying states of his sheep.

Then too, let all hearers listen especially to those things which more especially concern them and belong to them. Old men should isten to what belongs to them, young men to what is their portion. It is true, there is no doctrine that will not fit everyone present, since a young man will become an old man and require what now belongs to old men; but especially you should attend to those things which belong to you in the present. And you must not take it lightly or impatiently if the minister comes to particularize; it is your crown to be particularized. You take it kindly when you are invited to a feast, and the master of the feast not only sets out the whole lump but carves out one particular piece for you; so you ought to take it kindly when the minister sets out a particular portion to you. Yea, you should make your state known to him, or else you fail in your duty.

But though the apostle writes to different sorts of Christians in different ways, still he writes to all; from which we observe this point of doctrine.

Doct. It is the duty of all sorts and ages of Christians to be conversant in reading the Scriptures.

To what end does he write to old men, if old men do not read what he writes? And so with young men and babes. It was the charge put upon the very kings of Israel (Deut. 17:19), that they should read the book of the law all the days of their lives; and when they do not have opportunity to read, then let them meditate on the word (Ps. 1:2).

There is great use in reading the scriptures.
-1. It helps knowledge much (1 Tim. 3:15).

-2. It helps to make a right use of what we hear; yea, it sets such an edge on the word heard, that though the preaching was not completely effective, yet by reading they came to a lively faith (Acts 17:11, 12). Though the preached Word prepared their hearts and made them attentive, yet until they read and revised and meditated again on what they had heard, their faith was suspended. But after they saw the agreement of the apostle's public teaching with the written word, then many of them believed. God of course does not ordinarily beget faith by reading without hearing; but when we have heard, reading exceedingly quickens our spirits and faith.

-3. There is a further benefit from reading the word. A man shall thereby find himself framed to fear God, to be humble, etc. (Deut. 17:19, 20). The day that a man neglects reading the word of God, he shall find his spirit more loose and unbridled, because he does not stand in awe so much.

-4. It is a means to confirm us, and establish and help our memories, and stir us up to holy duties.

-5. It makes the word more ready for us in times of temptation. What a wonderful use our Saviour made of the word, when Satan tempted him. A man in temptation will need many passages of scripture (Eph. 5:17).

-6. Lastly, another use of reading the scriptures is that our joy may be full (1 John 1:4). Reading fills our hearts with comfort and consolation; not that reading is sufficient to salvation, for no ordinance roots out another.

Faith comes by hearing (Rom. 10:17); but though that especially begets faith, yet for other graces reading is of special use, at least to quicken and stir up grace. We do not read that God ever blessed reading alone to beget faith, for God does not usually bless it alone, but joined with hearing the word preached. In any congregation where there is only reading of the word, the soul that is begotten to God seldom proceeds from faith to the fear of God, humility, patience: not that there are not good Christians in such places, but because they stray from hearing. It usually fares with reading as with the eunuch; he did not know what he read until Philip declared the interpretation (Acts 8:30, 31).

But I say, you old men read, and you young men read, and you children read. It is a great fault to neglect it and give it wholly over to children, as a childish exercise; does St. John write only to babes? No, but he writes to young men and to old men, and therefore they too are to read what he writes. We shall understand the word better and remember it better; we shall be more stirred up to fear God and to keep his law; we shall be better furnished against many temptations, which otherwise might prevail against us. In a word, since he wrote to them that they might learn to walk as Christ walked, you may expect by reading the word, by laying it up, by praying for a blessing, to be helped to walk as Christ walked.

A. "I write unto you, fathers, because you have known him who was from the beginning."

Who are these fathers? They are opposed to young men and babes, and therefore he speaks of old men (1 Tim. 5:1-3). But why does he call them fathers? Not because they were his fathers to bring him to God, for before he had called them brethren; neither because they were his natural fathers; but he calls them so out of very reverence to their age.

Doct. It is the duty of all Christians, yea even of ministers, to carry themselves to old men as to their fathers.

This duty belongs to all Christians, as well as to ministers. God has special care to the reverence of old age, for he would have ministers to rebuke with all authority (Tit. 2:15), and yet he would not have them easily rebuke an elder (1 Tim. 5:1). Much less is a private person, who has less authority and commission, to deal roundly with elder years. In Lev. 19:32 he gives commandment to all men to rise up before the hoary head, and to reverence the person of the old man, and to dread the Lord; implying that the fear of God requires this duty. Who would say there is fear of God in those who do not reverence the persons of old men?

God has stamped on old men the image of his eternity, as on magistrates the image of his sovereignty. God himself is called the Ancient of days, so that an old man bears a faint trace of the image of God. Rich men carry the image of God's allsufficiency, magistrates of his sovereignty, and old men of his eternity.

Use 1. To reprove the rudeness of some young men who look at old men as base and contemptible. Isaiah speaks it as a sign of confusion (Isa. 3:5), when they see the hoary head pass by but do not rise up nor reverence him.

Use 2. It may stir up all young men to reverence old age, and that by a threefold respect. -1. By rising up before them (Lev. 19:32). -2. By showing them reverence in speech. Here St. John calls them fathers. -3. By silence. Do not put yourself forth in their presence, at least not until they have spoken (Job 32:6, 7).

Use 3. To teach old men, since God has put such honor and respect upon them, to think themselves bound to him. Shall he have such respect for your honor, and shall you not honor the Ancient of days? Do you desire all to rise up and express reverence to you, and not desire to come before God with reverence and speak reverently of his name? Further, take heed that you do not put dishonor on yourself by any unseemly practice. Noah had no sooner committed that shameful sin of drunkenness than his own child mocked him.

Doct. It is the honor of ancient men, of fathers, to know him who was from the beginning.

When they know the Father of eternity, the Ancient of days, it is an honor to them both before God and man. God is called "him who was from the beginning"; this is not to be understood in relation to time but to eternity. He does not say "with the beginning," but "from the beginning," before the beginning of the earth, from eternity. The knowledge of Christ is the honor of aged persons.

There is a twofold knowledge of Christ. -1. A speculative historical knowledge, only of the understanding (Acts 9:5).

-2. A practical saving knowledge of Christ. And there is a threefold difference between the knowledge of the understanding and the practical, saving knowledge of Christ.

-1. The knowledge that rests in the understanding is only by hearing or reading, but the other is given by the Spirit of Christ infused into us (1 Cor. 2:9, 10). We receive it partly by the enlightening of our minds, but partly by feeling the work of grace in our hearts (Phil. 3:10). Hence it is that this experimental knowledge excels the best knowledge that is gained by reading or hearing; whoever has it knows the worth and value of Christ.

-2. They differ in their effects. That knowledge which rests in the understanding breeds pride and carnal indifference (Isa. 47:10), and scandal and offense to the weak (1 Cor. 8:11). But this saving knowledge breeds: prayer (John 4:10); faith (Ps. 8:1); justification (1 John 2:2); obedience, innocence toward our brethren (Isa. 11:6-9), and eternal life (John 17:3).

-3. These two kinds of knowledge differ in the adjuncts. Saving knowledge is joined with a high esteem of Christ (Phil. 3:7, 8); yea, a man has liberty to rejoice in this knowledge, which he may not have in any other (Jer. 9:24, 25).

There are two things in the knowledge of Christ which old men have more than other men. Jacob expressed both in Gen. 48:15, 16. He knew by much experience the goodness of God; he had supplied him in all his wants and delivered him out of all his dangers. A young man cannot say as much. It seems not so savoury in a young man's mouth; but when an old man gives a recital of God's favor, this is the honor of old age.

Use 1. This will direct old men to take notice of their own state, whether they know him who was from the beginning. Has God's Spirit brought you to pray, to humble yourself, to obey, to be innocent? If so, happy are you; you are truly honorable.

Use 2. Let us not satisfy ourselves with any knowledge until we know him who was from the beginning. The study of antiquity is pleasing to many, especially to old men; but there is no knowledge like this, when you are able to speak of God's old mercies to you. Could you tell of all antiquities, this is nothing until you know him who was from the beginning.

"I write unto you, young men, because you have overcome the wicked one."

Why does he call them young men and not brethren, as he before called old men fathers? Because then he would not have distinguished them from the others, for all Christians are brethren one to another.

Observe their adversary, "the wicked one," and their victory, "you have overcome." This wicked one is Satan (1 John 5:18; Matt. 5:37; Matt. 13:19; Mark 4:15). He is called Satan, as he was once one of the noblest creatures, nobler than man.

Doct. The chiefest of the glorious creatures of God may in time become the chiefest of the wicked ones.

He is called "that wicked one." This implies: -1. That he excels in wickedness; his understanding is most blind, his will most rebellious, his affections most corrupt. -2. That he is the father of all sin (Matt. 5:37; John 13:2; "the father of lies," John 8:44). -3. That he takes pains to do evil, is industrious to do evil. He traverses the world, goes about continually doing evil (1 Pet. 5:8; Job 1:7).

But how does it happen that such a glorious angel has now become the wicked one? The causes of his fall were partly external and partly internal.

-1. God did not elect him to stand, as he did ordain some angels (1 Tim. 5:21); thus he was left to a possibility of falling, though not to a certainty or necessity.

-2. His condition as a creature gave occasion to his fall. Since God is infinitely good, his will is the rule of good; since Satan was a creature, God's will was his rule. But if he pleased, he might not attend to the rule and so might do evil.

-3. But the moving cause of his fall was inward, and that

was his proud nature. He was not created so, but he exalted himself (1 Tim. 3:6). This verse implies that he saw man made after the image of God; and he was a glorious creature attending on God himself, and thus was puffed up with his own glory and despised man who was to live upon the earth and dress the garden.

Use 1. This may teach young scholars not to please themselves in any gifts of nature, though ever so excellent; for even an angel who excelled in wisdom has fallen away and become that wicked one.

Use 2. It may teach them to take heed how they enter into the calling of the ministry in their younger years, especially before they are humbled. It was the cause of Satan's fall that he was puffed up with his office. It is a wonder to see how, when scholars are admitted into the ministry in their young years, how they despise the people and think themselves too good to condescend to peasants; but they prefer to exercise their gifts in the university, and so fall into the condemnation of Satan.

Use 3. Here you may see part of the image of Satan. Why was he called "that wicked one"? Because he excels in wickedness, and is the father of sin, and takes pains to do evil. Do you see men excel in wickedness, lead others to sin, and take pains in mischief? Then they bear the image of Satan upon them. When Paul saw Elymas hardened in mischief, leading others on, and taking pains to keep the deputy from the faith, he called him the child of the devil (Acts 13:10).

Use 4. If the devil has gotten this name by excelling in wickedness and drawing others to sin and taking pains to do mischief; then on the contrary, let us excel in goodness, strive to draw others on to God, and take pains in it. Those who do this are more like God their Father.

"Because you have overcome." All overcoming implies a fight; so when you read here that young men have overcome, it implies that they have strong wrestlings with Satan.

Doct. As Satan is an enemy to all mankind, so especially to

young men.

The apostle does not here write to fathers or babes that they have overcome the wicked one. But he chiefly encourages young men, which implies that it was a proper work for them. Observe all the temptations of Satan in scripture, and where you find one old man tempted by Satan, you shall read of ten young men. When did he set upon Eve? Immediately after her first creation. Our Saviour was not above thirty years old years old when Satan tempted him; Peter when tempted was young. We shall find few of God's saints failing any time except in youth; there were two exceptions, Noah and Solomon, who fell in their old days. Still less do we read of temptations to young children (2 Kings 2:23-25). Satan's chief assaults have always been against young men.

Why does Satan set chiefly upon young men?

-1. Because of their vigor of their nature; their courage, strength, and fervency. Satan strives to draw them on because he knows that if they get free from him, they will do him least and God most service, more than either old men or children, and therefore he strives fiercely to drive them on. Indeed God sometimes makes use of the weakest, but Satan always makes use of the stirring, quick spirits among men.

-2. Because Satan has most advantage to surprise them. There is no age so subject to temptation. The apostle says, "Flee youthful lusts" (2 Tim. 2:22); yet Timothy was not more subject to lusts than others, but rather was of a weak and sedentary nature (1 Tim. 5:23). But still Paul charges him to take heed of youthful lusts. Now if such a weak, quiet nature was subject to youthful lusts, then no age is so easy to be led into lusts as youth.

-3. Because it is the purpose of God to magnify his grace when corruption is strongest. Therefore God himself, to magnify his grace, lets Satan loose upon young men. So it was with our Saviour (Matt. 4). It is the purpose of God that where sin abounds, grace should much more abound (Rom. 5:20); therefore young men are most strongly assaulted, so that God may magnify his grace.

But why do the temptations of young men exceed all other ages? Because children have not yet come to the full lusts of youth, and old men are past them, so that young men are most liable to temptations and discouragements.

Use 1. This may teach young men to fear their states. If they do not have strong temptations, it is a sign the devil has strong hold already and so is in peace. But otherwise they are subject to spiritual assaults.

There are three temptations with which Satan commonly asaaults the sons of men. (a) Against their effectual calling. He persuades them it is yet too soon to look towards repentance, and they are more easily persuaded, being given more to evil company and to pleasures and delights than old men, and more impatient of counsel. (b) If God breaks through this, he puts them to question their faith and adoption. Are they indeed the children of God? Their strong lusts make them doubt it. (c) And if God breaks through this, the devil tempts them about their sanctification, going about to fill their hearts with unclean lusts. And if a man breaks through these, he has much cause to magnify God's grace.

Use 2. Since Satan's aim is chiefly at young men, let them strive to grow strong against him, so that the evil one may touch them not.

There are three special graces to help young men against the assaults of Satan: -1. Sobriety; be sober and vigilant (1 Pet. 5:8); take heed of intemperance and incontinence. -2. Stand fast in the faith (1 Pet. 5:9), not trusting to your own strength or courage, but relying upon God. While young men are confident of themselves, as Peter was, they fall; but if you stay yourself upon God, he will support you. -3. Humility. Treasure up this grace, so that you may not think too highly of yourself, for this is the folly of youth. "God resists the proud, but gives grace to the humble."

And there are three duties which I commend to young men. -1. Diligence in your callings. The lack of this overthrew David; when he was idle, Satan took advantage to tempt him to uncleanness (2 Sam. 11:1, 2). -2. Frequency in God's ordinances, in reading and hearing the word. The more you treasure up the word, the more power and strength you get, for this is the end of receiving the sacrament, to get strength against your lusts. -3. Be frequent in prayer, and that will help you much (James 4:7, 8). Complain of the slipperiness of your nature, of your weakness to withstand Satan's assaults, and entreat God to give you strength that you might hold out.

"I write unto you, young men, because you have overcome the wicked one."

Doct. Satan may be overcome, and is often overcome and disappointed, even by young men against whom he had the most advantage.

What is it to overcome Satan?

It is an expression borrowed from the victory of soldiers in war; and soldiers overcome their enemies by killing, spoiling, capturing, and by putting to flight.

Now Satan cannot be put to death; he is a spirit and not capable of physical death, only of the second death. And he may only be led captive by Christ (Eph. 4:8). But for the remaining two, young men may overcome Satan by spoiling him or by putting him to flight. Christ has taken the first spoil (Col. 2:15), but so may his young men spoil.

-1. Young men may put Satan to flight (James 4:7). It is possible for young men to stand and not to yield to his temptations; for though he has power to delude our senses and hurry our bodies about, yet he cannot capture our wills. Therefore stand, resist, give no place; and if you do so, he will flee from you for shame. He no longer has power to hold out, when he sees a man stand out against him. God has not given him liberty to pursue us unto death; but if we stand out against him, he will flee from us. So it was with our Saviour. First he tempted him about his sonship: "If thou be the Son of God, command that these stones be made bread." Second he tempted him to presumption, to cast himself down from the pinnacle of the temple; and then he tempted him with the glory of the world: "All these I will give thee, if thou wilt fall down and worship me." But because our Saviour still resisted his temptations, and Satan could not prevail, he departed. His very pride and insolence ake him scorn to trouble himself with any creature who disdains to be overcome by him; therefore he will depart.

-2. A young man may not only put Satan to flight, but he may also spoil him; that is, he may take advantage by his assaults to grow more wary, more holy, more obedient, and more fruitful; and so he spoils Satan. If a Christian enriches his spirit by the temptations he meets with, he makes a spoil of Satan, for the riches of the soldier is the spoil of the enemy. When young men stand fast and make a spoil of Satan, and grow more meek and humble and obedient, they shall the more overcome Satan. Job was strongly tempted by Satan to blaspheme God, but yet he stood fast; and not only so, but he took occasion to bless God (Job 1:21). So when Satan tempted him by his wife, see how he answers (Job 2:10). Michal tempted David by deriding him when he danced before the ark, but he grew more zealous by it (2 Sam. 6:20, 21). So they tempted John the Baptist to emulate Christ, but that stirred him up to magnify him more than he ever did before, and give the most honorable testimony of him (John 3:26-36).

How may young men overcome Satan? -1. By the blood of the Lamb; his power is quelled by the death of Christ. -2. By the power of the word that dwells in them (v. 14). -3. By the power of the Spirit, who is in them and is stronger than he who is in the world (1 John 4:3, 4).

Use 1. Since young men may and do overcome the world, this will teach them to make this their glory. Fight the spiritual battle; there is no gift in which you may so much please yourself, as in this (Prov. 20:29). What a shame it is for young men to show their strength in pouring down strong drink, and spend their strength upon women. If they were valiant in war, yet how much more an honorable fight it is to fight the Lord's battle, to over-wrestle our lusts. When a young man shall single out that grand captain, the Devil, and foil him in war, that is truly honorable. Remember, if Satan in a special manner strives to overcome you, stand out against him; resist him and do not yield to him. Examine what spiritual battles you have had with Satan; if none, then your case is not good.

Use 2. This may hearten the feeblest Christian not to be discouraged with conflicts. Many a soul says, "My corruptions are so strong, and my lusts so powerful, that I shall never be able to stand out against them and overcome them." But St. John here writes to young men whose corruptions were strong and violent, and yet he says, "You have overcome the wicked one."

Use 3. Of reproof to old men and women, if they do not overcome. Children have not come to the full force of lusts, and old men are past it; therefore they may be the more ashamed if they are given to voluptuousness and gluttony and gaming and lying and company-keeping.

Use 4. It exhorts all to do what we may do, though we cannot capture Satan or put him to death. In every temptation let us stand fast and put him to flight, and labor to spoil him by temptations. Let his temptations make you more humble and fruitful and obedient; this is the greatest honor of a Christian, to put Satan to flight and to spoil him thus.

C. "I write unto you, babes, because you have known the Father."

We have heard his words to old men and young men; now we come to his apostolic writing to babes.

Doct. Little children, even babes, may know God as their Father.

For the proof of this, I shall show it by examples. Though at first Samuel knew not, yet from that time forward he knew God (1 Sam. 3). See it in Josiah (2 Chron 34); and so in Timothy, who knew the scripture from a child (2 Tim. 3:15), and in John, who was full of the Holy Ghost from his mother's womb (Luke 1:15). And our Saviour bears testimony of little children, "Suffer little children to come unto me, for to such belongs the kingdom of heaven" (Mark 10:14). We may see that they were little ones, for he took them in his arms as we usually take children. The Anabaptists say that he does not mean children, but those who are of years though little children in grace; but this cavil is vain, for else his reason would have been vain. He might as well have said it of sheep as of little lambs, for they too are God's children; but yet he never mentions such, but only little children.

There are two reasons for the regeneration of little children.

–1. Their original sin. Those who are capable of sin are also capable of grace; and the greatest part of their sin is that they are without grace, whereas it is possible for them to have it (Luke 1:15; Ps. 58:3).

–2. Their interest in the covenant. They enter into a covenant with God even from their childhood. They brought their young babes to enter into a covenant with God (Deut. 29:10-12), and so they are capable of grace (Joel 2:15, 16). In times of great dangers to the land, God required little children and babes to humble themselves for breach of the covenant, which implies that they too were in a covenant.

So we see that little children may know God as their Father.

How soon do children come to be capable of this grace, to know God as their Father?

They are capable of the acts of grace as soon as they are capable of the use of reason. Yea, grace is capable of working more silently than reason. Though there can be no act of grace but what is from reason, they are capable of exercising grace and reason together sooner than we can discern it, yea even as soon as they can discern their natural father. Sooner than children can well use reason, they content themselves much with looking on the light and looking-glasses and other toys. So these little children have something in their hearts which pleases them, though they do not know what it is. Further, a parent can still a child sometimes by a silent gesture; so God can refresh the spirit of a child by some silent consolation which pleases the child, though it cannot express it. As soon as the child begins to know its natural parents, so soon it may begin to know God its Father; yea, there is no object so easily known as God, seeing he infuses to all enough light to know that he is God; and if the Holy Spirit strikes in, it may discern that he is its Father.

But how does the child express its knowledge of God as its Father? -1. In its silent thoughts, in some inward comfort which it cannot well express but which it feels to clear its spirit. -2. In affections. Children will show you love in God, joy in God, and fear of God. They are not averse to good duties nor forward to them, but they will listen though they do not know the meaning, and they have some delight and fear of God in them. They may be broken off from evil courses and be well pleased in God, and delight in his way. These things may be found in a child (I call them children until they are grown up to young men). And as a child soon discovers that he knows his parents, by smiling on them, crying after them, and delighting in them, so they will show you their knowledge of God by delighting in him, longing after him, and fearing his name.

Use 1. To reprove the sinful vanity of that proverb, "A young saint is an old devil." For if St. John acknowledges it as a great matter, and indeed writes for that reason, then surely it is no premonition of a future miscarriage. No, it is a sign that in old age they will know him who was from the beginning. But rather, if he is a young devil it is likely that he will prove worse; a young devil an old Beelzebub, but a young saint an old angel. A straight twig makes a straight tree; so if a child is well set and straight in childhood, he will grow more strong and compact when he is older.

Use 2. This refutes an error of the Papists, that is a presumption to say that a man knows his state in grace. Why, St. John writes it to all sorts, to old men, to young men, to babes, that they know their Father. If it is impossible or extraordinary, why does he take it as being so common? The woman who holds it impossible that a child should know its father, is a strumpet; so that church which holds that her children cannot know their Father, is a harlot. They worship so many gods that they know not of whose seed they are. If they were begotten of the seed of the word, we might conclude that they knew they knew him, because they would keep his word.

But they say this doctrine breeds presumption. I answer, no doctrine makes us more circumspect than to know that God is our Father; and if we grow secure in our sins, God will show that he is a Father to correct as well as to show indulgence.

What course may we take to instruct young infants?

-1. Teach them the principles of religion. "Train up a child in the way wherein he should walk, and he will keep it to the end" (Prov. 22:6); nurture him, or initiate him in the trade of his way. In the original it is, "in the mouth of his way," that is, at the beginning of his way. Set him right at the first in his way, and he will keep it to the end. If a traveler is set right in his way at first, it will help him better to keep his way all his journey; so set a child in a good way, teach him to cease from evil and to do well, and he will keep that way better in his age, as David says (Ps. 34:11-15).

-2. Teach them to read the scriptures and be conversant in them. Reading brings much benefit to little children.

-3. Bring them to church, and help them to remember something, and tell them the meaning of it, and encourage them, and that will make them delight in it.

-4. Give them a good example; let them learn no wickedness, no disorder, and no miscarriage from you (1 Chron. 29:9).

-5. God has sanctified seasonable and wise correction to children (Prov. 29:15; Prov. 22:15). It is a means to give wisdom, which is the fear of the Lord, and to drive away folly; and more, to deliver his soul from hell. But if you use correction without instruction, it is brutish (Prov. 6:23);

ver. 14 FIRST JOHN 165

therefore instruct them also, and withal use prayer and wait on God for a blessing.

1 John 2:14

"I have written unto you, fathers, because you have known him who is from the beginning. I have written unto you, young men, because you are strong, and the Word of God abides in you, and you have overcome the wicked one."

In verse 6 the apostle had exhorted all Christians to walk as Christ had walked. He amplified this duty from the antiquity of it (v. 7) and from the newness of it (v. 8). Then he mentioned one special duty, that of loving one another (vv. 9-11). And in v. 12 he laid down a motive, "because their sins were forgiven them"; and in v. 13 he divided those to whom he wrote into three sorts, pateres, neanionoi, paidia. Now in this fourteenth verse he repeats the same words almost.

Some think these words are a fault in the copy, as it is almost a vain tautology; but this is not likely. Sometimes repetitions in Scripture imply certainty, but I do not think that is here intended chiefly. I think the apostle, being about ready to press them to another duty in the next verse, here gives a reason to urge them to it.

Why does he not include babes here too, as in the verse preceding? Because they were not so easily carried away with the world. But he writes to old men and young men, who should not love the world since they knew God and had overcome tge wicked one. But to little children he writes, "Beware of false doctrines" (v. 18).

Doct. The saving knowledge of him who is from the beginning, of the Ancient of days, or of Jesus Christ, is able to wean even old men from the love of the world.

To know Christ and his worth, and our need of him, is a sufficient motive to wean old men from the world.

Two things there were which made wise, ancient men reluctant to embrace Christ and his gospel. -1. The antiquity of the heathen religion. Jesus Christ seemed a new God, only thirty-two or thirty-three years old, hated of all men and crucified. To commend such a God to them against their ancient doctrine, and to say that all must subject themselves to him, seemed strange. -2. The authority of heathen emperors who supported it.

To remove these two impediments, the apostle lays down a means and a reason. The means, "love not the world," implies that it was love of the world that made them embrace the ancient religion and reject Christ. That they might not love the world, he gives them a reason: "You have known him who is from the beginning, the Ancient of days," implying that all other religions are but novelties.

Use. This shows us a preservative against deluding our souls, against embracing false religion either on grounds of antiquity or authority. If old men follow it, yet this is no good reason, for St. John writes to old men, "Love not the world." And if the laws of man should go that way, yet if you rightly know Christ and him who was from the beginning, you will be kept from the love of the world. Thus no worldly things will keep you from embracing Christ and his gospel.

"I have written unto you, young men, because you are strong and the Word of God dwells in you, and you have overcome the wicked one."

Here are two causes of their victory over the wicked one; their strength and the abiding of the word in them.

I. Their strength.

Doct. Spiritual strength in young men is a grace highly acknowledged by God's servants.

The apostle here speaks not of bodily strength, but of the strength by which they overcome the wicked one, and he acknowledges this in them.

What is this strength? -1. It is the power of God's Spirit, by which a Christian is enabled to do all spiritual duties in the power of Christ. -2. It is a power of God's Spirit (2 Tim. 1:17; 2 Cor. 3:5); and hereby the Christian is enabled to do all spiritual duties (Phil. 4:13).

A Christian man, young or old, is able to perform every Christian duty; he is able to do all duties and suffer for Christ with power.

-1. This strength enables a man to do every Christian duty with strength, and to do so implies three things.

a. When a man comes to perform a thing in strength he performs it cheerfully (Ps. 19:5). Christ accounted it his meat and drink to do his Father's will (John 4:34), and it was his strength that made him do so.

b. Doing the will of God in strength implies a spirit of boldness and courage. Such a man is not fearful (1 Tim. 1:7; Acts 4:13; Acts 19:20).

c. Such strength makes a man do God's will diligently and constantly. An old man is soon wearied and soon slacks, but a strong man does his business diligently and constantly (1 Cor. 15:10). Let a child shoot an arrow with a weak hand, and it waggles; but if a strong man shoots it, it goes evenly. So if a weak man takes a duty in hand he soon begins to lag and fail, but a strong Christian does his duties constantly.

-2. Strength of grace appears in suffering patiently and joyfully under all things (Phil. 4:11-13; Col. 1:11). Therefore when a man is able to do duties with cheerfulness, and suffer with patience, he is endued with the power of the Spirit.

-3. There is a strength required for the overcoming and standing out against Satan, when a man is able not only to do and suffer valiantly, but also to hold out and resist all temptations (James 4:7) and to make an advantage of them (2 Sam. 6:20, 21; John 3:26). It shows much strength when a man can go on in power and vigour in the face of Satan's temptations.

But why does God vouchsafe this strength to young men and not to old men and children? -1. Because they are to

wrestle with stronger lusts, which old men have passed and children have not come to. Young men are sure to be faced with strong lusts (2 Tim. 2:22), and therefore God gives young men much strength to resist these strong temptations.
-2. The temptations of young men from without are stronger. They are more apt to be carried away with company and worldly business, and pleasures. Therefore that God might show his might in the face of the strongest challenge, he strengthens them; and indeed the devil loses more by one young young man who breaks off from him, than by six or seven old men, or twenty children.

Use. Let all young men labor for this spiritual strength. The strength of young men is their honor, to be able to outrun and outwrestle others; but what is that to being able to outrun the world and one's own lusts? What is it to outwrestle his adversary if he cannot outwrestle Satan, his temptations, and his own corruptions? For a young man to overcome the world and himself is a greater victory than Alexander could attain.

Here are means to help a young man to attain this spiritual strength and to grow in it.

-1. Obtain truth of grace. No man can be strong by outward performance only. A shadow of a man may look like a man, but it has no strength; truth of grace and power go together, and where there is no truth there is no power (2 Tim. 3:5). Therefore if we would be powerful in godliness, let us do duties with hearty affection. Do all things in obedience to God, and to do him service; and this very truth and sincerity will grow up to such strength that you may go further, conquering and to conquer.

-2. To get strength we must have a wholesome and good diet. If we would get spiritual strength we must feed on the ordinances of God and the word of God (1 Pet. 2:1, 2). No man can receive the word and sacrament with a good heart without growing stronger by it. Especially attend to it, and apply to your heart that part which belongs to you. Water it with your prayer, and look up to God for a blessing. If a young man feeds on these wholesome foods he will indeed grow strong. But those who seek after tricks of elegance and wit and speech, will be filled only with vain and empty notions.

-3. To get strength we must have exercise. Let a man daily exercise himself in grace, and he will grow up in the Lord and increase in spiritual strength (Gal. 5:16; Col. 2:6, 7). The more deeply a tree is rooted, the more fruit it brings forth; and so they who walk daily in a Christian course increase in strength. The one main duty which will strengthen us is walking in Christ, that is, not walking in our own strength. St. Paul was not able of himself to think a good thought (2 Cor. 3:5). "Without me you can do nothing." Therefore let us exercise our gifts in Christ, that is, to wait on Christ daily for the renewal of strength according to our daily tasks (Isa. 40:30, 31).

-4. To get strength we must purge out our corruptions (Rev. 2:5) as the body purges out sickness and pollution. There is need of daily repentance, which will cast out all noisome lusts and weaknesses, and make us able to perform duties in strength.

II. We have heard of the strength of young men. The second cause of their victory is because the word of God abides in them (v. 12).

Doct. Those young men who have their sins forgiven them also have the word of God abiding in them.

What is meant by the word of God abiding in them?

-1. He does not mean part of the word, but the whole word, abides in them; promises to comfort them, commands to bind them, threatenings to awe them, good examples to encourage them, bad examples to dissuade them. Therefore for men to be carvers and choosers of the word is not to have the word abiding in them. Herod would have some of John's words abide in him, but not all; and this is the commendation of St. John's young men, that every parcel of the word abides in them.

-2. When he says "the word of God," it implies that they

receive it as the word of God and not as the word of man (1 Thess. 2:13). A man receives the word, then, as looking at it all as of highest authority; no word of man shall stand against it, but all falls to the ground before it; it sways all.

-3. The word abides; this implies that this word did not flash in suddenly and continue for a time, but abides in them continually (John 5:35; Heb. 2:1, 2).

-4. It abides in you. This implies that the whole man receives the word; the judgment understands it, the will embraces it, the affections rejoice in it; the lips and mouth speak it; in the whole man the word abides, and that not for a time, but continually.

What is the reason why those who have their sins forgiven them, also have the word of God abiding in them? The reason is that those whose sins are forgiven them also have their eyes open to see the weight and danger of sin. The word has opened and affected the heart, and has made such deep impression that it cannot be rooted out (Ps. 119:93). Those promises which have comforted his soul, he shall never forget (Ps. 119:129); and hence he looks at them as sweeter than the honey and the honeycomb. Because he has found the word wonderful to humble him and to comfort him, therefore he still keeps it.

Use 1. This will try us, whether our sins are forgiven us or not. There is nothing more necessary to know, nor anything more comfortable; but how may we know it? Why, consider what place the word of God takes in you. If it abides in you, the whole word, there is no commandment which you would not obey, no threatening at which you are not humble, no promise you do not take as the word of God. Do you find your whole man submitting to it as the word of God? This is an evident sign of the remission of your sins; this could not have been if the word of God had not been wonderful to humble and comfort you.

But one will say, I have a brittle memory and cannot retain the word; therefore how can the word be said to abide in me? I answer, do you remember other things well, and not the word? Then it is dangerous. But if your memory is brittle in other things, then it argues the less danger though the word is also; for though it slips out of your memory, still it abides in your heart. Do you delight in it and desire more and more after it? If so, it may be said to abide in you.

Use 2. To exhort young men who have found their sins forgiven. God requires it of you, that you give up your heart to the whole word of God, to be wholly guided by it forever. If you ever drift loose from the word, you shall find the pardon of your sins drifting loose from your soul. Therefore let the word of God abide in you richly and plentifully, that you may have the comfort of pardon of sins.

Doct. Young men who have the word of God in them are strong young men.

-1. They are strong because the word of God abides not in the letter, but in power and efficacy. The word of God is mighty and powerful, and therefore it conveys strength and power wherever it dwells (Rom. 1:16). It is mighty to cast down the strongholds of Satan (2 Cor. 10:4), mighty to over-wrestle lusts, mighty to overcome the world (Ps. 119:9, 11).

Use 1. This will show us what poor weak young men they are, who have not the word of God abiding in them.

Use 2. If you desire to be strong indeed, let the word abide in you. Though Joseph was much tempted to uncleanness, yet he did not consent, for he looked at it as a breach of God's word. There are none so able to resist temptations as those who have the Word of God abiding in them; therefore if you would overcome pride and wantonness, let the word of God dwell in you; receive it in your judgment, in your will, in your memory, in your affections. Do not think it weakness, for it will be your strength. He who fears God does not fear any threatening of gods, and he who is taken up with God's promises does not regard all the flatteries of the world.

Doct. Those young men who have the word of God abiding

in them overcome the wicked one; and this is one reason for their victory, the abiding of the word in them.

There are three special temptations of Satan; against repentance, against faith, and against sanctification. And the word of God is mighty through God to repel all these.

-1. Against repenting so soon; but there is a word that binds him (Eccl. 12:1) and a word that threatens the contrary (Eccl. 11:9). There are promises (Prov. 8:17) and examples: Josiah, Timothy, and others resisted this temptation.

-2. Against faith. If a man gives up his heart to God and sets on a good course, yet he will make him live in pensiveness and fears and doubts. Against this too the word is powerful: there are commands to believe (1 John 3:23; 1 John 5:1; Matt. 11:28); there are threatenings if a man believes not (John 3:36); and there are notable promises to him who believes, and many notable examples.

-3. Against sanctification. If a man's heart is satisfied in the pardon of sin, Satan will tempt him with some base lusts which may defile and wound his conscience. Against this the word has: (a) Commands (1 Thess. 4:3; 1 Pet. 1:13-16; Matt. 5:48). (b) Promises (Rom. 2:6-8). (c) Threatenings to discourage him. (d) Examples to encourage him (Acts 24:16).

But how is the word so powerful, to overcome all the enemies of salvation? Because it is the sword of the Spirit, to cut asunder all lusts and temptations (Eph. 6:17). No man has more need of a sword to defend himself than young men have of the word to defend themselves and resist Satan. And it is not so much the letter of the word as the Spirit of the word that does this; the word cuts off all temptations; there is no place for invasion.

Use. This will teach us, if we desire to walk as victors in the world, to walk so as not to be beaten and kept off from either repentance or faith or sanctification. Let this be our care, to have the word of God engrafted in us; this is all our strength against temptations.

You will ask, How shall I get the word of God to abide in me? I answer:

-1. Be sure you keep your heart broken and clean, for then the word will abide there and will have rule and dominion (Isa. 66:2). If we receive the word with fear and reverence, this very reverence will overrule us. Why could not princes prevail against the Psalmist? Because his heart stood in awe of God's word (Ps. 119:161). So then that is an antidote against all temptations and persecutions. What if princes rise against you, even the prince of darkness and his angels? If the word dwells in you, it will help you to resist them. The word of God dwells in broken vessels; so then come to the word with your heart pure, resolved not to keep any lust (James 2:1).

-2. Look at the word as wonderful, as very effectual to do great things, and that will make you keep the word in you. Thus David speaks (Ps. 119:129). A sense of the great efficacy of the word will humble you and cleanse you, and will make you keep the word.

-3. Another means is to look up to God to send his Spirit, who will bring to mind those things you have need of and fasten them to your heart. Though you forget the word for the present, yet when you are tempted to a lust the Spirit will bring it to your remembrance (Isa. 30:21).

-4. Ponder the word of God in your heart. This was the practice of Mary (Luke 2:19), and it made her an eminent Christian.

-5. Confer the word to others. It is a great help to make it abide in you when you teach it to others, searching the scripture (Acts 17:11, 12).

-6. If you would have the word abide in you, give your soul up to a conscientious obedience of what you hear. If you resolve to keep it, it will mightily keep you against the world, against Satan, against your lusts. He who would keep his heart in a good frame must let his heart stick close to the word. Let them be stirred together, let them be riveted together, so that you may love the word of God and rejoice in it. Therefore if you desire to be a conqueror, let the word dwell richly in you (Col. 3:16; Isa. 11:9), so that you may grow up to abundance of knowledge; look at it as a wonderful word, and submit your soul to it.

1 John 2:15

"Love not the world, nor the things of the world."

The apostle had exhorted to many duties, as keeping the commandments and walking as Christ walked. Here he goes on to remove an impediment which might hinder all, and that is love of the world. He writes here to young men and old men chiefly, and to babes in v. 18.

In this verse we have a double prohibition of love; love to the world and love to the things of the world. This prohibition is grounded on a threefold reason: -1. The Father's love is removed from such. -2. Whoever is in the world is in either the lust of the flesh, the lust of the eyes, or the pride of life, and is not of the Father (v. 16). -3. The world is transitory, and the love of God is permanent.

What is the world? The world is taken four ways in scripture, and all four are pertinent to this place. It is used: -1. For the frame and fabric of the heaven and the earth, and all the creatures (Acts 17:24). So "love not the world" means "love not the created thing." -2. For the wicked of the world (John 15:19); and though he does not here intend them, yet we are to separate ourselves from them. -3. For the fashions and customs of the world (Rom. 12:2). -4. For those endowments and benefits which the world affords, as riches, honors, profits, and pleasures (James 4:4). The latter two are chiefly what the apostle aims at: "Love not the world," that is, love not the fashions and customs of the world; love not the profits and pleasures of the world.

But why may we not love the creatures? Are they not said by God himself to be "very good"? (Gen. 1:31) I answer, there are two sorts of love: a love of concupiscence, when a man loves the thing for the thing itself and desires to gain it; and a love of amity, when I not only desire to commune with it but to communicate good to it. The first love is here forbidden. When we love the world for its own sake and not for God's, when we desire it even though by it we are separated from God, and when we rejoice in it for itself, we are transgressing the apostle's commandment.

What is meant by "the things of the world"? Not the creatures, for they are included in the first expression, "the world" (Acts 17:24). It appears from v. 16 that by "the things of the world" St. John means the lusts of the world; not only lusting after women, but such an affection as carries us after any creature inordinately (Rom. 7:7; Gal. 5:17). He writes to old men and young men, "love not the things of the world," for such are most subject to it.

Doct. The world is not to be beloved of young or old.

St. James is sharp in this point (James 4:3, 4); he reproves as adulterers those who love the world. Those who are friends to the world are enemies of God.

But are not all creatures of God good, and should we not be merciful to our beasts?

He does not forbid mercy or love to beasts or creatures, but he would not have your love terminated in them and bounded in them; he would not have you rejoice or delight in the creature before you delight in God; for if you seek these things for themselves, the love of God is not in you.

What are the reasons we should not love the world? The world itself is at enmity against the Creator; ever since the fall there lies this vanity in the creature; it empties souls of grace and love to the Creator, and keeps them from God's ordinances.

-1. In hearing the word, if possible, the world will keep you back. Let God propound a feast of fat things, and one makes an excuse that he has hired a farm and must go see it; another has bought yokes of oxen, and he must go try them; and a third has married a wife, and he cannot come (Luke 14:18, 20).

-2. If a man breaks through this and comes to the

ordinances, he shall find that the world is a great enemy to him there (Ezek. 33:21, 22). It will seek to draw your heart after profits and pleasures, and as a result of them to make you scoff at what you hear, as the Pharisees scoffed at Christ.

-3. Further, if you should surmount this temptation and hear the word and attend to it, yet the world will so dampen you or choke you that all the seed will be smothered (Matt. 13:22). While we busy ourselves here and there in the world, the world is gone and grace is gone; this is the enmity of the world.

The man who is addicted to the world is more in slavery and bondage than the galley slave, whose heart is free though his hands may be bound and his feet shackled. Even the slave desires freedom from his slavery, but the worldly man is so busied in the world that not only his body but his mind and heart are captive to the world.

Use. This is a sign of trial. Do you love the world for itself? Do you think it well with you when you have the world, and not well when you do not have the world? Does all your contentment rest in the world, like the rich man in the parable? Then you love the world. But if you regard the world no further than it will help you in a Christian course, then it will never hinder you in the ways of God, and you do not love the world, but the love of God is in you.

Doct. There is in our corrupt nature not only a love to the world, but also a love to our own lusts.

"Love not the things of the world," that is, our own lusts, implying that there is in us by nature a love for the things of the world; that is, for the lusts of the flesh, the lusts of the eye, and the pride of life.

What is the lust of the flesh? It is a corrupt inclination by which our bodies seek sensual lusts and sensual objects; as meat and drink, which is intemperance; or women, which is incontinence; or pastimes and pleasures, which is voluptuousness. And they are called the lusts of the flesh because it is our flesh which sets us to seek them.

What are the lusts of the eye? There is a good eye, a bountiful eye, but an evil eye is called a covetous eye (Prov. 23:6). So then the lust of the eye is covetousness; and it is called the lust of the eye because the eye stirs us up to it. We need merely to behold them (Eccl. 5:10, 11), and immediately we fall alusting.

What is the pride of life? This is seeking our own carnal excellency, looking at ourselves only. Whether we do it in heart by conceit, or in speech by worldly boastings, or in conduct by a high attitude, it is the pride of life.

And we are ready to love all these; we are ready to love our own wantonness, our intemperance, our covetousness, our conceit. Would you think a man would be so wicked as to love voluptuousness or desire or selfrighteousness? Yes, or else St. John would not have been at such pains to forbid it.

It is evident that a man loves his lust, from these:

-1. From our aptness to take part with our own lusts when they are discovered or reproved. Thus Herod loved his Herodias and took part with her against John the Baptist (Matt. 14:3). When a man is angry with the minister rather than with his sin, that is a sign of his love for his lust. So Asa was wrathful when the prophet rebuked him (2 Chron. 16:10). Jonah was so in love with his own pride that he was displeased exceedingly when Nineveh was not destroyed, and was much displeased that God should reprove him for his frowardness. He loved this pride and anger in himself and pleaded for it when God asked him, "Do you do well to be angry?" He replied, "Yea, I do well to be angry even to the death." If a man pleads for his lust and stands out against reproof, that is a sign he loves that lust.

-2. From the slight regard we give to exhortations against our lusts. If ministers exhort, "Love not the world, nor the things of the world," we slight them and do not search out our lusts and mortify them; and thus it plainly appears that we love them. If a prince should send to a city and ask them not to harbor such and such traitors, but to seek them out and punish them; and if they should never seek them out, never look for them, would that not be a sign of their love to those traitors?

Use 1. This may show us the amazing depth of the wickedness that is in our hearts. We might think it wickedness enough to have this voluptuousness and covetousness and pride in our hearts, but this is nothing; we not only have these lusts, but we love them. Therefore this should teach us to abhor our own carnal state. Therefore let no man have a high opinion of himself, but let him labor to see the depth of the wickedness of his heart by nature (Jer. 17:9), for he not only has these lusts but loves them.

Use 2. It will teach us, whenever we renew our repentance and find any lusts in our hearts, to go a little deeper, and we shall find a love of those lusts in our hearts. As God said to Ezekiel, "Turn, and you shall see greater abominations than these," so we shall find it in our own hearts.

Doct. Young and old are to be weaned from the lusts of the world.

The love of Christians is not to be set on the lusts of the world. The Holy Spirit in scripture encourages restraint from these lusts (1 Pet. 2:11; 2 Tim. 2:22). St. Peter wishes us to abstain from them as if they wee some deadly poison that would stain and infect our souls. "Flee them"; this implies some great danger; flee from them, make no means to accomplish them (Rom. 13:14).

The scripture commands us to mortify our lusts (Col. 3:5). There lusts are called the members of the body, implying that there is a body of sin. Mortifying is a metaphor: when surgeons would cut off a member, they mortify it, either by binding it and stopping the flow of blood, or else by applying sedatives to stupefy it; and then they cut it off, lest it pollute and kill the whole body. So we ought to mortify our lusts, either by binding and restraining them from delight in any pleasure (Ps. 119:101; "my feet," that is, the inclination of my heart), or else by applying sedatives to subdue our lusts. One such sedative is the Spirit (Rom. 8:13); another is the threatenings of God; a third is the dangers of our lusts. Another special agent to mortify our lusts is the death of Christ; when we consider Christ dying for us, and ourselves dead in him, how can we live any longer in sin? (Rom. 6:1-6)

After mortifying the member, making it insensible of feeling, the surgeon cuts it off. So Christians must cut off their lusts lest they pollute them entirely (Matt. 18:8, 9). If our lusts were as near and precious to us as our right eyes, were they as convenient and necessary as our right hands, yet if they interrupted us in our callings it were better to go lame in our business and with reproach and shame in the world, than to be cast body and soul into hell. Cut them off, then; away with them, mortify them.

A similar scripture injunction is to crucify the flesh with the affections and lusts (Gal. 5:24). They who are in Christ have crucified the flesh with the affections and lusts; they have crucified the whole body of sin. They look at all their lusts as crucifying Christ, and they look up to Christ for the pardon and healing of sin, because pardoning and healing go together (Hosea 14:3, 4; 1 John 1:7, 8).

Why should all be weaned from lusts?

-1. Because of the enmity which these lusts have against God (Gal. 5:17). If they are enemies to God, then a Christian has reason to consider them his own enemies; and indeed he cannot love these lusts and God too. "He who loves the world, the love of the Father is not in him"; he is not fit for any duty. Every lust hinders spiritual duties, hearing the word, prayer, receiving the sacrament; any one lust tolerated or lived in, hinders all spiritual duties.

-2. Because of the enmity they have against our souls (1 Pet. 2:11). They fight against our souls; we must kill or be killed. Either mortify them, or they will mortify our souls; either capture them or they will capture us. Therefore if we would not have our lusts hinder our peace with God and eat out our grace, and interrupt our communion with God, let us love not the world nor the lusts of the world.

Use 1. It is not enough to abstain from outward gross sins; we must not love our lusts. We may abstain from the outward acts of sin, but yet our hearts may secretly delight in it; then we yet love the world. Therefore we must labor to cleanse ourselves from secret lusts. Circumcision was cutting off the foreskin of a secret member, and yet God would have another circumcision more secret, of the heart. We must circumcise our hearts. God took special care that he might have the kidneys and fat of the sacrifices (Lev. 3:3, 4); the kidneys and fat are our strongest desires and lusts; therefore when we offer sacrifice, we must come before the Lord and burn them. There is no savour so sweet in God's nostrils as the burning of our strongest lusts. The more our lusts stink in our nostrils, the more sweet smelling savour it is to God; and as long as our lusts smell sweet in our nostrils, we are loathsome to God.

Use 2. It is not enough to cut off some lusts, but we must cut off those we love most. If a man hates prodigality, you need not exhort him to frugality; and so one who cares not for pride may yet be covetous. If prodigality is your lust, do not cry out against another man's covetousness; and if you are covetous, do not stand out against another man's prodigality, but strive against your own covetousness. Let us look especially to those lusts which our hearts delight after.

"If any man love the world, the love of the Father is not in him."

Doct. It is not the having of the world, but the loving of it, that keeps our hearts from the love of the Father.

David's mountain was strong; Joseph had his will in Egypt; Abraham was rich. But though they had the world, yet they had not the love of the world (James 4:3, 4). It is not the lordship of the world, but the friendship of the world, which is enmity to God; for the time shall come that they who follow the Lamb shall be princes of the world.

St. James calls the love of the world adultery. A woman who makes herself a friend to another man and bestows that love on him which her husband only should enjoy, is an enemy of her husband. So a man who is a friend of the world is an enemy of God.

Why is this so?

-1. That love which we owe to God is so great that it cannot be divided to others. "Thou shalt love the Lord thy God with all thy heart, and all thy soul, and mind, and strength" (Matt. 22:37). Then we must love the world no further than it may help us in his service; if we love it more we sin against the great commandment. All our love and vigor is to be set in God; and if a man loves the world, he cannot thus love God. If he loves the world his chief care is for wealth and riches, and then he will perhaps look a little toward God. First let me bury my father; first let me stock my farm; first let me try my oxen, or enjoy my wife, and then if I have time I will come to the feast.

-2. A covetous or lustful or proud man, when he has the world and its lusts, is fully satisfied even without God (Ps. 17:8-14; Luke 12:19). The more he has of the world, the less he cares for God. The moon is at the full when it is opposite the sun; so with a worldly man.

-3. The love of the world will make a man part with God rather than with the world. He will rather part with grace and heaven than to leave the world; he would rather part with Christ than with his possessions, as the young man in the gospel (Matt. 19:16-22). "No man can serve two masters" (Matt. 6:24); God and this world are two masters, and he who serves God as he ought, has no time or strength to serve the world.

Use 1. This will discourage us all from love of the world. If a father should come to his child and say, "If you love such a man or woman, you cannot love me, and I shall take you for my utter enemy, and you shall never make it up again," would not any child part with any friend rather than be an enemy to his father? Any man who loves the world makes the world his god; therefore covetousness is called idolatry (Col. 3:5). A man's belly may be his god; the love of the world is directly against God. The love of God requires all your heart, soul, and strength, and therefore no part is left to be set on the world.

Use 2. This will exhort Christians to mortify their love to the world. You must either crucify your love to the world or to God; you cannot serve God and mammon.

What are our motives to mortify our love to the world? If a man can withdraw his mind from the world, he may be master of the field in any temptation that befalls him. What is the world? All that is in the world is either profit, pleasure or credit. Thus if you are weaned from your profit or pleasure in meat or drink or pastime, and if you are weaned from credit in regard to others, you shall bereave Satan of the weapons he fights you with. For how can he keep men back from religion if they will not be enticed by his credit and applause in the world? How can he hinder them from holy duties if they ignore his profits and pleasures? Therefore if a man could wean himself from them, he might easily overcome the wicked one. When Satan saw that Christ had nothing to do with these things, he left him.

Use 3. This will console every soul who, though he is busy in the world, yet does not love the world. It is not the having of the world, or having the lusts of the world, which makes us enemies to God, but loving them. So then you may have the world, and even have its lusts, and yet have God, if you desire to mortify them and crucify them. Only let God see that in your heart, and though you have many lusts in you against his will, these will not separate you from the love of the Father.

1 John 2:16

"For all that is in the world, the lust of the flesh, the lust of the eyes, and the pride of life, is not of the Father, but is of the world."

In the former verse the apostle dissuaded both old and young from the love of the world and the things of the world, that is, the lust of the flesh, the lust of the eye, and the pride of life. And he dissuades them from this by a threefold reason: -1. It evacuates the love of God in us (v. 13). -2. The lusts of the world are not of God but of the world (v. 16). -3. These lusts are not permanent, but pass away.

Doct. All the sinful dispositions and courses of the world are of these three sorts: either the lusts of the flesh, the lusts of the eye, or the pride of life.

This text is a sufficient warrant, though there is no other such division in scripture, for every word of God is perfect. All the sinful dispositions and ways of the world are one of the three classes, either the lusts of the flesh, the lusts of the eye, or the pride of life.

What is intended by these terms? The lusts of the flesh are such as are stirred up by the flesh and promise our bodies comfort. The lusts of the eye are such as satisfy the senses, namely covetousness; they are called lusts of the eye because the eye is only satisfied with them. The pride of life is the seeking after one's own carnal excellency when he looks only at himself and has a high conceit of himself.

But it will be asked, Are there not many sins which do not fall into this division?

-1. May not a man may grow contentious without being led by profit or pleasure or pride? No, really there is no contention which does not spring from pride (Prov. 13:10). A carnal seeking of his own excellence makes him contend.

-2. Atheism or superstition is said to have no profit or pleasure or credit in it; and what profit or pleasure or credit is there in swearing? I answer, both these proceed from disobedience, which is lack of fear and reverence of God; and what else is this but pride? When you see any man neglecting religion, it is from pride of heart. "The wicked, through the pride of his countenance, will not seek after God" (Ps. 10:3, 4); so superstition comes from pride, though it seems to be done with humility and devotion (Col. 2:23;

Micah 6:6-8). Do not come before God with your own inventions and seek to please him with them, for this is nothing but pride.

The same is true of profaneness. When Pharaoh said, "Who is the Lord? I know him not," it proceeded from pride (Exod. 9:17). So when men break the bonds of God's service and will not be held in, this springs from pride of heart.

-3. Indulgence to children, as David and Eli, who could not find it in their hearts to rebuke their children; does this spring from pride or profit or pleasure? Is it not rather meekness and mildness? I answer, such indulgence always proceeds from pride. "You have honored your children above me" (1 Sam. 2:29). When a man would rather see God dishonored than his children, or his children rather honored than God, this is a great measure of pride.

-4. What about timorousness, when a man neglects religion out of fear? Peter denied his master for fear; it was not pleasure or profit or pride. And where came the despair of Cain or Judas; did this come from pride? I answer, this too springs from pride of heart. Did not Peter's temerity come from his former self-confidence? God left Peter to such baseness of spirit; and when he preferred his own safety to his master, was not this pride indeed? So Pilate; what made him afraid of Caesar? Was it not love of his own safety? Did he not honor himself before God, and was that not pride? And why did Cain despair? Was it not because of his pride against his brother, envying his brother and preferring himself before his brother? And the despair of Judas came from pride of heart, because God was not in his heart; if he had no comfort in himself, he did not seek it in God but in a halter. This is pride, because he cannot endure the punishment of conscience which God inflicted; had he had an humble soul, he would have contended himself and looked up to Christ for pardon, as did many of those who crucified him. All temerity and baseness of spirit proceeds from pride; if a man is afraid of offending a great one, is it not because he is afraid of losing his honor in the great one's eyes, and is this not pride?

Use 1. Thus every man may learn what sin he is most given to, what corruption most defiles his heart, and which way his heart is most inclined; and this is needful. Would you know what sin most sways you? It is one of these: either the lust of the flesh, lust of the eye, or the pride of life; or if all of them, one overrules. Therefore see which of these bears most sway in your life. If your comfort and encouragement in God are damped and choked, it is because one of these three lusts is in you.

Use 2. This may exhort us to humiliation when we find one of these lusts working in our hearts. He who is addicted to pride may be given over to the world too, and look for pleasure and sensual objects. This should unfeignedly humble us, that such a mass of sin should be in us; there is not one sin in the world but what is in our hearts. St. James calls the tongue a world of iniquity (James 3:6). What a world of mischief is in our hearts. Therefore do not say, "I find no great power in myself to abstain from sin, but I have a good heart to God"; alas, there is no lust which is not found in your heart; all that is in the world is in you.

Use 3. This is a cause of much thankfulness to God, that he has restrained any of these lusts in you, and that you have not run into them with as much force as any man in the world. When you see any punished for adultery or murder, you may see it in yourself; our hearts had been subject to the same, if God had not held us back. Therefore we ought to be thankful to God.

Use 4. If there is in us such a world of wickedness, let us get a heavenly measure of grace which will countervail all these corruptions. Let us look for a new world of grace which will humble our hearts against our pride, which will make us liberal against covetousness, chaste and pure against the lusts of the flesh, so that this world of wickedness may not reign in us.

We are not to love these lusts because they are not of

the Father but of the world.

Doct. There is no lust in the world which can claim God as its author or fountain.

When David committed adultery, which was a lust of the flesh (2 Sam. 11:4), it was evil in the sight of the Lord. He pleased not God but himself in this. In other things he was a man after God's own heart, but in this after his heart. What made Joseph abstain from the same sin? Because he considered that it would be a great sin against God. God so hates covetousness (Ps. 10:3), which is a lust of the eye, that he hates both it and the covetous man (Isa. 57:17). So for pride of life (Prov. 6:18, 19, 1 Pet. 5:5). God wars against a proud man; he sets an army against him. And therefore, since God hates these, he cannot be the author of sin. It is manifest that these things do not spring from God, for he abhors them and punishes them (Job 34:9-12; Rom. 1:18, 19; Gal. 5:17).

But why can they not claim their origin from God?

-1. Because God is pure (Hab. 1:13); he is of pure eyes and so abhors evil. "What fellowship has light with darkness?" What fellowship have filthy lusts with a pure God, a covetous heart with a liberal God, a proud heart with the great God?

-2. From the hindrance sin offers in the service of God (James 1:13, 14). There is nothing in sin for which God should desire it, or respect it, or make use of it.

But it will be said, Does not the scripture itself say that God has his hand in sin? Did not Joseph's brethren sell him because of envy and pride, and does he not yet say that it was God who sold him? (Gen. 45:7, 8) Was it not for envy that the Pharisees crucified Christ, and yet was it not what God foreordained? And does not God say plainly that he will give David's wives into Absalom's hands? How is it then that you say that no sin is from God?

I answer, they are from the Father, but not in the sense in which they are from the world. They are not from him as an author or fountain, for the good God can work no evil. But yet there is no sin of which he is not the occasion, though he is the cause of none. All good things come from God as cause, all evil from God as occasion. The gospel is the gospel of peace, yet it is made to set men at variance and strife (Mark 10:29). This is not the proper work of the gospel, but of the corruption of men who use it for the contrary. The accidental work of God consists in three things: in leaving men to their own corruptions, in leaving them to Satan, and in giving them good occasions and objects which they pervert to sin.

-1. God hardened Pharaoh's heart; how? By leaving him to himself. Wax left to itself will grow hard; how much more the stony heart of man. As God does not rule and work in his heart, it grows hard.

-2. So God left Pharaoh to Satan by allowing Satan to help his soothsayers repeat the miracles of Moses (Exod. 7:12, 22). And because Pharaoh saw his enchanters do so much, he thought they were no better than his magicians.

-3. He hardens our hearts by many comforts, mercies, and outward blessings; and these often harden our hearts, as respite from judgment hardened Pharaoh's (Exod. 8:15), when it should lead us to repentance (Rom. 2:4, 5).

How did God tempt Absalom? First, by leaving him to his lustful heart; second, by leaving him to ill counsel; and third, by giving the kingdom into his hand, so that he took liberty to commit wickedness in lying with his father's concubines. Similarly, how did God work Joseph's sale into Egypt? First, by turning his father's love to him above his other brethren; second, by his dreams which stirred them up to capture and sell him. God only gave the occasions and objects, which all these abused to sin.

So with Adam's sin. God led him into a temptation, but it was of trial, not of seducement. He gave him a goodly tree, and its fruit fair to the eye, but the cause of all their woe was their own consent and mutability, which they might have resisted.

And for God's decree, though they did nothing but what God decreed, God's purpose never decreed that any sin should be wrought otherwise than as it is wrought by the propounding objects and occasions, and leaving them to themselves and Satan; but he never decreed to force any to sin. Therefore let God and his throne be guiltless; let iniquity rest on the wicked, but God's hand is not with it.

Use 1. This is a just refutation of the Papists, who say we make God the author of sin. We believe that there is no sin in the world which is from the Father, but all is from the world. Let no man say when he is tempted, he is tempted of God, for God finds nothing in sin to desire it. If God know that there will grow weeds as well as grain if he sends the showers, must he therefore restrain the showers? If the dunghill is made to stink by the sunbeams, shall the sun therefore not shine? The sun does not cause the stench, but the filth in the dunghill; so there is nothing in God's providence which works sin. If his providence turns many to sin, the fault is not in God's providence but in men's corruptions; he is as far from sin as the sun from stench.

Use 2. To reprove all foolish men who wrong God's providence. If they fall into sin, they impute it to destiny; what a profane thing this is, for a man to impute his sin to God. Was Absalom innocent because God gave his father's wives into his hands? No, but God punishes his sin before the people, because he had committed iniquity openly before all.

Use 3. To teach every man and woman to abhor these sins, all pride, gluttony, adultery, covetousness. God detests them and abhors them; they are not from him; therefore what have good men to do with them? Let those follow the lusts that are in the world, whose chief good is in the world; but you live as becomes God's servants.

Use 4. This may teach us to clothe ourselves with the contrary graces. If those lusts are not from the Father, surely the contrary graces are. Therefore deck yourself with humility; "God resists the proud, but gives grace to the humble" (James 4:6). Be heavenly-minded; "If you are risen with Christ, seek those things that are above." Alas, are these worldly things your highest things? It is a sign you are not risen with Christ. Deck yourself with sobriety, chastity, temperance, liberality, humility; walk thus, and you shall find rest to your soul.

Doct. The love of young men and old is to be weaned from that which is not from the Father.

If honor comes not from God, and people seek it, they cannot believe (John 5:44). What kept Joseph from the lusts of the flesh? God withheld his mistress from him. If God withholds a thing, it is not for us to put forth a reaching desire to it. Shall we take it unkindly that God withholds it?

So with Jephthah; when the king of Ammon contended with him, he told him, "What God gives us, we will possess" (Judg. 11:24). If God had not given it he would have usurped it, as the king of Ammon did; so if our God does not give us a thing, let us not reach after it.

But it will be asked, What does a man receive that is not from God's hand? Do not good and evil come from him? So if we are given to our lusts, is that too not from God?

I answer, It is one thing when God gives us a blessing in his providence, and quite another thing when he gives us a blessing in his ordinances. We may have many things by way of God's providence and yet have little comfort from them. It was his providence which gave David's concubines to Absalom, and yet he gave him little comfort in them.

You will say then, God's providence sends a bribe. But we must not reason thus; these trials are for obedience and not for seduction. If a bribe comes, God is trying you to see if you will take it; if a harlot presses on you, God is trying your chastity by this; it is his providence. But if God gives us a thing in an ordinance, either by his commandment or by our calling, that we may safely take (Heb. 5:4). God's commandment and our calling are God's ordinances. Whatever he calls us to receive, he ordains; and whatever he does not call us to receive, he does not ordain; so that whatever is ordained by God in his ordinance, that we may take, but whatever does not come by ordinance let us shake off.

Use 1. This will teach us to take heed of all unlawful honors and riches. Though they may comfort us a while, yet they shall do us no good if they do not come from God. We may not be afraid to receive any lawful honor or lawful pleasure, for God is the God of all comfort (2 Cor. 1:3). But though we may receive honor, yet we must not be ambitious. So riches are God's gifts, but let us not use ill means to come by them; and if we cannot come by pleasures without violating God's law, let our hearts not reach for them.

Use 2. This may quiet our hearts in the lack of all blessings which do not come from God. You see that you cannot have such riches, or such pleasures, or such profits; why then, wean your heart from them and be content without them. It is the wisdom of men to follow an occasion when they see God's providence leading to it; but if you see God's providence hindering it, it is not good for you, and therefore you must be content without it.

Use 3. This shows God's children what they may lawfully enjoy. You may lawfully love and enjoy anything which comes from the Father in his providence.

But how shall we know whether all our blessings are from the Father? Whatever we have obtained by prayer, it is a good sign that it is from God. But you will say, I have many things which I never prayed for, a wife and friends and honor and calling, and other things, that I have never prayed for; may I have comfort in them? I answer, a man may say he has a thing from the Father, when he has it by fellowship with Christ (Eph. 3:16-19). Many times God gives us things out of his love in Christ, which we never thought of; for our hearts are so shallow and empty that we are not able to comprehend what God is able to do, for he is able to do above all we can ask or think; therefore let us get hold of Christ, and then we need fear no blessing.

Thus much for the general. Now because these lusts are the springs of all the lusts in the world, therefore we will speak of them in particular.

I. The lusts of the flesh.

What are the lusts of the flesh? The lust of the flesh is an affection to satisfy the flesh, that is, the body.

-1. The body stirs up to intemperance, of which there are two parts, gluttony and drunkenness.

-2. The body stirs up to incontinence, whoredom and adultery.

-3. The body desires pleasure.

-4. The body desires ease.

Why does the apostle not speak to children here? They are usually not given to eat or drink more than needs, and are not tempted to inconstancy. Ease cannot be idleness in them, for their bodies are too weak to labor and their minds too shallow to study; but when they come to riper years, let them be employed in these.

A. The first lusts of the flesh are gluttony and drunkenness. The body distempered with meat is gluttony, the body distempered with drink is drunkenness.

-1. A man may sin in gluttony and drunkenness by having his appetite directed to an unfit object, as when he has a desire for those things which are harmful to him. If wine is forbidden by the physician, or salt meats to some persons, yet there is a lust in men's natures to crave these. It was a lust of intemperance in the old law to desire after any unclean meats (Lev. 8:31, 32; Isa. 65:4). Thus a man may sin in the object of his desire; such a lust was in our first parents, who lusted after a forbidden fruit because they saw it was fair (Gen. 3:6).

-2. This lust shows itself more in the measure of eating and drinking than in the nature of them. A man may exceed in measure in eating and drinking:

a. Beyond health, when it is not for strength (Eccl. 10:16, 17). A lawful amount of eating gives strength to the body; an unlawful amount takes it away. The same may be said of drinking; when the body is distempered and inflamed, and health hurt (Luke 21:34; Prov. 23:29-35), this is excess.

b. Beyond ability. When we covet meats and drinks beyond the measure of our estate, when we lust above our means (Prov. 23:20, 21), when by costly meat and drink we weaken our estates (Prov. 21:17), we shall surely come to poverty.

c. Beyond reason. When we eat and drink beyond the bounds of reason, so that we forget our business, this is a lust of the flesh. Lot was so drunk that he defiled his daughters (Gen. 19:33, 35), and Noah was so far drunk that he could not cover his nakedness. In Lot reason was wholly taken away, in Noah but partly; but whether partly or wholly, it is lust.

d. Beyond our calling. When a man eats or drinks so much that he is unfit for his calling, this is a lust of the flesh (Luke 21:34; Exod. 32). The meat and drink which should strengthen a man to follow his calling, prevents him from doing so; this is lust.

-3. If we are carried to meat and drink with no other end but to eat and drink and satisfy our appetite, this is a lust of the flesh, a satisfying of the flesh, and looking no further than to serve the body. This is often the failing of many who otherwise abhor drunkenness and gluttony. But ask them why they eat and drink, and they must confess it is only to satisfy their appetite. But the command is, do all to the glory of God (1 Cor. 10:31). We may satisfy our bodies, but we must not terminate all this in eating and drinking, for then it is a lust of the flesh. "Go and take your bow, and take some venison, and make me savoury meat, such as my soul loves" (Gen. 27:3, 4) Why? Only to please his appetite? No, but "that I may eat and bless you"; that being refreshed by your provision I may be strengthened to bless you.

B. Next follows incontinence, which is an inordinate affection to women (Matt. 5:28), and a lust to be avoided by all. Like the former, it expresses itself in three things: -1. In being directed toward a wrong object. -2. In exceeding above measure. -3. In not being aimed at a right end.

-1. Sometimes the heart is carried to beastly, unnatural lusts against nature and order; as with beasts (Lev. 18:23), with kindred (as when Amnon defiled his sister Tamar), and in women with men, or men with women before consent of parents.

-2. Even in conjugal affection it is lust when it exceeds measure, as when for it a man omits his duty to God or denies his profession. Sometimes a man has a good affection to religion, but the love of his wife carries him away (Luke 14:26).

-3. It is a lust of the flesh when they are so transported with affection that they look at no higher end than marriage itself (1 Cor. 7:29). The meaning of this verse is, let those who have wives not look at them for their own ends, but to be better fitted for God's service and bring them nearer to God.

C. There is a lust of the flesh which is a lust of inordinate pastime or pleasure, and God threatens this with poverty (Prov. 21:17). There is a threefold lust in pleasure also: in respect of object, in respect of measure, and in respect of end.

-1. Our pastimes are unlawful in respect of object if we make a pastime of everything, of such things as should be matters of devotion, sorrow, and humility. We may not jest in scripture phrase, nor may we make shows and pageants of scripture stories. So cards and dice, we may not make a pastime of them, for they are lots, an ordinance of God.

It is sometimes replied that there are religious lots, civil lots, and indifferent lots; divine lots are to be used only in devotion and solemnity, but we may take more liberty in the others. I reply that all lots are religious, whether they are about holy things (as choosing an apostle), civil things (as division of lands), or about any other thing (to determine a controversy, as they cast lots on Christ's garments). For swearing is calling God to be a witness, whether in religious, civil, or light matters; so all kinds of lottery, whether religious, civil, or indifferent matters, are in effect calling on God to dispose of the matter at hand. Thus casting a lot, though in matters of pastime or lightness, is a religious ordinance, because it appeals to divine providence, and is therefore to be avoided.

It is likewise unlawful to make sport of the judgments of God (Ps. 119:120). If you see God's judgments on another, make it not a pastime. It is thus not meet for great men to keep fools and madmen to make them pastime (1 Sam. 21:14, 15). So it is unlawful to make a mere recreation of hunting, since the enmity between the creatures came for our sins and therefore should be a matter of compassion.

-2. Our pastimes are unlawful in respect of measure when they are pursued excessively, as when men spend whole days and nights in pastime (Eph. 5:16), when men make an occupation of recreation, and when we abuse it in excess of affection.

-3. Pleasure is unlawful in respect of end when it becomes an end in itself. St. Paul says, "Whatsoever you do, do it for the glory of God." Again, it is unlawful when we abuse it in regard of gain. Though card-playing were lawful, yet to make a gain of it is reproved, for pastime should be for our delight. For a man to sell his pastime is filthy lucre.

D. The last lust of the flesh is the lust of idleness or ease or sleep, for it is the body that craves sleep and ease. Both young and old are to be weaned from it.

How is a man carried inordinately to ease or sleep? As before, in respect of object, in respect of measure, and in respect of end.

-1. It is unlawful in respect of object when we observe it at times which are unseasonable.

    a. When we are so drowsy that we cannot attend to holy duties, the very inclination to sleep is a sinful lust. This lust fell heavily on Eutychus (Acts 20:9). A heavy sleep fell upon him, and a heavy hand of God followed it, though he restored him; he would not have such assemblies scandalized.

    b. So if a man is drowsy in the duties of his calling,

this is a lust of the flesh. "He who sleeps in harvest is a shameful son" (Prov. 10:5). He shames himself and his master, and indeed the nature of his work requires that he should be at it early and late. He may of course take a little sleep to fit him for his work, but when the sun has risen and calls him to his business, if he loves his bed, this is a lust of the flesh. It is called deceit: "Cursed is he who does his work deceitfully," that is, with the deceit that comes from slackness, for so it is interpreted (Prov. 10:14). The metaphor is taken from a bow that is bent only slack, for it deceives (Ps. 78:57). A man who uses such a bow never reaches the mark he shoots at, because it is not strongly bent; so when a man's heart is not strongly bent to his business, he will never reach his purpose, and so it is a deceitful work. Cursed is he who aims at any business with a slack hand.

-2. It is an unlawful lust of the flesh when a man is carried to sleep above due measure (Prov. 20:13). Poverty comes on such a one suddenly and strongly. Most men's natures require seven hours' sleep, some eight, but that is the most. And if we observe, we shall find that the same illnesses arise from too much sleep as from lack of sleep; it makes the body drowsy and the brain dull, and the whole man unfit for anything.

-3. This love of sleep and rest is a lust of the flesh when it is not used to a right end. Now the end of all sleep and rest is to refresh the spirit and strengthen the body and help digestion, as the unbending of a bow makes it stronger. If a bow stands always bent, it weakens. Therefore so much sleep as may help digestion, and comfort and refresh a man's body and spirit, God allows; but when a man has grown to love sleep and ease, a little more sleep, a little more slumber, one ease after, and never looks how to employ it in God's service, he works toward a wrong end. He eases himself that he may be eased, and never looks further than ease and sleep, and so rests in the creature and never looks up to God, to whom all our ease and refreshment should tend.

God forbid that we should be like that fool in the parable, "Soul, take thine ease, thou hast much goods laid up for many years." We must not think that God has given great means and estates so that their owners may live at ease; why, even the angels are ministering spirits, doing their duties with diligence and cheerfulness; and Adam, who was lord of the world, was yet set to till the ground. From the highest creature to the lowest, all have employments appointed them by God.

The chief dangers of idleness are:

-1. It will bring you to poverty; you shall be suddenly a beggar, and that without remedy.

-2. It distempers your body and stomach.

-3. It makes your soul naked and ragged. The field of the sluggard is overgrown with thorns and thistles; all your impatience, vanity, idleness, dullness, unprofitableness in your life, springs from your sluggishness of heart. You have not stirred up your spirit.

-4. It will make you a brother to a great waster. You waste your outward patrimony and your patrimony of grace. When Peter had once fallen into drowsiness, how woefully he was bankrupt! "Simon, sleepest thou?" and we see temptation come on him suddenly and strongly.

-5. It will make God leave you to yourself; you curse both yourself and your business if you undertake to manage them without God's blessing. Therefore be diligent and strengthen your hands, and you shall find the blessing of God going along with you, prospering your estate and your soul.

These are the reasons why we should wean ourselves from these lusts; and may they be so many motives to dissuade us from them.

-1. These lusts are so many enemies to our souls (1 Pet. 3:11). They are the diseases of our spirits. If we satisfy any disease off our bodies, we feed it and make it worse; so we cannot satisfy any of these lusts without seeing them become stronger. The more you obey a tyrant and submit yourself to him, the more authority he claims over you; so if you once give yourself up to obey these lusts and let them reign, they will lord it over you and keep you in greater subjection (Rom. 6:12). Give way but once to a lust, and all the lusts in the forest will break in; make but one little crevice in the bank of the sea, and it will make it wider and overflow all. The more fuel you give, the stronger the fire of lust burns.

-2. The distempers brought on by lusts aggravate the spiritual diseases that Christians most complain of. It is the common complaint of Christians, "O, the deadness and dullness and hardness and coldness of my heart and spirit!" Why, the lusts of the flesh so overcharge our hearts, and make them so heavy, that we have no desire to do good (Luke 21:34). They are like lead at a bird's heels.

-3. If we seek any pleasure of the world for itself, it is a lust of the flesh to cling to the creatures. We shall find that none of these lusts commend us to God, neither meat and drink, nor pastime, nor sleep. If we affect anything for itself, it never commends us to God; but many a poor soul who lacks all these has far more fellowship with God than those who enjoy abundance of them. Thus a Christian should reason, Am I a whit nearer God for these? Why then should my heart seek them?

-4. They are all corruptible; but both the pleasure we seek and the bodies for which we seek it, are incorruptible. Therefore let us set our minds on incorruptible things.

The following means will help us against these lusts.

-1. Abstain from fleshly lusts (Rom. 13:14). It is a notable means of mortification to withhold blood from the member to be mortified. Then cut it off. Would you then mortify lust? Withhold from it the very things on which its life and feeling depend, and then apply the death of Christ and the threatenings of God; and so when it begins to stupefy, cut it off. It is better to lack all the sinful pleasures of this life than to be cast with them into hell.

-2. Refrain from bringing forth fruit of these lusts. The more a tree strikes into the earth and draws sap and strength, the more fruitful it grows; and let it once grow fruitful, and it will get deeper hold and grow so rooted that it will prove nigh impossible to uproot. So with sin; if you avoid all occasions, and yield not to satisfy the least of them, it will soon be gone. If a strange dog comes in, and if you feed him, he stands waiting for one piece after another; but if you beat him he is gone. So if lusts find that they cannot get one morsel, no yielding, from you, they will be gone where they can fine better welcome.

When you find any lust of the flesh rising in you, turn its strength to a spiritual end. If you have a craving to meat or drink, what does Christ say? "I have meat and drink that you know not of"; though he was very faint and hungry, yet when he saw a crowd coming, he did not attend to his meat and drink, for there was spiritual food, and that comforted and refreshed him. Are you troubled with lust for women? If God calls you not to marriage, turn the strength of your affection to another who is "white and ruddy, the fairest of ten thousand." The more you set your heart to consider how amiable and beautiful and excellent he is, the more you will find him to satisfy your heart, so that you will find little contentment in any other thing besides him.

-4. Walk faithfully and constantly in your general and particular calling. The reason a Christian grows carnal and sensual is because either in God's ordinances or his particular calling, he was not spiritually minded; walk in the Spirit and you shall not fulfill the lusts of the flesh (Gal. 5:16).

-5. Look after spiritual objects. When we are carried to delight in pleasures and pastimes, let us remember, "Blessed is the man whose delight is in the law of the Lord" (Ps. 1:1, 2). He recreates himself in that; such a man will be as a tree planted by the rivers of water, ever procuring nourishment from the ordinances of God and ever growing; but on the contrary, such a one who runs into occasions and fulfills his lusts shall be as a barren heath and parched wilderness, his leaf withered and his fruit blasted.

II. The lusts of the eye.

By the lust of the eye is meant covetousness, or inordinate desire for profit. Why does he call it the lust of the eye? Because the eye makes us covet it (as Achan, Josh. 7:21), and because the eye is in some measure glutted with the sight of it.

But why does he not speak of lusts of the ear? There is an itching ear (2 Tim. 4:3), and this the Athenians had. I answer that the eye is the seat of several faculties. -1. It is put in scripture for the understanding and imagination, for that is in the soul (Ps. 33:18). -2. The hope of a man is translated to his eye (2 Chron. 20:12). -3. Sometimes pity (Deut. 13:8). -4. Sometimes disdain, sometimes pride (Prov. 30:17). -5. The eye is often put for the desire of the heart, when the eye looks long after something (Matt. 5:28). It is true then that the desires mentioned are lusts of the flesh, a desire of melody, desire of news to satisfy curiosity, affection of vain preaching to satisfy the pride of life, and indeed the lusts of all outward senses as they satisfy the body. These are all lusts of the flesh; but a longing earnest desire after profit is covetousness, and this is a lust of the eye.

What then is the lust of the eye?

As before, when it is set on wrong objects, or in excessive measure, or to a wrong end. If the eye is set on wrong objects, the scripture calls it "a hasty eye" (Prov. 28:22, 23); a man of an evil eye hastens to be rich, never waiting for God's providence, as Achan, and as Ahab lusting for Naboth's vineyard. This is lust against piety, because our love to God should make us seek nothing but what we may lawfully enjoy, in subordination to his will and to employ it in his service.

-2. This lust of the eye is expressed in excessive measure, and this is called a greedy eye. A man will perhaps not get it but by honesty, but when he has gotten it he is never satisfied (Eccl. 4:8; Eccl. 5:9-11). The more a man has, the more he desires. In Prov. 27:20 the greedy eye or covetous heart is compared to hell and the grave.

The greedy eye offends against that inward contentment that a man owes to his soul, when he is so covetous that his heart is never satisfied.

When should a man think himself satisfied, and how far may he desire these things? We must be diligent in our callings, and we may desire wealth from God, partly for our necessity and expediency, partly to leave to our posterity; a man may desire wealth this far. But we are never to desire more than we can make good use of, and glorify God by. A man must be content to want as well as to abound; but when he is insatiably craving, and wants more when he has much and is not satisfied when he has most, that is a greedy eye.

-3. The lust of the eye is expressed in desiring wealth for a wrong end. When a man craves wealth for wealth's sake, never taking care to use it well, this I call a needy eye. God calls him to bestow some on church or commonwealth or family or friends; and what does he say? "I may have need of it myself"; and so for fear of future need he will not provide seasonably for family or church or commonwealth. He will part with nothing willingly unless he sees it is for his profit (Deut. 15:19). This needy eye was reproved in Nabal (1 Sam. 25:11), who thought his servants would lack and therefore would not supply David's necessity.

This needy eye trespasses against liberality and charity.

The ground of this evil eye is an evil judgment. It springs from a blind eye which in delusion thinks that wealth is good in itself, and places happiness in riches, and therefore desires wealth above all things.

Use 1. This discovers the true nature of covetousness. You will say, I hope frugality is not covetousness, and providing for children and family. True, but:

    a. Do you see your heart carried after wealth, though by such unlawful means as simony or deceit or sabbath-breaking? Then your heart is covetous. You haste so to be rich that you can neither stay for sermons or prayer or grace; certainly then your covetousness transports you, and you are the firstborn of hell.

    b. When gain does not come in, though you are diligent, you are not content; and if much comes in, yet you are not satisfied.

    c. When you have wealth, you take no care how to use it; you grudge to give anything to church or commonwealth or poor; you say, What if I and my children should lack? Why, truly this needy eye is covetousness; but when you take lawful pains, and it hinders you in no good duty; if God crosses you, you are content, and if God blesses you you are eager to be helpful to do good; then you are not covetous.

Use 2. This will exhort young and old not to love the world or the things of the world. You see how much these things trespass against piety and liberality and charity; they are the root of all evil (1 Tim. 6:10); not so much the breeding root as the feeding root of evil. It is called the root of all evil in three respects.

    a. It separates the man from God, the fountain of all good (Col. 3:5), and therefore it is called idolatry, because he worships himself in his riches (Ps. 49:18; Prov. 18:11; Matt. 6:24). Wealth makes him serve mammon rather than God (Deut. 13:16-18).

    b. It chokes the best seed of the word; sometimes keeping him from the word (Luke 14:19), or distracting him there, or choking the word afterwards.

    c. Covetousness exposes a man to every temptation of Satan; lays him open to Satan to be a slave to him; makes him apostatize, swear, lie, deceive, if he makes wealth his chiefest good.

If you belong to God, you will seldom find your heart cramped and God's face turned away, without your covetousness being involved (Isa. 57:17, 18).

The greatest remedy against covetousness is a contented desire (Heb. 13:5). But, you say, how shall I be content?

I answer, godliness is both great gain and contentment; until God gives grace the soul is never satisfied, but when the soul is endued with grace it is content in these outward things.

There are two things in godliness that breed content and satisfaction. -1. It makes God our portion; and then dry bread and cold water, with God's favor and mercy, is enough for us and our children (Ps. 16:5, 6; Phil. 4:11, 12). -2. It not only fills our hearts with God, but it turns the desire of the soul to God's ordinances. Godliness will make a man look at the word as more precious than gold (Ps. 119:27), and as a hidden treasure which he will part with all for (Ps. 36:6, 7; Ps. 63:1-3).

III. The Pride of Life.

The pride of life is an inordinate affection of our hearts for carnal excellency, i.e., to be great in ourselves and for ourselves. -1. A proud man contends with God about the cause and goal of his life. -2. He desires to depend on himself. -3. He makes himself the end. As he depends on himself, it is called self-dependence; as he seeks excellency for himself, it is called self-seeking.

A. When he depends on himself, he throws off the crown from God's head. There are four ways of doing this.

-1. Self-conceit (Rom. 12:3). When a man thinks soberly of himself, he is not so blind as not to see himself, nor so proud as to think above that which is fitting.

-2. Carnal confidence and presumption. He does what he does by his own strength and wit and pains; this is called arrogance. A man undertakes to carry through some business by his own strength (Jer. 10:23; Isa. 10:7-11; Isa. 37:12, 13). He boasts of his wisdom and power to do great things.

-3. Curiosity. When a man will thrust himself into that which he ought not, as Eve sought the fruit of knowledge, this is self-dependence (Col. 3:18).

-4. Self-fulness. He is full of himself and rests himself

in his present condition (Rev. 3:17), and thanks God it is well with him. He desires to be no better; and this is a lust of pride.

This sin is against God, from whom, to whom, and in whom are all things.

B. A second branch of this pride of life is self-seeking. "He seeks not God in all his ways" (Ps. 10:3, 4). He seeks not God's glory, but his own (Prov. 25:27). It is not good to eat much honey; so it is not good for men to seek their own glory. As much honey turns to bitterness, so if a man licks up too much of his own glory he turns it to his shame and confusion.

This self-seeking shows itself:

-1. In pursuing his own glory; he looks not to God's glory, but to his own. This is manifest in:

a. Ambition, when a man aims at his own glory and primacy. St. John reproved this in Diotrephes (3 John 9); and it was also ambition in seeking a government God did not appoint for them (Judg. 9:1-21).

b. Hypocrisy. This is another lust of pride in self-seeking, when a man in religious duties seeks his own credit and applause (Matt. 23:5). This is pride in hypocrisy (Matt. 6:1-16). From this comes self-rejoicing (Amos 6:1-6), as Herod rejoiced in the applause of the people (Acts 12:23).

c. Condemning and despising others. This is another lust of self-seeking, caused by regard to a man's own excellency (Luke 18:11), and this proceeds from making himself his own end.

d. Carnal boasting of himself, either in word or in manner (Prov. 27:2). It is boasting to magnify oneself in words; so in gestures of the eyes (Prov. 30:13), and in stretched-out necks (Isa. 3:16).

-2. So there is pride in world, as when men build to make themselves a name (Gen. 11:4; Dan. 4:20-27). So in strange fashions and apparel (Isa. 3:18-24). So pride is shown in feasting to show their own magnificence and riches, as Nabel, who fasted as a king (1 Sam. 25:36).

-3. There is another pride expressed when a man is crossed and frustrated, and this shows itself in:

a. Discontent. When a man has made himself his own end and is crossed in it, he is discontented, as Ahithophel when his counsel was crossed (2 Sam. 17:23). He was so discontented that he hanged himself. Though some do not grow so desperate, yet they vex and fret so that they cannot eat or sleep; whereas if we made God our end, we should be willing to do without what God denies.

b. Contention (Prov. 28:25). All contention comes from pride.

c. Indignation. When others take away their applause, they disdain and loathe it, as the Pharisees did when they saw Christ take away their praise (Matt. 21:15).

Now for our motives from fleeing pride. Chiefly they are:

-1. The proud man is an abomination to the Lord (Prov. 16:5). Shall we live in such a state that God cannot look at us without loathing and indignation? They contend with God; they depend on their own strength and seek themselves and are angry if crossed. Let them then use all means, but they shall never prosper, for God resists the proud; God will cross him at every turn.

-2. Pride of all sins cuts asunder the sinews of grace. What do the duties of Christianity consists in? Repentance, faith and obedience. Now repentance consists in loathing, abhorring, and being ashamed of ourselves (Job 42:5, 6; Dan. 9:7); but a proud man is far from this. For faith, the man who believes goes out of himself (Hab. 2:4) and depends on God. And for obedience, you see the commandment: Do justice, love mercy, and walk humbly with your God (Micah 6:8). But a man of a high spirit cannot bend to humility and self-denial.

Two means to wean us from pride are:

-1. Meditate on what you are; know yourself. Know what you are and what you tend to; dust you are, and to dust you must return. You have no dependence but on God; shall you then be full of yourself? God made all for himself (1 Cor. 7:17, 23); therefore we are not to aim at ourselves. Let us then consider our own insufficiency.

-2. Exercise yourself in those graces that are most contrary to pride. If you see your heart grow ambitious and vain-glorious and discontent, then weed out this lust. Renew your repentance in dust and ashes; loathe yourself; see your own unworthiness; learn to live by faith, depend wholly on Christ, and learn to be obedient. We are servants of God; it is not for us to look at our own ends, but to do all for God's glory.

1 John 2:17

"And the world passes away, and the lusts of it, but he who does the will of God abides forever."

To dissuade them from the love of the world, the apostle uses three arguments. Two have been noted already; the third is from the difference between those who love the world and those who keep the word. That which is eternal should not addict itself to temporary and transitory things. This argument then runs from the frailty of these outward things, and the constancy and eternity of heavenly things; therefore shun the one and seek the other.

Doct. The world and all its lusts are of a transitory and fading condition.

So says the text; and they are transitory in three respects.

-1. "The world passes away"; the shape and fashion of the world passes away. The word is taken from the presentation of the world as upon a stage; an actor seldom acts the same part a week together, and thus you shall never see the world or the creatures in the same state long. Now you shall see a man single; come later and you shall find him married; come yet again and you shall find him a widower; he is sometimes doleful, sometimes joyous.

-2. Even our joy in the world flees and passes away by little and little, even while we enjoy it. They are compared to flowers (Isa. 40:6, 7); even while they flourish they decay. What are all the comforts in the world but a nosegay, which for the present smells sweet and comfortable, but fades and dies even while we smell it.

Again, all the sorrows and vexations of the world pass away; sorrow abides not ever, and in the midst of it we may find some joy (Ps. 94:18, 19). Yet many times we add sorrow to sorrow; we think we shall go on in the bitterness of our souls all the day, as Hezekiah; but he was comforted (Isa. 38:15).

-3. One generation passes, and another (Eccl. 1:4); yea, the world itself shall be consumed (2 Pet. 3:10); those who inhabit it shall be consumed, and the elements themselves changed (Ps. 102:26).

How do the lusts of the world pass away?

The lusts of the flesh, the lust of the eye, and the pride of life, which are the sum of all the ways of the sons of men, pass away; all their lives are spent in pleasure or profit or credit, and all these pass away.

-1. They are often disappointed of the objects they aim at. A man pursues pleasure but finds sorrow; he pursues profit, but it fades away. It falls as the house of the spider (Ps. 112:10).

-2. They pass away, fade and wither, even while the man is enjoying them. He strongly desires a thing, but as soon as he has it he is weary of it. Amnon had a strong lust for his sister Tamar; but when he had fulfilled it he hated her more than he loved her (2 Sam. 13:15). When a bee has sucked something from one flower, it goes to another, and then to a third. We are soon weary of lusts; they are in no way able to satisfy the desires of our hearts.

-3. These lusts perpetually destroy themselves, and us with them. When we die, all our lusts die with us; therefore "the world passes, and its lusts"; they are all but for a season.

Use 1. Then let us flee the love of the world. This is the counsel of an aged apostle; when he was near a hundred years old, he spoke it out of his experience of heavenly things and vanity of the world. On this ground Solomon exhorts us not to set our hearts on the world; neither on wisdom nor riches, for "riches certainly make themselves wings and fly away like an eagle" (Prov. 23:4, 5).

Use 2. If we desire constancy in any condition, then let us not trust in riches or honor, nor in life itself; for they are all transitory. But entreat God to set your heart on everlasting things, on everlasting life and enduring pleasures and riches; for they flow from him (Ps. 16:11). These are an abiding inheritance, and they will stick close with us. The very fullness of earthly comforts breeds gluttony, and a man is dulled with them; they seem full of comfort until we get them, but once we have them we are weary with them. Grace, on the contrary, seems hateful until it is gotten, and then the more a man has the more he desires. Never did a Christian repent of his repentance or faith or godliness, for "godly sorrow breeds repentance never to be repented of" (2 Cor. 7:10). Then "labor not for the meat that perishes," but for that profit and pleasure and honor which endure forever (John 6:26, 27).

"He who does the will of God abides forever."

What is it to abide forever?

-1. It implies that the man is not of an unsteady temper, but of a constant and even frame of spirit and life. Mountains are not easily shaken or driven to and fro, but remain in their strength and place; so "those who trust in the Lord shall be as Mount Zion, that shall not be moved" (Ps. 125:1).

-2. He is said to abide forever because he abides in that state forever. There is a difference between constancy and perseverance. A man may said to go to London, though he goes in and out and does not keep an even pace; so he may be said to go to heaven if he aims at it and goes on as evenly as he can, and gets back in the way again if he once gets out.

What is it to do the will of God? The apostle uses this expression to oppose fulfilling the lusts of the flesh; so by it he means not only the will of God's pleasure, but the will of God's commandment. All the creatures do the will of God's pleasure, for they cannot do what God's pleasure forbids; but the apostle here means more. "Not every one who says Lord, Lord, shall enter into heaven, but he who does the will of my Father" (Matt. 7:21); that is, the revealed will of God (John 8:51).

Why do they abide forever?

-1. Because they are born of the unchangeable will of God (James 1:17, 18). The will of God is not dependent upon the creature, but free (Rom. 9:15); and therefore when God bestows any mercy upon a creature, he does it because he will do it. This puts the creature in an unchangeable condition.

-2. Because this will of God is vigorous and strong, and doing it produces strength in the Christian. The more a man does God's will, the more he is enabled and strengthened to do it (John 4:34). The more fruit a tree brings forth upwards, the more deeply it takes root downwards; so with a Christian, the more fruit he brings forth unto God, the deeper he strikes his root in Christ (John 14:21); and thus he may well be said to abide forever.

-3. He has a close union with Christ if he does the will of the Father, for Christ came for that end (John 6:38). He is to Christ father and mother and brother and sister (Mark 3:35). We are born of the same Father as Christ, of the same Spirit, and we do the same work; therefore if we do the will of God as children, then we are heirs and remain in the house forever (John 8:35, 36).

-4. God is always ready to hear the prayers of those who do his will (John 15:17). If we hear God, he hears us; if we listen to his commandments, he listens to our petitions; he is as ready to do our wills as we are to do his; with what measure we mete to him, it will be meted to us again (Matt. 7:2). God's way is the way everlasting (Ps. 139:24), and those who are in it shall abide forever.

But does not David say, "I am tossed to and fro as a grasshopper"? (Ps. 109:22-25) I answer, he speaks there not of his inward state, which was constant and even, but of his outward state, which was very inconstant. He hopped from one place to another, from mountains to woods, from woods to caves, from place to place like a grasshopper; but his inward frame was constant and even.

But was not his inward frame sometimes very uneven? Though he showed much kindness to Mephibosheth, and though he spared the life of Saul and was indeed striken in confor even cutting off his skirt, yet he afterward commits adultery and slays Uriah, and still afterward numbers the people. Does this not argue an uneven inward state? I answer, he may err through infirmity, as a man in a journey intends to go on yet loses his way through ignorance and carelessness; but when he knows it, he makes haste to get in the way again. So a Christian aims at a good course, but sometimes through heedlessness or ignorance falls into byways. When he knows it, however, he makes haste to recover himself. The reason he goes aside is that he does not do God's will, but his own will; and he recovers himself by repentance and firm resolve to obey God's will once more.

Use 1. This justifies the doctrine of the perseverance of the saints, and confutes the contrary opinion of their apostasy. Every Christian does the will of God, and he who does the will of God abides forever. He makes God's will his meat and drink; he feeds on everlasting food (John 6:27); he has known union with Christ; and therefore he fulfills God's will, and God will fulfill his desire.

Use 2. This forms a ground for directing all who would find comfort. If you follow the lusts of the world, you will not find it; for they do not last always. Therefore though a man prides himself in his youth or riches or lusts, they will not endure; the time will come when you will be weary of them. But would you abide forever? Then do God's will, and thus you shall choose that part which shall never be taken from you (Luke 10:41-42; Ps. 125:1, 2). Let a man be doing God's will, and he shall never die. There is no man who does not desire to have his estate confirmed to perpetuity. So then, all the lusts of the world continue only for a while; but if you would leave all for perpetuity, be doing God's will, and then you shall abide forever.

Use 3. Of consolation to every obedient Christian who breaks off from his own will and sets himself with all his power to do God's will. This is your comfort: you are in an everlasting way which leads to eternity. "He who does the will of God shall never fear death"; he shall stand as a mountain that shall not be shaken, which is a great blessing for a poor Christian.

But may not even the mountains be shaken and removed, as by an earthquake? May not Christians then be shaken and removed? Are they not tossed up and down in the world, and never in a settled condition? I answer, it is true that mountains may be shaken and removed (Isa. 54:10, 11), and Christians may be tossed in their outward states; but though the mountains are moved and the hills shaken, yet God's lovingkindness shall never depart from them.

Doct. The difference between the world and its lusts, and the children of God who do his will, ought to wean them from the love of the world and its lusts.

"Labor not for the meat that perishes"; for the meat which Christ gives is eternal and will nourish life eternal in us.

But what is this difference between the world and its lusts, and those who do God's will?

-1. The world and its lusts are transitory and fading; but he who does the will of God is strengthened as he does it, and thus is confirmed and supported to everlasting life.

-2. The world and all its lusts are bodily and sensual, and not heavenly. All the comforts and creatures support only sensual life in us; and what shall it profit a man to win the whole world (that is, gain a perfect sensual life) and lose his own soul? The world never feeds the spiritual life, but there is a spiritual bread which does feed to everlasting life. It is not possible for a body to nourish a spirit, nor for earthly things to nourish heavenly things; nor can a transitory thing feed everlasting life.

But why should this difference wean us from the love of the world and its lusts?

-1. Vanity is found in all these things; they are bodily and transitory, and thus it is impossible that they should nourish heavenly and eternal life (Isa. 55:2). Your soul in the midst of them will be as Pharaoh's lean cattle, hungry and empty of grace, void of all good things.

-2. These things will put corruption on our spirits, if we set our love and desires upon them. They will be as a running issue which will empty us of all goodness. Either they will draw us from coming to the ordinances, or else they will fill our hearts with cares when we have come; or else they will choke the word after we have gone, so that they draw our hearts away from spiritual food.

-3. Ever since the fall of our first parents, there lies a curse of God upon all the creatures (Gen. 3:17, 18). In cursing the ground God cursed all the creatures with it, so that there is now a disproportion between the creatures and man, for whom they were made. Thus the whole creation is subject to vanity (Rom. 8:20; Eccl. 1:2). How come we to grow so full of the creatures, and so empty of the Creator, when we are thus blessed? The cause is no other than a secret curse that lies upon all the creatures; for otherwise we should not grow so careless and stupid.

Use 1. Let us then take the apostolic injunction to heart and love not the world. There is no proportion between the world and a child of God; what proportion between transitory and everlasting things, between fading and permanent? These are bodily and carnal, and your heart is spiritual and heavenly; therefore it is for you to look out for other things that will abide. Why do you spend your substance for that which satisfies not? Once we have made the world our element, if we are lifted up out of the world to heavenly and spiritual things, we are like a fish out of water; we faint and gasp, and are weary, and must return to our mud again. Is this not a woeful case? But since even the lawful pleasures of this world are vanity and folly (Eccl. 2:2), let us be exhorted to wean our affection from them also; to walk among them as snares and take heed we be not trapped by them. All the blessings of this life are but curses, if you use them for themselves.

Use 2. Then let us be exhorted to lift up our hearts to more heavenly and spiritual things; let us lift up our souls to those pleasures and profits that endure forever (John 6:27). Labor for those pleasures which may truly satisfy your soul; desire God to lift up your heart from worldly to spiritual things, and then you shall find the word of God sweeter than honey and the honeycomb. Therefore do not feed on husks and chaff, but on spiritual things. Use them to make you desirous of spiritual things and more fruitful in religious exercises. So you shall find them helpful to you, and you shall draw near to God by them.

1 John 2:18

"Little children, it is the last time; and as you have heard that Antichrist shall come, even now there are many antichrists; whereby we know that it is the last time."

St. John writes to all sorts of Christians, old men, young men, and children, and he speaks one by one to them all. He wrote to old and young men, "love not the world"; but for babes, he does not write to them about the love of the world, for they are not easily subject to it. There is no age so flexible as a young child; if he is once set in a right way, and lives under faithful instructors, there is no danger to him. Therefore he writes to children here to beware of false teachers and cleave to sound doctrine.

First he sets out and describes these false teachers. -1. By their coming in the last time (v. 18). -2. By their apostasy; "they went out from us." (v. 19). -3. By the reason of their apostasy; "they were never of us" (v. 19).

Second, he gives them signs by which they may know them and discern them; and that is from the unction which they have received (vv. 20, 21).

Third, he gives a mark of antichrist; "he is a liar"; whoever denies that Jesus is the Christ is a liar (v. 22).

Fourth, he lays down some means to help them. -1. Look to your doctrine. -2. Cling to your holy unction; take special care to live righteously.

In verse 18 he plays the trumpeter, and warns the church that now is the last time and that many antichrists have come.

The words afford these points.

-1. These times were the last times.

-2. The church was then warned beforehand of antichrist.

-3. Many antichrists had already come in that time.

-4. The prophecy of the antichrist was partly fulfilled in the antichrists who had then come.

-5. Such is the condition of the last ages of the church that she cannot long be without some antichrist; for he says, "There are many antichrists, whereby we know that it is the last time."

Doct. 1. The days of the New Testament were the last times.

The times one thousand and six hundred years since have been called ἐσχάτη ὥρα, the last seasons; and this is no special phrase of St. John's, but is common with other places in scripture (1 Pet. 4:7; Acts 2:17; 1 Cor. 10:11). The apostles looked at themselves as living in the very last age of the world (Heb. 9:26; James 5:8, 9; Phil. 4:5).

Why do the scriptures call them the last days, since there have been fifteen centuries and more since then? I answer, the apostles did not mean that the last judgment was to come immediately, for when some Christians began to grow slack in their callings because they thought it would be vain, since the last judgment was so near, Paul seriously dissuaded them from expecting it so suddenly (2 Thess. 2:1-3). Thus, though he had said that the day was at hand, he would not have them imagine that it would come upon them immediately; fore he says that there must first be an apostasy. Thus we see that the apostles were not deceived, nor did they speak uncertainly. But why did they call them the last times?

-1. Because they are the last period of time before the last judgment.

a. The first period was from Adam to Moses, 2450 years (Rom. 5:14).

b. The second period of time was from Moses to Christ (Luke 16:16; Matt. 11:13). In the first age the church was not national, but was handed down from family to family. Moses then collected a national church of the Jews, bound together by the law, and excluded the Gentiles. He gave them the law written, and this continued till Christ's time.

c. The third period of time, or third age, is from Christ's time to the end of the world (Heb. 1:1, 2). It is the last time of the revelation of God's will, and we must expect no further revelation until the end. Though the church has seen many differences, yet there is one uniform doctrine which God has set up so that all may be saved. Christ has delivered his last will and testament, which cannot be reversed or amended (Heb. 9:16, 17). Thus if any comes and declares a new doctrine, let him be accursed; he is an antichrist.

-2. The apostle Peter stirred up his readers to several duties on this ground, that the end drew near (1 Pet. 1:13-16). But this would not be an argument for patience unless he had some inkling that it was true (James 5:8, 9; Phil. 4:5).

In what sense was the coming of Christ near in the apostles' time? -1. In opposition to former ages which were far off. -2. Because in God's account a thousand years are but as one day (2 Pet. 3:8, 9); yet God will come when the day of accomplishment arrives; he will not stay a day longer, for that would be to him as a thousand years. -3. Such is the faith of many Christians that what they see in a promise, they view as being already fulfilled (John 8:36; Rom. 4:11).

Use 1. If this gospel age is the last time, then we may certainly conclude that not so much time shall pass from Christ to the end of the world, as passed from Adam to Christ; for else how can they be called the last times? And if it was the last time in the first century, what is it now?

Use 2. If these are the last days, we must not marvel if we meet with perilous times, for such they are said to be (2 Tim. 3:1). Our day is the dregs of the last times; marvel not therefore if you see haters and scorners in these last times. When men once grow aged, they are cold and distempered; such is the spirit of these last times, froward against good, testy and malignant. Do not wonder at it, for these are the last times.

Use 3. If these are the last times, then how vain it is to expect any new kind of revelation; if any teach any other doctrine that what Christ has already revealed, he is antichrist.

Use 4. Of exhortation.

    a. To patience. James exhorts to a double patience: to be patient in bearing evil and to be patient in forbearing revenge. Be patient a while; the Judge stands at the door, and then all will be right (James 5:7, 8).

But some will say this is a cold encouragement to patience, to say that the day of the Lord is at hand. Look how long it has been promised, and yet it is far enough away! Yet when God's will is accomplished he will not stay a day; and if you have faith, you shall take the promise as ready to be fulfilled, so that you dare not take vengeance, no more than if Christ were immediately to come.

There is another kind of patience required on this ground, and that is patience to expect the promises God has made. We have need of patience for this (Heb. 10:37). Therefore he says, "Faith is the evidence of things not seen" (Heb. 11:1). Faith sees things afar off, as did the patriarchs.

    b. We are exhorted to watchfulness (1 Pet. 4:7), and there is a double watchfulness required. First, watchfulness against false teachers; the last times are perilous and dangerous. Second, watchfulness unto prayer; that is, watch every occasion, so that you may stand fast in these evil times. You will have need of prayer because of the many perils and evils in these last days.

Doct. 2. The church of God was forewarned of antichrists.

Our Saviour forewarns them of antichrists and false teachers (Matt. 24:24, 25), and John seems to have reference to this. So also the apostles were careful in forewarning them (2 Thess. 2:3-10; 1 Tim. 4:1-3; 2 Pet. 2:2, 3). So we see by the mouth of two or three witnesses this truth was confirmed.

There were three reasons for this warning.

-1. To prevent the misconceit that the people had, that the day of the Lord was near at hand and thus it was no time to settle to their callings (2 Thess. 2:1-3). To prevent this conceit, the apostle tells them expressly that antichrist must first come.

-2. That they might be better forearmed against such false teachers, for there should be damnable heresies (2 Pet. 2:1); therefore they were to prepare themselves against such heresies. Christ and the apostles were careful to forewarn them (Matt. 24:24, 25; 2 Pet. 3:17, 18). Unless you are well established in the truth, they will carry you away into error.

-3. That they might quicken the pastors of the church to lay sound foundations by establishing them in sound doctrine (Acts 20:27, 31).

Use 1. This shows us the great faithfulness of the great Shepherd of our souls, in foretelling us of wolves coming and in stirring up his apostles to do the like.

Use 2. It will teach both ministers and people to practice such duties. One purpose in writing is to establish them in sound doctrine, so that whatever false teachers say, Christians may not be seduced. Therefore let not women or children excuse themselves from the duty of studying the scriptures, for God looks that you should be grounded in the truth, so that no seducer may carry you away.

Doct. 3. In the days when St. John wrote this epistle, many antichrists had already come into the world.

What is antichrist? Anti signifies: -1. Opposition. -2. Substitution. -3. Equality.

Now antichrist includes all these. He is opposite to Christ; he is, secondly, a substitute or vicar of Christ. Hence the beast that came out of the sea had the horn of a lamb, as if he had the power of Christ. Thirdly, he carries himself as equal to Christ, and therefore dispenses those laws which no mortal may dispense, as allowing incestuous marriages and binding the consciences of men. Now it is a property of the law of Christ to sit in the conscience, so that he may well be called antichrist. But of the three he is most properly called antichrist in the first sense, for he opposes himself against God and Christ, and all emperors and kings. Here is the misery: he carries himself as a vicar of Christ, but yet he can oppose himself against Christ.

We find many such antichrists in St. John's time, as Simon Magus, Menander, Ebion, etc.

Use 1. This shows us the marvelous enmity of that wicked one. As soon as Christ had sown good seed, the evil one sowed tares. This was his subtlety, to sow errors before the truth could take firm root.

Use 2. Here we see the impudence of heresy, especially when it is set on fire of hell, that such monstrous opinions should be broached in St. John's time. And therefore we must not be surprised if heresies broach themselves broadside in the church. St. John was a son of thunder who shook them mightily, yet even against him were those darts shot. Therefore it must stir up Christians to ground themselves in the whole counsel of God; do you think such heresies will blush and cringe before us if they did not blush before St. John?

Use 3. Here we see that the truth of God is more powerful than the spirit of error. Though there were many heads of error, yet they all fell down before the doctrine of St. John, so that his epistle remained when they were all lost. Such is the power of truth that it dispels all errors.

Use 4. This confutes boasting of antiquity. Every ancient thing is not true, for then these false heresies had been true. Yet there is an antiquity which springs from the first founding of a thing, and that prevails here; and there is a secondary antiquity, which the tares in the parable possessed. Though they were sown the same day as the wheat, yet secondary antiquity will not justify them, but only that which comes from the institution of God.

Doct 4. In the coming of these antichrists, that which was foretold of the antichrist was in some measure fulfilled.

For otherwise St. John's discourse would have been irrelevant. Why then does he say, "You have heard that antichrist shall come, and he has come already"? Again, he argues from the last times to antichrist, and from antichrist to the last times; this reason would have no strength if it were not grounded upon this point. For proof see 1 John 4:3; 1 Tim. 4:1, 2.

But does not Paul say that antichrist shall not come until there is a general apostasy, and until that which withholds him is taken away? What then is "that which now withholds"? (2 Thess. 2:7)

The withholding agent was not the Roman Empire, for that was not taken away until many hundred years later; but the things which withheld him was the emperor himself. When the emperor Constantine moved from Rome to Constantinople, then the withholder was taken away. The splendor of the emperor, that monarch of the world, and the splendor of antichrist could not stand together; but as soon as the emperor had departed from Rome, antichrist began to be revealed. When all the bishops of the Christian world met together at the Council of Nicea, the Bishop of Rome (though invited by letter) did not come; pretending indeed the weakness of his body, but Bellarmine plainly tells us the reason. "It was not meet," he says, "that the head should follow the members; the members rather should follow the head. And if the emperor were present, it was likely he would take his place above the Pope, which was not meet, since the Pope was the spiritual head. Therefore because of this and some other inconveniences, the Pope in his discretion thought it meet to absent himself." At this time antichrist began to be revealed to the full; for though there were after that time some godly men in that seat, as Gregory the great and some others, yet the question is not of the person but of the place.

But Paul says that that which withholds antichrist must first be taken away, an John here says that many antichrists have come already. How can these two stand together?

Though the antichrist was not then revealed, yet the mystery of iniquity did then work in many men, when John wrote this epistle. Then men began to observe human traditions and to teach that the laws of the church must be kept as well as God's laws; and it is against this that John writes in his second epistle (vv. 5-7). Besides, some then exalted themselves above their brethren, as you may see in his third epistle, and thrust them out. This was the spirit which made way for the Bishop of Rome, exalting himself above other bishops, as the emperor was exalted above kings and princes. This mystery increased by degrees; but even in John's time his pomp began to go before him, and thus the way was made. The apostle therefore wrote against the pomp and spirit of antichrist which was then working, though antichrist himself was not so fully revealed as afterwards; and so it is plain that that which was spoken of antichrist was even then in part fulfilled.

Use 1. This confutes the church of Rome, who even yet cannot discern antichrist, but say antichrist is some individual person. But we say that antichrist is a state that has many forerunners and followers, and that the Pope himself is one of them.

But is the article ὁ not the sign of a certain singular person? Sometimes it is so, but yet not always; sometimes it signifies a state, as we say, ὁ βασιλεύς the King made this law, though not necessarily the present king, but any before and any who may come after. So we see in Matt. 13:3, ὁ σπείρων "The sower went forth"; not any one singular sower, but every sower of the word.

But again, does Paul not say that that wicked one must be revealed, whom the Lord will consume with the brightness of his coming? True, he shall continue until the coming of Christ, and shall be abolished by the spirit of his mouth; and therefore it cannot be said of any individual person, for no man can live from the Council of Nicea to the coming of Christ.

Use 2. Let us learn from this the close fellowship that is between antichrist himself and all who make way for him, as all heretics do. This must teach us not to keep any error or superstition, for there is a strong bond between antichrist and heresies.

Doct. 5. Such is the condition of the last times that they cannot be long without an antichrist.

Antichrist has come, and therefore it is the last time. Conversely, it is the last time, and therefore antichrist has come; there must be antichrists (1 John 4:3; 2 John 7). In these latter times, the Spirit speaks expressly that there shall be such (1 Tim. 4:1).

What then is the condition of the last times, that it is so prepared for an antichrist?

-1. There was an itching ear for new doctrine. Men inwardly loathed the truth and sought any new doctrine they could hear (2 Thess. 2:10-12; 2 Tim. 4:3, 4). Since men lusted with itching ears for new doctrines, therefore God sent such as would deceive; and if you survey the whole body of Popery, you will find it consists of such: either of curious speculations of the Schoolmen, by which they deceive scholars, and fables of the secular priests with which they idly amuse the common folk; and so they deceive the whole people.

-2. There was an abundance of knowledge. So now, when there is much knowledge and little grace, there is a world of pride (1 Cor. 8:11; 2 Tim. 3:1-8). For lack of faith with their knowledge, the time was fit to receive new doctrines (1 Tim.

4:1, 2). Much knowledge, no conscience; while some have neglected to keep their consciences clean, their judgment is unsound (1 Tim. 1:19).

-3. Men are always apt to go to the lowest cold after their spirits have been most warmed and heated. No men are so apt to catch cold as those who are very warm and hot. The apostles not only filled them with knowledge but warmed them with zeal and heat; now when their spirits are so warm, they are more subject to get cold and distemper. Every Christian finds it so. Let him be enlarged at the word or prayer, and ere long he will be more deadened. There is such a secret pride in the experience of God's favor that having received it we tend to rest in ourselves, thinking we have sufficient grace in ourselves. When we see our need of Christ, we depend only upon him; but when we are full, we depend upon ourselves, and so leaving Christ we get a great coldness and deadness of spirit. Thus it is with the church; when God sheds his spirit abundantly, they grow secure and depend upon themselves. One would have thought that generation which went in with Moses would have been most zealous, yet none was so full of idolatry until God stirred them up by their enemies. So in the apostles' time the church was very eager and zealous, but a few generations afterward their spirits were carried away with errors.

-4. Satan has much rage, because the time is short (Rev. 12:8). We shall always find the devil to imitate God. If God sets up a Christ, Satan will have antichrist set up, who may be not only a substitute but an enemy to Christ; as God had won the world by Christ, he would delude the world by antichrist.

Use 1. This will teach Christians not to be offended if they find a variety of seducing spirits in these days. A man would marvel to find so many opinions and agitations in such peaceable days, when religion is maintained; but how does this come about? God never gave generally more knowledge since the revelation of antichrist until now; but where there is most wisdom, Satan will be most active in seducing and corrupting that wisdom. Where there is more wisdom there is more curiosity and pride.

Use 2. Since many antichrists are and will be in these last times, let us labor to be established in the faith; and then no matter how the times are, we may keep our faith and our religion.

How may we be thus established? By going contrary to the followers of antichrist. Do not give yourself up to vain curiosity and speculations; if the Lord finds you humble, he will teach you in his ways. If you are warm and zealous, take heed that you do not grow cold (1 Chron. 29:18). And then, whatever the times are, your heart and judgment shall be established in the truth; but unless God gives you a good conscience with your knowledge, you will soon be perverted. And therefore I say to you, as St. Paul to the Ephesians (3:17-19), continue in a firm love of the truth, as well as in the knowledge of it.

1 John 2:19

"They went out from us, but they were not of us; for if they had been of us, no doubt they would have continued with us; but they went out that they might be made manifest that the were not all of us."

In verse 18 the apostle had instructed babes of the coming of antichrists. Now in this verse he describes them: by their apostasy, "they went out from us," and by their condition before, "they were not of us." The latter he proves by an argument, "if they had been of us they would have continued with us"; the former he amplifies by the reason why God gave them up to apostasy, "that they might be made manifest that they were not of us."

What is meant by the expression, "they went out from us"?

They departed from their doctrine in judgment, and from their fellowship in practice (Acts 2:42). -1. They forsook the truth which they once owned (2 John 9), and not in incidental points, but in such as caused them to deny both the Father and Son (1 John 2:22; 1 Tim. 1:19).

They went out "from us"; from whom? From apostles and ministers, from old men, young men, and children. They went out from all the true members of the church.

"They were not of us"; that is, they were never true members of our body. They were with us and among us, but they were never of us. The children of God are in the world but not of the world (1 John 4:4, 5); their minds are not on this world, their inheritance is not in this world; so on the contrary, the children of the world are in the church but not of the church.

The doctrines to be gained from the text are these:

-1. Some may be in the church and afterward depart from the church.

-2. Such as do thus depart were never members of the church.

-3. Those who are members continue always in the church.

-4. Those who depart manifest themselves not to be of the church.

-5. This departing from the church is a note of antichrist.

Doct. 1. There are some in the church who may depart from the church.

How does this come about?

-1. It comes from lack of thorough and entire fellowship with the Lord Jesus. Though they have much joy and comfort in the members of the church, yet it is but a land-flood. All that joy and grace may be dried up unless they partake of that fountain which never fails. If you see any departing from the church, they departed from Christ first (Dan. 11:34, 35), and have clung to him only in pretense. When a man halts between falsehood and truth, or between God and his lusts, he will be turned out of the way (Heb. 12:13).

-2. It comes from the stumblingblocks they meet with in the church. The first is persecution, which makes some offended (Matt. 13:21). The second is hard doctrine (John

6:66). The doctrine of purity seems hard doctrine to some of them; the doctrine of predestination offends some. Third, there are admonitions or reproofs to be dispensed to the members of the church. Now if they come with proud unmortified spirits, they will be offended at them. This was the cause of the apostasy of Simon Magus; when Peter rebuked him sharply, he could not endure it, but fell off and set up a false doctrine and lying miracles to subvert the apostles' doctrine. Some depart from others because they think themselves more holy than others (Isa. 65:5); either they give offense to others, or others to them.

Use. This shows us our duty not to rest satisfied that we are members of the church. We may live in the church and partake of the ordinances, and yet fall off. Therefore be sure that you give yourself up first to the Lord, and then to the church; for otherwise you will fall away. Therefore come with an humble and mortified heart and give up yourself to Christ, and then you will neither give offense nor be offended, and thus you will continue a member of the church.

Doct. 2. Those who depart from the church were never members of the church.

"They were not of us"; that is, not of those whose sins had been forgiven them, either old men, young men, or children.

What is the church, or who are the church?

-1. The church is called a company of saints, because they are holy in heart and practice (1 Cor. 1:2; 14:12). -2. The church is called an elect people. -3. They who are indeed of the church are such as shall be saved (Acts 2:47). As all those in Noah's ark were saved, so all those who are true members of the church.

Why does the apostle say that those who depart from the church were never of the church?

-1. Those who are true members of the church have near fellowship with the Catholic Church, and so are certainly of the number of the firstborn, written in heaven (Heb. 12:23).

Therefore Christ says that all his sheep hear his voice (John 10:27, 28), and none shall pluck them out of his hand. Those who are truly members of the particular church are likewise members of the catholic. My finger, which is a part of my hand, is a part of my whole body.

-2. These also have fellowship with the head Christ. All the true members receive nourishment from the head; therefore those who do not hold the head fall into vain speculations and so depart from the church (Eph. 4:15, 16; Col. 2:18, 19). And being knit to the head, they are joined in such bonds of the spirit and of ordinances that they all partake of one Spirit (1 Cor. 6:17; 10:16, 17; 12:13). Those who are truly thus knit cannot fall off.

Use 1. This reproves an error of the Romish church, for they maintain that wicked men may be true members of the church. They hold that many fall off who were yet members of the true church. We reply, they might indeed depart from their church, but never from any true church; if they do depart from the church, they were never true members of it; they were never of Christ's sheep. We say therefore that such were not true members, but parasites and superfluous excrements of the body; and therefore no wonder they fall off.

But you will say, there are some who continue faithful friends to the church, and never fall off from them. Have they not come who are ornaments and supporters of the church, and yet have no truth of grace in them; are they members of the church? I answer, they have the place of members, but they are not true members. A glass eye may be an ornament to the body, and a wooden leg may support the body, yet they are not true members. So such may be ornaments and supports of the church, but yet not true members. Though they cleave to the body, yet they are not joined by nerves and sinews, nor animated by the head.

Use 2. This will teach us what to judge of those men who have been once very zealous professors but who afterward drift from religion and fall off from the saints. They were never true members of the church. The church is compared to heaven, and Christians to stars; when we think we see a star fall, it is no star but a meteor.

Use 3. This may teach us never to rest in any fellowship or society of the church until we are knit by the Spirit to God and Christ. If we are thus, every ordinance knits us closer to Christ and to his members, and every conference quickens our affection to the church, and theirs to us.

Use 4. Here is a direction to all, what society to follow; even the highest society, that of the church, the company of saints. Therefore if you would aspire to the best society, you must not be a noisome humor, harmful to another; but be knit together in love; join to one another with one consent.

So for all members of the congregation; be doing good to one another, be knit together, for you are all members of the same church. Let no outward respect disjoin the members. You would think it a woeful thing to see a convulsion of the members, one limb pulled from another; so let no external respect hinder fellowship.

Use 5. This will console all who find their hearts knit to Christ by his ordinances, and to one another. You shall never fall off, you shall never depart one from another. And being added to the church, you are one who is appointed for salvation; they who are in God's tabernacle shall dwell one day in his holy hill (Ps. 15). They who are members of the church militant here shall be members of the church triumphant in heaven. Your name is entered among the general assembly and church of the firstborn, whose names are written in heaven.

Doct. 3. Those who are true members of the church keep continual fellowship with the church, and never depart from the church.

"If they had been of us," that is, of our fellowship which is with the Father, "they would have continued with us." God gives a man true fellowship with him by trusting in him, and he stands as a mountain or rock that cannot be moved

(Ps. 125:1). The reason is that God protects him in a special manner. God's protection stands as a hill about him, so that none can climb over God to come at him (1 Tim. 2:19). Such a man sets his seal that the Lord is true.

How does it come to pass that they always keep communion with Christ and with his members?

-1. They keep fellowship with Christ because of that covenant which Christ makes with all believers (Jer. 31:31-35). It is contrasted with a covenant that may be broken, so this covenant cannot be broken. Nothing may break it but sin, and "God will write his law in their hearts," and they shall not depart from him. This covenant is expressed either without condition, or with conditions which he will give us power to perform, or else with conditions which Christ will perform for us; and therefore it cannot be broken.

But is it possible that a covenant should be without condition? Is it not the very nature of a covenant to have a condition on both parts?

a. It sometimes requires none, as the covenant God made with Noah (Gen. 9:1-17). He made a covenant never again to destroy the whole world by a flood, and yet there is no condition expressed on man's part. Now the covenant of grace is like this covenant he made with Noah; it is absolutely without condition, that he will remember us with everlasting mercy (Isa. 54:8-10). So then whoever has made a covenant with God to cling to him in Christ, he will never cast them off, no more than he will drown the world.

b. But though God requires a condition, yet it is such as he himself will perform, so that we can never forfeit his covenant (Jer. 32:40). You will say, "God will never depart from us, but we may depart from him"; no, God will put his fear in our hearts so that we shall not depart from him. Though God requires faith, repentance, and obedience, yet he gives it to us, or else we have Christ as our surety (Heb. 7:22), and he has fulfilled all righteousness for us. Therefore if I or my Surety pays, as he has done here, there can be no breach of covenant made on our part. Though we are unfaithful and disobedient, yet Christ has undertaken for us.

-2. The grace which the Lord gives to every true member of the church is efficacious and lively. The Spirit which knits us to Christ and his members is an immortal seed (1 Pet. 1:23). It is that spring which springs up into everlasting life (John 4:14).

But may we cease drinking and perish of thirst? Could we do so, then Christ's well should not differ from Jacob's well, but if we drink of it we shall never thirst. Whoever draws back from Christ never had true faith (Heb. 10:39). No, this grace is expressed as overcoming all the enemies of salvation, Satan, the world, and the flesh (1 John 5:4; Rom. 6:14). "Sin shall not reign over you"; it may be remnant but not regnant; it may tyrannize over us and lead us captive, but it shall not carry us willingly. We strive to get loose from it. Now if sin once had dominion over grace it would have dominion over us as well, which cannot be.

Those who are true members of Christ never depart from him, but further, they also never depart from the fellowship of the church.

And what is the reason?

Such is the sweetness of the grace, life, and power which they have felt in the society of the saints, sweeter than which they will not find in any other company or in solitude, that it will make them cleave to the members of Christ and not depart from them (John 6:66, 67). They find such sweetness and fullness in God's house that they would rather be doorkeepers in God's house than dwell in the courts of princes without (Heb. 11:26, 27). He who has once seen God's face in his church regards not the wrath of men; and as for the pleasures of the world, he accounts the very reproaches of the people of God to be sweeter. The true church of Christ has found conjugal society with Christ, and what could move them to turn aside to other companions? (Cant. 1:6-8; Ps. 16:3).

But if Christians cannot fall away, what is the need of so many exhortations and threatenings to backsliders? (1 Cor. 5:5; 1 Cor. 10:5-11; Rom. 8:13). I answer: -1. These are not grounds for beliefing in apostasy, but means to keep us from apostasy. He who has appointed the end has also appointed the means. -2. Though true members cannot fall away, yet there are many hypocrites who seem to have fellowship with the church, and they may fall away.

But does not this doctrine breed presumption? Since they cannot fall away, what need they care how they live?

-1. This is a doctrine of presumption only to carnal men. We shall find no Christian more careful to please God and careful not to offend him than those who have most assurance of his love and fellowship (2 Cor. 5:4; Gen. 39:9).

-2. But if God's children do wax wanton, yet he has means to scourge them soundly, though he does not take away his lovingkindness. (a) Though the erring Christian may not lose grace wholly, yet he may lose the strength of his grace. (b) Corruption may grow strong. (c) He may lose the comfort of his grace. (d) He may meet with afflictions from men, as David did. Though God did not cast him out of heaven, yet out of his kingdom; after he had committed murder and adultery, he raised up his own son to rebel against him.

But did not Lot depart from the fellowship of Abraham and pitch his tent toward Sodom? I answer, yes, but: -1. This was dangerous for Lot. -2. It was with Abraham's consent, and there was necessity for it; they could not well live together, for they had such great estates. -3. This was not breaking fellowship with the church of Christ, for the church was not then in congregations but in families.

But what of the ten tribes? Did they not renounce fellowship with the church? True, but by this they rejected the covenant of grace and so had no fellowship with the church. But were there no good people there? The good people of the land left their possessions and went to Jerusalem, with the priests and Levites (2 Chron. 11:13-17). Rather than leave the fellowship of the church, they would sell all that they had to purchase such a pearl.

Use 1. This will reprove the errors of the Pelagians and Papists, who teach that even the true members of the church may fall away, not only for a time but finally and forever.

Use 2. This will show us the wonderful eminency of that grace and that covenant which we have in Christ above the grace and covenant which Adam had. Adam had grace which he might lose, and a covenant which he might break, if he chose; but we have grace which we cannot lose and a covenant which we cannot break. So true Christians have no reason to complain of Adam's fall, for they have a covenant which they can no more break than they can break Noah's rainbow.

Use 3. Do not be offended because of antichrists and backsliders. There are thousands who have fallen away within these few years; and why? Because they were not of us. As parasites and noisome humors, the body is better without them. Demas forsook Paul, and showed thereby that he was a hypocrite (2 Tim. 4:10); had his heart been right, he would not have left Paul for the whole world.

Use 4. Do you seek good company? If you desire company which may be for your everlasting comfort, then use this fellowship of the church. There was never any who once got into the fellowship of the saints, that would ever be pulled away from them. What company is there so sweet as Christian communion? Moses, who had been in princes' courts, yet found the communion of God's people sweeter than the sweetest pleasures of Egypt. It was the saying of a late faithful servant of God, Dr. Preston, "Though I leave my life, yet I shall not leave my company."

Use 5. This will console the heart which has ever had true fellowship with Christ and his church. Having loved you once, he will love you to the end (1 Cor. 10:13; 1 Thess. 5:23, 24; Ps. 37:23-25). Though we fall, yet the Lord upholds us by his hand (Rom. 8:25; Rom. 5:10; 1 Pet. 1:5). We are kept by the power of God to salvation; he embraces us with his everlasting arms; and if we do start aside and feed on an ill diet, he will humble us that he may save us at the last day.

Doct. 4. It is a note of seducers or antichristian teachers, to depart from the fellowship of the church.

"They went out from us, because they were not of us"; and so such were never cordial or hearty to the church. Therefore when you see any fall off, know it betrays an antichristian spirit (2 Thess. 2:3; 1 Tim. 4:1).

What is this separation?

-1. It is not a separation of locale, as that of Gad and Manasseh (Josh. 22:9, 10), but without a separation in fellowship (vv. 26, 27). This is not the kind of separation which makes an antichrist.

-2. Nor is it a departing in fellowship which falls short of the spirit of antichrist, though it deserves reproof (Gal. 2:12). Though Paul blamed Peter for a spirit of dissimulation, yet it was not such a spirit as comes of antichrist. Peter was a man of great zeal and courage, yet we find him here carried with fear. Therefore let Christians most suspect themselves where they least suspect themselves; let them look for infirmities where they think themselves strongest.

-3. But the separation of antichrist is such a departing from the faith, and separating from the church in doctrine, spirit, judgment, and affection as Paul speaks of: "In the latter days some shall depart from the faith" (1 Tim. 4:1). These fall off not only in place or fellowship, but in judgment, heart, and affection; that is a mark of an antichristian spirit (Jude 4, 5; 3 John 9, 10).

What are the reasons for this separation?

The new converts to the church continued in the apostles' doctrine and fellowship (Acts 2:42). Therefore when they break from the fellowship of the church, they depart from the apostles' doctrine, and so from Christ. Therefore to prevent denying of Christ, he gives them charge that they do not forsake assembling themselves (Heb. 10:25-29). A finger cut off from the hand is not only cut off from the hand but from the head too; so if men fall away from the members, they also fall away from Christ the head.

Use 1. Rightly applied, this doctrine will teach us what to think in case of separation. But it is much abused. The

Papists build on this place that they who separate themselves from the Roman church are antichrists. They say, any who break off from the fellowship of the church are antichristian; now what were Calvin and Luther but those who broke off from the fellowship of the church? Therefore they were of the spirit of antichrist, and were forerunners of him.

But it is not every separation from what is called a church that is a note of an antichristian spirit; it must be a separation from the true church. Now the church which John speaks of was the true church, for it was made up of those whose sins were forgiven. But if it is not a true church that they break from, it is no sign of antichrist Those who set their hearts to seek the Lord separated themselves from Jeroboam and came to Jerusalem (2 Chron 11:16). So the apostles separated from the church of the Jews which persecuted Christ, and constituted a Christian church. It is then not separation from a false church, but from a true, which is a sign of an antichristian spirit.

But it will be objected, on what ground did the Reformers fall away from the Romish church, or we in England? Did not the English church begin with the dispute of Henry VIII with the Pope? True, that matter of divorce moved him to fall away from the Pope; and indeed it was enough to cause him to fall away from the Pope, who would bind him to an unlawful marriage. But the whole body of Christendom had a threefold ground of separation which is just.

It may be just to separate when a church is heretical, yet that alone is not a sufficient ground. The church at Corinth denied the resurrection from the dead yet Paul calls them saints; so the Pharisees charged that none should profess Christ, and taught false doctrine, yet Christ charges his disciples to obey them because they sit in Moses' chair. Therefore error, even fundamental error, is not always a just cause.

But the threefold ground of separation from Rome is indeed a just cause: -1. It is a just cause of separation when a church is infected with blasphemy (Acts 19:19; Acts 13:

45, 46). -2. Idolatry is a just ground of separation (2 Cor. 6:16, 17). -3. Persecution is a just ground of separation (Matt. 10:23; Acts 8:1). Now all these have been met in the Church of Rome. -1. They have blasphemed and condemned as heretical, justification by faith and other fundamental truths. -2. They worship images, as of the virgin Mary, and as the bread in the Sacrament; what greater idolatry? -3. The world knows, and the blood of thousands of martyrs can testify, their horrible persecutions. As long as we are subordinate to them, we could not profess the true religion without loss of goods and life; therefore we have just cause to separate ourselves from them.

Use 2. This may also teach us that, if it is a sign of antichristianity to withdraw from the church, then it is a mark of true Christianity to stick close to the fellowship of the saints, in love, in duty, in admonishing one another, in counselling and reproving one another. Therefore take heed that you do not forsake this fellowship. All the oil that was poured upon Christ's head descended to the lowest skirts of his garment (Ps. 133); to the lowest member, to the meanest Christian. Therefore if you remove from Christ and his members, how can you look for any drops of his oil?

Now we come to the last point, the end of the departing of these men out of the church. "They went out that it might appear that they were not all of us."

Who propounded this end? It was not their intention to manifest themselves not to be of the church, but all heretics pretended that they aimed at a better church; they never intended to manifest themselves as enemies of the church. Neither was it the end of the church itself. The church did not cast them out, but it was voluntary defection; they went out of their own will.

Whose end was it then? Surely it was God's end, for he overruled their apostasy to the benefit of his church when he saw them warp from the fellowship of the church. God gives them up to apostasy, that he might make it appear that they were never sincerely of the church (1 Kings 12:24).

Doct. 5. It is the holy end that God aims at, in giving up seducing corrupt spirits to apostasy, that he might show that they were hypocrites while they lived in the church.

God punishes hypocrites with apostasy. Why? It is a fearful sin to forsake the ordinances of God and the covenant of the church; and why should God thus work?

-1. By this means God manifests the integrity and soundheartedness of his own servants. God would have his name sanctified by his servants; and it is never more sanctified than when their sincerity is approved while others fall off (1 Cor. 11:19). In winnowing time, when there comes a good wind, it carries away the chaff but the wheat lies firm and is cleansed. So God has a fan to winnow his church and cleanse out the chaff, that it may be more clean (Matt. 3:12).

-2. So that he might prevent the corrupting and seducing of his weak servants. Lest any should be misled by them, therefore God timely discovers them (2 Tim. 3:9). Though these had led away some simple women, laden with many lusts, yet they shall proceed no further. So careful is God, that when his church is negligent in casting out such, he gives them up to defection voluntarily.

-3. He gives them up to apostasy that he might preserve the purity of his ordinances and law (Mal. 3:3-5). As long as corrupt teachers live among men, they pollute God's ordinances, so that they are not pure and sweet. Therefore he takes a course to refine them from their dross. This was fulfilled in the time of John the Baptist, who came before Christ and discovered the Pharisees to be hypocrites who would renounce Christ (Matt. 3:7-9). And Christ himself said, "Woe unto you, scribes, Pharisees hypocrites"; so that by their defection the Christian congregations and ordinances were more pure and refined. Take away the dross from the ordinances, as from silver, and they shall come forth more pure (Prov. 25:4, 5).

-4. To exempt his people from many scandals and

aspersions that would be cast upon the church if these corrupt persons should live among them (Jude 12). That these spots might appear to be corrupt humours and not members of the body, it pleased God that they should depart and so carry away their spots and scandals with them, so that his church might not be defamed.

-5. A fifth end is that it tends to the just punishment of hypocrites. It is a just judgment of God to leave them to be discovered and revealed (Matt. 12:33). God will have the tree known by its fruit at length; there is no great difference between the crab and the good apple tree in the leaf or blossom; therefore it must be known by the fruit.

Use 1. This will teach us that even the falls of the sons and daughters of men are managed and ordered by the wise and good hand of God's providence. You see here a Hand going quite beyond all the ends of men. God has always claimed this for himself, to have a hand in the sins of men; not to work them, but to punish one sin by another. If God sees envy in Joseph's brethren, he stirs them up to sell him into Egypt (Gen. 50:20; 2 Chron 32:21; Isa. 10:5). God has a hand in the worst evils that have been in the church (2 Sam. 24:1; Acts 4:28), not as an author, but by accident and occasion he gives them up to such courses. If David is idle, God gives him up to adultery (2 Sam. 11:12); if Pharaoh vexes God's people, God leaves him to hardness of heart (Exod. 7:3). If Judas is covetous, God gives him to betray his master. If they are his servants, he does it to cleanse them; if wicked, to punish them.

Therefore let us fear that God who is not only able to cast both body and soul into hell, but also into sin (which is worse than hell) by propounding such temptations as may leave a man to run into desperate courses. Therefore do not give way to any sin, thinking to recover yourself; but fear lest God will leave you to run into worse.

Use 2. It will teach God's people not to wonder and be offended first, if they see men of good esteem and profession fall away; marvel not, for such were never of the church (2 Tim. 2:17-19; Prov. 10:25). Therefore do not be discouraged when you see others whom you thought better than yourself fall, for "the foundation of God stands sure." God keeps his church unspotted and undefiled, so that even Balaam could say, "How goodly are thy tents, O Jacob." Therefore if you see any in the church grow corrupt and defiled, it implies that they were never members of the church. But if God leaves his people to any scandalous course that casts shame on them (which is very rare), he gives them such unfeigned humiliation and broken-heartedness, and such chastisements, that they recover themselves; and thus all the world may see that neither the church nor God allows it. As they were patterns of sin, so they shall be patterns of repentance (2 Sam. 12:11).

Use 3. It may teach God's servants to make a holy use of other men's falls. Do you see professors fall into wicked courses? If you give no countenance to their sin, God hereby manifests that you are sincere and upright, and keeps you from being misled by their evil counsel and practice. Bless God that he wipes the stain from his ordinances and church by casting out such; and especially make this use: "Be not high-minded, but fear"; fear that God is able to cast men from one sin to another.

Use 4. This will exhort all to take special heed of hypocrisy. If we take up a course of religion and good duties, we think that God will be merciful to us; but let us see that we do it in spirit and in truth (Heb. 12:13; Lev. 10:3). God will certainly discover us. There was hardly any who died in hypocrisy who was not uncased before his death; there is nothing secret that shall not be revealed.

There are signs of this hypocrisy.

-1. A hatred of admonition. Herod was impatient of reproof and put John in prison (Matt. 14:3, 4), thereby admitting his hypocrisy.

-2. A disposition to praise wicked men and run with them (Prov. 13:20; Prov. 28:4). That is a forerunner of forsaking the law.

-3. Making no conscience of your tongue, but letting it run at random, to passion or railing or slandering (James 1:26).

-4. Living in known sin and delighting in it.

-5. Making use of religion for any other end than for God's glory. If you make religion a horse to carry you wherever you will, certainly you will fall (John 6:26, 60 66). Those who followed Christ for the loaves all fell away when the fragments were gone. When Simon Magus made use of spiritual gifts to get money, he was in the gall of bitterness and bond of iniquity. Therefore if you desire to have fellowship with God be sincere and upright.

1 John 2:20

"But you have an unction from the Holy One, and you know all things."

The apostle had instructed little children that antichrist would come, and he had described him (vv. 18, 19). Now in this verse and the next, he propounds some means to help them. -1. An unction within themselves, by which they know all their seducements and snares (vv. 20 21). -2. The corrupt and false doctrine of these teachers; who is antichrist but he who denies the Son? And this doctrine had perverted the unction which they had received (vv. 22, 23).

In the first means observe: -1. A benefit received, an unction. -2. The author, Christ. -3. The virtue of it; you know all things; you know the truth, and that no lie is ever of the truth.

"You have an unction."

Doct. There is not the least of the children of God who does not partake of an ointment of Christ; even the little children have it (v. 27).

There were three sorts of unctions in the Old Testament: of prophets (1 Kings 19:16), priests (Exod. 29:7), and kings (1 Sam. 10:1). Now since Christ has been ordained to be our king, priest, and prophet, therefore he is anointed (John 12:15; Luke 1:32, 33; Heb. 6:20; Heb. 7:24; Acts 3:22, 23). All other unctions were but types of him; therefore he is said to be anointed with the oil of gladness above his fellows (Ps. 45:7). He was not only gladdened himself, but all the ends of the earth were made glad by him; therefore he is called Christos.

Now because he was not a type, but the person typified, he was anointed with material oil, but with the Spirit of God who is the true unction (Acts 10:38; Luke 4:18; Dan. 9:24). Hence in Hebrew he is called Messiah, the same as Christ in Greek. We are anointed by the same unction. That which was poured on Aaron's head descended to his skirts (Ps. 133); so that Spirit which was poured on Christ's head descends to his lowest members (2 Cor. 1:21, 22). So then we are anointed by the Spirit.

Now we are said to be anointed by the Spirit as with oil, in a fourfold respect.

-1. Oil has been used for healing wounds (Luke 10:34); so when the spirits of men are wounded by the sense of sin, God pours in such an oil of his Spirit that he heals and binds them up.

-2. Oil has a suppling, softening, and lighting power. So God's Spirit makes us nimble and agile to every good work. In the eastern countries they used to anoint wrestlers and runners, to make them more nimble and quick; so the Spirit makes us quick and ready to run in the ways of God's commandment (Ezek. 36:27), and to fight and wrestle against our spiritual enemies, sin, Satan, and the world.

-3. Oil cheers the hearts and countenances of men. So the Spirit is an oil of gladness (Isa. 61:3); they who are continually anointed with it are no longer afraid of hell or Satan, but walk on cheerfully before God.

-4. Oil was used to consecrate all vessels; there was no

consecration of which it was not a part (Exod. 30:23-33). So through the Holy Spirit the children of God are no longer for themselves or for the world, but are consecrated to God and dedicated to him, as kings, prophets, and priests (Acts 2:17; Rev. 1:6).

That ointment which was poured on Christ above measure descends to every member of his church, healing their wounds, softening and suppling their souls, cheering their hearts and countenances, and consecrating them to be kings, priests, and prophets to God.

-1. Kings were chosen to be judges and to fight the Lord's battles. So in some measure every Christian has a power to judge (1 Cor. 2:15) and to fight the Lord's battles. He has such an unction that whatever case he is called to, he has a spirit of judging and discerning what is good and what bad, so that he does not stand upon any man's judgment. He is able to fight the Lord's battles, not against flesh and blood, for those battles were types and shadows, but against principalities and powers (Eph. 6:12-18); and so he is far above princes. These are great battles with Satan, and the world, and our own corruptions (1 Pet. 2:11), and so we should fight the good fight (2 Tim. 4:7, 8).

-2. The priest's office stood partly in praying, partly in teaching, partly in sacrificing. So God has given to every Christian a Spirit of prayer and teaching (Rom. 8:15; Jer. 31:31-33). So also they offer up to God a sacrifice of a broken heart (Ps. 51:17), a sacrifice of praise and righteousness (Ps. 4:5, 6; Rom. 12:1, 2). Yea, and sometimes the Lord gives them to sacrifice whole towns and cities to God, as Peter offered three thousand together. He takes them from sin and brings them unto God, so that they bring in heaps upon heaps to God. They are not poor kings and priests; truly if Christians knew their worth, they would not be so discouraged and cast down in the world.

-3. It was the office of the prophets to preach and pray. Further, they sometimes had a special revelation of God's secrets, and so now God reveals his secrets often to poor

Christians (Ps. 25:14; Matt. 13:11). Many a poor Christian is able to discern more than his minister. Apollos was an eloquent man, and mighty in the scriptures, but yet he found Aquila and Priscilla, tentmakers, who were able to instruct him more perfectly. The great mysteries of election, vocation, justification are hidden from the world (Matt. 11:25-27); but God reveals them to poor fishermen and to babes. It was likewise a spirit of prophecy to interpret obscure mysteries, and often God helps poor Christians to see more clearly into scripture than many great scholars.

This unction is from "the holy one"; that is, Christ, for he is often so called (Luke 1:35; Ps. 16:10; Dan. 9:24). Holiness is that by which we give God his own due; it is the fulfillment of the first table of the commandments, as righteousness is of the second. And Christ is called the Holy One because he was set apart not only from all unclean but from all common uses, and dedicated to the Lord.

Two things make a thing holy, a setting apart from unclean and common uses and a dedicating to spiritual and holy uses. So the sabbath and sacraments are said to be holy, and so Christ is properly said to be the holy one. As there is an antichrist, so is there a Christ; as they have a spirit of seducing, so he has an unction, a box of ointment which is able to confirm you and help you against all these.

Use 1. This will try every Christian whether he is a Christian or not, for he is not a Jew who is one outwardly (Rom. 2:27, 28). We would think ourselves deeply wronged if any should deny us to be Christians; but what is a Christian? One who is anointed to be prophet, priest, and king. Do you know the things that belong to your peace and heavenly knowledge? Do you find that you cannot war against your spiritual enemies? Do you find that you cannot pray or instruct others? Do find yourself unwilling or unable to discern things that differ? Then you have not the unction from the Holy One, and are none of his. But if you are able to fight the Lord's battles, to pray, to instruct others, to discern the mysteries of God, to subdue Satan, the world, and your own heart; if it is thus with you, you are a Christian, one whose praise is of God and not of man.

Use 2. Would you know where the church is? Every company says, It is in me. The Papists say, It is in me, and the Separatists, It is in me; the Protestants say, It is in neither of you, but in me. Why, where you have a company endued with this holy ointment, there the church is, and he who departs from it is of Antichrist. So then the question is, Where is this spiritual unction?

Use 3. For all you who have received this unction. It is not meet for kings and princes to be digging in the earth; it is not for priests and prophets to be ignorant and blind and dumb. Paul is confident that the meanest Christian is a judge (1 Cor. 6:1-5). What a shame it is for a Christian to be carried captive at every temptation. What a shame it is for kings to soil and besmut themselves. For Saul to cast away his shield was a vile dishonor; so for Christians to be soiled and carried away with every temptation, to cast away their shields as if they had not been anointed, is a great dishonor.

Use 4. This will teach every Christian who stands in need of healing or suppling for a stiff spirit. You need balm and oil for healing the wounds of your soul, and suppling and softening for your stiff spirit; and here is an unction that will heal your wounds and soften your heart. Entreat God that he would shed abroad his Spirit into your heart, that he would heal your spirit, soften your heart, and cheer your soul. Look up to the holy one, for he is able to pour floods of consolation upon you, and establish your soul in peace.

Use 5. Here is a ground of much consolation that God is pleased to bestow such a mercy, such a blessing as this upon us. How we are bound to Christ, for he is pleased to anoint us with the same ointment wherewith he himself was anointed. It is a ground of much consolation. Christians are often called to great employments which (if they look upon themselves) they see themselves altogether unfit for; but is not this unction able to make us kings and priests? We know where to find supply; and if God calls us to more employments, this is our comfort, that we have an unction which is able to fit us for every work that God shall call us to.

Use 6. To exhort every Christian not to rest contented in an empty name of Christianity, until you get this spiritual unction. The wise virgins had their oil continually ready and prepared when Christ came; the foolish virgins had some oil, some common gifts and graces, but they were spent and it was too late to seek for oil when the bridegroom came. So do not only hear the word, but labor to find some oil dropped into your soul, so that in storms you may find the life and comfort of the Spirit.

Now we come to speak of the virtue of this unction.

Doct. The little children of God, by virtue of the ointment of the Spirit of grace, know all things.

So v. 27. There is an abiding ointment, and so sufficient that they need not be taught more or better things than it will teach them.

A. Consider the subject, "you." This universality of Christian knowledge is amplified by the subject, "You know all things."

-1. They desire to know all things necessary for salvation (Acts 10:33). So great is the desire of God's children to know this, that they desire to know even the things that are most against them. Eli knew by Samuel's lingering that he had some terrible message; but yet he would know it, and he urged him by a curse to declare it. And when he had told him, yet he says, "Good is the word of the Lord" (1 Sam. 3:18). So a godly heart desires to know all the will of God, especially if it belongs to him, though it be ever so bitter. Few they are who are willing to know all things; especially if they are against them and cross their lusts; so Herod (Mark 6:12), so Isaiah's hearers (Isa. 30:10).

-2. As in their desire, so they know it in the preparation of their hearts. If God reveals his will at any time, they have hearts ready to hear it (John 10:4, 5). There is a virtue in them by which they discern between the truth of Christ and false doctrine; so the Bereans were more noble, because they received the truth with all readiness and fear (Acts 17: 11, 12). They searched the scriptures, so that the word fell into their hearts like good seed. But on the contrary, if any man consents not to wholesome words, but makes questions and contention about them, he knows nothing (1 Tim. 6:3-5) because he has a heart unprepared to receive it. But he who is ready to receive it, knows it; such a one knows all things.

-3. In regard to their humility and meekness of spirit, whereby they think they know nothing and are more foolish than any. Agur says, "I am more brutish than any man, and have not the understanding of a man" (Prov. 30:2, 3); yet as foolish as he was, he still exhorts them to learn their knowledge from the high one. Therefore seeing such a deep self-denial in him, the Holy Ghost ranks him with Solomon for wisdom, and puts his proverbs among his. The man who thinks he knows anything, knows nothing as he ought to know (1 Cor. 8:2); therefore he who thinks he knows nothing, as weak Christians do, such a one knows all things which God sees meet for him; and this sense of his own ignorance makes him still thirst yet more after knowledge.

B. For the act, "you know." "You know all things." Other men may know much, yet knowing they do not know, and understanding they do not understand (Prov. 9:12). He who knows not for his own soul's good, is not wise (Prov. 24:5).

-1. The Christian's knowledge is more clear. One sees a thing by candlelight, another by daylight; but a third, who sees at noonday, sees most clearly. So a Christian sees things not only by the dim light of nature, nor by the daylight of the word, but by the bright clear light of the Spirit, which clearly manifests things.

-2. His knowledge is more certain. He knows by his own experience the misery of sin and the excellence of grace. He knows how Christ was formed in him; he has conceived him in his soul, and so he knows all the motions and operations of the Spirit (Gal. 4:19).

–3. It is more particular. He can apply all he hears and reads to himself, how far this promise belongs to him. He thinks the command belongs to him, the threatenings to him, the promises to him; he thinks the word was penned for him. Another man hears and reads, and never applies it to himself.

–4. Their knowledge is effectual. It makes them ready to obey; "the law is a light to my feet, and a lantern to my path," says David. It is not a light to the understanding only, but a light to my steps, to my practice. All the understanding a Christian has is true knowledge. If a man should walk in a soil where he should certainly sink in and be swallowed up, would you say he knows the danger? It is a sign he knew it not. So if we meet with one of our acquaintance and he passes us by without observing us, we would say he did not know us.

C. What is it that they know? "All things"; that is, all things pertaining to life and godliness (2 Pet. 1:3). They do not know the motions of the heavens, the influences of the stars, the nature of the creatures, but they know all things belonging to life and godliness. First, they know all things belonging to life, all things that are expedient in their callings and places. Second, they know all things belonging to godliness; there is no fundamental point which is necessary to salvation, which God does not read to them.

Why must some know more than others?

–1. It is expedient that men in some callings should know more than others, as ministers (Jer. 3:15; Mal. 2:7). God has promised that "their lips shall preserve knowledge." So it is not enough for a magistrate to know as much as a private Christian, but he should know how to administer judgment, as Solomon prayed for wisdom (1 Kings 3:9, 12). So husbands should know more than wives (1 Pet. 3:7), and parents than children (Eph. 6:4).

–2. Sometimes it is expedient that God should limit knowledge in regard to the present condition of his people. If God sees that his children are puffed up with knowledge, he is pleased to leave them in much ignorance; but if he finds their hearts humble and prepared to hear, he delights to pour out his Spirit upon them (Ps. 25:9). As long as the woman had an empty vessel, the oil ran; but when it was full, it ceased. So as long as we come with empty hearts this oil runs upon them, but as soon as we think we have enough and rest content, our knowledge grows no more.

-3. There is expediency for the present in any business. A man may have present need of direction in some present business that must be done; if men have humble hearts and look up to God, the Spirit is pleased to whisper into their hearts, "There is your way, walk in it" (Isa. 30:21).

-4. There is a further expedience for the present condition of the church, for different things are expedient in different ages. It would have been a hindrance of many providences of God, if men had known the sinfulness of polygamy in the first ages of the world. Many Christians were ignorant of the death and resurrection of Christ, but after the ascension of Christ they had a clear knowledge of it. The days of the Old Testament were but as a dim light; now it is more clear (2 Pet. 1:19). The fathers of the church of old had little need for the Revelation of St. John; as the church now has need to know more than at other times, so God reveals himself accordingly.

D. Why do these know all things?

-1. The object of their knowledge has in him all things needful (1 Cor. 2:2). In Christ they have enough (Col. 2:9); therefore if you have Christ, will he not give you all other things needful? Since God has given us Christ, our head understands all things; and the head will be sure to guide the foot when it has need to go.

-2. Their teacher is God himself (John 6:45). Our children shall be taught of God (Isa. 48:17); and if God undertakes to teach us, he is able to do more than any other teachers. They may teach, but they cannot give a dullard wit; God can open our understandings and enlarge our hearts with wisdom, clearing the object, the medium, and the faculty (Ps. 119:

Use 1. This is a ground of singular comfort to any poor Christian, that whatever is needful for him or expedient for him, he has a teacher. Every poor Christian has a Counsellor within him, who teaches him all things, and this is better than the Urim and Thummim to counsel at.

Use 2. Here is ground of trial to all. Are you a true child of God? You may know it by your knowledge; do you find your heart prepared to receive Christ's voice? Do you discern of things that differ? And do you still think that you know nothing? Why then, certainly you are a child of God, and have received an unction from the Holy One. But if it is contrary with you, you cannot be assured that you have received an unction from the Spirit, and so the least in God's kingdom is greater in knowledge than you.

Use 3. It teaches every child of God what course to take to get knowledge, and use it, and increase it. If you want knowledge, give your heart up to God; labor for that spiritual eye-salve which will enlighten your eyes. One day's teaching in Christ's school is able to teach you more than you can learn all your lifetime from other teachers.

And if you have received this unction, make use of it; it is not for you to hide and smother this light; it is for you to consult at this oracle. And take heed by all means that you grieve not this Spirit, for then you shall find this ointment polluted. Therefore keep your heart empty and humble, hunger after the ways of God, and gladly receive his motions; he will be ready to fill an empty vessel and to guide an humble soul in his ways.

Use 4. Here we see of what use it is to consult with Christians in cases of difference, for the weakest Christian is able to discern more than the greatest heathenish philosophers or counsellors (1 Cor. 6:1-6). God provides that there shall be some differences in the judgments of his children, but in the main they shall hold no error hurtful. Therefore let us search more into this ointment, and let us labor for it more than ever. We never had more need of knowledge than in these days, and our children will have more. Therefore let us labor to establish them and ourselves in the truth.

1 John 2:21

"I have not written unto you because you know not the truth, but because you know it, and that no lie is of the truth."

These words are an answer to an objection that might arise from the former verse. They might say, If we know all things, what need you write to us? And if we know not, how can we be said to know all things? To these questions he answers in this verse, "I write unto you, not because you know not the truth, but because you know it."

Doct. The apostles' writings were rather directed to those who know the truth, than to those who know not the truth. It was not the ignorance of the truth, but rather the knowledge of it, that occasioned the apostles' writings.

Observe all the apostles' writings. They were never written to any country, or town, or person that did not know the truth before (Rom. 15:14; 1 Cor. 1:1, 2; 2 Cor. 8:9; Gal. 3:3, 4; Eph. 4:21; Phil. 1:6; Col. 1:12, 13; 1 Thess. 1:9; he writes to Timothy and Titus as to his natural sons in Christ; Heb. 6:9-11; James chap. 1; 1 Pet. 1:1-4; for St. John, the text; 2 Jn. 1; 3 Jn. 2, 3. Likewise the epistles Christ wrote to the seven churches of Asia; he wrote to those who knew the truth of Christ and professed his name). So then this is a universal truth: not the ignorance of the truth, but the knowledge of it, has occasioned the apostles' writings.

But why should they write to those who already know?

-1. God has not sanctified his writings for the conversion of the Gentiles, but for their establishment. The apostle here speaks of those who knew the main truth, though they were ignorant of many particular truths. If men are converted to the truth, and brought to prize Christ and walk in obedience, the apostles' writings will establish them in the truth; but we never read that they wrote to any kingdoms where they had not been themselves or sent. They wrote not to Persia, Spain, or France, but to places where they had been. If God had sanctified their writings to the conversion of the Gentiles, it had been more fit to write to such places where they were not likely to come. But we see that God has so ordered it that men should be called by the foolishness of preaching (Rom. 10:13-15) and not of writing; the work of conversion is wrought by the preaching of the gospel.

-2. God accompanied their preaching of the gospel with mighty signs and wonders, but we never read that God accompanied any of their writings with miracles. Tongues are not for those who believe, but for those who believe not (1 Cor. 14:22); that is, the miracle of speaking with divers tongues is not for believers but for unbelievers. Therefore we never read that their writings did any miracle, and so he never intended that they should convert.

Then are their writings in vain, since they are of no use in conversion? No, there are other uses of their writings.

-1. Sometimes their writings are used to put men in remembrance of what they have heard (Rom. 15:14; 2 Pet. 1:15).

-2. That they may be established in the truth and confirmed in the knowledge of it (2 Cor. 13:1; Phil. 3:1).

-3. To stir them up to the exercise of such truth as they knew, but were slack in performing it, as in liberality or in the ordinances; to stir them up to their first love (Rev. 2:4, 5), to stir them up to take heed of false doctrine (1 Pet. 2:13; 1 John 4:1; 2 John 8).

-4. To inform them in some particular truth which they were ignorant of. Some were afraid that the Day of the Lord was so nigh that they neglected their callings (2 Thess. 2). He tells Timothy how to behave himself (1 Tim. 3:15); so he informs the Corinthians how husbands ought to carry themselves toward their wives in case of desertion or persecution.

Use 1. This shows why little good has been done among

the Papists by any writings which have been written in defense of the truth. Among millions of Papists, it is hard to know whether any have been converted to the true religion after such evident demonstration and proof; and the reason is because writings do not profit those who know not the truth, but who know the truth; else why did not St. John write to Cerinthus or other heretics in that time?

Why then do our divines not spare their labor in writing? Though they do not write for conversion, yet their writings establish many in the truth, and stir them up to stick closer to the truth.

Use 2. You may hence see the reason why, among those who read the word of God diligently, without hearing the gospel, few or none are converted and brought to the true knowledge of the truth. Such people are fit to be led into Popery or heresy; and no wonder, for God never blessed the apostles' writings, even while they were living, to the conversion of unbelievers. Therefore we see the necessity of preaching in every congregation, or else the body will sit in darkness and shadow of death.

But you will say, what then of pagans? And what of those who live under dumb ministers? Are they all castaways? I answer by asking, Do you think it greater charity to tell them that they may be saved without a teaching minister, or to tell them that without a teaching ministry they live without God and without the law? We know that many who live in such places go abroad and light on good sermons, and so Christ is found where he was not sought. But men who go home from bare reading, their hearts go home as dead as their minister was dumb, so that you shall find many such people as ignorant as pagans and Turks.

Use 3. This serves for direction to those unto whom God has given a gift of writing; you may know where your writings will be of most use. If you write to some, thinking to convert them, it will be labor in vain; but to write to them that know the truth, may be of much use.

Use 4. It may serve to encourage all Christians to be

frequent in reading. To what purpose did the apostles write, if others read not? It is good to be reading. Put more fuel to a fire, and it grows hotter; so let people read after they have heard, and it will be very profitable. Therefore we see the great abuse of the Papists, who deny the reading of the scriptures in a vulgar tongue. Therefore let us be stirred up not to forbear the reading of the Scriptures, though we know the truth; if kings might not be excused (Deut. 17:19), much less private men.

Doct. 2. Those who have received from Christ the anointing of the Spirit, know the truth.

In 1 Tim. 4:3 he puts believers and knowers together, and believers are anointed with the Spirit of faith (John 8:31, 32). The stronger our faith, the stronger our knowledge of the truth; the weaker our faith, the weaker our knowledge.

What is "the truth"? The expression might be taken for the Lord Jesus Christ, and he is not to be excluded, but he is not principally meant here (John 15:6). And it is true that they who know Christ have received this unction (John 6:69). But here by "the truth" is meant the doctrine of the gospel (Eph. 4:21), which is called the truth in Jesus, the truth which teaches us to find Christ and to prize him. You know it in a special manner, "as it is in Jesus"; that is, first, in a crucified manner, and second, as it is in Jesus who raises us from death to life. It is sometimes called the word of truth (Col. 1:5; Gal. 2:4, 5); so then, you who know the truth know also the worth of Christ and the means to find him; yea, you know him in a crucified manner, in his death and resurrection.

What is "the knowledge of the truth"? Three things make up the knowledge of the truth: understanding it, approving it, and consenting to it not as a probable thing, but as an undoubted certain truth. And thus these babes know the truth: they understand it (Luke 24:45); they approve and consent to it, and follow it (John 10:4, 5, 27); and lastly, they receive it as a certain and undoubted truth (John 6:68, 69).

There is as much difference between knowledge and faith as between hearing and seeing. If I hear a thing from an undoubted testimony, I believe it; but when I see it myself I know it more evidently. Stephen believed that Christ sat at God's right hand, but when he saw it, he knew it certainly; so these babes by sight and experience know these things that they believe (Heb. 11:1).

What is the reason that babes come to know the truth by virtue of this unction?

-1. This Spirit is an eye-salve to make them understand. By nature we are slow and dull of understanding; but as soon as God has dropped in some of this spiritual eye-salve, we strongly see the deep things of God, yea, even those which we were dull to understand before.

-2. He vouchsafes wisdom to them, by which they embrace and approve the truth as the very truth of Christ. They have a spirit to believe it, and therefore they have knowledge of it.

-3. He gives them experience, so that their hearts feel as plainly as their understandings know. Nay, these babes get their understanding from the feeling of their hearts; they know the danger of sin and the worth of Christ, and this puts them to reach after Christ and look at him as the most excellent of a thousand, and so they come to find true fellowship with Christ (1 Pet. 3:8). Thus they know it not only by faith, but by experience, and so they know the truth as it is in Jesus. You may have men who, by hearing and study, come to know much of the ways of grace, the doctrines and points of divinity; yea, they may come to approve them and may convince an adversary, but yet this is not properly a knowledge of these things, but an understanding of them. A man who lacks this unction may say that he understands these and believes them, but he cannot say he knows them by any heartfelt work of God on his own soul.

Use 1. In the name of the Lord, this will exhort all who intend to receive the Sacrament to a conscientious care and endeavor to get knowledge. It is not a privilege of scholars, but even of very babes. Therefore if they have received this unction, let none excuse themselves, for if the apostle acknowledges it in babes, it may shame older people if they are ignorant of the rudiments of religion. There is no hope that you should find comfort in God's ordinances, either here or in the life to come, if you are ignorant of the truth (Isa. 27:11). Mark how the prophet prevents an objection: "he who made us will surely save us"; no, if you are ignorant, he who made you will not save you. Therefore if you would ever get any good to your soul, with all your gettings get understanding, for without it you may look for no mercy. And above all understanding get this wisdom which is infused by the unction of the Spirit.

Use 2. And let those who have gotten knowledge labor to grow up in it. Three things did Paul desire: (a) That their hearts might be comforted. There is nothing more useful for a Christian than comfort. (b) But when Christians have gotten comfort, it is easy for them to sit loose from one another, and not to regard one another. Therefore he also desired that they might be knit together in the bond of love. (c) Finally that they might grow up to fullness of knowledge.

We see it was a great matter of concern to the apostles that they might be brought to the riches of full assurance; and shall ministers thus be concerned for their people, and shall not the people themselves labor to grow up to fullness of knowledge? It would be a great conflict to a faithful minister to see people poor in knowledge, to have only a few remnants and shreds of knowledge; therefore let people labor for the riches of the full assurance of understanding, which is properly true knowledge.

Use 3. We see therefore how much parents and masters are to blame, if they are so far from having conflicts for the knowledge of their children and servants that they have no care to help them along. You are merciless parents and masters, if you do not labor to bring them on to the riches of knowledge; for without this they shall find no mercy nor favor from God.

Use 4. This serves as a sign of trial of our knowledge. If you know the truth in a right manner, then you have partaken of the unction of the holy one. This differs from all other knowledge:

a. In its cause. This knowledge is from God (Isa. 54: 13). The means of getting it is to attend diligently to the word (John 4:42) and the other means of grace. Private conference may bring men on to understanding of the truth; and when we come to the public ordinances, we arise to higher and full understanding, and riches of full assurance.

b. In its effects. This knowledge humbles men (Prov. 30:2, 3), and this knowledge works faith (Ps. 9:10) and obedience (Col. 1:5, 6). That knowledge which does not bring forth obedience is no true knowledge; none but this kind of knowledge brings forth sincere obedience.

"No lie is ever of the truth." These words afford us three doctrines.

-1. Every antichristian doctrine is a lie (for of that he speaks).

-2. No lie (that is, no antichristian doctrine) is of the truth, that is, flows from the truth of the gospel.

-3. Those who have received spiritual unction and know the truth, know also that no lie is of the truth.

Doct. 1. Every antichristian doctrine is a lie.

What is a lie in doctrine? Three things make up a lie. -1. The proposition does not agree with the thing we speak of. -2. It does not agree with the notion that we have in our minds. -3. We speak it with a purpose to deceive.

All these are found in every antichristian doctrine.

-1. These enunciations do not agree with the word of truth, for else they could not be a lie. The word antichrist shows that they do not agree with the spirit of Christ.

-2. These doctrines are contrary to the judgments of those who deliver them, and this may appear from the definition of a heretic (Tit. 3:10, 11). A heretic is one who is subverted in his error and is condemned of himself. A man may be an erroneous man, but he does not come to be a heretic until he is condemned in himself; that is, until he speaks contrary to his judgment. This appears when he will contradict himself rather than depart from his error; and when he is convinced, he falls to wrangling or blaspheming. These are all signs of speaking contrary to their own judgments.

-3. They deliver them with a purpose to deceive. "They lie in wait to deceive" (Eph. 4:14); that is, they plot how to deceive the consciences of men. Their trade is to deceive and cheat men.

Thus there is a threefold lie in every antichristian doctrine. -1. It is materially a lie; the doctrine itself is contrary to the truth. -2. It is formally a lie; they speak against their judgment. -3. It is efficiently a lie; they breed lies in others (1 Tim. 4:1, 2).

Why is every antichristian teacher a liar and his doctrine

-1. Because it springs from a lying spirit; not from a spirit of truth, but of lies. So the devil describes himself when he seduces false prophets (1 Kings 22:22), as "a lying spirit"; as if there were no more effectual way to seduce kings than by false teachers acted by the lying spirit. The devil does the same in all false teachers; he comes and is a lying spirit in them, with such show of truth that it deceives them; they take it for truth. "They shall come with deceitfulness of doctrine, and many false lying wonders, whereby they shall seduce many" (2 Thess. 2:10).

-2. Because these false teachers aim at a corrupt end in all their doctrine (Acts 20:30). Some do it in ambition, to draw disciples to themselves and not to Christ; such was Simon Magus, who gave out that he was the Christ who had suffered, and so drew many away after him. Others aimed to fill their bellies and to get gain and pleasure from their followers (Rom. 16:18). They serve not Christ but their own bellies, and for that end with fair flattering speeches they beguile for filthy lucre (Tit. 1:11,12). They aim at all the lusts of the world, ambition, sensuality, and filthy gain; and if their ends are so corrupt, their doctrine must be corrupt and a lie.

-3. They make sport and jest at deluding people. One would think there should be none so desperately wicked as to come into congregations and obtrude false doctrines and delude men, and then make a sport of it. It sports them to see how handsomely they circumvented such a man at such a conference (2 Pet. 2:13); this is matter of sport to them, to see how at feasts and meetings they could carry the whole table before them. What is their end? To make a fair show in the flesh (Gal. 6:12,13). They themselves regard not the things which they obtrude on others; they know that they are empty things, so this is manifestly a lie.

Use 1. This may teach us how to conceive of Popery, and to stir up in ourselves a holy indignation against it. You see that Popery is a lie and has deluded many. Machiavelli clearly discerned that their religion was but mere juggling to fill the Pope's coffers and to keep his kitchen warm by purgatory and pardons. But indeed this was his wickedness: though he discerned this, he sought not the true religion. And this is the evil of their religion, that it leads simple men to superstition and understanding men to atheism. If Popery is only cheating and juggling and lying, it should kindle in us an inward loathing of that religion.

Use 2. This teaches us how prone our natures are to receive such false doctrines (Ps. 58:3; Rom. 3:4). Every man's judgment is apt to take up that opinion which suits with his understanding; now by nature we are prone to lies, and therefore let us take heed to ourselves and watch more exactly. Heresy is a fruit of the flesh (Gal. 5:19, 20), and therefore it is no wonder if carnal ears are ready to take it up, since by nature the truth seems harsh to us.

Use 3. It must stir us up to embrace the doctrine of the gospel. The more your spirit loathes falsehood, the more you are to cleave to the word. If the whole bulk of Popery is but a heap of lies, and we are to detest that, so we are to love the truth of the gospel. It comes from the Spirit of truth, and the ends of it are contrary to antichrist. Its preachers aim to bring disciples to Christ; they look not at their own belly and gain, but to edify and do good to the church of God. Since therefore the religion of Christ is so pure, so peaceable, so self-denying, so free from cheating and juggling, therefore let us be more enamoured with it, embrace it, study it more, practice it more.

Doct. 2. No lie, that is, no heretical antichristian doctrine, is of the truth.

Out of false things we may sometimes draw falsehood and sometimes truth; but out of true principles you can never gather falsehood. Out of the truth you cannot conclude any lie, any false doctrine; thus no lie is of the truth.

A doctrine may be said to be of the truth, or not of the truth, in a double respect.

-1. As a cause (John 8:47). He who is born of the truth is true (1 John 3:19). So to be of the truth iymoohbe a child of the truth. Thus when it is said that this doctrine is not of the truth, we may understand that it is not born of the truth and that it is not bred of the truth.

    a. It springs not from the gospel of truth.

    b. It springs not from the Spirit of truth, but from a lying spirit.

    c. It springs not from the truth of their own hearts, neither from moral civil truth; they neither spring from the divine truth of the gospel, nor from the Spirit, nor from the moral truth in their own hearts. A man may speak not from the Spirit of truth in the word, and yet speak from an honest heart; but a heretic speaks not from the truth of his own heart (Tit. 3:10, 11). Thus these men's errors are not from ignorance or infirmity, but completely from the spirit of falsehood.

    -2. In correspondence to the truth. Every antichristian doctrine comes from the spirit of lying and murder, and such a spirit is the devil's spirit (John 8:48). Satan's intention is to lie and deceive, and murder men's souls; and that proceeds from the enmity between Christ and the seed of the serpent. Now the seed of the serpent is not only heretics but heretical doctrines, and they strive to root out one another (Amos 7: 10, 11; 2 Cor. 6:14, 15). Therefore they would not allow Christ to live, and therefore they persecuted the apostles, because they spoke the truth.

Use 1. This may exhort all professors of the truth to take heed of lying. If no lie is of the truth, then if you speak falsehood or lies, you walk not like the servants of God. Such words come not from the Spirit of truth, but from the lying spirit, the spirit of wickedness and falsehood. And what have the children of the truth to do with falsehood and false words and false dealings? And especially take heed of false doctrine, for it is not of the truth but of lies. Therefore have nothing to do with the spirit of falsehood, the spirit of Popery, or the spirit of separation, to draw you from the truth of Christ and from the communion of the church.

Use 2. If no heresy is of the truth, then certainly it will never be for the truth. No stream rises higher than the spring from which it comes; if such doctrine comes not from the truth, it will never rise so high as the truth. Never look for true dealing from a heretic who lies against the gospel and against his own conscience. Never believe any doctrine of theirs, for they aim at subverting; if they deal not truly with God, they will not deal truly with man.

Use 3. It may teach us that there is no safe reconciliation with these doctrines, yea no safe toleration, for no lie is of the truth. How you can reconcile night and day, light and darkness? There is as wide a difference between the truth and antichristian doctrines; therefore there is no safe toleration of them, but one of them will be rooting out the other; either lies or the truth will be banished.

Doct. 3. Those who have received the unction of the Spirit, they know that no error or false doctrine is of the truth.

They know it; not only think so but know it.

−1. It is contrary to that unction of the Spirit which they have received, and the doctrine. The Spirit of God in them teaches them to be humble, but the spirit of these false doctors is ambitious (2 Pet. 2:18). They speak great swelling words; this does not suit with the Spirit of God.

−2. It is contrary to their experience. If they come to speak of free will, his own heart tells him that he was reluctant to be drawn out of himself; he found that he could hardly be pulled out of his natural state; he knows that this is contrary to the truth. Let another say we are justified by works; you cannot persuade a Christian to believe that, for he knows his best righteousness is defiled (Isa. 64:6) and that when he has done what he can, he is but an unprofitable servant. When they tell him that there is merit and satisfaction in his works, yea supererogation, every Christian knows this to be a lie, and he knows that he deserves wrath for his best performances. He knows that he is no way able to satisfy God's justice or God's law, but only Christ can satisfy for him.

−3. They know the truth because they have received it from a messenger of truth.

−4. They know the truth by its affects.

a. By the peace and grace they find from the truth. No antichristian doctrine ever brought peace to their souls, and there is no truth where no peace is. Where you cannot find peace of conscience, that religion has no saving truth in it. If they find not the fruit of peace, they know it is not of the truth.

b. Another fruit of the true religion is liberty and freedom of spirit to come to God from Satan, from his lusts, from the world (John 8:32). Therefore if religion does not make us free to come to God, and free from the world and our own lusts, surely that religion is not of the truth. He speaks of those false teachers that they promise liberty, but they themselves are servants of sin (2 Pet. 2:19).

Use 1. This reproves all who are at an uncertainty in

their religion. They do not know which religion to take; they say they find reasons on both sides so probable, and there are some on both sides so corrupt that they know not which to take. Why, if it is so with you, you have not received the unction of the Spirit, for there is not the least of these little children who have received this unction who does not know the truth, and who does not know that no lie is of the truth.

Use 2. You who have taken up your religion, do you know your religion to be the truth and no lie? You may say you hope it is true because the king and state follow it; but do you know it to be true, and do you know every contrary doctrine to be a lie? If you do not, you do not know what you should. "I have chosen the truth" (Ps. 119:30); he does not say the state has chosen it, or others have chosen it, but I have chosen it let others choose what they will.

Use 3. It will teach all to grow up in discerning the truth, and that will reveal all falsehood. Suppose you should have one come to you and tell you that you frequent the ordinances and perform good duties only in the letter, but you ought to do them only when the Spirit moves you. Let a Christian decide if this is not a lie, and contrary to the truth and to his experience for we ought to pray continually. So if one comes and tells you that you ought not to read the scriptures, your own spirit tells you that you have as much need of the word as a child of his daily milk. Therefore let Christians learn to discern of the spirit of truth and error.

1 John 2:22

"Who is a liar but he who denies that Jesus is the Christ? He is antichrist who denies the Father and the Son."

In these verses (20-22) the apostle propounds some means to help them against false teachers: -1. By something within themselves, that unction in them. -2. By the grossness and falseness of the doctrine, which is called a lie and the teachers of which are called liars; who is a liar if they are not?

These false teachers are described in this verse: -1. As liars, and that so grossly that if they are not liars, there are none in the world. It is as gross a lie as any, so that these liars may stand in comparison with any. -2. As being revealed by their doctrine: who is a liar but he who denies that Jesus is the Christ? -3. By their name and nature. Their name is Antichrist, and their doctrine is to deny the Father and the Son; for if they deny the Son, they deny the Father also.

Doct. Antichrist's teachers are as gross liars as they who are the worst.

Who is a liar if not these? Let none be accounted liars if not they; they are equal to the worst. These words come home; and no wonder Christ called James and John the sons of thunder, for they spoke boldly and plainly.

Two things make a man a gross liar, equal to the worst: the perniciousness of his lie and the evidence of it.

-1. The perniciousness of it. It is a pernicious lie to speak against the government of a house or family, but there is no lie so pernicious as Popish lies. None do so much harm as the lies of antichristian teachers; they lie not only against their own souls but also to the hurt of others. They shall bring in damnable heresies (2 Pet. 3:1, 2), such doctrines that if men live and die in them, they shall be damned, and many shall follow their pernicious ways, and so they sell the souls of men. One part of the merchandise of the Romish whore is the souls of men (Rev. 18:12, 13); and therefore if there are any pernicious liars, who are more pernicious than those who lie against the souls and salvation of men? There are no greater cheaters than to cheat us of our Saviour, of our Father, of salvation.

-2. The evident falsehood of it. A man lies when he mistakes the truth which he might easily see, or even though it were harder to see; but if a man knows it to be false and pernicious, and yet lies against his knowledge and conscience, this makes the lie palpable and gross. Now these lies are not only contrary to the truth of the word and the experience of Christians, but also contrary to their own knowledge and conscience. They must needs be gross liars who lie in such weighty matters as salvation and that so evidently that he who runs may see their falsehood.

Use 1. Let us see the damnable state of all antichristian false teachers. They who not only hold but thrust on others damnable doctrines, by which they hasten their own and others' destructions, must needs be in a damnable state.

It is their tenet that no church is so safe to live and die in as their Catholic Church; and their reason is because among pagans and infidels you shall find nothing but horrible lies and blasphemies; and it is true. But among Christians is the safest living. If there are any liars among Turks and infidels, these antichristian teachers carry away the prize in lying; and those who are saved among them are saved because they secretly renounce their doctrine. Therefore let them not boast of our charity to some amongst them, for none are more pernicious and evident liars than they. Therefore let us flee from their doctrine, and cleave close to the profession of the truth.

Use 2. Let us take heed of antichristian doctrines, if they ever come among us; these are described to be the frogs that go about the world to seduce poor people. Be not deluded then; when they profess themselves to be patrons of the truth, the Spirit condemns them to be liars; and no lies are more gross and evident than theirs.

Use 3. It may serve to teach men not to be mealy mouthed in speaking plainly and homely. We must not be offended at the plainness and simplicity of the scripture. None is so plain as this apostle; he calls them liars in the Revelation, and beasts, and the whore of Rome.

Use 4. It may serve to teach us all to be abundantly thankful to God, who has delivered us from this lying false doctrine in which many of our fathers have perished; for there is no religion more gross and no blessing greater than to be delivered from such a gross lying religion. To be delivered from a gross sin is no such great matter, for the publicans and sinners came into the kingdom of Heaven sooner than the Pharisees, and yet theirs was the strictest sect. No mercy can be greater to any nation than to be delivered from this lying religion; and on this ground God urges obedience to the moral law, because he was the God who had brought them out of the land of Egypt, out of the house of bondage (Exod. 20:2).

Doct. 2. Antichrist denies Jesus to be the Christ; or, he who denies Jesus to be the Christ, is antichrist.

See 1 John 4:3; 2 John 7. The name Antichrist shows he is one who is against Christ, an enemy to Christ; he is called ἀντικείμενος, "he who opposes" (2 Thess. 2:4).

A man may deny Jesus to be the Christ, either grossly and assertively, or else cunningly and fraudulently. Some ancient heretics denied the manhood of Christ, and some the Godhead, and some palpably denied his office of mediation and redemption. But that false antichrist did not deny him palpably and grossly, for first, antichrist is said to work in a mystery (2 Thess. 2:7). Second, he shall sit in the temple of God (2 Thess. 2:4), so that he should keep some correspondence with Christ and his; and he fits as a member of Christ, for otherwise no church would receive him. Therefore if you find any in the church who deny Christ to be prophet, priest, and king to his church, that is antichrist.

I. Observe how their doctrine cuts asunder the whole work of redemption.

A. For his prophetical office, the Church of Rome denies it. Christ is anointed to be a prophet to teach his church by his word, and by his Spirit in his word, but they deny his prophetic office.

-1. The Lord teaches by the word; but they deny it:

a. By adding other unwritten traditions to the word of God as necessary.

b. By preferring the Vulgate translation as more authentic than the original languages.

c. By denying the use of the scripture to the common people, and telling them it is obscure and dangerous for them.

d. By suspending the authority of his word not upon the testimony of his Spirit, but on the Church of Rome; so that if you ask a Papist why they receive the Gospel of St. Matthew and deny that of St. Bartholomew, they say because the church has received the one and renounced the other; and so they make the scripture to depend on general councils, and especially on the Pope.

-2. The Lord teaches his church by his Spirit whom they evacuate:

a. By confining this Spirit to councils and to clergymen, and not to the common people.

b. By making it a conjectural thing, probable, but not of any certain knowledge.

B. For the priestly office of Christ, which consists, first, in offering sacrifice, and second in intercession, in applying his sacrifice.

-1. Now the Church of Rome denies his sacrifice.

a. By adding other sacrifices, and so making his not to be sufficient. They add two sacrifices: (i) The sacrifice of merits: first by works done as building of churches and monasteries, which they say satisfy for men's sins; and second they merit by suffering, as pilgrimages and purgatory, and so by indulgences and pardons. (ii) Their second sacrifice, worse than the first, is the Mass.

b. They evacuate the sacrifice of Christ by evacuating the redemption of Christ. (i) By making it not plentiful. Whereas the redemption of Christ is a plenteous redemption for both body and soul, they say he redeems us from eternal pains, but not from temporal, from purgatory. (ii) By making it not gracious; for they say the grace of redemption is applied to us not invincibly, but according to the will of the creature. (iii) By applying it not by faith but by works. (iv) They say a man cannot know his redemption by Christ surely and certainly, but only conjecturally and probably. (v) This grace they dispense not spiritually but elementally, by imposing it on sacraments; so that without sacrament, no grace.

 c. They evacuate his sacrifice by making it not eternal. He who has been washed in Christ's blood may finally fall away and become a reprobate.

 d. They make it not necessary for some, as for the virgin Mary.

 e. They say it is not necessary in respect to temporal punishments.

 -2. They evacuate his priestly office by discouraging people from coming to God in the name of Christ, but telling them to approach God by the mediation of the virgin Mary and some saints; they would have us direct our prayers to some saint, and so they deny the sole mediation of Christ.

 C. For his kingly office.

 -1 They deny his headship and his absolute sovereignty; they will not make election to be of free grace.

 -2. They deny it by setting up another head in the church, a Pope whom God never appointed. He who sets up another king without his consent, as good as denies the other king; there is as much dishonor to Christ in setting up a new head as in cutting off the true head.

 -3. They deny his kingly office in his great work of conversion, by making it to depend not on the sovereignty or prerogative of his kingly office, but on the liberty of our wills.

 -4. They deny his kingly office by defacing his kingdom, which is his body his church; they deface his church, his body, and transform it not into a Christian state, but antichristian.

 II. They deface the Church of Christ, whether militant or triumphant.

 A. The church militant.

 -1. As a catholic body.

a. They teach that the most erroneous, notorious livers, are truly members of the church. But we see that Christ's kingdom consists of spiritual people; they are but wens and ill humors.

b. They give false notes of the church, as antiquity, universality, prosperity, which may agree to some heathenish places.

c. They make the church infallible; and this they confine to the church of Rome, so that if Rome falls, the Church of Christ falls.

-2. For the parts of the church.

a. In a council. (i) They say a council is incapable of error. (ii) Yet they say it is subject to the Pope. (iii) They make the decrees and laws of councils to bind the consciences of men.

b. Or in the several parts. (i) For the head, the Pope: they set two heads on the body, and so make it a monster. (ii) For the middle members, the priests. First, they say they may not marry, and so are unclean. Second they exempt them from the power of civil magistrates, and so are an inordinate generation. Third, their regular priests as monks and friars are all of them abominable, not planted by God; they profess poverty and chastity, which exposes them to uncleanness and covetousness. (iii) For the lowest members, the laymen, whether magistrates or private men. For magistrates, they make them not heads, not even in their own kingdoms, but subject to the Pope. For the people, he can dispense with their oath of allegiance to their sovereign. From both magistrate and people he can withhold the scripture in the known tongue, and the cup.

-3. For the church militant in purgatory; they make a church God never acknowledged.

B. For the church triumphant. They make the saints as so many idols, in praying to them, visiting their relics making them partakers in Christ's mediation. Such a kingdom as this Christ would loathe, and such a kingdom any true Christian would detest.

So we see, though they do not deny his manhood or his Godhead, yet they deny him to be the Christ, that is, the Anointed for they wash off all his unction.

Use 1. This shows us the depth and danger of Popery. You cannot give yourself up to an antichristian doctrine without becoming an enemy to Christ. You take away his offices, you make him no Christ, no Saviour. Therefore let none say that Popery and the true religion can be reconciled; they may as well combine light and darkness as Christ and antichrist.

Use 2. It may encourage us to thankfulness that God has delivered us from this darkness, and has brought us to know the truth as it is in Jesus, the true king, priest, and prophet of his church. Therefore let us sanctify God in our hearts; let us walk as men that are redeemed and taught of him; let us learn to rest on him for pardon, for teaching, for direction and guidance.

Doct. 3. Antichristian teachers deny the Father and the Son.

He had said before that they deny the Christ; but now he goes further and says, "They deny the Father and the Son," because he who denies the Son denies the Father, there is such a close relation between them (v. 23). The truth of this appears in St. John's time, for some made themselves the Christ, and some God the Father, as Simon Magus and Menander made themselves the Christ and so took away the Fatherhood and the Sonship. Some again taught that the Father came down and took flesh, and was buried, and so often descended in cloven tongues, so that they denied the distinct persons of the Trinity.

But that great ἀντικείμενος, the Antichrist of Rome, he denies the Father and the Son.

-1. He denies the Son.

a. They deny his Godhead. They say we are in error to say that Christ is God himself, but that he is merely from the Father. They will not take the true sense, but they say that Christ has a derived Godhead; and so they make him no God. We say the person of Christ is from the Father, but his Godhead is the same with the Father. There are not three gods but one God; and if you make it a derived Godhead, you make three gods.

b. They as much wrong his manhood; for when they say the priest has a power to create, they take away his manhood for it is incompatible to human nature to make any living creature. And when in the mass they say, "Hoc est Corpus meum," "This is my body," they claim to make the body.

c. While they say that the whole body of Christ is in a thousand churches together, yet they say every communicant receives a whole Christ. Now if Christ has so many bodies, he is a monster; yea, they still say his body sits at God's right hand, a strange lie; are they not the greatest liars? The Christ they describe is no better than a fable and so they deny the Son; and in denying him, they deny the Father.

-2. But they deny the Father more directly, when they take away all assurance of favor with God through Christ, and say that it is presumption to be certain of the favor of God. Yet Christ says, "I ascend to my Father and your Father"; if he is the Father of Christ, he is the Father of all his members, and therefore if they take away all assurance of God's love as a Father, they deny the Father.

Use 1. This teaches us something concerning God.

a. It shows us a reference between the Father and the Son. (i) It is manifest then that they have a living and reasonable nature, for Father and Son is compatible only to rational beings, not to beasts and trees; therefore if we who are fathers and children have rational natures, much more God the Father and the Son. (ii) If there is this relation, then they are both of the same nature. A man does not beget a beast, but one of the same nature; and therefore when the Father begets the Son, it implies the Son is of the same nature with the Father, each of them an eternal being (John 10:32-36). (iii) If Christ is the Son of God, then he is equal with the Father; if he is the Son, he is God; and if God, there is not one superior and another inferior, but he must be equal with the Father.

But is not a father often greater than a son, and a son greater than a father? True, among men; but in the Godhead no person can be superior to another; there are no distempers nor misery.

b. As there is a reference, so there is also a distinction. The Father cannot be the Son in the same relation; nor can the Son be the Father in the same relation. This shows the error of Sabellius, who said that the same God the Father took upon him flesh and became the Son; but this is a horrible error, for the Father cannot be a Son to himself, nor the Son a Father.

Use 2. The same doctrine condemns the antichristian teachers; for though they say they teach the same with us, yet it is manifest that they deny the Son, for he who makes him a derived Godhead, makes him no God. And so when they say his body is in many places at once, they deny his manhood, for one cannot be many, and many cannot be one.

Use 4. It may teach us to magnify the mercy of God, who has delivered us from this lying doctrine which our forefathers lived in, and which it may be we would have followed as greedily. Therefore let us abhor their doctrine, and cleave to the truth, and walk in the truth of Christ.

1 John 2:23

"Whosoever denies the Son the same has not the Father."

Because he had said before that he who denies the Son denies the Father, he proves it now from the near relation between them. He who denies the Son denies the Father, and contrarily, he who acknowledges the Son acknowledges the Father.

Some doubt whether these words are in the Canon, but Beza testifies that he found them in four old good translations, and the Syriac translation reads it and the Vulgate Latin; and it is a common thing in this epistle to show one thing by denying its contrary.

Doct. According to our acknowledgement or denial of the Son we either have or have not the Father.

What is it to confess and to deny the Son?

To deny the Son is not only a dogmatic denying in doctrine or word, neither is confession only a dogmatic confession of him with the mouth. True, if in doctrine you deny the Son, you deny the Father also; and if you preach Christ in a true manner, you preach and confess the Father also. But there are more denials and confessions of the Son than in word, so it includes having the Son and the Father, and not having the Son and the Father (as v. 24).

Did not Peter deny Jesus, and yet did he deny God? Again, did not many confess Jesus, whom he will yet deny at the last day? Did not Judas and Demas profess Christ, and yet did not both deny the Father and Son?

In the scriptures there is a threefold denial and a threefold confession: in heart, in word, and in practice.

-1. A denial in heart. "The fool has said in his heart, there is no God" (Ps. 14:1); he does not mean natural idols, for he speaks of those who eat up God's people as bread. "Let him deny himself," said Jesus (Luke 9:23); he does not mean in word, that he must say he is not himself; but he must deny all worth in himself; he must deny all pleasure and gain. This is to deny a man's self, though he may not express it in words. So there is a denial of Christ in heart, when a man does not prize Christ and magnify him, nor see the worth and value of him; and this is to deny Christ.

-2. A denial in word openly (2 Pet. 2:1).

-3. A denial in manner (1 Pet. 2:8; Tit. 1:10). "They profess they know Christ, but in their works they deny him"

(Tit. 1:16). One who does thus, denies Christ and so denies the Father.

Suitable to this there is a threefold confession:

-1. In heart. "In all thy ways acknowledge him" (Prov. 3:5, 6); trust not in your own wisdom. To confess him then is to trust on him and depend on him in a man's heart.

-2. In words (John 1:20, 29). This kind of confession is mixed with holy boldness and holy humility. He is so humble that he denies all his own credit and life, and so bold that he dares confess Christ before kings and princes. We read of some who professed Christ, but it was secretly for fear of the Jews; here was lack of humility and boldness. Such lack of humility was in Peter; for lack of Christian courage, and for leaning to his own strength, he denied Christ in word, though in heart he did confess him.

-3. In life and practice. "In all thy ways acknowledge him"; not only in word, but in your outward course so that in all your walking you may acknowledge him and depend on some word of command or promise. "The grace of God has appeared to all men, teaching us to deny all ungodliness and worldly lusts" (Tit. 2:11-13). A man confesses Christ when he denies ungodliness and walks soberly, righteously, and holy, as one who looks for the hope of his appearing; and thus, in his very practice and life he acknowledges Christ.

What is it to have the Father or to lack the Father?

To have the Father is to have him as my Father, and to deny him is to renounce him for my Father. To have him is to have fellowship with him as with a Father, and to continue with him. When God commands us to have him for our God, and says, "Thou shalt have no other gods before me," he would have us to trust in him and depend upon him and to set him up as the God of all our peace and comfort and help. If a man thinks he has enough if he has God and nothing else, then he is said to have God. To have the wisdom and righteousness of God; and not to have God is to live without God in the world, without fellowship with him.

What is the reason why, according to our confessing or

denying of Christ the Son, we have or do not have the Father?

-1. God's wrath is dreadful against all who are out of Christ (John 3:36). If we do not confess Christ and show forth the virtue of Christ in our lives, the wrath of God has gone out against us, for sin makes God our enemy; therefore if we have not a mediator, woe unto us.

-2. There is a close relation between them: "I and my Father are one" (John 10:30; John 14:11). They are wrapped and folded up, one within another; deny one and you deny both.

-3. It was a great ordinance of God which set up Christ, that through him we might have access to God. Christ is the only way to come to the Father (John 14:6); if we would get God for our Father we must get Christ for our elder Brother.

But some of God's own servants have denied Christ with their lips; then did they not have the Father? As Peter.

-1. Even when Peter denied Christ with his lips, his faith did not fail him (Luke 22:31, 32); and if his faith remained, then Christ dwelt in his heart by faith; and if he had Christ, he had the Father. Though you see neither leaf nor sap in a tree in winter, yet there is life in the root; so there was faith in Peter's heart, even when he denied Christ with his lips. A man may in mouth deny Christ in some sudden temptation, and yet in his heart confess him; and in his mouth he will yet confess him again, and in his life, as Peter did. Thus his was not a total but a partial denying; in lips only, but not in heart or life.

-2. That denial was but for a time; afterwards he repented and confessed Christ constantly. According to his threefold denial he confessed him three times. Afterwards when Peter and John were charged and threatened to speak no more in his name, they would not smother him any more, but confessed him to the death. Otherwise this would be a constant denial in word, which is a fearful thing (Matt. 3:12).

Use 1. This shows the desperate danger, not only of all heretics who have doctrinally denied Christ, but also of the heathen who never knew Christ; none of them have God for their Father. It is a woeful conceit of some, that a man may be saved in any religion; but if we have not Christ, we have not the Father. So says the apostle: "Remember you were Gentiles and lived without Christ" (Eph. 2:11, 12), and so without God in the world. See then the danger of the Turks who deny God to be their prophet, and of the Jews who, though they hold to one God, yet denying Christ deny the Father. Take God out of Christ, out of the Trinity, and he is a mere idol. Let that move us to pity the state of those who have lived without Christ many generations.

Use 2. Hence you may see how much the Church of Rome is without the Father. They charge us for holding Christ to be autotheos, God of himself; they say he is "God from God," but not God of himself. They further deliver him to be a Christ whose body is in a hundred places at once; and so they deny the Son, entrenching upon all his offices; and in denying the Son, they deny the Father.

Use 3. It may teach us what to think or believe of all the saints of God before Christ. Does God say, "I am the Father of Abraham, Isaac, and Jacob"? Then you may certainly conclude that they had the Christ. "Your father Abraham rejoiced to see my day" (John 8:56); he saw Christ to come of his son, and therefore he rejoiced. So Moses wrote of Christ, so David knew Christ (Ps. 110:1, quoted Matt. 22:44). So the prophet prays God to be merciful to his people for the Lord's sake (Dan. 9:17), that is, for Christ's sake (Acts 15:11), for there is no other way to be saved. They saw Christ in all sacrifices and types; there is no other name under heaven to be saved, but by Christ.

Use 4. It may be a ground of trial, whether we have God for our Father or not. We say daily, "Our Father, who art in heaven"; but would we know whether he is so or not? If we deny the Son, we have not the Father; if we confess the Son, we have the Father; therefore let us inquire whether we acknowledge him in our hearts. If you are ashamed to confess him in your words, for fear of disgrace or danger, Christ will be ashamed of you. If your works deny him, if you care not whether your ways please him or not, you have neither the Father nor the Son, and so you lose your own soul. But contrarily, if you acknowledge him in your heart, trust and depend upon him, choose him, prize him, then in your heart you profess Christ and the Father.

Use 5. To console every soul who knows and professes Christ. Every poor Christian professes Christ and desires to live as may please him; and if you walk thus, you have both the Father and the Son; the Son for your Saviour, your king, priest, and prophet, and God for your Father. And if so, he will provide for you, and you shall lack nothing (Ps. 23:1-4). Therefore here is comfort in sickness; you have the God of health (Exod. 15:26). God is the life and length of our days (Deut. 30:20). If we have God, we have life, and health, and peace, and grace.

Now there are three graces by which we walk in an acknowledgement of Christ all our days.

-1. Faith in Christ. "I live, yet not I, but the life I live in the flesh, I live by the faith of the Son of God" (Gal. 2:19, 20). This faith is a grace much known, more talked of, but very little practiced. If we live without faith, we live without Christ; therefore live by faith in Christ. Look at yourself as unable to do anything without him; depend on him; live not for yourself but for Christ.

-2. Mortification, or self-denial. When a man denies his own lusts, his own honor, profit, and credit, and is content to be all in Christ; when he looks at outward things as talents he is to employ in God's service; when he is weaned from them and regards not much how they go, then he can get Christ and the Father. Christians should make it appear that their profit and pleasure and honor is not of this world, but in Christ. They should deny all these things. As faith makes you acknowledge Christ as your Saviour, so self-denial as your Lord.

-3. Zeal. This may show in us the power of the resurrection of Christ, when a man not only desires to do good duties, but to do them with life and power. God requires that we should be zealous (Tit. 2:11-14). Zeal is the life and strength of grace (1 Cor. 15:55). If at any time you find yourself without zeal, then you need the might of the Father; and if you need him, then you need the Son. Therefore you must seek Christ, and then you shall find a new spring of help.

1 John 2:24

"Let that therefore abide in you, which you have heard from the beginning. If that which you have heard from the beginning shall remain in you, you also shall continue in the Son and in the Father."

We see the apostle instructs them against antichrist's coming by foretelling his coming and by describing him. The means by which they shall know him is double: first, their unction, and second, the grossness of antichrist's lies.

Now we come to St. John's exhortation to use a special help against antichrist. He exhorts that that doctrine which they heard from the beginning should abide in them, and he presses this exhortation from a double benefit: first continuance both in the Son and the Father, and second, obtaining the promise of eternal life.

Doct. Perseverance in the doctrine of the apostles is a certain pledge of perseverance in grace, and attaining of glory.

Both these benefits are joined together. Perseverance in the apostles' doctrine is an undoubted pledge both of our fellowship with the Father and the Son and of our eternal life. He who abides in the doctrine of Christ abides in the Father and the Son (2 John 9). It is said of the primitive Christians that they clave to and continued in the doctrine of the apostles; and he tells us that they were such as should be saved (Acts 2:42, 47).

"Let that abide in you which you have heard from the beginning," that is, the doctrine which was preached at first by Christ and afterwards by his apostles (Luke 1:2).

How are we to let it abide in us?

There are three special graces by which God's word is said to abide in us. It is not enough for a Christian to have it rest in his judgment and assent. The devil himself knows and believes that antichristian doctrine is a lie, and he knows the truth; yet because he continues not in the truth, he has neither fellowship with the Father nor with the Son nor any hope of salvation. Therefore there are more special graces by which the word is said to continue in us; as David says, "I have hid thy word in my heart" (Ps. 119:11).

-1. Faith, which receives the word not as the word of men but as the word of God (1 Thess. 2:13). Men then receive the word aright when they believe it, and when they think it effectual to salvation and able to save their souls (James 1:21). When we receive it as the word of life, when we receive it as our stock and portion, then it dwells in our hearts by faith. Let a man receive the word as true only, and not as good, and it will not continue in him. The devils receive it as true, but do not receive it as good; they think it mischievous to them, and therefore they get no good by it.

-2. A holy awe and fear of this word. Unless the word awes us and rules in our hearts, we have no fellowship with it (Ps. 119:161). In this verse the heart is taken for the conscience; in the Old Testament we read not of the word conscience. Though David's heart stood in awe of princes as when he cut off Saul's skirt, yet it was the word that over-awed him so that he would not hurt him. This awe of the word over-awes that authority we might use to evil; so when Job had it in his hand to do wrong, yet the fear of God kept him from doing any wrong (Job 31:13-15), even to the least servant or maid he had (Jer. 32:40).

-3. Obedience keeps the word in our lives, and our lives in the word (Ps. 119:32). If a man takes liberty to live sometimes in the word, sometimes beside it, he will break off from fellowship. Herod kept an awe of John for a while, but in his life he would not exercise it; therefore he shakes off John and his word, and cleaves to his lust. Thus the word abides in us by faith, fear, and obedience.

What is meant by continuing in the Son and in the Father? -1. It implies communion between them; a man cannot continue in them without communion with them. -2. It implies perseverance in them forever; thus he who has the word abiding in him, has fellowship with the Son; he has Christ for his Saviour, Brother, King, Priest, and Prophet; and he has God for his Father, an all-sufficient God blessing him with all blessings.

He shall persevere in this state forever.

What are the reasons why such continue in the Son and in the Father?

-1. The intercession of Christ (John 17:20-22), without which we neither could have fellowship with them, nor eternal life. Christ himself has prayed for this, and yet prays, and he is heard always (John 11:42); therefore when he prays that all who believe in his word may be one with him and with the Father, we may know that they shall have union with them, and glory everlasting.

But was not Christ's intercession for himself sometimes not heard? Did he not pray that the cup might pass from him? I answer, -1. He prayed against it, and yet did drink it; but he prayed conditionally, "if it be thy will"; and therefore he had his desire, because he fulfilled God's will (Heb. 5:7). -2. He prayed not so much that he might not taste of it, as that he might not be overwhelmed by it; and so he was supported by his eternal Godhead, so that he was saved in death and from death. Therefore since Christ has prayed for our union with him, and eternal glory, we shall attain it.

-2. The effectual power of sound heavenly doctrine. It is the power of God to salvation; it is the arm of the Lord (John 12:38); it is the glorious ministration of the Spirit (2 Cor. 3:8; 2 Cor. 10:4, 5; Jas. 1:21). This doctrine then is the ministration, the mighty power of God, to convey to us the Spirit of God, which gives us fellowship with the Father and the Son, and eternal life. The breath of the word breathes the Spirit of God into us, and makes us live spiritually here and gloriously hereafter.

Use 1. This may show us what a hard thing it is to persevere and abide in the doctrine of the apostles, as appears from the strong exhortation. One would think that the honesty and purity of the word would prevail with us to abide in their doctrine; but we see that is not enough, but the Holy Spirit uses as strong motives here as any can be. He knows the world might overreach us; some come and tell us that if we continue in the word we shall lose our friends and goods, and maybe our life, and why then should we be so strange? Seeing then that the world makes such a large offer to withdraw us, he therefore gives a far larger offer, such an offer as the world cannot give; he outbids the world, and even promises fellowship with the Father and the Son, and eternal life. Therefore that we might be established against all the subtleties of the world, he offers us promises which will eternally establish us in the truth.

Use 2. This exhorts us to take hold of this doctrine while we have it. If we preach no other doctrine but what has been delivered from the beginning, we have fellowship with the Father and the Son, and eternal glory. Why then, let us cleave to this word, abide in it, receive it with faith and fear, and express it in obedience. "Lord, thou hast the words of eternal life"; therefore where should we go from it? (John 6:68; Prov. 19:16). What encouragement it would be to keep a pill, if the physician should say, Keep this and you keep your life, lose it and you die. Truly such is the word of Christ; keep it and you keep your life, but if you despise the commandment, no matter how you live, you shall certainly die. This is the promise, that if we receive and keep this word, we shall not only keep a long life, but even a life forever and ever. This is more than the world can give; this is an argument that countervails all other arguments.

Use 3. To console all who lose anything by keeping the

apostles' doctrine; whether they lose goods or friends, or life or liberty, here is a comfort that over-balances all discomforts.

Two things chiefly discourage a Christian. He may either lose fellowship with the church and be excommunicate, or else he may lose his natural life. Here is comfort against both. Though you are excommunicated from society with the church, yet you shall keep fellowship with the Father and Son. The blind man gave such a strong testimony to Christ that the Pharisees cast him out (that is, excommunicated him, John 9:34); well, when Christ heard that he was cast out, he found him out. And so, though this poor man was cast out of the church by a wrong excommunication, yet he had fellowship with Christ. Further, Christ came and instructed him, though he was cut short from instruction in the public ordinances; and he never spoke more powerfully and effectually. He gave him faith to believe and grace to worship him. Though in a good cause a man should be cast out of the society of the church, yet he shall find closer communion with Christ.

And likewise a man by professing Christ may be delivered up to the powers, and so lose his life. Why, this is the promise, even eternal life; he may lose a temporary life, but he shall gain an eternal one.

Doct. Primary antiquity is a certain note of divine and apostolic verity.

He says here, "it was from the beginning," and he appeals to the doctrine which was delivered from the beginning of his time, that is, from the first promulgation of the gospel. Thus prime antiquity, that which the apostles first taught, is a note of the truth. "Inquire for the old way," that is, the good way (Jer. 6:16); he complains that they had strayed from the ancient ways, and had gone into by-ways (Jer. 18:15), and he complains of it as if thereby they had forgotten God. Therefore when St. John would describe the gospel, he calls it an everlasting gospel (Rev. 14:6); and when God would confute the people for leaving him, he convicts them of novelty (Deut. 13:6-11); they followed other new gods.

But why is prime antiquity the note of divine and apostolic truth?

-1. Because antiquity is the image of God. Every truth is an image of God; while Satan stood in the truth, he had the image of God. When a doctrine teaches the truth, it comes to the image of the Ancient of days; it is the same truth now that was from the beginning of the world.

-2. Because God takes special care to plant and water the church with pure doctrine. Satan is up early to do mischief, but God is up before him to do good. As soon as God made a world, he made a church, and gave them truth. Though Satan was a liar from the beginning, yet God taught him truth before he was a liar; "the good seed is first sown, and then comes the envious man and sows tares."

-3. Because all errors are aberrations from the way of truth. Therefore there was some way of truth before there was a way of error. When our Saviour would refute the error about divorce, he says, "From the beginning it was not so."

Use 1. This may be a trial between the Popish and Protestant religions. They boast much of antiquity, and claim to fetch it from the apostles' times. But yet if they fetch it from the prime antiquity, from the times of the apostles, yet we will not yield it to them; for John himself would not fetch his antiquity from the latter part of his days, but from the first promulgation of the gospel. Our Saviour says, "It has been said of old," and yet it was not truth (Matt. 5). Error may come as soon as the truth is sown, but yet it does not have prime antiquity, for Satan was a liar from the beginning. For our religion, if we cannot fetch it from the apostles' first doctrine, and from the prophets and apostles of old, we will renounce it; but when we can bring the seal of the prophets and apostles for all our doctrine, we have a sure note of the truth.

Use 2. It confutes the common cavil against professors. They accuse them of newfangledness; they say, "none of your fathers or ancestors walked in this way"; but nonetheless it is the way of Christ and his apostles. Sin is a new way, a new strange thing.

1 John 2:25

"And this is the promise he has promised us, even life eternal."

Doct. Eternal life is given by promise.

Gal. 3:18. Heirs of eternal life are called heirs of promise (Heb. 6:17) because they are heirs of that promise which was made to Abraham (Rom. 4:13, 14).

Why is it given by promise?

-1. Eternal life was granted to Christ and through him to us (Gal. 3:16). Therefore so that eternal life might be by Christ, it is needful that it should be by promise (2 Cor. 1:20).

-2. It is by promise so that it might procure those two great benefits, honor to God and peace to his children. Had we pled it by the law, we would have pled it by debt; but God provided that grace should be free, and therefore by promise.

-3. This gives us peace of conscience. Had we been under the law, every failing would make us doubt; and therefore, that our hearts might be settled, he has given it to us by promise (Rom. 4:16).

Use 1. Here is a strong refutation of Popish merits by the works of the law in their own persons; why, then it is not of grace nor of promise. That is the true reason why they deny certainty of salvation, because they hold it from the works of the law; therefore there is no peace of conscience in their religion. If it is of the works of the law, then not of grace; and if not of grace, then not of promise; if not of promise, then not of Christ. If they are bound to obey the whole law, they cannot be sure they will not break it; if they keep it, yet they know not whether they shall persevere to the end, and so no peace. It is as impossible for a man to attain salvation by works as to be his own savior.

Use 2. Hence learn the way to attain peace of conscience and assurance of salvation. Claim it by promise, and it is sure to you. Do you see corruption and rebellion, and do you see the lack of this and that grace, and therefore are you in doubt? Why, you should claim salvation by promise. That which makes us doubt is a secret cleaving to the works of the law; but we must not look so much at what we do as what we believe, not so much at what we work as at what Christ has wrought for us.

But you will ask, "How shall I know whether I have this faith?" I answer, If God has given you a heart to distrust self and to be humbled and look after Christ; if you prize Christ and desire him above all blessings, this is true faith. If your faith has emptied you of yourself, to go out to Christ as the most sweet and comfortable thing, I say you have that faith which conveys Christ to you, and Christ conveys the promise, and the promise conveys eternal life.

Use 3. This will teach us to magnify the grace of God, who has thus devised a way for our salvation; he therefore has given it to us by grace, that it might be sure.

1 John 2:26

"These things have I written unto you concerning them that deceive you."

To help young Christians beware of antichrist, the apostle had given them some instructions and some means. Now in this verse, and to the end of this second chapter, he discusses the two special means he had prescribed: his writings (v. 26) and their unction (v. 27). Therefore he exhorts them to abide in Christ (vv. 28, 29).

In verse 26 we have: -1. St. John's writing to these babes, and his purpose in it. -2. A description of false teachers, seducers. -3. A description of their act and work.

Doct. There is good use to be made of the scripture against false teachers, even with those who do not lack the unction of the Spirit.

"These things I have written to you," you who have received the spiritual unction; otherwise St. John's writing and their reading would have been in vain. Paul informs the Corinthians of false teachers (2 Cor. 11:13; Gal. 5:12; Phil. 3:2; Col. 2:8). All these places show that the Spirit thought it meet to instruct even Christians against false teachers.

But if their anointing teaches all things, why were the scriptures written? Need a man give light to the sun?

There is a double use of the scriptures.

-1. To confirm the witness of our own conscience. A Christian's heart witnesses against false doctrines, but when the Holy Spirit not only witnesses in our hearts but in his word too, in the mouth of two or three witnesses every truth is established (2 Cor. 13:1).

-2. There is use in them to help our own spirits. Though my spirit rises up against such false teachers, yet I might be deceived; therefore, that I might discern the truth of my own spirit, I must try it by the word. A good man may know what spirit he is of (Luke 9:55) in some things; therefore that we may discern the truth of our own spirits, we must try them by the word.

Use 1. This will teach us the corruption of the spirits of those who say after they have once received the spirit of regeneration, they need not the scriptures. Therefore they neglect reading, as the Enthusiasts and the Anabaptists, who will neither read nor pray except when the Spirit moves them.

To this purpose they abuse a notable place (2 Pet. 1:19). They say we do well to attend to the scriptures until the day dawns and the day-star arises in our hearts, but afterwards there is no further use of them. But "until" is not always a word of restraint; you do well to do it before and after also. When it is said, "Michal had no child till the day of her death," it does not imply that she had any then, but that she never had any. It is a vain conceit to reason in this way. "Give diligence to reading and exhortation till I come" (1 Tim. 4:13); would he have him leave off when he came? No, but he would have him always continue so doing; so then that place rather exhorts them to attend to the scripture continually, even after the day dawns in their hearts, rather than restraining them from it.

Use 2. It exhorts us in these seducing days to be diligent and frequent in reading the scriptures, because they are written to help us against seducers. If a friend should write us to beware of such cheaters, we would give heed to what he wrote; but we have letters sent from far, even from heaven, to warn us of seducers. And our friend sets down their marks and the means by which we may avoid them. Therefore let us be reading his epistles, and let us observe what they direct us to.

Doct. 2. The children of God are to look at false teachers as deceivers (2 John 7; 2 Cor. 11:13; Rom. 16:17, 18).

What is meant by a deceiver?

A deceiver is one who, upon pretense of what is good and true, puts us off with what is counterfeit and naught. These false teachers have deceit in their doctrine (Eph. 4:4) and in their persons (2 Cor. 11:13).

Use 1. This may stir us up so much the more to hate and detest them, and to watch seriously against them. A man hates a deceiver worse than a robber; he would rather lose his purse by violence than be cunningly cheated out of it. The reason is that a man who takes your purse only wrongs you of your money, but the other deprives you of your money and also makes a mock at it. So these deceivers not only deprive us of the truth, but through cunning delusions they overreach us and laugh us to scorn (2 Pet. 2:14).

Therefore let us try all things and hold fast to that which is good (1 Thess. 5:21). If we heard that there were counterfeit money abroad, and cunning fellows who would undermine us, we would look more carefully to ourselves. There are indeed deceivers abroad, who will not only deceive you of your purse and goods, but of your faith, the gospel, and salvation. Therefore how circumspect and careful we ought to be. It is an amazing sluggishness of spirit, when we know there are so many false teachers now in the land, and yet it is a wonder to see how raw we are in the scriptures, how unapt to answer anything out of the scripture if we were put to it. Therefore do not only receive the truth from the credit of your ministers or of your own spirit, but be certain it is warranted from the word, that we may be ready to render a reason of the hope that is in us.

Doct. 3. Sometimes in reproving and confuting false teachers, it is seasonable to conceal their names.

St. John does not say, These things I write to you concerning Cerinthus or Ebion, but he passes by their names and says, "These things I write to you concerning deceivers." In some places they are not described or named (2 Cor. 11:13; 1 Cor. 15:12; Gal. 1:7; Phil. 3:2; Jude 4); yet sometimes he names them (1 Tim. 1:20; 2 Tim. 2:17; 2 Tim. 4:14).

It is seasonable to conceal their names: -1. When there is any hope of their conversion. We should not exasperate them too much, because the contention is not so much against their persons as against their doctrine and practice. -2. When it is good that both they and their doctrine should utterly perish and be forgotten (Gal. 5:12).

It is seasonable to express their names: -1. When they are excommunicated, as Hymeneus and Philetus. -2. That others may beware of them (2 Tim. 4:14, 15).

Use. This may teach us to forbear personal invectives in our writings. A wound in a good man's name is a wound in the apple of his eye. A man who has his eye hurt, sees you not; so if you strike a man on his good name, it is hard for him to hear anything afterward from you.

Doct. 4. The desire and endeavor to deceive, is deceit. Those who have a desire and purpose to deceive are indeed deceivers, though they actually seduce not (2 John 7; Rom. 16:17, 18; 2 Cor. 11:13), as he who lusts after a woman commits adultery (Matt. 5:28). Because a man has a long look in his heart to deceive, he is a deceiver. You read of some who trod under foot the blood of Christ (Heb. 10:29), which is impossible, for Christ is in heaven; yet if a man do what in him lies, it is as if he did it all.

This is true because God accepts the will for the deed, whether in good or evil (2 Cor. 8:12). Therefore it was provided in the law that if any man bore false witness against his neighbor, it should be death, because he would have taken away his neighbor's life if he could. If there is a will to deceive in a man, it is as if he did deceive. The poor woman is said to cast more into the treasury than they all (Luke 21:3, 4), because she had a will to do it, and put herself forth to her utmost ability; so if a man puts himself forth in what he can to deceive, he is yet a deceiver though he never reaches it. Though it is impossible the elect should be seduced (Matt. 24:24), yet it is his desire and endeavor to do it, for God has communicated to men more will and desire many times than power to accomplish; therefore if there is a will to it, the hindrance is not on man's part but on God's.

Use 1. This will teach men to make as much conscience of their wills and desires, as of their acts. Men are apt to excuse themselves in respect to the will, if the act is not done; but did you desire it and go about it? If you had a mind to do it, then it is as done, because God sees what is in your heart. There was the desire of your soul and the endeavor of your hand; that it did not come to pass is from God.

Use 2. This will be a sweet comfort to God's servants who cannot do the good which they would. They have a mind to profit by the word, to read and pray as they ought, but they cannot. I say, if there is a willing mind, if the desire of your soul is toward God, if your endeavor is to do it, it is certainly done, though you cannot now reach it. Abraham spared his son, true; but that was because God held his hand (Gen. 22:12). Because he went three days' journey, and came to the place

God had appointed, and built an altar and bound him, and would have slain him — though he spared him when God called from heaven, yet God accounts it as if he did it. So if a man had many corruptions in his heart, yet if he uses all means to mortify and crucify them, yet if he cannot get the victory over them as he desires, yet God accounts it as if they were mortified. When David had a mind to build a temple to God and prepared abundantly for it, though God forbade him, yet he says it was well that it was in his heart, and therefore God will build him a house (2 Sam. 7:11). He accepted the will for the deed.

But then may we easily flatter ourselves and say, I desire that my soul and all mine might do well? I answer, if a man has a willing mind to do a thing, it will much comfort him if he does it, and it will grieve him if he cannot perform it. You say you would have yourself and all yours do well; but is it your greatest grief that you cannot effect this, and would it be your greatest comfort if you could? Then God accepts your desire. But if a man has only lazy desires, so that if it goes well, well and good; but if not, he is not much troubled; then there was no right desire.

1 John 2:27

"But the anointing which you have received from him abides in you, and you need not that any man should teach you. But as the same anointing teaches you of all things, and is truth, and is no lie; and even as it has taught you, you shall abide in him."

Doct. Every child of God, even the least and meanest, has received the unction of the Spirit.

We heard of this before in v. 20. But something is to be considered in the varying of the words. In that verse he said they had it; here he says they have received it of him.

Doct. The children of God receive the Spirit from the Father and from Christ (John 14:16, 17; John 16:13).

God's sending and our receiving are related (2 Cor. 1: 21, 22). God's giving and our taking mutually agree to one another; sometimes God the Father is said to send the Spirit, and sometimes God the Son. It is God who sends it, but Christ has prayed that he would send it (John 14:16, 17); and by his death and ascension he has purchased and procured the Spirit for us (Acts 2:32, 33).

The reasons why we must receive this unction from God and from Christ are:

-1. What we have by nature is a spirit of error and falsehood and corruption. We have no unction from the first Adam, no spirit that heals and softens and cheers us; we have no spirit to anoint us, but rather it besmears us and daubs us with base lusts. Therefore if we have any spirit of grace, it is needful that we should receive it from the second Adam.

-2. We receive it from the Father, because by Christ we are made sons, and therefore we need the spirit of sons (Gal. 4:4-6). All of us are like Christ his eldest Son. God's Spirit is the mark by which he owns us; it is the earnest we have (Rom. 8:14), that we might be comforted; and therefore he is called the Comforter (John 16:7). An earnest penny is part of the payment, of the same nature with the whole; this Spirit is part of the payment which we shall then receive in abundance, though now in a small measure. We now have little love and faith, etc., but he will make perfect love, perfect knowledge, and perfect strength.

-3. That Christ should give it is shown from his death, by which he has purchased it (Gal. 3:13, 14). By his ascension he shed abroad his Spirit in our hearts. As Elijah was ascending into heaven, he spread his mantle upon Elisha, who was thereby clothed with a double spirit; so when Christ ascended into heaven, he spread abroad his mantle as it were, his Spirit, by whom every Christian is clothed with the Spirit of Christ, with the Spirit of gladness and holiness.

Use 1. This shows the wonderful love of God, even to the least and meanest of his servants. He not only gives us his

Son to be our Redeemer, but his Spirit to be our Sanctifier, so large is his bounty. No wonder then that he gives us health and peace and friends and means and maintenance, for if he gives us his Son and his Spirit, will he deny us lesser things?

Use 2. This teaches God's children not to be proud of any spiritual gift that God gives us (1 Cor. 4:6, 7). If all we have we have received, what have we to boast? And let us not insult others, for they may receive the spirit of unction as well as we; Paul did, though he was a persecutor. Much less should we despise weaker Christians than ourselves; what if they have received but a little measure of faith and love and patience? That little is so much that it seals them up to eternal happiness; they have received so much that they are invested with the garment of Christ. Therefore let there be no striving or contention or contempt among brethren, since all have received this unction.

Use 3. Have you received the Spirit? Then walk in him, rooted and established in him (Col. 2:6, 7). Why have you received him if not that you may pray and preach, and buy and sell in this Spirit? Therefore let everyone so walk that he may express that he has received the Spirit of God (Gal. 5:25). Put forth the life of the Spirit in every employment.

Doct. 2. The Spirit which the children of God have received from him, dwells in them forever.

It is an indwelling and abiding Spirit (John 14:16, 17; 1 Cor. 3:16; 1 Cor. 6:19; Eph. 2:20-22). The Spirit of God builds a tabernacle in you and dwells in you.

-1. The Spirit is said to abide in us because, since it has knit us to Jesus Christ, we have become his flesh and bone. Now it is both a dishonor and unseemly for Christ to have any lifeless dead members; therefore that God might make us serviceable unto him, he continues his Spirit to us so that he may enliven us.

-2. The same reason that moves God to give his Spirit in our conversion will also move him to continue it to us. We have as much need to be like God in our whole course as at first, and we have as much need of assurance of glory. The same God who begins the work will also continue it to us (Phil. 1:6).

Use 1. Here is a ground of trial of our states. If we have no spirit but the spirit of the old Adam, the spirit of pride and malice and covetousness, truly this is not the Spirit of Christ which Christ purchased for us by his death and ascension. But suppose we had some of the Spirit of God, the spirit of wisdom as Ahithophel, the spirit of joy as Herod, the spirit of zeal as Jehu, the spirit of fear as Felix had, yet we have not this unction of the Spirit unless it dwells in us.

But some may say, Alas, what then will become of me? It may be now I can pray, but ere night I am wholly unable; I am now enlarged, now straitened; I have now a spirit of zeal and courage, but soon all is cold and weak and dead. So David said he had made the word his delight (Ps. 119:24), but yet he said his soul cleaves to the dust (v. 25), and prays to God for quickening.

I answer, though this Spirit is said to abide, yet he does not always abide in the same measure, nor in the same measure of expression. But though there are several garments, yet the soul is never naked. A man does not always have his holyday garments sweetly perfumed, but sometimes homely, mean garments; so Elijah was clothed with zeal when he slew Baal's prophets, yet afterwards he remitted of it. But yet he had the Spirit of God on him; he was not naked, though he was not clothed with the Spirit in such a measure. Even so sometimes we have even poor ragged homely garments, and much of our nakedness appears; and sometimes again when God has greater business for us to do, he clothes us with better, richer garments, a greater measure of the Spirit. But though we have not the same measure, yet always some garment of the Spirit rests on us; we are not left naked.

Use 2. This may exhort us, if we have this Spirit dwelling in us, to use him honorably and courteously as an indweller. He has come from far, even from heaven, from our Father, and he brings joy and comfort with him; therefore let us give him honorable entertainment. He is sent to guide us in all our ways, to be a pledge of our eternal inheritance. He came not for a day, but to dwell with us forever (John 14:16). Therefore take heed of grieving him (Eph. 4:30); he comes for your good and benefit, for your redemption.

How shall we keep ourselves from grieving the Spirit? -1. God has given him to guide you; therefore look that you are guided by him. If you entertain him kindly he will comfort you, but if you grieve him he will grieve your spirit. -2. Be careful to nourish him. Do not starve this guest; neglect not the word and ordinances, which are the food of the Spirit. "Quench not the Spirit, despise not prophecy" (1 Thess. 5: 19, 20); as if the despising of prophecy were the quenching of the Spirit. Therefore feed the Spirit of God; do not withdraw food from it, do not prefer outward things before it. -3. Take heed especially of living in any known sin, for that dampens and deadens the Spirit. Therefore David woefully complains, "Restore unto me the joy of thy salvation" (Ps. 51:8-12), as if it were quite gone; his very bones were broken, not of his body, but of his soul (i.e., the strength and staff of his spirit). The Spirit is like fire; every gross sin is like water cast upon it; it quenches it.

Use 3. Here is a ground of much consolation to God's servants. You can never say you dwell alone and lack company; you cannot lack good company if the Holy Spirit dwells in you. Christ says, "I am not alone, but the Father is with me"; so a Christian may say, I am never alone, for the Spirit of God dwells in me. He is an indwelling and abiding Spirit.

Doct. 3. The anointing of the Spirit teaches us all things.

It teaches all things needful to salvation, needful to life and godliness (2 Pet. 1:3), and needful to our places, callings, and ages. We have heard of this more fully before (v. 20).

Doct. 4. The anointing of the Spirit is so plentiful and sufficient that we need not be taught better things, nor in a better manner, than the Spirit teaches.

Jer. 31:32. Not that we do not need magistrates or ministers, but he speaks comparatively: "you shall not be helped as much by any instructions without the Spirit, as with the Spirit"; the Spirit shall declare the truth in Jesus.

-1. The Holy Spirit teaches fully (1 Cor. 3:9-11). The spirit of a Christian is inquisitive concerning all things, and the Spirit helps him to search even into the deep things of God.

-2. The instruction of the Spirit is plain and clear (1 Tim. 4:1; John 16:25). Christ spoke in parables, but after his ascension the Spirit revealed things clearly.

Three things form a clear discerning: the object must be clear, the medium clear, and the eye clear. Now the Holy Spirit plainly reveals the counsels of God, and then opens our judgments to discern it, and then clears all the mediums, so that a Christian may plainly discern.

-3. The instruction of the Spirit is a certain instruction. There is hardly any truth which a Christian cannot tell by experience. A woman who is with child feels such qualms and distempers that she knows she is with child; so they who have had the Spirit in their hearts and have perceived his motions, they know more clearly than any other.

-4. The Spirit teaches us most profitably; for such is the dexterity of the Spirit that he tells you what use you are to make of such a scripture, such a sermon, such a providence, such an affliction. "I am the holy one of Israel, who teach you to profit" (Isa. 48:17). Let the minister speak ever so powerfully and plainly, yet the heart of man cannot discern it and profit by it unless the Spirit strikes in with it.

Use 1. This reveals the vanity of the Popish doctrine which would not have men trust their own spirit, but follow the judgment of the church. This is a poor instruction; what if the spirit of the church becomes apostate? What has become of all the famous churches of Asia and Greece? Have they not warped from the truth? Therefore if men would follow the spirit of the church, they might fall from the truth. But you see how St. John magnifies the instruction of the

Spirit; you need not that anyone teach you otherwise than the Spirit within you witnesses.

But may not a man's spirit be a delusion; must we trust every private spirit? I answer, though it may be in a private man, yet it is not a private spirit, but the same spirit common to the whole body of Christ. His Spirit is not limited to public persons or ministers, but goes to all the members of Christ. So though it is in a private man, it is a public spirit; the Spirit breathes where it lists, and wherever it breathes, none need teach more or better.

Use 2. If God's Spirit is so sufficient, then let us make use of the Spirit to discern falsehood and to know the truth. Let us not rest in what ministers or parents or masters teach, but what the Spirit teaches; one day's instruction of the Spirit will lead you into more knowledge than a hundred sermons.

Use 3. Look that you keep the Spirit in good order. If you grieve the Spirit, he has no comfort to teach you. Parents or masters take no delight in teaching their children or servants when they take no heed to what they teach them; but if the Spirit sees you willing to hear and listen, he teaches you with delight. If you grieve God's Spirit by sensual lusts, the Spirit will be so discouraged that you shall find his instruction very thin and weak; and if he sees you do not intend to make use of what he teaches, he will have little delight to teach you.

Use 4. This reproves them who will content themselves in ignorance by saying that they are not book-learned, and therefore not much is expected from them. If you give your spirit up to God's, his Spirit will teach you all things; he will teach you without book as much as shall be needful for you.

Doct. 5. The Spirit of God in the hearts of his servants is not a spirit of delusion, but of truth.

They might say, "Every man will boast of his own spirit; we know there are many lying spirits abroad; how shall we know we have the true Spirit?" Why, he says it is not a lying spirit, but a true; and so our Saviour calls it a Spirit of Truth (John 16:13; John 14:16, 17).

-1. It is a true Spirit because it makes us true men, whereas by nature we are full of falsehood and lies (Rom. 3:13).

-2. It reveals the truth of God in a true manner; it teaches such things as agree with the scripture, the word of truth.

-3. It is given by the God of truth, and therefore must needs be true.

-4. Because it teaches nothing but what it receives from Christ, and Christ teaches nothing but what comes from the Father, the God of truth (John 12:49, 50); therefore it must be true.

But you will say, How yhall I know that my spirit is not a spirit of error and delusion? There was a lying spirit among Ahab's prophets (1 Kings 22:22-24), and he cunningly conveyed himself as an angel of light; how shall a child of God discern the true spirit from a spirit of delusion? I answer, they who have received a spirit of error may be deluded by a spirit of error; but they who have received the Spirit of truth cannot be deluded by a spirit of error.

But how shall we know that we are not deluded, and that our spirit is a spirit of truth?

-1. By the testimony of this spirit. There is such a clear light in the Spirit that he will reveal himself plainly enough (1 John 5:3).

-2. You shall find that the Spirit of God is ever suitable to the Word of God; that spirit which teaches you other things than the word, or withdraws you from the word, that spirit is a delusion. The word begat us, and a Christian loves to be sucking at it.

-3. It is a spirit of truth if it makes you conformable to Christ, meek and lowly as he was, going about doing good as he did. That is the proper work of the Spirit, to make us holy as he is holy, meek as he is meek, pure as he is pure.

-4. We may discern the Spirit by his fruits. A tree is known by the fruit; good fruit comes not from a corrupt spirit. Any corrupt spirit so confounds and troubles the spirits of men that they cannot bring forth good fruit. But the Holy Spirit is so meek and plain that it does not disturb nature, but perfect it. On the contrary, a bad spirit does not perfect but corrupts nature (Gal. 5:19-23). It is a sign an evil spirit was upon Zedekiah, that he was so boisterous and rude and impatient (1 Kings 22:24); but God's spirit is meek and humble and lowly.

Use 1. This teaches us to see the excellency of a Christian above other men (Prov. 12:10). The way of a Christian is the way of truth and goodness, but the ways of the wicked are deceitful, and will certainly seduce us; but a Christian has fellowship with the Spirit of truth.

Use 2. It must therefore stir men up to labor to be partakers of this excellent spirit, this Spirit of truth. The way of righteousness will not deceive us. Many times by following the Spirit we run into dangerous ways; the way of truth is a straight narrow way, but it is a safe way. Keep your way, and it will keep you.

Use 3. This is a ground of comfort to all who have received this Spirit; it will not deceive you. If God's Spirit were not in you, you were of all men most miserable; but we have a Spirit that will not fail us. Polycarp said, "These eighty-six years I have served Christ, and he never deceived me; therefore I will not leave him."

Doct. 6. The anointing of God's Spirit teaches us our perseverance in Christ, i.e. assures us that we shall abide in him.

"The Spirit bears witness with our spirits" (Rom. 8:16, 17). Two Spirits bear witness, God's and ours, and both co-witness our adoption. Our spirit is our renewed, regenerate spirit; for God's Spirit would not join with our corrupt spirit, but with our renewed spirit, and this makes us become the sons of God. Besides this renewed spirit of ours,

God's Spirit itself witnesses. The other indeed was the fruit and effect of God's Spirit, but God's Spirit itself is a lively and comfortable witness, which speaks more clearly and fully than the created graces of God in us.

-1. This peace that God's Spirit immediately pours into the heart is without understanding (Phil. 4:7); and the witness which God's Spirit gives to our hearts, makes us never to doubt it as formerly.

-2. It works in us joy unspeakable and full of glory (1 Pet. 1:8). There is such a witness as fills our hearts with glorious consolation (Rom. 14:17), and this fills our souls so that we taste the firstfruits of heaven. "In his light we see light" (Ps. 36:9).

-3. Sometimes when we are preparing for some great trial, then God sends some more special help of his Spirit. It was thus with our Saviour when he was to be tempted forty days; immediately before he had a testimony from heaven, "Thou art my beloved son." So when God has any great temptation for us, he pours down more enlargement and comfort of the Spirit. When Christ came to be crucified, he was a little before gloriously transfigured; and when he came riding to Jerusalem, exulting and rejoicing, he went to be crucified. Often in the midst of tribulation (Rom. 5:3) and often after afflictions and conflicts, God comes to comfort us with happy enlargements (1 Pet. 4:14); not only a spirit of grace but a spirit of glory, as on Stephen (Acts 7:60).

The Spirit in scripture is given three names, all of which witness this truth.

-1. He is called the Comforter (John 14:16, 17), especially because he comforts our hearts by assuring us that we are sons and daughters of God, and heirs of life. Else his comfort were not above the world, for the world can comfort us in temporal things; but here is a comforter who far transcends the world.

-2. The Spirit is called the seal and earnest of our inheritance (Eph. 1:13, 14; Eph. 4:30; 2 Cor. 1:21, 22). Now a seal has a threefold use: (a) It has a use to keep secret or to distinguish. (b) Not only so, but to confirm us in all leases, bonds, covenants; so the Spirit not only keeps us sure and distinguishes us from all hypocrites, but seals us by confirming the happiness of our present and future state. (c) On the seals of princes their person is portrayed. So this Spirit is the very character of God's image, and it fashions us after the image of God.

-3. He is called an earnest. Now an earnest has three uses: (a) It binds and assures a man. (b) An earnest is part of the payment, though small in regard to the whole; so the Spirit of grace is part of the payment, and shall remain with us until the full payment. (c) It abides with us after the whole payment.

Use. This may serve to comfort the hearts of all who have received the unction of the Spirit. They have an assurance of their state of grace here and glory hereafter.

But then how does it come to pass that so many Christians are troubled? There is a double reason.

    a. Sometimes by imaginary causes, when there is no such cause. (i) Desertion. We think we have quenched and grieved the Spirit, and therefore it has left us. Indeed God does not assure us that the Spirit shall abide with us in a full and glorious measure, but yet we may know that some fruits of it shall remain. (ii) Sometimes outward crosses and afflictions make us doubt, as David (Ps. 73:13). (iii) Sometimes melancholy may so distemper us that we will hardly be persuaded of that which we have no reason to doubt.

    b. There are some real causes. (i) Any known sin, which breaks the very bones (Ps. 51:8) and deprives us of the vigor of the Spirit. (ii) The high prizing of earthly contentments, and exceeding delight in them, which much benumbs and dims the light of the Spirit. When a man so prizes this pearl, he keeps it with him in comfort (Matt. 13:44-46). (iii) The proud frame of our spirit hinders our peace. We are all naturally of proud lofty spirits, and if God does not see us humble and meek, his Spirit will not so easily converse with us (Isa. 57:15). (iv) Suspending our peace upon our own performances is a great impediment, because then we cannot pray so enlargedly, nor hear so profitably as we have sometimes done; but we deceive ourselves, because we do not look for peace and justification from grace but from the works of the law (Rom. 5:1). By these means we grieve the Spirit, blur the seal, and dim and dull our peace and comfort.

1 John 2:28

"And now, little children, abide in him, that when he shall appear, we may have confidence and not be ashamed before him at his coming."

The apostle had written to different ages and given different instructions. Now in this verse he turns his speech to all Christians in general, for here it is τεκνία, "little children," and not παιδία, "babes"; and he promises that they should abide in him.

There are two parts: an exhortation to all to abide in Christ, and a reason or encouragement taken from the benefit that shall arise.

Doct. 1. The promise of perseverance in the state of grace does not open a gap to carnal liberty, but rather gives us cause of encouragement to abide in Christ.

He had promised that they should abide in him; now he does not say, Therefore take your ease, take no care, for you are safe. No, but he says, Abide in Christ. In other places of scripture, when the clearest promises of grace and perseverance are laid down, there is exhortation to careful obedience. Though you cannot fall finally, yet "let him that standeth take heed lest he fall" (1 Cor. 10:12, 13; Phil. 2:12, 13); not a carnal fear, but such a fear as is opposed to carnal confidence and pride. Paul triumphed in his good state (Rom. 8:35-39); but did this make him carnally secure? No, he is now more vigilant and careful than before (1 Cor. 9:26, 27). Confidence breeds not negligence but rather diligence; the more assurance he had, the more vigilant he was. So you, little children, even now you have a promise to abide in Christ; therefore abide in him.

-1. This will nourish those graces by which we cleave most to Christ. Faith feeds on these promises; as it is bred by them, so it is nourished by them. Now the more faith you have, the more you purify your heart (Acts 15:9). No promise promises perseverance to us in our own strength, but all are made in Christ, and therefore they make a Christian cleave closer to Christ.

-2. These promises breed hope in us, and this hope makes us purify ourselves, as Christ is pure (1 John 3:1-3). A maid who knows she shall be married such a day, will it make her the less careful to adorn herself? No surely; so those who hope to meet the bridegroom at the last day, do they go and soil and defile themselves with base lusts? No, they adorn and beautify their souls the more. Those maids who were to go in to King Ahasuerus spent twelve months in purifying themselves (Esther 2:12).

-3. These promises increase love in us. The more beautiful God is in his promises, the more the love of Christ constrains us.

Use 1. To confute Popish spirits, who say the doctrine of perseverance breeds security. They say, why do you press people to abide in Christ when they can do no other? It is true, if these new promises were put into old bottles, they would breed security in us; but a spirit who is taught to believe in Christ is made the more watchful by it (1 Cor. 15:58).

Use 2. This may stir all up to abide in Christ, and for that end to make use of the promises (Ps. 116:9-12). Since God has freed your soul from darkness and ignorance and bondage, why, walk holily therefore in the sight of the Lord. There are none more dissolute and careless than those who are uncertain of their salvation.

Doct. 2. It is the duty of all Christians to abide in Christ.
-1. "If you abide in me, you shall bring forth much fruit"

(John 15:5); no Christian can bring forth any fruit without Christ.

-2. If you abide in him, it keeps you from sin (1 John 3:6).

-3. Abiding in Christ is the means to have our petitions heard (John 15:7).

-4. Abide in Christ, and you abide in eternal life (John 15:14, 15).

How may we abide in Christ? -1. If his word abides in us, Christ abides in us (1 John 2:24; 2 Chron. 25:16). -2. All your strength depends on Christ; therefore live in his grace. -3. Be fruitful in Christ; make use of him to grow in grace. -4. If at any time you turn from him, return to him speedily, so that by repentance you may renew your covenant (Jer. 3:1).

Use. To reprove the apostasy that is sometimes found in professors. Though many dead branches are cut off, yet the vine is perfect and has living branches. Some are members, some only imperfect, and some adhere to Christ only by external graces, as Judas and Jehu. These may be cut off, and we see how woeful their case is; they wither and are cut down (John 15:6) and are cast into the fire. They have committed two evils (Jer. 2:13); it had been better that they had never tasted of Christ or known him (Jer. 18:14-16).

Doct. 3. Those who abide in Christ, do with boldness expect and without shame receive him at his coming.

This is plain in the text. The reasons are:

-1. From the causes. What makes men afraid of his coming? Either knowing it shall go ill with them, or not knowing it shall go well with them. The cardinal said he would rather have his part in Paris than his part in Paradise; the one he was certain of, the other uncertain. But those who abide in Christ know that it shall be well with them at that day (Ps. 23:3-5). Why is Paul bold? Because he knows he shall receive a crown of righteousness at his appearing (2 Tim. 4:7, 8).

-2. From the effects of their confidence.

a. They love the appearing of Christ; since it is

therefore manifest, they look for it with confidence (2 Tim. 4:8).

b. As they love Christ's appearing, so they pray for it (Cant. 8:14), and therefore it is a sign that they expect it with confidence (Rev. 22:20). Did you ever know any malefactor write to the judge to hasten his coming to trial? No, but they would rather prevent his coming; if they hasten his coming, they are confident it shall go well with them, and at his coming they are confident of being freed. Many afflictions and vexations lie on God's children as so many bolts; therefore they desire the Lord to hasten his coming, to rid them of all their misery and revenge them of their enemies.

c. As they are confident, so they are not ashamed. They profess his name here without shame, and therefore Christ will not be ashamed of them at that day.

Use 1. This reproves and refutes a Popish doctrine of uncertainty of salvation; how could Christians love and pray for Christ's coming if they did not know it would be well with them at that day? This love and desire shows that they are confident of their good state.

Use 2. To try whether or not you abide in Christ. See how you seek the coming of Christ; are you bold and confident at the mention of the last day? Are you reverently bold, and do you love and pray for his coming? This is a sign that you abide in Christ. But if hearing of it strikes terror into you, and you would gladly put it off, surely you are not in Christ. The day of judgment is a day of marriage to the godly, and therefore the spouse longs for it; but to the wicked it is a day of execution, and therefore they tremble at the thought and hearing of it.

But how does it come to pass that many a godly soul fears and trembles at death? Were not Hezekiah and David afraid of it? (Ps. 30:9) God's children may be afraid to die in two cases: -1. When they have loosely and negligently laid up the evidences of their states. If a man who goes to court has no case for himself, he desires the trial to be put off. -2. When they know they have lived somewhat loosely, and their hearts have run awhoring from God by some carnal delights. Such a man would fain gather himself up better before death. So David was in some grievous disease, and was conscious that his spirit was not perfect; therefore he prays, "O spare me a little, that I may recover myself before I go hence and be no more seen" (Ps. 39:13).

But both these fears differ from wicked men's fear. Wicked men tremble because they have no evidence at all; but a godly man knows he has evidences, yet he has them not so ready, and therefore he desires to be deferred.

Use 3. This may stir us all up. If we desire to live comfortably and die gloriously, we should be careful to abide in Christ, for otherwise we will die both with fear and shame. But if we abide in Christ, we may with boldness look death in the face. Therefore abide not in your natural state, civil honesty, but abide in Christ.

Use 4. It is a profane saying of some, that religion makes men cowards and never famous warriors. Does that make us cowards which makes us look death in the face, and judgment also? Were those cowards who have looked fire and fagot and torments in the face? Therefore it is not religion, but lack of religion, that makes men cowards.

1 John 2:29

"If you know that he is righteous, you know that everyone who does righteousness is born of him."

In the former verse he had exhorted all to abide in Christ, and that from an argument of their boldness and confidence at the day of death and judgment. Now in this verse he proves that such may have boldness. They that are born of God are children of God, and may lift up their heads with joy at his coming; a child is not afraid but glad at his father's coming. But how do they know they are born of God? Why, they that do righteousness are born of God, but those that abide in Christ do righteousness. How does that appear? If Christ is righteous, it is evident that such as do righteousness are born of God.

Doct. 1. Jesus Christ is righteous.

This is clearly set forth in scripture (Isa. 53:11; Matt. 27:19, 24; Acts 22:14; 1 Pet. 3:18). But what are the reasons why he is righteous?

-1. He is righteous because of his sinless conception and birth; he was not begotten as other men, but the Holy Spirit overshadowed the virgin.

-2. Because of his innocent life. He fulfilled all righteousness (Matt. 3:15; Heb. 4:15). Satan could find no sin in him to take advantage of (John 14:30).

-3. Because of the necessary effects of his righteousness. He must be righteous: (a) To overcome the sorrows of death. One sin would have kept him under death (Acts 2:24, 25), but by his innocence he overcame death. (b) That he might be a holy High Priest to us and a perfect Sacrifice for us (Heb. 7:26, 27). Had he not been innocent and harmless, he could not have been so. The priests in the law were to be without blemish (Lev. 21:1-7) to show that the great High Priest should be so. Likewise the offering was to be without blemish (Lev. 22:19), and therefore it is requisite that Christ should be so (Heb. 9:4). (c) It was needful that he should be righteous, because his righteousness is to be imputed to us for righteousness. (d) That he might work inherent righteousness in us, so that we might do righteousness. Had Christ been blemished in one sin, he could not have begotten us righteous to God.

What is it to be righteous? Holiness gives God his due; righteousness gives man his due. But when righteousness is put alone, it implies giving due both to God and man. So Christ gave to Caesar what was his due, to the Pharisees their due, and to everyone his due.

Use 1. This is a wonderful ground of consolation to every poor soul who is burdened with a sense of his own unrighteousness. Though we are unrighteous, yet Christ is righteous, and what is lacking on our part is supplied on his. Elihu gives this comfort to a man in extremity of body and soul (Job 33:23), to declare where his righteousness is found. That is, it is not to be found in himself; God will say of such a soul, Deliver his soul from going into the pit, for I have received a ransom. Though we have cause to utter the complaint of Isa. 64:6, yet if we know Christ is innocent and pure and holy, why then his righteousness is imputed to us. So every soul that is conscious of his own unworthiness will say, as the good thief, "Do you not fear God?" (Luke 23:40) If a man fears before God and trembles at his wrath, Christ will say as he did to the good thief, This day you will be in Paradise, or at least have right to it.

But you will say, Christ is indeed righteous, but what is that to me? Do all wicked men receive righteousness from him? Alas, I have nothing to move God to impute his righteousness to me! I answer, if you can but find this in your heart, that you fear God because of your sins and are humbled — why then if Christ is righteous, you need not fear his coming; for his righteousness shall veil your unrighteousness, and your state shall be happy.

But was not Judas afraid of the horrors of hell, when he had betrayed Christ? Did he not fear sin, and was it not a terror to his soul? Judas was indeed afraid of that sin, but he was not afraid of all sin, for then he would have been as much afraid of taking his own life as of taking his Master's. He feared the horror of that sin, but not of all sin. But take a man fearing God for all sin, and fearing other men's sins, as the good thief, and looking at Christ's righteousness; this surmounts all danger at death, and we may expect death and judgment with comfort and joy.

Use 2. It is a ground of comfort likewise to those who have found comfort heretofore in the righteousness of Christ, but who now doubt of their state. Why? Though you fail in many things, yet look up to Christ He is pure and righteous; and so being clothed with his righteousness, we may lift up our heads with comfort. This Paul comforted himself in, that he counted all dross and dung in respect of the righteousness of Christ (Phil. 3:7-9).

Doct. 2. Those who work righteousness are born of Christ (1 John 3:10).

This is manifest from four reasons.

-1. From the weakness and impotence of nature to bring forth a righteous work (Rom. 8:3, 4; Rom. 7:18; Rom. 3:10, 12). All of the famous heroes among the heathen were but splendid sinners. God's people had corrupted themselves, and the Spirit of God was not upon them (Deut. 32:32, 33). Their sweetest works were like the grapes of Sodom and Gomorrah, which are fair to the eye, but if touched vanish away; there is a fair outside, but no nourishment. None are so opposed to Christ as men of best natural abilities (Acts 17:32; Acts 13:50; Rom. 11:17, 20; Phil. 3:6). Though Paul was clean in his own and others' eyes, yet he persecuted the church of God; there is no power of nature which can reach to a supernatural work (Rom. 6:16-20).

-2. From the impotence and weakness of common graces (Matt. 12:33; Heb. 9:14). Until Christ's blood has sprinkled our consciences, all our works are but dead works. Every work that is spiritual must spring from faith (Gal. 3:14; Rom. 14:23), and its end must be the glory of God (2 Cor. 10:17). Nature never works higher than its own glory. Let Saul prophesy, let Jehu set upon reformation with great zeal, let Herod hear John the Baptist gladly; yet all these detain the truth in unrighteousness.

-3. From the fact that abiding in Christ is necessary to perform every good duty (John 15:5). He does not say, "Without me you can do no great matter," but, "Without me you can do nothing."

-4. From the resemblance between Christ and the workers of righteousness. There is such a resemblance between them as between father and son (1 John 3:2). We are the seed of Christ, and are made like him; a child is known to be born of such a man by its look, speech, and manner (Isa. 9:6).

How are we said to be born of Christ? Though he is our elder brother, yet he is sometimes called our Father. We are born of his seed, his word and Spirit, and we resemble Christ as well as the Father (Rom. 8:29).

Use 1. This reproves the doctrine of the Jesuits and Franciscans, who hold that by strength of common graces a man may receive justifying grace when it is offered. A man must be born of God if he will do so good a work; it is therefore a doctrine contrary to the word of God.

Use 2. Those who are in a state of nature or common grace should not rest there.

Use 3. Those who are born of God should make use of their new birth. Walk in the life of the new birth, or else you do nothing (Gal. 2:20). We must do all out of the strength of the new birth. If the sun should shine into our houses, and if we shut up all the doors and windows to keep it in, we shut it out; so we must keep the windows of our hearts open to Christ.

Use 4. Have respect to works of righteousness.

Doct. 3. They who know that Christ is righteous, they know also that everyone who does righteousness is born of God, a child of God.

What is it to know Christ to be righteous? It does not consist in understanding it, conceiving it, and acknowledging it, for Pharaoh could say, "The Lord is righteous" (Exod. 9:27), and yet he could not come to say that God's people were righteous and born of God. Certainly the centurion said that Christ was a righteous man (Luke 23:47); and yet we do not read that he joined himself to the disciples of Christ. Therefore to know that Christ is righteous, is to acknowledge him by divine faith; and those who do thus do know that he who does righteousness is born of God.

Three things are implied in this.

-1. No man knows Christ to be righteous but he who is sensible of his own unrighteousness. Before his calling Paul thought himself righteous and unblameable; but when he saw that Christ was righteous, he saw that he himself was unrighteous (Phil. 3:6-8); therefore he thought all his own righteousness loss in respect to Christ's. His education, his profession, his wisdom, his zeal, his privileges, he counted all loss to win Christ.

-2. It implies a sensible experience of the righteousness of Christ, pacifying our consciences and purging them from dead works; for Christ's righteousness does both. None know Christ to be righteous but those who know that by his righteousness they have their consciences quieted and purified. They are free from the guilt and uncleanness of an evil conscience; they know that they are such grievous sinners that if Christ were not righteous, they could never look for pardon.

-3. They find the power of Christ's righteousness purging their consciences from dead works (Heb. 9:14). All our works before were dead, but now by the blood of Christ we are purged from them and quickened to do him living service. Though a man may have a good opinion that Christ was a good man, and that he was both God and man, yet none know it but those who have provoked God so woefully that if Christ their mediator were not righteous, they could have no hope of pardon or mortification. Only these know it certainly by experience in their own souls.

But how do these know that they work the righteousness of God?

-1. They know him by experience of their own spirits. They know themselves that they have never wrought a work of righteousness until they were born of Christ. All their works before were for the world or for self-love; therefore if they find a man denying himself, not looking at his own ends, going out of himself, not relying upon himself nor aiming at his own ends, they know such a one to be born of God, or else he could not do so. Not one natural man comes off with a good work (Rom. 3:10, 12).

-2. They know it from the life of Christ which breathes and works in every work of righteousness; they know their own spirits would not reach it.

Why is our conversion called a new birth? In itself it is only an alteration in qualities, not in substance; but it is called a new birth or regeneration, for two reasons.

-1. Because it changes the whole man. In generation there is a whole change from one thing to another; so in regeneration there is an alteration of the whole old man into the whole new man; a new heart, new judgments, new affections.

-2. It is the mighty power of God. In regeneration there is more than any work of parents; it could not be without a special concurrence of God's mighty power. So in conversion there must not only be a change of some qualities, but a mighty power in changing us wholly from our old state to a new.

Use 1. This reveals the fond pagan ignorance of those who do not know that they who do righteousness are born of God. We should account him who denies Christ to be righteous, to be no Christian but a very pagan; and if you do not know that they who do righteousness are born of God, you do not know that Christ is righteous. Therefore this shows the great error of those who malign God's servants; for surely if they knew that they were the children of God, they would not oppose them or injure them. And if they do not know that, they do not know that Christ is righteous. They cast them out in pretense of God's glory (Isa. 66:5), but they shall know that they are born of God, and they shall be ashamed that they did not know it before.

Use 2. This may serve as a ground of trial. Do you know that they who work righteousness are born of Christ? Many a poor soul can testify it of others, though he will not say it of himself; but you could not have known that others were born of Christ unless you had known it yourself. Therefore let it comfort you.

But may not a carnal man see plainly by common illumination that such are God's servants? Is there not a broad difference between them and others? True; and so far as they know that Christ is righteous, so far may they know that those who work righteousness are born of Christ. But these have no true knowledge that Christ is righteous, but only an opinion; and they may afterward doubt of this opinion. But if you know it, then you see it by experience of his righteousness pacifying your conscience and purging it from dead works. If you do not know experimentally that Christ is righteous, you cannot know experimentally that they who do righteousness are born of God.

Use 3. Here is a notable encouragement to all who are born of God, to work righteousness. If you work righteousness, every righteous man shall know that you are born of God, and shall testify it of you; not that I would have men practice righteousness for their credit.

But may not a man do many works of righteousness, as prayer and alms, and yet do them for his own ends and profit? I answer, though Christian charity is apt to think the best, yet none will say they know that you are born of God until you deny yourself and your own ends, and until you do things in virtue of Christ, and walk constantly in a Christian course. Therefore walk humbly before God; do things in the power of Christ; and if it come that your ends and Christ's ends cannot stand together, and if you willingly leave your own way and take Christ's, though it cost you much — why, this will be your encouragement: everyone who does righteousness will know that you are born of God.

Use 4. This will discourage every man from evil ways. If Christians know that they who do righteousness are born of God, then they will know that they who do unrighteousness are born of the serpent. If they see that you work for your own ends and by your own gifts, not by virtue of Christ, they may wish you well, but they know that you are not born of Christ. A worldly man cannot rise higher than his own ends; a thing rises no higher than the original it comes from; therefore let this discourage you from working unrighteousness; for if you do, you will be known to do unrighteously, and not to be born of God.

1 John 3:1

"Behold, what manner of love the Father has bestowed upon us, that we should be called the sons of God: therefore the world knows us not, because it knew him not."

"They that work righteousness are born of God." Knowing how apt we are to pass over such a mercy without serious and humble acknowledgement, he stirs us up to consider this mercy.

He removes a double objection. -1. We meet with none who acknowledge us as sons of God. -2. What with corruptions and afflictions, we have much ado to persuade ourselves that we are sons of God. To the first John replies, Not everyone acknowledges this, but only they who work righteousness; not the world, because they know not Christ. To the second he answers, Now we are the sons of God. Take us in our strongest corruptions and afflictions, we are God's sons; but it does not appear what we shall be. When he appears, we shall be like him, free from corruption and affliction, for "we shall see him."

Here are: -1. The manner of God's love to us; we are called his children. -2. The exhortation to behold this love. -3. The removal of an objection.

It is a great and wonderful love of God, that we are accounted and called his sons. "Behold, what manner of love!" It is such a love as cannot be said how much (Matt. 8:27; Luke 1:29). Speaking of quickening us to our new birth, the scripture says it is a rich mercy, great love (Eph. 2:4, 5; Tit. 3:4, 5; 1 Pet. 1:3).

Why is it such a great love?

-1. Because of our amazing unworthiness of such a favor. We have a fourfold unworthiness.

    a. Prodigal riotous waste of original righteousness. Adam was the Son of God by creation (Luke 3:38), but he sold it for an apple; more profane he was than Esau, because Esau sold it for necessity and hunger, whereas Adam did not. Now for God to give us a new stock, to set us upon our feet again, argues wonderful love and mercy. The prodigal's father had bestowed a portion upon him, and he spent it riotously; now he freely and rightly acknowledges, "I am unworthy" (Luke 15:21). Might not every son of Adam say as much?

b. Our estrangement from God and enmity against God, before we are called the sons of God (Col. 1:21). Even if a man should adopt a child, would he adopt a stranger or an enemy?

c. Every child of God was once not only an enemy to God, but a harlot. Suppose a king should marry his firstborn to a harlot who was his enemy, and press him to take her: would not this seem strange? We were harlots, running awhoring after our pleasures and profits; what a depth of love it is for God to offer us his Christ, his only Son in marriage to us; what manner of love is this?

d. There is nothing that God could expect from us. Many a man will match his daughter with one who has not so much means, if he is an understanding man and able to manage his estate. A man will say, "Had I such a man in hand, I would set him in such a course that he would thrive and do well"; but how much shame and dishonor have we been to God. David's adultery and murder, Noah's drunkenness, Lot's incest, Abraham's lie, which a heathen king could check him for — what a discredit God has by us.

-2. Because of the little need God has of us. Men usually do not adopt if they have children of their own; God had a natural son, Christ, and the angels are his sons by creation. Christ was God's Son, in whom he had pleasure.

-3. Because of the great difficulty which must be surmounted before we could be the sons of God. Christ must come from heaven, and be humbled even to the death (Gal. 4:4, 5). God denies his natural Son, abases him.

-4. Because of the excellent benefits we are called to.

a. We call God Father. Is it a light matter for the God of heaven and earth to be called your Father, since you are but a man? (1 Sam. 18:23).

b. Christ is your brother (Heb. 2:11, 12).

c. You partake with him in the Spirit, the Comforter (John 14:16, 17; Rom. 8:14, 26, 27; Ezek. 36:27). Whereas before you had but a rough-hewn spirit, God sheds his own Spirit abroad in you, makes you a partaker of the divine nature, so that you should have eternal life.

d. Provision as a son here, as an heir hereafter. God provides spiritual and temporal means (Deut. 8:11-18). God nurtures us, washes us Ethiopians, and gives us an inheritance (1 Pet. 1:3, 4).

Use 1. This refutes all good opinions that men have of themselves. They do not know that God has no need of us; they do not know what Christ paid for us; they do not know what a great mercy it is to have God for our Father (2 Cor. 6:17, 18). They do not know what manner of love it is.

Use 2. This reproves a great unworthiness of God's children, and a shameful dishonor they put upon him, when they are ashamed to call him Father. This is the case of many of God's servants when they come in bad company; they cover themselves with a veil of carnality. What do we lose by calling God Father? Does not God rather lose by calling us children? This was Peter's sin, and it cost him many a bitter tear (Matt. 26:75).

Use 3. This should teach all the children of God to love God with all their strength and might. We can never abound too much in love (1 John 4:19).

Use 4. Here we may learn how much we are bound to love our brethren. Let us enlarge the bowels of our affections, and let us think we can never sufficiently love them. If the king favors any man, every man will be looking at him and always seeking his favor.

Use 5. This teaches worldly men how much they wrong themselves in depriving themselves of this manner of love, when they content themselves with other things.

"Behold!" This implies presence, evidence, eminence. There is something in the object and in the act.

For the object. -1. What we behold is present; we cannot behold what is absent. -2. It is evident and sensible; no one can behold a spirit or the wind. -3. It is a thing of weight, excellent and eminent (John 1:29; Ps. 133:1).

For the act. Beholding implies to look with the eye, to consider a thing, and to fix our eyes upon it.

Why would God have us behold his love?

-1. For his own glory. There is nothing in which God shows more of his glory (Rom. 9:23; Eph. 2:4, 5).

-2. So that we might better support our spirits against the discouragements we meet with from the world, which knows us not.

-3. So that we may be persuaded to love God, and strengthened to doing and suffering (2 Cor. 5:14).

Use 1. This reproves men's squint-looking. They do not look at God's love, but at themselves and at their own corruptions and afflictions. It is a wonder that God's children should pore only upon corruptions, and not consider what love it is for God to discover them and pardon them.

Use 2. It reproves a Popish opinion which looks at our adoption and spiritual state as doubtful and uncertain (Eccl. 9:2). Why then are we bidden to behold it? Can a man behold that which is not seen? If a man is bidden to behold, the thing is present and sensible.

Use 3. To lift up the hearts of all God's people, to fasten their meditations much upon the love of God. We read such passages as, "He who works righteousness is born of God," but we are ready to pass over such things. Therefore St. John says, Stand still and behold; look at it as a present benefit, and rest not until you see it present and evident. Look closely at this; when you find it, stand and behold what God has done for you. Though you meet with a world of corruptions, temptations, discouragements, remember this above all: God will not allow those he loves to lack support.

But if this love is present, evident, and sensible, how does it happen that the world does not know of it? The apostle sees this objection and answers, The world knows you not because it knows him not. The world does not know the children of God (John 17:2). Had they known them to be children, they would not have killed them. It was a sign Ahab did not know God, for he did not know Elijah, the chariots and horsemen of Israel, their strength, stay, and protection from God.

What is meant by "the world"? Not the whole body of the creation, nor only reasonable men, but that part of the world that is destitute of God's Spirit.

-1. These are called the world because they are born of the world and in the world (John 8:23; 1 John 4:5); born of corrupt nature, defiled with the world.

-2. They have their portion in this world. A man is said to be of that place where his means lies (Ps. 17:14).

-3. The world is the object of all their thoughts and affections.

-4. They are the greatest part of the world (1 John 5:19).

-5. The world is called by the name of wicked men; it borrows its name from them (2 Pet. 2:5).

What is meant by not knowing God's children?

-1. Knowledge is taken for discerning. Many times they do not discern who are the children of God.

-2. They do not acknowledge them. If a friend of old acquaintance should pass by and give no sign of acknowledgement, we would say that such a one did not know us.

-3. They are ready to do them ill (John 16:2).

Because they know not Christ, they know not you (1 Cor. 2:8; Acts 3:17; John 15:21; John 16:2, 3). If a man does not know the face or head of a man, he knows not any other part, for there is no part so easily discerned as the head. Christ is the head of his members; if they knew not him the head, they will not know us the members.

John had told us before that if we know Christ to be righteous, we know that they who work righteousness are born of him; but the world is ignorant of Christ's righteousness.

-1. They look at God as righteous yet merciful, and so they expect him to save men out of Christ. Therefore they think God does not require so much obedience as is found in the lives of God's people.

-2. The world looks at God as righteous, yet a respecter of persons.

-3. It is the conceit of men that God blesses the good with prosperity and the wicked with want and adversity; so did Job's friends.

-4. They measure God's righteousness to reach no farther than the sins of the second table of the commandments, forgetting the stricter righteousness of our Saviour (Matt. 5:20).

-5. If any are so enlightened that they know God requires service to himself, they content themselves with performance of duties, without engaging their hearts and lives (Ps. 51:6).

-6. Some who are best discerning, find some desires after the word, some affections in prayer and fasting. They perform duties not only to men but to God, and they do God service zealously. Where is the defect in this? Being ignorant of the righteousness of God, they go about to establish their own righteousness (Rom. 10:3, 4); they know God requires righteousness with zeal, and yet they know not the righteousness of Christ. They think that doing good duties zealously will serve them at the day of judgment. They never knew what need they had of Christ to cover their imperfections, and to help them perform good duties. Hence they persecuted Paul, who knew the righteousness of Christ better than they.

But does it not sometimes fall out that evil men know good men? Herod knew John. -1. Sometimes a hypocrite may discern a righteous man, but then they are more than mere worldly men (1 Cor. 12:1-3). There must be some works of the Holy Spirit. -2. There is a defect in all such knowledge; they cannot discern them of weak grace and many corruptions, but eminent men they may. Herod reverenced John and despised Christ.

Use 1. This refutes two Popish opinions. (a) They say that

the church of God is always visible to the world. If we say that it is not, we say no more than St. John says. (b) They say none can know himself to be born of God. St. John makes it the property of a worldling not to know the children of God; much more not to know himself to be a child of God (Gal. 6:10).

Use 2. It reproves all the uncertain walks of God's servants, or those who profess themselves to be. Either you are worldly, or your brethren; else they would know you to be a child of God (1 Thess. 1:4).

Use 3. It is a ground of trial of a man's state. If you do not know that they who fear God are born of him, you are still of the world; you do not know Christ if you do not love them, nor seek them, nor lend a helping hand to them.

Use 4. This teaches us that God's children are hidden and unknown to the world. A man who is wealthy and conducts himself meanly, we say such a man is a hidden man; he is worth thousands. God's people are worth millions, but they are hidden men; the world knows them not. If a pearl falls into the dirt, you cannot discern it; but wash away the dirt, and you shall see it sparkle.

Use 5. It should teach God's children to moderate the affections of carnal excellence and acceptance in the world. It is a leaven of hypocrisy and pride, which many times infects the hearts of God's people. They would be something. But the world knows you not. Be willing to go as unknown men in the world (John 5:44). Shall the hand or foot take it ill that it is not known, when the head was not known?

Use 6. It should work in God's children an inclination to forgive wrongs and injuries; if they knew you better, they would use you better (Luke 23:22-25; Acts 3:17).

Use 7. It may teach the world not to flatter themselves in doing ill to God's servants; you think it is out of wisdom, but it is indeed out of ignorance, and because you do not know Christ and his righteousness.

1 John 3:2

"Beloved, now are we the sons of God, and it does not yet appear what we shall be: but we know that when he shall appear, we shall be like him, for we shall see him as he is."

In the last verse the apostle answered an objection against his consideration of the love of God which he had shown them. The objection is taken from the ignorance of the world. It is objected that the world knows no such excellency in them; to this he answers that this ignorance of theirs arises from their ignorance of Christ.

A second objection arises from the doubts that they themselves have of their states, because of those many temptations and afflictions which they meet in the world. To this he answers: -1. Even now they are the sons of God. -2. Though now their state is hidden, yet it shall appear. -3. He confirms this, that they shall appear when Christ appears. And that he confirms from their own knowledge, for they shall see him as he is.

Let us consider:

-1. Their states: "sons of God."

-2. The hiddenness of their present and future states.

-3. What they shall be like, viz. Christ, which is set out by the testimony of their own knowledge. And he strengthens all by a sweet compellation, "beloved."

Doct. 1. The sons of God ought to be the men of our love and delight (3 John 1, 2, 5; 1 Pet. 2:11; Phil. 4:1).

We see his deep affection toward them; he looks at them as born of God, and therefore he calls them "beloved" and "dearly beloved."

In love there is first a desire to be united to them, and second a communication of good to them. First, if a son of God is to choose company, he will choose those who fear God (Ps. 119:63, 79). Second, this love desires to communicate good to the thing loved. "Do good to all, but especially to the household of faith" (2 Pet. 1:7; Ps. 60:1, 2). So whether we desire union or communion of good company to any, we should chiefly desire it to the company of believers. This was David's grief, that he could not enjoy the company of good men (Ps. 120:3-5).

Why are we to love them?

-1. Because of God's singular love to them (v. 1).

-2. Because of their love to God. When others are cold in their affections, Christians should love those who love God, who has loved them so dearly (Ps. 139:21, 22).

-3. Because of the truth that is in every Christian believer (2 John 1, 2). If a man loves gold, he loves to have true gold; so if we love any, let us love them in whom is truth. There is not one in a thousand who has truth in him; you shall find them loving no further than may be to their own ends. But Christians love one another for the sake of the love that is in them.

Use 1. This should teach ministers with what affection they should speak to their people when they call them beloved. This ought not to be a word of mere civility, but their hearts should go with it. How can they call them dearly beloved when they come to them only once a year?

Use 2. If we would approve the truth of our hearts before God, let us love all who are born of God, as St. John did. Look at all believers as the sons of God, and look at them as beloved, if they walk in the truth.

Use 3. This may be a reproof to all who estrange themselves from Christians. There are some who will not malign and oppose them, yet if they are poor they estrange themselves from them. But St. John calls any beloved in whom he finds the truth of grace. There is no Christian who does not have something for which he ought to be beloved.

Doct. 2. Both the ignorance of the word about God's children, and our obscurity and weakness in the world, do not hinder our present good state in the world.

"Now we are the sons of God"; now that we are afflicted in the world (Isa. 54:11). Though the children of God be afflicted and weather-beaten, yet God has promised blessings to them which may make them blessed in the world (vv. 13, 14; Isa. 43:3, 4). Though we are led through the water and fire of affliction, yet in the midst of all our troubles, when we are passing through, the Lord promises that he will be with us and that he will be our comfort in the midst of persecution and temptation.

Thus you see how dear and precious God's children are in his sight. When David saw the prosperity of the wicked, then he began to think he had cleansed his heart in vain; but soon after, when he went into the sanctuary of the Lord, then he saw that the Lord set them but in slippery places. Therefore no matter how it seems in our eyes that it goes well with the wicked, let us not despair: God will guide his children by his counsel, and afterward receive them to glory. The apostle says, "Your life is hid with Christ in God" (Col. 3:3, 4).

Why is our state good, though in obscurity and weakness?

-1. We are like the Son of God, Christ Jesus. He was in such a poor condition that he had not where to lay his head; and yet all this while he was the Son of God, in whom he was well pleased (Matt. 3:17). And as it was with Christ our head, so we may expect it to be with us his members (Rom. 8:29). If God saw it meet that his son should be thus afflicted in the world and drink of such a bitter portion of God's wrath, let us not think we shall go to heaven and partake of those heavenly mansions which Christ has prepared for us, without also drinking of the same cup that he drank of. Let us account ourselves happy that God will so esteem us as to make us his sons.

-2. God's love is free to men. First, he does not esteem of them according to their outward luster (1 Sam. 16:7; Ps. 22:6). This latter scripture is meant of Christ. Second, he does not esteem of them according to their inward state (Ezek. 16:15-18; Deut. 7:7, 8). Though there is much pride and stubbornness of heart found in God's children, and sometimes even against God, yet all these inward corruptions do not hinder our future glorious state.

Use 1. This should teach the children of God to be content with their states. They are indeed apt to think that if the world is ready to put many injuries upon them, and to persecute them with such hatred, they are not God's children; or else they murmur and grieve within themselves. As for the men of the world, they are in prosperity; they suck water out of a full cup, their eyes bulge out with fatness, and they have more than they can wish. But David can tell them that when he went into the sanctuary, he saw that God had set them in slippery places. And then (v. 22) he condemns himself for his ignorance.

Use 2. This should teach the children of God not to misjudge of themselves about their inward states. Some of them will be ready to doubt and say, Surely I am not a child of God, because I find much pride in my heart, and much rebellion and corruption in my spirit. Surely if I were born of Christ, I should be like him. But what says St. John here? We are the sons of God even now, though there is much unbelief in our hearts, and much weakness and many corruptions within us.

But how shall I know that I am the child of God? The answer is laid down in verse 3. "Every man that has this hope in himself purifies himself as he is pure." Though he sees much filthiness in his spirit for the present, yet he labors to purge himself from time to time, and is ashamed of his hardness of heart and unbelief. He has so long stood out with God, but now he is sensible of his own misery and wretched state, and he strives daily to get out of it. Therefore laboring to purify himself as Christ is pure, he is the child of God.

"But it does not appear what we shall be."

Doct. 3. The future glorious state of God's children is for the present a hidden state (Col. 3:3, 4).

It is said to be hidden because it is hidden with the veil

of corruption, temptation and affliction, which overshadow our future glorious state. A Christian many times has many desertions in his spirit; many temptations from the world, the devil, and his flesh; many corruptions in his nature, as hypocrisy and lukewarmness; and much behavior which is unbecoming to the gospel of Christ. And therefore in regard to all these, well may his present state be said to be hidden.

But why does God allow it to be hidden?

-1. That they may be like Christ the head. Though Christ was without sin, yet he was counted a sinner, yea a conjurer, a friend of publicans and sinners (Heb. 4:15). But as for God's servants, they are ofttimes taken with many gross sins, and God will have them overshadowed with much weakness, so that the glory of his grace may be seen in their weakness, and also that they might not be too much lifted up with the conceit of their own worth (2 Cor. 12:7, 8). If God had purged and cleansed us from all our sins, then we should not have believed that our hearts were so desperately wicked as indeed they are; and we would not see God ever going along from day to day to purge and cleanse our hearts. As God did not make the whole fabric of the world at once (though it was not impossible to him, God Almighty), but in six days, so he deals with his children in creating a clean heart in them. First he allows their hearts to be a rude and massy lump, full of darkness; and then God sends his Holy Spirit into their hearts, and it illuminates them and drives away those black clouds of darkness and ignorance. And then he breathes in the sweet air of his Spirit, so that a man may perceive the gracious providence of God leading him along in his Christian course.

-2. That they may have a better toleration in the world. If God should allow them to be perfectly holy in this world, the men of the world would not allow them to live among them long (Deut. 7:22). As our eyes cannot endure to behold the light of the sun, so wicked men cannot endure to see the candlelight of grace in God's children.

-3. That God might keep his people in exercise. God will

have the Canaanites remain among the Israelites so that they might be stirred up to stand upon their guard and watch, and that he may have their graces exercised.

Use 1. To teach the children of God not to judge of their spiritual state by outward appearance, but to judge righteous judgment; that is, to judge as the thing is in itself, and not according to what befalls a man in his outward or inward state. Sometimes a wicked man meets with lesser temptations than many of God's children. But God judges according to the heart (Luke 16:15, 16). What if there is a lust of pride or arrogance in the best of God's children? What if the Canaanites are powerful within them, and they have much labor to get from among them? If they only endeavor to keep themselves pure and unspotted from the world, to purge themselves as Christ is pure, they shall at length come to a blessed and happy state in the heavens.

Use 2. To console God's children. Though our future condition is hid, yet it is safe enough, for it is laid up with Christ in the heavens. "If in this life only we have hope in Christ, then we are of all men most miserable." If the Christian should have no more joy and happiness than he has in this life, then the vilest wretch in the world is more happy than he. But our happiness does not depend on our present condition.

Use 3. This should teach the children of God to sit down contented with their present state. Though they do not enjoy so many pleasures, riches, honors, and esteem, as many men of the world do, let them be content; it will appear what they shall be. They shall be kings and princes, and therefore it must be their daily care and labor to be fitting and preparing themselves for that kingdom, to be purging themselves as Christ is pure.

Doct. 4. When Christ shall appear in glory, then shall our glorious state appear with him (Col. 3:4).

This glorious state, which consists in our likeness to Christ, shall appear in our bodies, in our souls, and in our outward states. For in all those Christ shall be glorious, so shall we see him as we are capable (1 Cor. 13:12).

-1. In our bodies. The apostle says:

a. "The body is sown in corruption, and it is raised again in incorruption." While we live in this world our bodies are subject to many sicknesses and diseases. But in the life to come there shall be no noise of corruption heard of; our bodies shall then be so hardened and strengthened that they shall be in no way capable of corruption or change. Yea, the bodies of wicked men shall be so hardened that they shall not again return to the matter of which they were first made, but they shall be so hardened forever as to subsist under everlasting torments. But the bodies of the godly shall be so strengthened as to receive an eternal weight of glory.

b. "It is sown in dishonor, but shall be raised again in glory." If our bodies were made ever so comely and favorable, yet they would be changed and made subject to putrefaction. But in the world to come, we shall be as the sun in the kingdom of our Father (Matt. 13:43).

c. "It is sown in weakness, but it shall be raised again in power." Old men here need a staff to sustain their feeble joints; but at the day of Judgment we shall need no staff, for then we shall be stronger than the strongest who ever lived.

d. "It is sown a natural body, but it shall be raised a spiritual body." Our bodies here must be sustained with meat and drink, or else they cannot continue; but there we shall stand in need of none. Our meat and drink shall be to do the will of our Father which is in heaven. Our bodies now are subject to gravity, but then they shall be made so light that they shall ascend and pass from place to place even in a moment; we shall be quick to dispatch the business we are sent about.

-2. As our bodies shall be changed, so also shall our souls. Now our souls are much starved and polluted with ignorance, pride, wantonness, impatience, and other infirmities, but then we shall be perfect in strength and knowledge (1 Cor. 13:12). Now while we live here, our souls are as it were drowned in sin (Ezra 9:6), but then we shall not have any combating or striving between the flesh and the Spirit, but then the Spirit shall in all things have rule. Now we are full of imperfections, so that the good duties that we perform even in the best manner we can, are full of much frailty and weakness. Now our natural affections do often whirl us about and carry us away from the performance of good duties, but then it shall be our constant course to be performing good duties. We shall then know our Christian friends and acquaintances, and rejoice mutually together (John 4:36).

-3. We shall be like Christ in our states. (a) Then will our Saviour say, "Come, ye blessed" (Matt. 25:34-40). (b) Then will our Saviour lay open before our eyes all our good performances (Luke 12:2; Eccl. 12:14; 2 Thess. 1:10; Matt. 6:1-15; 1 Cor. 4:5). (c) We shall sit on the throne of God, and shall judge the world and the angels (1 Cor. 6:2, 3).

-4. We do now count it a great mercy and matter of great joy to see the face of Christ in the gospel, in his ordinances; how much more will it be joy unspeakable to see Christ face to face! And if seeing Christ in the gospel and in his ordinances transforms us in some manner into his likeness, then how we shall be transformed into his image when we shall see him face to face! (Heb. 12:23) It shall then be our meat and drink to do our Father's will.

-1. The first proof of the doctrine is taken from the day of Christ's coming to judge. It shall be our marriage day. Now we are only betrothed to Christ; we are now so coy that Christ has much ado to get our good will; the ministers of Christ travail in birth for us, and when they have gotten us to give our consent, it is their labor to fit us and trim us for that day (2 Cor. 11:2).

-2. Although we are but unprofitable servants when we have done all we can (Luke 17:10), yet Christ at that day will give us a reward (2 Thess. 1:6-10; 2 Tim. 4:7, 8; 2 Cor. 4:17, 18).

Use 1. This will be a great consolation to us when we shall know of our departure hence. It shall be for the better, and not for the worse; then we shall be every way perfect, and then we shall receive our rewards according to our deeds (Rev. 20:12).

Use 2. This should exhort us all to be fruitful in every good word and work, knowing our labor shall not be in vain in the Lord (1 Cor. 15:8).

Use 3. This exhorts us to patience. Though we meet with much hard dealing here, yet let us gird up our minds with patience, for there will come a day which shall pay for all, when Christ shall reward every man according to his works (Rev. 2:16, 17; 2 Tim. 2:11, 12).

Use 4. To exhort everyone who would see a joyful and a comfortable end, and a crown of glory in the world to come, to have a care that he becomes the child of God here (Rom. 8:11). Make your choice now whether you will have Christ and a base, miserable life, or cleave to this world and be in endless torments forever hereafter. If those virgins who were brought to the king had twelve months' time for their purifying, then how we ought to be decking and purifying ourselves all our lives, so that we may be taken up into the presence of the king of heaven (Esther 2:6-12).

Doct. 5. We know we shall know him, because we shall see him; and seeing him shall make us like him.

John is confident of this (John 19:27). What are his reasons?

-1. The prayer of Christ (John 17:24); and whatever he prayed for, his Father heard him (John 11:41, 42).

-2. Our state here. We are now only espoused to Christ. As princes send ambassadors into far countries to make matches for their sons and daughters, so the Lord Jesus sends his ministers to us, to win us to him and to get us betrothed to him; and his coming to judge shall be our marriage (1 Thess. 4:17).

Use 1. This is a ground of much comfort to all the servants of God in the midst of temptations and distresses (John 19:25, 27).

Use 2. This should be an encouragement to all who think they shall never see good days after they have set foot into the ways of God. Certainly you shall have one good day; here is one promised in the text. We shall see him when the marriage day comes, and see him as he is in great glory. Therefore we strive after perfection here, for if we become not the children of God here, we shall never see his face with comfort in the world to come.

Use 3. This exhorts us to prepare to meet Christ in person. If a man had come to speak to a prince, would he not have care to make himself handsome? Therefore what care should Christians have, for they are to come into the presence of the King of heaven.

Doct. 6. Beholding and seeing Christ face to face shall fashion us to be like him, for we shall see him as he is (1 Cor. 13:12; Heb. 11:27).

This seeing Christ invested Moses with such glory and strength that he feared not the fierceness of the king; and so should the full assurance of seeing Christ in his kingdom arm us against all discouragements and whatever the world may lay upon us.

What is it to see Christ face to face? It is the clear and perfect knowledge of God, which proceeds only from Jesus Christ, for "no man has seen God at any time" (1 Tim. 6:16; John 4:14); and this is opposed to the sight of Christ in the world (2 Cor. 3:13-17). Under the Old Testament they saw Christ through a veil of ceremonies (2 Cor. 3:13); in the New Testament we see Christ as in a glass of God's word, sacraments, and Christian communion. Afterwards we shall not only see him without ceremonies, but without ordinances also; we shall then see Christ face to face. Further, then we shall see Christ's manhood and all the glory he had before the world (1 Cor. 13:12; John 17:24).

How shall this make us like him? -1. We see him in the glass of the gospel (2 Cor. 3:18), and so we grow from one measure of grace to another. If the gospel will do this, much more the presence of Christ's body. -2. Look at Moses; when he saw God's back parts, his face shone (Exod. 34:29); so our face much more. -3. We shall see what Peter, James, and John saw when Christ was transfigured (Matt. 17:2-5; Prov. 27:17). A man may learn something from the countenance of a Christian. When Christ only looked at Peter, it was enough to move him to repentance.

Use 1. This comforts those who find benefit by the ordinances. If you find good by the ordinances, then how much better you shall be by seeing Christ face to face. A Christian fears death, judgment, distresses, because he does not see Christ.

Doct. 7. God's children know this much, that when Christ shall appear, they shall be like him, and they shall be made like him by seeing him as he is (Ps. 17:15).

How do we know this? Partly by the testimony of the Spirit of God, who reveals the deep things of God (1 Cor. 2:9,10), and partly by our own experience of the efficacy of God's ordinances in this life. If we are better for seeing Christ in his ordinances, then how much more when we see him face to face?

Use 1. This refutes the doctrine of doubting. We shall not only persevere, but we know it. This assures us of perseverance, that we shall never fall away. We know we shall persevere, and knowledge is of a certain conclusion.

But how may we come to such a knowledge? We should labor to be like Christ in his word and sacraments, and in Christian communion. If we find that every ordinance makes us like Christ, then the sight of Christ much more.

Use 2. This should encourage us to bless God, who has redeemed us from darkness of error. If they who write against this doctrine had seen Christ in his ordinances, they would have believed it.

Use 3. Those who have seen God in his ordinances, let them meditate thus: Though they are obscured with the veil of affliction, temptation, or persecution, yet they shall hereafter be made like Christ. By seeing Christ Zaccheus was made the son of Abraham, and was ready to part with all. Moses saw Christ in a bush, and feared not Pharaoh.

1 John 3:3

"And every man who has this hope in him purifies himself even as he is pure."

In these words you have a description of a child of God. -1. He is one who has hope in Christ. -2. This hope is set forth by its proper work, purging. -3. Here you have the pattern or rule according to which it purges: "even as Christ is pure."

Doct. 1. Every child of God has hope in Christ, to be made like him at his appearing.

Every man who is begotten again is begotten to a lively hope (1 Pet. 1:3-5). A hypocrite's hope is dead; it has neither comfort nor power in it to cleanse or purge. When they doubt of the life of a child in the womb, though the parent is very wealthy, yet the child has not a lively hope of his possession; but if the child be born alive, then there is hope. So if we are not born again, all our hopes of eternal life are vain (1 Cor. 15:19). It is the property of the Israel of God to hope in their God (Ps. 130:7).

What is this hope? It is a patient, certain, and grounded expectation of all those promises in Christ which by faith we believe to belong to us. It is a sure and patient expectation.

There are two acts of hope: expectation and waiting. This is not an expectation of mere opinion, but a sure expectation. The apostle puts both together (Rom. 8:25; Heb. 6:11, 18, 19). An anchor is a sure and steadfast stay to the ship, so that though it waves up and down, yet it shall not drift. And so a Christian's hope is like an anchor to stay the soul; the object of hope is the accomplishment of the promises to come, and so it differs from faith. No man hopes for that which is present or past, but for that which he sees not (Tit. 2:13, 14; Heb. 11:1). Faith looks at all promises as present; faith believes that the promises are true, and then hope stirs itself up to look for accomplishment, and it waits if God tarry long (Rom. 5:5). It is a sure hope, for never was any man disappointed; and yet hope, though it is sure, is not without all doubting. Every true Christian has this hope.

The reason this hope is given is that God's children might not be tossed and hurried up and down the world. A child of God is never carried far; an anchor sticks in the foundation (Heb. 6:18, 19). While we hold on our hopes, and they are fastened to Christ, we have strong consolation; hereby we are kept from dashing against rocks and sands and shores. Here is the difference between an anchor and hope; an anchor is fastened in the earth, and hope is fastened in heaven.

Use 1. This will show you the dignity and honor of a Christian. He is a man of great hopes; he will not give his hopes for the best man's state in the world. He has a steadfast hope of being like Christ when he sees him. Though the clothes he now wears are mean, yet he hopes to be clad in Christ's righteousness; and though his house be mean, he hopes for a house not made with hands. This is his anchor, and this will hold when we fail.

Use 2. This may be a ground of trial. What are the hopes you build upon? There is a double difference between the hopes of a godly and a wicked man. (a) The wicked man's hopes are groundless; he has no grounds, only hopes. (b) It is fruitless (Job 8:11-14). The hope of a hypocrite is without ground, like a rush or flag without water or mire. Hope without a promise lacks water to nourish it. A spider's web looks like a curious work; but it is drawn out of its own bowels and is soon swept away; so a hypocrite has no hope but what he spins out of his own bowels. He builds upon present or future duties; his hope is fruitless; it yields neither comfort nor self-purging. A true Christian rejoices in tribulation, but a hypocrite is overthrown with it (Rom. 5:2, 3).

Take away prosperity from a hopeful hypocrite, and perhaps his hope may hold still, for he may hope that friends will do something; when he is sick, he hopes to recover; when he fears death, he hopes for another life; but when death comes, all his hopes are crushed. But a godly man hopes in death; he hopes for God's goodness, and his hope will never fail him or make him ashamed.

Use 3. Hope and knowledge of the same thing may well stand together. In the former verse he says, "we know"; here, "we hope." A man's hope does not cease in another world; for do not the saints believe that their bodies shall rise again? And do they not hope for it? (Rom. 8:23-25) They know the perpetuity of their states, and yet they hope for it (2 Cor. 11:1-3).

Use 4. This should stir us up. If we would have a comfortable and safe death, let us not go to sea without this anchor of hope. The world is full of perplexities; carry your anchor about with you; see your hope well wrought, and you shall be safe. Mariners do not go to sea without an anchor, but perhaps sometimes the storms may be so great that they are forced to cut the cable. But if you have an anchor pitched in heaven, you shall be safe. A woman in childbed may be put to distress, but hope will carry her through.

How may we get this hope? -1. We can never come to it until we are out of hope with any goodness in ourselves. -2. We must attend upon God in his ordinances, so that he may work faith in us; and where there is faith, there will be hope, for hope is built upon faith.

How shall we carry it about with us? We must look at it as a mercy and stay ourselves upon our anchor. Look afresh at the promises and believe them, and you shall have hope enough. That which makes us unquiet is because we have not visited the promises in many a day, nor renewed our faith in them.

Doct. 2. Every Christian who hopes to be like Christ hereafter in glory, purges himself to be like Christ in grace here.

The lively hope of a Christian is set forth by the lively fruit of self-purging (2 Pet. 3:12-14; Tit. 2:11-14).

How does this hope purify us?

-1. By the holy meditations it suggests to the heart of every hopeful Christian.

    a. A Christian who knows he has long been imprisoned in the fetters of corruption, and knows he shall shortly be called to appear before God, it makes him put off all superfluity of uncleanness and put on the garments of holiness. Shall I come before Christ dressed in pride and wantonness? Can a maid forget her ornaments when she is to be married? And can a Christian forget the ornaments which befit him for such a kingdom?

    b. The more a Christian is purged and purified, the greater shall his glory be (2 Pet. 2:10-12).

-2. Hope purifies by setting to work some graces which cleanse and purify. (a) Repentance is a grace which purges our hearts from sin (Ps. 130:1-4). (b) Faith purifies our hearts (Acts 15:9). If God stirs up our hearts to wait on him, we may certainly know that he will do so as we have desired; else our hope would make us ashamed. "Remember now thy word unto thy servant, in which thou hast made me to trust" (Ps. 119:49). (c) Meditation upon the graces in Christ transforms us into their image (2 Cor. 3:18). There is such a power in the promises of God that they fashion us like Christ. (d) Hope cleanses us by giving us hearts fastening on the word, and applying it; and the word applied has a strong power to cleanse even young men (Ps. 119:9). (e) This hope has a power to stir us up to faithfulness, by persuading us that our labor shall not be in vain in the Lord; and this faithfulness sets God awork to purge us, that we may bring forth more fruits (John 15:2). But when God sees us stand at a stay, and wax barren, then he is ready to cut us down that we may not encumber the ground.

-3. Hope to be made like Christ in glory hereafter makes us abandon those impediments which hinder our purification (1 Cor. 5:6). When he says that everyone who has this hope purifies himself, it implies that it is a continued work; he makes it a part of a Christian's daily work.

"He purifies himself"; he does not say from what. He leaves it indefinite; he includes all and excludes none (James 1:21). This hope purges the whole man, the understanding, will, and affections (2 Cor. 7:1; 1 Thess. 5:23). Then it may well be called a lively fruitful hope.

a Hope comes to all the ordinances of God with expectation that it shall find benefit from the word, prayer, and good company. Hope waits on God for good in every ordinance, and then it never goes away empty; it strives to prepare the heart before it comes, and to cleanse it from all filthiness.

Use 1. This shows us the amazing loathsomeness of sin. If sin were not an excrement, why should we purge it out? We purge out nothing but filthy loathsome things; and therefore when it is said to purge, it implies that sin is loathsome.

Use 2. Here we discern the soundness of our hope. Do you find your heart daily striving to cleanse yourself? If not, your hope will make you ashamed. If your hope does not set you to work every day to cleanse your heart, truly your hope is nothing but a vain delusion, and nothing will sting you more at the last day, when you shall hope for heaven; you shall be cast out of God's presence.

Use 3. Let it teach all Christians, if they would not be ashamed of their hopes, to make their calling and election sure. Let their hopes make them purge and cleanse themselves. And let not Christians think it is enough to purge themselves; they must purge their families. A Christian must allow none in his family to be uncircumcised. God would have killed Moses because he had one uncircumcised. Magistrates must cleanse their towns and places where they live. When good Josiah was to celebrate the Passover, he set himself with all his heart to purge Jerusalem and Judah.

Doct. 3. The purity of Christ is the pattern of every Christian's purity (1 Cor. 11:1; Heb. 12:12).

Set before you a pattern, a cloud of witnesses. He who abides in Christ ought to walk as he walked (1 John 2:6).

Why should every Christian make Christ the pattern of his purity? -1. Because of the end of God's predestination. "He has predestinated us to be conformed to the image of his Son" (Rom. 8:29). And God in all things requires that we should grow up to the fellowship of the stature of Jesus Christ. -2. Because of the perfection of our pattern. All other patterns of godly men will fail us in some things; but Christ is a perfect pattern, and he will fail us in nothing.

What are our motives and means to gain this perfection?

A. For motives:

-1. As soon as you slack this care, your hope, faith, and grace grow weak. If our bodies do not void excrements for many days, we think some disease lies on us. How can we have a healthy soul when we do not purge our corruption many a day?

-2. Is it not uncomely to see the head made of gold, and the members partly of brass, clay, and dirt? So if we would be comely, let us be pure as he is pure.

-3. It is very grievous to the Spirit of God that we should be no better since he has dwelt so long in us. When Christ had been long with his disciples, and they had not been bettered by him, he upbraids them, "O foolish and slow of heart to believe! How long shall I be with you?" It was a grief to Christ that he should be long with his disciples and they not grow up to strength of grace.

But does not virtue consist in a golden mean? Yes, but in a mean between two extremes. You may exceed the bounds of righteousness and so be unrighteous; but you cannot exceed the degrees of righteousness, for Christ says, "Be perfect as your heavenly Father is perfect." Can you then be too pure and holy? No, you cannot, though you were as full of grace and holiness as Christ himself.

-4. If you desire to be a worthy partaker of the sacraments, then labor to purify yourself. The reason why many a Christian comes to the sacrament and finds no comfort is because he grieved the Spirit of God before he came, by neglecting to cast out those obstructions which hinder the influence of the head to the members (1 Cor. 11:27-31).

B. For means:

-1. Be persuade that you are not in a safe state until you have grown up to some good measure of purity. You would think that man in a poor case, who should live 200 years and yet who for lack of evacuation should live in sickness and weakness. And so a Christian is in an uncomfortable state unless he purges himself.

-2. Be very watchful over your ways.

-3. Use the ordinances of God constantly. Say not after conversion, It is no matter whether or not I am always in God's ordinances, but only at times, when the Spirit moves me. But let us labor to become not idle hearers, but faithful doers; let us labor to see our spots and deformities, and strive to purge them. Let us labor to practice new duties as they are renewed to us.

Use 1. This should teach us to reject the company of men who inwardly loathe the name of Puritans. Alas, if they cannot endure the name of purity in poor weak Christians, how would they hate the purity of Christ? If they cannot endure the brightness of a candle, how will they endure the brightness of the sun? And yet they say they love Christ; but if they have not purity, how can they? And if they love not Christ, they are accursed forever.

Use 2. This reproves those who, though they do not hate purity, yet think themselves very well if they exceed the worst sort of men. They are no whoremongers, nor thieves, nor deceivers. Alas, if there is in them no more than moral honesty, they shall come far short of heaven.

Use 3. This reproves the Romish church, for they think ordinary Christians are not bound to so strict a pattern as their regular Christians. Did ever any of them reach higher than Christ? And is not every Christian exhorted to set Christ as a pattern?

Use 4. This reproves another sort of Christians. If they

have but such a measure of grace as assures them to be in a state of grace, they never look further; they look out for themselves in the world, as if they might rest in what is behind and never press forward to what is before them. But this is contrary to Paul. Know, O Christian, that it is not enough to get truth of grace and some purity, but you must grow pure as Christ is pure.

Use 5. If we would maintain our hope to be made like Christ hereafter, let us strive to this exactness of purity. Let us purify ourselves as he is pure. If you would be a hopeful Christian, you must be a growing Christian; grow up to the measure of the purity of Christ. Decay in your growth, and you decay in hope.

1 John 3:4

"Whoever commits sin also transgresses the law; for sin is the transgression of the law."

In these words, and in the following to ver. 7, he uses four motives to stir us up to self-cleansing.

-1. The danger of committing sin, as proved from the proper definition of sin. It is the transgression of the law.

-2. The end of Christ's coming, which was to take away sin.

-3. The pattern of Christ, who was without sin.

-4. The practice of those who have any fellowship by union with Christ. Whoever abides in Christ does not sin.

Doct. It is and ought to be a sufficient motive to every hopeful Christian to abstain from sin because it is the transgression of the law (Numb. 14:41).

The Rechabites were commended because they kept their fathers' commandment. And he hereby convinces the Jews of rebellion, that the sons of mortal men should make more conscience of obeying their dead fathers than his people make of his laws (Dan. 9:11; Neh. 9:34, 35; Rom. 2:22-24; James 2:9, 10).

Why should this be a sufficient motive? Because of the nature of God and the nature of the law.

A. The nature of God.

-1. The great Lawgiver looks at every sin as an abrogation of his ordinances. He who walks in his law confirms it, sets his seal to it (Deut. 27:26). They who break it would make it of no force. This is one act of high rebellion against God (2 Sam. 12:9).

-2. God pronounces wrath and displeasure against every transgressor (Jer. 7:19; 44:4-6).

-3. God takes it as a dishonor to the power and efficacy of his word. God looks at it as more unruliness in a man to break the bounds of his law, than for the sea to break its bounds (Jer. 5:22, 23).

-4. God takes delight in the keeping and keepers of his law (1 Sam. 15;22). He delights more in obedience than in the cattle of a hundred hills. "My son, give me your heart" (Prov. 23:26). That is more acceptable than all the sacrifices.

B. The nature of the law itself.

-1. It is holy, just, and good; therefore it is abominable to transgress it, for this is a sin against holiness, justice, and goodness.

-2. It is vigorous and efficacious, offering life to the obedient (Ps. 19:11; 1 Tim. 4:8; Ps. 119:1-6) and death to the disobedient (Gal. 3:10; Isa. 59:1, 2).

Use 1. This will reprove those who are afraid to break man's laws for fear of penalty, but are not afraid to violate and break the holy and righteous laws of God. This argues a most rebellious and revolting heart. Such are not hopeful Christians.

Use 2. This will teach and exhort ue to make conscience of all our ways, and to take heed to our paths, lest we transgress the law and sin against God. If we turn away our ears from hearing God's law, even our prayers are abominable (Prov. 28:9). This should keep us from secret petty sins, for though man sees not, yet God sees and will punish (2 Sam. 12:11, 12). If we think to get honor, profit, or pleasure by sin, we deceive ourselves. Is it not as grievous a thing to have our soul wounded by our darling child as by our mortal enemy? It is all one to be stabbed with a pen knife as with a sword. Every sin wounds and rents our hearts. Let us abstain from all sin, for even the least sin is the transgression of the law.

Use 3. This refutes those who think the law is not given to the regenerate. The apostle here encourages hopeful Christians not to transgress the law.

But does not the apostle say that we are not under law but under grace? True, but he means that we are not under the covenant of works, but of grace (Ps. 119:97).

But does not Christ's passive obedience free us from the curse, and likewise does not his active obedience free us from the commanding power of the law? Yes, Christ has done this, and therefore those that are in Christ fear not death by their disobedience, nor look for life by their obedience; but we look to the law as a rule of obedience, that we may walk according to God, and show that we live by endeavoring to keep his commandments.

"For sin is a transgression of the law." This is a perfect definition of sin; transgression is the genus, the law the species. In scripture, by "law" without addition is meant the law of the ten commandments.

If a man sins against the law of nature, is that not a sin? True; but in effect and substance it is the same. Though the law of nature was more dimly and darkly known, Moses' law was but a new draft of the law of nature in innocence. Heathen lawgivers, philosophers, and poets have expressed the effect of all the commandments save the tenth (Rom. 2:14, 15).

But again, was it not a sin to transgress the ceremonial and judicial law? To the Jew it was. The ceremonial law was but an exemplification of the second commandment, and all the judicial law only explains the second table. The judicial is included in the moral law; the ceremonial stood in force until Christ died.

Thirdly, is it not a sin to transgress the gospel? Is not unbelief a sin? (John 16:9) Is not a new obedience required in the Gospel? (John 14:21; Ezek. 36:27) I answer that the commandments of the gospel can all be reduced to the commandments of the law; for God commanded perfect conformity and obedience to his whole will, not only that which was revealed but that which would be revealed later. If God commanded David to bring music into the temple (2 Chron. 29:25), though Moses spoke nothing of it, yet Moses did express this, to hear and obey God in all things (Deut. 18:18). God commanded to hearken to Christ; Moses darkly and hiddenly delivered the substance of the gospel, partly in the ceremonial law, partly in the sacrament of circumcision and the passover; Christ was veiled under them (Rom. 10:5-8 with Deut. 30:12-14).

Transgression is anomia, a lack of law and absence of it; as when a man speaks and acts without law.

Why is sin a transgression of the law? Consider the end for which God gives the law; it is to be the means of perfection (2 Tim. 3:16, 17). Sin is called error from the law (Isa. 63:17) "He who wanders out of the way of righteousness shall rejoice among the dead" (Prov. 21:16).

Use 1. Of refutation.

    a. This refutes the works of Popish supererogation, which are held forth as better and more perfect than the law, for the law never commands such things. Such are those monkish vows of perpetual virginity and voluntary poverty: if these are above the law, then they are transgressions of the law (Isa. 1:12, 13). Will a man be wiser than his maker, holier than the lawgiver? (Josh. 1:7, 8) To devise a worship better than God has appointed is worse than to fail in breaking God's law. The latter is mere impotence; the other is arrogance, casting aspersion on God's wisdom.

    b. They further hold some sins to be venial in themselves, some mortal. But if they are sins, then they fall under the curse: "The wages of sin is death."

    c. They also hold that original sin in the regenerate

is no sin; but David says that he was conceived in sin; and original sin wherever found is a transgression of the commandment.

d. They also say that man's law binds the conscience, and the transgression of man's law is sin. We answer and grant that they bind when they are grounded on God's laws, but not otherwise. If the breaking of men's laws is a sin, then the keeping of them were a virtue; but this is hypocrisy (Isa. 29:13). We must be subject for conscience' sake.

e. This verse also refutes those who hold that infants are without original sin. The scripture says they are conceived in sin.

f. This reproves the familists, who hold that godly and regenerate men are in no wise subject to the law, but are freed from the condemning and commanding power of it. But if they sin, then certainly they are transgressors.

Use 2. Of instruction.

a. All the sins and good things found in the whole Bible are to be ranked within the compass of the ten commandments.

b. All nations are under the law.

c. The law and gospel thus mutually agree. The law of Moses is included in the gospel, and yet the law and gospel are not confounded together. The Gospel requires that in the way of thankfulness we should keep the commandments of God (Ezek. 36:27).

Use 3. Of exhortation. This should discourage us from all sin and encourage us to labor to purge ourselves of it. All sin is the transgression of the law of God. Let not pleasures, profits, or credits allure us to sin against God. We must take heed how we meddle with what we have no law for. We must prove all our paths by the stony tables of God's law (Ps. 119: 105). Obedience is the fulfilling of the law, and has great recompense of reward.

1 John 3:5

"And you know that he was manifested to take away our sins; and in him is no sin."

These words contain the second and third reasons why the hopeful Christian should purge himself as Christ is pure. The second reason is taken from the end of Christ's coming into the world, which was "to take away our sins." The third argument is taken from the pattern of Christ's righteousness, for "in him is no sin."

Doct. The end of Christ's coming into the world was to take away our sins.

By 'being manifested' we must understand Christ's coming in the flesh (1 Tim. 3:16). He came for this end, to take away our sins (John 1:29).

What did Christ do for us to take away our sins? He became our surety; he willingly took upon him the burden of our sins (1 Pet. 2:24). Christ took away our sins by imputation. In the old law, every man was to lay his hand on the head of the burnt offering and confess his sins, and by that means their sins were taken away (Lev. 16:21, 22). So now in this time of the gospel, we must lay hold on Christ by a true and living faith, claiming him as our Saviour (2 Cor. 5:21).

Thus Christ takes away our sins by justifying us from the guilt, and by sanctifying us from the spot and stain of them (Ezek. 36:25; 1 John 1:9). This he does three ways.

-1. By his death he overcame the principal enemy of our salvation, the devil (Heb. 2:14). He has overcome the world, which was strong to carry us captive by flattery and fear (Gal. 6:14). He has crucified the body of sin and corruption in us (Rom. 6:6).

-2. He sent ordinances into the church to cleanse us (Eph. 5:11-16; Isa. 27:9). The fruit of afflictions is to purge away sin.

-3. He has sent his Holy Spirit into our hearts to change us, a Spirit of faith purifying (Acts 15:9), a Spirit of hope and love (1 John 3:3; Gal. 3:14). We receive the Spirit of grace, which makes God's ordinance effectual to cleanse us.

Use 1. To instruct everyone who is afflicted in conscience for sin, and who knows not how to be eased and purged. It is not fair buildings, music, and merry company that will take away sin. This course will make you worse. But this you must do: consider to what end Christ was manifested and sent into the world; was it not to take away our sins? You will say, But I do not find this wrought in me; I find the world and the lusts of my heart prevailing against me. What then? Christ takes away the burden and debt of sin by undertaking to accept and bear them (1 John 2:2; Matt. 11:28). The Father has laid on Christ the iniquity of every weary and broken soul. Therefore let us get to Christ and confess all our iniquities, and leave them upon him, calling on him for grace and mercy.

Use 2. To comfort those who depend upon Christ for mercy, and have confessed their sins to him. If he has taken away sin, it is done effectually (Heb. 10:1-10).

Use 3. To teach every soul who believes that Christ came to take away our sins, to renounce and abhor all sin and to cleanse themselves from all filthiness of flesh and spirit. Let us not take Christ's coming in vain, but give all diligence to purify ourselves as Christ is pure.

"And in him is no sin." This is the third reason, taken from the spotless innocence of Christ.

Doct. Christ is spotless and pure from sin.

Pilate, the malefactor, and the centurion acknowledged him to be so (Luke 23:22, 41, 47; Heb. 4:15; John 18:38; 1 Pet. 2:21, 22; 1 Pet. 1:19, 20). But why is he so?

-1. Because of the purity of the divine nature. If there had been sin in the human nature of Christ, it might have been said that God was a sinner.

-2. He must be faultless that he might fulfill all the legal types and sacrifices, which were to be without blemish.

-3. We needed such a Saviour (Heb. 7:26, 27). If he had offered sacrifice for himself, he would have needed a Saviour to redeem him; if he had not been without sin, he would have been swallowed up by death.

But does not the scripture say none is clean who is born of woman? (Job 25:4) True; yet Christ was not born by carnal generation, after the manner of men, but by the Holy Spirit.

Use 1. To show a difference between the first and second Adam. The first Adam was a sinner and propagated sins; the second Adam was without sin and propagated righteousness (Rom. 5:19). We must not rest in a carnal generation, for our natural birth is polluted; until we are born of him in whom is no sin, we cannot be blessed.

Use 2. To console those who feel themselves burdened and pressed down with sin. Though we are sinful and laden, and compassed about with it, yet in Christ is no sin or spot in nature, heart, or life. He came to fulfill all righteousness, and paid to God all to the utmost farthing. Righteous is Christ, both in life and death; what is lacking in us is supplied in him.

Use 3. To teach us all not to judge ourselves more sinful and miserable than others because we are evil treated in the world and afflicted of God. Thus it was with Christ; it is our happiness to do well, though we suffer evil (1 Pet. 2:21).

Doct. The spotless innocence of Christ is and ought to be an effectual motive to every hopeful Christian, to purge himself as Christ is pure (1 Pet. 1:16; Matt. 5:48).

-1. This is evident from the end of God's predestination of us (Rom. 8:28, 29); and God works all things according to the counsel of his will (Eph. 1:11).

-2. From the end of Christ's spotless life and death; he left us an example to follow in his steps (1 Pet. 2:21, 22). If we sin, we sin against the end of Christ's coming.

-3. From the close fellowship between Christ and us. He is our head and husband; therefore we must labor to be conformable to him (Eph. 5:25, 26).

-4. Christ takes pains to cleanse and heal us, so that he might present us without blemish to God. This is the scope of all his holy ordinances, and of Christ's shedding his blood.

Use 1. To reprove all who take pleasure in sin and, when they are reproved, justify themselves by saying that all are sinners. We must purge ourselves as Christ is pure, and in him is no sin.

Use 2. To stir up all the children of God to conform themselves to Christ in life and death (2 Cor. 7:1). Let us not sin against God's predestination and Christ's blood; let us not be a dishonor and grief to our head, and take God's ordinances in vain.

How shall we do this?

-1. Believe steadfastly in the Lord Jesus Christ for justification, and get his blood sprinkled upon us to cleanse us for sanctification.

-2. Set the pattern of Christ before us, and wisely behold it and view it. This will be effectual to mold and fashion us according to it (John 1:16). There is a supernatural power in Christ, looked upon by the eye of faith, to transfigure us into his likeness (2 Cor. 3:18). There is a power in the sight of Christ to convey his Spirit to transform us.

-3. Deal effectually with our own hearts, and pray to God for grace, that our souls may abhor and disallow and condemn all sin in us (Rom. 7:14-16). Let your judgment disallow it, and let your will abhor and hate it; and then it is not you who do it, but sin that dwells in you. God looks at sin as your enemy, and pities you.

1 John 3:6

"Whoever abides in him sins not: whoever sins has not seen him, neither known him."

The fourth reason why every hopeful Christian purifies himself is taken from the constant practice of hopeful Christians.

Doct. Every hopeful Christian who has constant fellowship with Christ does constantly avoid sin.

To abide in Christ implies two things: communion with Christ and continuance in it.

-1. We have fellowship with Christ, first, by the free donation of God. We are members of Christ by God's counsel and purpose; our sins are imputed to Christ, and his righteousness is imputed to us (John 16:14). Second, we have fellowship by a communication of his Spirit, causing us to receive him, and thus we are joined to him by faith and love (1 Cor. 6:17).

-2. This communion with Christ is indissoluble and everlasting (John 8:31, 32). Those who continue not, never had fellowship with Christ as his disciples (Jer. 31:34).

"Whoever abides in him sins not."

-1. He never sins to death (1 John 5:18). He does not commit the sin against the Holy Ghost.

-2. He does not live in sin. He does not make it his course and employment. He may slip and go astray, but he turns into the way again. Living in sin is made all one with continuing in sin (Rom. 6:1, 2).

-3. His judgment and conscience do not allow sin, but abhor it; therefore it is not his sin, but the sin of his rebellious and carnal part (Rom. 7:14, 15). He judges and condemns himself and grieves for it, and hates what he does; and therefore he is said not to sin.

The scriptures show a cleft nature in the Christian; yet by this text he sins not.

-1. There is the flesh and the Spirit; his will and conscience is more sanctified than corrupt. In the state of innocence the will was the weakest, but in regeneration God has made it the firmest and best. God has provided that the hedge should be stronger where it was broken.

-2. Being the most predominant faculties, the will and

judgment lead and rule the whole man. A clear fountain will purge itself and run a clear stream; so will the will and judgment, being the fountain of all our actions.

-3. If these faculties are for God, God accepts the whole man according to them. If there is a league between two kings, and offenses are committed by some subject — yet though the rulers punish such, the league is not broken. Thus the sins of the godly are punished even though they remain children of God.

But if this be so, why does God bitterly and sharply reprove his people for sin? To bring them to a better sight of sin and judgment, to shake us out of a lethargy and numbness. But when he has once awakened us and caused us to judge and loathe ourselves for our sins, God looks at us as righteous. Thus the diseases and distempers of judgment and heart are pitied and healed. As the stone in the reins distempers men, so the stone in the heart distempers the heart and judgment. God looks at this as the disease of his children.

Use 1. This shows a broad difference between those who are born of God and those who are not. (a) Those who sin unto death are not born of God. God keeps his from that sin. (b) Nor are those who take pleasure in sin and made a trade of it, since God's children do not do so. (c) If men live in secret sins, against knowledge and conscience, they are not yet born of God; their will and affections are not with God but against him.

Use 2. To teach us all to put a favorable construction upon the failings of God's people. We must not believe everyone who reports evil of them. When those who are born of God commit any great sin, their repentance is as exemplary as their sin, as is seen in David and Peter.

Use 3. To comfort those Christians who find their judgments and wills upright, hating and abhorring the sins they commit, complaining and shaming themselves for them. If the judgment and heart are with God and against sin, God looks at them as not sinning. But this must not make us secure and careless of repenting and being grieved for sin.

Doct. The exemplary walking of the children of God ought to be an effectual motive to every Christian not to walk in the ways of sin, but to purge themselves.

-1. When the apostle discourages men from wearing long hair and women from shearing their hair, the argument he uses is, "We have no such custom" (1 Cor. 11:16); which would be of no force unless the examples of God's servants were an effectual motive to stir us up to the same ways (1 Cor. 14:33). There is a decency in all church of God, and therefore he pleads against their confusion. "Let all things be done decently and in order" (1 Cor. 14:40). This is a reason why we should wait upon God, because it is good in the eyes of the saints (Ps. 52:9).

-2. God commands it. God has set this as the royal way (Phil. 3:17). This is the highway to heaven; God would have all to walk in the trodden path of his people.

-3. It is a matter of comfort to our own souls. It will excuse us from many doubts of our own hearts, and many slanders which might be cast upon us. If a member of your body has a motion not guided by the body, you look at it as a palsy.

-4. We put a discomfort upon our brethren when we walk in ways contrary to them. They walk in a blameless course; if we walk in sinful ways, we put heartbreak upon them. When the apostle saw men walk in ways contrary to God's, it was the grief of his heart (Phil. 3:17-19).

Use 1. This is a notable comfort to every soul who stands uncertain what way to take. Walk in holy ways like God's people. Do not think they are strange and solitary ways; no, if you walk in good ways you shall not go alone, for all good company has gone this way. Some will go to much effort to be in good company; why, walk in a way free from sin, and in it you shall have good company, and in it only.

Use 2. To dissuade us from sin; gird up your loins from it. When we walk in the ways of sin, none go that way but bad company, and it will be an argument against us (Matt. 7:23).

Use 3. To guide us to a wise observation of the ways of

godly men. Though every godly man has his failings, for which he blushes before God, yet all of them have something in their ways by which you may purge yourself. All of them come closer to Christ in something than you; there is something in which they purge themselves more than you. God has always been wont to guide his servants into ways of innocence. If God guides them into good ways, then follow them.

But you will say, May I not be deceived?

-1. True, sometimes God's people go wrong; Aaron and the congregation danced around the calf (Exod. 32:19). The people of God took up a custom of carrying the ark in a cart from the heathen, when the shoulders of the Levites should have carried it (1 Chron. 13:5-7). So it is true that the generality of God's people might go wrong; but though they do go astray, do not take them at their starts, but in their latter courses; for they are good. Though David and the people went wrong, yet presently they saw their error.

-2. Look at the pattern of God's people so that you weigh them in the balance of the sanctuary. Have your wits exercised in the scripture, so that you may discern of their ways and follow them so far as they go right.

Doct. All who sin had never a clear sound knowledge of the Lord Christ, and have never seen him.

Sight implies clearness and certainty. He speaks of the knowledge whose ground is experience, word, Spirit (Phil. 3:10); whose fruit is obedience (1 John 2:3); and whose end is salvation (John 17:3). Men who have had an experimental knowledge of God have such a spirit within them that they cannot sin (Gal. 5:17). If they do, their conscience will so smite them that they will be glad to get rid of it.

Use 1. To refute the doctrine of the Papists, who say that a man who is in Christ may fall away. St. John here refutes them: if they sin, they never knew him.

Use 2. If we would rivet this comfort in our souls, let us keep our hearts innocent from sin.

Use 3. To console the soul who has formerly seen Christ's death purging sin in him. Though we are weak and think we shall not hold out, yet God will keep us from sin and comfort us against the aspersions cast upon religion by the sins of professors. Whoever sins has never seen Christ.

1 John 3:7

"Little children, let no man deceive you: he who does righteousness is righteous, even as he is righteous."

The apostle had shown that all hopeful Christians cleanse themselves from sin. It might be objected, We have teachers who teach otherwise. The apostle meets with this and answers, "Let no man deceive you."

In his answer are three parts:

-1. A loving compellation, "little children," which includes babes, young men, and old men.

-2. The exhortation, a warning against deceivers.

-3. Two doctrines contrary to them: "He who does righteousness is righteous," and "He who commits sin is of the devil." He proves these by three reasons: the practice of the devil, the purpose of Christ's coming, and the practice of those who are born of God.

Doct. It is the duty of all sorts of good people to take heed that they be not deceived in judging who are righteous men.

The question was, Who was righteous? The false teachers said a man may be righteous and yet live in sin. We must as much beware of counterfeit righteousness as of dogs (Phil. 3:2); they are not so apt to bite men as these are apt to do the church hurt.

Why must we view this as a duty?

-1. Because of the easiness of being deceived by the pretenses of righteous men in all ages (Gal. 2:4). Under the mask of righteous men walk many who are unrighteous.

-2. Because of the necessity that lies upon us to have communion and fellowship with them (Ps. 16:3; Gal. 6:10), doing good offices to them (1 John 4:7, 20). Yea, we are commanded to walk in their steps (Phil. 3:17).

-3. Because of the danger of walking with unrighteous men (Prov. 17:15; Prov. 4:14, 15). This we may easily do unless we know them.

Use 1. To reprove all who think that all they live among are righteous; why then was this exhortation? How could a man be deceived if all were righteous? (Numb. 16:2, 3)

Use 2. To teach us all to pray to God that we may grow up in a spirit of discerning. There is an instinct in the servants of God by which they are able to relish the spirits of one another. A dog will scent out his way with more dexterity than a man can reason it out. A man may be able to open the whole law, but when he comes to discerning, he may yet know not who is righteous and who is not.

Use 3. As we grow righteous ourselves, we shall better discern others. A woman who has conceived will more easily discern another; so when you feel the work of righteousness in your own heart, you may comfort yourself that you are righteous, because you love God's children.

But you will say, How shall I know who is righteous? A righteous man is known by his righteous ways. St. John does not speak here of what makes a man righteous, but what declares him righteous. The Jesuits grant this; if a tree brings forth grapes, it is a vine; if figs, a fig-tree.

What is it to do righteousness? It is the contrary to what it is to commit sin; that is, to walk in God's commandments. A man does righteousness: -1. When his heart and judgment are for it. -2. When God's laws are his rule of righteousness. -3. When his end is righteousness. -4. When it is a burden and grief to do unrighteousness, and he recovers himself.

Use 4. To avoid the doctrine of justification by works. He does not say that good works make a man good, but that we may know a man is righteous by his righteousness. He says this to prevent them from thinking that the habit of righteousness makes us righteous. Imperfect righteousness cannot make us perfectly righteous (Isa. 64:6; 1 Cor. 13:8-12), neither in the covenant of works nor of grace. In the covenant of works, not the habits of grace but works of righteousness justify; and in the covenant of grace, we are justified by faith without the works of the law.

Use 5. Here is a sign of trial of our own righteousness and that of others. When in ordinary course we give God and man their due, when we go about good duties in God's name and for his glory, then we are righteous.

But may we not do it to stop conscience, or so that we may be well thought of? You may do so, and yet be sincere. I may please both men and my own conscience. If you please men, will you not still stick to God? If you do good duties freely, constantly, and humbly, though you do them to satisfy your conscience or to please men, yet you are righteous. So you may judge of other men. It is not enough to do good duties, but they must do them with affection. If they cling to God, though for their own ends, yet they are righteous.

1 John 3:8, 9

"He who commits sin is of the devil, for the devil sins from the beginning. For this purpose the Son of God was manifested, that he might destroy the works of the devil. Whoever is born of God does not commit sin; for his seed remains in him, and he cannot sin, because he is born of God."

Against the wicked principles of the false teachers, the apostle arms them with these two principles of Christian religion: he who does righteousness is righteous, and he who commits sin is of the devil.

"He who makes sin his work, makes himself the child of the devil." So it is in the original.

What is it to commit or work sin? In many things we sin all (James 3:2). Yet a man is said to sin, even when his ordinary course is a righteous and good way, when he makes a trade of sin and when he justifies or excuses himself in his sin.

But in a proper sense a man is said to commit sin:

-1. When he imagines, devises, or plots sin.

-2. When he acts it, by travailing in birth as a woman with child, and by bringing it forth in due time (Ps. 7:14). "He who does not righteousness is not of God." Of whom then? Of the devil (John 8:44). To be of the devil is to have him as a father, to be begotten of him, as Elymas, who would have kept the deputy from the faith (Acts 13:8-10).

Use 1. Here we may see what parentage we are of. What is our business in the world? If it is to follow the lust of our own hearts, to regard our profits and pleasures, and if we delight in sin and malign what crosses us, we are children of the devil. The scripture does not call a man a child of the devil if he is merely natural, deprived of grace and prone to sin; but men are called the children of the devil when they are in the bosom of the church, and see the way they should walk in, and yet are resolved to do evil and to take pains in it; and if any reprove them, they are at enmity with them.

Are they then damned? No, it is possible for them to become better (2 Tim. 2:25, 26). They may be delivered out of the snares of Satan. But God never does this without deep conflicts, so that it may be seen that there has been strife between Michael and his angels, and the devil and his angels.

Take a man merely natural, and it is an easy matter to bring him home (Jude 22, 23). There is more opposition against grace when the devil has come into the heart and has joined with sin. The devil cast a thought into Judas' heart to betray Christ (John 13:2); he did not consent to it immediately, but after he had eaten the sop, Satan entered into him (v. 27). The devil had possession of him before, setting his heart to covetousness, but now he has a farther possession, leading him to betray Christ. The devil finds us flesh and blood at the first, and tempts us to sin; if we begin to run to him, then he enters and sets us in that way. When a new temptation comes, and we consider whether to do it or not, if we break off we are the better, and we get strength against sin. But if we yield and commit sin willingly, then we are the children of the devil.

Let us take heed of pleasing ourselves in any sin. If we have committed sin willingly, and if the devil comes with full sail into our souls, now if we lie down in peace, we shall be the children of Satan. This is to give our souls and hearts to the devil. A sin of rebellion is not of ignorance, but through depravity of will (1 Sam. 15:23). When a man resolves to sin against God, this is a sin of witchcraft. As in witchcraft a man or woman gives his soul to the devil, so when a man commits sin willingly, he gives his soul to the devil. You would think it strange to be called a witch; therefore do not rest in this condition.

How shall we get out of it? -1. Henceforth resolve that through the strength of God's grace, you will never commit any sin again. -2. Listen more diligently to the word of God; give up your heart to God and his word (2 Cor. 8;5). -3. Lay open all your rebellion, confessing your sins and rebellions to God; tell him how and where you have rebelled against him (1 John 21:9).

Use 2. To magnify the freeness of God's grace which has delivered us out of darkness into light and from Satan to God, when we have sinned against knowledge and conscience.

But how may we know that he who sins is of the devil? The apostle gives us three reasons.

-1. Because the devil sinned from the beginning.

-2. Because Christ came for the contrary end.

-3. Because the practice of every child of God opposes sin (v. 9).

Doct. 1. The devil keeps a constant and continual course of sinning from the beginning to this day.

The word διάβολος signifies an accuser; yet that is not

his only word, for he is sometimes called Satan, an adversary. One of his ordinary works is to accuse the brethren.

-1. Sometimes he does accuse God to us, as he did to Adam. "Does not God know?"

-2. He accuses God to the conscience of a poor sinner, that God has cast him off forever.

-3. Sometimes he accuses us to God as he accused Job. "Does Job fear God for nought?" (Job 1:9, 10).

-4. He accuses us to those who are in God's place, as to the magistrates. And he accuses us to other men; he puts slanderous speeches in the mouths of others without any ground or cause.

How is he said to sin from the beginning? It implies that he transgresses the law by a constant act; he sins daily and provokes others to sin; that has been his constant course from the beginning. "From the beginning" is not meant from his first creation, for it is evident that he stood until the sixth day; otherwise God would not have said that it was all very good.

There are five things in which Satan has sinned from the beginning, and in these he transcends all sinners.

-1. He was the eldest sinner, the first in sin.

-2. He is the most industrious sinner; he comes from compassing the world (Job 2:2).

-3. He is the father of sin (John 8:44). If a man can utter any vain word, any sinful practice, it is from the devil, because he watches over the ways of men; and he is always casting in blasphemous thoughts against God and envious thoughts against our brother.

-4. Every sin he has committed has been a sin against the Holy Spirit; for that sin requires illumination and malice of heart, and Satan has both.

-5. He transcends others in the perpetuity and constancy of sinning. He is called an unclean spirit. When he lies, he speaks of his own accord (John 8:44). If at any time he speaks true, it is by the overruling hand of God.

Use 1. Satan has the law of God in his heart; for otherwise he could not sin, because sin is the transgression of the law. Satan at first had the image of God stamped upon him; he was created in holiness and righteousness, having all the commandments of the first and second table written in his heart. The fallen angels, with Satan at their head, are called sons of God (Job 1:6); but through sinning against holiness and righteousness, they transgressed the law of God.

Use 2. It confutes the Anabaptists, who say that sin enters into the world by parents, not through propagation but through imitation only; from which it follows that children do not sin until they are capable of imitation. But then why does David complain that he was born in sin?

Use 3. It exhorts us all to a threefold duty. (a) It teaches us to walk more circumspectly against Satan, for he knows all the ways and methods of the sons of men; therefore we have need to pray daily, "Lead us not into temptation, but deliver us from evil." (b) It teaches us to loathe sin and all its ways. You cannot walk in a way of sin without having Satan for your companion. (c) Take heed especially of continuing long in any sin. Many there are who not only now and then fall into sin, but always walk in it. Do they not truly imitate the devil in this?

Use 4. This may teach God's servants never to be weary of well-doing. The devil is not weary of sin; he is always employed in it, and yet he is not weary. It is his meat and drink to sin and to draw others to sin. And if Satan finds such pleasure in sin, then you may find more comfort in well-doing. If he is not weary in aggravating his own sin and misery, then let us not be weary in getting grace and peace to ourselves and others. Do not believe him; he is your enemy.

Doct. 2. The end of Christ's coming into the world was to dissolve and loose the works of Satan.

This was expressly foretold: "The seed of the woman shall break the serpent's head" (Gen. 3:15), that is, the projects and plots of Satan. The head is taken for the dominion and power which he has in our hearts.

What is it to loose and dissolve? It implies that the work of the devil was tied in knots. Satan had bound us with a threefold knot. (a) He had tied our nature to sin, so that we cannot partake of mere nature without partaking of his corruption (Gen. 6:5; John 3:6; Rom. 7:14). (b) He has bound one sin to another. Partake of one sin and you partake of all (Deut. 29:19). (c) If we partake of sin, we shall inevitably partake of punishment (Rom. 6:23; Gen. 2:17; Gal. 3:10).

How did Christ's coming into the world loose the works of Satan? By being manifested we must understand the whole work of Christ's mediation. By his innocent birth, holy life, and righteous and holy suffering, Christ has procured pardon of sin. And since he has gotten that, sin and punishment are dissolved.

But may not our natures be corrupt, though our sins are pardoned? (Gal. 4:4, 5) The same Spirit that makes us cry "Abba, Father" (Rom. 8:14-16) also leads us into all ways of holiness and righteousness. Hence our ways are healed, and our course of sin is broken off (Luke 19:48). Yet we are still bitterly entangled with the corruptions of our own hearts (Hos. 4:8, 9).

Use 1. To teach those who live in any sin that this is a sign they are of the devil. They tie those knots which Christ came to loose.

Use 2. To try our hearts, whether or not we are indeed born of God. Would you know whether Christ came effectually for you? If he did, then he has untied those knots and snares.

Use 3. To exhort us to several duties. (a) Take heed of all sin, and do not allow any in yourself. If you do the work of Satan, you dissolve the work of Christ. (b) If you find your soul entangled, labor to dissolve the work of Satan. Now none can dissolve it but Christ, but he came to this end; so therefore let us make our complaint to him. And because this will not serve unless we give up ourselves wholly to be ruled by him, therefore let us resign our souls up to him, wholly to be wrought upon by the word of God. (c) We may comfort ourselves, if we have given ourselves up to Christ. If we see that Christ has begun to pardon our sins, to cut us off from sin and to mortify it, he will perfect this good work (Deut. 32:4; Rom. 16:22).

Doct. 3. The seed of God in the hearts of God's children preserves them not only from sin, but from possibility to sin.

In verse 9 are three things:

-1. The course of a child of God; he does not commit sin.

-2. The cause of it; the seed of God is in him.

-3. This is amplified from the impossibility of sin which is in him by his new birth.

What is this seed of God? The word of God is an immortal seed, and that not in the letter, but in the spirit (1 Pet. 1:2). A man is born again when the word and Spirit have begotten him to the image of God. He is born when the word and Spirit have done the work of seed. Many a man knows the word is true; the devil knows the word well enough; but the word is seed when the soul of a man not only receives it, but conceives by it, and is framed to the will of God. Being thus born of God, he is always his child. When a man is transformed into the image of God, his judgment and heart are stamped with the image of God; he delights in God and in his way, and in his children. His judgment and heart are carried that way; they are all for God. His heart is given to God (Prov. 23:26). The seed of God's word is not in a natural man (John 2:24, 25), but is in a child of God (Ps. 119:11; 1 John 2:27).

Why does the seed of God, both word and Spirit, remain in the children of God? There are three reasons.

-1. The word had mighty power in his soul when he was first begotten and born of God. It so affected and terrified that no earthly comfort was able to satisfy his heart; he had been so overwhelmed with fears and doubts that he will be afraid to sin as long as he lives.

-2. The word and Spirit have strong possession in the heart. They abide in the whole man, but especially in the conscience and will. "I do not allow what I do; but what I hate, that do I"; this shows that the word has taken such fast hold of his judgment and will that both are for God (Ps. 119: 111; Jer. 32:40).

-3. This seed makes a great change in the heart of a child of God. It makes him, a wild olive, to be a sweet olive. "A good tree cannot bring forth evil fruit (Matt. 7:18).

But there is a seed of corruption in us; cannot we bring forth according to that? True, there is an old man; but he is crucified. If we sin, we do not trade in sin, for our judgments and hearts are against it. When some lawless lusts have carried us captive, and we complain of them to God and desire that they were cast out, God does not look at them as ours (Rom. 6:14; Ps. 119:29, 30).

Use 1. To refute all doctrines of the apostasy of saints. They say that those who are born of God may come to sin totally and finally. This error fights against a double doctrine of the apostle. First he says, "Whoever is born of God, the seed remains in him." If a man can shake out the Spirit, how does it remain? Second, the text says there is no possibility of sinning, but they say he may sin.

It may be objected that he cannot sin while he is a child of God, but he may cease to be a child of God. I answer, he cannot sin, and sin is the only means by which he may be made no child of God.

It may be objected again (as by the Papists and their divines) that liberty of will is restrained by such a doctrine. The will cannot be free unless a man may will a thing or not.

I ask whether a child of God forbears a sin willingly or not. We say willingly; if a child of God walks in innocency from sin, he can do no otherwise. But their doctrine is that a man's will is not free unless a man may do a thing or not do it. What do they think of saints and angels in heaven, or God himself? Do they have free will or not? I hope none of them can sin, yet they do good most freely.

Well then, in what does liberty consist? First, in doing a thing without restraint; but more, in following a man's own judgment and reason.

Use 2. To try our own hearts, whether we are born of God or not. If we are, our ordinary course is good; we dare not sin, know not how to go about it. That seed which is in us sets our hearts and judgments aright (Gen. 39:9). Other men may think it strange that we cannot do as they do. This is a good evidence that we are born of God.

Use 3. See what to judge of those who have made a profession and yet fall away. They were never born of God, for then they could not have sinned.

Use 4. This may be a ground of much comfort to every child of God. He will preserve us spotless and blameless. Here is a double comfort. (a) He looks not at your course as sin, if you are humbled for it; and he will take a course to mortify it. (b) You can never lose the savor of God; if you are once begotten, you can never be unbegotten. You are begotten of an immortal seed, and therefore cannot die.

May this not be a doctrine of presumption? For then a man may live as he desires. I answer, suppose a physician should give us the apple of the tree of life, that we should never die; but yet he bids us take heed to a diet, for though we could not die, yet we should have such pains and diseases that we would wish death rather than life. So God will make the best of his servants know what it is to wax wanton against him, and make them curse all the occasions that lead them to sin.

Use 5. This should teach us who have received any seed of God, to take heed that we sin not. And therefore let us inform our judgments aright, out of the Word of God (2 Tim. 1:3), so that we may come to sound judgment and wisdom. One error of judgment will shake you much in your way (1 John 5:18).

1 John 3:10

"In this the children of God are manifest, and the children of the devil: whoever does not do righteousness is not of God, neither he who loves not his brother."

Here is a manifest difference between the children of God and the children of the devil. The signs of difference are twofold: general, they do not do righteousness, and particular, they do not love the brethren.

Doct. The children of God and the children of the devil are not so much alike that there may not be found a manifest difference between them, even in this world (Gal. 5:19; Matt. 7:20).

If there were not a manifest difference, it were not so necessary for God to charge his ministers to walk with a divided affection toward them (Jer. 15:19). If the difference had not been so manifest, God would not have blamed them so justly (Ezek. 13:22).

If you say this is peculiar to ministers, Levites, so that only they may judge who is clean and who is not, and not private Christians, I answer that God makes it a badge here of those who shall inherit heaven and have fellowship with God there (Ps. 15:4). This shows we should put a sign of difference not merely between good and bad, but even between bads. Some sin ignorantly, others more absolutely (Jude vv. 20-23).

How does this manifest difference appear? A double sign of it is given in 1 Cor. 12:10.

-1. It is a spiritual gift of discerning. He speaks concerning what gifts and what measures a man has, and wherein the strength of a man's gifts lies (1 Cor. 2:15). Although he cannot discern every man's special gifts, what he is most fit for, yet plain and manifest things he discerns, and also between moral and spiritual, between things of God, and Satan, and the world.

-2. The second manifestation of this difference is the inclination of the end of each. "By their fruits you shall know them" (Matt. 7:20; Gal. 5:19).

But cannot a hypocrite pass so that he may not be discerned? What of Judas? He was not discerned for a long time; for every one of the disciples at the Supper began to suspect himself (Matt. 26:22). Again, God's people sometimes carry things weakly, and the pulse of God's grace beats weakly, as if no life and strength were in them (1 Kings 19:17, 18; Ps. 12:1).

I answer, sometimes hypocrisy is spun with so fine a thread, and so well dyed, that you can hardly discern a difference. And sometimes grace is so low in the heart that you cannot discern it. This is true, but it is but for a time. Judas was at length plainly known to have been a thief. Jannes and Jambres can do miracles as well as Moses and Aaron, but in time they shall be discerned (2 Tim. 3:8, 9). Lay hands suddenly on no man; for if he proves not pure, you shall be partaker of his sins, and all the harm he does (1 Tim. 5:22, 25). Some men's sins lie open beforehand, i.e. before the judgment of the church; others follow after, but they cannot be hid; God will have them made manifest in due time. There is nothing so secret that it will not be made manifest (Luke 12:2). If you put leaven into five pecks of meal, it will not always lie hidden, but will in time break forth.

Use 1. Of reproof to good men and bad. After a while in sin, we do not know ourselves. It was a dangerous sign of a man's separation from God if, after so long a time of the apostles' preaching, he did not know what was in him (2 Cor. 13:5).

Use 2. This reproves the Popish doctors, who say that no man can discern his own state. They allege from Eccl. 9:2 that a man cannot know by outward things whether he is in God's favor or not. But if a man comes in a sheepskin, I shall take him to be a sheep (Matt. 7:16-20).

Use 3. To teach everyone to take heed of a devilish spirit, or any unrighteous course of life. Though a man may hide it long, yet at length it will be known. It is as impossible that a man's lack of love should be known, as for a man to keep fire in his bosom and it not to break out (Ps. 36:2-4).

Use 4. To exhort all who are born of God, not to smother grace. God would have your grace manifest, and that to edify. Do not content yourself with household Christianity, but manifest to the world of what spirit you are. It was commendable in Mary, when she was stirring with child, to visit her cousin Elizabeth (Luke 2:6). If God has wrought any grace in our hearts, it is well to manifest it.

"He who does not righteousness is not of God."

Doct. Not only commission of sin, but negligence of a Christian course of life, is a manifest sign of a child of the devil.

Every tree that brings forth not good fruit is cut down and cast into the fire (Matt. 3:10). "There is no fear of God before their eyes" (Ps. 36:1) How does this appear to David? "He has left off to do good, he does not shun evil; but if an evil matter comes in his way, he sets himself to work it" (Ps. 36:3, 4). He does not study as David did, "What shall I render to the Lord for all his benefits?" (Ps. 116:12) He who does not set himself in a good course is not the child of God, but of the devil.

-1. His ways bear the image of Satan. He was set in a good state, but he ceased to do good and set himself in a course which was not good.

-2. The seed of God is necessarily fruitful wherever it is (Ps. 1:2, 3). A child of God is working in his mind and heart, and always doing good.

-3. He puts a hindrance upon some who would do better if it were removed (Acts 13:8-19). The devil is always an impediment of good. If a man can do good and does it not, he cumbers the ground; therefore cut him down (Luke 13:7-9).

Use 1. To reprove the ignorance of those who imagine that if they do nobody any harm, God will accept them. But if it goes badly with them, what will become of whoremongers and adulterers? Can you say you have devised good and watched for an opportunity to be doing good? This is a comfort to you. But do not comfort yourself merely in your innocence from evil, without doing good.

Use 2. To teach us all, if we ever desire an evident mark to ourselves that we are children of God, to become doers of righteousness. It is the seed of God which sets you to work. God requires that we should be doing good with our means, so that when we go hence we may say, as our Saviour, "Father, I have finished the work thou gavest me to do." Rehoboam did evil in the sight of the Lord, because he did not prepare good in his heart; he studied not to do good (2 Chron. 10:13).

"Neither he who loves not his brother."

Doct. Not only the hatred of a brother, but the lack of love to a brother, is a sign of a child of the devil (John 13:35).

-1. This may be seen from the constant practice of God. Is there any of those whom he has adopted, whom he loves not? (Matt. 10:42) And observe the contrary practice of Satan: there is no child of God from whom he is not estranged.

-2. Those who love not their brethren have no knowledge of God (1 John 4:8). He has not the experience of God's love, and God is love. When the sun shines upon a stone wall, though it is cold, yet it reflects the heat back again. So there is none who has felt the warmth of God's love upon his soul, but though his heart were cold before, yet he reflects it upon all.

-3. All brethren are in the same condition. He who loves not his brother because he is a brother, loves none at all. He who does not love one of a man's children, because he is born of the man, loves none of them. A man may hate a brother for some sinister reason, as Joseph's brethren; but it was a certain sign they were not born of God. And they who did not love Joseph for his goodness' sake, could not love Jacob or Abraham.

Use 1. Here is a manifest difference between the children of God and of the devil. If there is any brother whom you love not, from whom your heart is girded up, you are not born of God. I know provocations may weaken affections and turn the stream so that it shall not run so fully nor so strongly; yet a child of God takes a course to remove matters of enmity, and he considers himself bound to hate himself for neglect of his brother. A man may be angry toward those he loves, yet without sin. But this lack of love will do more injury to your spirit than the injury your brother does to you. When anger is over, love returns again.

What is it not to love a brother? We have seen that there are two things in love: communion with them and communication of good to them. In some things a man desires communion with others; in other things, though he desires not communion with them, yet he desires communication of good to them. But when both are lacking, there is no love.

Use 2. This should exhort us to stretch our love universally to every soul. It is better to bestow your love upon some base hypocrite than to restrain it from some poor Christian. You cannot neglect one Christian without hazarding your whole general state. In judgment of charity, if they abstain from gross sins and do good duties, we should think well of them; and we had better lose our love upon them than neglect a child of God (Ps. 35:12, 14). And indeed our love is not lost, for it shall return into our bosom. It is a sign I love a man, if I love his picture; so though a man should be a hypocrite, yet if we love the show of grace, it is a sign we love grace indeed.

1 John 3:11

"For this is the message that you heard from the beginning, that we should love one another."

In the former verse the apostle had given us two manifest differences between the children of God and of the devil. He proves the latter mark to be;a manifest difference. This is a message and an ancient one which we have received of God. The duty of brotherly love is proved by its promulgation as a message, and by its adjunct, "from the beginning."

Doct. When we read or hear the word of God, we should look at it as a message sent from God.

-1. We should so consider it because of the purpose of scripture. "Whatever is written, is written for our instruction" (Rom. 15:4). There are not in scripture some things for men of talents, and other things for meaner men, but all things are for our comfort and instruction. If I read threatenings, commandments, promises, they are all a message to me; though every threatening does not belong to me, yet it does so far as to keep me from sins. And so, though promises do not belong to you who are not in the state of grace, yet it is good for you to know them, so that these promises may break your heart, to see what mercy you neglect.

-2. Because of the office and calling of the penmen of scripture (Mal. 2:7; 2 Cor. 5:19).

Use 1. To direct those who hear or read the word. God calls the king to read it once a day (Deut. 17:19). If you take up the Book of God, you take a bundle of messages; as if God should ask you, "Understandest thou what thou readest?" You will have read it in vain if you do not look at it as a message. We are more ready to receive the message if it comes from great men or friends.

Use 2. In hearing or reading the word, we have a twofold duty. (a) To receive all with reverence (Judg. 3:20; Acts

10:33). (b) To consider how far it pertains to us. Though all scripture is for my comfort to know, yet I must apply it to myself, so far as it concerns me; I must receive it as the bread of my portion, and chew upon it. God requires that we mix the word with faith (Heb. 4:2).

Use 3. This should teach us to obey the word of God. It is a message from God; therefore do not take it ill from the messenger's hands, nor cavil at it.

Use 4. This should exhort all to get Bibles, if they have none; and if they have them, to read something every day. There are two ways of communion between God and ourselves: when we speak to God in prayer, and when God speaks to us in his word. It is a fearful thing when there is such strangeness between God and us that he should seldom hear us, and we seldom hear him.

Doct. The love of another is an ancient message that God has sent us, and has continued to send us from the beginning.

He does not say "in the beginning," but "from the beginning," which implies a continuance of it (1 Thess. 4:9). Thus God complains of Cain, "Why are you angry with your brother?" (Gen. 4:6) When Abraham's and Lot's herdsmen were ready to fall out, this message from heaven was sent by Abraham a prophet, "We are brethren" (Gen. 13:8). This continued to Moses (Lev. 19:18). Our Saviour is instant in preaching this love (John 13:34), as are Paul (Rom. 13:8,10; 1 Cor. 13:4-7) and Peter (1 Pet. 1:22).

We have the strongest reasons to urge us to mutual love.

-1. God's love to us. He walks in tender love to us, and therefore he never writes a letter to us without bidding us to love one another. "See that you do not fall out by the way" (Gen. 45:24). It is an argument that we are born of God, if we love one another.

-2. The great use of this grace. It is necessary above all graces; it is the bond of perfection, which knits all together in a family or in a congregation (Ps. 133:1-3).

-3. Love covers a multitude of sins, both in me and others (1 Pet. 4:8; Cant. 8:7).

-4. Love is the fulfilling of the law (Rom. 13:10). When a man walks in love, love will carry him through every good duty with cheerfulness and comfort.

Use 1. This reproves all strangeness and enmity among members of a family or congregation. If God sends this message and we receive it not, there is no fellowship between him and us, but a spirit of strangeness or the breach of the whole law. If a man does not come to church in love, he never profits by anything, neither by word nor sacraments.

Use 2. Whatever we learn, let us learn above all this lesson so anciently taught us, so often pressed upon us.

1 John 3:12

"Not as Cain, who was of that wicked one and slew his brother. And why did he slay him? Because his own works were evil, and his brother's righteous."

In the tenth verse the apostle makes lack of love to the brethren a manifest difference between the child of God and of the devil. This he proves: -1. Because to love our brother is the message of God. -2. Because he who lacks love is of the devil. This he proves by the pattern of the eldest son of the devil; as he did, so will his younger brethren do. Here is a pattern of hatred of our brother, Cain. He is described by his spiritual origin, "of the devil," and by the cause of his hatred, "because his brother's works were good and his evil."

Doct. The example of any not loving his brother should be an effectual motive to us to love every brother.

Consider the hatred of Cain for his brother.

-1. It was causeless (Ps. 69:4). They hated Christ without a cause (John 15:25); so Cain hated Abel (Gen. 4:7).

-2. It was impious and wicked. He had just cause to love,

and against that just cause he hated him for his righteousness.

-3. It was a deadly hatred, such as would not be slacked without blood.

-4. It was implacable (Gen. 4:8), for no counsel would abate the mood of his malice. God asks Cain, "Why is your countenance so cast down?" The good counsel which God gave him was as bellows to blow up his wrath.

-5. It was a hypocritical hatred, for it is likely that in God's presence he had smoothed over his countenance and speech. Yet when he got his brother in the field and had opportunity, he slew him.

Use 1. This dissuades us from the hatred of any Christian soul. If there is but one Abel whom we hate, it will translate us into the brotherhood of Cain. Therefore either love your brethren, all of them, or be as Cain.

But one will say, I do not slay my brother, though I hate him. I answer, it is no thanks to you if your malice is curbed and restrained.

Use 2. To teach us all, if we desire to be free from hating our brethren, to love goodness for goodness' sake. Aquila and Priscilla would lay down their necks for Paul (Rom. 16:4). If a man loves the light well, it is a sign of good eyes; so if we love to see many lights about us, it is a sign our eyes are good (Acts 11:22, 23). If we were evil, we would wink and shut our eyes.

1 John 3:13

"Marvel not, my brethren, if the world hates you."

Having told us of Cain's hatred to his brother, the apostle takes away an objection. It might be said that Abel was so innocent it was a wonder that he should slay him. But he bids them not to wonder at it.

Doct. It should be no surprise if the world hates God's children.

By 'world' he means worldly men:

-1. Because their original is in the world (John 8:23; John 15:19).

-2. Because they are the greater part of the world (1 John 5:19).

-3. Because they are wholly taken up in worldly business, in mind, heart, speech, actions (Phil. 3:19). They serve the god of this world (2 Cor. 4:4, 5). They have their portion in this world (Ps. 17:14). Such men hate God's children (Mark 13:13; Luke 6:22).

Why do they hate them?

-1. Because of ignorance of them: the world knows you not (1 John 3:1).

-2. Because of the separation of God's people from the world. "I have chosen you out of the world" (John 15:19).

-3. Because God's servants desire to draw others out of the world, and this they cannot endure.

Use 1. To reprove the unthankfulness of the world, that will requite evil for good and hatred for good-will. The world has its standing for their sakes (2 Kings 3:14; Acts 18:9-11). If your worldly state prospers, it is for the sakes of God's people (Gen. 30:27; Gen. 39:5; Gen. 19:22). God would have poured out his wrath, had not Moses stood in the gap (Ps. 106:23).

Use 2. To teach us not to enter upon Christianity if we cannot swallow bitter pills. If the hatred of the world is too churlish for your stomach, keep your heart and hands from it (Luke 14:26).

Use 3. This will comfort God's people. Though the world hates them, yet they are only the world; they have no higher breath than the world.

"Marvel not."

God's people are apt to marvel at this for three reasons:

-1. They know not the cause (Ps. 69:4).

-2. The hatred is sometimes extreme and deadly.

-3. It is new and rare.

Let the world know that God's people have more cause to think strange of the world than the world of them; they give the world no cause to hate them (Acts 17:6).

Doct. God's children are not to marvel at the world's hatred.

-1. God has appointed you to it (1 Thess 3:3); he has done it for many ends. How else could you show forth your patience? How could you be kept from bad company? God will lay bitter pills to the breasts of the world so that you may be weaned from it (Ps. 119:115).

-2. Many times the world does it out of ignorance; therefore we may take it better that we are ill dealt with. A king takes it not ill to be badly dealt with at strangers' hands.

-3. The world hated Christ; therefore it is no marvel if it hates us.

-4. This hatred is no new thing; it has continued from Cain.

-5. If you were in the world's case, you would do the like. Therefore marvel not (Tit. 3:2, 3).

Use 1. Do not lay down religion for fear of the world's hatred. This is not the way; do not fear the hatred of the world.

Use 2. This should teach God's servants to walk more circumspectly, humbly, lovingly. If a man were to walk among his friends, he would care the less; but if he lives among his enemies, he will look to every step. As soon as you trip, you shall have mouths open against you. Therefore Daniel's course was notable; he so walked that they could not tax him (Daniel 6:1-5).

1 John 3:14

"We know that we have passed from death to life, because we love the brethren. He who loves not his brother abides in death."

The apostle lays this down as a second reason why they should not marvel, that they have passed from death to life; implying that they who know they have passed from death to life need not marvel if the world hates them.

Doct. God's people have passed from death to life.

God's people are opposed to the world; they are translated out of the world (John 5:24). They are redeemed out of the world by death. Death and condemnation are synonymous. By death is meant death for sin and death in sin; the natural state in which a man lives while he is in this world. It is called a state of death in a fivefold respect.

-1. All death presupposes life to go before: we do not say that a stone is dead. Death is a privation of life. A man who has no life but what the world gives is dead, because he had life, at least in possibility, in the loins of Adam (Eph. 2:3).

-2. Death is a separation of the soul from the body. We are said to be dead (Gal. 2:20) because our souls and bodies, which are capable of life, are separated from the Lord Jesus, the fountain of life (Eph. 2:12; Eph. 4:17-19).

-3. Life is a power to move oneself in one's own place. When we see a thing move itself, we say it has life. A man may do many things, yet not from an inward principle, as Judas and Jehu (Matt. 27:18, 19; 2 Kings 10:15, 16). Is this life? There are some motions from common grace, but it is not spiritual life unless it aims at spiritual ends and upon spiritual grounds. A man must be humbled for sin because it is displeasing to God. Judas was troubled in his conscience, but not for sinning against God; for then he would not have grieved God further by hanging himself. It was not an inward motion and voluntary. So Jehu did it to establish his own kingdom; he did not regard the commandments of the Lord (2 Kings 10:30, 31).

-4. He is called dead in regard to being bound to eternal death, as a condemned man is counted a dead man (John 3:36).

-5. In regard to the power required to make him alive (2 Cor. 5:17).

Conversely, the state of grace is called life.

-1. We have received fellowship with the living Christ; he lives in us, and we in him (Gal. 2:20; John 15:1).

-2. We have an inbred power in ourselves to move upon spiritual grounds and for spiritual ends (Rom. 8:2). We have passed from death to life, from the hatred of our brethren to love of them. There are these steps: (a) A man is a poor man. First, he is in debt; second, he has nothing; third, he has a hard creditor, and last, he has no surety. (b) He begins to mourn bitterly for this his state. (c) He becomes meek. (d) He hungers and thirsts, and prays for grace, and cannot be satisfied without it. (e) He begins to be merciful; he pities every soul that is in a state of nature and under a spirit of bondage. (f) He is pure in heart, he abstains from sin, and does God's commandments. (g) He is a peacemaker; he is at peace with God and with his own conscience; and now he labors to make others at peace. (h) He will now suffer persecution for righteousness' sake. (Matt. 5:3-10)

Use 1. This shows all the works of the heathen as dead works. Some of them are famous for courage, justice, and other virtues, but all these are but dead works. God's pure martyrs have not suffered for their own glory, but for God's.

Use 2. It refutes a main ground of Popery, the doctrine of free will, which gives a man power to be converted when he will. If a dead man can rise from death to life, then may a man dead in sin come to the life of grace.

Use 3. We may observe our state from this. We come to church; we repeat sermons; we do many good duties. Would we know whether our life is a dead life or not? Let us consider on what principles we do these good duties. If we do them because they are pleasing to God, if we have respect to all God's commandments, and if there is a change in our hearts which makes us willing, this is a sign we have passed from death to life.

Use 4. To teach us not to rest in our natural condition, for then we are but dead men (1 Cor. 13:2, 3).

Use 5. This may be a comfort to every soul who has passed from death to life; God is his God, and he shall never come into condemnation (Matt. 6:22, 23; John 5:24).

Doct. The love of our brethren is a known and undoubted evidence that we have passed from death to life.

We have seen that love consists in two things, desire for communion and for communication of good. A man in nature prizes his brethren and will do more for them than any other; so it is in grace (Acts 4:37; Acts 2:42, 44; Phil. 2:1, 2). We must seek to be of one heart (Eph. 4:3-6). There must be brotherly equality if we are brethren. You are of one Father (Gal. 3:26), one mother, one seed (1 Pet. 1:23), one inheritance (1 Pet. 1:4). We will desire to communicate brotherly offices to the inward man (Rom. 12:9, 10) and to the outward man, if need be (Acts 2:44).

Why is this an evidence we have passed from death to life?

-1. Because of the natural proneness in our nature to strangeness and envy. We do not naturally seek any man's good but our own, or so far as our own ends reach.

-2. Because every man's heart seeks liberty. Now a man delights only in the company of those like himself, because otherwise he feels not free. If God's people are the men of your delight and counsel, if you are never so well as with them (Ps. 115:15; Ps. 16:3), this is a sign you have passed from death to life.

-3. Because of our great distance from the love of our brethren. How many steps there are before we come to it (Matt. 5:3-10).

Use 1. To try our own states, whether we are in death or life. It is one of the plainest and most evident notes in scripture (Gal. 6:10). If our love runs in an equal channel to all men, and if we know not God's people, we do not know Christ (1 John 3:1, 2).

But do not many, who are yet not the children of God, love and honor God's children? (Gen. 27:29; Acts 5:13) True, but they did not join with them; thus they were not born of God.

Use 2. To reprove the doctrine of doubting Papists, who say a man cannot know himself to be in a state of grace. They say that here by knowledge is meant conjectural knowledge, not certain knowledge. But this is a contradiction. A man lies if he says he knows a thing and is not certain of it. There is no peace of conscience in this religion.

Use 3. To exhort those who do not yet know that they have passed from death to life, to labor to love the brethren (Prov. 13:20).

Use 4. To console every soul who has nothing in the world but this, they love the brethren. This is a thing upon which you may build a certain knowledge that you have passed from death to life, and thus you may take comfort.

"He who loves not his brother, abides in death." In the former words the apostle implied that the world was in death for lack of love. And lest any should think that he only implied it and did not directly express it, here he sets it down expressly.

Here is a description of a man who loves not his brother. He is in death, and he abides in death. By 'death' is meant the same as in the former part of the verse; 'abiding' not only implies being in that state, but continuing and residing in it.

Doct. The lack of love to any of our brethren is a sign of abiding in the state of damnation, or in an unregenerate and carnal state.

He does not say, "he who hates," but "he who loves not"; and he does not say "brethren" but "brother"; any or every brother. "Offend not one of these little ones" (Matt. 18:6). Christ's little ones are those who have little grace and great corruption.

Why is this a sign of damnation?

-1. Because a lack of love is found in such a one toward God; and that is an argument of being in a state of death. If a man loves God in obedience to his commandments, he should love his brother by the same commandment. The commandment which requires me to love one brother also requires me to love all. Break one commandment and you break all (James 2:10, 11), for he who gave one gave all. Whoever neglects offices of love to one has no love to any, nor to God. It is a note of sincerity that a man hates all sin as well as one (Ps. 119:101, 104). So it is an argument of love when there is no brother or sister to whom we do not enlarge our affections (Gal. 3:28). So much lack of love, so much hypocrisy.

-2. Because of the bitter or deadly root of no love to this or that brother. It springs either from his infirmities in himself, or from spiritual injuries to us.

a. From infirmities in the other.

(i) The first root of this is the condemnation of the generation of God's people. If a man may condemn this or that man for this or that corruption, he may come to condemn the best of God's servants, because the best of God's servants may be in the same failings for which you hate such a brother. The greatest of God's servants have shamefully fallen, as David, Peter, Lot, Noah.

(ii) The second root is the enmity against God's free justification of sinners. Take away this and you take away all Christian religion. If you love not a brother because of some infirmities, you overthrow the free justification of God's grace to a sinner. For God who justifies the greatest, has justified the least as well, as freely and as fully; and will you justify some and condemn others? God condemns none (Rom. 8:1, 33, 34). If we believe in the free justification of sinners, then let us imitate our Father who is in heaven, and let us justify those whom he justifies.

(iii) If there is the least spark of grace in his heart, all his corruptions are his enemies, and he has many. What love is this, when a man would love a man if he had no enemies, but when he has enemies he cannot love him.

(iv) The more naked, unseemly, or deformed any member is, the more the body cares for it, to heal it if possible, to cover it if not; if we lack this, it flows from lack of a member-like spirit (1 Cor. 12:23, 24).

b. Sometimes neglect of our brother springs from some personal injury done to ourselves. This springs from lack of forgiveness of our own sins; for we pray for forgiveness upon this ground (Matt. 6:12, 15). Our Saviour gives this as a reason above all; there is no surer argument than this. If I, who have but a little spark of grace, can forgive injuries, shall not the great Ocean of love much more forgive me? (Matt. 18:27) God will never have us to think that if we cannot forgive one injury, he will forgive us a thousand.

Use 1. This shows the dangerous and fearful state of a man who dares live in envy and malice against his brethren. A man thinks he has a just cause; he will not receive the sacrament nor allow them. What a poor thing is this! You have not your sins forgiven; you do not love God, nor any Christian soul in obedience to God. A Christian dares not allow himself to hate any brother, but looks at hatred as an enemy to his soul.

Use 2. It exhorts every Christian to enlarge the bowels of his affection to every brother. "I am a companion to all who fear thee" (Ps. 119:63); he does not pick and choose (Ps. 66:16). If he does good to all men, he does especially to the household of faith (Gal. 6:10).

Use 3. It is a ground of thankfulness to God, who has taken such care for weakest Christians. For lack of love to such, God will either discharge a man as a hypocrite, or else his own corruption shall take him by the throat and make him believe that he shall hardly get pardon of sins.

1 John 3:15

"Whoever hates his brother is a murderer, and you know that no murderer has eternal life abiding in him."

Doct. He who hates his brother is a murderer.

As he who looks upon a woman to lust after her has committed adultery, so he who hates his brother is a murderer.

-1. He wraps this up and enfolds it in his heart, as the seed of a tree is in the root even though it breaks not forth. So sin has its seed in the heart (Matt. 15:19). No murder could spring from the heart if it were not there already. A fountain could not flow over unless water were in it (Prov. 4:23).

-2. Hatred commits a foul murder. To give offense is to destroy our brother; now whoever hates his brother makes no scruple of giving offense (Rom. 14:15; 1 Cor. 8:11).

-3. It is a foul murder because it withdraws many good offices. A man shall be unwilling to do any good office either for soul or body. Ill-will never speaks well nor does well.

Use 1. This teaches us the spiritualness of the word of God. It transcends the words of men. They never reach farther than speeches and actions; they make no laws for the hearts of men. But the word of God has special regard to the heart (1 Sam. 16:7). As soon as God saw hatred in Cain's heart and countenance, he reproved him for it.

Use 2. Here we may see a just reason for referring all sins and virtues to the ten commandments. Before God, unadvised anger is killing (Matt. 5:21, 22); so lust is adultery (5:28).

Use 3. See the wisdom of God in putting such foul names upon the beginnings of sin, to make us afraid. He puts bad words upon the seeds of sin.

Use 4. This should be a means to cleanse us from all hatred of our brother; look at it as an ugly and loathsome vice. If there is a spirit of envy in your heart, though you do not lift up your hand against your brother, this is murder.

Doct. It is a known truth among God's children that every murderer is devoid of eternal life (Rev. 21:8).

This is evident from two considerations.

-1. The injury done to God's image. If a man deface the image of a prince, it is a crime; then the defacing of God's image is a more heinous one (Gen. 9:6).

-2. The ancestry of all murderers. He makes every

murderer of the posterity of Cain (v. 12) and of Satan (John 8:44). Now because a man kills his brother out of the seed of the serpent, a devilish and malignant spirit, therefore he has not eternal life abiding in him.

But is there no possibility that a murderer should be saved? What of David and others in their carnal state? David did indeed kill, and God followed him with judgments and afflictions (2 Sam. 12:8-10); but upon repentance God forgave him his sin. As for those who have murdered in their carnal states, if God gives them hearts to be humbled, then the blood of Christ is of a louder cry than the blood of Abel (Heb. 12:24). St. John speaks not of every murderer, for some do it against their judgments and hearts; but others, if they repent not, have not eternal life (1 Cor. 6:9).

Use 1. To stir up every Christian who has his hands in blood, to have recourse to the blood of the covenenant for the pardoning and healing of his sins. The sin on Levi held him longest, to bring him to repentance. Jacob blessed him in a curse (Gen. 49:7, 28); God preserves us with curses, which put us in mind of our sins and make us walk sensibly of them; therefore let us renew our mournings for our hatred.

Use 3. Those who love their brethren are not only out of abiding in death, but already have everlasting life abiding in them. If you see any hatred spring in you, you are taken with a dead palsy. You cannot bring out a good word or good countenance. So much hatred, so much death; so much lack of love, so much lack of life.

1 John 3:16

"Hereby perceive we the love of God, because he laid down his life for us; and we ought to lay down our lives for the brethren."

These words are part of the exhortation St. John uses to all Christians to love one another. He uses many arguments. He tells us:

-1. It is a sign we are translated from death to life.

-2. It is dangerous to hate our brethren.

-3. We should remember the exemplary and strong love of Christ.

-4. Such hearts are empty of grace, when there is no love of their brethren.

Doct. The death of Christ for us is the manifestation of his love to us.

This manifestation makes it a certain and known truth that he loves us (Rom. 5:10; 1 John 4:10). He gave his Son to be a propitiatory sacrifice (Eph. 2:4, 5; Gal. 2:20).

-1. See the greatness of Christ's self-denial. That which commends love is this: to bestow great matters and to come off freely with it. "Greater love has no man, than to lay down his life for his friends" (John 15:13); but Christ did it for his enemies (Rom. 5:6).

-2. It further magnifies his love if we consider the great benefits we receive, as reconciliation, pardon of sins (1 John 4:10), adoption of sons, the favor to be accepted as his sons and daughters.

-3. Our corruptions are dead and mortified (Heb. 9:14; Gal. 1:4). We are crucified to the world, to all objects that draw us to sin.

-4. We receive Christian liberty, that by virtue of Christ's death we should be delivered from the curse of the law (Col. 2:13), from the enmity we stood in against the church (Eph. 2:14-16), from hell and fear of death (Heb. 2:14); that we should have liberty to call God Father, to enter into his sanctuary, to have confidence that our prayers are heard, to have assurance when we die that we shall enter into the holy place, that we shall have right and liberty to the creation (Rom. 5:1-3). The greatness of this benefit will appear if we consider how miserable our state had been. If Christ had not done this, we would yet have been in our sins, under the guilt of them, and in horror and anguish of spirit (Heb. 12:19).

-5. Consider how freely God has done it. We gratified

him with no kindness. Some will recompense a small kindness with a great reward (Rom. 11:35). But all we have done has been to abuse every mercy of God to his dishonor (Col. 1:21).

Use 1. This reproves such weakness of God's servants in time of temptations, that they can see no love of God because he does not gratify them with something in this life. God's servants do many times lack necessities which the world abounds with; therefore David had cleansed his heart in vain (Ps. 73:13). But what if God's servants never see good days? Yet here is abundant, rich, and inestimable love, that when you were enemies, strangers, children of wrath, Christ died for you. God has shown you more love than the angels (Heb. 2:5).

Use 2. To teach those who abound in outward things, not to content themselves in them (Eccl. 4:2). We can perceive neither love nor hatred by those outward things (Ps. 17:14). But labor to say that God has laid down his life for you, for else you cannot say he loves you.

Use 3. It teaches us that the death of Christ was not the cause of God's love. God's love is more ancient than the death of Christ. Where shall we lay the foundation of God's love but in eternity? He has loved me and given himself for me (Gal. 2:20).

But does not God attribute his love to the death of Christ? (1 John 4:10; Rom. 3:24, 25; Eph. 2:14, 15; Col. 1:21, 22) In a double respect Christ's death is said to make this reconciliation. Hereby he has slain the enmity and hatred on our part, that we might be no more enemies to him. Further, Christ by his death has made a way whereby God might show his love to us; while sin was in the way he could not show it. Many a father bears a tender affection to a child, yet he will not seem to regard him. He shuts him out of doors, and though he is intreated, yet he thinks it not good to express his love. He will have his child humble himself and acknowledge his faults. He will send someone else to persuade the son to humble himself. So God sends his Son out of love, to take a course to show us favor, notwithstanding his justice.

Use 4. Let us then behold God's love, so that we may be able to say freely that we perceive the love of God. Do not rest in any spiritual duty nor in any common gift until you know that Christ died for you.

You will say, How shall I know this? Some will say that Christ died for all, and so all may know. True, the sufficiency of Christ's death reaches to all, but none can say Christ died for him until he finds in his soul some fruits of the death of Christ.

Use 5. To encourage God's servants to expect offices of love from God to us and ours all our days. He has given his Son; what would you have more? (Ps. 84:11) Lay hold of this love of God, and plead with him upon his love. All blessings are wrapped up in his son (Gal. 4:4). As God sent his Son in fullness of time, so he will send every other mercy.

Use 6. To teach us to abound in love to God and to his children, and hatred against sin. Give up all to God; work for him; suffer for him.

Doct. Christian men ought to be ready to lay down their lives for their brethren.

The apostle extols the love of Aquila and Priscilla, as if all the church and himself were bound to those who were so ready to lay down their lives (Rom. 16:3, 4). He himself looks to be poured out as a drink offering (Phil. 2:17).

-1. Consider the example of our blessed Saviour. He laid down his life for us, and this is worthy of imitation.

-2. Add to this Christ's command, which binds us to imitate this (John 13:34).

-3. Consider the near fellowship of our brethren with Christ. We fulfill the sufferings of Christ for his body (Col. 1:24). He calls them Christ's sufferings, for Christ suffered in him and he for Christ in his saints.

-4. The subordination of God's most eminent servants to the church of God. As Christ is for God, so Paul and Cephas are for the church. God has subordinated the lives of his servants to the church, and the church to Christ, and Christ to God: Christ is the head of the church, and the church is the head of the members (Phil. 2:17).

-5. The rule of love God has given in ancient times. We must love our neighbors as ourselves (Lev. 19:18). Many a Christian will lay down his life for himself; therefore he must in some cases lay down his life for the church. A man will lay down his life for his own salvation and for honor; therefore how much more for God and for the honor of religion.

In what cases is a man to lay down his life? The apostle means that we should be ready to do it for the service of the church, if it cannot be otherwise.

-1. In heat of persecution, to confirm the faith of the people of God. They would perhaps be ready to doubt if he should withdraw himself, though he might escape; a minister or eminent person is bound to go before in sufferings. So, if Paul is to be poured out as a drink offering, every drop of his blood poured out, if it is for strengthening the faith of weak Christians, he rejoices (Phil. 2:17). The stronger must lay down their lives to confirm the faith of the weaker.

-2. There may be a case in which the weaker are to lay down their lives for the stronger. Aquila and Priscilla were ready to lay down their life for Paul's; they thought it better to expose themselves to the utmost extremity than that Paul should be hurt. I must not spare my own life, if it will be serviceable to God and the church (2 Sam. 21:16, 17; 2 Sam. 18:3).

-3. When we perceive it would much advance the glory of God if we should perish rather than our brethren. Paul could wish himself accursed for the Jews, even his soul for a sacrifice (Rom. 9:2, 3); thus Moses (Exod. 32:32).

-4. When a man sees that the wrath of God is kindled against others for his sin, he must rather offer himself to death than have evil come upon those who are with him (Jonah 1:22; 2 Sam. 24).

Use 1. We learn here to justify ourselves and others. If we should be called to lay down our lives to suffer for our brethren, here is a direction how to suffer (Phil. 2:5). God has given us a commandment to love our brethren as ourselves. Also, God has subordinated the members of his church to the body itself.

Use 2. Though it is lawful to flee in time of persecution, yet if it cannot be without weakening the church where we live, we must in heart live and die together.

Use 3. When ministers are called by God for the service of any congregation, let them not hold themselves back for fear that they may cut short their days. Either never take such a charge, or count that you must hazard your life for the people of God, unless on trial it appears that you may do more good in some other place.

Use 4. It reproves all who are so far from laying down their lives that they will not lay down their estates for their brethren's necessities (1 Sam. 25:11). How shall such ever persuade themselves that Christ died for them?

Use 5. This is a ground of deep thankfulness, that Christ should not only give Christ to die for us, but also would have Christians fitted to lay down their lives for their brethren.

1 John 3:17

"But whoever has this world's good and sees his brother have need, and shuts up his bowels of compassion from him, how dwells the love of God in such?"

Doct. There dwells no love of God in the man who, having this world's goods, stretches not out his hand to help the necessity of his brother.

What is it to have the world's good? In the original it is "the life of this world," this world's living; that is, whereof to maintain his life. A man many times has little means to help, but if he has not bowels to work for him, how dwells the love of God in such a man?

How may we know the love of God does not dwell in such a man?

-1. From the nature of love. Such is love that God dwells in it (1 John 4:26). There is no affection in which God reveals himself more than in love. Love is bountiful, ready to be doing good, succoring others in their need (1 Cor. 13:4).

-2. From the nature of brethren.

a. They are more worthy than our estate. One of their souls cost more than all our estates, yea more than the world. How dwells the love of God in us if we love the world more than our brother?

b. Look at our brother as a member of Christ, hungry, thirsty, naked, homeless. We would love Christ if we saw him thus (Matt. 25:40), and they are members of our own body (1 Cor. 12:25, 26).

Use 1. Of instruction, to give rules to order our lives aright or to perform any work of mercy.

a. Who shall relieve his brother? He who has the world's goods; he who can live; he must open his heart and hand. This therefore will reach not only to men's superfluities, but they must withhold only enough to live (Eph. 4:28). We must not only labor for ourselves, but to give to him who has need (2 Cor. 8:3-5; Luke 8:3; Luke 21:34; John 12:6; John 13:28, 29).

b. To whom shall we be helpful? To every brother who has need. (i) Beggars who are unable to labor, and would gladly labor, must be relieved (Luke 16:20, 21), or those who, though they do labor, yet cannot get a living (2 Thess. 3:10). (ii) A brother who has need (Eph. 8:18; 1 Tim. 5:4, 5); those who are poor indeed, who have neither hands, friends, nor maintenance. A man is said to be in need not only when he is utterly cast down, but when he is falling. (iii) We must aid every brother, one as well as another.

c. With what shall we be helpful? With this world's good (Eccl. 10:1). When we have unjustly gotten, we must restore (Prov. 5:16, 17).

d. When shall we be helpful? When we see our brother

has need, then we may see it bestowed ourselves. It is a vanity to leave alms after our death, to be bestowed by others (1 Sam. 20:15; 2 Sam. 16:4, 19). If we give alms while we are alive, we shall have the benefit of them; "the loins of the poor shall bless us." When we are dead, their prayers will do us no good (Luke 16:8, 9).

Use 2. To reprove those who are close-handed and close-hearted. Though a man should do something for company's sake, and out of vain glory, yet if he does not give out of love and compassion, how does the love of God dwell in him?

Use 3. Here is comfort to poor men who are in need. God so far takes their case that he thinks there is no love of God in him who helps not his brother; not that people should be idle and sturdy.

1 John 3:18, 19

"My little children, let us not love in word, neither in tongue, but in deed and in truth. And hereby we know that we are of the truth, and shall assure our hearts before him."

Exhorting us to brotherly love, the apostle uses various arguments. His third argument is taken from the security of conscience of men who love in truth. But a man may say, I may be deceived; to this St. John answers, If our hearts condemn us not, God will less condemn us.

Doct. The love of Christians to one another ought not to be verbal, or in word only, but in deed and in truth; not in tongue, but in truth of inward affection and deed and performance (Ps. 16:2, 3).

He does not confine his love to them, but indicates it in his whole being; every part in him expresses love to them. David's love to Jonathan passed the love of women in affection and in action (1 Sam. 18:3); he loved him as his own soul.

Why is our love commanded to be in deed and truth?

-1. Because lip love is unprofitable; it will neither do

you nor your brother good. It is an empty love (James 2:15, 16). This will do our brother no good; to pity his nakedness will do him no good, nor us either; because as our love to our brother, so is God's love to us. No man can assure himself of receiving God's real and hearty love unless he loves his brethren really and heartily.

-2. This verbal love is unsuitable to God's love toward Christians (Luke 1:78; Isa. 55:3). His is a hearty love and real (John 13:10). He loves his enemies (Rom. 3:8; Rom. 8:32).

Use 1. To reprove all love which falls short of reality. Some even fall short of lip-love; they cannot afford their brother a good word or a good work, when they know a word in season might be of much use.

Use 2. Likewise does it reprove those who give good words, but their hands are withered; that comes from withered affections. "He says, Eat and drink, but his heart is not with you" (Prov. 23:7, 8; 2 Pet. 1:27). Peter shows every man lacks ability to love his brother, if his heart is clogged with any base lust of envy, covetousness, or wantonness. If there is any kitchen lust, it will not endure this heavenly fire.

Doct. The sincerity of our love to our brethren is the security of our consciences and states before God.

Use 1. To reprove the Popish doctrine that it is impossible to have a certainty of salvation. The apostle says here, "We assure our hearts before God."

Use 2. To exhort us to love our brethren in sincerity, and to grow up in it. A man may give all that he has, and yet not know love. Get your heart purified from all lusts. The word of God will purify you (Ps. 119:9). You shall find a fresh spring of love bubbling up and streaming forth, and though your brethren cannot recompense it to you, yet you shall have peace.

Use 3. Here is a means to seal confidence and belief of heart. Cleanse your heart from sin, which hinders brotherly love.

Use 4. To comfort those who love the brethren heartily. You may be sure of your good state.

1 John 3:20, 21

"For if our heart condemn us, God is greater than our heart, and knows all things. Beloved, if our hearts condemn us not, then we have confidence toward God."

Doct. According to the verdict or testimony of our consciences, God will save us or condemn us at the last day.

If our hearts condemn us, God knows more against us to condemn us. By "heart" here is meant conscience, for St. John here speaks a Hebraism. The Old Testament does not have the word "conscience," only the new (Prov. 15:15; 2 Sam. 24:10). If our conscience records that we are innocent, God in heaven will record it (Tit. 3:10, 11).

Conscience has a fivefold work.

-1. It is an observer and spier of what a man is and what he does (Prov. 14:10). Another does not know what a man is, but he himself does. Conscience is a good companion of the good, the worst companion of the bad. "A good conscience is a feast" (Prov. 15:15). There is good company where a good conscience is.

-2. Conscience is a register of what we have done long ago. "Whereto your heart is privy" (1 Kings 2:44); he means his conscience (Gen. 42:20, 21).

-3. Conscience is a witness, and will either accuse or excuse (Rom. 2:15); excuse in well-doing, accuse in ill-doing (Heb. 13:18; Rom. 14:12; 2 Cor. 1:12).

-4. Conscience is a judge, either to clear or to condemn (1 Cor. 4:3; Gen. 20:5).

-5. It is an executioner of what God gives in judgment and sentence. It goes before God's judgment and witnesses (Matt. 27:4, 5); but after God's sentence and his word, conscience executes it (Rom. 8:15). Then conscience pours upon us horrors and terrors, which are a forerunner of hell, differing only in measure and endurance. Conscience does this to godly men upon some occasions, as to David, when he had numbered the people (2 Sam. 24:10). This is called pricking of heart (Acts 2:37; Prov. 18:14).

Why does God put such a faculty into man?

-1. That he might manifest his being. There is no stronger evidence of God's being; for to whom does it witness? Is it not to God? Before whom does it condemn, or to whom is it an executioner, if there is no God?

-2. To manifest his own providence. We must not think that God does not care for things below; why is conscience afraid or comforted, if God does not look into conscience?

-3. That he might magnify his justice. God proceeds in his judicial course without any witness but conscience. If God has none to bear witness, how shall he magnify his justice in condemning secret sins?

-4. To magnify his mercy. If God is angry with a man, it is an advantage to the man to know it (Acts 9:6; Heb. 9:14). As conscience determines here, so will God determine in another world. Conscience is God's vicegerent, set up in the throne of a man's heart. If conscience is our companion, God much more (Ps. 139:2, 3).

Use 1. This is a sign of our present state, and of what God will do to us if we live and die thus. What does your conscience testify? If your heart assures you that you love your brother (2 Cor. 1:12), that you have been humbled for your sins, conscience has been an executioner, and yet it has come with pardon sealed to you, with the broad seal of heaven. If you see one spark of sincerity in yourself, God sees more.

But may not a man's conscience be deceived? (Rom. 3:17; Luke 18:9-14) True, conscience sometimes bears false witness (Tit. 1:15, 16). If a man has a defiled conscience, it will deal falsely. As it is many times with a jury, ignorance of law or false evidence makes them bring in a false verdict; but send them back again, and show them better evidence and the law, and their verdict is true. So conscience often brings in a false verdict through ignorance of the law of God, or through partiality.

Does your conscience speak bitter things? Consider what the grounds are. If they are such as argue you dead in trespasses and sins, then know that God calls you from heaven to repentance. If it tells you you are a hypocrite, consider what grounds it has.

Use 2. This is also a ground of serious humiliation to the heart of every man whose conscience upon due examination still accuses him.

Use 3. To teach every Christian who has found that he has passed from death to life, to be afraid to commit any sin. And comfort your soul: if conscience acquits you, then willl God much more.

Use 4. Let us always labor to be doing some good, for we have a companion who hears and sees all, and a register that notes every good word or work.

The apostle does not tell us, "If our hearts condemn us, God will condemn us much more." Instead he gives a reason, describing God first from his greatness and second from his knowledge.

Doct. God is better acquainted with our hearts and ways than ourselves (Ps. 19:12).

The Psalmist means sins not only secret and hidden from others, but from our very selves (Ps. 139:12; 2 Kings 8:11-13).

But how does God know us better than we ourselves?

-1. God has omniscience, all-sufficient knowledge (Heb. 4:13). Our thoughts are anatomized before him, as if every vein and sinew were laid open. He divides between the marrow and the bone (John 21:12; Rom. 15:11). Though hell and destruction be both covered, set before the Lord they are both open (Job 26:6). "Hell and destruction are before the Lord; how much more the hearts of the children of men?"

-2. God made our hearts, gave us power to move, think, purpose. He knows what is in us (Job 38:36). If God gave understanding to the heart, he knows much more what is in the heart (Ps. 33:13). Again, God has fashioned our hearts; therefore he knows them (Ps. 99:10).

-3. Consider the providence of God. We have our motion in him. A mill moves from the miller, because he has caused it to do so; but the motion of the mill is not in the miller, for it can move without him. As a mill moves by the breath of the wind, so we by the breath of the Lord; as there is not a turning in the mill except from the wind, so there is not a turning of our hearts without him (Prov. 21:1).

-4. Lastly, it is proved by the deceitfulness of man's heart (Jer. 17:9, 10; Prov. 3:17). Our hearts make us believe we are rich and have need of nothing, when indeed we are wretched and miserable, poor, blind and naked (Prov. 30: 2, 3). Sometimes we are more foolish than any man, and have not the understanding of a man; while we walk in a sinful way, they make us believe we are in God's favor (Luke 18:9). When we are in a good state, and when God would have us walk cheerfully in him, our hearts will cast a thousand discouragements upon us; they will sew pillows under our elbows, so that we may sleep quietly; but when we go to try our hearts by the word of God, then they will fall out with us indeed (2 Sam. 15:1-6).

Use 1. Take heed of all secret sins. Not only those hidden from men, but such roots of sin as are hidden from yourself, yet cannot be hidden from God. Take heed of sins which are so subtle that you cannot know whether they are sins or not; sins which our own souls know not of. If a man would be kept from presumptuous sins, he must cleanse the inward and hidden frame of his heart.

How shall we cleanse our hearts? Pray to God with David to cleanse us from sins which we know not (Ps. 19:12). We have confessed the sins which we know by ourselves, and those which the world knows by us, but we must make a new reckoning for sins which we know not of. Second, let us not trust our own hearts, but the word of God (Ps. 119:9). The word of God says there are such sins in every age; therefore we must pray to God to help us against them. Third, let us keep our hearts with all diligence, observe every winding and turning, and take heed of occasions which provoke our hearts to any way of sin (Prov. 4:23).

Use 2. This shows the impossibility of the good state of those who look to be justified by habits and works. It is the happiness of God's servants that they do not look to be justified by the perfection of their hearts.

Use 3. If we find that our hearts do not condemn us, let us trust our hearts no farther than we prove them by the rule of God's Word. If God has helped you to look up to Christ for the pardon of your sins, and you flee from sin, it is an argument that your sins are pardoned, because you could not else hate sin (Ps. 119:6). But on the contrary, if we find our hearts condemning us, our hearts are full of self-love.

Doct. Those who have peace with their own consciences, have boldness with God.

If we have peace with our hearts, we have not only peace with God, but boldness (Eph. 3:12). When God has been pleased to give us fellowship with him in Christ, that we have the ministry of the gospel revealed to us, then we have boldness (Phil. 1:20). He who has this hope shall never be ashamed before God or men (Rom. 5:1, 2). This rejoicing is a companion of boldness.

In what does this boldness consist?

-1. In liberty of spirit to ask those things at God's hand that are meet for us. This we may do with boldness and liberty: "Let us go boldly to the throne of grace" (Heb. 4:16); he means in prayer. A Christian who has for his high priest the Lord Jesus Christ, who has reconciled him to God — to him God's throne is not a judgment seat but a mercy seat, and he begs mercy to help him in time of need. We may safely expect that God will not deny what we ask (Phil. 1:6). The apostle tells us by his own example, whenever he prayed for them his heart was warmed with joy, and he was confident God would grant what he prayed for. "We come to a throne of grace"; that is, we may always speak as favorites with God.

-2. In boldness in dangers that may befall in this world or another. We walk fearlessly and securely against the fear of danger (Ps. 23:6). This is a bold saying.

-3. In expectation of all good things, whether we pray for them or not. God many times will have more care for us than we for ourselves. Paul was in a strait; he knew it would be better for him to be dissolved and to be with Christ, yet better for the church if he should stay in the flesh; and he is confident he shall stay with them to their joy (Phil. 1:24, 25; Acts 20:23, 24). There was a readiness of heart in him, to carry all things that he might rejoice in all (1 Cor. 1:12).

How do we obtain this boldness?

-1. From justification by faith. "We rejoice in tribulation; hope never makes ashamed" (Rom. 5:1-5). The soul is never at peace until by faith it receives and applies Christ's righteousness (Acts 14:5). A man who owes another money, and knows not how to pay him, is ashamed to come into his sight.

-2. From sincerity of sanctification. Though a man has assurance that his sins are pardoned and that he is a child of God, yet if he walks crookedly in his own ways, his conscience will be so perplexed and distracted that he will think every hand of God comes as a judgment (2 Cor. 1:12). But here is his boldness: he has walked in simplicity and pureness. A man is fearful and ashamed when he has dealt doubly either with God or man, or walked in some way of impurity of heart. David's bones were broken; he could not stand upright (Ps. 51:8); he could not look God in the face. When God gives a man to walk in simplicity without guile and in pureness without uncleanness, then a man may walk boldly and with joy; otherwise he walks like a cripple.

Use 1. This reproves an old cavil that religion makes men dastards and cowards. No, rather lack of religion. If men had but purity of heart and good conscience toward men, they would fear no dangers (2 Cor. 1:12).

Use 2. To refute all Popery. They cannot be bold, because they cannot know God to be their Father. They do not keep a good conscience, and where there is no good conscience, there is no boldness. Wicked men indeed may be bold through ignorance or through abundance of natural mettle and courage; this indeed may be found in Papists, but it was also found in heathens.

Use 3. This is a ground of trial of a man's peace (Luke 11:21). You are in peace: do you pray boldly? Do you expect God to answer you? How do you look danger in the face? (Prov. 28:1, 2) In danger you know that Christ has borne all; many things befall you, but you are confident that all shall be for your good.

Use 4. This teaches us the true way of boldness. St. Augustine praises God that he can think of his former evils without fear. If you would do thus, strive with God that he would sprinkle your soul with the blood of Christ. If you have found peace of justification with God, labor for peace of sanctification. Let no rebellious lusts be in your soul, but complain to the Lord and fight against them.

Use 5. This affords much consolation to a child of God who walks in simplicity of a good conscience. If God has given you a heart to loathe all wickedness and abandon all occasions of sin, there is a boldness springing in your heart.

1 John 3:22

"And whatever we ask, we receive of him, because we keep his commandments, and do those things that are pleasing in his sight."

There is a double benefit from assuring ourselves that we are of the truth. First, if our hearts condemn us not, God will much less condemn us, but we have boldness toward God. Second, all our prayers are accepted in the presence of God. This he proves from an argument taken from the practice of all who have peace: they keep his commandments.

Here is a privilege of those who are at peace with God: they may assure themselves that their prayers are heard. Here is also a reason of this: they keep his commandments.

Doct. According to our hearing of God's commandments, so he hears our prayers.

As we regard God's word, so he regards ours (John 9:33). The Pharisees' question to the blind man was what he thought of him who opened his eyes. He thought he was a prophet, because God hears not sinners. Let us keep God's word, and he will keep our prayers to fulfill them (John 15:7). God's word abides in us when in our judgments we approve of it, and in our hearts we cleave to it, and in our lives we practice it. The word of God does not abide in us unless it rules as becomes the word of God (Zech. 7:13; Prov. 28:9).

Why must we hear God's commandments?

-1. God uses a rule of equity in dispensing himself (Matt. 7:2). As we dispense ourselves to him, so does God dispense himself to us. This is a general rule of God's walking with men. With what measure we mete, God will measure to us again. If we let no word of God fall to the ground, but let our conscience stand in awe of it and our hearts cleave to it, God will let none of our prayers fall to the ground.

-2. The Spirit helps us to keep the commandment. God accounts that we keep the commandments when our judgments approve them all (Ezek. 36:26, 27; Rom. 8:15). The Spirit helps us to pray, and it asks things according to the will of God, and he knows the meaning of the Spirit. He who prays not in the Spirit is a barbarian to God.

-3. God bears love and respect to those who keep his commandments. It is the way to become God's favorite (John 14:21, 23).

Use 1. To show us the cause of the fruitlessness of our prayers at times. God does not hear us because we hear him not. If our prayer falls to the ground, then surely God's word has fallen to the ground. A good prayer and a bad life can never meet (James 2:20). If we live in aweless respect to God's commandments, he hears not our prayer.

Use 2. To comfort every soul who makes conscience of his ways. If you walk with a care to fulfill God's will, he will fulfill yours. Those who give themselves to walk as Christ has walked, may have this comfort (John 11:32; Ps. 119:5, 6). Petitions which are long delayed and seem to be most strongly denied, are fulfilled. Daniel's prayer was heard the first day, but was not answered then (Dan. 10:3, 10-12). A petition is granted in heaven and a course taken to accomplish it, but yet there must be a time to bring it about (Deut. 5:25, 26). Though God delays our prayers, yet even then he grants them (Prov. 21:10; Jer. 17:10). We have an end always in our prayers, and we prescribe means to God; he many times denies the means in displeasure, but gives the end. So in Paul, God would not remove the messenger of Satan, but he did by it what Paul would have done, i.e. gave free passage to the Spirit (2 Cor. 12:7, 8).

The second benefit is the acceptance of all our prayers in the presence of God, amplified by an argument taken from the practice of those whose hearts do not condemn them before God. They keep his commandments and do that which is pleasing in his sight. Those who keep God's commandments receive whatever they ask of God. But those whose hearts do not condemn them, keep God's commandments. Therefore they too receive whatever they ask.

Doct. Those who keep God's commandments keep a good conscience and God's favor together. They have peace at home and in heaven.

-1. They have peace at home in their own conscience. "We have a good conscience in all things, desiring to live honestly" (Heb. 13:18); that is, to keep God's commandments.

-2. As they keep a good conscience on earth, so they keep favor in heaven. Thus it was said of David that he did that which was good in the sight of the Lord (1 Kings 15:5); he had a care to keep God's commandments. Thus did Asa (2 Chron. 14:2); Hezekiah (2 Chron. 29:2); Josiah (2 Kings 23:25; 2 Chron. 34:2).

What is it to keep God's commandments? It is not barely to keep them in our minds and memory, but: -1. To keep them as one would keep his highway. -2. To keep them as a man would keep his jewels (Prov. 6:20, 21). -3. To keep them as the apple of our eye (Prov. 7:1-3). -4. To keep the commandments as we would keep our life. Now, "skin for skin; all that a man has, will he give for his life"; so we should lose our lives and all we have for God's commandments.

The reason for our peace is that God's commandments are suitable to the conscience of a Christian. You please a man when you do what is according to his will; and what is good in God's sight? That which is according to his commandments. The commandments of God are a living image of his will. God is a God of pure eyes (Hab. 1:13); he hates wickedness (Ps. 5:4). A man is said to be made after God's own image when he is righteous and holy. The apostle exhorts us to put on the new man, which after God is created in righteousness and true holiness (Eph. 4:24). Holiness is the sum of the commandments of the first table, righteousness of the second.

Use 1. Hence we may try our consciences, whether they are good or not; for upon the goodness of our conscience depends the peace of this world and the other (Heb. 13:18). Examine yourself: Do you keep God's commandments as a man would keep his way, the apple of his eye, his life or soul, and his jewels? If not, you do not have a good conscience.

Use 2. It exhorts us all to take the right way, to keep God's commandments and to keep a good conscience.

What shall we gain by this? "In keeping God's commandments is great reward." You shall keep a good house at home and favor in heaven. A good conscience is worth keeping; it will uphold your heart against all discouragements you shall meet with in the world, and you shall have peace with God by keeping his commandments. You shall keep a good conscience, which is a continual feast. The peace of a good conscience is the greatest blessing in the world; nothing in the world can take it away. Therefore above all things have a care to keep it, for it will be more joy to you than all worldly contenentments (Ps. 4:6, 7).

1 John 3:23

"And this is his commandment, that we should believe on the name of his Son Jesus Christ, and love one another, as he gave us commandment."

In this verse he shows you what this commandment is, by keeping which we obtain the grant of our prayers. "This is his commandment, that we believe in the name of his Son Jesus Christ, and that we love one another."

Doct. Instead of loving God with all our hearts, the first and great commandment now is that we believe in the name of the Lord Jesus.

When the Holy Spirit would rank all the commandments under two heads, he reduces them to these two.

-1. Instead of loving God with all our hearts, we must believe in Jesus Christ.

-2. Instead of loving our neighbor as ourselves, we must love our brethren, as Christ commands. Christ made the former the greatest commandment (Matt. 22:36-39), but the apostle John sums up the commandments in these two. He does not say, "these are the commandments," but "this is the commandment": as much as to say, there is nothing more commanded by God. "Keep a pattern of wholesome words" (2 Tim. 1:13); what words? "Faith and love in Christ Jesus."

What is meant by the name of Jesus Christ? "There is no other name under heaven given among men, whereby we must be saved" (Acts 4:12). Not the letters or syllables of the name, for it is superstition to believe there were virtue in the letters or syllables of the name Jesus. What Peter means is, there is no other person under heaven whereby we can be saved, but only him who is named the Lord Jesus. Abraham called upon the name of the Lord (Gen. 13:4), that is, upon the Lord. The apostle says, "At the name of Jesus every knee shall bow" (Phil. 2:10). So Isa. 45:24. In Rom. 14:11 you may see what is meant by the name of Jesus, and what it is to bow at the name of Jesus. To bow to or worship the name of Jesus is to worship the person of Jesus. He ads the name of the Lord Jesus, however, because we do not believe in Christ by those attributes given to him, but it is by Christ himself that we are saved. If we did not consider him as a priest, a prophet, and a king, he could not have saved us; these offices of Christ are the name of Christ.

What is meant by believing in his name? There are three acts of faith in believing in the name of the Lord Jesus.

-1. To be persuaded of his goodness and promises. Doubting is opposed to faith (Rom. 4:20). Doubting and persuasion are acts of the mind.

-2. Faith is an act of a man's will, by which he trusts on the name of the Lord Jesus. Not to believe in God is not to trust on God for his salvation (Ps. 78:22). There are two things in God's promises, truth and goodness. The understanding believes the truth; the will accepts the goodness. These are acts about a promise.

-3. There is a true faith, but yet weak, which does not reach to those and yet reaches to believing in his name, and therefore it has salvation by his name. This is when a man can abide by the Lord, and will not go away until he blesses him, like Jacob (Gen. 32:26). This is the same as drawing near to God (Ps. 73:28). A man draws near to God when he is willing to forsake all his lusts, and can find no satisfaction in earthly things, but only in the Lord.

The truth of the doctrine is proved by four reasons.

-1. It is a work of greater honor to God to believe in the Lord Jesus Christ than to love God when we know him to be our friend. When a Christian first begins to believe in Christ, he does not take God as a friend, but as an enemy. Now to cleave to God when he is an enemy is more than to love God when he is a friend to us. For a soul to throw itself on God when he is terrible and seems as an angry God, and not to let him go till he shows us mercy, is a notable thing. The faith of a weak Christian is more notable than the love of a strong Christian. The one has had the experience of God's love, but the other never felt the warmth of God's Spirit in his heart.

-2. This magnifies the grace of God, because the soul who believes in Christ relies on Christ for every blessing. He does not trust on the best graces he has received; he does not trust on his own faith, but he trusts in Christ for the favor of God, and he believes that for his sake every promise shall be fulfilled. This great commandment gives God and Christ all the honor.

-3. By faith we rest upon God for all the good we stand in need of (Rom. 4:16).

-4. Because of the wickedness of our nature, it is impossible for us to love God before we trust him, and before we are persuaded that our sins are forgiven. The end of the commandment is love, but from where does this love come? "From faith unfeigned" (1 Tim. 1:5; John 14:1). Christ's disciples were much troubled because he was to leave the world; but he comforts them, saying, "Believe in God, believe also in me"; but let no man think to believe in God before he believes in Christ (John 14:6).

Use 1. This reproves a sinful error of the doctors of the church of Rome, who say that faith may be severed from love. They say a man may believe in God and yet not love him; but that is contrary to this great commandment. We no sooner believe in God than we love him.

Use 2. To exhort every soul, if they desire to do anything pleasing to God, to make this their greatest duty: to believe on the Lord Jesus. Faith and love are correlatives. Let no man flatter himself that he is born of good parents, that he lives in the bosom of the church, and that he enjoys God's ordinances; but let him trust in the name of the Lord Jesus Christ (Ps. 9:10).

Use 3. Believing on the name of Jesus Christ is a divine thing. Christ is no creature, but equal with the Father.

Use 4. To comfort every soul that believes in the name of the Lord Jesus. He fulfills this great commandment. Is this not a great comfort to a man who knows there is little that he can either do or suffer, but yet this he is persuaded of, that he abides in Christ Jesus and trusts in God.

Doct. The second great commandment is that we love one another.

-1. Because of the large extent of it. All the duties or offices of love which we perform to man are comprehended in this, "Thou shalt love thy neighbor as thyself. Love is the fulfilling of the law" (Rom. 13:19). Forbear to love your neighbor, and you break all the commandments of God.

-2. Because whatever we perform without love is unprofitable. Without faith no duty profits (Heb. 4:2), and likewise without love we cannot profit our brethren (1 Cor. 13: 1-3), and neither can we profit ourselves. The apostle exhorts that all be done in love (1 Cor. 8:1; 1 Cor 16:14).

-3. Love makes all other duties honorable to our brethren. By love we should serve one another (Gal. 5:13). Love makes a nurse very careful about her child; you shall not have so much service from any servant as from a nurse; she does it freely and readily. Love will make us serviceable without measure.

Use 1. Let us all have great respect to this commandment. If it is a work of love, it is that which God requires. By love we perform all the commandment of God at once. Whatever a man does without love, profits neither himself nor his neighbor. Whatever duty you perform to any brother, if you do not do it out of love, you will soon be weary of it. The truest-hearted duty is performed in love. Therefore let us avoid occasions which hinder us from loving one another, as strangeness, enmity, wickedness, and self-love.

Use 2. Let us love our brethren in obedience to God's commandment; this must be the rule of our love. Many cankers there are in love, which this love in obedience to

God's commandment heals: as carnal love, faithless love, immoderate love, self-seeking love, licentious love, and inconstant love. Every love not in obedience to the commandment will be consumed by these.

Use 3. Let us love the Lord our God so much the more, because he is careful to lay this commandment on us; though a stranger, an enemy, a wicked man, God cannot endure the rank breath of hatred.

"As he has commanded us."

Doct. The rule of our love to one another is not as we love ourselves, but as Christ has loved us (John 13:34; John 16:12).

Indeed the rule in the Law was, "Thou shalt love thy neighbor as thyself" (Lev. 19:18). But now there is a new commandment, so called because it is given by a new rule.

-1. Christ denied his own ease and pleasure, that he might save us from pain.

-2. He denied himself in his own profit. He laid down his own soul (2 Cor. 8:9). He laid down both earthly and heavenly profits, that we through him might be rich.

-3. He denied his own honor. Being in the form of God, he yet made himself of no reputation to save us from reproach.

-4. As if all this had been too little, he denied his own life and laid it down for us (John 3:16).

What is the reason for this difference, that our love to our neighbor must be so great above the love to ourselves?

-1. Because there was no cause for denying ourselves in innocence, but now man is fallen; he cannot raise up another without stooping himself. Two men go together; if they both go upright, they may go hand in hand, but if one is fallen and not able to rise, the other must stoop down and toil to get him up. God has raised up some sooner than others; therefore we must take up our fallen brethren.

-2. Now God requires love in a more exact pattern and measure, because he has now given a higher and more exact pattern. We have the pattern of Christ, who forgave us ten thousand talents; therefore we ought to forgive our brethren a hundred pence.

Use 1. This should stir up all Christians to walk now in a higher frame of love than formerly they were accustomed. We walked then in a lower way, to love our brother as ourselves. We said, I will do for my brother all I can, but I must not prejudice myself, my estate, my credit, or my life. But now "we who are strong ought to bear the infirmities of the weaker" (Rom. 15:1, 2). Now we must have the same mind in us which was in Christ Jesus (Heb. 2:4-16, 2 Cor. 11:7, 8). Paul abased himself that they might be exalted, and denied himself of many comforts so that he might help them. As Christ laid down his life for us, so must we for our brethren in many cases (1 John 3:16).

Now for more particular direction: (a) A man ought to deny his own expedience for his brother's necessity (Neh. 5:18). (b) He ought to deny himself in outward things to supply his brethren in spiritual things. Thus Paul. (c) If a man is in a private condition, and his brother is of public use to the church, he ought to deny himself to maintain and succor him; as they said to David, "You are worth ten thousand of us." Thus Aquila and Priscilla (Rom. 16:4, 5).

Use 2. This should teach you who are of higher state to help your poor neighbors who have fallen into want, not through prodigality or riot but through God's hand. You must not say, I must look to myself and my children first. This was the old rule, but now we must deny ourselves and our own experiences, and be continually doing good in obedience to this commandment. It was a royal saying of David, "Shall I offer a sacrifice of that which cost me nothing?" (2 Sam. 24; Heb. 13:15, 16). When God blesses you with many a pound, will you offer to God a sacrifice that cost a penny, or a thing that has cost you nothing? It is for you to bless God who has enriched you with such abundance, and say with David, "What shall I render to the Lord for all these goods?"

Doct. There is no more effectual means to obtain our petitions than by growing up in practicing these two commandments; in believing on the name of Christ and in loving our brethren.

In Mark 11:22-26 you have both joined together. Let a man pray in faith and waver not (James 1:8). When a Christian is tossed with doubtings and distractions, he shall rather drown his prayers than bring them to the bosom of Christ Jesus. Job's friends were godly men; but because they did not deal well with Job, God professed he would not hear them. Lack of love to our brethren damps our prayers before God. Though our persons are accepted,; yet our prayers shall not be.

Why is faith so necessary?

-1. Faith makes our persons acceptable to God. God hears the young ravens and lions when they call upon him; he rather hears their misery than their prayer, but faith makes the person acceptable. "By faith Abel," etc. (Heb. 11).

-2. Faith purifies the heart (Acts 15:9; Ps. 66:18).

-3. Faith furnishes the heart with graces which make our prayers amiable. There are four graces requisite in prayer, and all are wrought by faith.

    a. Faith produces reverence to God. A man without faith does not consider before whose presence he stands; he considers not that God is near to hear his petitions. But faith is the evidence of things not seen; it makes us come before God with reverence and godly fear (Heb. 11:27).

    b. Faith breeds in us humility, by which we come before God with a sense of our unworthiness of the least of God's mercies, and an inability to ask anything according to his will.

    c. Faith works fervency and earnestness of spirit, that we will give God no rest (2 Sam. 15:16). Effectual fervent prayer is called a prayer of faith, for: (i) Faith puts life into every duty (Gal. 3). (ii) Faith lays hold of the promises of God in Christ, and we urge and press God upon his word.

(iii) Faith makes us very sensible of our wants, and therefore we cry very hard for help.

d. Faith works in us a holy confidence that what we ask God will undoubtedly grant.

This is meant of faith in the Lord Jesus. There are three things in the name of the Lord Jesus which faith lays hold on.

-1. Faith lays hold on the offices of his mediation. There had been no hope of acceptance unless there had been a Mediator to reconcile God and us (1 John 2:1, 2; Heb. 4:14-16). Though we should find many weaknesses in ourselves, yet with confidence we may draw near to God, seeing we have a High Priest who is touched with our infirmities. He is the great Master of requests, who is in such favor with God that he never presents up a prayer to God without returning an answer; and thus we need not go away with sad hearts (John 16:23, 24).

-2. Faith looks at Christ as him in whom all the promises are yea and amen (2 Cor. 5:20).

-3. Faith lays hold on all the attributes of God, set on work by Christ for our good; so that if we look for wisdom, grace, or power, they are all set on work for the good of his church. "The name of the Lord," that is, the attributes of God, "is a strong tower; the righteous flee to it." How? By faith.

How is the love of our brethren such an effectual means for obtaining our prayers?

-1. Love enlarges us to forgive injuries done to us, and that moves God to forgive us our trespasses. To forgive is a work of love.

-2. Love is ready to give (Acts 10:4). God was ready to give ear to the prayer of Cornelius, because he was ready to give alms.

-3. There are those to whom we can give little, but yet there is a good opinion and esteem to be given of them. Now this is a fruit of love, to esteem well of our brethren and to judge charitably, and this prevails with God to have a good regard for our prayers. If we are estranged and alienated from our brother in ill conceits, we shall find God estranged to us. This was the fault of Job's friends: they had a hard opinion of him, for lack of love, and this provoked God against them. God will accept no prayer as long as he sees in us a low respect for our brother (Matt. 5:23, 24).

Use 1. To exhort us in the Lord, when we go about any such duty as prayer, to present it to God in the spirit of faith and love. They are special graces, and without them no prayer can be accepted. Let us only labor to grow up in these two, faith toward God and love toward our brethren, and then whatever we ask shall find acceptance with God.

Use 2. To console every soul that comes with any measure of faith and love before God: we shall not put up any petition without finding God ready to answer it.

1 John 3:24

> "And he who keeps his commandments dwells in him, and he in him. And hereby we know that he abides in us, by the Spirit which he has given us."

The apostle had told us of a magnificent privilege from keeping God's commandments (v. 22), and that is obtaining the grant of our petitions (v. 23). In the latter verse he tells us what commandments they are. Now in this verse he lays down another benefit which we have by keeping God's commandments, and that is fellowship with God. God dwells in us and we in him.

This verse consists of two parts:

-1. The benefit of obedience to God's commandments: God dwells in us and we in him.

-2. The means by which we know that God dwells in us: that is by himself, for a Christian might else doubt it.

Doct. An obedient Christian keeps mutual, entire, and constant fellowship with Christ.

To keep them as commandments implies obedience out

of a sense of superiority in the commander and inferiority in the person commanded. He who keeps the commandments in such a manner has true fellowship with God: God dwells in him, and he dwells in God.

Our keeping of God's commandments is a means to keep fellowship with God (John 14:23). God will come and keep house with us, and refresh and comfort us. If a Christian grows up in obedience to Christ, then Christ his Husband will lop off his superfluous branches, so that he may bring forth more fruit than he did before. He will comfort us with the consolations of his Holy Spirit: he will come in and sup with us (Neh. 8:10). The more comfort, the more strength. Comfort comes from "confortare," to strengthen; the more strong a Christian is, the more cheerfully he performs Christian duties, as the sun is said to come forth like a giant, rejoicing to run his race (Ps. 19:4). A weak man soon faints and is weary, but a strong man goes through his business cheerfully.

Use 1. This reproves a Popish clamor. They say Protestant Christians can do no good works, because we deny all merit in them; as our Saviour teaches us, "when we have done all we can, we must say we are unprofitable servants." As Jacob confessed, "we are less than the least of his mercies" (Gen. 30:1). Is there no use of good works except in merit? Is there no use of gold because it does not justify us? Is not this encouragement enough for us to be doing good works, that by them we maintain mutual, entire, and constant fellowship with God? Yea, we say that God will recompense us at the last day, though not for our works, yet according to our works. We do not merit anything at God's hands by our good works, because we receive strength from him to perform them.

Use 2. This will show every Christian just ground of encouragement to keep him close to God's commandments. In keeping them there is great reward. For thus we keep in Christ Jesus, and we keep mutual, entire, and constant fellowship with the Father; and so we shall find him as a husbandman taking pains with us, keeping us from evil, and cleansing us from those corruptions which will make us stink in his nostrils; and this he will do because he sees us taking pains and employing that stock of graces which he has bestowed on us. By this means God will make our lives comfortable, and will multiply graces in us in a great measure, and will give us more strength to make us yield more obedience to him.

Use 3. To reprove those Christians who walk loosely with God, who do not keep God's commandments; such Christians fall short of that great reward which God promises.

Use 4. To comfort Christians who have regard to the commandments of God, and who desire to walk more closely with God on God's holy day. Such shall have God dwelling with them and working all their works for them; God will play the good husbandman about them; he will prune from them all loose distempers that hang about their souls; and by this means they shall come before him with Christian boldness and confidence.

"Hereby we know he abides in us, by the Spirit which he has given us."

In the second place we come to speak of the means by which we may discern that God dwells in us, and that is by the Spirit that he has given us.

Doct. The Spirit of God bestowed on us is an evident sign of Jesus Christ's dwelling in us.

He does not say "we believe," though this is a great saying; yet faith is the evidence of things not seen. But he says, "we know it."

What is that Spirit which is an evidence of Christ's dwelling in us? Did not the Spirit of the Lord come upon Saul, and he prophesied? (1 Sam. 10) Yet it is not said that Christ abode in him, for "the Spirit of the Lord departed from Saul, and an evil spirit from the Lord troubled him" (1 Sam. 16:14). How then may we be sure that we have not received the Spirit in vain?

I answer, there are many degrees of God's Spirit which may be given to a man, and yet which are no evidence of God's dwelling in him or he in God.

-1. There is a Spirit of illumination, by which a man may prophesy, as Saul did. But a man may have this Spirit of God and yet fall away, so as to sin against the Holy Spirit (Heb. 6:4-6).

-2. There is a Spirit of administration of church or commonwealth (1 Sam. 11:6).

-3. There is a Spirit of power, to do many wonders (Matt. 7:22, 23). And yet Christ acknowledges that he never knew them; they never abode in Christ, nor he in them.

-4. There is a Spirit of renewal of many affections. (a) Zeal, as in Jehu: "Come and see my zeal for the Lord" (2 Kings 10:15, 16); and yet he took no heed to walk in the law of the Lord (vv. 31, 32). (b) Joy, as in Herod (Mark 6:20) (c) Humility, as in Ahab (1 Kings 21:29) (d) Fear, as in Felix (Acts 24:25).

What then is the Spirit by which we know that we keep God's commandments and have fellowship with him? It is the Spirit of life which is in Jesus, which frees us from the law of sin and death (Rom. 8:2). This is the Spirit of adoption (Rom. 8:15), of grace and supplication (Zech. 12:10).

But how does this Spirit differ from the others? Were they not the Spirit of God? It excels in this: the former Spirits of God rested only upon the outwards of a man, as his tongue, memory, and affections; but this Spirit bids defiance to all the enemies of his salvation. The heart and will, which are the castles in which Christ abides, are given up to Christ (Prov. 23:26). God requires the heart; if we give the heart we give all (Prov. 4:23). Life springs not from good affections nor good actions, but from the heart.

What does this Spirit do more in my heart than the other? How shall I know that the Holy Spirit has gotten possession of my heart? If the Spirit of God has taken possession of your heart, it lifts up your heart to prize the Lord Jesus above all other things in the world; it makes you willing to do and suffer God's will with patience; it will cause you to resign yourself and your desires to the Lord Jesus, so that all your affections and your whole heart are for the Lord. If Paul now sins, he does that which he would not (Rom. 7:16, 17). Having given us this Spirit, we dwell in Christ and he in us (1 John 4:13), because by this Spirit we keep his commandments. If we keep his commandments, it shall go well with us and with our children after us forever (Deut. 5:29).

The reason why the Spirit's presence is a certain sign is the covenant of grace, by which he has promised everlasting fellowship to those who keep his commandments (Jer. 32:40; Isa. 55:2, 3).

But it may be said, This will perhaps make us believe, but it will not make us know what we believe. Trinity in unity, unity in trinity; we believe this, but we cannot know it. Yet you say here that we not only believe but know. I answer, there is a difference between faith and knowledge. A man may believe a thing is true because he does not doubt the authority of it; but knowledge is of a certain conclusion. We know a thing to be so, partly by faith, partly by sense and reason; for though faith believes things before we know them, yet when faith has laid hold on the promises, it sets reason to work. This Spirit of God works in us an evidence of our abode in Christ, for:

-1. This Spirit of God works peace of conscience, which passes all understanding (Phil. 4:7). Though it does not always abide, yet it keeps garrison always; it bears witness to a man that Christ is in him and he in Christ.

-2. It works a change in all Christians. It changes them from the power of Satan to the power of God (Gal. 5:19-21). And though the peace of conscience and consolation of the Spirit do not always abide, yet the Spirit of regeneration and sanctification always abides and changes the whole man (2 Cor. 5:17). Before a carnal and fleshly spirit rested upon us, but now the Spirit of grace and glory, which makes us relish Christian communion and Christian society. The Spirit always abides, and so we know that Christ abides.

But though we think there is a thorough change, may it not be of the outward man only? I answer, Consider how it changes your heart. Is your heart with God and wholly for God? Do you long for peace with God? Would you not forego it if you had it, for all the world? Is the word of God more precious to you than your appointed food? Then no profit, pleasure, or preferment shall hinder you from following Christ.

Use 1. To reprove a Popish opinion that no man can know whether Christ abides in him or not. But why does St. John then say, "Hereby we know"? And he speaks to old men, young men, and babes, to try themselves. These condemn the whole generation of the just. A woman who cannot tell her child who its father is, is a strumpet, and so is the Church of Rome.

Use 2. It reproves others who think it unimportant. Some think it not worth the knowing, others think it not proper to know whether Christ abides in them or not. Such have no care to make their calling and election sure. St. John says it is possible, and a thing worth seeking after, and also very expedient.

Use 3. This should exhort all Christians to try and examine themselves, whether they are in the faith or not (2 Cor. 13:5).

Use 4. To exhort us to give up our hearts to God, so that his fear and love may rule our hearts, that these outward things may not take up our affections (Rom. 8:9, 14).

Use 5. To comfort God's servants who give up their hearts and lives to God. You have laid your salvation not on sandy but on sure ground, if you have built it upon divine testimony, even the Spirit of God.

1 John 4:1

"Beloved, believe not every spirit, but try the spirits whether they are of God, because many false prophets have gone out into the world."

This chapter consists of two parts:
-1. A preservative against false teachers (to v. 6).
-2. A renewed exhortation to brotherly love.

He touches by the way on trial of spirits, for he had said, "Hereby we know that he abides in us, by the Spirit which he has given to us." Now, lest the people of God should be deceived by the spirits of their ministers, he bids them to try their spirits, and that by the Spirit which Christ has given them. "For he who is spiritual discerns all things" (1 Cor. 2:15).

These words are an exhortation to the people of God, how to order themselves toward the spirits of their ministers: the exhortation is laid down negatively, "believe not every spirit," and positively, "but try the spirits." The negative and affirmative duty are both confirmed by a reason: "There are many false prophets gone out into the world." This shows that he speaks chiefly of the trial of their ministers, or else they may be deceived in their judgment; as if a friend should bid his friend take heed what piece of gold he takes, because there are many slips and counterfeits gone abroad.

St. John bids his hearers not to believe every spirit. Hence observe:

Doct. Every minister is carried away with one spirit or another.

Else why does he exhort them to try the spirits? He speaks of ordinary prophets, who are subject to the judgment of the people (1 Cor. 14:23). As for Paul, he was an extraordinary prophet (1 Cor. 4:3).

What is meant by prophecy? Such a gift as a man may

attain to by use: hence ministers are called prophets. Though they cannot foretell things besides the scripture, yet they may foretell things out of the scripture, and thus you may see that God is with them of a truth. Every good prophet, so far as he prophesies according to God, is carried by the Holy Spirit; but when he does not speak according to God, he is carried with an evil spirit (Numb. 11:25, 26). "An evil spirit came upon Saul" (1 Sam. 18:10); so that every spirit prophesies either by the Spirit of God or by an evil spirit. An evil man may sometimes prophesy well, and then it is by the Spirit of God that comes upon him, as Balaam. Conversely, a good man is ordinarily led by the Spirit of God, but sometimes he is transported by an evil spirit, and then he speaks not by the Spirit of God; he perverts the word, and he misses the text and application. Peter will tell our Saviour, "This thing shall not be unto thee" (Matt. 16:22); but what says Christ to him? "Get thee behind me, Satan." When any minister comes to preach, one spirit or other comes upon him; therefore well does St. John say, "Believe not every spirit."

What is the spirit of the prophets? There are three things in a man, body, soul, and spirit (1 Thess. 5:23); the soul of man is the breath of God, by which he is made a living creature. By spirit is here meant the inclination of the mind, which is called a spirit in many places, as a spirit of fornication, a spirit of slumber, a spirit of jealousy. Every good or evil inclination is called a spirit: "Be renewed in the spirit of your minds" (Eph. 4:23); that is, the disposition of your minds.

Why is an inclination of mind called a spirit?

-1. It always comes from some spirit.

-2. It has force in it, to bow the will one way or another.

What kinds of spirits are there? "Try all things," says the apostle, "and cleave to that which is good" (1 Thess. 5:21). There are three sorts of spirits, of the world, of the Devil, and of God. Every minister is led by some of these, but of each one of these spirits there is a great variety.

-1. Sometimes the Spirit of God comes upon a man as

it did on the seventy elders (Numb. 11:25, 26). The Spirit of God is like the spirit of new wine, which ripens the wits; so when the Spirit of God comes upon a man, he better understands the word of God and the hearts of the people. "The Spirit searches all things, yea, the deep things of God" (1 Cor. 2:12). There are two sorts of deep things of God: some lie hidden in the word of God, some in man.

-2. There is a spirit of the world, which does not breathe to unite the hearts of God's people. This is a spirit of pride.

-3. There is the spirit of the Devil, which guides a man into error in his doctrine, as Peter. This spirit searches not the deep things of God, but of the devil; this spirit seeks to make the hearts of those sad, whom he would not have made sad (2 Cor. 11:2, 13-15); to pervert the scripture; and to drive out the care of God's service and the power of godliness.

Use 1. This should instruct ministers, when they come into the presence of God and enter into the ministry, to labor to prevail with God, so that they may be acquainted with the deep things of God and that they may lead the people of God by the still waters of comfort and consolation. Such a minister will go out conquering and to conquer, and prospering and to prosper.

Use 2. This should instruct the people of God to search the scriptures daily, so that they may be better able to try the spirits of their ministers. Labor also to try your own heart.

"Try the spirits."

Doct. The people of God should first try the spirits of their ministers, before they trust them.

"Beloved, try the spirits"; as if he would take them by the hand; try how they relish Christ, whether they show forth the mighty power of God in human frailties. "Despise not prophecy; try all things, hold fast to that which is good" (1 Thess. 5:19-22). By trying all things you shall keep your heart from quenching the Spirit.

-1. By trying the Spirit you put honor upon him A man does not try a small piece of money; but if he suspects a great piece to be counterfeit, he will try that.

-2. In so doing you shall keep your heart from damping the Spirit. When the noble men of Berea had heard Paul preach, they searched the scriptures daily, whether such things as he preached were true or not (Acts 17:11). Finding his doctrine true, they believed it.

What is it to try the spirit of a minister? They must try the spirit of a man's person, calling, doctrine, applications.

-1. There may be a false spirit of a man's person (Matt. 7:15, 16).

-2. Try the spirit of their callings. Christ says to John and James, "You know not what spirit you are of" (Luke 9: 55, 56), and yet they were pillars of the church (Gw . 2:9). You know not what spirit you are proving, you do not know what your calling is. It is the same as Mine; not to destroy but to save.

-3. Try the spirit of their doctrine. Peter received the keys of the kingdom of heaven; was he therefore kept from error? No, he spoke with a good spirit in the morning and with a bad spirit in the afternoon.

-4. You must try the spirit of their application. Bad ministers will misapply the word of God; they will make sad the hearts of the righteous, whom God would not have made sad (Ezek. 13:22). Thus also may good men misapply the word, as Job's friends (Job. 42:6-8); they spoke from a spirit of truth, but not from a spirit of righteousness. When you shall see a man go on in wicked courses, it is not time to apply the promises, but rather threatenings; and so you must not apply threatenings to a wounded conscience, but promises; else you do not speak aright from God.

What is it to believe a spirit? -1. To acknowledge and be persuaded of its truth (Heb. 11:13). -2. To apply the promises to oneself wisely (Eph. 3:17; 1 John 1:21). -3. To trust in it. Two things are in a promise, truth and goodness; we must be persuaded of both (Ps. 119:44).

Why must we try every spirit?

-1. Because great danger may befall the child of God by neglect of this duty. The prophet of God, not knowing whether another prophet spoke in the name of the Lord or not, hearkened not to his word; therefore a lion slew him (1 Kings 20: 35-39). By the contrary another was saved (1 Kings 13:15-25). Further, there is danger in regard to the prophets themselves (Matt. 7:15; 2 Pet. ch. 1, 2, 3; Rev. 18:13).

-2. It is easy for prophets to delude God's people. (a) Because there are great stores of false prophets (1 Kings 22:21-23); a man is easily deceived by a multitude. (b) They may delude by their calling; many men think their minister must be right. (c) They delude through hypocrisy (Matt. 7:15).

Use 1. To refute the doctrine of the Church of Rome. They would keep men in ignorance, thinking it to be the mother of devotion.

Use 2. This may stir up all the people of God to search the scriptures, so that they may discover the spirits of their ministers. Though he is a man who fears God, try his every word; follow him from first to last. If you do not try the word, you will not trust it; it will be to you as water spilled upon the ground.

Doct. Many false prophets, even in the days of St. John the apostle, had gone out into the world.

What is a false prophet? Not everyone who teaches false doctrine, for we know in part and prophesy in part (1 Cor. 13:9-12). Therefore in part we may prophesy falsely. A false prophet then is one who preaches some doctrine that overthrows the doctrine of the Christian faith, and who seduces others to believe false doctrine (2 Tim. 2:17, 18).

-1. A man is a false prophet who preaches such doctrine as cannot be delivered without peril, without damnation unless he afterwards repents (2 Peter 2:1-3). Such are called ravening wolves (Matt. 7:15); they destroy both the souls and bodies of those who believe them; they root up the church of God like wild boars.

-2. They seduce others to believe the same. They sell men's souls for nought; if possible they would deceive the very elect (Matt. 24:24).

-3. They are convinced of their errors, and yet they will not yield (Tit. 3:10, 11). These are to be rejected, being perverted; and they sin, being condemned by their own souls.

But does not God have power to restrain these false prophets? True; but God will have not only divisions among Christians so that the spirits of his faithful ones may be discerned, but he will also have heresies; first that they may be tempted in judgment as well as in affections, and second that those who are approved may be made manifest. By the wind you may see the difference between wheat and chaff.

Use 1. If in St. John's time there were many mists of errors, this reproves men who, when they see variety of opinions in religion, sit down and do nothing until all men are agreed. Does St. John make this use of it? Shall we take our ease until there are none but true teachers? No, but rather let us try the spirits of our ministers, because many false prophets have gone out into the world.

Use 2. This teaches us not to wonder that many false prophets have gone out, if they went out in those days, in the light of the gospel. There is not now such power of godliness in the hearts of professors, but Christians now are given to much worldliness, and many rest in security; therefore wonder not, though the face of the earth be overspread with heresies.

Use 3. This should teach professors to take heed of opening a door to false prophets. Take heed of ignorance in your judgment, of ambition, and of sensuality; this is the smoke of the bottomless pit.

Use 4. Try the spirits of false prophets in these days. Take not up every instruction at the first blush, but try them. There are many spirits of false prophets. (a) You shall find in Popery a spirit of presumption, doubt, despair, hypocrisy; every point in Popery is carried on some of those wings. They teach that a man cannot be assured of salvation; this is doubting; yet a man may merit salvation; this is presumption. They worship stocks and stones. (b) There is a doctrine of faith and free grace which undermines the doctrine of Jesus (Rom. 8:2, 3). The doctrine of free grace is maintained to free a man from prayer, preaching, and any Christian duty that God has ordained to maintain grace in a man. Does not David pray God to create a new heart in him, and to renew a right spirit? (Ps. 51:10) Therefore a man ought to pray that he may have the Spirit of God quickened in him; this doctrine of faith and free grace secretly withdraws a man from the ordinances of God. (c) Lastly, there is a spirit of common Protestants who fashion their religion according to the world. They have respect only to their profit and ease; they follow the course of the court and country.

1 John 4:2

"Hereby you know the Spirit of God. Every spirit that confesses that Jesus Christ has come in the flesh is of God."

It is not rightly translated "come," for many false prophets did believe that Christ had come in the flesh, as the disciples of Balaam, and the Nicolaitans, and Hymeneus and Philetus. But it should rather be translated: "confesses the Christ that has come in the flesh"; that is, Christ veiled over with human frailties.

Doct. The people of God may well discern the spirits of their ministers by the confession which they make of Christ come in the flesh.

What is it to confess? There is a threefold confession in scripture:

-1. To acknowledge the truth, doctrine, and worship of Christ, even before rulers (Matt. 32:35). To confess is to profess, to bear witness of the grace of Christ.

-2. To confess a man's ministry (1 John 1:2).

-3. To confess by our work (Tit. 1:16); that is, by our life and works to confess him to be a Saviour (Matt. 1:21).

What is it for the spirit of a prophet to confess Jesus Christ? By spirit is meant here an inclination of mind, as before. When the bent of both soul and body, the inclination of the whole man, holds forth Christ Jesus, that is the mighty saving power of Christ revealed in human infirmities. Paul desires to know nothing (1 Cor. 2:3,4), that is, to express nothing in his life and doctrine but Christ Jesus revealed in the flesh, in human infirmities. Was any doctrine weakly delivered? In body, perhaps (2 Cor. 13:3-5; Gal. 4:13-15); but in his life he showed such a mighty power of Christ that they looked at him as an angel of God.

But how is a good confession a mark of discernment?

-1. This cannot come from man's nature, for man's spirit comes short of it (Phil. 2:20). Every man seeks his own; Demas has forsaken Christ and embraced this present world (2 Tim. 4:10). Some men look too high; they look to their own profits in the world, and account seeking to save souls a matter too low for them; if they preach, they preach only some moral discourse, which sends away those who are looking towards the ways of grace. The mighty saving power of Christ Jesus is not to be found in their ministry.

-2. It is not from the spirit of Satan, for this spirit far exceeds his spirit. He cries down Christ Jesus (Ezek. 13:22); he speaks with envy against Christ. Since then this effect is produced neither by the spirit of man nor by the spirit of Satan, it must needs be the Spirit of God which confesses Jesus Christ come in the flesh.

Use 1. To teach God's people to be well acquainted with the Lord Jesus, or else they will not be able to discern the spirit of their minister. It is a sinful vanity of God's servants to express their carnal excellencies before men; the apostle complains of it in the Galatians, that they desire to make a fair show in the flesh (Gal. 6:12). God does put honor upon many Christians, and gives them carnal excellence, but they must beware of darkening the power of the Lord Jesus.

Use 2. To try our states. Does our manner hold forth the Lord Jesus in human infirmities? God is not pleased with our human excellencies; we best please him when we show forth the hidden man of the heart.

Use 3. If there were so many false prophets in St. John's time, then this reproves the Papists who are burdened with traditions. They much adore venerable antiquity, as they call it; it is true indeed that "a hoary head is a crown of glory," but only "when it is found in a way of righteousness."

1 John 4:3

"And every spirit which confesses not that Jesus Christ has come in the flesh, is not of God. And this is that spirit of antichrist, whereof you have heard that it should come; and even now already it is in the world."

Doct. The spirit of every prophet who does not hold out the mighty power of Christ veiled with human frailties and infirmities, is not of God but of antichrist.

He does not say every prophet or every person, for a good prophet may express much weakness. But he says "every spirit"; if any spirit shall not acknowledge Christ come in the flesh, such a spirit is of antichrist.

-1. If a man does not express the truth of the Lord Jesus in his ministry, but breathes such error as overthrows the Lord Jesus, he is not of God (John 14:17; John 16:15). If a man speaks truth, not saving truth but only moral truths; if he does not press the saving power of the Lord Jesus; if he reveals Christ in moral writings, in tinkling cymbals of man's wisdom, if his spirit relishes nothing but affected eloquence, his spirit is of antichrist.

-2. Do you see the spirit of a prophet savor of ambition, pomp, and delicacy? This is the spirit of Popery; this does not hold forth the Lord Jesus.

-3. If a man's doctrine holds forth the Lord Jesus in a

tyrannical manner, making hearts sad whom God would not have made sad, he does not hold forth Jesus Christ.

How is it certain that such a spirit is a mark of antichrist?

-1. Because the whole carriage of the frame of spirit is contrary to the spirit of the Lord Jesus; for though he was veiled with human frailties, he was yet the way, the truth, and the life (John 14:6). Christ came riding upon the colt of an ass, not with any outward magnificence. When the people would have made him king, he escaped out of their midst.

-2. Because it makes cold the spirits of the people; it makes iniquity to abound (Matt. 24:11, 12).

-3. Because while ministers pump out the doctrine with heathenish rights, they have a special care to feed themselves, as Demas.

Use 1. This should teach ministers what frame of spirit they should hold forth when they take upon them such a holy and heavenly profession. If they would approve their hearts to God and his people, they must hold forth the Lord Jesus Christ in human simplicity. Though men cannot well try the doctrine of their ministers, yet they may try their spirits.

Use 2. Here is a ground of much consolation, when a man's heart can bear him witness that God has given him a spirit of saving truth; not to deliver his doctrine in carnal excellence, but in human simplicity.

Use 3. This reproves men of an antichristian spirit, who content themselves with outward flourishings; they know what harm they do to the church of God in so doing.

Use 4. This directs the people of God narrowly to watch the spirits of their ministers, if they would be freed from Popery, not seeking flourishing eloquence, nor him who has a tyrannical spirit, or him who delivers only moral truths.

Doct. The spirit of antichrist had come into the world in St. John's time; and also in St. Paul's time as well.

He speaks of the mystery of iniquity, which antichrist did work even in his time (2 Thess. 2:7). There are three things in the body of Popery, a spirit breathing in its doctrine, worship, and discipline; the same was visible in the apostles' time.

–1. For the doctrine.

a. There was a spirit of error in their foundation. It wrought mightily at that time in their hearts, so that men dared not trust the grace of Christ; but the apostle utterly inveighs against such, saying, "Either trust God for all or nothing" Gal. 5:3-5). Distrusting grace, or depending on something in nature and grace, are the rocks upon which so many souls suffer shipwreck in religion at this day.

b. There is a spirit of arrogance, contempt for magistracy and government (Jude 8), looking at the Pope as the sun in the firmament. This also was flourishing in the apostles' time.

–2. There is a spirit that breathes in their worship.

a. A spirit of superstition (Col. 2:18). Men at that time worshipped angels, as the Papists to this day; but they have more angels and saints, to which they cling rather than to Christ (1 John 5:21).

b. There was a spirit of hypocrisy, a show of religion, without the mighty power of the Lord Jesus shown in any performance. They had many things to draw their bodies (Col. 2:23). They dared not come to the Lord Jesus, but they must have some saint or angel to come to him by; they invented courses which the Lord did not require, and the apostle calls this a show of religion, which is hypocrisy. To them it may be said, "Who has required this at your hand?" They observe days and months and years, as did the Galatians; and the apostle was afraid he had bestowed his labor upon them in vain (Gal. 3:10, 11).

–3. What was the spirit of their discipline and government?

a. They sought primacy. The apostles had no sooner been removed out of the world than this spirit began to spring up; yea, while some of them lived (3 John 9).

b. That spirit which sought and exercised tyranny, casting out of the church ministers who were more faithful

(3 John 9, 10). Diotrephes would not receive John himself, nor his brethren; nor would he allow those who would. That spirit has been in the Church of Rome from that day to this. A second part of their tyranny was in imposing upon them unprofitable courses, unprofitable because they perished in the using (Col. 2:20-22).

c. There was a spirit of covetousness in ministers; they did not savor the things of God, but relished wealth and ambition (Jude 11). They followed the ways of sin, as Cain did.

The way of Cain consists in three steps: First, hypocrisy; he offers a sacrifice. Second, wrath, when he saw his brother's sacrifice accepted, being offered in faith, and his not. Third, bloodshed. Such was the spirit of Popery in Queen Mary's days.

Some walk in the ways of Balaam, the ways of covetousness, putting stumbling-blocks before the people, and that for covetousness' sake. Thirdly, some have the gainsaying spirit of Korah; they gainsay the ordinances of God.

Use 1. See the diligence of Satan to sow tares, even in the apostles' times. Therefore ministers should watch diligently over their people, so that no such spirit should be sown in their hearts. Satan will creep in by dissension; therefore ministers and people should have a special care of dissension; for if it creeps in, then soon you will have your worship shut up, and then there will be a woeful waste of religion.

Use 2. See the impudence of heretics who dare look God in the face and rise up among his many bright and glorious lights in the apostles' times; but let no Christian be discouraged by this, but rather the more encouraged to contend and strive for the faith of Christ.

Use 3. If we would be growing up in grace from day to day, let us take heed of the spirit of antichrist, of taking up a worship which God has not commanded. Let us take heed of hypocrisy, a spirit of Popery, a show of devotion. Let us walk steadfastly in that religion which we have received.

1 John 4:4

"You are of God, little children, and have overcome them, because greater is he who is in you than he who is in the world."

In the former verse you had a sign of the spirit of teachers; so in these verses you have a sign of the spirit of hearers, a sign taken from the victory which good hearers have gotten over bad teachers. A good hearer is not overcome by bad teachers, but he soon finds them out and overcomes them. This is argued from a double cause.

-1. They are of a higher offspring than corrupt teachers.

-2. Their spirits are stronger and more excellent than the spirits of worldly teachers. "Greater is he who is in you than he who is in the world."

"He who knows God hears us." There is another sign of good hearers: they heard good teachers. And on the contrary, "He that is not of God hears us not." You see here:

-1. A difference between good and bad teachers, good and bad hearers. Good teachers and good hearers are of God, and contrary, bad teachers and bad hearers are of the world.

-2. A combat between good and bad teachers, and a victory also: Good hearers overcome bad teachers.

-3. The issue of the conflict: good hearers overcome.

-4. The cause of their victory, which is the divine descent and excellence of their spirit: greater is he that is in good hearers than he that is in bad teachers.

-5. A congratulation: "little children, you are of God."

Doct. There are in the church of God two sorts of teachers and two sorts of hearers: some of God, some of the world.

Why are good teachers and good hearers said to be of God?

-1. They are of a divine original; they are born from on high, from the seed of the eternal God. "I am from above," says Christ (John 8:23); and those who are regenerate are also descended from God. Those who have no higher offspring than flesh and blood are of the world.

-2. They savor and relish the doctrine of God (Rom. 8:15). They who are of the Spirit of God savor the things of God; those who hold forth the mighty power of God veiled in human frailties, they are of God.

-3. He who is of God has a place in the church of God (1 Cor. 12:28). God sets the members of Christ in the church; this is a work of God (v. 18). There is no member of Christ whom the Lord has not set in his place; all men in the world cannot fit one member to the body; it would be both unprofitable and burdensome unless God join it to the body. So all the men in the world cannot put one member into the spiritual body unless God puts it in. Indeed those who are of the world have a place in the church too, but yet they are not of the church; they are superfluous humors (Matt. 15:13). As it is never well with the body until the noisome humors are purged out, so the church will never be well until those superfluous humors are cut off.

Use. This should teach us all not to comfort ourselves because we are members of the church, and live under the ministry of the gospel; we must not rest here, for all this while we may go no further than flesh and blood. We may live civilly and diligently in our calling, and yet have no higher place in the church, no higher offices than worldly. Are we the better for this? Let us labor to be not only in the church but of the church; to be in that place where God has set us; to derive sap and strength daily from the root Christ Jesus. We must thus try our hearts and the hearts of others, and unless this frame of spirit is in us we are not true members of the church.

"And you have overcome them." They overcome, therefore there is a conflict.

Doct. Godly hearers and worldly teachers have a conflict (Jude 3).

Jude shows them that when corrupt teachers break into the church, he would not have godly hearers sit down, but contend and wrestle earnestly for the faith. Paul stirs up Timothy to war a good warfare, to hold faith and a good conscience (1 Tim. 4:18, 19). This shows that there are two things for which goood ministers and people contend with worldly ministers and people, viz. faith and a good conscience.

How is this conflict fought between bad ministers and good people?

-1. When bad ministers contend with good people to pervert their faith (2 Tim. 2:18, 19) or to destroy their good conscience. If they see good Christians making conscience of keeping the sabbath or performing family duties, or abstaining from sin, bad ministers will do as much as they can to pervert their faith and to destroy their good conscience. Now the people of God contend for both.

a. They wrestle with God for a better faith and a better judgment (Rom. 15:30, 31); if for Paul, then much more for themselves.

b. They observe those who corrupt their faith, and so they are better armed against them (Rom. 16:17, 18) and so are better able to overcome.

c. Good hearers admonish bad teachers to look better to their doctrine (Col. 4:17) and conversation.

d. If none of these prevail, they argue with them and deal seriously with them, as the man born blind (and therefore no great scholar) reasoned with the Pharisees about Christ (John 9:7-34).

e. If all this will not prevail, then they avoid their doctrine (Matt. 22:3, 4) and their leaven (Luke 12:1).

-2. When there is a conflict, the godly have a care either to remove altogether from their congregations, or else to depart from them on the Sabbath day. The Levites left their suburbs and possessions and came to Judah and Jerusalem

(2 Chron. 11:14), and those who could not sell their possessions, took horses and rode where the word was faithfully and sincerely taught. And so men who live under bad ministers should take their horses and ride to places where the word of God is faithfully taught; not that people must go from their ministers when they preach the word of God in truth.

Use 1. This shows how much people are left without excuse, when they are ignorant and graceless when their ministers are so. The worse your ministers are, the more you should contend to hold fast faith and a good conscience. You must not plead that you are unlearned; are you more ignorant than the blind man? If you would show yourself to be a Christian, you must hold forth faith and a good conscience.

Use 2. To exhort people to contend with their ministers when they are not of God.

"You are of God, little children, and you have overcome them."

Doct. As there is a conflict between godly hearers and worldly teachers, so godly hearers overcome.

Whoever is born of God overcomes the world (1 John 5:4); not only the world of vain-glory and reproaches, the world of covetousness, injury, and losses, but the world of false teachers also.

In what does this victory consist?

-1. In trying and examining their doctrine, and finding it to be false. If he discovers him he overcomes him (Rev. 2:2); by this means he puts them to shame, as those who have lost the field.

-2. In standing fast in the doctrine of God's truth and liberty of Christian profession, whatever those false teachers say. Resist the devil and he will flee from you (James 4:7); so those false teachers are overcome if you do not yield to their doctrine.

-3. When God's servants grow so much more fervent, resolute, and zealous Christians, so much more do they see themselves opposed. When David danced before the ark of the Lord, Michal the daughter of Saul laughed at him; but says David, "I will yet be more vile" (2 Sam. 6:20, 22).

-4. A man gets ground when he is able to prevail either by avoiding them or by being content to suffer under them. When a man cannot overcome them, by being faithful to the death he overcomes evil with good.

What are the assurances we will prevail?

-1. The blood of Christ, with which we are sprinkled (Luke 1:74), delivers us from our enemies (v. 68). They overcome by the blood of the Lamb (Rev. 12:11). Christ has triumphed over them openly (Col. 2:13, 14); so that we come to fight with wounded enemies. Christ has broken the serpent's head; we come to finish the victory that Christ has begun for us. Were the Devil and ungodly teachers set loose in their great strength, they would be too strong for us; but now their teeth are broken.

-2. The mighty power of God that dwells in God's children. St. John says, "I write unto you, young men, because you have overcome the wicked one." They are so ballasted with promises and threatenings that they do not sin against God. If the devil or the world promise them earthly things, they have many and better promises.

-3. The glories of him who dwells in godly hearers, which are greater than him who dwells in wicked teachers. Who is he that is greater in them? It is the Spirit of God (Eph. 1:22; 1 Cor. 3:16). The Lord dwells in his children by his Spirit; he is greater than he that dwells in the world.

How is he greater? In all those things by which men achieve victory (Isa. 26:5). To win a victory three things are required, wisdom, strength, and watchfulness.

-1. Wisdom. David says, "I have more wisdom and understanding than all my teachers" (Ps. 119:98-100). God had so taught him by his word that he came to get more understanding than his old teachers. He does not speak this in arrogance, but only to comfort himself thereby. God teaches wisdom secretly (Ps. 51:6).

-2. God puts a renewed strength and power into their souls, by which they are mighty to overcome all their enemies (Eph. 6:10) and by which they are able to do and suffer all things (Phil. 4:13).

-3. They are greater in watchfulness, without which they fall. They never lack wisdom and strength. Though it is the fault of God's servants to wax fat and to kick up the heel against God, and to forget the great things he has done for them, even at this time he who is in them is greater than he who is in worldly teachers; for though they fall, yet they rise again, and get greater strength, and overcome mightily (Mark 14:37, 38). When God's servants put on a careless spirit and do not make use of their wisdom and strength which they have received, they come to be soiled; yet there is a seed in them by which they overcome all their enemies, yea and themselves also.

How does a man overcome at his first conversion? God puts forth such a mighty arm of watchfulness, wisdom, and strength, that he overcomes the devil (Luke 11:21). Thus he overcomes the world (Gal. 1:4; John 15:19). He is crucified to the world, and the world to him; he crucifies the flesh with the affections and lusts (Gal. 5:24), so that he looks at them all as ignominious and deadly enemies. If Christ shows himself thus strong when a man begins to grow, what will he do when Christians grow stronger in wisdom, grace, strength, and watchfulness!

Use 1. This reproves everyone who excuses himself and thinks he may lawfully grow worse under bad and worldly teachers. Has a worldly teacher overcome you? What a shame it is for a Christian man who has the seed of God in him, to allow himself to be overcome by worldly teachers. It is an ill sign for Christians to grow worse because of bad teachers; it is a great shame that God should give place to the devil, and that the children of God should give place to the children of the world and of the devil.

Use 2. This should teach all God's children to war against all worldly teachers, with the wrestlings of God, with strong wrestlings, and not to give over the conflict. They are upon certain grounds of victory. If you only stand out, you shall overcome, for Christ has overcome, and his promises and threatenings are greater than those of the world and of Satan.

Use 3. Here is a ground of consolation and assurance to God's children of perseverance; for if anything could separate them from God, then it must be either the world, the Devil, or lusts of their own flesh. But none of these can.

1 John 4:5, 6

"They are of the world: therefore they speak of the world, and the world hears them. We are of God. He who knows God hears us; he that is not of God does not hear us. Hereby we know the spirit of truth and the spirit of error."

What is it to be a worldly teacher?

-1. Teachers are said to be of the world because it is their natural frame and temper to be worldly (John 3:23). There are several descents of ministers: some have no other spirit than that which they draw from their parents, but the Spirit of God comes down from God upon some ministers and makes them walk by another rule than worldly men do.

-2. Worldly men savor the things of the world. If a man is of a divine spirit, he relishes divine matters, as saving the souls of God's people and freeing them from the danger of sin; but a worldly teacher relishes preferment and housekeeping; his spirit reaches no higher.

-3. The ends of worldly teachers are worldly: first, to draw away disciples after them (Acts 20:30) and second, to have respect to their wages of unrighteousness. They love only to live in pleasure and to keep a good house (2 Pet 2:13); but godly ministers labor to make disciples for God (Matt. 28:19, 20).

What is meant by the world? The world is a mass of

mankind which lies in a state of corruption; those who fell in Adam and never rose again (John 15:19). Wicked men are called the world:

-1. Because they are but flesh and blood (John :6).

-2. Because they savor those things that are of the world; every man speaks of matters in his own element.

-3. Because most of the world are such (1 John 5:19). The world lies in wickedness; it takes up its rest therein.

-4. Because they have their portion in this world (Ps. 17:14). But a child of God looks for another inheritance, immortal and undefiled (1 Pet. 1:4).

Those who are of the world would not have their conscience troubled; they would go home in peace and possess their goods in peace. But those who are of God relish the things of God. They cannot relish worldly teachers, because they do not speak to the conscience nor show how to lay hold of eternal life; and if they do speak of heavenly matters, they speak with a cold affection. But when a godly minister preaches in a heavenly manner, being moved by a godly principle, his conversation is in heaven (Phil. 3:20). He talks of heaven.

Use. If ministers would know their own spirits, let them consider what doctrine they deliver, what end they aim at, and what their hearers are; and by this means they will easily discern their own spirits.

1 John 4:7

"Beloved, let us love one another; for love is of God. And everyone who loves is born of God, and knows God."

In the words there is, first, an exhortation to mutual love among ministers and people, and secondly, a threefold reason to press this upon them. The reason is taken: -1. From the origin of their love, that is, "from God." -2. From the state of those who love: "they are born of God, and know God."

-3. From the evil state of those who do not love: "they do not know God." This is proved by an argument from God's nature: "for God is love."

Doct. Godly ministers should exhort themselves and their godly hearers to mutual love, both the people to love their ministers and the ministers to love their people.

When our Saviour was about to leave the charge of the souls of his people to Peter, he asked him three distinct times whether he loved him (John 21:15-17), so that out of his abundant love to Christ he might feed his sheep (1 Thess. 5:13); esteeming him, they would love him for his works' sake (Heb. 10:24). The apostle exhorts them to provoke one another to love (Heb. 13:1). Whatever happens, he would have brotherly love to continue; so St. Peter exhorts (1 Pet. 1:2).

Why is this the duty of ministers?

-1. Because a covenant stands between ministers and people; they are partakers of one baptism, members of one and the same body (1 Cor. 10:17; 1 Cor. 12:27). Therefore they should enlarge themselves one to another (Eph. 4:16). They should love one another because God has incorporated them into one body.

-2. Because they do not receive mutual edification unless all is done in love, for edification is wrought by love. Knowledge puffs up, but love edifies; therefore let all things be done in love. Mutual love is both profitable and comfortable.

-3. Lack of love lowers a minister's spirit (2 Cor. 12:20). It saddens him when he sees the people envying one another. When the body is full of swellings and inflammations, the medicines and plasters laid on do not heal; a man must first allay the inflammations. So when a minister sees swelling among his people, what he preaches is spilled on the ground.

-4. If people do not walk in mutual love, the minister shall lose his portion from them (1 Thess. 5:13); he shall lose his estimation among them, for they will not profit by any ordinance of God, but will wax cold.

Use 1. This exhorts ministers to make it their main and principal work to allay swellings, and to knit together all the members of a congregation in one spirit, and mutual love, as God knits them together in one body. All graces fall short of edifying where love is lacking (1 Cor. 13:1, 2).

Use 2. To exhort the people of God to receive this exhortation of love, and not to allow any dissension to be found among them.

Doct. Our love springs from God; this should move ministers and people to mutual love.

Love is the chief lesson Christ gave to his disciples when he went out of the world (John 13:35, 36; 2 Tim. 1:13). A man may as soon lose his inheritance in the Lord Jesus, as his love to his brethren. If God sets love in my soul and man unsets it, I shall destroy the work of God in my soul.

Use 1. Take heed of wrath; if love is of God, then whence is hatred? It is from the enemy of God (Eph. 4:26, 27).

You will say, "I do not hate my brother"; but yet you will have nothing to do with him. When a man does not seek communion with his brother, nor communication of good to him, he hates his brother.

Use 2. If we would have any comfort in our hearts, we must have a care that nothing which falls between us and our brethren should take away our love from them. If we allow a fire of wrath to kindle in us, we do as much as in us lies to destroy our own souls.

Doct. Love to our brethren is a pledge of our birthright (John 13:34).

-1. It is the nature of God, and by this means we partake of the divine nature (Rom. 5:5).

-2. Love is a fruit of faith, by which we receive Christ (Gal. 5:6).

Use 1. This condemns all who are of such deep prodigality as to allow love to decay. If you lose so much of love to your brethren, you lose so much of your love to God, and so much of the evidence of your inheritance.

Use 2. Preserve your love to your brethren, and you preserve your inheritance; your brotherly love is a pledge of your inheritance.

1 John 4:8

"He who loves not, knows not God; for God is love."

Doct. According to our love or lack of love to our brethren, such is our knowledge or lack of knowledge of God.

The apostle bears witness of the Corinthians that they abound in knowledge and that they fall short in no gift (1 Cor. 1:5); but yet he complains that there is schism among them (v. 10). Therefore there may be knowledge of God and yet lack of love to our brethren.

What is it then to know God?

-1. The knowledge there spoken of is a knowledge that enlightens the understanding, that puffs up and swims in the brain; it does not sink into the heart and affections.

-2. There is a knowledge that reaches to the heart and life of a man; a man is said not to know when he does not acknowledge. "The Lord knows the way of the righteous" (Ps. 1:6); that is, approves and delights in their way. What a man does not regard, he is said not to know (Matt. 7:23).

-3. There is a knowledge that expresses itself in action. "Know the God of your fathers" (1 Chron. 18:). The sons of Eli did not know God; though priests, yet they knew not the way of religion, because they were wicked children without yoke. They were not acquainted with the ways of the Lord (1 Sam. 2:12).

But how is love a sign of knowledge?

-1. God's nature is both in his attributes and works. Both express in abundance that those who know God love their brethren; for no attribute so much expresses the nature of God as this of love.

-2. If we know God and are acquainted with God, there will be some likeness between God and us; if we see God loving godly ministers and hearers, so will we (Gal. 6:10).

-3. The love of God makes an impression in our hearts (Rom. 5:5). Our hearts are like a stone wall on a cold day; the wall is cold, but is warmed on a sunny day.

-4. What caused you to love God? If you love him because he pardons your sins and saves your soul, a man may do this by a spirit of false love; but he who loves God truly will love him for his goodness not only to us, but to others.

Use 1. This is a ground of trial for our love and fellowship with God. If you find in your heart an unfeigned love to godly ministers; if you make God's servants the men of your delight, you need no better evidence from heaven that you are beloved of God.

You will say you are acquainted with many godly ministers and good men. I answer, consider whether you love them for your sake, because they may be helpful to you (which is self-love), or for their goodness' sake, for their likeness to God, for their graces and virtues. This is a sign you love them not for your sake but for God's.

Use 2. This exhorts every soul which desires fellowship with God, to be acquainted with God and to love the brethren. According to your love to your brethren, such is God's love to you; if there is any strangeness in you to any brother, this will make God strange to you.

1 John 4:9

"In this was manifested the love of God toward us, because God sent his only begotten Son into the world that we might live through him."

The second argument to move us to brotherly love is the example of God the Father's love to us.

A third argument is taken from the benefit we receive when we walk in love among ourselves. The benefit is twofold:

-1. We have fellowship with God; we see the face of God and find God dwelling in us (vv. 9-16).

-2. We grow up to perfection; without love there is no growth of grace (vv. 17-21).

In the words of this verse we have then an argument to love our brethren, and this argument is taken from God's love. In it there are five parts:
   -1. The manifestation of God's love.
   -2. The object, "toward us."
   -3. The evidence thereof, "because he sent his Son."
   -4. The place to which he sent his son, "into the world."
   -5. The end, "that we might live through him."

Doct. God not only bestows love upon his people, but it is his pleasure to manifest it as well (Rom. 5:8; Ps. 98:2, 3; Isa. 52:10).

There is the mighty power of God by which he overcomes all our sins, by which he redeems us. "All flesh shall see the salvation of our God" (Luke 3:6); yea, more than all flesh, for it is manifested:
   -1. To the angels (Luke 2:13, 14).
   -2. To men's consciences (Rom. 5:8; Gal. 2:20).
   -3. To the rest of mankind (Rev. 3:9).

Why does God manifest his love to us?
   -1. To promote his glory. The high praises of God were in the shepherds' mouths (Luke 2:14). Jerusalem shall be comforted, because God will make bare his arm in the redemption of his people (Isa. 52:9, 10).
   -2. If God did not reveal our salvation to us, it would be no comfort to us; but when it is manifested, it is a ground of joy.
   -3. It is a means to draw many men to the unfeigned love of God, who might otherwise be left in darkness (Zech. 8:23). When the love of God is manifested to the children of men, it raises them up to seek God (Cant. 5:16). Therefore the daughters of Jerusalem are provoked to seek Christ Jesus with the rest of his people. This encourages those who are in the ways of grace, and discourages those who are in the ways of sin.

Use. This should teach the servants of God not only to bear a hidden love, but also a manifest love to Christ. Now indeed men need not be ashamed to manifest their love; but if times grow hard, then men will come to Christ by night, as Nicodemus did. But if God would manifest his love to your conscience, he requires that you should make it known to the world. If we are ashamed of him in the world, he will be ashamed of us before his Father (Mark 8:38). Joseph of Arimathea was a disciple secretly for fear of the Jews; but when the body of Christ hung on the cross, he came in boldly to Pilate and begged it. Though it was slow coming on, there was truth of grace in him; and where there is danger indeed, every man will put himself forth to bear witness to the truth.

Doct. God loved us before he sent his Son to reconcile us to himself.

His sending Christ into the world was out of free love (Rom. 5:8; John 3:16). Christ died to make an atonement for us; he did not come unsent, but was sent before he went (Heb. 5:4, 5).

But does not the scripture say that the death and blood of Christ are the grounds of our reconciliation? (Rom. 5:10; Rom. 3:24, 25) How could God love us before?

-1. Though God loved us before, yet we did not love him; thus reconciliation was needed. There must be a mutual fellowship in reconciliation (2 Cor. 5:16). The blood of Christ did not so much reconcile God to us as us to God; that we seeing the blood of Christ shed for us, might be stirred up to love God. Out of the abundance of his compasssion he takes a course to bring us to him.

-2. Though God bore love to us before, yet his love was secret; he did not break forth into a manifestation of his love to us until he sent his Son into the world, though he loved us with an everlasting love (Jer. 31:3). Because of his justice he could not manifest it to our conscience until he had given his Son, the Lord Jesus Christ, to die for us.

What kind of love was it which God bore to the world in

that he sent his son? (Tit. 3:5) Was it his love toward all mankind, the whole race, or a peculiar love which he bore to the people of the election of grace?

The Arminians say that he bore a love to the world, and this love was general to all before the sending of Christ, and therefore all may be saved. The truth is that God bore a love to the world, a φιλανθρωπία reaching to all, but he bore an ancient love to his own people. Had he borne a general love only, all men might have perished; for if God sent his Son that whoever believed should be saved, was it in the will to believe or not? Yes, they say; he gave them means, but they might will or not. If this was a general love, then there was a greater love than the sending of Christ, which is contrary to scripture. "Greater love hath no man than this, that a man lay down his life for his friends."

Use 1. Let us magnify the love of God to us in Christ. We esteem much of ancient love; like ancient wine, it is the best. God loved us before he sent Christ, before the foundation of the world was laid (Jer. 31:3). This love was without cause on our parts, for we were enemies to him.

Use 2. This exhorts us to accept this love. Shall God send his ambassadors (2 Cor. 5:20), and shall we still stand out against God?

Use 3. If God so loved us, we ought to love one another.

Doct. God sending his only begotten Son into the world, is a manifest token of God's love to us.

-1. God not only sends us bodily bread every day, but the bread of eternal life; not so much the gift as the Giver himself.

-2. Consider on what terms we stood with God when he sent us his son. Even then we provoked him to his face, and were enemies of his majesty (Rom. 5:8).

-3. God looked not at the angels, but the seed of man. He passed over angels and left them in chains of darkness (Heb. 2:16); but of man he said, "Shall he fall and not rise again?"

-4. We were strangers and enemies to God, dead in

trespasses and sins, and so we did neither desire nor deserve love, yet us he has reconciled (Col. 1:21; Eph. 2:4, 5).

-5. Consider Christ who was sent. Had it been a morsel of daily bread, it had been a great mercy; but in Christ he sent a horn of plenty, a horn of salvation (Ps. 89:18; Luke 1:69). Consider Christ not as a servant but as a Son, and a well-beloved Son in whom he was well pleased; and such a son as thought it not blasphemy to think and say he was an equal with God (Phil. 2:5, 6).

-6. Consider where God sent his Son: "into the world." Our salvation could not be wrought in heaven; it was no place for suffering, no place for a man to be born. Therefore it was needful that he should come down to earth.

-7. The world did not put on Christ that honor which was due to him, but rather dishonor; a crown of thorns.

-8. The more the world knew him, the more they hated him; in heaven they adore and honor him, but "you have known me and hated me," he says (John 15:18).

Use 1. Learn hence to acknowledge the divinity of the nature of Christ; he is called the only begotten Son of God, therefore of the same nature with God (Phil. 2:5, 6).

Use 2. This shows you the love of the Father for us, in that he sends his Son to be a ransom for us. When all other signs fail, if God gives you his only Son, that is a true token of his love (Eccl. 9:1).

Use 3. This shows us the woeful misery that we naturally lie in, when Christ must come down from heaven or else we could not have been saved; no man or angel could do it.

Use 4. This should stir us all up to accept this love of God. We would accept a small gift from a prince; shall we not accept such a gift from God?

Use 5. To persuade us all that if God gives Christ, he will deny us nothing (Rom. 8:32). We may go boldly to the throne of grace, and he will fill our mouths.

Use 6. This should cause us to return back again to God manifest pledges of our love to him. Let us give body and soul to God, since he has not been wanting in his love to us.

Does not love require love? (Ps. 116:12) Let us train up our children to know God, and draw as many as we can to know God. There is no greater dishonor to God than to refuse this manifest love.

Doct. God sent Christ that we might live by him (John 1:10, 11).

What is the life that Christ came to procure for us?

-1. A life of God's favor in justification, sanctification, and consolation; that is the chief life for the soul of a Christian, the manifestation of God's love to his conscience. Though God loved us before he sent Christ, yet we did not know it. "In his favor is life" (Ps. 30:5); take away the sun and we die, let the sun shine and we live. Let God take away the sunshine of his favor from us, and we can neither pray nor preach, nor live a life of holiness (Prov. 16:14, 15; Rom. 8:2; Eph. 2:4, 5). There is enough life in Christ to procure us life.

-2. There is a life of glory, of which it is said that Christ gives eternal life to his sheep (John 10:27, 28; 1 Cor. 15:4, 5; John 5:24, 28, 29). Those whose souls receive life by the word of the gospel, their bodies shall rise to eternal life.

How did Christ procure us this life? By his death. While we were yet enemies, we were reconciled by the death of Christ (Rom. 5:9, 10). We received life of grace and holiness by this means.

Why does Christ quicken?

-1. It was impossible that our corrupt nature should fulfull any law of God (Rom. 8:4; Gal. 3:21).

-2. The glory of Christ requires that as the Father quickens, so he should also (John 5:21).

Use 1. This shows us what our condition is without Christ. If God sends Christ so that we might live through him, then in God's sight without him we are dead; we are like thorns that give a blaze, but we lie down in sorrow (Isa. 50:11). Christ is our life; without him we can do nothing.

Use 2. Let us try our states, whether we can say that

God sent Christ into the world and manifested his love to us. Do you live in God's sight? Without Christ we are dry bones; until we can say we live in Christ, we cannot say we have the sense of God's favor.

Use 3. It teaches those who have any evidence of life in Christ (John 10:10) to come into God's presence as dry bones; entreat God that he would speak the word, so that those dry bones may live.

Use 4. To teach all who have received this manifest token of God's love, to acknowledge the Lord Christ to be their life. "For me to live is Christ" (Phil. 1:21); now Paul is crucified (Gal. 2:20), and now for him to live is Christ. Now every day he lives he expresses Christ.

1 John 4:10

"Herein is love, not that we loved God, but that he loved us and sent his Son to be the propitiation for our sins."

Doct. The love of God to us was not procured by our love to him, but by his own good pleasure; he loved us because it pleased him.

In these words we have the freeness of Christ's love; he loved us freely, because he loved us when we did not love him. We did not begin in love to him, but he to us; and therefore he pardoned our sins.

What is the love that God bore to us before we loved him?

There is a threefold principle of love which God magnifies and manifests to his people before they love him.

-1. That love by which he chose us to life, and to redeem us by Christ (2 Tim. 1:9); and the choice to life was not according to works but free grace.

-2. God's love in redeeming us by Christ was before any love of ours to God (John 3:16).

-3. His love went before us by effectually calling us. He drew us; drew us out of presumption, then out of despair.

How may we know that God's love preceded ours?

-1. By the difference between the care of God's love and ours. Self-love is so riveted in our hearts that we cannot love any unless it is for our own ends; a natural man loves no one any further than tends to his own profit or pleasure. But a Christian is enlarged to all God's children; he loves them all; and the reason for this is that he knows such to be incorporated into the same body with him. We should never have loved God unless we had found his love to us.

But a Christian freely performs many offices of love to those who do not love him. True; but this is because he knows God can abundantly recompense it. He sometimes may lay down his life for the truth and for his brethren; but he knows that Christ has done this for him before.

-2. By the eternity of God's love (Jer. 31:3). Now an everlasting love can have no cause. The cause is always before the effect; no temporal thing can be the cause of an eternal love.

-3. By the end of God's love, that he might bring us to walk in love (Eph. 1:4; Tit. 2:14). The love of God to his people of old is a fit precedent and example for all his children (Deut. 7:8, 9; Deut. 9:4-6).

Use. This refutes a Popish and Arminian conceit that God chooses none to life apart from foreseen faith and good works. But then he would have chosen none to life. This is a mercenary love.

Use 2. It exhorts all to begin early to love God. Though we begin ever so soon, God has preceded us (Rom. 11:35). It was an early love of Josiah, when at twelve years of age he sought after God; but God's love was up before him. You cannot be before him in your love, though you begin as soon as you are born.

Use 3. To teach old people, if God has gone before them with love long ago, to love him in return; and to be humbled for lack of love to God, who has loved them so long. Let us acknowledge the freedom of God's love. By God's testimony Job was a man that feared God and eschewed evil. Says the

Devil, Does Job serve God for nought? No, but though God stripped him of all, yet he had shown such marvelous love to his soul that he had just cause to love him forever, even if he had not bestowed upon him one dram of wealth.

Use 4. This should teach God's children to be as faithful in loving his servants as he was in loving them; to love them freely and do kindness to them freely (Ps. 16:2, 3).

Use 5. Here is comfort to God's servants who have tasted of this love. He who loves you freely, loves you forever, for his love does not stand upon condition. If he loved us when we were enemies, will he hate us when we are acquainted with him and reconciled? We shall not, though ever so bad, be worse than we were before; and if he loved us because he desired to love us, his love will forever remain.

Doct. The sending of Christ for our sakes was a fruit, not only of his love, but of his free love (Rom. 5:8, 4).

"Herein is love"; "God so loved the world" (John 3:16); which implies that there was a love of God which moved him to send Christ before we believed, so that believing on him we might have mercy and salvation.

What is a free love? Love is said to be free in two respects:

-1. When it is granted without any merit or desert on the part of those to whom it is granted; and then it is much greater when there is not only lack of merit but demerit. If men deserve our love, it is not free; but God's love is so free that he sent his Son into the world to redeem us, when we did not deserve redemption but rather wrath (Col. 1:21).

-2. Love is said to be free when it is without condition, so that nothing on our parts shall take away his love: "he will remember their sins no more" (Jer. 31:34).

But why then is faith required? (John 3:36) True indeed, there is a condition required; but of what sort? It is this: the same God who requires the condition, promises likewise that he will work the condition; thus it is free love.

Again, is not faith a supernatural gift? Can men justly be condemned then for not having it, if it is beyond the power of nature to reach unto it? I answer, the reason men are condemned is that light has come into the world, and men loved darkness rather than light (John 3:36).

Why was free love required to save us?

-1. Because of the state in which we lay before Christ was sent into the world. We were then strangers and enemies (Col. 1:21). We were not fit to receive mercy, much less to deserve any.

-2. God did this that the glory of his great name might appear (Eph. 1:5-7; Deut. 7:8). God did not love us because we were many, but because it pleased him to love us. The same day that Adam sinned, he and his posterity should have died (Gen. 3:15). But the benefit that the godly have is that we might live and that we might all come to the knowledge of his grace (2 Pet. 3:9; Rom. 2:4, 5); so if it be asked why God is patient to the world, it is for Christ's sake (Exod. 33:1-5).

-3. God sent Christ into the world so that by his suffering his elect might suffer; that by his growing they might grow; and by his dying they might die (Col. 2:29). There is a difference in the way Christ died for the world and for the elect. He so died for the elect that he prayed his death might be effectual to them (John 17:9, 20, 21); he does not pray for the world.

Use 1. This refutes an error of the Papists, that Christ loved the world without difference; that God sent his Son for the one as well as for the other. They say God does not bestow his love without condition; this we deny.

Use 2. This teaches us who have pardon of sins, to acknowledge God's love in sending his Son freely (Rom. 5:8).

Use 3. To teach those who have not found reconciliation with God, what course to take to be reconciled. Get the Lord Jesus to be propitiatory sacrifice for you (1 John 2:2).

Doct. Christ was sent by his Father to be a propitiation for our sins.

What is a propitiation? The word signifies four things.

-1. It signifies a pledge, satisfaction, or redemption; a ransom (Numb. 35:31, 32; Heb. 12:24). The blood of Christ spilled for our sins speaks better things than the blood of Abel; his blood cried for vengeance, Christ's cries that I might receive a ransom.

-2. It signifies a gift to appease wrath (Gen. 32:20).

-3. It signifies a surety to undergo wrath for another man (Prv. 21:18; Rev. 12:11).

-4. It signifies a covering, not such a covering as a garment, but a covering as a plaster; the word signifies resin or pitch (Gen. 6:14). This keeps the ark from the injury of the water. As the physician applies a covering to a wound to purge it, so God sent Christ to plaster us, to purge away the filth of our souls.

Why was Christ our propitiation?

-1. Other things could not take away sin (Heb. 10:1-10; Ps. 40:11). The blood of bulls and beasts could not satisfy God's wrath.

-2. There was a great disproportion between all other things and the price of atonement. By our sins we had provoked God to infinite displeasure; therefore the gift which must appease God's wrath must be infinite, and that is Christ.

Use 1. This shows the wonderful wisdom, justice, and grace of God that have met together. First, it was God's wisdom that he took such a course as would reconcile us to himself. When no creature would serve the turn, God sent his Son to suffer for us. Second, we see the grace of God, that he would send his Son to be a propitiation for us, and to drink up all the dregs of his Father's wrath for us. Third, this shows the exact justice of God: though he is infinitely compassionate and gracious, yet he will be satisfied. And yet rather than that the creature should perish in suffering, God in his infinite wisdom devised a means by which all our sins could be done away.

Use 2. This sets forth the amazing, miserable state into which we had plunged ourselves; so great that all the men in the world and all the angels in heaven could not have delivered us.

Use 3. This shows us what course to take to have our sins pardoned. If God has sent his Son to be a propitiation fo our sins, we must take the same course that they did of old (Lev. 4:4). We must confess all our sins and offer up Christ, and pray that Christ's blood may speak better things than the blood of Abel.

Use 4. Here is a comfort to all souls for whose sins Christ is a propitiation. He now makes the Father reconciled to them, and well pleased with them.

1 John 4:11

"Beloved, if God so loved us, we ought also to love one another."

This is the conclusion of the argument stirring us up to love one another. Here heaven and earth meet as it were in one exhortation.

Doct. Such love of God to us is a pattern of like love in us to our brethren.

How did God so love us? As is described in the two former verses.

-1. With a manifest love (1 John 4:9; Gal. 4:4).

-2. With a bountiful and large love; he spared not his Son, but sent him out of his bosom into the world.

-3. When we did not love God, when we were enemies and strangers, he cast about to see how he might reconcile us to himself by sending his Son. This is free gracious love. So we should love one another, in manifest, bountiful, gracious love (Eph. 5:1, 2).

Why is God's love to be the pattern of ours?

-1. Consider the subject and object of this love.

a. Consider us as children of God. Children should be like the parents; therefore the apostle presses the argument from our near conjunction with God (Eph. 5:1) and from the resemblance that ought to be between God and us (Matt. 5:44, 45). As we seek to approve ourselves as children of such a gracious, tender-hearted Father, let us be so to our brethren.

b. Consider us as loved of God. There is an equity required in our giving and receiving. As we have received, so let us give (Matt. 10:8). Should we be rigorous to our brother, when God is so gracious to us? (Matt. 18:33, 34)

c. Consider the just recompense of love we owe to God who has loved us. Where we sow more seed, we look for a more plentiful harvest (Matt. 25:28). Not to give God his own with interest is injustice in us. The members of the body serve to help the body; therefore pour God's love upon all his saints. David inquires if there are any left of Jonathan's house, that he may show him "the kindness of the Lord" (2 Sam. 9:2); as if he had been bound to it by the Lord.

-2. Look at those who are to be loved; since they have received such love, we are to love them from the firmness of God's love to them, which we cannot reverse; therefore they are to be beloved by men and angels (Numb. 23:20). It is a vain thing to hate where God has loved. When Isaac had blessed Jacob the younger brother, though Esau entreated him and sought it with tears, and though his own affection went that way, yet he could not reverse it (Gen. 27:33, 34).

-3. Consider the danger that may befall us if we do not love where God has loved. The wrath of God had gone out against his children (2 Chron. 19:2, 3) because they had loved where God had hated; so when we hate where God has loved, the wrath of God has gone out against us. Jehoshaphat joins in league with Ahab, God's enemy; and God's wrath goes out and falls upon his children; his eldest son proved a persecutor. So if we are straight-hearted where God has loved, God's wrath will go out against us, and will find out either us or our children.

Use 1. This reproves all enmity or strangeness that is found in God's people toward the brethren. When God's people are young beginners and newly come on, they think they can never love Christ or his servants enough; but St. John implies that in his old age he had need of this exhortation. Through love of the world, themselves, and their lusts, the people of God grow cold in their love to God and his servants. This is one reason why we call in question our hopes of eternal life, because we do not love our brethren.

Use 2. To exhort us to put the will of our heavenly Father in execution. Christ showed us an example in his life and death, and urged it upon his disciples. As God loves us manifestly, graciously, and bountifully, so should we love our brethren (Prov. 27:5; 1 Cor. 16:14). Be bountiful in your love, and so you shall enjoy peace and comfort to your soul.

1 John 4:12

"No man has seen God at any time. If we love one another, God dwells in us; and his love is perfected in us."

In these words the apostle stirs us up to brotherly love, and that from the benefit of it, which is twofold: first, fellowship with God (vv. 13-16), and second, the perfection of his love in us (v. 12). The fellowship we have with God is invisible: "No man has seen God at any time."

How can we love God, since we never saw him?

We never saw our own souls, nor ever shall; yet we know that we have such, and without them we could not subsist.

Doct. Our fellowship with God and Christ is not outward and visible, but inward, and consists in love.

"No man has seen God at any time" (John 1:18); no man has had speech face to face with God the Father; the only begotten Son who lay in the bosom of the Father has revealed him. He dwells in that light that no eye can attain unto, whom no man has seen nor can see (1 Tim. 1:16). His light is so glorious that no man can behold it (Exod. 33:10).

What is it that Moses saw when he saw God's glory? He saw God in a glorious resemblance; he saw him in his attributes, which so affected Moses that his face shone (v. 35).

And as the outside was glorious, so was the inside of Moses greatly enlarged. Thus the disciples saw Christ (Matt. 17: 1-5), and were so affected that they knew not what they said.

Why can we not see God's face and live?

-1. Because of the frailty of flesh and blood. The presence of God would swallow us up; we are not capable of beholding Father, Son, or Holy Spirit; when we are in heaven, we shall be changed.

-2. Because of the sinful corruption of human nature. His glorious presence, which is a consuming fire, would consume us. When Isaiah saw God in a similitude, then he said, "Woe is me, for I am undone, because I am unclean" (Isa. 1:5); he was afraid for his life, though he saw God only in similitude.

Use 1. To teach us how to understand many places of scripture which speak of God manifesting himself to any. Do not understand God the Father, but Jesus Christ assuming a human body, or a similitude of God's glorious attributes.

Use 2. Be willing to put off mortal infirmities, for so we shall see God face to face (Phil. 1:23; 2 Cor. 12:1-5).

Use 3. To try whether we have communion with God or not. (a) You never heard God the Father nor the Son. God now delivers all his counsel in his word by his Son, and in the word we may have familiar, affectionate communion with God (Heb. 1:1). (b) We may find God revealing himself to our hearts and consciences (Ps. 73:24, 25). That is the chiefest joy; other fears and cares leave us (Heb. 11:27).

Use 4. It stirs us up to love our brethren. We have not seen God at any time, yet we have communion with him; and God loves his people; in communing with them we commune with God (Ps. 16:2, 3). The Papists ask for images; can there be any better resemblance of the Father than the image of the Son, and in loving and having communion with those who bear that image? They kill his living images to honor dead images. But the greatest love we can show to God is to love his image in his servants.

Doct. Where love dwells, God dwells, for God is love.

What is it for God to dwell or abide in us?

God is said to dwell not where he is, but where he loves to be, and so does a man. Now God loves to be where love is. Being a God of peace, he loves to dwell in a place of peace, or else he dwells not. Though we go to hell, he is indeed there; but yet he does not dwell there (Isa. 57:15). God loves to dwell where peace is, and keeps that peace which passes understanding.

There is a twofold peace that passes understanding: -1. The peace of the soul whose sins are pardoned (Phil. 4:7). -2. The peace of the soul whose sins are mortified. Now where God is, where God keeps the soul, there is peace that passes understanding, both pardoning sin and mortifying corruption.

When Jacob was with Laban, and Joseph in Potiphar's house, all was well; much more will all be well where God himself is.

-1. "God is love"; where sparks fly out of the chimney, there is fire; so where you see love in the lips, behavior, and heart of a man, there is the presence of the blessed God.

-2. Consider God's operations.

a. Where God dwells he pardons sin and purifies the conscience, or prospers the outward man; and there is a spirit of love in that man's heart. Where God freely pardons, there is much forgiven; and where there is much forgiven, there is much love (Luke 10:43, 47).

b. He purges filth. If our hearts are purified from uncleanness and sinful distempers, the heart runs clear in love, and there God dwells (1 Pet. 1:21). But if the heart is full of mud, it will run foul in hatred.

c. He works love. If we love our brethren, it must be from the love of God in us. If there is love, it is from God; if there is hatred, it is from the devil. Where Satan dwells, he will set all on fire; all hatred and wrath is from hell, and it will so kindle that it will consume one another.

Fire from hell does not warm; it scorches (Eph. 4:17). If we give way to sinful wrath, we give place to the devil.

Love cannot be from the devil; it is not from the world (James 4:4), and it is not from our flesh (James 4:5). Therefore it must spring from God, who makes peace, pardoning our sins and mortifying our corruptions.

But may there not be peace where Satan is? (Luke 11:21) His peace is a false peace, for the wrath of God lies upon him; he is as it were asleep when a house is on fire.

There may be much true-hearted love among men who have nothing but the light of nature; shall we say that God does not dwell there? I answer, the Spirit speaks not of civil love, but of such a love as God dwells in, pardoning and mortifying sin, which he never does in natural men. There may be found good nature in men, but the love which evidences pardon and healing of sin is not found in natural men; this love differs from carnal love.

-1. This love reaches not to the body only, but to the soul (Lev. 19:16, 17). If we do not love the soul of our brother, our love is not true love.

-2. Christian love reaches to strangers and enemies, as well as to neighbors and friends. Good-natured love may reach to strangers, but not to enemies.

-3. Christian love will be stronger to our brethren than worldly love. Though Christian love may be damped, yet it will overflow. A little thing will stop good-natured love that comes from a little fountain; but Christian love springs from heaven, and no man can make a dam to stop it.

Use 1. To try God's fellowship with us, whether God dwells in our hearts or not. Where God once dwells, he always dwells (John 10:27, 28). Who shall put him out? He is stronger than all.

Use 2. This should teach us all to walk in a frame of brotherly love, to abound in tenderness of spirit to one another's souls; not to provoke one another to wrath and seduce one another from ways of salvation, but to be helpful to one another in our spiritual state. God is where he is loved, and he loves to be where love is; wrath, malice, and hatred smoke him out of doors. A man performs no duty pleasing to God while wrath is in his heart.

Doct. The love of God is perfect in those who love in brotherly love.

"His love is perfect in us"; he does not mean that love which God has shed abroad in our hearts, for that love of God is perfect in every man; but he means the love by which we love God. If our love is not lacking to our brethren, our love is perfect toward God.

What is meant by perfect?

-1. Sometimes the word means sound and unfeigned. Amaziah did not do that which was good in the sight of the Lord with a perfect heart (2 Kings 18:3), that is, without rottenness and hypocrisy.

-2. It is sometimes the same as entire; a child is said to be perfect when he has all the parts of a man, though not in full size and proportion as yet. This perfection is opposed to that which is maimed. So that love is perfect which is entire to God and man (1 John 4:21; Micah 6:8). This is perfection of spirit (Rom. 13:10). Therefore the apostle says that he who loves has fulfilled the law; the chiefest of the three graces is love (1 Cor. 13:12). We do God more honor by faith and hope, but we edify the church more by love. God requires our love of him to be expressed by doing good to the sons of men (1 Cor. 13:1-3; Matt. 25:34); all the love that we would show God must be poured out upon our brethren.

-3. Sometimes it shows perfection of degrees, which he means here. Though no man is perfect in all degrees, yet he is more and more perfecting; he is on the growing hand (Eph. 4:15, 16). As no member can grow in the body unless it is knit to the body by joints and sinews, so in the body of Christ (Col. 3:14); love is the bond that knits us together to God and our brethren (1 Cor. 1:8; 1 Cor. 13:1-3).

-4. A thing is perfect when it is expert (Ezra 7:8). A loving Christian is a perfect Christian. You cannot set him to any good duty without seeing him skilled in it; love oils the wheels of his affections and sets him on that which is helpful to his brethren. When Christ set Peter to feed his lambs, he first asked him whether he loved him or not (John 21:15-17). If a man goes about a business with ill-will, he always bungles it.

-5. A thing is perfect when it is durable. Our love is more durable if it is nourished with love to our brethren; this will make it not only grow and continue, but also abound forever (Eph. 2:4-7). If love continues not, the church will not continue.

Use 1. Here is a sign of the truth of our love. We must have as great a care of the truth of our love to our brethren as of faith and repentance. If your love is closed up from your brethren, then your love is very unsound or very sick. So much failing in your love, so much failing in your spiritual life. Faith works by love (Gal. 5:6), and that avails much with God. As our love works, so works our faith.

Use 2. It exhorts us all to the love of one another, for by this means God dwells in us, and his love is perfected in our hearts. As you desire therefore that your love to God may be found entire, and thriving in your soul, give yourself to the unfeigned love of one another; edify one another in love.

Use 3. Here is comfort to all who know they are of a loving heart; their love to God is perfect. You may know your love to God is perfect, if your love is sound to your brethren.

1 John 4:13

"Hereby we know that we dwell in him, and he in us, because he has given us of his Spirit."

They who love their brethren have a twofold benefit: they have God's Spirit dwelling in them, and they know it.

Doct. To those who love one another, God has given of his Spirit.

What is meant by this, giving of the Spirit?

It implies that God has given us that Spirit of grace that accompanies salvation. Moses' spirit was not diminished though God communicated it to the seventy elders; God did cause it to be enlarged in them, for they were in the place of magistracy with him; so, whoever loves dwells in God, and communicates the same spirit of love to their brethren, so that they walk by the same rule and aim at the same end. "The fruit of the Spirit is love" (Gal. 5:22). They who walk in love have received of the Spirit; they have received of the Holy Spirit, for the Spirit lusts against envy (Judg. 9:22, 23).

Use 1. It teaches us that there is no love to be found towards our brethren except among spiritual men; for if we love one another, there is a Spirit of God in us. Where the Spirit is not, there is no love. Love is not a fruit that grows upon thorns, or on such a stock as nature brings forth, the old olive.

But do not many of God's servants bring forth sour fruit which will neither benefit themselves nor others? How then is it said that God's Spirit is in them? I answer, they have sour oil distilling from the old stock, for there are many branches in us that suck sourness from the old stock. Though there is a spirit of love in God's children, yet many times it does not run forth; but when you see Christian love expressing itself, it springs not from nature but from the Spirit of God.

Use 2. To comfort any soul who finds his spirit suppled with any compassion. If you can find your spirit mourning for the evil case of your brother, it is a sign that God's Spirit is in you.

Use 3. Let us labor to preserve our hearts in brotherly love, for love is a fruit of the Spirit of God. If we desire that God would forever keep us in a good state and that his Spirit should not be grieved by us, we must keep this Spirit of love, that is, the Comforter; when we grieve the Spirit of God, that is grief enough. If the Spirit that is in us be uncomfortable, how great is that discomfort.

Doct. Those to whom God has given of his Spirit of love, maintain mutual, entire, and constant fellowship with God; and they know it.

God dwells in us, which is more than to have God dwell with us. If God only dwelt with us, it would signify much happiness; but this is more, for God to dwell in us. We are not only near one another, and branches of one another, but one body with another; he abides in us as the head, we in him as the members.

What does he mean by knowing it?

This act of knowledge is more than an act of faith; men may believe more to be true than they know; "by faith we understand the world was made" (Heb. 11:3). Faith understands a thing to be done, and thus we are persuaded of its truth. But if it is not evident by sense and reason, we cannot know it; the meaning is, we have evident sense and evident reason for it.

How can we be certain of our fellowship with God if we have this Spirit?

-1. From the evidence of sense. When God has shed abroad into our hearts a spirit of love, we shall see and feel the savor of God shining in our hearts, the mercy of God pacifying our souls; so that now we do not only believe the promises belonging to us, but the feelings of God's love is a manifestation of God's grace. "If any man love me," says Christ, "and keep my word, my Father will love him; and we will come in to him and make our abode with him" (John 14: 21, 22). As we grow in love, so the comforts of God's Spirit grow in us. The ground of this argument is God's nature, for he is love; God is not said to be faith or hope, but love; and the more any man has received of love, the nearer he comes to God, and the readier he is to be doing good offices and to be helpful.

-2. From the cause of love. "God dwells in us, and we in him," because we have received a Spirit of love. We could not receive a spirit of love if we had not received a spirit of faith (Gal. 5:6). We could not love our brethren if we did not have faith to believe in Christ: now where faith is, there Christ dwells (Eph. 3:17).

Use 1. To console loving Christians; they have manifest experience and knowledge of God's love. The benefit of a loving spirit is this: it keeps fellowship with God, and that entire fellowship. A loving man does not only believe that he has fellowship with God, but he knows it; he has evident reason for it.

Use 2. To those who lack the goodness of the promises. They are not aware of God's favor; they have no sensible experience of it. They may be persuaded that God will show them mercy at the end, but yet they do not know it. If you will know the fellowship between God and your soul, then pray more that the Spirit of love of love may dwell in you; as your love grows, so shall you grow in sensible experience of God's love to you. God crowns faith with trust, confidence, and assurance; but he crowns love with experience. If you lack an experience of God's love, then think surely there is some weed of envy, wrath, and hatred; if you cleanse your heart from this, you shall have not only assurance but experience.

Use 3. This refutes the Papists, who say a man cannot know that God dwells in him. This is an evident sign that they have neither faith nor love. If they have faith, they would have assurance; if love, they would have experience.

1 John 4:14

"And we have seen and do testify that the Father sent the Son to be the Saviour of the world."

Doct. Those who love one another have seen and do bear witness that the Father has sent his Son to be a Saviour of the world (John 13:4, 5).

This word "sight" is more than believing, for the apostle puts a difference between them (2 Cor. 4:3). We believe that Christ sits at the right hand of God, but we have not seen it, When he says, "we have seen," he would have you know that they have had experimental knowledge. All sight is an act of sense and leads to a certain knowledge. When the woman of Samaria saw that Christ was the Messiah, and when he had convinced her of her sins, she left her waterpots and ran into the city, and said to the men, "Come see a man who has told me all that ever I did; is not this the Christ?" (John 4:20) And when the Samaritans were warmed with his words, they besought him to stay among them, and many of them believed in him (vv. 39, 40). So much sight of Christ, so much love.

How do such bear witness of the Father?

They have knowledge of God's love to themselves. The Lord has sent his Son into the world to save the world; and if the Lord has sent his Son to save us from his own wrath, shall we bear wrath and malice towards those that are his? A Christian will be ashamed that his heart should be wrathful and malicious; he will be reconciled to his brethren. When a Christian walks in love, he has seen the Saviour of the world, and has known him; that makes him love his brethren, because God sent his Son to save them. Thus he bears witness.

Contrariwise, if a man refuses to love his brethren, he denies that God sent his Son to save them. God has promised to withhold no good thing from those who fear him (Ps. 84:11); and if we withhold any good thing from our brethren, we bear witness that Christ did not come into the world to save them.

Use 1. This should teach us to lay down all wrath and hatred, and to be discouraged from harboring any hatred; for else you proclaim before God, angels, and men, that God did not send his Son to be a Saviour. Shall Christ come to save his people from the wrath of God and from the devil, and shall he not free his people from my wrath? Either make Christ a whole Saviour, or else make him no Saviour at all.

Use 2. To console those who love all men, but especially those who are of the household of faith. Such a man has seen that God has sent his Son to be a Saviour of the world. And such a man may be persuaded that God has forgiven him his sins.

1 John 4:15

"Whosoever shall confess that Jesus is the Son of God, God dwells in him and he in God."

The 14th and 15th verses contain an argument to prove that God's love dwells in us. The proposition is laid down in ver. 14, and the assumption in v. 15.

Doct. The confession that Jesus Christ is the Son of God is a true note or pledge of our mutual, entire, and constant fellowship with God.

They have entire fellowship, because they do not only dwell with one another, but in one another, as members in the body and branches in the root. So this is one mark of true Christianity: where this confession is, there is true fellowship with God (Matt. 16:16, 17; Luke 23:42, 43). He who overcomes believes that Jesus is the Son of God (1 John 5:5); none can truly say that Jesus is Lord but by the Holy Ghost (1 Cor. 12:3).

But who does not profess Christ? Did not the Pharisees admit that he was the heir, though they killed him? (Matt. 21:38) The devils professed that they knew Jesus (Mark 1:24); does God dwell in the devil, or the devil in God?

I answer, it was something in the days of St. John for a man to confess that Jesus was the Christ. Then men dared not, for it was a new doctrine and had universality and antiquity against it, and often persecution and the sword. But now it is persecution to deny it; it is now no thanks for men to confess that Jesus is the Son of God. The devils believed this, but they did not confess him truly; and good men will distrust this point, because the devil confesses this. The devil was convinced of the truth of this, but yet it was no argument of his dwelling with God, because he did it fraudulently. Likewise the Pharisees believed it and were convinced in their consciences, but yet they did not confess him openly (John 7:13).

What is it to confess that Jesus is the Son of God?

It is not only an act of judgment, neither is it barely an act of the lips. This is no such sign of our fellowship with God. God does not take that for a true confession, when a man does confess him with his lips but denies him in his works (Tit. 1:16; Isa. 29:13). But this confession is twofold: with the heart and with the life.

-1. With the heart. (a) First, there is a looking to Christ for salvation, and this is an evident pledge of God's dwelling with us and we with him (Isa. 45:22-25; Rom. 14:11; Phil. 2:10, 11). No man can look to God as a God of his salvation without being saved. This is the proper work of faith. (b) The second is a penitential confessing. When Peter had convinced the Jews that Jesus was the Lord, they were pricked in their hearts (Acts 2:36, 37). For a man to confess that he is the Lord and never to be troubled that he afflicts him, nor never to look for salvation by him, argues that there is no truth, no heartiness in that confession. But when the heart is humbled for all the wrong it has done to Christ, this is an evidence of hearty confession.

-2. In the confession of our life there are two parts. If I confess Christ to be the Son of God, I do not only take him to be my Saviour, but to be my Lord and Governor (2 Cor. 10:4, 5; Heb. 5:9). We obey Christ in thoughts, in speeches, affections, and conversations (1 Pet. 3:14, 20). When we suffer as Christians and are not ashamed of the cross of Christ, but answer as did the three children (Dan. 3:17, 18) — this is the grace of a Christian.

But what of Peter, when he swore that he never knew Christ? Yet he did believe, for it pricked him so at the heart that he wept bitterly, and afterward with constant courage he confessed Christ.

Use 1. This refutes all contrary religions. You see what becomes of all the nations of the world who do not believe Christ to be the Son of God — they have no fellowship with God, nor God with them. There is no other name given by which we shall be saved, but the name of the Lord Jesus Christ.

Use 2. Of trial. Would you know whether God dwells in you or you in him? Do you confess that Jesus Christ is the Son of God; do you look up to Christ for salvation? (Isa. 45: 22) Do you find your heart pricked when you sin against Christ? If you are an obedient child of God, you shall enjoy entire fellowship with God.

Use 3. To comfort those who have prevailed with their hearts and lives to make such a confession. So shall you be sure to have God dwelling in you, and you in him; and so shall you not go from home, wherever you go.

1 John 4:16

"And we have known and believed the love that God has to us. God is love; and he who dwells in love dwells in God, and God in him."

These words contain a third argument to prove a proposition laid down in v. 12. "They who love one another, God dwells in them." The argument is taken from the knowledge and faith that such have of the love that God has toward them. They who have known and believed the love of God dwell in God and God in them; but they who love one another know and believe the love of God. Therefore:

Doct. Loving Christians do discern the love that God has to them, by knowledge as well as by faith.

"We have known and believed the love that God has to us." This love is wrapped up in the bosom of the Father, and no man can discern either love or hatred by any outward thing. But yet this love is manifested by faith and knowledge. Faith and knowledge are both acts of the judgment, for both are the knowledge of a certain truth. It is not divine faith unless it is of a truth.

How then do faith and knowledge differ?

Faith is the judgment of a certain truth, but certain by

divine testimony, whether of the Spirit or of the word. The apprehension we have of a truth by the authority of a divine testimony is faith; but knowledge is the judgment of a truth certain, not only by a divine testimony, but either by sense or by evident reason. Most of the rules of practical art are known by experience or by evident reason; mathematical rules are gathered by certain principles of evident reason. Therefore those who love one another have a certain persuasion of God's love to them by some divine testimony, and that is faith; or else we know it, and that implies that it is evident by sense or by evident reason, or by both, as indeed by them all. "We know the love of God to us." Loving Christians discern by faith the love of God to them, by the testimony both of the word and of the Spirit of God.

A. For faith. There is a twofold testimony of God by which we believe the love of God to us: the word and the Spirit.

-1. The word is twofold: a word of doctrine and a word of promise.

The word of doctrine is threefold.

    a. There is a word of doctrine which teaches us the fruit of faith (Gal. 5:16). If therefore we find love in our hearts, then surely there is faith in us, to believe the love of God to us.

    b. There is a word of doctrine which teaches us the efficacy of love; it fulfills the law (Rom. 13:10). Therefore if God gives a man a testimony that he loves his brethren, then he has an inclination to keep the whole law, and so consequently God's love is assured to him.

    c. There is a word of promise that assures us of our comfortable state (1 John 2:10; Matt. 10:41, 42). If therefore we find love in our hearts, God will give us of his light (so 1 John 4:12).

-2. They are further assured of God's love to them by a testimony of the Spirit. Now the Spirit witnesses by its fruits, and one of these fruits is love (Gal. 5:12).

B. For knowledge. We know that he has loved us for divers reasons.

—1. By sense. If a man loves God and is loving to the children of God, God delights to reveal himself sensibly to such a soul (John 14:21-23). The more tender our affections toward our brethren, the more we shall grow up in a sense of God's favor to us. As we mete to God, God will mete to us: if we close up our hearts to our brethren, God will not manifest himself to us; but if we abound in love to God's saints, God will abundantly reveal his love to us (Ps. 16:3-6).

—2. By experience. Frequent observation of things by sense breeds experience. Now when a man is of a loving heart, God not only gives him a taste of his love, but he often renews the sensible feeling of his favor, and that breeds experience. From the constant expression of God's love to him, Paul finds that Christ lives in him daily (Gal. 2:20); and by daily actions he finds that Christ loves him and gave himself for him. Now none of the apostles expressed so much love as Paul (2 Cor. 11:26-30); and God more manifested himself to Paul than to the rest of the apostles.

—3. A loving Christian knows the love of God to him by evident reason, by artificial arguments which convince his judgment of God's love to him.

a. From the change and frame that is wrought in his heart when he is once brought to love his brethren. Paul exhorts them to be loving and gentle to all, for "we ourselves were sometimes foolish, disobedient, and hating one another" (Tit. 3:2, 3). The frame of our natural temper lusts after envy and emulation (James 4:5), as the sparks fly upward. Therefore if we find this temper subdued so that we can think well and speak well of our brethren, and do good offices to them, this is an evident argument that God has shown love to us; or else we could never have so freely loved others.

b. From the knowledge which others have of our abiding in Christ, because they see us expressing love to his saints. "By this shall all men know that you are my disciples, if you love one another" (John 13:35). If you see men forward and ready in helpfulness to their Christian brethren, all men will say, Surely he is one of that company. If therefore others may know us to be disciples of Christ by this, may we not much more know it ourselves?

Use 1. To refute some Popish tenets.

a. Bellarmine says that faith is rather defined by ignorance than by knowledge; for, says he, faith is the evidence of things not seen. But we see that faith and knowledge may well stand together; yea, we first know a thing before we can believe. When Stephen saw Christ sitting at the right hand of God, did he then not believe it? For that place (Heb. 11:1) is not a definition of faith, but a description of faith by one of its effects (v. 12) — it makes things evident which we never saw. By faith we believe the world was created, though we never saw it. Thomas' feeling and seeing Christ did not hinder his faith but helped it (John 20:27, 28).

b. Bellarmine and most of their writers say that a certain knowledge is not actually faith but presumption. Certainly their error is presumptuous; for does not the apostle plainly say, "We believe and know the love that God has to us"?

Use 2. This may be a strong incentive to us all, to be abundant in love and tender-heartedness to one another. Little does a man know how he disturbs the peace of his own conscience when he disturbs another man's peace. A man may wrong his brother, and go out as at other times and think all is right as before, but he knows not that the Lord has departed from him. Why is the heart so straight and heavy? Because our bowels have been shut up towards our brethren, and therefore God shuts up his favor and helpfulness from us.

"God is love, and he who dwells in love dwells in God, and God in him." These words contain a fourth argument to prove that those who love one another have mutual and entire fellowship with God, as he had said in v. 12. The words contain two parts:

-1. The nature of God: "God is love."

-2. The condition of those who dwell in love: they have mutual, entire, and constant fellowship with God. Not only do they dwell with one another; they also dwell in one another.

Doct. God is so loving that he is love itself.

God is love in a threefold sense:

-1. He is the only adequate object of love. He is altogether lovely; every part of him is wholly delectable, altogether lovely. In scripture the object of love is sometimes called love. The church is called Christ's love (Cant. 4:6), that is, the object of his love; so God is the only object of our love (Ps. 73:25). In the creature there is something lovely and something not; but not so in God. There is nothing in God but what is wholly lovely.

-2. God is called love because he is the fountain of love. As Christ is called wisdom (1 Cor. 1:30) because he gives us wisdom, so God is called love because any love in us comes from his love first to us (1 John 4:19). And so if any show love to us, it is from God's love toward us.

-3. God is the subject of love; he is a God full of love and mercy. We cannot, except figuratively and metaphorically, call a wise man wisdom, or a wall whiteness, but merely wise or white. But here God transcends all creatures. We may properly speak of God in the abstract: God is love. We may say as truly that God is love as our Saviour said that he is a spirit: that is, it is not a quality in him, which he may or may not possess, but love is essential and natural to him. God's love is in himself.

This implies the simplicity of God's nature. God is not compounded, but free without mixture; he is without all causes besides himself; he is of himself, from himself, by himself, and for himself. And as he is not compounded of causes, so he is not compounded of subject and adjunct. Man is one thing, and his learning and wisdom another thing; but God and his wisdom are not two distinct things; God and his love are the same. There is no reason for this truth, because he is above reason. There are reasons for his works, but not for his nature.

Use 1. This may exhort us all to be willing to forego any blessing in the world for the love of God. Many are discouraged from Christian ways because they shall lose the love of friends by it. But it may be otherwise, for if a man's ways please the Lord, he makes his enemies to be at peace with him, and then much more his friends. But suppose at one clap you should lose the love of all your friends; yet you shall not lose by it — you shall gain more by God's love than you shall lose by the loss of all other love.

Use 2. To teach all godly men to strive to be as God is. We cannot be so loving as to be love itself; but we should strive to be like-minded with God, to be altogether abounding in love. "Let all things be done in love" (1 Cor. 16:14). God is of that nature, and would have his children so (Matt. 5:48). There is no righteous work that we can perform righteously while there is lack of love in our hearts (James 3:20). The word is full of power, but it never had power to save any who did not receive it in love.

Use 3. If God is love, then the Devil is hatred; and the more we live in hatred, the more we walk in the Devil's ways and make ourselves firebrands of hell.

Doct. 2. Constancy in love is an evident mark of our mutual, entire and constant fellowship with the God of love.

-1. Because of the nature of God. From this the apostle infers it: "God is love," not only the object but the fountain of love. All the well-placed love in the creature is from God. Carnal love is neither of God nor from God; but where there is true spiritual love, which is indeed called charity, God communicates himself to such a soul as the root to the branches. God is present wherever true love is found, even in the presence by which the Holy Spirit lives in the soul, and dwells there forever (Gal. 5:22; John 15:34, 35).

-2. Because of the fitness and aptness that is in such a soul to grow up by every ordinance (Eph. 3:17, 18; Col. 3:14). Love is of an edifying nature (1 Cor. 8:1). Let love admonish, reprove, or exhort — it edifies much, especially if it is received in love, where there is love on both sides, both in speaker and hearer. Love puts life into every ordinance.

-3. Because God delights to communicate his love more abundantly where he finds men walking in love. No creature partakes of the boundless love of God but those who are grounded in love (Eph. 3:17-19). Let us abound only in faith toward Christ and love toward our brethren, and we shall have a large measure of God's love dispensed to us. According to the capacity of the receiver, so is the thing received. And no grace is of so enlarging a nature as love; so if we abound in love, we become of a comprehending nature, able to comprehend the height, and breadth, and length, and depth of God's love toward us.

Use 1. This exhorts us all not only to the love, but to the constant love of our brethren. You shall have constant and abiding fellowship. We should not only grow in love, but grow rooted in love; let no grace be so eminent in you as love. If God had said he dwells in wisdom, how it would have provoked men to study for wisdom; but God dwells not in knowledge nor in honor and riches, but in such a house as the poor and ignorant may build, a house of love. Therefore above all endowments and gifts of soul or body, have a special care to grow rooted in love.

God dwells in love. There are four places where God is said to dwell: in the highest holy place, in an humble heart (Isa. 57:15), in our hearts by faith (Eph. 3:17), and in a loving heart. If you would know where God dwells, it is in one of three graces, humility, faith, or love. Set up a loving heart, and God will dwell there forever; whereas, if you sleep in wrath, the devil rests with you.

Use 2. To console every loving heart. If God has given you a heart to love your brethren with true spiritual love, God dwells in your heart; and more than that, you dwell in God's heart. If you had testimony of no other grace, yet if you can find a hearty love in you, you have a tabernacle for the Most High to dwell in.

1 John 4:17

"Herein is our love made perfect, that we may have boldness in the day of judgment: because as he is, so are we in this world."

These words depend on v. 12. He had promised a double benefit to those who love one another: God dwells in them, which he proved by four arguments, and God's love is perfected in them, which he enlarges in these following verses.

He gives two arguments. They who are in the world as God himself is, may have boldness in the day of judgment; but they who love one another are in the world as God himself is; therefore they may have boldness in the day of judgment. Further, they who may have boldness in the day of judgment, in them is love perfected. But loving Christians may have boldness in the day of judgment. Therefore the love of God is perfected in them.

Doct. Those in whom is found perfect love to God and their brethren, they may have boldness in the day of judgment.

This Paul confirms (2 Tim. 4:7, 8). He is confident that God would give him a crown of righteousness, for he has fought a good fight and finished his course. He had abounded in love to God and man, which is our righteousness, to give God and man his due. And this crown of glory God will give not only to him, but to all who love his appearing. "Mercy rejoices against judgment" (James 2:13); this is a fruit of love, for mercy is nothing else but love having compassion on our brother's distress. We see what encouragement Christ gives his sheep because they showed him kindness in being kind to his brethren (Matt. 25:24-41).

Whence comes their boldness?

-1. From the esteem the Lord Jesus bears to them. They have found Christ dispensing himself to them not as a judge, but as a Saviour; for else they could never have loved him nor others. Now they who are to meet with a Saviour have cause of boldness in that day; or if he comes as a judge, it is as a judge to plead their cause, right their wrong, and take vengeance on their enemies.

-2. A loving Christian has a further ground of confidence in his heart, that the day of Christ's appearing shall be as the day of his marriage (Cant. 3:10). Now they who love one another are espoused to Christ here by their effectual call; but the day of judgment is as the marriage day. Those who are in marriage love, how they desire and long for the marriage day! And so do all true Christians, who have kept their hearts chaste to Christ; how they pray for the hastening of that day. That day is called the day of refreshing (Acts 3:19), and it is the work of ministers to make a match between you and Christ, so that at that day they may say, as they present you to Christ: Lo, here am I, and the children whom thou hast given me (Isa. 8:18; 2 Cor. 11:1-3). It is therefore the day of the comfort of God's ministers and servants, and therefore a day of boldness.

-3. It is a day of much comfort and boldness because then they shall be freed from all discouragements, from all persecutions and malignities, from slanderous tongues and hard speeches, from all fears and sorrows; more, from all temptations and corruptions. This must needs give boldness to them; it is a day of universal freedom from all sin (1 John 3:2). We shall then be like him in grace and glory and in freedom from all evils.

Use 1. To reprove a gross error in Popery, which is, that no man can be certain of his salvation in the day of judgment; but this is the doctrine that John here delivers. Is it not a word of boldness and confidence that Paul has? (2 Tim. 4:7, 8) True, they say, Paul was an extraordinary Christian, yea, a saint; but he adds, "not for me only, but for all them that love his appearing." If Christians were not confident in that day, how is it that they so earnestly desire it? "The Spirit and the Bride say, 'Come,' and let him who reads say, 'Come,' and everyone who is athirst says, "Come.' This shows plainly that they do not look at it as a day of terror and uncertainty, but as a day of boldness and comfort.

But have not many of God's servants been afraid at the face of death? I grant that a man's nature may shrink at death, though he knows that he has been a faithful servant and is not afraid of judgment; for death is an enemy to nature, though a friend to grace. Paul himself desires to be clothed with glory, but yet is loath to be unclothed of his body (2 Cor. 5:12). So Christ told Peter that they would lead him where he would not, meaning to martyrdom (John 21:18); which implies that if he could have shunned martyrdom with a good conscience, he would have avoided it, because it is an enemy to nature. This natural fear is often aggravated by temptations and doubts, as Satan commonly at such times takes away all matter of comfort, so that the spirit will startle at death. Hezekiah and Job were both unwilling to die. But this hinders not; a man of perfect love may have boldness in that day, though in the day of desertion, when it is stricken with temptations and corruptions, it may be afraid. Take David—though he is afraid when God hides his face, and cries out, "What profit is there in my blood" (Ps. 30: 7-10), yet in his right temper he is constantly persuaded of Christ's love to him (Ps. 3:6). It is not only eminent Christians, but everyone whose love is perfect, who may have boldness in that day.

Use 2. This shows the dangerous state of those whose love to God and their brethren is not perfect. If they whose love is perfect may have boldness, then those who never sought God or his favor, never loved the fellowship of his servants, in that day where shall they appear?

But are not men who never troubled themselves with religion, scornful men, as little afraid of death and hell as the best Christians? (Isa. 22:14, 15) That which the Papists condemn as heretical presumption in God's servants, may be called profane presumption in such men. Indeed it proceeds from their profound ignorance and deadness of their hearts, if they have never once felt the wrath of God nor the terrors of hell. But if they once come to see that day, then they shall call to the mountains and hills to cover them from the wrath of the Lamb.

Use 3. If you would live comfortably and die peaceably, take this ready way. Be perfect and sincere in your love to God and his saints, and that will breed in you marvelous boldness against that day, when the Lord Jesus shall come to be admired in you and glorified in all his saints. So much perfect love, so much boldness.

Use 4. To console all loving Christians, who walk sincerely towards God and their brethren. You go up and down with a spirit of boldness. Whereas others call death the most terrible of all terrible things, you shall look at it with confidence; when others are cast down, you shall be lifted up.

"As he is, so are we in this world." In these words he proves that those in whom such love is perfect, may have boldness in the day of judgment.

Doct. Those who love one another are in this world as God himself is.

Paul advances the same doctrine, "Be kind one to another, tender hearted, forgiving one another, even as God for Christ's sake has forgiven you. Be followers of God, as dear children" (Eph. 4:32, 5:1). They who walk in love walk as Christ himself did. He was kind and helpful to the sons of men, forgiving injuries and giving liberally to all men. So is God in this world; all his paths are mercy and truth. In his love he promises, in his love he performs; so that they who walk in love walk like God in this world. When Adam stood in innocence, God loved him abundantlly; and when he fell, he would not let him lie, but in love sent his Son to redeem him. So let men walk lovingly towards all, and if their love to you decay, yet stretch out your hand of compassion to help them.

We may know that we are as he is, if we love one another, because a universal frame of righteousness is expressed in the spirit of love. All the attributes of God's mercy, wisdom, goodness — all proceed from love. In his love he made us, in love he chastens us. Love is the fulfilling of the law (Rom. 13:10); and if it fulfills the law, then it fulfills all the righteousness we owe to God and man.

Use. This is a notable encouragement to Christians to grow up in the grace of love. He who is perfect in love, is in this world as God himself is. Many think the duties of religion are hard and intricate, but to a loving heart all is easy. Let there be but love in the heart, and every duty both to God and man will come off easily. If you observe, you shall find men in the world busying themselves in some perfection — to be perfect in wisdom, learning, or honors — and these things they labor hard after. Why, go home and labor as hard after love, strive to be eminent in love, and you shall get more by that than they can get by all their endeavors.

Doct. They who are in this world as God himself is, they may have boldness in the day of judgment (Matt. 18:33-35).

Suppose a man should live in this world with a confidence that all his sins are forgiven him, and in the meantime he grows hard-hearted and bitter against his brethren. If before he had good assurance of the pardon of his sins, yet he shall find such horror and anguish that he believes all his sins still lie open and liable. If we lack love, we cannot have boldness in the day of judgment. Christ had so furnished his disciples with love that thereby they abounded in much service to him and his; and being men of love, they should not be afraid of Christ's coming, but then he bids them lift up their heads with comfort (Luke 21:28).

What is this boldness?

-1. Boldness is that which mortifies fear and shame. If a man is fearful, what boldness is there? But this boldness makes a man look at death and judgment without fear.

-2. Boldness removes shame (1 John 2:28). When he shall appear, we may have boldness and not be ashamed; therefore a man who is like God in this world is neither afraid nor ashamed in the day of judgment.

Why do we enjoy this boldness, if we are as God is?

-1. Because that which might be matter of fear is removed. That which makes a man afraid at that day is because he is not like God. God is of pure eyes, and they are altogether unclean; and indeed Christ will command such workers of iniquity to depart from him. But a loving Christian is not a worker of iniquity, but a worker of love, a worker of mercy and righteousness, and so God accepts him.

-2. This spirit of love clothes us with those duties and works which God most recompenses at that day. God will then crown men with glory, not because they are wiser and richer than others, but because they saw him hungry and gave him food, naked and clothed him. "Mercy rejoices against judment"; and there God will be abundantly merciful, to recompense every work and office of mercy.

-3. There is no cause of shame, for where there is a resemblance of God there is cause of joy. God acknowledges his own image, and will perfect it at that day, for love ceases not. A man may have learning and riches and honors, and be ashamed at that day; but if we are clothed with love, we shall never be ashamed.

Use. Labor therefore above all graces, to clothe yourself with love. A loving Christian is a courageous Christian; when other men's hearts shall quail and tremble for fear, and shake like the leaves of a tree, then a loving Christian may lift up his head with joy (Isa. 7:2), because then he knows his love shall be consummated. And when others are ashamed of their riches, learning, and honors, he is not ashamed of his love — a loving Christian is safe and bold both in life and death. He who neglects this duty of love, God and his conscience will take him by the throat and exact the due debt, because he walked with a private spirit in the public world; whereas if we do but walk in a spirit of love and helpfulness to our brethren, neglecting our private respects, the devil and our consciences will find nothing to accuse us of, but we shall meet death and judgment in the face, without fear or shame.

1 John 4:18

"There is no fear in love; but perfect love casts out fear, because fear has torment. He who fears is not made perfect in love."

In v. 17 he proved that those who love one another may have boldness in the day of judgment. This he proved:
 -1. From the likeness to God (v. 17).
 -2. From the contrast between fear and love, "there is no fear in love," which he proves by an effect of love, "perfect love casts out fear," and therefore the two cannot stand together. This he proves by a double argument from fear. a) Fear has torments; therefore love, a peaceable grace, casts out fear. (b) He who fears is not perfect in love; therefore he who is perfect in love fears not.

Now in this 18th verse, note:
 -1. The state of a soul troubled with fear, and that is a state of torment.
 -2. The unsound and uncomfortable condition of such a soul: he is not perfect in love.
 -3. The remedy for this state: perfect love casts out fear.
 -4. The exemption of perfect love from all fear.

Doct. 1. A fearful conscience lies in torment.

"Fear has torment"; he speaks of the fear of death, but especially of judgment; where that fear is, there is torment. The word translated torment, kulasin, is elsewhere so translated (Matt. 25:46). The torment here spoken of is such a torment as hell is, not in measure but in kind. Let us see what the scripture speaks of this torment in several descriptions and metaphors.

 -1. This torment is sometimes called pricking of conscience (Acts 2:37). Though but a little while before they had scoffed at the apostle (2:13), yet now they were struck with such torments that they knew not what to do.

 -2. It is called a wounding of the spirit (Prov. 18:14); a

wound is a larger gash than a prick, and so implies more anguish, fear, and shame.

-3. It is compared to the sting of a scorpion (Rev. 9:5). The Jesuits so sting men with torments of hell and horror of conscience, and God gave them not power to heal themselves again; hence they thought everything little enough to satisfy their torments.

-4. The wrath of God in the soul is compared to venomed arrows (Job 6:4).

-5. It is called the rending of the heart (Joel 2:13), when the heart and thoughts are so torn and distracted that one thing will not hang by another.

-6. David calls this melting of spirit (Ps. 119:28), as if the heart were like wax and God's wrath like burning fire; therefore a man in this case is in a bitter state (Job 13:26; Isa. 38:15). For this the soul is troubled (Ps. 77) and sorely vexed (Ps. 6:3).

Why does a soul in fear lie in torment?

-1. Consider the effects of this fear. (a) This fear sometimes brings men into trembling of body. (b) If it continues, it leads often to inward consumptions of body (Hab. 3:16; Ps. 30:4, 5). (c) Sometimes it causes terrible dreams which amaze and affright (Job 13:14). (d) It causes weariness of life, so that a soul long exercised with this kind of fear cries out in bitterness and heartily wishes for death (Job 7:15).

There are worse effects than those proceeding from this fear, when Satan sets on against us. (a) Sometimes Satan so follows us with fears and horrors, so that though a man be of a large measure of patience, yet he is able to fear no longer, but breaks out in impatience, "Cursed be the day that ever I was born" (Job 3:1-3); and this is a sinful effect. (b) It breeds in some a fleeing from the presence of God. They dare not read nor pray; they are afraid the earth should swallow them up, and God suddenly consume them; so Cain, pursued with horror of conscience, fled from the presence of God, from Adam's family, from the church. (c) This fear sometimes brings destruction, when the soul is so wearied with sense of horrors, with cares and watchings, that the brain grows frenzied, so that you can do them no good until God puts in his help (Ps. 88:15, 16). (d) Sometimes upon this fear follows despair; the soul is persuaded that it shall never see the light of God's countenance again, but that it shall be utterly cast off (Ps. 3:6, 7; Ps. 77). (e) From this sometimes follows self-murder, as in Judas (Matt. 27).

-2. Consider the properties of this fear. (a) It is incomprehensible; when Job would express it, he could not tell how to set it forth, but, "O that my afflictions were laid in the balance!" "Is there any sorrow like my sorrow?" (Job 6:2, 3; Lam. 1:12, 13) (b) It is insupportable; "A wounded spirit who can bear?" (Prov. 18:14) The stoutest heart is not able to stand under it. (c) It is immoveable; nothing in the world is able to remove it; no balm can cure the conscience but the blood of Christ.

-3. Consider the causes of this fear. (a) The sense of God's wrath here and the expectation of greater wrath hereafter (Ps. 90:11). (b) A terrible expectation of violent fire, to consume God's adversaries (Heb. 10:27).

-4. Consider the subject of all this fear and torment, and that is the conscience and heart of man, the judgment and will. Before the will was most tough and obstinate of all the faculties, but these torments make it soft and tender; therefore it is said that Josiah's heart melted at the hearing of the law (2 Chron. 34:17). Raw flesh is especially sensitive to fire; so the tender raw conscience is anguished with this fire of God's wrath.

Use 1. To stir up all who have any friends exercised by this fear, to pity and have compassion on them. To him that is afflicted, pity should be shown by his friends; to do else is to forsake the fear of the Almighty (Job 6:14). Some seamen on their first voyage can pity those who are seasick and tossed, but afterward they grow more unfeeling; so when Christians first launch out themselves into this troubled condition, they could have pitied others in the same case; but through custom men forsake the fear of the Almighty.

Job never cried out for help in the loss of his children or estate, but when God's hand touched his soul he called upon all who feared God to pity him. Indeed God is very careful with those who show compassion upon them; if he ever sends them comfort, he will likewise restore comfort to their mourners (Isa. 57:7, 8).

Use 2. From those who are thus afflicted, learn to be sensible of your state, and do not think this state desperate, for this torment may be healed; and therefore let us labor in this case to seek for healing. Is a man in torment, and will he not seek for help?

How may you help yourself? Confess your sins to God, consider that it is an evil thing that you have forsaken him and cast aside his yoke; use the ordinances, the word, the sacraments, Christian communion; bow your heart to wait on God patiently; and prize and nurture the least expression of his mercy to your soul.

Use 3. To those who have been in such a case and have gotten out. Take heed of relapses; for if we start back again, God will make us know what an evil and bitter thing it is to fly back from God. When David made bold with his sins, what woeful horror he fell into. Therefore take heed, lest by sinning you fall into this torment again.

We come now to the second part of the text, which is the unsound condition of a soul which lies in fear.

Doct. 2. A fearful conscience is void of true-hearted love.

"He who fears," viz. death and judgment, "is not made perfect in love." The fearful are reckoned among the most notorious sinners and firebrands of hell (Rev. 21:8). Therefore surely they are not sound-hearted.

There is a double fearfulness.

-1. Of the day of judgment, death, and wrath.

-2. When a man is afraid of displeasing men; when he dares not do a thing, be it ever so right and good, for fear of displeasing men (Prov. 29:25).

But a child of God fears not, though he walk through the midst of the shadow of death (Ps. 23:4).

Why do the godly not fear, and why is fear a sign of lack of love?

-1. The ground or root of fear is unbelief, for faith breeds confidence and boldness. "We have access with confidence through faith in him" (Eph. 3:12); and therefore that which breeds fear is unbelief. St. John puts the fearful and unbelievers together (Rev. 21:8). A heart that believes not God's faithfulness or goodness is a fearful heart.

-2. The effect of this fear is to drive us from God. Men possessed with this fear at the last day shall cry to the mountains to cover them from the presence of the lamb (Rev. 6:17). So when Adam had sinned, he hid himself from the presence of the Lord.

-3. The object of this fear is the expectation of some terrible evil. Therefore if the creatures look at God as terrible and to be feared, it is a sign they are not sound in love; for they who love Christ also love his appearing.

-4. Consider the adjunct of fear. Fear brings torment and stinging with it; but love brings peace, joy, and comfort. Therefore this properly argues that where fear is, the heart is not sound.

But then how does it come to pass that some who are of loving spirits are full of fear and terrors? So Job (Job 6:4); so Heman; so Paul (2 Cor. 7:5). If such glorious saints were so fearful, were they also unsound? I answer, there may be such fears even in God's saints who have experienced his love to them; but this fear differs much from the fears of unsound hearts.

-1. The fears of the godly spring not so much from the expectation of death and hell, as from some inward trouble for lack of God's favor (Ps. 80:3, 4). It is for want of the light of his countenance that they so grieve. Now here is a great difference, for there is always a spirit of love mixed with these fears, for it is the love of God that they most desire; on the contrary, a wicked man is not so much affected by the lack of God's favor as by the sense of wrath and judgment, and expectation of future evil.

-2. In the midst of a godly man's fears there is an intermixture of many secret supports and comforts (Ps. 94:18, 19). But a man of an unsound heart has no intermixture of comfort; he drinks of the cup of God's wrath, not mixed with joy and comfort, but full of terror, grief, and discomfort (Ps. 75:8).

-3. There is a difference in the effects. A wicked man's fears drive him from God. Adam and Cain ran from the presence of God; Saul sometimes seeks David's harp, sometimes a witch; Judas runs to a halter; but the fear of the godly drives them to use the right means to run to God, to keep closer to him. Jehoshaphat feared exceedingly, and therefore set himself to seek the Lord (2 Chron. 20:3). Though God seems very angry, yet they will throw themselves into his arms; they run to the horns of the altar, and if they must perish, there will they die. Indeed it argues more love to cleave to him when we see less cause.

But are not many wicked men unafraid of hell? True, there are such boisterous spirits that neither fear God nor man; they are not afraid of hell, and yet they are far from any soundness. Their fearlessness differs from the boldness of Christians. (a) It is without root, whereas the true boldness of Christians proceeds from faith in Christ (Eph. 3:12; Rom. 5:1-3). (b) It is without fruit, whereas the boldness of the saints makes them reverence God and fear sin the more. They are not more fruitful by it, but more licentious.

Use 1. This teaches all who would possess a spirit of boldness and confidence, to maintain sound love to their brethren. Indeed every fear that befalls God's servants proceeds either from bemudding themselves with the world, or from lack of love to their brethren. Would you be cheerful at death? Grow up in love to God; acquaint yourself with him, and be at peace; and join the love of your brethren, or else his coming will be uncomfortable. If you fall out with your brethren, no wonder your heart is afraid of God's coming and you would gladly have God defer it a while. Therefore labor to cleanse out all enmity and lack of love.

Use 2. To console all who find their hearts uncomfortable, though they are sound in love to God and their brethren. Consider whether there is an evil root of bitterness in you; and if you find your heart free from envy, wrath, and hatred, then consider what good offices you do. Labor not only to be sincere, but to grow up to fruitfulness; and if you find that your fear is for want of God's favor, rather than for hell and wrath, this is not the fear of hypocrites, but proceeds only from lack of experience.

Use 3. It is a ground of much comfort to those who are fearless of death and judgment, and those who are sound in love. If you find your fearfulness arising from longing after God, and if it make you fruitful, you have a just ground of fearless boldness; you are sound-hearted in love.

Use 4. Let us labor for that grace that will help us against all fears and doubts.

We have formerly heard of the torment of fear and the hypocrisy of fear. Now the third thing is the remedy of this fear. "But perfect love casts out fear."

Doct. 3. True hearted love to God casts out all fear of evil from the hand of God.

Though at first the conscience of a young Christian may be fearful of the wrath of God and judgment, yet as love grows, fear is being cast out. "Perfect love casts out fear"; he does not mean perfect without imperfection, for we know in part, and prophesy in part, and hence love in part; but he speaks of love perfect without hypocrisy and dissimulation. True-hearted love fears no evil from the hand of God.

This love casts out fear, cleansing the heart as a man cleanses a pit. He cannot do it all at once, but he is constantly casting it out until it is all cleansed. Fear is a deep pit, compared to sinking into deep mire. Now love comes to cast out this fear, but it is not done the first hour; little by little we get rid of all fear. Truly it does not cast out the fear of God, for the more we love him the more we fear him; but it casts out all tormenting fear. It casts out the fear of the day of judgment, and so consequently of God's wrath. The apostle prays that the Lord would direct their hearts into the love of God (2 Thess. 3:5); and what is the fruit of that? "And into the patient waiting for Christ." When a man's heart is once directed to the love of God, he is prepared to wait for the coming of the Lord Jesus (Jude 21). The same may be said of keeping our hearts in love to our brethren.

How may we know that perfect love casts out fear?

-1. Because of the proper nature of love; it thinks no evil (1 Cor. 13:5). This is the proper work of love in the heart; it bows the heart to take all that God does in good part. Though we find much disquiet and anguish and torment, yet love makes the soul take all in good part, so that it thinks no evil of God.

    a. The soul thinks thus: though I feel much pain and anguish, yet I cannot but think it well that God should apply such corrosives to my festered wounds.

    b. The soul takes it well that God shows him all the danger of sickness or death; that he shows him part of hell, and awakens him before he comes there. It is a great mercy that I have yet time of mercy, that hell has not swallowed me up but that he has given me so fair a warning to prevent it.

    c. A loving soul takes God's dealing in this kind in very good part, as being a notable preservative against many sinful distempers he would have fallen into. It considers that by these anguishes he drives it from the world, and from putting God off until later times; for fear and anguish make us seek God speedily.

    d. The soul takes it in good part that by these fears of conscience he is brought better to attend on sermons, to be conversant in the scripture, to like good company. Though all these do not cast out tormenting fear, yet they make all to be taken in good part, and by them the soul grows more meek and lowly, and thus to find rest to his soul; and then he is not in torment.

-2. Because of the effects of true-hearted love. It stirs a man up to seek him whom his soul loves, and the very seeking prepares the heart to rest; for such a soul, when he has found Christ, will not let him go until he is possessed of his love, whereas the soul that lacks love runs away from God.

-3. Love of God makes us afraid of all sin and careful to obey in all things. All who love God hate sin; love makes us hate sin and desire to keep God's commandments (John 14:23); now both these lead to tranquility (Ps. 79:10, 11).

There is a double ground of comfort to those who begin to hate evil out of love to God. First, the Lord preserves them; second, light is sown for them, which in time will sprout up to manifest comfort. Love likewise provokes us to be fruitful in goodness; and if we are so, Christ promises that he will reveal his savor and similarity to us (John 14:23).

Use 1. To direct those who deal with troubled spirits. Let them apply comfort where they may. A man comes and complains bitterly of the burden of his soul; as yet there is no sure ground of applying comfort, but when you can discern any fruit of love in his expressions, if you find him taking all in good part, and blessing God that by this means he is pleased to break them off from their own sinful ways and draw them closer to himself, then you may safely apply comfort; but otherwise, if you see men murmuring against God's hand, why truly they have the fear that has torments. This is true love, to love God when he is angry, and to take it well that God should deal frowardly with a froward heart.

Use 2. For those who find their hearts overwhelmed with fears and doubts, and yet are unwilling to come to this frame of spirit. Let it convince them that they have deserved more than this, so that they may take it all well; and then if they are possessed of God's love in this, and apprehend it, there is way for comfort and peace.

Use 3. For you who find disturbance and anguish of soul; it may be a ground of consolation and direction to you. You find your heart pricked with the torment of sin; consider how you find your heart inclined to God. Does your soul say to God in your deepest anguishes, "Thou art just in all that has come upon us; thou hast done righteously, but we have done foolishly" (Neh. 9:33)? Do you take it well and bless God that in very faithfulness to your soul he has afflicted you? If you submit yourself to God, willing to be turned any way, why then there is a spirit of love in you, which in time will cast out all fear. There are now seeds of light and joy sown, which ere long will sprout forth to your endless comfort.

Use 4. This may teach those whose consciences are tormented, what course to take for comfort. (a) Look at God's good providence to you, in trying you and proving you, that he may do you good at the latter end. (b) As you have cause to take all in good part, so learn to seek him carefully. Take heed of sin, and do what good you may; strive to be more fruitful in good services to God and offices of love to your brethren, and certainly this unfeigned love will lead to peace.

Use 5. Hence see the estrangement of wicked men from the way of peace (Rom. 3:17). (a) They cannot think that torment and fear should be the way of peace, if they see a man in this state. (b) They would put off such fears with merry company; but if they see such a man seeking God earnestly and hearing the word carefully, they cannot think this is the way of peace. "Salvation is far from them" (Ps. 119:155), because they are far from it.

"There is no fear in love." We come to the fourth thing.

Doct. 4. A heart possessed with the love of God is dispossessed of fear of evil from God.

He speaks of the fear of death and judgment; so much love in our hearts, so much freedom and boldness against the day of judgment. Once we take God as our Shepherd and love him and follow him, though we walk through the valley of the shadow of death, we need fear no evil (Ps. 23:4). David makes solemn proclamation of a parable, a dark mystery and yet a word of wisdom and understanding. What is the parable? "Why should I be afraid, when the iniquity of my heels does compass me about?" That is, the iniquity of my footsteps, the fears and dangers which follow at my heels. Yet why should I fear? A heart possessed with the love of God is dispossessed of fear of evil from God (Ps. 3:6).

How may we be convinced of this truth?

By the nature of fear and of its removal. Fear is a troublesome dread of the expectation of some evil; and to remove it, two things must be done. There must be no evil towards the man, and he must know this.

-1. There is no evil towards him who fears God (Ps. 9:10). Indeed sickness may befall him, and reproaches, and imprisonments; but whatever befalls that is evil, it shall not come nigh him.

-2. As no evil is towards him, so he knows that it shall not befall him (Ps. 56:3, 9). So a Christian finds not only security from danger, but knowledge of it too. Yea farther, the child of God knows that all those things that are accounted evil shall turn to his advantage (Rom. 8:28; Phil. 1:19).

How do they know that no evil shall befall them?

-1. From the love of God shed abroad in their hearts (Rom. 5:1-6).

-2. From the presence of God for them in their worst sins: and then who can be against them? (Rom. 8:31)

-3. From the interest they have in the blood of Christ, who has cleansed them from all their sins; so they know that God will follow them as a deliverer from their sins, and though burdened with many sins, yet they fear not (Ps. 44:5).

-4. From the knowledge they have of all the promises as belonging to them; these are a stay and support to their souls (Ps. 56:3, 4, 10, 11).

-5. From the knowledge they have of the integrity of their consciences, which is as a brazen wall against all evils.

-6. The prayers of themselves and other Christians are for them, so that through them no evil shall befall them (Ps. 56:9; Phil. 1:19).

-7. They are emboldened against dangers by the support of God's Spirit in their worst times (Phil. 1:19; Ps. 5; Ps.

46). God is a present help in the time of trouble; when trouble is near, God is nearer; as Elisha saw the mountain full of chariots and horsemen (2 Kings 6:17).

Use 1. This is a notable ground upon which is built that heavenly truth of the perseverance of the saints, a bulwark against apostasy. If a loving heart is without fear of the day of judgment, he is without fear of falling away.

You will say, True, as long as he keeps perfect in his love; but may he not fall off from his love and so from his good state? I answer that the apostle says, "there is no fear in love"; and if there is no fear, then there is no fear of falling away.

Use 2. To direct poor souls against troubles and fears of heart. If we would be quit of all those cares and griefs, let us grow up in love to God and to the brethren, for there is no fear in love. Therefore cleanse your heart from all hatred of God, learn to take all his dealings as proceeding from his love to your soul; look at all those fears and anguishes he puts you to, as wholesome for your spirit; and the very apprehension of God's love to you in these will quiet your conscience and scatter those fears. Likewise grow up in love to your brethren; lay aside all wrath and revenge, and be tender-hearted and merciful to them; and thus growing in love, you shall grow in fearlessness.

Use 3. This shows the fearful state of a hateful heart. If there is no fear in love, there is nothing but fear in hatred. What is the reason why natural men are so afraid of death and judgment? Why, because they have hateful spirits, whereas a loving soul prays for the hastening of the day of judgment. Yea, this hateful disposition is more dangerous to the soul than any sin besides. Let a godly man be defiled with many sins and frailties; yet because he maintains a loving heart to God and his people, these sins do not eclipse his boldness. Though the iniquities of David's heels compassed him about, yet he asks, "Why should I be afraid?"

Use 4. To console every loving heart. If you find your heart possessed with love to God and his saints, so that there is none in heaven or earth that you desire in comparison to him, and the saints are the only men of your delight; if you are afraid, you are much too severe. If you discern God's love in your heart, bid farewell to groundless fears. Though you often trip and fall in your Christian course, yet these are not grounds to fear, but to love God the more for pardoning these failings, and to hate sin the more.

1 John 4:19

"We love him because he first loved us."

These words depend on the words of ver. 17. He had said that those who are sound in love may have boldness in the day of judgment. This he proves:

-1. From the resemblance between God and a loving heart.

-2. From the contrast between fear and love. "There is no fear in love," which he proves: (a) From the effect of love: "perfect love casts out fear." (b) From the adjunct of fear: "fear has torments," therefore love, a quiet and peaceable grace, cannot stand with it. (c) From the unsoundness of fear: "he who fears is not perfect in love." (d) From the cause of love, which is God's love to us. Love makes us look at God as good and merciful to us, and therefore love casts out all fear of evil from the hand of God.

In ver. 19 observe two parts.

-1. The freedom of God's love to us: he loved us, not because we loved him, but he first loved us.

-2. The root and spring of our love to God is God's first love to us.

Doct. 1. The love of God to us is altogether free, uncaused and undeserved on our part.

God did not love us because we had done him any service of love, but he loved us before we loved him. He did not call us according to our works, but according to his free purpose and grace (2 Tim. 1:9). He did not set his love upon Israel nor upon us because we were more in number than any people, for we were the fewest of all people, but because he loved us (Deut. 7:7, 8; Deut. 9:4, 5).

How may we know that God's love is free?

-1. If there is any cause on our parts, he loved us either out of foreseen faith or foreseen good works; but not from either of these. Not from foreseen faith, for it is the love of God to us that produces faith (Acts 13:48); nor from our good works, for we are his workmanship, created in Christ Jesus to good works. Good works did not cause God's ordaining us to life, but God's ordaining to life causes good works, so that faith and good works are not causes but fruits of God's love to us.

-2. Because of the eternity of God's love to us (Jer. 31:3). Now if God's love is eternal before the world was, then it was not for our sakes, for we were made after (Eph. 4:5). Nothing temporal can be the cause of that which is eternal; our love and faith began in time, but his love was eternal.

But though our love and faith began but now, did not God foresee it from eternity and therefore set his love upon us? I answer, it is all one with God to have respect to that which now is or that which shall be hereafter. If a man serves a master because he saw that he would have abundant recompense, his service is as mercenary as if his recompense were present, if he loved himself and not his master. Therefore when God loved us, it was not for anything we did or were foreseen to do; for then he would have loved us because we first loved him.

Further, in scripture account that which comes after is not the cause of that which went before. To Abraham and his seed were the promises made, not by works or obedience to the law, for the law was given four hundred years after (Gal. 3:17); and therefore the apostle argues that God had no respect for it. Thus what we have done four thousand years after the world was made cannot be the cause of God's love before the world was (Rom. 9:12-14). If the apostle had not excluded foreseen works in the ninth of Romans, his argument would have been of no effect; for he speaks not only of what was then, but of what would be afterwards, and found nothing to be the cause of God's love.

Use 1. To refute those who make God's love to us depend on our love to him. They expressly blot out this scripture when they say that one is beloved of God for his foreseen faith, which is to say that God loved us because we first loved him, which is expressly contrary to this text. We must seek the cause of love in God, and not in ourselves.

Use 2. This may teach us to love God early. You can never begin too soon, but he has gone before you. What a shame it is for men to defer this until their old age. God was up early to manifest his love to you, and will you not begin to love God until you are going out of the world?

Use 3. To those who have already given their love to God. Let them learn to maintain their love and increase it. A man thinks highly of an old friend (Prov. 27:10); why, God is the most ancient that you ever had.

Use 4. To console those who have experience of God's love towards them. If God loved us before we loved him, when we were strangers and enemies, then surely he will not cast us off for our infirmities in our after lives. It may be that we are sinful; but God did not love us for our goodness, neither will he cast us off for our wickedness. Yet this is no encouragement to licentiousness, for God knows how to put us to anguishes and straits and crosses, and yet to reserve everlasting life for us. Did God cast off his servants for their failings, none would have been saved; for all have failed in many things, and abused God's grace; but God knows how to heal such distempers and yet reserve his mercy to us. If he loved us before we loved him, then as he was first in love, so he will be last.

Use 5. This may teach us to be free in our love to God and our brethren: freely we have received, freely let us give (Matt. 10:8). God loved us when we loved him not; so though men do not precede you with love, yet precede them;

and if they provoke you, be steadfast in your love; be like God in your love. Be content to part with all for him; for shall we be able to give more for God than he has given for us?

Doct. 2. The preceding love of God to us is the effectual cause of our love to God.

How does it do this?

-1. By setting us a pattern of love; but that is not all, for all have read and heard of the great love of God to us.

-2. By working something in us which makes us to love him. "With lovingkindness I have drawn you" (Jer. 31:3); and this is not only a moral drawing, as a horse is drawn by a lock of hay, which is a leading rather than a drawing; but God's drawing us is not only by propounding fitarguments, but by a physical or rather hyperphysical work of his Spirit; he makes us, the unwilling, willing to follow him. Objects do not give a new heart, but this God is said to do (Ezek. 36:26). God gives us a new heart by striking us with shame and horror for our sins, so that we are brought to grieve heartily for them; and when he has drawn us to the suburbs of hell, then he shows us the glad tidings of salvation, and gives us a believing heart to long after them, to embrace them, and to assure ourselves of them.

How may we know that God's love is the cause of ours? Because of the efficacy of his gracious work. There is no work of God in us which does not work in our hearts the like work. If God chooses us for himself, then we choose him for our God. God's election of us stamps in us an election of him. Has God purchased us at a high cost? Then we learn to purchase him at a high cost, though it be at the loss of all we have. God calls us sons; we call him Father (Hos. 2:1-3). When God says to a soul, "Seek my face," it answers, "thy face, O Lord, I will seek" (Ps. 27:8). If God will not turn away from us, we shall not turn away from him (Jer. 32:40). If God loves us, then we learn to love him.

Use 1. This reproves the Papists and Pelagians, who have

attributed the efficacy of grace to other causes. If you would ask the Pelagians of old and their followers at this day, why Simon Peter accepts God's love while Simon Magus refuses it, they would say that the one was willing to accept the offer, the other not. Well then, if the efficacy of grace depends on our wills, then we begin first. Many of the Papists say the same, but the more moderate among them say that the grace offered was sufficient for them both; but God offered it to Peter in a fit time and place when his heart was free from temptation, but it was offered to Simon Magus at a time when his heart was carried away with the love of money. But the true cause is that God first loved Peter; and that made him love God again. If God should stay for a fit time, men's hearts will always find some evasion; he would never find it. Christians can tell how God took hold of them when their hearts were most undisposed to it. Tell them of promises ever so fair, they cannot be brought to embrace them unless God mightily draws them to them; but we love God because by his love he has brought us to that which of ourselves we could never have been brought to.

Use 2. Would a man know whether God loves him or not, which is a thing most needful? No man can know it by these outward things, which fall alike to all (Eccl. 9:1). If you ask how your hearts stands before God, I ask you whether you can find it in your heart that you love God; if so, the text will tell you that God loves you.

But who does not love God? Does not everyone? I answer, do you find your heart choosing God above all things in the world? You could not thus choose God unless he had first chosen you; if you find that you would be content to purchase Christ at the loss of your dearest comforts, then you may know that God has loved you and been willing to part with Christ for you.

Use 3. To console those who find in their hearts that they do love God. If you find that you would be willing to part with all for his sake, why then surely God so loved you first, that he will rather part with anything than you

(Isa. 43:4). If you would know whether God loves you with a love unto life, labor to love him with a living love. This should stir us up to love God more than we ever did.

1 John 4:20, 21

"If any man says, I love God, and hates his brother, he is a liar; for he who does not love his brother whom he has seen, how can he love God whom he has not seen? And this commandment we have from him, that he who loves God should love his brother also."

These words continue the discourse begun in v. 12, in which he uses two motives to stir us up to love our brethren.
-1. The fellowship such have with God (vv. 13-16).
-2. The soundness of God's love to such (vv. 17-21).
In these two verses he argues this truth by the contrary, viz. that those who hate their brother have an imperfect, unsound love. This he proves by a double argument:
-1. He has a greater occasion to love his brother than God; therefore if he loves not his brother, he loves not God, for he sees his brother daily.
-2. He has great cause to love his brother, which is the same as his cause to love God, viz. God's command. And therefore if we love God out of obedience to his law, we should love our brother out of obedience to the same law.

Doct. 1. Hatred of a Christian brother is an undoubted sign of hypocrisy of the profession of our love to God.

If any man says in heart, tongue, or practice that he loves God, and yet hates his brother, such a man is a liar; that is, he expresses not the truth (1 John 3:9-11). This is part of the message of God, that we love one another.

The profession of a Christian is a profession of his subjection to the gospel of Christ; and the gospel holds out five principal ordinances: prayer, the apostles' doctrines, the sacraments, mutual communion, and discipline. Now if a man professes subjection to the gospel, he professes subjection to these five ordinances. The apostle delights in this word, 'profession' (Heb. 3:1), and commends it in Timothy that he had made a good profession before many witnesses (1 Tim. 6:12). Consider what every one of these ordinances express about brotherly love.

-1. Prayer. (a) In prayer we call God "Our Father"; and if he is our Father, then all his children are our brethren; and if we do not respect them as our brethren, we renounce God as our Father. (b) In the same prayer we desire God to forgive us, but no further than we have hearts to forgive our brethren; therefore if we will not forgive our brethren, we are not true professors.

-2. The apostles' doctrine. (a) In hearing the word, we are to come like new-born babes, desiring the sincere milk of the word; that is, free from all malice and emulation, as babes are (2 Pet. 2:1, 2). Therefore if a man comes to the word with a heart full of envy and emulation, he professes himself a Christian but deceives himself. (b) It overthrows the gospel, because this is one of the great commandments of the gospel, to love one another (Matt. 22:36-40). Therefore if a man professes himself a hearer of the law, and so of the gospel (for he who renounces the law also renounces the gospel, for the gospel establishes obedience to the law, Rom. 3:31), and does not yield obedience to this particular commandment of the gospel, he is a liar.

-3. The sacraments are seals of our love. In baptism we are baptized into one body (1 Cor. 12:13), and in the Lord's Supper we ars all partakers of one bread and one Spirit (1 Cor. 10:17). If therefore there is a different spirit in us, we are not of the same spirit and do not work by the same spirit.

-4. Private communion calls for love; David said, as does every true Christian, "I am a companion to all who fear thee" (Ps. 119:63). He does not only say he is a well-wisher or favorer to such, but more, he is a companion of them. Therefore if we are so far from making them our companions that we can hardly be brought to favor them, we renounce subjection to the ordinances of the gospel.

-5. This is one of the main ends of discipline, to see that no offense be given from one to another (Matt. 8:15-20). If therefore a man offends his brother and is not willing to be reconciled, he renounces subjection to a main ordinance of the gospel.

Use. To teach Christians, if they would be honest, true-hearted men, to let there be no Christian brother in the world of whom they cannot say that they love him. If there is any whom you neglect, and cannot have fellowship with, why, there is no soundness in you. It is better that you should love a hundred hypocrites than hate one Christian brother. If God gives you a heart unfeignedly loving every brother, if you make them your companions and the men of your delight — why then, if he who says he loves God and hates his brother is a liar, then he who doubts whether he loves God and yet unfeignedly loves his brother, may be sure that he loves God. If you can find in your heart true love to your brethren, though your profession be but weak and poor, yet it is sound and sincere. So much love, so much sincerity; so much lack of love, so much hypocrisy.

Doct. 2. The sight of our brother is a stronger inducement to love him, than any who hates his brother can have to love God.

For some might say, I cannot love my brother because he is full of weaknesses and failings, yet I can love God, for I have more cause. The apostle tells you that the sight of your brother is a greater occasion to love him than any who hates his brother can have to love God. It is true indeed that he has more cause to love God than his brother; yet he who hates his brother shall find less cause to love God than to love his brethren.

By 'sight' is meant not only viewing with the face, but having familiarity and fellowship with your brother; having daily intercourse and commerce with him. This greatly furthers love.

Why is sight so important to love?

-1. There is strength in daily commerce together to procure love. Our brother does many things in our sight which may justly win our love; we see many good things in him, many good offices which he does to us and we to him, which much increases our love. The more we see our brethren and communicate good to one another, the more we love them.

-2. A man has little cause to love God, if he hates his brother; a man who is estranged from his brother is much more estranged from God. (a) He has no faith in God, for faith works by love (Gal. 5:6). (b) He can have no sense of God's love, for God never reveals sensible love to those who have no love to their brethren; and then how can we love God if we have no sense of his love to us? (c) Much less can he have experience of God's love to him, for he never had it. (d) You will say he might love God for many bounties and providences toward him. But what reason can he have to think that God gives these in love? Therefore he will have no cause to love God. If he finds in his heart no reason to love his brother, he will find less reason to love God.

But what if his brother has done him wrong or given offense? God never gave any. I answer, if he has wronged you and you see him daily, pity him the more; strive to heal it and redress it; if you cannot do it, you cannot hope that God would ever pardon you.

Use. To stir us up out of our sinful lust of hatred toward our brethren. Though we may think we have more cause to love God than them, yet truly we shall find that if we are willing to part with our brother, we shall be more willing to part with God.

Doct. 3. True and sincere profession of Christian religion yields obedience to one commandment as readily as another.

He who loves God should love his brethren also. Why? Because God has commanded the one as well as the other.

"I shall never be ashamed when I have respect to all thy commandments" (Ps. 119:9). He does not say when he keeps them all; we all fail in that; but when he has respect to all. So a Christian cannot keep all God's commandments, but he may have respect to all, and profess with David, "I hate every false way" (Ps. 119:128).

-1. The same Lawgiver gave all the commandments. He who breaks one breaks all (James 2:10, 11). If in obedience to God's law you love him, then in obedience to the same law you will love your brother also.

-2. There is a close affinity between the commandments. They are like the links in a chain; break one and you break all. If a man does not love his brother, how can he love God, or worship him, or keep his sabbaths? He who has no respect to all of God's commandments, has respect to none.

Use 1. This gives us grounds for trial of our sincerity. If God gives you a heart to respect every commandment, your profession is true and sincere, though you cannot say that you keep them aright. But contrary, if you shake off the bonds of these commandments or break but one willingly, you have no truth of God in you.

Use 2. To console all who find this frame of heart and yield obedience to God. God himself testifies that your profession is sincere, and so you shall never be confounded, when you have respect to all God's commandments.

Use 3. To exhort all who would have a testimony of the sincerity of their profession; let us make conscience of every commandment of God, and so we may have a sure ground of our sincerity.

"And this commandment we have from him, that he who loves God should love his brother also." (v. 21)

Doct. 4. The same commandment that requires love to God, requires love to our brethren also.

God requires no man to love him without also loving his brethren. It is one of the great commandments of the law; neglect love to your brethren, and you neglect love to God likewise (Matt. 5:23, 24). God would not accept a service to himself without reconcilement to our brother; so God will not accept any office of love to himself if we do not come in love of our brethren. God would wait for his service, and would have us wait, until we are at peace with our brother; not that our love to God should not be greater, and in case of competition, God will be loved even with the hatred of our brother. "The wrath of man works not the righteousness of God" (James 1:20). A man can do no righteous service to God if he comes in wrath.

Why can he not?

-1. There lies a close relation between God and our brethren. God looks at his people as his children, as his spouse, as his members; and therefore he will often bear longer with injuries to himself than to his members. Pharaoh was a heathen prince; yet God did not charge him for his horrible idolatry and filthy abominations, but winked at these things. But when God's people were evil treated by them, Moses' message was, "Israel is my son, even my firstborn; and if you refuse to let him go, I will slay your son, even your firstborn" (Exod. 4:22, 23). "Saul, Saul, why persecutest thou me?" The injury done to them redounds to God himself; they are as dear to him as the apple of his eye (Zech. 2:8). How long did God endure the heathen monarchs of Rome, until they fell sore upon the church? Above seven hundred years, though in idolatry; but when the emperors grew hot against the Christians, God would endure them no longer. "Touch not mine anointed, and do my prophets no harm."

-2. God takes delight in the sincerity of your service; "let all things be done in love" (1 Cor. 16:14). What is done in love is a hearty sincere service; and if love is lacking, either a man performs no service, or else it is not done in truth. God is a God of truth, and is most impatient of such halting performances; he requires truth in the inward parts, whether in duties of service to himself or man (Ps. 51:12).

-3. God takes care to preserve love unfeigned to himself, that it might be preserved spotless. God will still keep in us a diligent care to love our brethren. As long as a man walks in love and keeps a constant fellowship with the saints, that long he keeps a constant fellowship with God himself; but let a man fail in his love to his brethren, and he falls off from God and so runs into grievous apostasy and spite of the Holy Spirit; and next to hypocrisy, nothing is more odious to God than apostasy. Therefore if you would put honor on God and maintain his Spirit in you, take heed that you do not neglect brotherly love. If we neglect this, we are in the way to total apostasy.

-4. God takes delight that all his servants should wear his garments and be known as his disciples. Now if God had only left us to faith in Christ, all this might have been and yet we never had been known what we were; but because God would have it known that there is a generation of men calling upon his name and serving him in truth, he would never have them come abroad without this cognizance to their brethren, "By this shall all men know you are my disciples, if you love one another" (John 13:35). Therefore if a man throws away brotherly love, he throws away the profession of Christianity; he is no Christian.

Use 1. To teach us that the love of our brethren is not an evidence of perfection or supererogation, but a duty of necessity lying straight upon all men; if they love God they must love their brethren also. We think we may love our brother as long as he loves us, but if he comes between us and our profit we will fall off from him; why, if we love those who love us, what do we more than others? (Matt. 5:45) But we are bound to love our brethren by a commandment.

But what if our brother's face toward us is changed? Still the commandment of God has not changed. Indeed we are to express our love according to the occasion; it is one thing to comfort, another to reprove, but both are acts of love. There is no commandment of God which when broken does not bring a curse (Deut. 27:26). Therefore if I love not my brother I fall under a curse; we cannot wrong our brother without doing great wrong to God and wrong to our own souls.

As soon as Cain hated his brother and slew him, he went out from the presence of God and dwelt in the land of Nod, a land of agitation; wandering prayers and wandering performances does a hateful soul put up. When David had once wronged Uriah, what poor work he made; he then makes nothing of the destruction of a worthy subject, though before he had been scrupulous of cutting an enemy's skirt. But as soon as a man expresses hearty love to his brother, with good deeds and prayer, he shall find that as he is reconciled to his brother God will be reconciled to him; as he lifts up a cheerful countenance on his brother, so will God upon him; and he shall plainly find that in keeping this great commandment is great reward.

Use 2. To teach us to love God so much the more, for he has had such special care that no man withdraw his love from us. This is marvelous love, that God should take it so ill that any should offer injury to you. How this should shame us, that we should sit so far from God, and slight him and wrong him, since he is so careful that none should wrong us.

1 John 5:1

"Whosoever believes that Jesus is the Christ is born of God. And everyone who loves him who begot, loves him also who is begotten of him."

These words contain a third argument to confirm a truth delivered in 4:20: the profession of love to God, without the love of our brethren, is but hypocrisy. In this verse the argument is drawn from the nearness of our brother to that God whom we profess to love. If our brother is begotten of God, then we cannot love him who begot without also loving him who is begotten. And our brother is indeed born of God. This latter proposition is proved by his faith: "whoever believes that Jesus is the Christ is born of God."

In this verse there are two parts:

-1. The safe and comfortable state of every believer. He is born of God.

-2. The necessity that lies upon those who love God. They must love the brethren also.

Doct. 1. Faith in Christ Jesus is a certain and universal work of regeneration.

What is it to believe on Christ? Do not the devils believe and tremble?

-1. To believe that Jesus is Christ is to be persuaded that God has anointed him to be king, priest, and prophet of his church; as a priest to sacrifice himself for us, as a prophet to direct us and reveal his will to us, and as a king to govern and to rule us.

-2. Believing is not only an act of the understanding, for the devils believe believe that Jesus is the Christ, the Messiah, and that he is prophet, priest, and king over his church. Therefore in this believing there is more than a mere persuasion, namely,

a. A particular application to my heart, that he is priest, king, and prophet to me.

b. Where this faith is, it works such a frame of heart in me that I trust on him alone for my salvation. In his blood I look to be pardoned; in his prophetical office I look to be guided; and I look to him as a king to subdue my rebellious heart.

This kind of faith is a certain mark of regeneration:

-1. Because no other cause remains for a man to look up to him as the Christ, the anointed of God; this is above the reach of flesh and blood, and this kind of faith makes a man blessed (Matt. 16:16, 17). The state of nature reaches no further than this: flesh and blood looks to satisfy by the works of the law; and this was the stumblingblock of the Jews, that they sought righteousness by the law (Rom. 9:3). The principle was given to Adam, "Do this and live"; this still cleaves to us by nature, and this is the religion of all the nations, to be saved by the works either of the natural or moral law.

-2. Suppose you convince flesh and blood that its righteousness is unclean, and that there is no salvation except in Christ; yet a natural man will not be persuaded that Christ did all this for him. In anguish of soul he runs to merry company, to the world, to the gallows, rather than to Christ for help. Therefore if a man be brought to believe on him as his Saviour, and to look to him for salvation and to trust him for it, it is an evidence of regeneration.

Thus by negative argument it is clear that faith is a mark of regeneration, for no other cause could have wrought this effect. But for positive argument, faith is a mark of regeneration:

-1. Because of the mighty power of a living faith. St. John does not here speak of a cold dead faith, but of a lively and powerful faith; now where such faith is, it makes us live (Hab. 2:4). By faith we live a life of justification and sanctification; faith looks not at its own works for satisfaction, but to him who justifies the ungodly (Rom. 4:4-6).

-2. Faith looks to the promise for strength. When he

goes about any Christian duty, he goes about it not in his own strength, but he derives strength from Christ: "without me you can do nothing." He relies on the promise for help, for comfort, for acceptance (Hos. 14:8, 9); he does all in the name of Christ, that is, in his life and power, and looks for acceptance in the name of Christ only.

-3. If he suffers under the will of God, and lies under heavy temptations and afflictions, he waits on God and lives by his faith. He knows that he shall come and will not tarry (Heb. 10:36, 37), and in the meantime he lives by faith, that is, quiets himself in dependence on Christ and expectation of his promise.

Use 1. To refute a Popish doctrine that God's people profess no other faith than what may be common to hypocrites and devils; and therefore they disclaim justification by faith, because if faith justifies, then the devils and hypocrites may be justified. The apostle, however, speaks of a faith that flesh and blood cannot attain unto. Therefore that which they call Catholic faith, to believe doctrines because propounded by their church, is a fiction; the devil believes better than they, because he takes the word of God to be true. But to believe this by a true and lively faith is a belief whereby we are born of God.

Use 2. To try our faith. You say that you believe Jesus is the Christ. Very well; has your faith regenerated you? Has it brought you into subjection to God's will? Do you live by your faith? That is, do you walk by the commandment for your rule, and do you depend on the promises of God for strength? If you are to suffer for God's will, do you wait patiently for strength, and quiet yourself in Christ? Then your faith is a regenerating faith.

Use 3. Would you become a son of God, born of him? Here is what course you must take. Faith is the door by which we enter into this happy state; there is a power in faith not only to justify but to sanctify. Therefore if you are convinced of your filthy unclean state by nature, and if you look to Christ for cleansing; if you find your heart submitting to God's will and depending on him for strength; and if you can wait for him though he hides his face, this is the way to regeneration. If you were told that in the corner of such a field there lay abundance of treasure, and yet you live in penury and want and never go to dig it up, every man would think you were not persuaded of the truth of the report. So if you say that you believe on Christ, and yet never to look to him for salvation and help, who will be persuaded that you believe him to be the Christ, the anointed of God?

Use 4. To console every believing soul. We are ready to call in question our regeneration and adoption; but if God gives us hearts to believe that Jesus is the Christ, and to search out the treasure that is in him, and to trust in him daily for help and comfort, then we may be of good comfort; our faith is then a sufficient testimony that we are born of God.

"And everyone who loves him who begot, loves him also who is begotten of him."

Doct. 2. Every Christian who is filled with the love of God as a father, is enlarged also with love to his brethren as those who are begotten of him.

This doctrine is not delivered in these express terms anywhere else in scripture, but something like it is found in John 20:17, "I ascend to my Father and your Father." He acknowledges his Father to be their Father reconciled in him, and he looks at them as his brethren. Thus acknowledging God as his Father, the Christian bears a child-like love to him, and by the same affection he is carried to love his brethren as those who are begotten of God.

-1. He takes them all to be his brethren, and looks at God as their father as well as his. He who looks at God as his Father and yet does not regard God's children as his brethren, is a liar; he who loves his father loves all his children, because they are his brethren of the same blood and of the same womb.

-2. Our brethren have the image of God stamped upon

them, and therefore we look at them as of the same temper as ourselves, as partakers of the divine nature with us (2 Pet. 1:4).

-3. If we look at God as our Father and believers as his sons, then we cannot conceive but that they are beloved of God, and that God pities them as a father does his children (Ps. 103:13). If we love God the Father, we must love his children for the sake of the love that God bears them. It was an argument of David's integrity that he hated those who hated the Lord (Ps. 139:20, 21); so it will be a sign of your sincerity if you love those who love the Lord and are loved by him.

-4. Do you find many weaknesses in the children of God? Yet look at them as children of a father who loves them, though they walk in contrary steps, and you cannot but love them for God's love toward them. When the kings of Judah walked in evil ways, yet the Lord spared them for David their father's sake (1 Kings 15:3, 4). Though Abijam's heart was not perfect with God, yet for his father David's sake God gave him a lamp in Jerusalem. So let us do. When Jehu came to Jezebel and commanded her to be thrown down and slain, he yet sends forth his servants, saying, "Go now and bury that cursed woman, for she is a king's daughter" (2 Kings 9:34). An idolatrous king; nonetheless, because a king's daughter, bury her. The children of kings and princes, even idolatrous kings, must be respected for their blood's sake. And how much more respect will God have you to put upon the poorest and uncleanest servant of God. They are not daughters of the king of Sidon, but sons and daughters of the king of heaven; and though they have many failings and sins in them, yet do them offices of love because they are kings' sons and daughters, even born of God.

Use 1. This excludes all from the love of God whose bowels are shut up from Christians as their brethren. What a poor case this world is in, that the more any express the nature of God, the more they hate them. But you can never look up to God and say, "Our Father," if you despise and neglect your brethren. If you show a lack of love to those who are begotten, you show lack of love to their Father who begot them.

Use 2. To exhort us all to this brotherly love. If God uses so many exhortations and arguments to stir us up to this duty, it shows that we are very backward in it, and that our spirits lust to envy (James 5:5, 6). And this is an especially good means to help us to this duty of love, by looking at them as born of God, and so partakers of the same faith, partakers of the same divine nature, children of the king of heaven. Jehu could respect the daughter of a king, an idolater and enemy to the state; so, though you should not see the Spirit of God on them, yet love and respect them; bury their infirmities, for they are kings' sons. Go to his children whom you see degenerate from him, and tell them, "I am sorry you should take such courses as are not meet for the children of such a good Father; I beseech you to carry yourself like his children; be holy as he is holy"; and this is a true act of love.

1 John 5:2

"By this we know that we love the children of God, when we love God and keep his commandments."

The apostle has exhorted us to the unfeigned love of our brethren; now he proceeds to a word of direction, how we may know whether or not we love them. "By this we know."

It was the scope of the apostle to write things by which their joy might be full (1:4); and with his exhortations he mingles marks and signs, so that they might know their state and thus have fullness of joy. Now, because love of our brethren was a course of full joy, therefore he tells us how we may know this. To satisfy some weak Christians that might be doubtful, he tells them that we know we love God's children when we love God and keep his commandments.

In the words there are two parts:

-1. The expedience of our knowledge of our love to our brethren; this is implied, for else he would not have laid down marks to know it by.

-2. The marks of discerning our love, which are two: love of God and obedience to the commands of God.

Doct. It is needful to a Christian's comfort, not only to love God's children but to know that he loves them.

The scope of his writing was to fulfill their joy. As a means of this he teaches us this main duty to love our brethren; and not only so, but signs how to know it. God teaches us to profit (Isa. 48:18); and then surely if he take such pains to teach us this point, it is a way of profiting; and therefore to walk in the knowledge of our love to God's saints is a profitable way.

-1. It will give us assurance of our good state before God, and of God's protection of us in such a state; and therefore if we know this, we know we are in a good estate. The love of our brethren is an undoubted argument of our passage from death to life (1 John 3:14). Therefore knowing this must needs give us comfort; it not only gives us evidence, but it manifests to others that our state is good (John 13:35). Now if we did not know our love, we should lose this comfort; but if we know that we walk in love, we might know what other men know, that we are disciples of Christ.

Further, by this knowledge of his love to the brethren, a Christian may know that God will preserve and maintain him in that comfortable state, because he finds his heart knit to those who are knit to God (Ps. 16:1-3).

-2. The Christian may expect prosperity from God in such a case. "They shall prosper who love her" (Ps. 122:6). Therefore if God gives us to know that we love him and his servants, we know we fall under a covenant of promise; for God said to Abraham, "I will bless them that bless you," and they of faith are blessed with the faithful Abraham. But conversely, "Let them be confunded and turned back, who have ill will to Zion" (Ps. 129:5-8). If we do not love our brethren, everything shall go cross against us.

-3. A man's spirit has confidence and comfort in his dealings with men, when he knows that his heart sincerely loves them (2 Cor. 1:12). He knows that he has paid his debt of love (Rom. 13:8), paid it in the full and with good coin, and this satisfies his heart.

Use 1. This reproves the hollowness of men when they content themselves with the love of their brethren, but are not solicitous to know whether that way is a way of love indeed. We have so much self-love and false love that we may easily deceive ourselves. Those who take their love upon trust have not so much wisdom as those who pay money; they count it before they pay it. Why, every day we have a debt of love to pay; let us be careful therefore to pay it in sound coin. God requires not only that we should love our brethren, but that we should know it.

Use 2. To direct ministers not only to lay down duties to people, but to lay down signs also, so that they may know when they have fulfilled them. This was St. John's practice, and he does it to add to their joy.

Doct. 2. The love of God and the keeping of his commandments, is an undoubted evidence of our love to our brethren.

-1. Because a man who does not keep God's commandments will be apt to sit loose from his love to his brethren as he sits loose from obedience to God. Herod heard John the Baptist gladly, but when he clave to Herodias he despised John and imprisoned him, and at last beheaded him. There is such a close relation between the keeping of God's commandments and the love of our brethren, that a man cannot sit loose from the one without sitting loose from the other.

-2. The love of God is an evidence that we love our brethren, for if a man loves not God he loves not his brother, unless for self-respect, on earthly grounds. Laban would by no means part with Jacob; was this great love? No, he did it because he found an advantage to his estate.

Use 1. Here is a ground of trial, whether our love to our brethren is unfeigned or not. What is your feeling toward

God? Do you look at his law as your way? Would you keep his commandments as your most precious jewels, as your life? If it is thus with you, your love is sincere and unfeigned. Otherwise your good opinion of religion will not assure your good state, unless the love of God and obedience to his commandments is found in your heart. If we love them in obedience to God and his commandments, it is an evidence of our sincere love.

Use 2. To those who desire to know that they love their brethren. Be constantly careful of your obedience to God's commandments, and love him, and then you may be assured that your love to your brethren is sincere. Maintain obedience to God, and you maintain love to your brethren.

Use 3. To comfort God's servants who desire to have good evidence of their unfeigned love to their brethren. If God gives you a heart to love God and keep his commandments, if your love has this inscription on one side, "Love to God," and on the other side, "Obedience to God's commandments," it will prove sound and current before God.

1 John 5:3

"For this is the love of God, that we keep his commandments; and his commandments are not grievous."

In v. 2 he had given a double mark of our love to our brethren, love of God and obedience to his commandments. Now because a Christian might be doubtful whether he loves God and commandments, he replies in v. 3, This is the love of God, that we keep his commandments, and they are not grievous.

Doct. The keeping of God's commandments and the easiness of that yoke, is an undoubted sign of our unfeigned love to God. If we are willing to bear the yoke of Christ and account it easy, that evidently argues that the love of God in our hearts is sincere.

This Christ teaches his disciples: "You are my friends

if you do whatever I command you" (John 15:14). Friendship argues integrity of love. In friendship there is a mutual covenant, a mutual communication of good to one another; so there is a certain community of all things, for things are common among friends. So he who keeps God's commandments looks at God's law, and makes it his counsel and delight, and is ruled by it. Again, God communicates his attributes to him, which is more than a parent can do to his child; but God looks at Christians as his friends, communicates his counsels to them, and grows in acquaintance with them.

But does not commanding suggests service rather than friendship? Does a man command his friends? I answer, to do it as a duty of necessity is indeed a servant's condition; but to do it out of love's sake is an act of friendship. Further, a man is not said to keep the commandments when he only strives to keep them himself, but when he draws others to the same obedience. Friends have all things common, and they do not desire that any who belong to them should be enemies to their friends. So God looks at it as a part of Abraham's friendship that he would command his children and servants after him, and they should keep the way of the Lord (Gen. 18:17, 19). We see his care about Isaac, that God would establish his covenant with him; and he brought his whole family to be circumcised. So David professes, "O Lord, I delight in thy law" (Ps. 40:8); a sign they were not grievous to him. Love makes us delight in the thing beloved.

Why is this such an undoubted argument of our love to God?

-1. Because God's law is strict and pure, and cross to our nature. Here two opposites meet: God's prerogative to have our thoughts brought into subjection (1 Cor. 10:4) and the creature's liberty (Ps. 12:4). Now as these are so cross to one another, for a man not only to submit himself to God's commandments, but to do it willingly and out of love; why, this is such a yoke that were it not for the mighty power of God's love prevailing in our hearts, it could never be done.

Hence God's people are said to be a willing people (Ps. 110: 4), and the Spirit of God is a spirit of liberty (2 Cor. 3:17). It is evident that God's Spirit is there when we do God's commandments with freedom and willingness.

-2. Because they have had experience of the burden of sin, they to whom God's commandments seem easy. For this is certain: the more welcome sin is, the more unwelcome God's commandments; the more we delight in sin, the less we joy in God's commands. But when once sin is wearisome to a soul, then Christ's yoke is easy and his burden light (Matt. 11:28, 29).

-3. Any state but a state of love is insufficient to reach to this obedience; much less to render it easy and light. By nature a man is not subject to the law of God, neither indeed can be (Rom. 8:7, 8). And though we may do much by common gifts, as Jehu and Herod did yet unless there is soundness of love within, you shall never prevail with Jehu to cast out the golden calves or with Herod to put away Herodias. It must be the love of God within that brings us to keep his commandments willingly and heartily.

Use 1. Here is a ground of trial for our states. Do we love God? If we would be assured of our love for God, as we all have need to be, let us consider whether we keep his commandments. Further, do we desire to bring our children and family to the same obedience, that all our family may be God's friends? And if this seems easy, and we delight in it and think it our happiness to make every thought subject to Christ, this is a sufficient testimony of the sincerity of our love. But conversely, if we shake off God's yoke and desire to have our thoughts and tongues at liberty, then we are none of God's friends.

If a man loved his master, and liked his service well and desired to stay with him, he might have his ear bored, so that all his master's commandments might sink better into him; and this must argue his great love for his master. David alludes to this: "my ears hast thou opened" (Ps. 40:6); or, as it is in the original, "digged." He dug through all obstructions and made him willing to listen to God's will; a loving servant becomes a friend. So, if we might have liberty to get loose from God, and yet if we would rather abide in his service, let us give our ears to God to be bored, and give up not only ourselves but our whole family to be God's bondservants.

Use 2. To teach all who love God to take heed that love for others draw them not to break any of God's commandments. This is plain: if love to man makes us break any of God's commandments, then we love him better than God.

Use 3. To encourage natural men to give up their hearts to God's commandments and not to think them burdensome and intolerable. For if you had but the love of God in your heart, God's commandments would be sweeter than the honey or the honeycomb. No, his commandments are not grievous; and if his commandments are pleasant, what are his promises and rewards?

Use 4. Would you have God's commandments seem easy to you, and not burdensome? Why, grow up in the love of God; meditate upon his goodness and promises and mercies, and so you shall grow up to love him; and the more love, the more willing obedience. A man never loses his first works without losing his first love. Let him renew his first love, and he shall renew his first works (Rev. 2:4, 5).

1 John 5:4, 5

"For whatever is born of God overcomes the world; and this is the victory that overcomes the world, even our faith. Who is he that overcomes the world, but he who believes that Jesus is the Son of God?"

In v. 3 the apostle had made an evidence of the love of God, to keep his commandments and to do them with ease. This he proves by an argument (v. 4) that the removal of the impediments of God's love in such a heart results in overcoming the world. To those who overcome the world, God's commandments are an easy yoke; but they who are born of God overcome the world; therefore God's commandments are an easy yoke to those who are born of God. It is the love of the world that hinders our obedience to God's commandments.

Doct 1. Every regenerate Christian is a victorious Christian, a conqueror of the world.

Every Christian who has the least pittance or shred of true grace, has a mighty power in him to overcome the world. It was a famous thing of old to be conquerors of the whole world, as the Babylonian and Roman monarchies were; but St. John testifies here that every Christian is lord of the whole world (1 Cor. 3:22, 23). He has it there by gifts, but here by conquest; he overcomes the world, so far as it is an enemy to grace. Indeed, in themselves the comforts of the world are good and useful, but as far as they have a snare in them, he overcomes them (1 John 4:4). The honors of the world have a snare in them to puff up our hearts (2 Chron. 26:16), as do its profits (Matt. 13:22, 23) and pleasures (Luke 8:19).

Now, how does a regenerate Christian overcome this?

-1. He abides constant in his Christian course, notwithstanding the flattering or threatening of the world, so that he will not be seduced by any of these snares. Paul would not give place to such seducements, no, not for an hour (Eph. 6:11, 13). That is part of a man's victory, to hold his own and to keep his standing, and not to flit; such a man is never said to be overcome while he keeps his standing.

-2. He not only holds his own, but he resists his enemies; he musters up all the forces he has to resist the temptations of the world (James 4:7). Stand out against temptation, and you overcome it, as did Joseph (Gen. 39:7-9).

-3. To overcome a temptation is to make a good use of every temptation and to get ground by it, that the more he is invited by a temptation the more earnest he is against it, and the more forward in his Christian course. When Michal reproved David for his unseemly dancing, as she thought, he answers, "I will be yet more vile." So when John's disciples stirred him up to envy Christ, what says John? "He must increase, and I must decrease." He is the bridegroom; it is my glory to see him glorious; so that he drew them on the more to honor Christ when they sought the more to debase him. The more we are tempted to covetousness, wantonness, or emulation, the more liberal, chaste, and humble let us grow. This is to overcome a temptation, to enrich ourselves by the spoil of our enemy; this the apostle calls more than a conquest, and us more than conquerors (Rom. 8:37).

What is the reason why every Christian is a conqueror, and more than a conqueror?

-1. Christ's victory over the world (Rom. 8:37). Christ has overcome the world (John 16:33); therefore I am to wrestle with a wounded, pinioned enemy. Christ has led captivity captive; I come to contend with a captive world, and so I overcome through Christ who has loved me. It is the death of Christ that has crucified the world to me (Gal. 6:14). Therefore I come to fight with a crucified enemy.

-2. The mighty power of God's word working in a Christian's heart (1 John 2:14). The commandments of God and his promises do so rule in his heart that no flatterings of the world, no commandments of men, can oversway him.

-3. From the Spirit of God dwelling in them, which is greater than the spirit of the world (1 John 4:4). The Spirit does so mortify him to the world and so quicken him to grace that he overcomes the world.

But did not Demas forsake Paul and embrace this present world? (2 Tim. 4:10) Have not many for the love of the world erred from the faith? (1 Tim. 6:9, 10) How is it true then that every poor Christian overcomes the world? I answer, truly the world does prevail with many professors, but then they were never truly born of God, as Demas and Judas, and Ananias and Sapphira.

But does everyone who is led away with the world have no shred of true grace in him? Let us here take heed of condemning the righteous. It may easily happen that sometimes the true servants of God are so filled with the world that they have much ado to take pains about edifying themselves or keeping peace with God. But yet though a true Christian is led captive by the world, yet if he is born of God the Spirit of God will at length let him see his error; and then he will mourn for it, and oppose and resist it to the death. The seed of God will keep some life of grace in him.

Use 1. This shows the hypocrisy of those who are carried wholly captive with the world; they were never truly born of God. Some illumination may make them blaze a while, but they vanish away at length.

Use 2. This shows us the amazing danger of the world. We think it a happy thing to have our treasuries full and our houses well furnished; but would a man think himself rich if his house were full of enemies? Truly such is the world; it carries us into the deep, and drowns us with many sinful lusts. Therefore the more we have of the world, the more wary let us grow of keeping the world shackled, so that it may not hinder us, but help us to more freedom. The more sea-room a mariner has, the better he sails; so let Christians who have much of the world, learn to be more free for God.

Doct. 2. It is the faith of a Christian that helps him to overcome the world.

-1. Because faith enlightens the mind to see things in another manner than the world sees them. Faith lets us see things as they are. Faith lets Moses see that to be called God's son is better honor than to be called the son of Pharaoh's daughter. Faith lets him see that the afflictions of God's servants are better than worldly pleasures. Faith lets him see that God's wrath is more to be feared than the king's. Faith is of a discerning nature (Heb. 11:1); it makes evident to a Christian that which others see not.

-2. Because faith translates us into Christ. Christ, dwelling in us by faith, enables us to overcome the world.

-3. Because faith has a power to purify our hearts (Acts 15:9; 2 Pet. 1:14) from the lusts of the world. Faith looks at

God as our portion, and therefore regards not the profits of the world. Further, it cleanses us from voluptuousness. Faith lets us see more joy and pleasure in God's favor than in all the contentments of the world. Third, it establishes our hearts in God's fear (Prov. 29:25); and therefore it makes us not to be afraid of the wrath of men. It thus fences us in on every side from the world.

-4. Because faith laid hold on the promises (2 Pet. 1:5). Now God's promises have a power to take off our minds from the world. Faith believes the promises of God's protection and provision and goodness, and therefore makes us not to regard the world.

Use 1. To teach a Christian never to go without the continual exercise of his faith. The world will still be drawing us away, either after pleasure or profit, or else discouraging us with fears and dangers. Faith alone is able to overcome them; therefore live continually by faith, depend upon Christ, look up to the promises, and you shall be too hard for the world.

Use 2. Comfort to every faithful believer. If faith overcomes the world, then it will overcome Satan and your own lusts; and thus you shall persevere.

Doct. 3. To those who have overcome the world, the yoke of God's commandments is easy.

By the world is not to be understood the creatures, but things in the world which have a snare in them. There are many comforts in the world that are apt to draw our minds from God. Again, there are many discomforts and dangers, which are enemies to grace. To him who has overcome these, the yoke of God's commandments is easy. The world was crucified to Paul (Gal. 6:14). When he hears that bonds and afflictions await him, he cares for none of these things; he can fulfill his course with joy for all these. Then surely his task is not a grievous yoke, but joyful.

Why is the world a hindrance?

-1. Because it gives Satan weapons in every temptation.

Whatever temptation comes from Satan or from our own corruptions, it finds no arguments to persuade us but those taken from the world; so that if you have once overcome the world, no temptation will lay hold on you. There have been many who have been willing to partake of Christ; but when Christ bids them part with all, they go away sorrowful. Seeking worldly honor and glory hinders them from seeking God's glory (John 12:42, 43); how can they believe if they receive honor from one another? (John 5:44)

Use 1. Bear a crucified affection to the contentments of the world, and then God's yoke will not seem heavy.

    a. Though the commandments be great and heavy, yet as a man is, so is his strength. When a man has gotten victory over the world, he has gotten Christ in his soul, and so through the strength of Christ he is able to prevail (1 John 4:4). And withal there abides in him the mighty power of God's Spirit and God's word, which affords him mighty strength.

    b. There is a weakening of the enemy. All Satan's weapons are taken away when a man has overcome the world. Could a man stand on the stars, he would see the stars to be huge immense things and the earth to be a small point. But if we stand here below, we look at the earth as a great thing. We think worldly honors and preferments great dignities because we stand below; but if God lifts us above the world, we have our eyes enlightened to see the greatness of God's favor, Christ's blood, and heavenly things; and then those earthly things seem small. Therefore if we would walk in an enlarged frame, let us esteem earthly things as small matters, worth little regard, and account heavenly things as worth our highest esteem.

"Who is he that overcomes the world, but he that believes that Jesus is the Son of God?"

Doct. The faith that overcomes the world is faith in the divinity and sonship of Christ.

When Peter had made his profession that Jesus was the

Christ, the Son of the living God, what says Christ to this? "Blessed art thou, Simon" (Matt. 16:16-18). This confession made Simon to be a rock, and upon this rock of Peter's confession, Christ built his church; so if you ask upon what foundation the church stands, it was upon this faith; and against this faith the gates of hell and all the judicial power thereof shall not prevail.

What is it to believe that Jesus is the Son of God?

-1. To believe that the Jesus whom Judas betrayed and the Jews crucified, is the Son of God.

-2. To believe that he is the Son in whom God is well pleased (Matt. 3:17).

This faith overcomes the world because it cannot be attained by any human means, but only by a heavenly revelation from God the Father (Matt. 16:16). And in the age when St. John wrote this, there was no human reason to induce us to believe it. (a) All antiquity of the Gentiles was against it. They had heard of Jupiter, Apollo, and Hercules, but Christ was a new god to them (Acts 17:18). (b) All authority was against it (2 Cor. 2:8). None of the princes of the world knew of it. (c) The universal consent of all the habitable world was against it, except only a small handful of people who believed him to be the Son of God. (d) There was something founded in reason against it. For a man to look for salvation from a poor carpenter's son, from a despised man; one who was excommunicated and crucified, and could not save himself; this was more than flesh and blood could reach.

But now we have all the arguments to prove him to be the Son of God, which they wanted. We have the antiquity of many hundred years; we have authority on our parts, and the universal consent of the whole Christian world; and we have reason enough, since in so many ages so many wise and great men have consented to this truth. And therefore it is less wonder now to believe Jesus to be the Son of God.

What then? Is St. John's argument of no force now? Yes, its force is still valid. It is no great matter to believe Jesus to be the Son of God upon human credulity of antiquity, universality, or human reason. That is not the faith that overcomes the world; but it must be such a faith as is wrought in our hearts by God himself, and this faith differs from human credulity.

-1. Every man who believes Christ to be the Son of God by this divine faith, looks up to him for salvation. "Look to me and be saved, all ye ends of the earth" (Isa. 45:22).

-2. If we look at Christ as the Son of God, this faith has an efficacy in it to work in us contrition and mourning for our sins (Acts 2:37; Zech. 12:10). To those who believe thus, Christ is made the author of eternal salvation (Heb. 5:8).

-3. A faithful soul derives mighty power and virtue from Christ to overcome the world. When you look at all the world and its comforts, and compare them to Christ, you shall find them to be so vain and empty that there is no comparison (Ps. 73:25; Matt. 16:24). What is there in all the world that would be equal with Christ?

Use 1. To encourage a Christian soul against all temptation. For if this faith overcomes the world, then it will overcome Satan and the corrupt lusts of your own heart, and therefore it cannot be overcome. If it were possible that our faith could be extinguished, then it would not be true that faith overcomes the world. Therefore if a man lose his faith, such faith was never true.

Use 2. It teaches us the exceeding danger of love of the world. How many are there who rise early and sit up late, who spend their whole care and pains to get worldly wealth. Do you think this a safe condition? If such a man is overcome of the world, then he does not believe that Jesus is the Son of God; and can such a ma be a Christian?

But were good men never overcome of the world? What of Peter? What of Lot? What of those who repented in persecution, both under the Roman monarchs and in Queen Mary's day in our country? A godly man in a combat may be overthrown, yet not overcome; often a wounded soldier gets the day. Though Peter were wounded at that day, yet he got up again; and though afterward he was charged not to preach in the name of Jesus, he overcame all (Acts 4:19). Indeed, if a man is thrown down, and there he lies, and takes no care to get up again, you may look at him as no true believer.

Use 3. To console those who profess and maintain that Jesus is the Son of God. You may assure yourself that the world shall never overcome you. Look up to him as your Saviour; so look to him as to mourn for your sins, and obey him as the eternal Son of God. Keep this faith in exercise, and you shall not be overthrown; or if you are, it will so raise you up and recover you, that you shall overcome at the last.

1 John 5:6

"This is he who came by water and blood, even Jesus Christ; not by water only, but by water and blood. And it is the Spirit that bears witness, because the Spirit is truth."

In the former verse he had shown that the faith which overcomes the world is faith in the divinity and sonship of Christ. Now in these words he describes Christ, the object of our faith, in two ways: by his manner of coming, "by water and blood," and by the witness borne to him: general, "the Spirit," and particular, in heaven and on earth (vv. 7, 8).

Christ came fully furnished for the work of our redemption: he came by water and blood. By water is not meant their legal obligations, for he speaks of a water which bears witness that Christ is the Son of God to this day, and these do not. By this water therefore is meant the clear water of sanctification (spoken of in Ezek. 36:25, 26), with which our Saviour Christ came abundantly furnished, to be our Redeemer. By blood is meant the blood of his sufferings.

Doct. Jesus Christ came to execute his office by the water of sanctification and by the blood of redemption.

It is he who came to overcome the world and to redeem us. How? "By water and blood." But why by both?

-1. So that he might fulfill the types of the law. In the old law no priest might enter upon his office on pain of death, without first washing his hands and feet (Exod. 30: 19, 20). This shows how careful we must be to come with clean hearts and hands to God's service; and it showed that when the Lord Jesus Christ was to take upon him his priestly office, he should come free and spotless from all sin; and he did so, so that no guile was found in his mouth. Pilate his judge testified of him, "I find no evil in him."

Further, as they came by water, they might not enter into the holy place unless they were first sprinkled with blood. This showed that it was needful that Christ should come by his own blood to expiate our sins (Heb. 9:7-12).

-2. He needed to come by water, so that it might be shown that he was not expiating his own sins (Heb. 2:25-29). Had there been found the least sin in Christ, all the blood he spilled would have been little enough for himself. Had he been unjust himself, he could not have redeemed us (1 Pet. 3:18). But being just himself, there was no need that he should die for himself, but for us.

-3. It was needful that he come by blood to make atonement; for without shedding of blood is no remission (Heb. 9:22). Had he been ever so completely sanctified, yet this alone would never have made atonement. He came by blood:

    a. That by his blood and sufferings he might purchase out of his Father's wrath a church unto himself (Acts 20:28). And by that blood not only the elect but all the creatures are purchased, at least to be serviceable to the church (2 Cor. 3:22, 23).

    b. That he might make atonement for our souls. It makes atonement not only between God and us, but also between Jews and Gentiles (Ep. 2:17-19).

    c. That he might procure not only God's favor, but this fruit of it, the remission of our sins (Matt. 26:28).

    d. That by the price of his blood he might procure the

inhabitation of his Spirit to us, so that our consciences might be purified (Heb. 9:14). The blood of Christ cleanses us from all sin (1 John 1:9); and that is done by putting in us a spirit of grace, which purges us from all uncleanness and sin, and adorning us with the contrary graces of piety, humility, patience. Christ by his cursed death for us has procured a Spirit of grace for us, which purifies our consciences from the guilt and from the stain of sin (Heb. 9:14).

e. That he might confirm his new covenant, the New Testament, to us (Matt. 26:28). Now without the death of the testator no testament is in force (Heb. 9:16-21); it is accounted a sacrilegious thing to violate the testament of the dead; so with Christ, for a man to call any of his promises into question is a sacrilegious violation of his testament.

f. That he might keep in us everlasting nourishment to feed on in our hearts (John 6:56). His blood is his wine to cheer us, that by the comfort of his blood and mediation applied to our souls we might have nourishment to sustain ourselves in the worst times. This is meat indeed and drink indeed. Our souls cannot feed on pleasures and profits; spirits must feed upon spiritual things. They are beggarly naked souls who have nothing but lands and riches to feed on; the soul's food is only spiritual things. And if the ordinances yield you any comfort, it is because the blood of Christ has sprinkled them and made them effectual (Heb. 9:19). The blood of sprinkling makes them effective to us.

Use 1. This teaches us that a poor Christian who believes in Christ may overcome the world, because he believes on one who came by water and blood. Therefore whoever believes on Christ is so sprinkled with the blood of Christ that he is redeemed from the world to become the servant of God, and he has all the promises of God which encourage him against all difficulties, and so he is assured of heavenly glory; thus he looks at the world as a thing little to be regarded.

Use 2. To stir up all who desire to get victory over the world, to labor to get faith in Christ Jesus; for he is abundantly furnished with helps and means for our redemption, fit to sanctify us by the water of sanctification, fit to sprinkle us with the blood of redemption. But if we do not believe on Christ, we shall be continually slaves to the world. Hence it is that worldlings take such content and comfort in the things of this life, and are so discouraged at the loss of them; this is a plain sign they lack faith to overcome the world.

Use 3. To try what portion we have in Christ. What do we feed on? If we have a part of Christ, there is a Spirit of God within us to comfort us; we find the ordinances sprinkled with the blood of Christ to feed on; we have better promises than the promises of the world. It is poor nourishment for spirits to feed on the husks of this world; but a Christian finds the blood of Christ the only food to his soul, and the world is his servant, not his master. But if we have no higher matters to feed upon than the profits and contentments of the world, why then we are truly not Christians.

Use 4. To console those who renounce the world and esteem Christ to be worth more than all the world. Your hope is not frustrated; you believe on one who came by water and blood; though you be unclean and your works defiled, yet he came to water to purge and cleanse you; and though your heart is full of many sinful lusts, yet you trust on one who can make atonement for you by blood, to procure his Spirit and to give you when you die an open entrance into the most holy place.

"It is the Spirit that bears witness, because the Spirit is truth." By the Spirit is meant the Spirit of God inbreathing the word, and in the conscience of God's people; both are here included.

-1. The Spirit breathing in the scripture is one of the chief testimonies borne to Christ (John 5:39); and therefore this witness may not be omitted.

-2. By the Spirit is meant the Spirit as it breathes in the consciences of God's people; for though the Spirit is strong in the scripture, yet how shall I be certain of the truth of the scripture? By the same spirit in my heart. It is the Spirit in our hearts that witnesses to the truth in the scripture (John 3:33); and therefore it is called a seal (2 Cor. 1;20).

What is that which the Spirit witnesses?

Some understand it that the Spirit bears witness to its own truth; the Spirit bears witness that (not because) it is true; as the sun, if there were no other testimony of its presence, would be known by its own shining.

But the apostles does not speak of the Spirit's witness to its own truth, but to the truth that Jesus Christ came by water and blood; and therefore the witness here spoken of is the Sonship of Christ, and of his powerful coming; and to this the Spirit bears witness.

Doct. The Spirit of God breathing in the scriptures and in the conscience of God's people, bears witness to our souls that Jesus Christ came to save us by the water of sanctification and the blood of redemption.

In the scripture is not the saying of the prophets or apostles which bears such authentic testimony, for Christ received not the testimony of men (John 1:33); but what captures the world to the belief of their testimony is the testimony of the Spirit breathing in them.

What is that Spirit that breathes in the Scripture, that bears such strong witness to Christ? It is not by might or power, but by the Lord's Spirit (Zech. 4:6) that any building of grace is built. There is in the scripture a spirit of power and a spirit of perfection.

-1. Of power (Luke 24:49). It is that power which fell on them at Pentecost, so that their words remit sins, and bind and ease the conscience (1 Cor. 14:24, 25; 2 Cor. 13:3-5). When the Spirit breathed in the apostles, though their outward man was base and weak, yet their words were mighty and powerful, even as Christ was most full of power when he was most debased.

There is a threefold power in the scriptures. (a) There is a mighty power in them to convince men of their sinful state and of their need of Christ (John 16:8, 9). (b) There is a power to comfort the hearts of God's servants in a sense of his favor (Rom. 8:15). Hence the Spirit is called the Comforter (John 14:15); and when the soul finds this success, it witnesses that no writings are like them, to cast down to hell and lift up to heaven again. (c) There is a Spirit of power in the scripture to cleanse us from all defilements, to purify our hearts, to overcome the world, to strengthen us against all temptations and discouragements. Breathing in us, the Spirit lets us see that Christ came fully furnished for our redemption (Phil. 4:13).

-2. In the scripture there is a Spirit of perfection, by which the man of God may be perfect, throughly furnished unto all good works (2 Tim. 3:16, 17). There is no calling for which a man may not find abundant directions in the scripture. The heathen moralists have written much concerning our behavior towards men, and little towards God; a man may fulfill all their precepts, and all the laws of men, and yet live as a hypocrite and die a reprobate. Therefore if a man finds a word which, when he understands it, he finds sufficient to lead him in all his ways and bring him to heaven, this shows its divine perfection. What the scripture once delivers is absolutely perfect, and this Spirit bears witness to it.

Though the Spirit should breathe ever so strongly, yet if we have not the evidence of it in our hearts, we shall not know it in truth. Now the Spirit breathing in our consciences is a Spirit of peace and purity, springing from Christ's blood and water.

-1. Christ came by blood, making peace. The Spirit of peace persuades our consciences of the true virtue and power of Christ's blood; had it not been for Christ's blood, we would have been like Cain living in Nod, in continual agitation and without peace; but Christ's blood speaks peace.

-2. Christ came by water as well as by blood, bringing peace. This coming by water is witnessed by the Spirit of sanctification, and there is in this Spirit a threefold work suitable to this water. (a) A spirit of refreshing. As water refreshes the dry and thirsty soul, so does the water of the Spirit allay the heat and scorch of God's wrath. (b) As springing water washes and cleanses as it goes along, so does the Spirit of God wash us with clean water (Ezek. 36: 25); if it is troubled with some obstructions, yet it will overflow them and run clear. (c) Water has a power to make trees fruitful about it (Ps. 1:3); so the water of life gives a Christian such supply of strength to his heart, that he is strong and fruitful. Whatever God or man requires, he is in some good measure enabled to perform it.

So by the breathing of the Spirit within him, a Christian soul can plainly discern that Christ came by water and blood.

Use 1. Here is a just reproof to Popery, that places the groundwork of our faith upon the testimony of the church. But may not the whole church err? Did not the whole Jewish church so dangerously err as to consent to crucifying Christ, and may they not as well err in putting on us false scripture? Are not all men subject to errors? Therefore a Christian dares not build his faith upon human testimony, for their testimony can give only human credulity. But a Christian believes the scriptures because the Spirit of God breathes in them by such a spirit of power and perfection; and God's Spirit breathes in him such peace that he knows Christ came by blood, and such power that he knows Christ came by water. Let it not be objected that this makes the scripture to depend upon our own private spirit, for this is not a private spirit, but the same spirit that breathes in the scripture, which witnesses to our conscience the truth.

Use 2. To teach Christians never to rest in any scripture they read or in any minister they hear, before they have examined things by the testimony of the Spirit. Not the saying of men can assure you of this, but the Spirit of God in the scripture. If you do not discern this Spirit in you, your faith is not divine faith but only human.

Use 4. Here is consolation in the testimony of the Spirit. The world will tell you it is but a delusion and fancy; but be not deceived, for "this spirit is truth," and it witnesses your true faith. Only trust not your private spirit, which does not agree with the Spirit breathing in the scripture, for both are to be joined together — the Spirit breathing in the scripture, and the Spirit breathing in our hearts.

"Because the Spirit is truth."

Doct. The Spirit of God bearing witness in the scripture and in the hearts of God's people, is a Spirit of truth (John 14:16,17; John 16:13).

Why is it called a spirit of truth? Not only because he is one of the persons of the Trinity, and therefore his witness must be truth, but rather:

-1. Because he speaks nothing but what he hears of the Father and of the Son (John 16:13). What they apprehend and judge, he testifies the same (John 8:26); he speaks it without change and alteration.

-2. Because he speaks a testimony, not a shadowing or typical representation. Moses spoke by types, which obscured the truth; but what the Holy Ghost speaks is evident truth, without veil or covering (2 Cor. 3:17,18).

-3. Because of his effects. The Spirit not only speaks but works truth in the hearts of those to whom he speaks; by speaking truth he works truth in the heart, so that they who receive the testimony are of the truth (John 3:9; 2 John 1, 2).

Now they who receive the testimony of the Spirit that Jesus Christ has come by water and blood, they are cleansed from the world, from dissimulation and hypocrisy, and so are made of the truth.

Use 1. If this Spirit, bearing witness to Christ's coming, is a Spirit of truth, then whose who have received the Spirit of truth need not be afraid that they are led by a spirit of delusion; they believe that Jesus Christ came by water and blood. The way of the righteous man cannot deceive him (Jer. 20:10, 11).

But how may we know that this Spirit does not deceive? (a) It bears witness of itself, as well as of other things; the sun shows itself as well as making other things visible. (b) The Spirit bears witness by the work it frames in the hearts of God's servants. The testimony of the Spirit so pacifies and purifies the Christian's conscience that he plainly sees that this is the very Spirit of God, which is manifest by its fruits. (c) The testimony of the Spirit in the word and in the hearts of God's children so agree in everything that they are evidently the same spirit. Though the Spirit is more strong and evident in the scriptures and perhaps weak in our hearts, yet always in the main aim and end they agree together. (d) If it is suitable to the scripture, it conforms us to the image of Christ. The Spirit of Christ makes you meek and lowly as he was; draws you from earthly objects to a divine frame. The Spirit which fashions us like Christ is of God.

Use 2. To reprove God's servants who have found the blood of Christ pacifying and purifying their hearts, if their souls doubt and refuse the testimony of the Spirit. They say that Satan may transform himself into an angel of light; true, but Satan cannot pacify the conscience, much less purify it, since he is an unclean spirit and loves to draw others to impurity. Therefore if the spirit within you draws you on to walk in truth and to frame your heart according to the image of Christ, it is evident that it is a spirit of truth.

Use 3. To comfort all who have put their trust in Christ upon the testimony of God's Spirit witnessing to them that Christ came to save and heal them. Though our hearts and feelings are deceitful, yet this Spirit of God which breathes in us is a Spirit of truth. A spirit bringing peace without purity may be a delusion; a spirit bringing purity without peace may be a delusion; but peace and purity together do evidently manifest it to be the Spirit of God.

Use 4. If you have found a spirit of peace or purity, be very careful to discern whether it comes from God or not. If you have found much peace and you walk in simplicity and godly sincerity, this Spirit is of God (2 Cor. 1:12). But if your peace makes you more licentious and careless, you may never conclude that spirit to be of God. Herod's spirit of joy was a spirit of delusion, because it was not a spirit of purity (Mark 6:20). Herod and David both fell into the same lusts; how shall we know which of them had the Spirit of God? Herod so favored his lust that he destroyed John for reproving him; but David listened to the prophet, and humbled himself and repented; and therefore doubtless his spirit was of God, because he pursued purity. The soul who favors its lust and takes its part against God, has not God's Spirit in it. If either our peace or purity is lacking, we do not have a testimony of God's Spirit; but the spirit that speaks both is a spirit of truth.

1 John 5;7

"For there are three that bear record in heaven, the Father, the word, and the Holy Spirit; and these three are one."

Christ the object of our faith is set out, first, by the manner of his coming: "he came by water and blood" (v. 6). Second, by the testimony given him of his coming, which is double, three in heaven and three on earth.

In this verse the heavenly witnesses are set forth: (a) By their number: three. (b) By their place: in heaven. (c) By their work: they bear witness. (d) By their names: the Father, the Son, and the Holy Spirit. (e) By their unity: these three are one.

Doct. There are three Persons, yet but one God, that do bear witness to the divinity of Christ and to the plenteous salvation wrought by him.

Who are these three Persons, and why are they so called?

-1. The first person is the Father, so called: (a) Chiefly because he is the Father of Christ (1 Pet. 1:3), partly by eternal generation, as he is God; partly by adoption, as he is man. (b) He is the Father of all the elect (1 Pet. 1:3, 5; John 20:17).

-2. The second person is styled the Word, as in John 1:1 and Rev. 19:13. This is a title seldom given Christ except by John, although some understand Heb. 4:12 of Christ. Christ is called the Word in a fourfold sense. (a) He is a word of wisdom, for λόγος is not only προσκορῆκος but ἐνδιαθήτις reason. Now reason is essential to a human soul; so Christ is the like to his Father; he is the wisdom or reason of his Father (Prov. 8:23, 24). (b) He is a word of representation; he is the living image of God (Heb. 1:3); he is the character of the Father, as a seal is stamped in wax. (c) He is a word of revelation (John 1:18), declaring God to us and revealing God's will. It was the Lord Christ who appeared to Adam and Moses and Abraham and Gideon, and the rest of the patriarchs. As a word expounds our reasoning and reveals our will, so it is Christ, the word of God, who reveals the will of God to us. (d) He is a word of promise (Heb. 11:39), promised of old but not revealed till the last days.

-3. The third witness is the Spirit. Every person in the Trinity is a holy Spirit (John 4:24), yet it is more particularly attributed to the third person because he works so powerfully and effectually. The action and life of the creatures we attribute to their spirits; so God's action to his Holy Spirit.

So we see that there are three persons who bear witness to the divinity of Christ; and if three, there is a difference between them. Now there is no difference but a personal difference (Heb. 1:3); so that the Father is one Person, the Son a second, the Holy Ghost a third; yet these Persons are but one in nature, and so they are one in witness. "The Lord our Lord is one God" (Deut. 6:4); it is possible that there should be more than one God. Nature itself abhors more infinites than one; if there were more gods than one, how could they be all self-sufficient without one having the perfection of another?

What is it that they witness to? They all witness Christ to be the Son of God; and they witness that he came by water and blood.

-1. The Father testifies this by that voice that came down from heaven, "This is my beloved Son in whom I am well pleased" (Matt. 3:17). He bore further witness to his works (John 6:30-37).

-2. Christ bore witness to himself by his ministry as often as occasion offered (John 8:14-18). He also bore witness by his works (John 5:36) and by his resurrection, which declared him to be the Son of God with power (Rom. 1:4).

-3. The Holy Spirit bore witness of him, first, by descending upon him in the shape of a dove; second, by convincing the world of sin because they did not believe on him, and third, by sealing up this truth to the consciences of men (Eph. 1:13).

Use 1. To refute the Jewish heresy which denies the trinity of the Persons, and others who denied the unity of the Godhead. All such heresies are here condemned. There are three, and yet the three are one.

Use 2. Learn here a just groundwork for our faith. All which we believe concerning Christ has sufficient testimony for it. It is written in the law that at the mouth of two or three witnesses every word is established. Now we have six witnesses, three in heaven and three on earth. If we believe not Jesus to be the Son of God, we make God a liar, because we believe not the testimony that he has given of his Son.

Use 3. Let us learn not to take up a truth on a slight report; God would not commend any of his work to us unless he had confirmed it by three witnesses. Therefore do not believe single reports, even from good men, but confirmed by witnesses; let God be true and every man a liar (Rom. 3:15; Jer. 9:2-5).

Use 4. If all the three persons of the Trinity agree together in the witness of this truth, then we see what manner of men we ought to be in our witness. As the Persons in the Trinity are three, and yet their nature such that they are one, one holiness, one goodness, one truth; so let all who worship him, though their persons be different, yet be one in spirit. It was the last solemn prayer that Christ put up for the church, that they all might be one in him, as he was one with the Father (John 17:8, 9, 20, 21). He prays that they might be one that thereby the world might believe that God had sent him; as if dissensions among brethren would bear witness to the world that God did not send his Son to be our Saviour.

Paul calls for this duty of union (Eph. 4:3, 6) upon this ground, that there is but one God, and one Christ, and one faith (Acts 4:31, 32). And indeed all the dissensions of the world have sprung from this ground, that they do not all worship one God or believe that God is one. The apostle accounts that if we profess one God, the unity of God should be more powerful to unite us than anything in the world should be to divide us. If we allow the world to be more mighty to make dissension than God to make unity, we make the world our idol.

1 John 5:8

"And there are three that bear witness in earth, the spirit, and the water, and the blood; and these three agree in one."

Doct. The spirit, the water, and the blood are three principal witnesses on earth which bear witness to the Sonship of Christ.

They are principal witnesses, for he compares them to the three witnesses in heaven.

What are these three witnesses?

-1. The Spirit breathing partly in the scripture, partly in the conscience of men.

a. The Spirit breathes in the scriptures, for they in a special manner bear witness to Christ; they are called testaments. Such witnesses indeed they are, that no other witness is to be received unless it is in harmony with theirs (Gal. 1:7, 8). It is not Paul or Peter that testifies this, but the Spirit breathing in them; otherwise Christ receives not the testimony of men; nor indeed does the conscience of a Christian receive the testimony of any man unless he finds the Spirit breathing in him. This Spirit breathing in the scripture is a Spirit of power and perfection. (i) The Spirit of power in the scriptures is shown, first, in convincing men (John 16:9); second, in comforting those who are dejected (Rom. 3:16); and third, in strengthening us against temptation (1 John 2:14). (ii) There is in the scripture a Spirit of perfection, so that if we have the testimony of the scripture, we have no need of any further witness (2 Tim. 3:16, 17).

b. There is a Spirit that bears witness in our hearts that Jesus is the Son of God, and that Spirit is the same that breathed in the scripture; so that when we are hearing or reading, the Spirit sets it home to our hearts and souls, so that we are convinced, comforted, or strengthened to every good work and duty that God requires. Now this Spirit fully persuades us that Jesus is the Son of God, for it goes beyond the power of all created things. No created power is able to convince a hard heart, or comfort a dejected spirit, or strengthen us in our Christian course; therefore if we find a Spirit in us which enables us to do all this, the soul rests satisfied without any need of further witness that Jesus is the Son of God.

-2. Water bears witness to this. By water some understand the water of baptism, and indeed that gives strong testimony to Christ; but because water is said to be a representation of this Spirit, therefore by water here may be understood the water of sanctification, the Spirit of God sanctifying and regenerating us. Besides the Spirit of God which at times fills us with unspeakable joy of the Holy Spirit, there is also an ordinary work of God's Spirit, cooling and refreshing us, as water does, and making us fruitful in our Christian course. Those great occasional enlargements of God's Spirit do not always abide with us in that measure, but this water is a spring in us, continually affording us something which evidently witnesses this truth (Tit. 3:5; John 4:14).

a. In this water of God's Spirit we find a power to cleanse us from our lusts, as running waters cleanse channels and sinks (Ezek. 36:25). When I see something in me confirming me to Christ, that water bears witness that Jesus is the Son of God.

b. There is a power in water to cool and refresh us; when God sheds abroad his Spirit in us, there is something that cools us from the heat of God's wrath (Isa. 44:3).

c. This water is of a mighty power to make us fruitful (Ps. 1:3). A Christian watered by the Spirit of God, draws much moisture and life from every ordinance of God, and brings forth fruit in due season, according to his calling (Ezek. 30:26, 27).

How does this water bear witness that Jesus is the Son of God? Because all the virtue that it has to cleanse, comfort, or sanctify us, springs from faith in the testimony that Jesus is the Son of God. When we walk in the strength of our own spirits, we grow dry and barren; and this is because we suck our own graces, and so soon draw ourselves dry. But a Christian who has the water of sanctification, let him do all in the name of Christ, and suck life from him daily, and he shall be sufficiently enabled to do every duty that God requires. When this water no longer runs fresh and full, then we must renew our daily dependence on him; if we did so daily, we should always find it full sea in our hearts.

-3. Blood is a third witness on earth, and that is the blood of his sufferings. It bears witness:

a. By pacifying our consciences (Heb. 12:24). There is a louder cry in the blood of Christ to pacify our souls, than in the guilt of sin to bring wrath upon us; and this is so lively a testimony that a Christian knows were it not for the blood of Christ, all the things in the world would not have quieted his conscience.

b. The blood of Christ purchases us to become his (Acts 20:28). Now when we can find ourselves the purchased ones of God, the peculiar people of God, this blood of purchase witnesses that it was the Son of God who redeemed us from the world and our own corrupt hearts.

c. This same blood bears witness that Jesus is the Son of God, because it is a blood of purity sprinkled upon every ordinance and creature; everything was purified by blood (Heb. 9:19-23). This blood of Christ on everything makes it pure. "To the pure all things are pure"; his calling and company, his meat and drink do not ensnare him as they do other men. Were it not for the blood of Christ, our very graces would corrupt us; it is the blood of Christ that makes them all useful and good.

Doct. These three witnesses, the Spirit, the water, and the blood, are in one.

Not only in this witness, but they are all one for one work; that is, they all consent to one truth. Further, they all conspire in one work of our redemption, for one would be of small use without the others.

Use 1. To establish our hearts that Jesus is the Son of God; and so to believe it that we may overcome the world. It is not enough to believe this upon the authority of the state, of parents, or upon the universal consent of men; for this is no part of divine testimony, and this belief will never help you to overcome the world. This is the testimony of the church of Rome, but these human testimonies will beget only human faith.

Use 2. To try whether we believe this truth aright or not. If your faith is built upon the testimony of the Father, the word, and the Spirit, upon the testimony of the Spirit breathing in the scripture and in your own conscience, upon the water of sanctification and the blood of redemption, it will stand.

Use 3. This reproves that Popish doctrine that a Christian can never have any certain assurance. If a Christian has six such strong witnesses, and divine, will they not breed more than probable conjecture? Six honest men's testimonies would breed more than probability; and do not God the Father, Son, and Holy Spirit breed assurance in their testimonies?

It is a dishonorable thing to God to think otherwise.

Use 4. To console everyone who has found this witness in him; that Jesus on whom he depends will help him to overcome the world.

Use 5. Let us keep our hearts and ears always open to these testimonies. Two things hinder this testimony; the noise and tumults of worldly business fill our hearts and hands so that we cannot hear what the Spirit speaks, or else the noise of our lusts so fills our souls that we cannot listen to the peace which Christ's blood speaks. Therefore we should always keep our hearts and ears open and free from tumults of the world and the noise of our own lusts, so that we might hear what God's Spirit testifies to our own hearts.

1 John 5:9, 10

"If we receive the witness of men, the witness of God is greater; for this is the witness of God which he has testified of his Son. He who believes on the Son of God has the witness in himself; he who does not believe God has made him a liar, because he believes not the record that God gave of his Son."

Having spoken of the three witnesses and of their testimony, St. John exhorts us in these verses to receive the testimony of these witnesses. He does this by four arguments:

-1. The argument from the lesser. If we receive the witness of men, how much more ought we to receive the witness of God.

-2. From the divinity of their testimony. Whatever these six witnesses speak, their testimony is not from the earth but from God.

-3. From the nearness of this testimony in the heart and conscience of every believer. It is to be credited because it is an inward testimony that we feel in our own hearts.

-4. From the dangerous condition of those who do not receive this truth; they do no less than make God a liar. All these bear witness from God, and therefore if we do not believe them, we make God a liar.

Doct. The three witnesses in heaven and the three witnesses on earth are all divine and inward testimonies in the hearts of believers, and therefore far more to be credited than the witness of all men in the world.

That they are divine witnesses is no question, for they are the three Persons in the Trinity and yet are but one God (Deut. 6:4). Therefore their testimony must be divine. But the question is, How do these bear witness in our hearts to this truth? How does the believer have all these witnesses in himself?

-1. As the Father is the fountain of the Godhead, so his work is a work of almighty power, and that it is which speaks in the believer. None come to Christ unless the Father draw them (John 6:44); so he draws none except by the same power by which he sent Christ, and that was by his sovereign authority.

If God drew us only by the cords of men, we should break through all, as the Israelites did (Hos. 11:4). But when God shakes our hearts by an almighty power, and lets us see the danger of our state, and afterward enlightens us to see the ways of salvation, then he draws a man on to Christ. All the world cannot persuade a natural man of his dangerous state, but he is persuaded of his good nature and good heart toward God. And even if he is convinced of his danger, all the world cannot persuade him that any promise belongs to him. Therefore God must put forth an almighty power of a Spirit of adoption, whereby he is brought to believe the promises. Before he had only a human credulity, but now he believes it from a testimony within himself (John 6:45).

-2. The Son of God bears witness in our hearts of this truth by speaking freedom and liberty to our souls from the guilt of sin (John 8:36). Whereas before we were bound to our sins and lusts, Christ comes and sets us free from all, so that now we serve not ourselves or men, but the Lord Christ; and by this a Christian knows that surely Christ is he Son of God, because he has made me a son myself.

-3. The Spirit bears witness to this truth: (a) By convincing our hearts of it (John 16:9). (b) By working a spirit of faith and joy in believing (John 14:16, 17). Hence he is called the Comforter. (c) By giving us a spirit to make us overcome the temptations of this world and the lusts of our own hearts (2 Tim. 1:7; 1 John 4:4).

This testimony is divine because it is the revelation and will of God himself, and because it is above all human power to draw us and convince us thus, and strengthen and comfort us against all temptations.

What of the three witnesses on earth? They likewise bear witness to this truth in our hearts.

-1. The Spirit, that is, the Spirit breathing in the word, has such a mighty power to enlighten and quicken and strengthen a soul, that whatever the Spirit speaks in scripture it also witnesses in our souls (1 Cor. 14:24, 25).

-2. Water bears witness in our hearts to this truth; when the water of sanctification cleanses, cools, and refreshes the conscience of a man, and makes him fruitful in his Christian course, that is plainly a divine testimony. It surpasses all the power of the creature thus to pacify and quiet the conscience; it is only the Spirit of God that is able thus to pacify a guilty soul, to cleanse an impure heart, and to make dry barren stocks fruitful. This is a divine work of God's Spirit.

-3. The blood of Christ witnesses this truth: (a) By being sprinkled on our consciences and so speaking peace to us; this is a divine work. (b) By purifying every ordinance and creature. There would be no virtue in any ordinance unless the blood of Christ sanctified it for our use.

Now this testimony is of greater force than the testimony of all the sons of men together. Three things are needful in a testimony: it must be certain, evident, and effectual.

-1. This divine testimony is more certain than all the

testimonies of the world. (a) God is greater in knowledge and so knows more than men can. (b) He is greater in truth; men may err, but God cannot lie (Tit. 1:2, 3; Rom. 4:2).

-2. This testimony is more evident. Evidence depends on three things: a visible object, a good eye, and a clear medium. Now God makes this truth evident in all these. (a) He lets us plainly see the danger of sin, and the virtue and worth of Christ's blood. He reveals his Son to our hearts (John 3:12; Gal. 1:4, 6). What the gospel speaks of his Son is plainly revealed, and thus he makes the object visible. (b) He opens men's eyes to discern it, to long after it, to taste of his virtue and power (Acts 26:18; 1 pet. 2:3; 1 Cor. 2:14, 15). A natural man sees nothing of this work. (c) He clears the medium; that is, the word and sacraments, prayer and Christian communion. Whereas before we looked at them as beggarly elements, of little power and worth, after God has once enlightened us we see the power and virtue of God in them as plainly as if we had been touched by sunbeams.

-3. This divine testimony is more powerful and effectual than any human testimony (Heb. 4:12, 13; 2 Cor. 10:4, 5). The ordinances of God are mighty and effectual through God, so to change and renew our hearts that no human power is able to reach them.

Use 1. To refute two doctrines of the Romish church.

a. That the last groundwork of faith is the testimony of the church. Ask them if they believe Jesus to be the Son of God; they say yes. Ask them why; because the scriptures say so. Ask them why they believe the scripture; from the testimony of the church, they say. So their best faith is only human credulity. But ask a true Protestant why he believes Jesus to be the Son of God; he tells you that the scriptures say so. Ask him why he believes the scriptures; he says, not because the church believes so, but because he has a testimony within himself.

"What?" they say; "you trust a private spirit of your own?" No; his private spirit is common with him to all believers ever since the world was; and that spirit is no other than the Spirit of God that breathes in all his children. Besides, he has other witnesses in his heart, the Spirit, the water, and the blood; and this is a divine testimony, greater than the witness of all the world.

Here then is a double error of theirs: grounding their faith upon the church's testimony, and blaspheming the Spirit of God as a private spirit. That doctrine which lifts the church from Christ and builds it upon the testimony of the fathers and the schoolmen, overthrows the foundation; for other foundation can no man lay than that which is laid already, which is Jesus Christ.

b. It refutes another uncomfortable doctrine of the Romish church, that a man cannot by divine faith have assurance of his state in grace and salvation. They say that all divine faith is general; the scriptures say that he who repents and believes shall be saved, but the scripture nowhere says that I believe. But we say, besides the testimony of the scripture there is a threefold witness in heaven and a threefold witness on earth, all witnessing this truth; and since they are divine and my faith is divine, I believe on him and shall be saved.

But then how does it come to pass that this witness is so low sometimes that we can hardly discern it? This is because we sometimes grieve the Spirit of God, so that he delights not to reveal himself to us; but this is our own fault, for we black this evidence and cannot read it. But if we maintain and cherish it, it will be a strong testimony to our souls.

Use 2. Would you know whether your faith is pure? If it is, it will convey a double trinity of witnesses into your heart, witnessing that Jesus is the Son of God and that he came by water and by blood. Most men's faith is built upon antiquity and authority; but the devil has better grounds than these. If you find this truth confirmed to you by the testimony of God's Spirit within you, this faith will hold trial.

From the change of phrase in v. 10, believing on the Son of God and believing God, observe:

Doct. True faith which believes God, believes also on the Son of God.

What is it to believe God?

-1. To believe that there is a God.

-2. To believe that every testimony God gives is true (Acts 27:25).

Now to believe that there is a God and that his word is true, are acts of the understanding; but to believe on God is not only an act of the understanding but of the will, for I trust on him and roll myself upon him. It is expressed by laying a stone upon a foundation (1 Pet. 2:5, 6). Christ lies as the cornerstone of his church; every living stone lies upon and depends upon him, and that is to believe on God. "Let not your hearts be troubled; you believe on God, believe also on me" (John 14:1). So much belief, so much less fear; and so much fear, so much less faith. The devils believe and tremble, but he who believes on the Son of God fears not. This faith is a resting on him, for a man may have faith and yet not rest on Christ.

Are there degrees then in belief? Yes, we may distinguish three degrees.

-1. "He who abides in the secret place of the Most High shall abide under the shadow of the Almighty" (Ps. 91:12). There are two things in God which are the secret place of the Almighty. (a) His attributes of mercy, goodness, patience, and the like. (b) His truth. "Thou hast exalted thy word above thy name" (Ps. 138:4); the word of God comforts more and commands more than any attribute without the word; so that the name of God, his attributes and promises, is the secret place of God in danger. A Christian runs into it and is safe.

-2. But if this were all, it would exclude from faith all whose faith is not grown to this quietness and rest, for it is many a day before we come to such quietness and rest. No Christian ordinarily doubts of God's power and ability, but he doubts whether God is willing to put forth his power for the salvation of one so sinful and wretched. The poor leper came to Jesus and said, "If thou wilt thou canst make me clean"; he believed his power but doubted somewhat of his will; yet he comes to him that he might be willing.

-3. There is a weaker faith than this; that is, when a Christian comes even to doubt the power of God. He thinks that God is not able to show him mercy, because he has said that the sin against the Holy Spirit shall never be forgiven, and the Christian is afraid he has committed this sin. A poor man comes to Christ to beg help for his son (Mark 9:22); Jesus says, "If you can believe, all things are possible to him who believes." And what says he? "Lord, I believe; help thou my unbelief." He believed that God was able to help him, and yet not certain of it either; and yet this faith procured this blessing from God.

How then can this be called believing on Christ, when the heart is not grounded in him nor rests on him? I answer, there is a faith in Christ when the heart does not rest on Christ but is only grounded on him, or rolls itself on him, which may be done while the heart is yet in motion. Sometimes it rolls one way, sometimes another; yet such a man believes on Christ, for he is rolling toward him so that he might lie on him. "Commit your ways to the Lord" (Ps. 37:5); in the original, "roll your ways upon the Lord"; lean your soul that way; roll toward him so that you might rest upon him. "Trust in the Lord with all your heart, and lean not to your own understanding" (Prov. 3:6); a man may be said to lean upon the Lord, when he is not yet settled upon him.

When is a man said to lean on Christ?

-1. When he is persuaded that God is able to help him, yet doubts of his willingness; and yet comes to him, leans toward him, desires his help. The woman with bloody issue comes to Christ doubting neither ability nor will; "If I but touch the hem of his garment, I shall be made whole" (Mark 5:25); this was leaning upon Christ. But the poor leper had not come so far as to assure himself that Christ would do it; but he believes his power and uses the means to make him willing; says he, "Lord, if thou wilt, thou canst make me clean."

-2. A man may be said to lean on Christ when he believes neither willingness nor power, but yet he desires God to help his unbelief. This is a rolling on Christ; "if thou canst do anything, help us." This kind of rolling on Christ is called coming to Christ; this is yet not resting on him, but a man is a believer if he only comes to Christ (Matt. 11:28), for Christ promises to refresh him, and Christ refreshes none but believers (John 6:35, 37, 67). If a man is coming to Christ, humbled for his sins and persuaded that God is able to help him, and if not he yet prays God to help his unbelief, this is coming to Christ, and this is faith. If a man tells you that in such a field of yours there is rich treasure; if you believe him, will you not dig it up? If you let it alone, it is a sign you doubt the truth of the man's report. So God tells you that all the treasures of life and grace are laid up in Christ; this is the record that God gives of his Son. Now if we believe this record, we will use all good means to attain this eternal life; but if we do not use the means to get this treasure, we make God a liar by acting as if his record were not true.

Use 1. This reproves the dangerous sin of those who neither rely on Christ nor roll towards him. St. John tells us that such a man makes God a liar; it is a fearful thing for mortal men to make the God of truth a God of lies. If we make him a liar, we make him no God at all; if we live in unbelief we live in atheism.

Use 2. Let this stir us up never to rest until we have brought our hearts to rely upon Christ, to lean on him, to roll towards him. If we do not do this, we are atheists; therefore if we desire to make God a God of truth, let us not rest until we find our hearts relying on him. If was a notable resolution of David, in the midst of all his troubles, that he would not give himself rest until he had prepared an habitation for God; so let us never cease rolling and coming toward

Chrit until at length we find ourselves resting upon him.

How may we bring our hearts to rely and lean upon God? (a) Come to places where you may have means of grace. Faith comes by hearing (Rom. 10:17). (b) Roll off your heart from all your sins; come out of your sinful corruptions, roll yourself out of your bed of carnal security (2 Cor. 6:17, 18). (c) Roll yourself so far from all worldly comforts that you do not set your heart upon them (Ps. 62:10) nor on great friends (Ps. 146:3). (d) Cast your meditation on the mighty power of God, which is able to heal such untoward hearts as yours. (e) If you doubt of God's will and are not confident of his ability, pray that God would give you a believing heart.

Use 3. If you have rolled yourself on Christ, do not rest in rolling, for there is no rest to be had in it; but labor to come to establishment and rest in Christ; sit down in quietness and confidence. If a stone is uneven, it will not lie sure upon the foundation; sometimes doubts make us uneven, or pride makes a great swelling; therefore we must lay down all our high thoughts and lie level with Christ, for he is meek and lowly; besides, all hatred and malice is an uneven swelling in our hearts, and how then can they lie smooth in the building? Let us therefore pare off all these swellings of heart, and so being made smooth and even, we shall lie sure upon the foundation.

1 John 5:11
"And this is the record, that God has given to us eternal life, and this life is in his Son."

In vv. 7, 8, St. John had declared the three witnesses in heaven and three on earth, which bear witness to the divinity of Christ. He exhorts us (vv. 9, 10) to receive their testimony. Now he tells us what this divine record is; and it is threefold.

-1. We have an heavenly gift, eternal life.
-2. This life is given to us by Christ.
-3. This life is given only to believers.

Doct. Eternal life is the gift of God.

Two things are to be opened: first, that the life given us by God in Christ, is eternal life; second, that this eternal life is the gift of God.

A. This is eternal life (John 3:16).

-1. It is eternal because it was given to us before the foundation of the world; it is more ancient than the world or man's fall. This was not only purposed in God's counsel, but was manifestly promised before the world began (Tit. 1:2). The Trinity then concluded that the Lord Jesus Christ should be made head of all. Therefore it is said, "He chose us in Christ before the foundation of the world" (Eph. 1:4). And therefore since God chose us as members of Christ, he promised to Christ that he would give us all eternal life (2 Tim. 1:9). There was not only a purpose of God, but a declaration of the same to Christ (John 17:6; Rev. 13:8). And this gift is more ancient than our actual vocation; we were given to Christ before we were called to the fellowship of his Spirit and adoption of sons (John 6:39).

-2. It is called eternal life because its fountain and principles are eternal. The word of God was revealed from eternity, and of this word we were begotten (1 Pet. 1:23). We are born of the Spirit, and this Spirit in us is a fountain of living water, springing up to everlasting life (John 4:14).

-3. The continuance of this life is to everlasting. "He who believes in Christ shall never die, but have everlasting life" (John 3:36; John 5:24); and this eternal life is a record which God has given us of his Son.

B. This life is a gift of God (Rom. 6:23). All the life we have is God's gift; there is a fourfold life, and all is given to us by God.

-1. The life of justification is a free gift (Rom. 5:15). We all lay dead in sin, and the pardon of these sins is the very life of our souls (Col. 2:13).

-2. There is a life of holiness whereby we live to God, life for his ends and walk by his rule; and this life is the free gift of God (Eph. 2:4, 5).

-3. There is a life of consolation (1 Thess. 3:7, 8); this life is given by free grace (2 Cor. 1:4, 5). When God so comforts a poor soul, he is to be looked at as the Father of mercies and the God of all consolation.

-4. There is a life of glory, which God has given us by Christ (Rom. 6:23).

How may we know that this eternal life is God's gift?

-1. If our natural life is God's gift, how much more this spiritual and eternal life (Job 10:12). Now if Job's natural life and ours was a gift of God, as it was, how much more is eternal life the gift of God.

-2. There is nothing by which we could merit this life, and thus it must needs be a gift. Four things are necessary in merit. (a) You must go before the other in giving; but who has given to God first? (Rom. 11:35) And if we give God his own, how can we merit? (1 Chron. 29:13-15) (b) It is required that we give freely, not of due debt or recompense. If we but do our duties, what do we merit? (Luke 17:9, 10) When we have done what we can, we have done no more than our duty; and how then do we merit? (c) What merits at God's hands must be perfect and pure, without spot. Now our best righteousness is defiled (Isa. 64:6; Exod. 28:38). If God did not accept our best offerings in Christ's holiness, he might justly reject them. (d) There should be something proportionate between the work and the reward. Now what proportion is there between natural life and spiritual, between our life of nature and the life of glory? Our sufferings, the highest part of our obedience, are not worthy to be compared to the eternal weight of glory (2 Cor. 4:17). Indeed they work for us a plentiful recompense of reward; but this is through the free gift of God.

Use 1. To reprove the Popish doctrine of merit. If eternal life is the free gift of God, then the life of grace is not given to us by merit. If it is gift, then we pay no price for it. Was this natural life given us of merit? Who would say he has merited to be a man, rather than a beast, a serpent, or a toad? And how can we say that our eternal life is of merit?

God's servants do not think God indebted to them for their service; but they never think themselves more indebted to God than when he enables them to do most service. They say with David, "Who are we that we should be able to offer thus willingly?" (1 Chron. 29:14). If the king will send a pardon to any malefactor on earth, he acknowledges it to be of the king's free grace and royal compassion; but yet the synagogue of Rome will not acknowledge God's pardon to be of free grace. God's people acknowledge that they are all but dead dogs before God, and were it not for the free grace of God they would never have seen life.

Use 2. If you desire to see life, and that life forever, look up to God to derive it from him. "Every man is a friend to him who gives gifts" (Prov. 16:6); and this is God's free gift. Shall we think it our happiness to do service to a prince, though he have but earthly honors to bestow, and shall we neglect God who has such great gifts to give? Shall we neglect this great gift of eternal life, and more respect the poor comforts of the world than him, in whose hands is our breath and life?

Use 3. To try whether we have this eternal life or not. (a) Consider whether there is any eternal life shed abroad in your heart or not; have you found pardon of sins? Whereas you saw your soul as a dead dog for lack of this life, now has God justified you from your sins? Then the life of justification is eternal life; if he has once pardoned your sins, he will remember them no more (Jer. 31:33). (b) Have you found a spirit of life in you to obey and serve the Lord? (Rom. 8:2) Why, this is eternal life which will never decay (John 17:3). Has God shed abroad the comfort of his Spirit into your heart, which is better than life? (Ps. 63:3) This is eternal life; though it may sometimes be overwhelmed, yet it shall spring up again, as trees after winter. But if you find none of these works in you, then you have no life.

Use 4. To console those who have received this life. If we have found the life of justification in the pardon of our sins, the life of holiness in Christian obedience, and the life of comfort of God's Spirit, this is a life that will never decay. This is the record of God himself, that this life which he has given us is eternal life; it was given us before we were born, and will he take it away after we are born? If it is eternal, how can it decay? Sinful lusts are dead lusts, and what has eternal life to do with dead lusts? Keep your hands off a sinful, carnal life, but lay fast hold on eternal life (1 Tim. 6:12). Get sure possession of it, and let neither Satan nor the world wrest it out of your hands.

"And this life is in his Son."
Doct. The eternal life that God has given us is laid up for us in Jesus Christ (John 11:25, 26; Col. 3:3; John 14:6).

This life is fourfold, of justification, of sanctification, of consolation, and of glorification. All these are laid up in Christ (Jer. 23:6; for all together, see 1 Cor. 1:30). Our life is hid with Christ in God (Col. 3:3); it is sometimes under a veil of corruptions, sometimes under a veil of afflictions, but yet it is laid up in Christ.

How is our life said to be laid up in him?

-1. Because he has received it for us from God the Father (John 5:21, 26; 1 Thess. 5:9, 10). He has appointed us to salvation through Jesus Christ, so that whether we live or die, yet we may live in Christ.

-2. Because Christ purchased this life for us. The Father has not only appointed us life, but he has appointed it through the death of Christ. He has come that we might have life and have it more abundantly (John 10:10); and this he has done by giving his life for us.

-3. It is laid up in Christ as one who prepares it for us, and us for it. It is he who makes us fit to be partakers of the inheritance of the saints in light (Col. 1:12); whereas before we were unfit, now he has adorned us and made us fit spouses for himself. And as he thus prepares us for eternal life, so likewise he prepares a place for us (John 14:2, 3).

-4. It is reserved for us principally in himself, notwithstanding that it is communicated in part to us daily (Jude 1).

Conversely we are said to be preserved in Jesus Christ to life; all our life of grace here and of glory hereafter is preserved in Christ.

-1. Because all the claim of eternal life is laid up only in him, we neither desire nor beg any pardon of sin, or any grace or comfort or glory, but through Jesus Christ. The claim of eternal life is wholly in him; for through him God has promised those kinds of life.

-2. As he reserves the claim of it in his own hands, so he reserves the security of it in his own hand. A father, doubting how his son will spend his estate, puts not into his hands the writing or evidences, but keeps them in his own hands. So God saw our first parents prodigally waste away the life he communicated to them; and therefore never since would he put it into our own hands, but reserved it in the hands of Christ. Therefore it is by faith, that the promise might be sure (Rom. 4:16). If our salvation had stood upon our own works, the promise would have been sure only as long as we kept our obedience; but we are unsettled, and so we would have been at a stand sometimes, not knowing whether we had life or not. Therefore he has laid it up in Christ, that it might be sure.

-3. The possession of this life is reserved for us in Christ. Our justification is complete in Christ here; but our life of holiness is but imperfect, and we have only some beginnings of the life of consolation here (Phil. 4:7; 1 Pet. 1:8). But sometimes all these except the first are lost, and then it lies in Christ, as the sap in the root in winter. Thus in him we rejoice always (Phil. 4:4), and our eternal life is reserved in him (John 14:2, 3; Eph. 2:5).

-4. The life of glory is now laid up for his saints to be manifested in the last day (2 Thess. 1:10); at that day he will dispense it to his servants, to the admiration of all men.

Why has God laid up this life in his Son?

Because it was impossible to lay up life for us in the law

or in the first Adam (Gal. 3:21). The law that Adam had in paradise could not have secured our life, for we might forfeit it by our own fall; nor could Adam himself give us this life, for in Adam all died (1 Cor. 15:22); and therefore Christ alone could restore us to life and glory.

Use 1. God did not first give us life and then provide Christ to maintain it in us; but he first appointed Christ, that in him we might have life (Eph. 1:3, 4). He has chosen us in Christ; Christ is the firstfruits of all the life we enjoy; he loved Christ and in him loved us. He gave him eternal life that he might give it to whom he would (John 5:26). He first crowned him with glory, that he might glorify us.

Use 2. This teaches us the dead state of all men by nature. If all our life is laid up in Christ, then those who lack this life lack pardon of sins, and holiness, and comfort, and eternal life (Eph. 2:11, 12; Eph. 4:19). Let natural men look at themselves as dead men; all their best comforts are but as the crackling of thorns. They may warm themselves for a while with the sparkles of their own fire, but at length they shall lie down in sorrow (Isa. 50:11). By nature we have no hopes of eternal life; we must be regenerated to this hope (1 Peter 1:3, 4).

Use 3. This may teach all who live in a dead state, to look out where they may have life. Do not look into your own hearts; there you shall not find life; look not into the world, for it is not able to give you life; but get Christ and you get life. Wisdom says (viz. Christ the wisdom of his Father), "Who finds me finds life, and all who hate me love death" (Prov. 8:35, 36).

Use 4. To console all who have found their parts in the Lord Christ. If you have found him, you have found life, pardon of sin, peace of conscience, and life eternal (Rom. 5:1). Having found him, you have a life of holiness laid up in him. Though you lack zeal, wisdom, patience, you may enjoy them from him; and though you find your heart sometimes drooping under heavy discouragements and afflictions, yet in him you may rejoice always. We may comfort ourselves the more that our life is not laid up in Satan's hands, for then we should never finger any of it; nor in our own hands, for we should lose it at every hand; but in Christ, and reserved safely for us in him.

1 John 5:12

"He who has the Son has life; and he who has not the Son of God has not life."

This verse contains the third record that God has given us of his Son, and that is the subject to whom this eternal life is given. He who has the Son has life, and he who has not the Son has not life.

Doct. Upon our having or not having Christ, depends our having or not having life (Prov. 8:35, 36; Eph. 2:11, 12).

Why does our life depend upon having Christ?

-1. Because the creature is insufficient to give life (Heb. 10:1, 4). Though we should die for our sins ourselves, yet we could not satisfy for our sins, because we could never overcome death; neither can our obedience to the law give us life (Gal. 3:21, 23). Yea, Adam in innocence was taught to look for the preservation of his life out of himself, and therefore he was to eat of the tree of life; the life he then lived could not have been in himself, but he must eat of the tree of life, a type of Christ. How much less could fallen Adam keep this life in him?

But why is the creature insufficient to give life?

-1. A precious price was to be paid for our life (Ps. 49:8). The redemption of souls is precious, and it is beyond the power of the creature. It was only the obedience of Christ as suffering to the death that could give a sufficient price for us, and none but Christ could do it.

-2. Our life of sanctification and consolation proceeds from the Spirit of God within us, springing in us to everlasting life (John 16:7; John 4:10). Now it is only Christ who can give us this life; it is he who must ascend to heaven and send down the Comforter; it is he who sets open this living fountain.

-3. Eternal life is difficult, far above all human reach. No man is able to deliver his soul from the grave (Ps. 49:7, 8). Death is the passage to eternal life; for a man to die and afterwards raise himself up, is above created power (John 11:24).

-4. The good pleasure of God has appointed that in Christ should all fullness dwell (Col. 1:19; Col. 3:4). All the springs of life flow from him only; there is no life to be derived from any other fountain.

What is it to have Christ? We are said to have Christ four ways: by way of service, by way of purchase, by way of covenant, and by way of acceptance.

-1. By way of service or worship. A man is said to have God if he worships God. As some princes are chosen by the people's adoration, so we have God by adoring God. "Thou shalt have no other gods before me" (Exod. 20:3); that is, you shall worship no other gods but me. The worship of God is performed in our minds, in our wills, in our lives.

-2. We are said to have Christ by purchase; this is partly expressed in the parable of the pearl (Matt. 13:46). But how are we to purchase him? Are we not invited to come and buy, without money and without price? (Isa. 55:1) True; if a man would give all the treasures of his house for Christ, they would be despised (Cant. 8:7). When Simon Magus offered money for the gift of the Holy Spirit, Simon Peter tells him, "Your money perish with you" (Acts 8:19). Yet in three cases we must part with money, or else we shall not purchase Christ.

    a. When the Lord requires it by special command, as he did the rich young man. Upon this point Ananias and Sapphira also lost Christ, because they kept back some of the price (Acts 5:1-4).

    b. When in times of persecution a man cannot have Christ with peace and purity, unless he is willing to part with all for him. Sometimes unless a man is content to be spoiled of all his goods, he cannot have liberty of conscience.

c. Sometimes by laying out money we may win Christ, as in case we need a good ministry among us and cannot have it unless we are willing to lay out money for the gospel; this the apostle calls sowing to the Spirit (Gal. 6:8). By laying out money a man provides things needful for him; so when a man lays out for spiritual uses, he shall of the Spirit reap life everlasting.

In these three cases money must be parted with; and yet if you think money can purchase Christ, you are not worthy of him. But there is another sense in which we are said to purchase Christ.

a. Christ must be purchased by parting with all those strong lusts that keep us from Christ. Having bidden us buy without money and without price (Isa. 55:1), the prophet tells us then what it is that we must spend for Christ: "Let the wicked forsake his ways, and the unrighteous man his thoughts" (55:7).

b. Sometimes we must be content to part with the ordinances themselves. If we cannot enjoy the ordinances of God in purity, without sin, let us part with them all. When the priests could not enjoy liberty in their callings under Jeroboam, without offering sacrifices to the golden calves, they left all and came up to Jerusalem, where they might enjoy God's ordinances in purity (2 Chron. 11:14); and as the priests did, so did the people (11:16).

c. We must part with all our good gifts and good possessions and good natures for Christ. "If any man seems wise in this world, let him become a fool that he may become wise" (1 Cor. 3:18); we must lay aside all carnal wisdom and reasonings, and be content to be counted fools, that we may win Christ.

-3. We are said to have Christ by way of covenant (Isa. 49:8). "Gather my saints together to me, those who have made a covenant with me by sacrifice" (Ps. 50:5), and then "I am God, even your God" (50:7); and so the tenor of the covenant runs (Gen. 17:17; Deut. 29:10-13; Deut. 26:17, 18).

This covenant is made by sacrifice (Ps. 50:5), in which they promised before the Lord to be obedient to all that the Lord would command them. Moses sprinkled the people and said, "Behold the blood of the covenant which the Lord has made with you"; this implies that when we make a covenant with God, we confess that death is our just portion, and therefore we look up to Christ, that his blood sprinkled on us might impart life to us. This is to make a covenant with God.

There is a threefold covenant that passes between men in civil society in this world. -1. There is a covenant between prince and people (2 Chron. 23:16). -2. Between man and wife (Matt. 2:14). -3. Between friend and friend, as David and Jonathan made a covenant together (1 Sam. 20:16). Now God makes a covenant with his people in all these ways. As a king he rules and defends us, and we as his subjects promise to be at his command and to obey him. As a wife promises to be for her husband alone, and he for her only, so the church promises that she will be for Christ alone, and he for her (Jer. 3:14; Hos. 3:3). The covenant of friendship implies not only subjection and affection, but communication of thoughts and counsels to one another, and to do all things out of friendship and love, heartily and readily (Ps. 25:14, 22; Ps. 32:8; Ps. 119:5, 24).

-4. We have Christ by way of acceptance. "To as many as received him he gave power to become the sons of God" (John 1:12). To receive him is to receive him into a house or temple, as may be gathered from the preceding verse; "he came into his own," eis ta idia, his own place or home. When we thus receive him, as into his own place, we have him.

How do we receive Christ as into a temple? In three ways: -1. By preparing a way for him to come into his holy temple (Mal. 3:1). -2. When Christ has come into our hearts, if we would keep him there, we must see that there is no common or unclean thing found there (2 Cor. 6:16-18). This temple is a holy place; therefore put away not only unclean but common things. All your affairs must be dedicated to the

Lord. -3. To receive Christ into his temple is to look well to the charge of God's holy offerings. God would have every man in particular to take the charge of his holy things on himself, and not to put it off on others. Let everyone keep his charge, offer up his daily sacrifice and his service for the sabbath. All God's offerings must be taken care of, and if we do thus, God will rest in his holy temple forever (Exod. 15:2).

What is it to have the Son? There are three things implied in having the Son.

-1. Not resting in any of the benefits of Christ, but chiefly seeking to have the Son himself. Yea further, a true Christian who seeks Christ seeks him without respect to profit, gain, or happiness, either here or in this life. He does not seek the ordinances to profit himself, but to find Christ in them.

A child of God is said to have the Son when he has the Spirit of the Son (2 Cor. 3:17). Having spoken before of a Spirit of ministration and grace, Paul says, "The Lord is that Spirit"; not only because he is the giver of it, but because there is a secret union between Christ and his Spirit, so that if you have the one, you have the other (Rom. 8:9). He who has the Son has the Spirit of the Son (Gal. 4:6), and is made conformable to his image.

There is a twofold Spirit by which we are knit to Christ and Christ to us: a Spirit of union and a Spirit of liberty.

-1. He who has fellowship with Christ has a Spirit of union, by which he is made one with him. Christ prays that all believers may be one "as we are one" (John 17:21); God in Christ by the Spirit, and Christ in us by the same Spirit; and thus "of his fullness we all received, and grace for grace" (John 1:16). We are predestinated to be made like the image of Christ (Rom. 8:29).

There is a threefold conformity and likeness between Christ and us, and that is wrought by the Spirit. (a) We are like him in his nature (2 Pet. 1:4). By the precious promises we are made partakers of the divine nature, so that we are meek as he was, lowly as he was, innocent and harmless as he was; the Spirit of God stamps the same image on us that was on Christ (John 1:16). (b) There is a conformity in offices: he has made us priests, kings, and prophets to his Father (Rev. 1:6). (c) There is a conformity in states. In this world our Saviour went through a double state, of humiliation and of exaltation. Such is a Christian's state: "Many were the afflictions of the righteous" (Ps. 34:19); there is his humiliation; "but the Lord delivers him out of all"; there is his exaltation, for by those deliverances he makes them glorious. "Since you seek a proof of Christ speaking in me; as he was crucified through weakness and yet lives in me by the power of God" (2 Cor. 13:4); even so we are weak with him, that is, in outward show. Yet when Christ was most debased, he showed forth most power; so a Christian has God's power most magnified in him in his greatest debasements and weaknesses; never is he more glorious than when most debased. Hence those strange phrases: we are dead with Christ (Col. 2:20), risen with Christ (Col. 3:1), crucified with Christ (Rom. 6:6); that is, by the same Spirit of Christ in us, we are so knit with him that we are made of the same state with him; as he was weak and base, and yet glorious, so are we.

-2. There is a Spirit of liberty. Nothing better expresses the temper of the Son than a Spirit of liberty (2 Cor. 3:17; John 8:36). His liberty is a real liberty. (a) Liberty from the fear of sin, of hell, of the grave, and of all his enemies. (b) Liberty from the dominion of sin. (c) Liberty from being servant unto men (1 Cor. 7:23). Though they should be subject to their masters, yet now they should not serve them in a slavish manner, but with freedom of spirit in obedience to Christ, heartily and readily. (d) The Spirit of God that sets me free from the service of men, makes me free to every duty of God. The Spirit that set me at liberty from Satan will make me run in the ways of God's commandments with an enlarged heart.

-3. We are said to have the Son when we have Christ not

only for our Saviour, but for our Prince; for God exalted him to be both Prince and Saviour (Acts 5:31). It would be a dishonor for God to save those whom he cannot rule; to deliver them from Satan and yet leave them in their sins. God sent his Son not only to save but to rule us.

In two ways we are said to have Christ as our Prince:

a. When we resign up ourselves in obedience to him; when we have not a thought within us that is not subject to him (2 Cor. 10:4, 5; Prov. 12:5). But whose heart is so right that every thought is subject to the will of Christ? Do not we all have many vain thoughts within us? (Jer. 4:14). I answer, he will not have these vain thoughts lodging in him. They may indeed rush in upon him, as sturdy beggars into a house, and they would be masters; but a Christian does not allow them to lodge there. He does not rest until they are thrown out; they find no welcome in his heart.

b. To have Christ as our Prince is not only to serve him, but to give him princely service (Mal. 1:8). Let us not serve him with blind and lame sacrifices, but with the best and fattest. Crucify your fattest and dearest lusts to him; let him have your best parts and best affections. Righteous Abel brought to God the firstlings of his flock, and the fat thereof (Gen. 4:4). So let God have your first years and the strength of your affections; do not give him your decrepit old age. Says David, "I will not offer to God that which cost me nothing" (2 Sam. 24:24).

"He that has the Son has life." Thus if we find signs of life in us, we may with certainty conclude that we have the Son as well. Our spiritual life may be discerned three ways: by the causes, by the effects, and by the properties.

-1. For the causes, the Holy Spirit gave us three causes of our spiritual life.

a. God's own good pleasure. "Of his own will he begot us" (James 1:18). St. John proves this by denying all other causes (John 1:13): "not of blood"; that is, not of parentage, for godly parents may have wicked children; "nor of flesh"; that is, not of corrupt nature; "not of the will of man"; that is, not of the will of our best friends, who desire it and pray for it, unless God sets in with his good pleasure. This is an evident sign of the life of grace. A natural man thinks well of himself, that he has always had a good nature, and his friends could say nothing against him. But a regenerate Christian acknowledges that he had no heart to goodness by nature, but he acknowledges with Paul, "When it pleased God to call me by his grace and to reveal Christ in me, then I lived" (Gal. 1:15, 16); but not before. A living soul never attributes anything to his good nature, when it pleases God to call him to his grace.

 b. A word of promise. All who are from Abraham's loins are not children of Abraham, but only the seed of the promise, as Isaac. And lest you should think it belongs to Isaac only, he makes it common to all the elect (Gal. 4:28).

 c. A third cause of life of the Spirit of God (John 3:6). The Spirit is shed abroad into the heart of every regenerate man, so that he has not the same spirit he had before. Now a man's spirit is the bent and inclination of the soul (Eph. 4:23). The soul and the body are the same as before; but now they have new thoughts, judgments, and affections, so that their heart is far from earthly things, and set on heavenly things. "All things have become new" (2 Cor. 5:17); a new heart, new conference, new employment, new company, a new spirit for the whole man. He who finds it thus has life.

–2. A second sort of signs is from the effects of this spiritual life.

 a. Justification or pardon of sins is a principal part of our spiritual life (Ps. 32:2, 3). And this is called justification to life (Rom. 5:18). A condemned man's pardon is the life of the man; so the pardon of our sins is the life of our souls. Now this has three effects: (i) An inward peace of conscience, some inward satisfaction that he never found before. (ii) A serious and constant care to preserve that life and peace, so that you will let all go rather than the peace of your conscience. (iii) The sign which our Saviour gives: "Her sins are forgiven her, because she loved much" (Luke 7:47). He who loves much has much forgiven him.

b. Sanctification, both in heart and in life. First, in the heart. (i) In the conversion of a sinner; he is taken up with two contrary emotions; joy that God should have such mercy on him, and yet grief and sorrow for his sins by which he has offended so merciful a God. (ii) In the duties of worship there is another combination of affections, and that is joy and fear: "Rejoice before him with trembling" (Ps. 2:11). When grace is lively and stirring, a Christian comes with holy fear and awesomeness, and yet none come with more joy and holiness. (iii) Take a godly man in tribulations, when he is most oppressed with afflictions; then is the heart most joyous. This was an argument for the sincerity of the Thessalonians: "Receiving the word in much affliction and joy in the Holy Spirit" (1 Thess. 1:6). No tribulation is joyous to nature, and yet Paul says, "We rejoice in tribulation" (Rom. 5:3). (iv) There is a mixture of affections in his dealing with men. You shall find a Christian very patient, and yet without all forbearance; very patient, and yet by no means bearing with evil (Rev. 2:2); injuries upon himself he endures with patience, but injuries against God he will by no means bear. (v) You will find gentleness and meekness mixed with much austerity and stiffness. (vi) There is a modesty mixed with magnanimity, a thing not easily found in moral virtue. Paul looks at all his outward privileges as dross and dung in comparison to Christ (Eph. 3:8); yet this modest man reacts with all boldness when the magistrates had whipped him and his companions, and would have sent them away; says he, "No, but let them come and fetch us" (Acts 10:37). (vi) There is another mixture of emotions in a Christian, busy diligence in worldly affairs and yet a dead-heartedness to the world. For a man to rise early and sit up late, follow his work hard, take much pains, is not a thing to be despised (Prov. 10:14; Prov. 31:27); but yet the same person must be dead to the world; his heart must be set on things above. These things are not his life, for that is laid up in Christ.

Second, we come to the outward effects of sanctification, as they are expressed in the life of a Christian, and they are comparable to the effects of natural life. The effects of natural life are principally five: motion, feeding, growth, purging, and the begetting of its kind.

(i) Motion. If a man has a spiritual motion in his proper place, it is a sign of spiritual life. Sometimes an unregenerate man reaches out of his place, reaching to higher matters and more ambitious thoughts than his calling leads to; these spring not from an inward principle of grace, but from levity of heart. It is one thing to move to spiritual duties out of an inward inclination and affection to them, but another thing to move out of levity or desire of eminence; it is one thing to move to them out of love, another thing to move to them out of respect, credit, or profit.

(ii) Feeding. Christ himself gives this sign. "Whoever eats my flesh and drinks my blood has eternal life" (John 6:54). This is not meant of the sacrament, for it was not then instituted, but of Christ himself. But when God has instituted ordinances, this is a sure sign of life if in every ordinance we feed on Christ, on his blood. He who feeds not, lives not; he who forbears his meat and forbears it long, cannot live.

(iii) Growth. That which lives grows, until it comes to full maturity; and then it either stands or begins to decay. But a spiritual life grows up to full perfection, and then it continues in that perfect state forever in heaven (Eph. 4:11, 12; Col. 2:19; 1 Pet. 2:2; 1 Pet. 3:18). If a Christian grows, he lives. True, a Christian may by some corrupt lusts waste his best graces, like a thief in a candle; but if he is a living Christian, he strives against them. He considers from where he has fallen, and recovers himself and does his first works (Rev. 2:4).

(iv) Repentance is the purge of the soul; it expels out evil lusts, and then we do more at the last than at the first (Rev. 2:17). Life has an expulsive power to expel that which is dangerous to it.

(v) A fifth act of life is the begetting of its kind. Though nature is weak at first, it soon grows up to this ability; so grace, as it grows, has a mind to beget others. The woman of Samaria ran to all her neighbors and told them she had met with one who had told her all that ever she did: "Is not this the Christ?" (John 4:29) Try yourself by these signs.

-3. This life may be discerned by the properties of it. These are principally three.

a. Wherever life is, there is some warmth. When Elisha had stretched himself over the dead child, the flesh began to wax warm (2 Kings 4:34). So the presence of the Spirit united to the soul of man is the cause of all spiritual heat (Rom. 12:11). Therefore the Spirit is compared to fire (Matt. 3:11; 1 Thess. 5:19).

b. Where life is, there is some pliableness and flexibleness; a dead carcass is always stiff. The wisdom that is from above is gentle and easy to be entreated (James 3:17).

There are four things in this pliableness. (i) First, the living Christian is easily pleased with any endeavors (1 Pet. 3:8). If a man is froward and hard to please, it is a sign he is stiff and dead. (ii) If he is offended, he is easy to be entreated (James 3:17). It is a sign of a reprobate to be implacable (Rom. 3:1). (iii) If he has offended another, he is willing to yield to that man whom he has offended; so much stiffness, so much deadness. (iv) There is this gentleness in every living Christian: he is willing to deny himself upon unequal terms. When he might stand upon his right, yet he yields his right rather than see any offense grow; so Abraham did to Lot (Gen. 13:8, 9). If we find it thus, we are loving Christians; but if men are difficult to please, and will not yield but stand upon their right to the utmost, then they are in a deep faint or dead.

While the body is alive it is pleasant; a dead carcass is very unsavory. Every living Christian is a sweet savor to God; his words are savory (Col. 4:5, 6; Eph. 4:29). His works are savory in the nostrils of God and man (Eph. 5:10). But if your speech and manner are unsavory and profane, are you not then carnal? But a good Christian so conducts himself that the bowels of the saints are refreshed by him.

Use 1. This shows us the dangerous condition of every soul that has not Christ. He has no life; if we are without Christ, we are dead in trespasses and sins (Eph. 2:1, 5). By nature we have not this kind of life.

Use 2. Let us mourn for our friends who yet lie in the state of nature. Have you a child, or wife, or friend who is in the state of nature? Look at them as dead children and dead friends; how bitterly we should mourn for them (Zech. 12:10).

Use 4. To condemn the church of Rome, which thinks that by nature men have free will to lay hold on Christ. I would ask them, when they lay hold of Christ, whether or not they have Christ before. Before they receive him, they obviously have him not; and if they have him not, they are dead men, and how shall they lay hold on Christ?

Briefly, let us consider motives and means to lay hold on Christ.

-1. For motives: (a) The sweetness of life. (b) If we have Christ we have life, and that in abundance. You have all the promises, for in him they are yea and amen (2 Cor. 1:20). And all the blessings of God are yours, both spiritual (Eph. 1:3) and temporal (1 Tim. 4:8). If you have Christ, the world is yours; you have all things (Rom. 8:32).

-2. For means: (a) Consider how dead and lost you are by nature. Christ came to call those who feel themselves lost (Luke 19:10; Matt. 9:12, 13). (b) If you know any sin in yourself, rid your hands of it. (c) Seek the Lord while he may be found (Isa. 55:6). Only seek him, and he will be found. How are we to seek him? By longing and thirsting after him, and by seeking him in the means of grace, and by seeking him in prayer.

1 John 5:13

"These things have I written unto you who believe on the name of the Son of God, that you may know that you have eternal life, and that you may believe on the name of the Son of God."

We now come to the beginning of the conclusion of this whole epistle. St. John sets down: -1. The persons to whom he writes, "you who believe." -2. The end for which he writes these things. The end is twofold: that you may know that you have eternal life, and that you may believe on the name of the Son of God.

These words afford three notes.

Doct. 1. This epistle of John was written and delivered to believers only.

This is evident not only in this text but in other places in the epistle. He wrote it to those who by reading it might attain to full joy (1:4). It is also evident by recounting the sorts of persons to whom he wrote: babes, young men, and fathers (2:12-14), who were all believers (4:4). All his epistles were written to believers, as were those of the other apostles and of our Saviour. This gives us just occasion to inquire: -1. Why they were written to believers. -2. Why to them only.

He writes to believers to give them special help and benefit. The benefits of these epistles were:

-1. Teaching (2 Thess. 2:2).

-2. Putting them in remembrance (2 Pet. 1:22, 23).

-3. Stirring them up to practice what they knew (2 Pet. 1:2, 3).

-4. To humble the spirits of those who were puffed up (2 Cor. 7, 8).

-5. That they might be strengthened in their faith (1 John 5:13).

-6. That their hearts might be filled with joy (1 John 1:4).

-7. That their writings might be the foundation of the

faith of all Christians to the end of the world. These epistles have furnished matter for the preaching of the ministers, and by them the men of God are fully furnished, made perfect to every good work (2 Tim. 4:16, 17).

He writes to believers only. These writings will be of little help or use to others until they are brought to believe. It is with the apostles' writings as with prophecies and not miracles: miracles are for those who believe not, though they may confirm believers; but believers should attend chiefly to prophecies. Faith comes not by reading, but by hearing; had God ordained that reading should be effectual to the conversion of men, he would have confirmed it by miracles, as he did the preaching of the apostles. Again, had their writings been sanctified for the conversion of men, they would have sent them abroad to the most remote places of the world, where they were never likely to come; but we see they did not, but rather took pains themselves to go about the world (Rom. 10:15-18).

But did not God sometimes bless the law to the conversion of men? (Deut. 31:10-13) And why should not the reading of the gospel be as effectual now, since it has more power than the law?

–1. The reading spoken of in Deut. 31 was a solemn reading at the year of solemn release, which was but once in seven years. The reason for this was that the year of release typified our redemption by Christ; therefore to denote that God could give an extraordinary blessing to the reading of the law, and to show that those were to be released by Christ, they read with understanding and profit. But you do not read that God blessed the ordinary reading of the law to this end.

–2. He does not speak of bare reading, but of expounding and applying it; for we read that they did so at that very feast (Neh. 7:73; 8:4-9).

Use 1. This may show us why so many good books written by learned and godly men, have so little prevailed to convert any of the Papists. There are few or none converted by our writings; and no wonder, for the writings of the apostles themselves were not sanctified to this end. Writings have always been useful to convince, to establish, to satisfy, to comfort; but none have prevailed to convert any.

Use 2. The same may be said of our reading ministers. Look at congregations where they have only readings; you shall find them as ignorant of Christ and empty of grace as if they had never heard of such things. Let this not be called uncharitable; is it more charitable to flatter you in your woeful condition to your destruction, or to tell you of your danger? "Israel had been without the true God and without a teaching priest" (2 Chron. 15:2, 3). It is likely that they had the law read in their synagogues; this they could not be said to be ignorant of, but yet they are said to be without God, because they had not a priest to teach.

Use 3. Let all believers be diligent to learn of the writings of St. John and the other apostles. Shall the Holy Spirit have a hand to write, and shall we not have a hand to receive or an eye to read? How much then is the church of Rome to blame, for they lock up those writings from the people that they may not hear them, except in an unknown tongue which they understand not! Sometimes the priests understand not the Latin they read; much less can they expound it.

Use 4. Is the word of no profit or benefit to carnal men? Yes, surely it is. (a) By hearing it expounded they may be brought to faith. (b) The reading itself is useful to beget knowledge, to stir up their memories, to quicken their desires. (c) The word read discovers what sin is, and thus they are kept in civil confirmity and made moral men. But let them be diligent in hearing the word preached, for where reading prevails not, hearing may (Rom. 10:17).

Use 5. Let all believers not only read, but expect and look for those benefits before mentioned. If you do not find those benefits by reading, you read unprofitably and take God's ordinance in vain.

Now for the ends of St. John's writings, which were two: that they might know they had eternal life, and that they might believe on the Name of the Son of God.

Doct. 2. Those who believe on the name of Jesus Christ may come to know they have eternal life by reading the epistles of John.

-1. He sets before them where eternal life is to be found, and that is in Jesus Christ (v. 12).

-2. He directs them to certain means by which they may obtain eternal life. (a) Confession of sins (1:9). (b) Looking up to Christ as our Propitiation and Advocate (2:1, 2). (c) Walking in the light (1:8, 9).

-3. He gives certain signs by which we may know whether we are in a state of eternal life. (a) Walking in the light (1:7). (b) Keeping his commandments (2:3). (c) Purifying ourselves from sin (3:3). (d) Loving our brethren (3:14). (e) Having boldness toward God (3:21).

Use 1. This may be a just refutation of that Popish doctrine that we cannot know we have eternal life; if that were true, St. John's end in writing these epistles is disappointed; and not only St. John, but the Holy Spirit himself is deceived. This doctrine of doubtings is a sufficient discouragement against their religion. That church that trains up herself and her children to be ignorant of their Father, is not the true spouse of Christ, but a harlot. The church of Rome has mixed herself with so many false gods that she knows not of whom her children are begotten.

Use 2. It condemns their excluding the common people from reading the scriptures. If by them we may come to know Christ and have eternal life, then in taking them away you take away a principal means of salvation.

Use 3. If you are doubtful of your state, above all the writings of the apostles read this epistle. This was the main scope of St. John, that their joy might be full and that they might know they have eternal life. Here you shall find a good groundwork of your good state.

Use 4. Let us know what we have profited by reading. It is

a usual thing to content ourselves with reading a chapter and praying every morning, and our conscience is not satisfied if we omit it. But a man may read and pray and yet get no good; if you would read profitably, read that you may know that you have eternal life. In reading learn to search out diligently the knowledge of your state.

Doct. 3. It was one of the holy ends and scope of the holy scriptures, that believers might believe.

St. John wrote his gospel for this end, that they might believe (John 20:31). Though believing had already been wrought, yet they who believe need to believe more. The word is the mighty power to lead believers from faith to faith (Rom. 1:17); that is, from one degree of faith to another.

Why must believers believe? Why must faith increase?

-1. Defects are found in believers, and they need to increase and grow up to supply these.

a. They need to grow up to the belief of some principles which they did not believe before; as many of the apostles did not believe the resurrection of Christ. The Thessalonians thought Christ would come suddenly, and therefore began to lay aside all diligence in their outward callings (2 Thess. 2). The Galatians were lacking in believing justification by faith, and therefore Paul writes to them.

b. Sometimes there is something wanting in the habit or grace of faith. Paul prays that the Colossians might be rooted and established in the faith (Col. 2:7). A young plant may be weak and easily rooted up; so a Christian may have some rooting in Christ and yet lack sound roots and firmness of faith.

c. Faith may be lacking in the sense of it. A Christian may have attained a great measure of lively faith, and yet be in doubt whether he has faith or not; he needs more faith to be assured that he has faith. Paul trusted that he would long continue with the Philippians, for the furtherance and joy of their faith (Phil. 1:25). So we sometimes need to be brought further, from faith to joyful faith.

d. Faith needs to be increased in its acts, which are persuasion and trust in Christ. When Peter walked on the water, he was persuaded that Christ would save him; but when he was afraid and began to sink, Christ reproves him, "O you of little faith" (Matt. 14:30, 31). So with the two disciples who went to Emmaus: "We trusted it had been he who should have delivered Israel"; implying that they now were afraid they had been deceived. And what says Christ? "O fools and slow of heart to believe" (Luke 24:44).

e. Faith needs to grow in fruits. One fruit of faith is love (Gal. 5:6). Now a Christian may leave his first love and lose his first works (Rev. 2:2, 3); therefore a Christian needs to grow in the increase of the fruits of faith, that his last works may be more than the first.

-2. There is a marvelous power in scripture to supply all those defects, whether preached, conferred about, read, examined, or meditated on.

a. The scriptures preached are the power of God unto salvation (Rom. 1:16, 17). Their writings are good helps this way, but yet their personal presence and preaching are much more effectual. Therefore Paul prays that he might come to the Thessalonians, that he might perfect what was lacking in their faith (1 Thess. 3:10, 11).

b. The word conferred about is very effectual to increase faith. When the two disciples were conferring together and their hearts were sad, Christ comes in with them and warms their hearts, so that their faith was confirmed; and they returned to Jerusalem and told the disciples, "The Lord has risen indeed." Now they had no doubt of it. And you know of Philip's conference with the eunuch, which brought him to believe with all his heart.

c. The word read is of such force that by reading you may believe (John 20:31). By reading the scriptures, believers are established in the faith.

d. When hearers bring things to the balance of the sanctuary, this examining increases faith. Yea, it sometimes begets faith in those who believed not before, as in the

Bereans (Acts 17:11, 12). Many times when a Christian hears the word of God, he is not well persuaded of what is taught; but let him meditate on it and examine it, and often the word examined works and increases faith, when the word preached did not.

e. The word meditated on is of special use to increase our faith, to make us more comfortable and fruitful, and rooted in our faith (Ps. 1:3, 4). When a man delights and meditates in the word day and night, he shall be like a tree planted by the riverside, well watered, well rooted, and fruitful in every season. In every condition of life he brings forth seasonable fruit.

Use 1. Here we may try a faithful minister and a faithful Christian. When St. John had begun faith in them, he would not leave them so, thinking that God would perfect what he had begun, and thus he could leave them and turn to others. His care, and the care of every faithful minister, is to be desirous to grow in faith and to confirm and establish others in the faith.

So for Christians. It is a sign of a good heart not only to labor for truth of faith, but also for growth of faith. A man needs a great deal of faith to be plenteous in love, and to heal offenses as Christ requires. We have so many temptations to meet with that above all we need to take the shield of faith (Eph. 6:6), the shield that covers the whole body.

Use 2. It reproves the sacrilegious, ungodly, and uncharitable practice of the Church of Rome, which takes away the scripture from the people. St. John writes these things that they might believe; then take away the scriptures, and you make them no better than infidels.

Use 3. For you who do believe. Be frequent in reading the word, for it was written to you, that you might believe. Meditate on it day and night. To the king himself, whose employments were greatest, the Lord laid a charge to read the book of the law all the days of his life (Deut. 17:14). And much more is every private man bound to it. Take away the word, and you take away the fuel of your faith.

1 John 5:14, 15

"And this is the confidence that we have in him, that if we ask anything according to his will, he hears us. And if we know that he hears us, whatever we ask, then we know that we have the petitions that we desired of him."

In v.13 the apostle had mentioned a purpose of his writing, that they might believe on the name of the Son of God. Now he exhorts Christians to this duty (vv. 14-16) by three arguments.

-1. The confidence such may have of the hearing of their petitions (v. 14).

-2. The certain knowledge they may have that their prayers are granted.

-3. The prevalence of our prayers with God; as we shall be assured of the granting of our petitions, so we shall thereby obtain life for our brother, if he has not sinned a sin unto death.

Doct. If we pray according to God's will, God will grant it according to our will.

Notable is that encouragement Christ gave to the woman, "Great is your faith; be it unto you even as you will" (Matt. 15:26). As if God would let such into his privy treasury and grant them what they desired.

What is it to pray according to God's will?

-1. When we pray for things which are agreeable to God's will, viz. his revealed will; we should ask nothing but what he commands us. In the Lord's Prayer Christ tells us what he would have us pray for; for those things we have warrant to pray.

-2. When, whatever we ask, we ask with submission of our wills to God's will. So did Christ himself (Matt. 26:39).

-3. Whatever we pray for, God commands us to ask it in Christ's name. This requires two graces, humility and faith.

a. Humility of spirit in prayer is expressed in four acts. (i) We acknowledge ourselves less than the least of God's mercies (Gen. 32:10), so that if God should grant us nothing we would justify God. (ii) We pray in a sense of our insufficiency to think a good thought, much less to pray according to God's will (2 Cor. 3:8; Rom. 8:26). (c) A man prays in humility when he does not desire God to satisfy any of his sinful lusts, but that God's will may be done (Matt. 26:39). (d) To pray in humility is to make mention of no mediation except that of Christ. The Gnostics made a show of humility, as not being so bold as to have immediate access to God, and therefore they put up their prayers through the mediation of some angel (Col. 2:18); but to go lower than God allows is pride of heart.

-2. To pray in the name of Christ is to pray in faith. Now faith is also expressed in four acts. (a) Faith directs us to put up our prayers only to him on whom we believe (Rom. 10:14). But we believe only in God; therefore neither saints nor angels, nor the mother of Christ, are to be prayed to, but we are to pray to our Father only (Gal. 4:5, 6; Rom. 8:15). (b) Faith makes us come with childlike confidence to God our Father: first as our heavenly Father in Christ, and well pleased in Christ as loving us himself (John 16:36), and second, as a Father Almighty, full of goodness, readier to give than we to ask. (c) A third act of faith is for a man to come truly cleaving to Christ, not debating whether it is best to leave our lusts or not, whether it is better to become a Christian or not. This wavering cannot stand with faith, for by it one becomes a double-minded man, with a heart for God and a heart for the world; sometimes for God, sometimes for his own lusts. Let not this man think that he shall receive anything (James 1:6-8). (d) A fourth act of faith is to believe that what we have asked according to God's will, he will certainly grant (Matt. 11:24). As far as you have asked with submission to his will, so far he will grant you according to your will. Though he defer, yet know that your prayers are heard; he will either grant what you ask, or what he knows will be better for you and as welcome to you. God looks not so much at the petition as at the end you aim at in asking such a blessing; and that he will grant even when he seems to deny us our petitions.

Christ was heard in what he prayed for (Heb. 5:9). How was he heard? Did he not drink the cup he prayed against? True, but yet he was heard:

-1. Christ's will was that his Father's will might be fulfilled, not his; in this he was heard.

-2. It is said he was heard in that he feared; though he did drink of the cup, yet he was saved from those fears and terrors that overwhelmed him.

-3. The main end of Christ's prayer was that his church might be redeemed, which God granted; so God granted the end of his petition, though not the thing itself.

So Moses prayed earnestly that he might go over and see the good land; God told him he should not go over, yet God let him see that good land as well as if he had gone over. Even when God is displeased with our weak and unworthy prayers, as he was with Moses (Deut. 3:22-28), yet then he knows how to grant what we aimed at. And this magnifies the name of Christ, that though in our own name we should never find acceptance, yet in Christ's name he will grant our petitions.

We pray according to the will of God when we pray according to his will revealed in our hearts (Jude 20; Eph. 6:18). Now we pray according to God's will revealed in the Spirit in three ways.

-1. When the Spirit raises our hearts to reach forth with longings and breathings after the blessings we want. Thus Hannah poured forth her soul unto God (1 Sam. 1:15). She expressed not so much in words as in the reaching of her spirit after the blessing she prayed for. "With my soul within me I have desired thee" (Isa. 26:9); as if there were another Spirit within his spirit. When we pray in a greater measure of strength than our own hearts could reach to, such a prayer is of the Spirit.

-2. When we pray with fervency and earnestness (James 5:16). This is called wrestling and striving with God (Rom. 15:30). When our hearts are so set on God's favor that they will not let go until they have prevailed with God (Gen. 32: 10, 24, 25, 26), this is to pray with the Spirit.

-3. We pray in the Spirit when we persevere in praying and are importunate with God. This is expressed by the importunity of the widow who prevailed with the unjust judge (Luke 18:1-10). Shall a sinful judge, a mortal man, be prevailed upon by a poor widow, and shall not God much more avenge his elect that cry to him day and night? You may think God does not regard your prayers, but he is more troubled with your prayers than this judge was troubled by the widow's cries, so that he cannot rest until he has fulfilled your desires.

Why are our prayers answered when we ask in the name of Christ?

-1. Because when we pray according to God's will, he fulfills his own will when he grants our petitions. It is God's will that we should pray so, and God's will must be fulfilled.

-2. Because when we pray according to the will of God in the name of Christ, our prayer is Christ's prayer. When you send a child or servant to a friend for anything in your name, the request is yours; and he who denies your child or servant denies you. So God can no more deny a prayer put up in Christ's name than he can deny Christ himself (John 16:23, 24).

-3. Because the Spirit intercedes in such a prayer. A prayer put up in this way is the prayer of the Holy Spirit, and God knows the meaning of his Spirit (Rom. 8:26). God knows that our prayers would be weak and cold unless there were another Spirit besides our own. Therefore if he discerns his own Spirit in our prayers, he cannot deny his Spirit; and further, as the Spirit makes intercession for us, so Christ himself prays for us (Rom. 8:34). He takes up all our prayers for us as the great Master of requests, and does so perfume them and take all weakness out of them that he presents them as a sweet odor unto God (Rev. 8:3).

Use 1. Let us learn to pray well.

a. Be certain that you are not of a wavering double mind (James 1:6-8); partly for God and partly for yourself. Pray with a single heart (Acts 11:21). That is: (i) Give up your heart wholly to God. (ii) Be careful to keep all his commandments; for as we hearken to God's commandments, so he will hearken to our prayers.

b. Have respect to pray according to God's will in faith and humility.

Use 2. If you do pray according to God's will, be sure that God will grant your petition according to your will. God has spoken it, and therefore he will not deny it.

Doct. Those who do believe on the name of Christ for salvation may come to have confidence and knowledge of the hearing and having of all their petitions.

How do these two great benefits, confidence and knowledge of granting our prayers, spring from what St. John has written in this epistle? Four things concur in this confidence, all of which are mentioned and insisted upon by St. John in this epistle.

-1. Our adoption is expressed by St. John (3:1). He marvels at the admirable love of God in looking on us poor earthworms, and raising us up to be sons and daughters of God. So this is the first ground of our confidence in prayer, our adoption (Gal. 4:5, 6; Rom. 8:15). To whom may a son come more boldly than to his father?

-2. Christ's advocation breeds confidence in us (2:1, 2). Christ pleads with his Father on our behalf for the hearing of our petitions, and for the granting of what we want. An advocate puts the petition, which may be rudely drawn by a man, into the form of a law, and so it holds before the judge; so Christ does with our prayers. He puts them into a right form, and so pleads for us.

-3. The atonement or propitiation of Christ is another

be afraid that his prayers shall never be heard, as he is so sinful and unclean, St. John assures us that he is the propitiation for our sins. He is not only an advocate but a propitiation, to make atonement for our sins so that they shall not hinder our acceptance.

-4. The anointing of the Spirit, by which we know all things (3:20) is another ground of much confidence. Though we are blind and dull, and know not what God does for us in our prayers, Christ like an advocate sends down his Spirit, and lets us know how all things go. This unction teaches us all things (1 Cor. 2:12).

How does the Spirit show us the hearing of our petitions?

-1. By helping us to pray. We know our own hearts are dead and strait, not able to put up any good prayer; therefore if the Spirit comes like oil, and makes us pray affectionately and sensibly, we know a prayer well made cannot speed ill. A prayer made by God's Spirit must be heard, for God knows the meaniing of his Spirit (Rom. 8:26).

-2. By putting in us a persuasion of faith, that what we pray for God will answer (Matt. 11:23, 24). And so God gives us an Amen in our hearts.. David was in a sore trial and affliction (Ps. 6:8); he prays to God. Then what says he? "Away from me, all you workers of iniquity; for the Lord has heard the voice of my weeping." In the midst of his mourning this unction fills him with a persuasion that his prayers will be granted.

-3. This Spirit works as a Spirit of hope, and this stirs us up to patient waiting on God, until he answers. When God gives us spirits to wait on him, he seals up to us the grant of our petitions. If I put up a lawful petition to a wise prince and he bids me wait for it, I count it granted; so if I put up a prayer and God gives me a heart to wait for it, I may be sure he will grant it.

-4. This Spirit is a Spirit of fear (Ps. 145:9). Do you walk in your Christian course depending upon Christ, reverencing his name and ordinances? Take comfort then; for God will fulfill the desires of those who fear him (Jer. 32:40).

If he gives us a reverent heart that keeps us from departing from him, and if he promises not to depart from us, then he will be near when we call upon him; and this is from the unction of the Spirit which makes us profit in all our ways (Isa. 11:2, 3).

-5. This is a Spirit of obedience, and obedience gives us good assurance of the hearing of our petitions (3:21). For as we listen to God, so God listens to us (Prov. 28:9; Judg. 9:7). If we say, "Speak, Lord, for thy servant hears" (1 Sam. 3:5), then what we speak God will hear. An obedient Christian is a powerful petitioner, mighty in prayer.

Use 1. This will take our hearts from confidence in any worldly thing, and encourages them to believe on the name of Jesus Christ. This gives us not only salvation but a confidence that our prayers will all be heard.

Use 2. If you believe in Christ, here is a method by which you may be sure of the grant of your petitions. (a) Be sure of your adoption, for that breeds much assurance in prayer. (b) Meditate much on Christ, for he is your advocate and atonement for your sins. (c) Labor for a Spirit of faith and hope, fear and obedience; and so you shall grow up to confidence and knowledge that your prayers are granted. Many a Christian falls short of this confidence because he does not consider who helps him with his prayers, who makes intercession for him; or else he is lacking in some of those graces, and so his prayers are full of doubtings.

Use 3. To console all who believe on Christ; whatever we ask according to his will, he hears us. How comfortable then is the condition of a believer. Be his wants ever so great, if he can but pray well, he may go on comfortably.

1 John 5:16

"If any man see his brother sin a sin which is not unto death, he shall ask, and he shall give him life for those who do not sin unto death. There is a sin unto death; I do not say that he shall pray for it."

These words contain a third motive to stir us up to believe on Christ, and that is from another benefit which we shall be able to bestow on our brethren. Our prayer shall give them life.

Observe in the words:

-1. A promise to those who shall pray for their brother who sins a sin not unto death: he shall give him life.

-2. An exception restraining a man's prayer: the sin unto death.

-3. The prevention of an objection (v. 17). All unrighteousness is sin, and the wages of sin is death (Rom. 6:23). And therefore this promise is of no effect, for every sin is a sin unto death. To this St. John answers that there is yet a sin not unto death. True, every sin deserves death, but every sin does not cut off all hope of recovery. Christ said of Lazarus that his sickness was not unto death (John 11:4); yet he died. Christ meant that his sickness was not irrecoverable, because he was raised to life again. So every sin is unto death, but every sin is not irrecoverable; a man may be raised to it out of life.

Doct. A believing Christian is not to hide his eyes from beholding and observing the sins of his brethren.

"If any man see his brother sin"; he may see it and ought to see it. Paul did not turn away his eyes from seeing Peter's dissembling (Gal. 2:14), but took note of it and reproved him. "Take heed lest there be in any of you an evil heart of unbelief" (Heb. 3:12, 13); he speaks not only of a man's self, but of his brother; and therefore he propounds a collective means to help them, "exhorting one another" (Heb. 10:24).

-1. Our first reason to perform this duty is the love we owe to our brethren. God requires larger love toward our brethren than toward our oxen or asses, and yet God requires that if we see them lying under their burden, we should help them up (Deut. 22:4). Much more our brethren's souls; if we see them going astray or sinking under the burden of sin, we should raise them up again.

-2. The love we owe to ourselves. We shall reap a benefit by it: we shall learn to keep better watch ourselves, when we see our brethren fall. We must not by their falls grow high-minded, and pride ourselves that we are not so bad as they, but we are to fear (Rom. 11:20).

With what eyes should we look at the falls of our brethren?

-1. Not with a partial or hypocritical eye (Matt. 7:3-5). We must so look at the mote in their eye as to see a beam in our own. We would see as great sins in ourselves, or greater, if God did not restrain us, for we all have the same root of evil, and would break out into as bad distempers as any if God did not hold us back.

-2. We must not observe them with a censorious eye; we love to be prying into other men's sins, not to heal them but to censure them. St. James reproves this: "Be not many masters" (James 3:1-3); that is, be not of a master-like spirit, not busy in other men's matters.

-3. Do not look at them with an envious, malicious eye. Jeremiah complains of this: "All my familiars watched for my haltings" (Jer. 20:10), watching for an advantage to undermine their brother.

-4. Let us abhor the wanton eye, which is twofold. (a) A man is not humbled at the sight of his brother's sins, but puffed up by them, like the proud Pharisee (Luke 18:9, 10); he built his comfort on the falls of others. (b) A man sees his brother's sin with a wanton eye when he thereby grows to imitate him. God complains of Judah for this; though she saw what her treacherous sister Israel had done, and that God had therefore cast her off, yet she feared not, but went and played the harlot also (Jer. 3:7, 8).

What use should we make of our brethren's falls?

-1. Let their falls affect us with a holy fear and jealousy of our own hearts, for we have a deceitful heart, subject to the like. Paul would have the church at Rome make this use of the fall of Israel (Rom. 11:20).

-2. Look at them with an eye of pity for your brother; if he is astray, bring him back; if he lies under the burden of sin, help him up; and if you cannot have opportunity to speak to him, yet pray heartily for him. That is the frame of heart of every loving Christian, to be compassionate of his brother's misery.

But does not the Holy Spirit say that love covers a multitude of sins? (1 Pet. 4:8) True, but how does it cover them?

-1. With a mantle of wisdom; not so as to skin over their wounds, but to cover them that they may be covered before God and man (James 5:19, 20). God would have us cover them not with a mantle of flattery, but with a healing plaster that may cure them.

-2. With a mantle of faithfulness; that is, not to blaze them abroad, not to reveal their infirmities any further than to help them. Ham told his brethren of their father's nakedness (Gen. 9:22, 23), but in a scornful manner; besides, he might have covered him himself and never told them, and therefore Noah made him a curse. God requires that if we are able to heal an infirmity ourselves, we are to let it go no further; if not, then let us get the help of others, not in a scorning manner, but in a spirit of grief and holy fear.

-3. Let us cover them with a mantle of compassion; if they turn again and repent, let us be ready to forgive them, as God for Christ's sake has forgiven us (Luke 17:13, 14; Eph. 4:2).

If a man thus observes other men's sins, will he not be counted a meddler and a busybody? True, we shall be busy, but yet not where we have nothing to do. God lays this charge upon us; if we keep the bounds named before, we do not go beyond our commission.

Doct. 2. Upon the sight of our brother's sins, a faithful man is to pray for him.

"If any man see his brother sin a sin not unto death, he shall pray for him, and shall give him life." He shall be an instrument to convey life to him; or God, moved by his prayer, shall give him life; it is all one. When the Israelites had committed a great sin, so that God in his displeasure had threatened to destroy them, yet at Moses' earnest request he spared them (Deut. 9:15-21). Job prayed for his friends, and the Lord accepted him. Stephen's prayer made way for the conversion of Paul.

Why will such a prayer obtain life and peace?

-1. Because God takes pleasure to knit the members of his body together. There is no better means thus to knit them than to make them useful one to another (1 Cor. 12:21, 22).

-2. Because Christ's ointment is poured on the head of every believer, and all his saints partake in his intercession for others. What is said of Christ (Rom. 8:34) is also said of our prayers (2 Tim. 4:1; James 5:15).

"There is a sin unto death; I do not say he shall pray for it." These words contain an exception to his former direction; he does not command us to pray for the sin unto death. From this we may infer that there is a sin unto death.

Indeed every sin is mortal, none venial (Rom. 6:23); all deserve death, but yet there is a sin unto death which not only deserves death, but certainly and inevitably procures death.

Doct. There is a sin that not only in itself is deadly, but that irrecoverably procures everlasting death (Matt. 12:31, 32; Mark 3:22).

What is this sin unto death? Two things concur in it: illumination in the mind and malice in the heart. The apostle joins them together: if they sin willfully (maliciously) after they have received the knowledge of the truth (which is called enlightening, Heb. 6:4), there remains no more sacrifice for sins (Heb. 10:26).

-1. There must be illumination in the mind. Such a knowledge of the truth is required as that which comes from the illumination of the Holy Spirit. When once a man is clearly allowed to see the truth of God's word and the goodness of his grace, and after this he sins willfully, there is no more hope of mercy.

-2. There must be malice in the heart. That is included

in its name, the sin against the Holy Spirit (Matt. 12:31, 32). Here is indicated the object they sin against, the Spirit of grace; and here is the manner, it is done with spite and malice against the known truth. They are said to do despite to the Spirit of God (Heb. 10:29); now this is not only contempt and despising, but it is joined likewise with malice and scorn. That sin is unpardonable, as our Saviour testifies (Matt. 12:32; Mark 3:22).

Why is this sin so unpardonable?

-1. Because of the mighty strong power of Satan in such a man. This sin is committed when seven worse than himself have entered in, after the knowledge of the truth and reformation of many things (Luke 11:24-27). When a man has been so enlightened that he has cast out many sinful lusts, if after this he makes way for Satan again by voluntary and willful commission of sins, then Satan enters with seven other spirits worse than before.

-2. Because of the nature of this sin. It is not a sin of ignorance, for lack of knowledge; not a sin of infirmity for lack of strength; nor is it only a sin of presumption, for that may proceed from boldness rather than malice; but a sin of malice is far worse than any of these.

-3. Because of the glory of God's grace. It is the glory of grace to extend to pardon and heal all sins besides; there is no sin of ignorance or infirmity which grace cannot heal. The most presumptuous it can humble; but if a man maliciously despises the Spirit of grace, God is most jealous of the glory of his grace, and will not have it abused by them.

Use 1. To refute some ancient tenets about this sin. The schoolmen say it is one of five sins: either despair, or presumption, or opposing the known truth, or envying the graces of others, or obstinate purpose in sin, or final impenitence. But many of those may be found in those whom God afterward received to mercy. There has been despair even in God's own servants (Ps. 31:22). And as for presumption, Nathan charges that David had despised the commandments of the Lord. Herod put John in prison and to death, and Darius cast

Daniel into the lions' den, both against their conscience; and yet neither of them sinned against the Holy Spirit, for they were both sorry for it. For envying the graces of others, it was found in Joshua (Numb. 11:28, 29). For obstinate purpose in sin, it is found in everyone who sins presumptuously (2 Sam. 24:1-4). For final impenitence, that is not the sin against the Holy Spirit, because St. John then would not have given order not to pray for them, for final impenitence cannot be discerned until death, and so his direction would have been but frivolous.

Augustine taught this sin to be envy and final impenitence. Origen taught it to be any sin after baptism. The Novatians took up the same tenet; but that it was an error is evident, for Peter sinned after baptism, and so are all the sins of God's children; if these were sins against the Holy Spirit, who could be saved?

Again, some conceive that this sin is very rarely found and difficult to discern; but then why does St. John write to common Christians not to pray for them? This is a sign they may be found and discerned.

Use 2. If we would live long and see good days, let us take heed of opposing and maligning the known truth. Many have conceived that this sin has hardly been found in the world, except in open enemies of Christ. I wish it were so rare. Are there not too many in the world who have been enlightened and convinced of the truth of God, and yet rise up against it with open spite and disdain, and persecute God's servants with malice and scorn? Is not this sin found too often in the church? Indeed many of our Saviour's persecutors did it out of ignorance, and our Saviour's prayers were effectual for them, "Father, forgive them, for they know not what they do." But there were others who knew him to be the heir, and yet said, "Come, let us kill him" (Matt. 21:38). And for these there remains no more sacrifice.

Use 3. Let all the servants of God strengthen themselves against this sin, and use all good preservatives against this sin unto death.

a. Keep constant fellowship with God's servants, and forsake them not; for that is the rise of the sin (Heb. 10:25). As long as God keeps in your heart a love for his people and a reverent esteem of his grace, it is impossible that you should fall into this sin.

b. Be diligent to add one grace to another, for so you shall make your calling and election sure, and shall never fall (2 Pet. 1:5, 10; Ps. 73:27, 28).

c. Deck your heart with an humble and awesome respect to God and his ways (Prov. 28:14; Jer. 32:40).

d. Take heed of turning aside to crooked ways (Ps. 125:4, 5). One sin will lead to another. "Make straight paths for your feet, lest that which is lame be turned out of the way" (Heb. 12:13).

Use 4. To those who fear that they have committed this sin, which is the case of two sorts of Christians.

a. Those who, having found much enlargement, afterward fall into deadness and slack-heartedness, and all is damped. It is true that a man may grieve the Holy Spirit by vexing and despising and damping it, but yet this is not the sin against the Holy Spirit unless it is done with spite and scorn.

b. Those who have indeed sinned against their consciences and wronged their own souls, and brought much mischief upon themselves; but yet a man may sin against his conscience and not sin against the Holy Spirit. It may be done out of infirmity or boldness, as Peter's and David's sins were, yet not out of spite or malice; therefore if you fear you have committed this sin, your fear argues that you have not committed it, for you are afraid and sorry for it.

"I do not say you shall pray for it."

Doct. We have no warrant to pray for the sin against the Holy Spirit, the sin unto death.

Though Paul bids us pray for all men (2 Tim. 2:1), yet St. John excepts those who have sinned this sin; and Paul himself is so far from praying for them that he prays against them, that they may be rewarded according to their works (2 Tim. 4:15). "I would that even those were cut off that trouble you" (Gal. 5:12); he wishes they were utterly cut off from church and commonwealth.

These false apostles would have overthrown the gospel of Christ and brought in another gospel; and because they were all alike, the apostle discerned them to be in a state of damnation, as enemies to the cross of Christ (Phil. 3:18, 19). At first they preached the gospel, but afterwards turned to earthly things, and began to magnify themselves and vilify the apostles; and therefore he looks at them as dogs. "If any man love not the Lord Jesus Christ, let him be anathema maranatha" (1 Cor. 16:22); this is the greatest curse that can befall a man.

Why then are we not to pray for them?

-1. Because they do despite to the chief means and helps of prayer. One is the Spirit of grace, for the Spirit of grace is the Spirit of supplication (Zech. 12:10). The Spirit is so grieved that it will not assist us in any prayer we make for such (Heb. 10:29).

-2. Because they despise the name of Christ, the other help in prayer. Upon these two wings our prayers fly up to heaven. Now those who sin against the Holy Spirit make a scorn of Christ; they trample his blood underfoot, and put him to an open shame (Heb. 6:6); they put him to an open and exemplary punishment, as the most notorious malefactor. To such there is no hope that Christ should lend his name as a mediator.

-3. Where Christ is not a sacrifice for sins, there he cannot be expected to make intercession. But to these there remains no more sacrifice for sin (Heb. 10:27). If the sacrifice of Christ does not reach to such, then he will never make intercession for them.

-4. If we pray for those who are professed enemies of God and Christ, we do not show ourselves to be God's friends but his enemies; and therefore our prayer will do them no good and ourselves harm.

Use 1. To teach us that the sin to death may be discerned even by common Christians; for else why does he write this to common Christians, to all believers in general?

Use 2. Let God's people learn the nature of this sin, lest they pray unawares for those for whom their prayers shall do no good. If you see professors who have tasted of the grace of God, afterward opposing and maligning his ways and his servants, in this case save your labor in praying for them; your prayers will do no good, but harm.

But how may we discern when they commit this sin against the light and knowledge of the truth?

If they express in their speech and conversation that they seek Christ and the ways of his grace, and say they are convinced that those ways are the right ways, and yet maliciously oppose those ways, then do not pray for them. The Pharisees knew Christ to be the heir, and yet tried to kill him (Matt. 21:28); and in the meantime they said he was a conjurer, and cast out devils through Beelzebub the prince of the devils; therefore Christ tells them that their sins would never be forgiven them.

Use 3. This shows us the desperate condition of all who commit this sin. Therefore let us take heed of all sins against conscience, of all presumptuous sins and sins of boldness, for they lead to this great transgressions (Ps. 19:13). And to be kept from presumptuous sins, let us take heed of secret sins.

Use 4. If we are children to parents, or wives to husbands, or subjects to kings, who sin against the Holy Spirit, yet we may do civil service and offices to them. If a prince shall sin this sin, his subjects ought not to depose him but to do him offices of service. If there is any tie of nature, a man may do them civil offices. This confutes that desperate doctrine of the Romish church, that whoever denies the Pope to be the supreme head of the church is to be excommunicated, and then no man is bound in allegiance to him, but whoever shall slay him shall merit salvation.

Use 5. Learn here to discern the nature of peremptory

prohibitions. He says, "I do not say he shall pray for it." But some might say, Neither does he say you shall pray against it. But he makes this a strong prohibition; "I do not say"; I give you no commission, no warrant. Such is the manner of scripture prohibitions. "Who has required this at your hands?" (Isa. 1:12) "I commanded them not, neither came it into my heart" (Jer. 7:31); implying that it is a most peremptory prohibition that God's word does not command it. If there is nothing for it, there is enough against it; for this is our direction, that we are to do only what God commands in his word. We must add nothing nor take away anything.

EDITOR'S NOTE: Here ends John Cotton's exposition. To make our commentary complete, however, we have added brief remarks by John Calvin, covering this concluding section of chapter 5. Calvin's comments are subjoined on the following pages.

v. 17. "All unrighteousness is sin; and there is a sin not unto death."

This passage may be explained variously. If you take it adversatively, the sense would not be unsuitable: "Though all unrighteousness is sin, yet every sin is not unto death." Some take "all unrighteousness" for complete unrighteousness, as though the apostle had said that the sin of which he spoke was the summit of unrighteousness. I, however, am more disposed to embrace the first or the second explanation; and as the result is nearly the same, I leave it to the judgment of readers to determine which of the two is the more appropriate.

18. "We know that whatever is born of God sins not; but he who is begotten of God keeps himself, and that wicked one touches him not."

If you suppose that God's children are wholly pure and free from all sin, as the fanatics contend, then the apostle is inconsistent with himself; for he would thus take away the duty of mutual prayer among brethren. Then he says that those sin not who do not wholly fall away from the grace of God; and hence he inferred that prayer ought to be made for all the children of God, because they sin not unto death. A proof is added: that everyone born of God keeps himself, that is, keeps himself in the fear of God; nor does he allow himself to be so led away as to lose all sense of religion, and to surrender himself wholly to the devil and the flesh.

When he says that the wicked one touches him not, reference is made to a deadly wound; for the children of God do not remain untouched by the assaults of Satan, but they ward off his strokes by the shield of faith, so that they do not penetrate into the heart. Hence spiritual life is never extinguished in them. This is what it is not to sin. Though the faithful indeed fall through the infirmity of the flesh, yet they groan under the burden of sin, loathe themselves, and cease not to fear God.

"Keeps himself." What properly belongs to God he transfers to us; for were any one of us the keeper of his own salvation, it would be a miserable protection. Therefore Christ asks the Father to keep us, intimating that it is not done by our own strength. The advocates of free-will lay hold on this expression, that they may prove from it that we are preserved from sin partly by God's grace and partly by our own power. But they do not perceive that the faithful do not have from themselves this power of preservation of which the apostle speaks. Nor does he indeed speak of their power, as though they could keep themselves by their own strength; but he only shows that they ought to resist Satan, so that they may never be fatally wounded by his darts. And we know that we fight with no other weapons than those of God. Hence the faithful keep themselves from sin, as far as they are kept by God (John 17:11).

v. 19. "And we know that we are of God, and the whole world lies in wickedness."

"We are of God." He deduces an exhortation from his previous doctrine; for what he had declared in common as to the children of God, he now applies to those he was writing; and this he did to stimulate them to beware of sin, and to encourage them to repel the onsets of Satan.

Let readers observe that it is only true faith that applies to us, so to speak, the grace of God; for the apostle acknowledges none faithful but those who have the dignity of being God's children. Nor does he indeed put probable conjecture, as the Sophishs speak, for confidence; for he says that we know. The meaning is that, as we have been born of God, we ought to strive to prove, by our separation from the world and by the sanctity of our life, that we have not been called in vain to so great an honor.

Now this is an admonition very necessary for all the godly; for wherever they turn their eyes, Satan has his allurements prepared, by which he seeks to draw them away from God. It would then be difficult for them to hold on in their course, were they not so to value their calling as to disregard all the hindrances of the world. Then, in order to be well prepared for the contest, these two things must be borne in mind: that the world is wicked, and that our calling is from God.

Under the term 'world' the apostle no doubt includes the whole human race. By saying that it lies in the wicked one, he represents it as being under the dominion of Satan. There is then no reason why we should hesitate to shun the world, which contemns God and delivers up itself into the bondage of Satan; nor is there a reason why we should fear its enmity, because it is alienated from God. In short, since corruption pervades all nature, the faithful ought to study self-denial; and since nothing is seen in the world but wickedness and corruption, they must necessarily disregard flesh and blood that they may follow God. At the same time the other thing must be added, that God is he who has called them, that under his protection they may oppose all the machinations of the world and Satan.

v. 20. "And we know that the Son of God has come and has given us an understanding, that we may know him who is true, even in his Son Jesus Christ. This is the true God and eternal life."

"And we know that the Son of God has come." As the children of God are assailed on every side, he (as we have said) encourages and exhorts them to persevere in resisting their enemies, and for this reason, because they fight under the banner of God and know certainly that they are ruled by his Spirit; but he now reminds them where this knowledge is especially to be found.

He then says that God has been so made known to us that there is now no reason for doubting. The apostle does not dwell in this point without reason; for unless our faith is really founded on God, we shall never stand firm in the contest. For this purpose the apostle shows that we have obtained through Christ a sure knowledge of the true God, so that we may not fluctuate in uncertainty.

By 'true God' he does not mean one who tells the truth, but him who is really God; and he so calls him to distinguish him from all idols. This 'true' is in opposition to what is fictitious, for it is ἀληθινός and not ἀληθής. A similar passage is in John 17:3: "This is eternal life, to know thee, the only true God, and Jesus Christ whom thou hast sent." And he justly ascribes to Christ this office of illuminating our minds as to the knowledge of God. For as he is the only true image of the invisible God, so he is the only interpreter of the Father; as he is the only true guide of life, yea, as he is the life and light of the world and truth, as soon as we depart from him we necessarily become vain in our own devices.

And Christ is said to have given us an understanding, not only because he shows us in the gospel what sort of being the true God is, and illuminates us by his Spirit, but because in Christ himself we have God manifested in the flesh, as Paul says, since in him dwells all the fullness of the Deity, and in him are hid all the treasures of knowledge and wisdom (Col. 2:9). Thus it is that the face of God in a manner appears to us in Christ; not that there was no knowledge or a doubtful knowledge of God before the coming of Christ, but that now he manifests himself more fully and more clearly. And this is what Paul says in 2 Cor. 4:6, that God, who formerly commanded light to shine out of darkness at the creation of the world, has how shined in our hearts through the brightness of the knowledge of his glory in the face of Christ.

And it must be observed that this gift is peculiar to the elect. Christ indeed kindles for all indiscriminately the torch of his gospel; but all have not the eyes of their minds enlightened to see it, but on the contrary Satan spreads the veil of blindness over many. Then the apostle means the light which Christ kindles within in the hearts of his people, and which when once kindled is never extinguished, though in some it may for a time be smothered.

"We are in him who is true." By these words he reminds us how efficacious is that knowledge which he mentions, even because by it we are united to Christ and become one with God; for it has a living root, fixed in the heart, by which God lives in us and we in him. As he says, without a copulative, that we are in him who is true, in his Son, he seems to express the manner of our union with God; as though he had said that we are in God through Christ.

"This is the true God." Though the Arians have attempted to elude this passage, and some agree with them at this day, yet we have here a remarkable testimony to the divinity of Christ. The Arians apply this passage to the Father, as though the apostle should again repeat that he is the true God. But nothing could be more frigid than such a repetition. He has already twice testified that the true God is he who has been made known to us in Christ; why should he again add, "this is the true God"? It applies, indeed, most suitably to Christ; for after having taught us that Christ is the guide by whose hand we are led to God, he now, by way of amplifying, affirms that Christ is that God, lest we should think that we are to seek further; and he confirms this view by what is added, 'and eternal life.' It is doubtless the same that is spoken of as being the true God and eternal life. The relative form, οὗτος , usually refers to the last person. I say then that Christ is properly called eternal life; and that this mode of speaking perpetually occurs in John, no one can deny.

The meaning is that when we have Christ, we enjoy the true and eternal God, for nowhere else is he to be sought;

and secondly, when we become thus partakers of eternal life, because it is offered to us in Christ though hid in the Father. The origin of life is indeed the Father; but the fountain from which we are to draw it is Christ.

v. 21. "Little children, keep yourselves from idols. Amen."

Though this is a separate sentence, yet it is as it were an appendix to the preceding doctrine. For the vivifying light of the gospel ought to scatter and dissipate not only darkness, but also all mists, from the minds of the godly. The apostle not only condemns idolatry, but commands us to beware of all images and idols; by which he intimates that the worship of God cannot continue uncorrupted and pure wherever men begin to be in love with idols or images. For so innate in us is superstition that the least occasion will infect us with its contagion. Dry wood will not so easily burn when coals are put under it, as idolatry will lay hold on and engross the minds of men when an occasion is given to them. And who does not see that images are the sparks? What! Sparks do I say? Nay, rather torches, which are sufficient to set the whole world on fire.

The apostle at the same time speaks not only of statues, but also of altars, and includes all the instruments of superstitions. Moreover, the Papists are ridiculous, who pervert this passage and apply it to the statues of Jupiter and Mercury and the like, as though the apostle did not teach generally that there is a corruption of religion whenever a corporeal form is ascribed to God, or whenever statues and pictures form a part of his worship. Let us then remember that we ought carefully to continue in the spiritual worship of God, so as to banish far from us everything that may turn us aside to gross and carnal superstitions.

www.ingramcontent.com/pod-product-compliance
Lightning Source LLC
Chambersburg PA
CBHW050131240426
43673CB00043B/1631